Sociology

Paul B. Horton

Chester L. Hunt

Western Michigan University

Sixth Edition

McGRAW-HILL BOOK COMPANY

New York	London	Paris
St. Louis	Madrid	São Paulo
San Francisco	Mexico	Singapore
Auckland	Montreal	Sydney
Bogotá	New Delhi	Tokyo
Hamburg	Panama	Toronto
Johannesburg		

Sociology

1 2 3 4 5 6 7 8 9 0   HALHAL   8 9 8 7 6 5 4 3

ISBN 0-07-030443-2

Library of Congress Cataloging in Publication Data

Horton, Paul B.
Sociology.

Bibliography: p.
Includes indexes.
1. Sociology. I. Hunt, Chester L. II. Title.
HM51.H64   1984   301   83-12052
ISBN 0-07-030443-2

This book was set in Palatino by Monotype Composition Company, Inc.
The editors were Christina Mediate, Anne Murphy, and James R. Belser;
the designer was Joan E. O'Connor;
the production supervisor was Charles Hess.
The photo editor was Inge King.
The cartoon drawings were done by Frederick J. Ashby;
new drawings were done by Fine Line Illustrations, Inc.
Halliday Lithograph Corporation was printer and binder.

COVER PHOTO CREDITS
Appearing on cover from left to right:

Uta Hoffmann, Owen Franken/Stock, Boston, Inc.; Jacques Jangoux/Peter Arnold, Inc.; Erika Stone/ Peter Arnold, Inc.; Louis Goldman/Photo Researchers, Inc.
Bernard P. Wolff/Photo Researchers, Inc.; Clyde H. Smith/Peter Arnold, Inc.; C. Vergara/Photo Researchers, Inc.; Borgo S. Lorenzo/Stock, Boston, Inc.; Owen Franken/Stock, Boston, Inc.
Michael George/Photo Researchers, Inc.; Helene Slavens/Peter Arnold, Inc.; F. B. Grunzweig/Photo Researchers, Inc.; Erika Stone/Peter Arnold, Inc.; Fred A. Anderson/Photo Researchers.

CHAPTER-OPENING PHOTO CREDITS

1. © Jan Lukas/Photo Researchers, Inc.; 2. © Beryl Goldberg; 3. © Victor Engelbert/Photo Researchers, Inc.; 4. Ginger Chih/Peter Arnold, Inc.; 5. Gloria Karlson; 6. Terry Evans/Magnum Photos; 7. Michael Putnam/Peter Arnold, Inc.; 8. © Jim Anderson/Woodfin Camp & Assoc.; 9. David Sheffield/Woodfin Camp & Assoc.; 10. © Christa Armstrong/Photo Researchers, Inc.; 11. Elliott Erwitt/Magnum Photos; 12. Stuart Rosner/Stock, Boston, Inc.; 13. © John Chao/Woodfin Camp & Assoc.; 14. Inge Morath/ Magnum Photos; 15. Evelyn Hofer/Archive Pictures; 16. © Katrina Thomas/Photo Researchers, Inc.; 17. © Steve Kagan/Photo Researchers, Inc.; 18. © Eric Kroll/Taurus Photos; 19. Hugh Rogers/ Monkmeyer Press Photo Service; 20. © Jim Anderson/Woodfin Camp & Assoc.

To
Talcott Parsons,
C. Wright Mills,
and
Erving Goffman

Contents

Contents

PART THREE *Social Organization*

PART FOUR *Social Stratification*

PART FIVE *Social Change and Social Policy*

Preface

What should an introductory sociology textbook try to do? First and most important, we believe it should capture the interest of the student and demonstrate both the process and challenge of scientific observation and analysis of social behavior in a readable and interesting way.

Second, an introductory so-ciology textbook should seek to cultivate in the student the habit of scientific analysis of social data. Unless students gain a sophisticated aware-ness of their own ethnocen-trism and some ability to ob-jectify their observations, the sociology course has failed in one of its major objectives.

Third, an introductory soci-ology textbook should present the basic concepts and de-scriptive materials of sociol-ogy clearly and intelligibly. These should be illustrated so vividly that they "come alive" and become part of the stu-dent's thinking vocabulary. Concepts should be learned not simply as definitions to be memorized but as accurate, descriptive names for the ways people act and the things people build. Concepts are far more than a professional vocabulary to be used in advanced studies: They are even more important as tools for identifying and understanding a process or idea. Many sociology students will find that the introductory course is a terminal course as well, and the basic concepts should be tools for continuing social observation and analysis.

In this textbook we have tried to do these things. Whether we have succeeded is for the reader to judge. We have generally avoided esoteric sources in favor of others more easily available to most students. We have often used literary and popular sources for purposes of illustration. We have done this to emphasize that sociology is the disciplined observation and analysis of everyday life and that the concepts and insights of sociology are applicable to all that goes on around the student.

We note that some recent textbooks contain very few footnotes or citations. It is true that footnotes and citations *do* clutter up a book. But we believe that students should constantly be reminded of the evidential basis for the conclusions of sociology. There-

fore, we have documented heavily in order to present sociology as a scientific and scholarly discipline, not as an exercise in popular journalism.

We have sought to incorporate recent research in this new edition but have not slavishly deleted significant earlier research and theory simply to gain a more current dateline. We seek to describe new and controversial developments in sociology analytically and objectively, in the belief that advocacy and espousal are not proper in an introductory textbook.

We have tried to minimize the overlap with other sociology courses. This textbook is not an encapsulated encyclopedia of the entire sociology curriculum. We have intentionally not emphasized "social problems" material, in the belief that the introductory course should concentrate upon principles and concepts and should leave specialized topics and problem-oriented materials for later courses.

In this sixth edition we have deleted very few topics, but many sections have been rewritten in condensed form to make room for new topics and materials. We have somewhat reordered the chapter sequence, have reorganized some chapters, and have

given greater attention to the interactionist and conflict perspectives.

The accompanying *Study Guide and Source Book* has again been revised by Bruce J. Cohen. Many students find it helpful in study and review, as a source of related materials and as a yardstick to measure their mastery of the text materials. An *Instructor's Resource Manual,* prepared again by Bobbie Wright and Steven Severin is again available as a teaching aid. Other supplements include a Test Bank keyed to the Micro Examiner System.

We owe a debt of appreciation to many people: to a number of our colleagues for helpful suggestions; to the sociologist-reviewers, George H. Benziger, Erie Community College; David Brinkerhoff, University of Nebraska; Brindaban Chaubey, Shippensburg State College; Richard Della Fave, North Carolina State University; Thomas E. Drabek, University of Denver; William Egelman, Iona College; Larry Horn, Los Angeles Pierce College; Dennis McGrath, Community College of Philadelphia; James Orcutt, Florida State University; James C. Petersen, Western Michigan University; Marcella Rainey, Black Hawk College; Laurel Richardson, The Ohio

State University; C. Edward Roy, Brevard College; Bobbie Wright, Thomas Nelson Community College; and Lloyd R. Young, Southwest Missouri State University, for their candid criticisms of our manuscript; to McGraw-Hill editors and staff members for their dedicated competence; and to Frederick J. Ashby for his imaginative line drawings.

Paul B. Horton
Chester L. Hunt

Preface

PART ONE

Sociology and Society

We are uncertain whether our prehistoric human ancestors knew that they lived in a *society,* but we suspect that they did. From cave excavations and rock paintings we know that they lived in family groups, laid out their dead for burial, and apparently believed in an afterlife. But of the rest of their social life, we know practically nothing.

For at least as long as we have had written language, we have speculated about the nature of the human animal and the societies it builds. But only within the past few generations has there been any systematic study of human societies, ancient or modern. Social scientists have developed a number of procedures through which they try to find verifiable knowledge about the social behavior of the human animal. People have sought knowledge from many sources, some dependable, some undependable. Sci-

ence as a method of finding dependable knowledge about society is discussed in Chapter 1, "Sociologists Study Society." All phenomena can be studied scientifically, but the techniques of study must be fitted to the materials studied. Just how sociologists use scientific methods in sociological investigation is discussed in Chapter 2, "Fields and Methods of Sociology."

1

1 Sociologists Study Society

3

Sociology: The intellectual discipline concerned with developing systematic, reliable knowledge about human social relations in general and about the products of such relationships. . . .

(Thomas Ford Hoult, *Dictionary of Modern Sociology*, Littlefield, Adams & Co., Totowa, New Jersey, 1969, p. 307.)

Sociologists study human society and social behavior by examining the groups that people form. These groups include families, tribes, communities, and governments, as well as a great variety of social, religious, political, business, and other organizations. Sociologists study the behavior and interaction of groups; trace their origin and growth; and analyze the influ-

ence of group activities on individual members.

(Occupational Outlook Handbook, 1980–1981, U.S. Department of Labor, 1980:431)

Sociology is the taking of what everyone knows and putting it into words that nobody can understand.

(Anonymous)

For thousands of years people's common sense told them that the earth was flat, that big objects fell faster than small ones, and that character was revealed in facial features; yet today we know none of these is true. Today, science is replacing common sense as a source of dependable knowledge.

SOCIAL SCIENCE AND COMMON SENSE

When we do not know where our ideas come from or what they are based on, we sometimes call them "common sense." If we call them common sense, we do not have to prove they are true, for then others will join us in the collective self-deception of assuming they have already been proved. If one presses for proof, one is told that the idea has been proved by experience. The term "common sense" puts a respectable front on all sorts of ideas for which there is no systematic body of evidence that can be cited.

What often passes for common sense consists of a group's accumulation of collective guesses, hunches, and haphazard trial-and-error learnings. Many common-sense propositions are sound, earthy, useful bits of knowledge. "A soft answer turneth away wrath," and "birds of a feather flock together," are practical observations on social life. But many common-sense conclusions are

based on ignorance, prejudice, and mistaken interpretation. When medieval Europeans noticed that feverish patients were free of lice while most healthy people were lousy, they made the common-sense conclusion that lice would cure fever and therefore sprinkled lice over feverish patients. Common sense thus preserves both folk wisdom and folk nonsense, and to sort out one from the other is a task for science.

Only within the past two or three hundred years has the scientific method become a common way of seeking answers about the natural world. Science has become a source of knowledge about our *social* world even more recently; yet in the brief period since we began to use the scientific method, we have learned more about our world than had been learned in the preceding ten thousand years. The spectacular explosion of knowledge in the modern world parallels our use of the scientific method. How does this scientific method operate?

SCIENTIFIC OBSERVATION— THE BASIC TECHNIQUE OF SCIENTIFIC METHOD

Science is based upon *verifiable evidence*. By "evidence" we mean factual observations other observers can see, weigh, count, and check for accuracy. Scientific observation is not the

Common sense tells us:	Scientific investigation finds that:
Men survive hardship and exposure better than women.	Women survive hardship as well as or better than men.
Colds are caused by chills and wet feet.	Colds are caused by viruses, although exposure may lower resistance.
One's character shows in one's face.	There is no dependable association between facial features and personality characteristics.
A person who cheats at cards will cheat in business.	Honesty in one situation tells little about one's behavior in a different situation.
Spare the rod and spoil the child.	Serious delinquents usually have been punished more severely than most nondelinquents.
The genius or near-genius is generally delicate, impractical, unstable, and unsuccessful.	The genius and near-genius group is above average in health, emotional adjustment, and income.
Blacks are especially talented in music but inferior in intellect.	There is no convincing evidence of racial differences in innate capacities.

same as just "looking at things." We have all been looking at things all our lives, but this does not make us scientific observers, any more than a lifetime of swatting flies makes us entomologists. How does scientific observation differ from just looking at things?

Scientific observation is accurate. The scientific observer tries to make sure things are exactly as described and avoids jumping to conclusions. Novelists may fantasize and politicians may exaggerate, but the scientist must try to be accurate.

Scientific observation is precise. While accuracy refers to the truth or correctness of a statement, precision refers to degree or measurement. No respectable social scientist would say, "I interviewed a lot of people, and most of them feel that things are terrible," and claim this was a scientific investigation. (How many people? What measuring instruments? How "terrible"?)

Since scientific writing is precise, scientists avoid colorful literary extravagances. Tennyson's lines, "Every moment dies a man; every moment one is born," is literature not science. If written with scientific precision it might read, "Every 0.596 seconds, on the average in 1980, died a person; every 0.2448 seconds an infant was born." Literary writing may be intentionally vague, stimulating the reader to wonder what is meant (e.g., was Hamlet insane?), but the dramatic sweep of the novelist and the provocative imagery of the poet have no place in scientific writing.

How much precision is needed? A billionth of an inch is too large an error for a nuclear physicist; for a social scientist studying crowded housing, a measure to the nearest square foot is satisfactory. Scientists seek *as much precision as the situation requires*. If conditions of observation do not permit such precision, the scientist must qualify judgment until more precise observations can be collected.

Scientific observation is systematic. Conclusions based on casual recollections are unreliable. Judgments which begin with, "I've talked to a lot of people and . . ." should be classed as conversation not as research. Unless observations have been collected in an

Evidence consists of verifiable facts.

Objectivity is the ability to see
and accept facts as they are, not
as one might wish them to be.

organized, systematic program, they are likely to be spotty and incomplete.

Scientific observation is recorded. Human memory is notoriously fallible. Suppose a professor says, "Women usually don't do as well in this course as men." Unless this professor has computed average scores for men and women students, he is saying, "I have recalled the grades of hundreds of students, mentally computed averages, and found the male average score to be higher." The utter absurdity of such a statement shows how untrustworthy are all conclusions based upon recalling unrecorded data.

Scientific observation is objective. This means that, insofar as is humanly possible, observation is unaffected by the observer's own belief, preferences, wishes, or values. In other words, *objectivity* means the *ability to see and accept facts as they are, not as one might wish them to be.* It is fairly easy to be objective when observing something about which we have no preferences or values. It is fairly easy to study objectively the mating practices of the fruit fly, but less easy to view the mating practices of the human being with objective detachment. On any matter where our emotions, beliefs, habits, and values are involved, we are likely to see whatever agrees with our emotional needs and values.

To be objective is perhaps the most taxing of all scientific obligations. It is not enough to be willing to see facts as they are. We must know what our biases are if we are to guard against them. A *bias* is simply a *tendency, usually unconscious, to see facts in a certain way because of one's habits, wishes, interests, and values.* Thus, a "peace demonstration" is seen by some as a courageous effort to save the world from collective suicide, while others see it as a misguided effort to replace hard-headed realism with idealistic mush.

Seldom are "the facts" so undebatable that bias does not distort them. *Selective perception is a tendency to see or hear only those facts which support our beliefs and overlook others.* Many experiments have shown that most people in a social situation will see and hear only what they expect to see and hear. If what we expect to see isn't there, we see it anyway! This is dramatically shown in a famous experiment [Allport and Postman, 1947] in which observers were shown a picture of a roughly dressed white man holding an open razor and arguing violently with a well-dressed black man who was shown in an apologetic, conciliatory posture; then the observers were asked to describe the scene. Some of them "saw" the razor in the black man's hand, where they expected it to be. Others perceived it correctly, but in passing on a description of the scene (A described it to B, who described it to C, and so on), they soon had the razor in the black man's hand, where it "belonged." Even though they were not emotionally involved in the situation, had ample time to study it, and were making a conscious effort to be accurate in what they saw and reported or heard, the observers' unconscious biases still led many of them to "see" or "hear" a fact that wasn't there.

Some common threats to objectivity, then, are vested interest, habit, and bias. Objectivity does not come easily to an observer, but it can be learned. One can become more objective as one becomes aware of personal biases and makes allowance for them. Through rigorous training in scientific methodology, through studying many experiments and noting many examples of objective and nonobjective uses of data, an observer may eventually develop some ability to cut through many layers of self-deception and to perceive facts with a greater degree of scientific objectivity. The scientist also has another powerful ally—the criticism of colleagues. The scientist publishes research so that it may be checked by other scientists who may not share the same biases and who come to the problem with a different point of view. This process of publication and criticism means that shoddy work is soon exposed, and scientists who let bias dictate the uses of data are open to severe criticism.

Scientific observations are made by trained observers. A billion people watch the sun and moon sweep across the sky, but more sophisticated observers know that is not exactly what happens. Untrained observers do not know what to look for or how to interpret it. They do not know the pitfalls which lead to inaccurate observation, nor are they fully aware of the tricks their own limitations and biases may play on them. Startling reports of weird phenomena generally come from uneducated, unsophisticated persons, and are discounted by the experts. When some remarkable observations are reported, the scientist will want to know: (1) What is the observer's general level of education and sophistication? Is this person a member of a superstition-ridden folk group, or of a well-informed and somewhat skeptical population? (2) What is his or her special knowledge or training in this particular field? Does this observer have the knowledge to tell whether this event has a perfectly natural explanation? Thus, the biologist among the ship's passengers is less likely to see a sea monster than are the members of the crew, and the meteorologist sees fewer UFOs than people with no special knowledge of atmospheric phenomena.

In recent years public interest in psychic and occult phenomena has exploded. A book claiming that plants have consciousness and are responsive to human feelings has been a best-seller [Tompkins and Bird, 1973], although scientists are generally unimpressed [First, 1973], and there are no authenticated reports that anyone has yet "hated" the crabgrass out of the lawn. A one-time stage magician, Uri Geller, has attracted great attention as a psychic and has even impressed a team of physicists at Stanford Research Institute [*Science News*, July 20, 1974, p. 46]. But physicists and other scientists, whatever their credentials as scientists, are *not* trained observers of sleight-of-hand deception. Stage

---

We have reported before on Bigfoot and Bighead, and now it is Skunkfoot who joins the company. A 7-foot monster, described by *The Globe* as having "an unbelievably bad case of body odor," has reportedly been terrifying the residents of Chesapeake, Virginia, near the Great Dismal Swamp, where the creature presumably resides. One man who claims to have seen it a dozen times says, "To give you an idea of how bad it smells, imagine falling into a cesspool up to your shoulders." To make matters worse, the tabloid *Weekly World News* adds that the creature is "amorous," causing local women to "live in terror." One witness, Sherry Davis, says that she thinks the creature is attracted to women. "Maybe it oozes out of the swamp at night and goes prowling the woods looking for a female," hypothesized another terrified resident. Almost all of the witnesses have been women, prompting Mrs. Davis to add that she is afraid to walk alone now, for fear of being "carried off into the woods by that thing."

(*The Skeptical Inquirer*, Vol. VI, No. 3, Spring 1982, p. 13.

How should the critical student evaluate such popular sensationalist accounts as this? Why are they so readily believed by many people?

magicians consider scientists as easy to fool as anyone else, and generally dismiss Geller and other psychics as showmen with no psychic powers [Weil, 1974; Randi, 1975, 1982; Gardner, 1981]. Obviously, a "trained observer" must be trained in the particular kind of observation he or she is conducting.

Many events happen without any scientific observer on the sidelines. If each sea monster broke water before a panel of ichthyologists, and each revolution were staged before a team of visiting sociologists, our knowledge would be far more complete. But for many phenomena the only reports we have are the casual impressions of untrained observers who happened to be there; these reports may be interesting and possibly useful, but must be interpreted most cautiously by scientists.

Scientific observations are made under controlled conditions. Laboratories are popular with scientists because they are handy places to control variables such as heat, light, air pressure, time intervals, or whatever is important. A *variable* is anything which varies from case to case. For example, people vary in height, weight, age, sex, race, religion, education, occupation, income, health, behavior characteristics, and many other things.

We have a scientific experiment when we *control all important variables except one*, then see what happens when that one is varied. Unless all variables except one have been controlled, we cannot be sure which variable has produced the results. If we wish to study, say, the effects of phosphates on plant growth, all other factors—seed, soil, water, sunlight, temperature, humidity—must be the same for all the sample plots; then the varying amounts of phosphates on different test plots can be held responsible for different growth rates. This is the basic technique in all scientific experimentation—allow one variable to vary while holding all other variables constant.

There are complicated statistical procedures for *multivariate analysis* which enable the re-searcher to work with two or more variables at a time. But this is only a refinement of the basic procedure of holding all other variables constant in order to measure the impact of the one (or more) under study.

Failure to control all variables is a most common error in scientific method and accounts for most false conclusions. For example, a number of studies several decades ago concluded that the employment of mothers increased child delinquency. But these studies failed to control for the variables of social class and family composition. A sample of working mothers who were mostly poor, uneducated, often widowed or separated, and living in wretched neighborhoods, was compared with a sample of nonworking mothers who were more prosperous, better educated, and living with their husbands in good neighborhoods. No wonder they found strong association between maternal employment and child delinquency which more recent research does not fully confirm (See Chapter 10). Failure to control some variable—social class, education, age, and occupation are common ones—has invalidated many research studies.

Since laboratories are such convenient places to control the conditions of observation, scientists use them whenever possible. But much that is important cannot be dragged into a laboratory. Volcanoes and earthquakes can-

Spiritualists can conduct a very convincing seance in their own stage setting.

not be staged in a test tube, nor can we study the courtship process very realistically by herding couples into a laboratory. Both physical and social scientists frequently must observe phenomena in their natural setting. Techniques may range from lowering a bathysphere to the ocean floor to giving a questionnaire to a group of army recruits. If we remember that the basic scientific procedure is the conducting of accurate observations, while laboratories, instruments, and computers are merely *tools* of observation, this difference in technique will not confuse us.

The scientific critic will trust a reported observation only insofar as the conditions of observation have been controlled. On this basis scientists are skeptical of the claims of spiritualism and mind reading. Spiritualists can conduct a very convincing séance in their own stage setting but are loath to attempt a séance where the room, furnishings, and lighting are controlled by the scientist. The professional mind reader is very convincing in a theater setting but is unwilling to attempt a reading under scientifically controlled conditions. Until spiritualists and mind readers make demonstrations under conditions which preclude the possibility of deception, scientists should dismiss them as either entertainers or frauds.

Is it not strange that most of those who claim to foresee the future are performing in shabby carnivals and nightclubs instead of raking in millions in Wall Street? Why has no professed mind reader ever won a world chess or bridge championship? Although there are occasional newspaper reports of some psychic having "solved" a crime, is it not significant that police departments and intelligence agencies do not routinely employ psychic detectives? Although many exposés of the tricks of psychics, mentalists, fortune tellers, astrologers, and spiritualists have been published [Barber and Meeker, 1974; Abell and Singer, 1981], their popular following today

seems greater than at any time in recent history.[1]

In these several respects, then, scientific observation differs from looking at things. We spend our lives looking at things, and this activity brings us much information, many impressions, and numerous conclusions. But these conclusions are clouded by accident of coincidence, by selective memory, and by personal bias. Therefore, before accepting any generalization as true, the critical observer wants to know what it is based upon. Is a conclusion based upon a systematically collected body of scientific evidence, or is it an offhand reaction to haphazard observation?

THE SCIENTIFIC METHOD OF INVESTIGATION

The scientific method (some would prefer to say scientific methods) includes a great deal. The scientist must accumulate considerable background information on the problem. Then he or she formulates a *hypothesis*. This is a carefully considered theoretical statement which seeks to relate all the *known* facts to one another in a logical manner. The hypothesis is then tested by scientific research. For example, the hypothesis that cancer is a virus disease is based upon a great deal of observation; it relates known facts in a logical manner, and is now being tested through many research projects. Eventually a hypothesis is confirmed, rejected, or revised, and in this manner a science grows.

There are several steps in scientific research. They are easy to list but not always easy to follow:

---

[1] An academic journal, *The Skeptical Inquirer*, founded by the Committee for the Scientific Investigation of Claims of the Paranormal (Box 29, Kensington Station, Buffalo, N.Y. 14215), accepts articles which either attack or defend astrology, psychic phenomena, and other exotic belief systems. Since it accepts only articles which meet acceptable scientific standards of evidence and logic, most of its articles are critical rather than supportive.

Sociologists may observe social events as they are taking place.
(*United Press International*)

1 *Define the problem.* We need a problem which is worth study and which can be studied through the methods of science.

2 *Review the literature.* It would be a waste of time to repeat the errors of other research scholars. A survey of whatever research has been done on this problem is in order.

3 *Formulate the hypotheses.* Develop one or more formal propositions which can be tested.

4 *Plan the research design,* outlining just what is to be studied, what data will be sought, and where and how they will be collected, processed, and analyzed.

5 *Collect the data* in accordance with the research design. Often it will be necessary to change the design to meet some unforeseen difficulty.

6 *Analyze the data.* Classify, tabulate, and compare the data, making whatever tests and computations are necessary to help find the results.

7 *Draw conclusions.* Was the original hypothesis confirmed or rejected? Or were the results inconclusive? What has this research added to our knowledge? What implications has it for sociological theory? What new questions and suggestions for further research have arisen from this investigation?

8 *Replicate the study.* The seven steps above complete a single research study, but research findings are confirmed by replication. When another scholar repeats the study, using a different sample, the original findings may or may not be confirmed. Only after several confirmations, and no disconfirmations, can a research conclusion be accepted as generally true.

A Research Exercise

Let us see how a research study might be designed and completed. First, we need a

AN EXAMPLE OF A REPLICATION STUDY

Recent research by Phillips suggested that publicized suicide stories triggered a rise in suicides, some of which were disguised as motor vehicle fatalities (MVF). The most striking finding of his research was a 31% jump in California MVF on the third day after publicized suicide stories. Yet, until they are replicated, we do not know whether these results are limited to: (1) California, (2) the time period studied (1966–73), or (3) the method of analysis used. In this research note we replicate Phillips's California analysis with Detroit metropolitan data for 1973–76. We use two different statistical techniques to insure that Phillips's findings are not an artifact of his method of analysis. We find a 35%–40% increase in Detroit MVF on the third day after the publicized suicide story. Our replication suggests that Phillips's most striking result—the third-day peak in MVF—is not limited to a particular geographic region, time period, or technique of analysis.

This is a research *abstract,* a very condensed summary of a research study which immediately precedes the full article in many research journals. This one preceded Kenneth A. Bollen and David P. Phillips, "Suicidal Motor Vehicle Fatalities in Detroit: A Replication," *American Journal of Sociology,* 87:404–412, September 1981. Copyright © by the University of Chicago. Reprinted by permission of the *American Journal of Sociology* and the author.

research problem. How about, "Does the commuting student miss much by not being on campus?"

As stated, this question covers too many topics. We need something more limited and more specific. How about, "Do commuting students suffer academically by not living on or near campus?"

The review of the literature, the second step, may turn up very little, but the card catalog and the relevant indexes should be checked. For this question the *Education Index, Social Science Index,* index to the *Chronicle of Higher Education,* and possibly the *New York Times Index* would be good prospects, also *Sociological Abstracts.* Every possible heading should be checked, such as higher education, colleges and universities, college students—housing, academic progress, and any others that turn up as likely subheadings. This search of the literature is extremely important.

The third step is to formulate one or more hypotheses. One might be, "Commuting undergraduate students receive lower grades than undergraduate students living on campus" or "living off but within one mile of the campus." Other hypotheses might be that commuting students "earn fewer credit hours per year," or "take part in fewer college activities," or "have fewer friends among other students."

Planning the research design is the fourth step. All terms and categories must be designed. The variables to be controlled must be decided. We must be sure that the two groups we compare are similar in all important respects except residence. We must select sources of data, kinds of data sought, and procedures for collecting and processing them. If a research grant is to be sought, all this information must be included in the grant application.

The fifth step, the actual collecting and processing of data according to the research design, is often the most exciting part of the project. In this instance the data on each person would be made "computer sensible" (prepared for computer processing) and fed through the computer, which is programmed to make the desired computations and comparisons.

The sixth step is to analyze the data. What contrasts between the two groups appear on the printout? Often, during this stage, some unexpected surprises will suggest additional hypotheses, and the data will be fed through

Personal interviews are one kind of sociological data. (*Teri Leigh Stratford/Photo Researchers, Inc.*)

the computer again for additional computations.

The seventh step is the drawing of conclusions. Were the hypotheses confirmed or disconfirmed? What further study is suggested by this research? What difference does it all make? Finally, other scientists will undertake replication studies.

This basic procedure is the same for all scientific research. Techniques used will vary according to the problem studied, but the same basic method is central to all sciences.

Not all research involves this formal model of hypothesis framing and testing. Some research involves analysis of data already collected, and some involves library research of published sources. But anything involving the careful, objective collecting of verifiable evidence in the search for knowledge is scientific research.

NORMATIVE METHODS OF INVESTIGATION

The term *normative* means "conforming to or supporting some norm or pattern." The scientific method of investigation consists of stating a question, collecting evidence, and drawing conclusions from the evidence, however surprising or unwelcome they may be. The normative method, by contrast, states the question in such a way that the conclusion is implied, and then looks for evidence in support of this conclusion. This is the method of "investigation" which most people use most of the time, and which even scientists sometimes fall into. For example, the question, "How does the traditional family thwart emotional growth?" (or, conversely, "How does the traditional family promote emotional growth?") really states a conclusion and asks for evidence to support it. Most popular thinking and a good deal of scientific research is normative, for it is a search for evidence to support a conclusion already assumed. Much Marxian scholarship is normative, for it begins with the conclusion that class oppression is the cause of most social ills. Much conservative scholarship is equally normative, for it begins with the conclusion that most social ills stem from the personal defects and failings

No crank wants, or will accept, an honest criticism of anything. He has solved the "problem," whatever it is, and is looking for an endorsement. . . . Whatever else cranks may be up to, after one deals with several it becomes clear that they are not really interested in doing science. They are not prepared to accept the rough-and-tumble of scientific criticism; any criticism is regarded as provocation and a threat.

(Jeremy Bernstein, "Scientific Cranks: How to Recognize One and What to Do Until the Doctor Arrives," *American Scholar*, 47:13, Winter 1977–1978.)

Studies of twins are one way of separating what is inherited from what is
learned. (*Rita Freed/Nancy Palmer Photo Agency*)

of the individuals involved, and the actual
"research" consists of an effort to identify
these failings. The findings of normative research are not necessarily "wrong," but they
are always incomplete, because the researcher
looks for only the kinds of evidence which
support the preconceived conclusion.

SOCIOLOGY AS A SCIENCE

A science may be defined in at least two ways:
(1) a science is a body of organized, verified

knowledge which has been secured through
scientific investigation; (2) a science is a method
of study whereby a body of organized, verified knowledge is discovered. These are, of
course, two ways of saying much the same
thing.

If the first definition is accepted, then sociology is a science *to the extent that it develops
a body of organized, verified knowledge* which is
based on scientific investigation. To the extent
that sociology forsakes myth, folklore, and
wishful thinking and bases its conclusions on
scientific evidence, it is a science. If science

is defined as a method of study, then sociology is a science *to the extent that it uses scientific methods of study.* All natural phenomena can be studied scientifically, if one is willing to use scientific methods. Any kind of behavior—whether of atoms, animals, or adolescents—is a proper field for scientific study.

During human history, few of our actions have been based on verified knowledge, for people through the ages have been guided mainly by folklore, habit, and guesswork. Until a few centuries ago, very few people accepted the idea that we should find out about the natural world by systematic observation of the natural world itself, rather than by consulting oracles, ancestors, or intuition. This new idea created the modern world. A few decades ago we began acting on the assumption that this same approach might also give useful knowledge about human social life. Just how far we have replaced folklore with knowledge in this area will be explored in the chapters which follow.

THE DEVELOPMENT OF SOCIOLOGY

Sociology is the youngest of the recognized social sciences. Auguste Comte in France coined the word "sociology" in his *Positive Philosophy,* published in 1838. He believed that a science of sociology should be based on systematic observation and classification, not on authority and speculation. This was a relatively new idea at that time. Herbert Spencer in England published his *Principles of Sociology* in 1876. He applied the theory of organic evolution to human society and developed a grand theory of "social evolution" which was widely accepted for several decades. Lester F. Ward, an American, published his *Dynamic Sociology* in 1883, calling for social progress through intelligent social action which sociologists should guide. All these founders of sociology were basically social philoso-

phers. They proclaimed that sociologists should collect, organize, and classify factual data, and derive sound social theories from these facts, but very often their own method was to think out a grand system of theory and then seek facts to support it. So while they called for scientific investigation, they did relatively little of it themselves. Yet they took the necessary first steps, for the *idea* of a science of sociology had to precede the building of one.

A Frenchman, Émile Durkheim, gave the most notable early demonstration of scientific methodology in sociology. In his *Rules of Sociological Method,* published in 1895, he outlined the methodology which he pursued in his study *Suicide,* published in 1897. Instead of *speculating* upon the causes of suicide, he first planned his research design, and then collected a large mass of data on the characteristics of people who commit suicide, and then derived a theory of suicide from these data.

Courses in sociology appeared in many universities in the 1890s. The *American Journal of Sociology* began publication in 1895, and the American Sociological Society (now the American Sociological Association) was organized in 1905. Whereas most of the early European sociologists came from the fields of history, political economy, or philosophy, many of the early American sociologists had been social workers, ministers, or ministers' sons; and nearly all were from rural backgrounds. Urbanization and industrialization were creating grave social problems, and these early sociologists were groping for "scientific" solutions. They saw sociology as a scientific guide to social progress. The early volumes of the *American Journal of Sociology* contained relatively few articles devoted to scientific description or research but carried many sermons filled with exhortation and advice. For example, a fairly typical article in 1903, "The Social Effects of the Eight Hour Day," contains no factual or experimental data but is entirely devoted to a recital of all the social benefits which the writer assures us will follow from the shorter working day [McVay, 1903]. But by the 1930s the several sociological journals were well filled with research articles and scientific descriptions. Sociology was becoming a body of scientific knowledge, with its theories based upon scientific observation rather than upon armchair speculation or impressionistic observation.

PERSPECTIVES IN SOCIOLOGY

In order to study anything, one must begin by making some assumptions about the nature of what is studied. For example, the ancient Greeks believed that the universe was run according to the whims of the gods. By contrast, all scientists assume that the universe is orderly, and operates in certain regular ways which we may be able to discover. Thus, Newton developed the laws of gravity after observing that apples always fall down, never up. A working set of assumptions is called a "perspective," an "approach," or sometimes a "paradigm." What are some of the perspectives used in sociology?

The Evolutionary Perspective

The evolutionary perspective is the earliest theoretical perspective in sociology. Based on the work of August Comte (1798–1857) and Herbert Spencer (1820–1903), it seemed to offer a satisfying explanation of how human societies originate and grow. After a few decades it fell from favor, and is now once again becoming fashionable.

Sociologists using the evolutionary perspective look for patterns of change and development appearing in different societies, to see whether any general sequences can be found. They might wonder, for example, whether Chinese Communism will develop in the same way as Russian Communism, which gained power three decades earlier, or whether industrialization will have the same

effects upon the family in developing countries that it seems to have had in Western nations. While not the major perspective in sociology, the evolutionary perspective is an active one.

The Interactionist Perspective

The interactionist perspective suggests no grand theories of society, since "society," "the state," and "social institutions" are conceptual abstractions, while only people and their interaction can be studied directly.

Symbolic interactionists such as G. H. Mead (1863–1931) and C. H. Cooley (1846–1929) concentrate upon this interaction between individuals and groups. They note that people interact mainly through *symbols*, which include signs, gestures, and most importantly, through written and spoken words. A word has no inherent meaning. It is simply a noise, but it becomes a *word* when people reach agreement that this noise carries a special meaning. Thus "yes," "no," "go," "come," and thousands of other sounds became symbols as a meaning is attached to each. Although some meanings can be exchanged without words, as all lovers know, most meanings are exchanged through spoken or written words.

People do not respond to the world directly; they respond to meanings they impute to the things and happenings around them: a traffic light, a lineup at a ticket window, a police officer's whistle and hand signal. An early sociologist, W. I. Thomas (1863–1947), coined the phrase, *definition of the situation*, noting that we can act sensibly only after we decide what kind of situation it is [Thomas, 1937, p. 9]. If a man approaches with right hand extended, we define this as a friendly greeting; if he approaches with clenched fists, we define the situation differently. The person who misdefines situations and tries to run when he should make love, or vice versa, is a stock comic figure. But in real life, failure to define behavior situations correctly and make appropriate responses can have unhappy consequences.

As Berger and Luckmann state in their *Social Construction of Reality* [1966], society is an *objective reality,* in that people, groups, and institutions are *real,* regardless of our perceptions of them. But society is also a *subjective reality,* in that for each person, the other persons, groups, and institutions are whatever that person perceives them as being. Whether most people are pretty nice or pretty nasty, whether the police are protectors or oppressors, whether corporations serve common interests or selfish interests—these are perceptions which persons form from their own experiences, and these perceptions become "the way it is" for persons holding them.

Modern interactionists such as Erving Goffman [1959] and Herbert Blumer [1962] emphasize that people do not respond to other people directly; instead, they respond to whatever they *imagine* other people to be. In human behavior, "reality" is not something that is just "out there" like the curbs and sidewalks along the street; "reality" is constructed in peoples' minds as they size one another up and guess at the feelings and impulses of one another. Whether a person is a friend, an enemy, or a stranger is not a characteristic of the person; that person is, to me, whatever I perceive him as being, at least until I change my perception. Whether he is good or bad is measured by my perception of him. Thus, I create reality about him in my own mind, and then I react to this reality that I have constructed. This "social construction of reality" proceeds continuously as people define the feelings and intentions of others. Thus the "people" with whom we interact are, to some extent, creatures of our own imagination. Whenever two groups, such as workers and management, arrive at sets of firmly held opinions about each other, such a "social construction of reality" has taken place. In like manner, situations are defined by us, and become part of the "reality" to

which we respond. Whether a new rule is a protection or an oppression is measured by our definition of it.

This does not mean that *all* reality is subjective—that it exists *only* in the mind. There *are* objective facts in the universe. The sun, moon, and stars are real, and still would be "out there" even if there were no humans to see them. Human beings are real; they get born and they die; they take actions which have consequences. But a fact has no meaning of itself. *Meanings* are given to facts and to human actions by human beings. The symbolic interactionist perspective concentrates upon what meanings people find in other people's actions, how these meanings are derived, and how others respond to them. The interactionist perspective has brought a great deal of insight into personality development and human behavior. It has been less helpful in the study of large groups and social institutions.

The Functionalist Perspective

In this perspective a society is seen as an organized network of cooperating groups operating in a fairly orderly manner according to a set of rules and values shared by most members. Society is seen as a stable system with a tendency toward equilibrium, that is, a tendency to maintain a balanced, harmoniously operating system.

In the functionalist perspective, with Talcott Parsons [1937], Kingsley Davis [1937], and Robert Merton [1957] as the most prominent spokesmen, each group or institution fulfills certain functions and persists because it is *functional.* Thus, the school educates children, prepares workers, takes children off their parents' hands for part of the day, and provides spectator sports events for the community, among other things.

Behavior patterns arise because they are functionally useful. On the American frontier, where there were few inns and fewer people with money for them, a hospitality pattern developed. The traveling family were welcome guests of the nearest settlers wherever night fell upon them. The travelers brought news and a break in monotony; the host provided food and shelter. As the frontier became settled, the hospitality pattern became unnecessary and it declined. Thus patterns arise to meet needs and pass when the needs change.

Social change disrupts the stable equilibrium of the society, but before long a new equilibrium is regained. For example, large families were desired throughout most of history. Death rates were high, and large families helped to ensure some survivors. Especially in America, with a continent to fill, and with never enough hands to do the work, large families were functionally useful. They provided workers, companionship, and old-age security and were good for both the individual and the society. Today, in a crowded world with a lower death rate, large families are no longer a blessing. In other words, large families have become dysfunctional and threaten the welfare of the society. So a new equilibrium is approaching in which, instead of high death rates and high birth rates, we shall (hopefully) have low death rates and low birth rates. Thus, a value or practice which is functional at one time or place may become dysfunctional—interfering with the smooth operation of society—at another time or place.

If a particular social change promotes a harmonious equilibrium, it is seen as functional; if it disrupts the equilibrium, it is dysfunctional; if it has no effects, it is nonfunctional. In a democracy political parties are functional while bombings, assassinations, and political terrorism are dysfunctional, and changes in political vocabulary or party insignia are nonfunctional.

Functionalists ask such questions as, "How does this value, practice, or institution help meet the needs of the society?" "How does it fit in with the other practices and institutions of the society?" "Would a proposed change make it more or less useful to the society?"

The Conflict Perspective

Although it stems from the work of many scholars, the conflict perspective is most directly based upon the work of Karl Marx (1818–1883), who saw class conflict and class exploitation as the prime moving forces in history. Largely ignored by sociologists for many years, the conflict perspective has recently been revived by C. Wright Mills [1956, 1959], Lewis Coser [1956], and others [Aron, 1957; Dahrendorf, 1959, 1964; Chambliss, 1973; Collins, 1975]. Where functionalists see the normal state of society as one of stable equilibrium, conflict theorists see society as in a continuous state of conflict between groups and classes. Although Marx concentrated upon conflict between classes for ownership of productive wealth, modern conflict theorists take a less narrow view. They see the struggle for power and income as a continuous process but one in which many categories of people appear as opponents—classes, races, nationalities, and even the sexes.

Conflict theorists see a society as held together through the power of dominant groups or classes. They claim that the "shared values" which functionalists see as the glue holding society together do not really form a true consensus; instead this is an artificial consensus in which the dominant groups or classes impose their values and rules upon the rest of the people. According to conflict theorists, functionalists fail to ask the question, "functionally useful to *whom?*" Conflict theorists accuse functionalists of a conservative bias, in that functionalists assume that this "harmonious equilibrium" is beneficial to everyone, whereas it benefits some and penalizes others. Conflict theorists see the harmonious equilibrium of society as an illusion held by those who fail to see how the dominant groups have silenced those whom they exploit.

TABLE 1-1
TWO MAJOR PERSPECTIVES IN SOCIOLOGY

Perception of:	Functionalist theory	Conflict theory
Society	A stable system of cooperating groups.	An unstable system of opposing groups and classes.
Social class	A status level of persons sharing similar incomes and life-styles. Develops from different roles persons and groups fill.	A group of people sharing similar economic interests and power needs. Develops from the success of some in exploiting others.
Social inequality	Inevitable in complex societies. Due largely to different contributions of different groups.	Unnecessary and unjust. Due largely to power differences. Avoidable through socialist reordering of society.
Social change	Arises from changing functional needs of society.	Imposed by one class upon another in its own interest.
Social order	An unconscious product of people's efforts to organize their activities productively.	Produced and maintained by organized coercion by the dominant classes.
Values	Consensus on values unites the society.	Conflicting interests divide society. Illusion of value consensus maintained by dominant classes.
Social institutions: churches, schools, mass media	Cultivate common values and loyalties which unite society.	Cultivate values and loyalties which protect the privileged.
Law and government	Enforce rules reflecting value consensus of the society.	Enforce rules imposed by dominant classes to protect their privileges.

Conflict theorists ask such questions as, "How have the present patterns emerged from the contest between conflicting groups, each seeking its own advantage? "How do the dominant groups and classes achieve and maintain their position of privilege?" "How do they manipulate the institutions of society (schools, churches, mass media) to protect their privileges?" "Who benefits and who suffers from the present social arrangements?" "How can society be made more just and humane?"

Comparison of the Perspectives

Which is the best perspective? This question cannot be answered, for none is "right" or "wrong," but each is a different way of looking at society. Just as international relations can be viewed either as a state of war interrupted by intervals of peace or as a state of peace interrupted by intervals of war, so society may be viewed either as a condition of cooperation containing elements of conflict or as a condition of conflict containing elements of cooperation. Thus each perspective views society from a different vantage point, asks different questions, and reaches different conclusions. Evolutionists focus upon the similarities in changing societies; interactionists focus upon the actual social behavior of persons and groups; functionalists focus more heavily upon value consensus, order, and stability; conflict theorists focus more heavily upon inequality, tension, and change. For example, in the study of class inequality, evolutionists look at the historical development of class inequalities in different societies; interactionists study how classes are defined and how people perceive and treat members of their own class and of other classes; functionalists note how class inequality operates in all societies to distribute tasks and rewards and to keep the system operating; conflict theorists focus upon how class inequality is imposed and maintained by dominant classes

DISORDER AT CEREBELLUM UNIVERSITY

Last week a faculty-administration committee, without any consultation with students, issued a new set of grading procedures. After several days of grumbling, an angry mass of students gathered yesterday on the commons, surged into the administration building, ushered out the president, deans, and other officers, told the secretarial staff to take a holiday, and barricaded the doors. The police were called and . . .

How to study this social event from—

The evolutionary perspective:

What is the history of student-administration confrontations?

What established patterns, if any, does this follow?

How is this event an outgrowth of earlier situations?

The interactionist perspective:

How do rules get made and changed?

Who gets the authority to change the rules, and how?

How do the "good guys" and the "bad guys" in this confrontation get named?

How did tension build, and what roles were played as the confrontation spirit developed?

The functionalist perspective:

What are the reasons for this policy change?

What purposes might it serve for the university? For the students?

What purposes does this confrontation serve for the student activists?

What will be the effects of this confrontation?

The conflict perspective:

Why was student input not invited before this policy change?

Who benefits and who is penalized by this policy change?

Why do faculty and administration want this change, and why do students oppose it?

for their own advantage and at the expense of the less privileged.

For most topics of study, there are some aspects for which each of the perspectives can be useful. For example, consider the development of the modern university. The evolutionary perspective might focus upon the procession of scholarly needs and arrangements, extending over several thousand years, which eventually led to the development of the modern university. The interactionist perspective would note the ways in which scholarly needs have been defined at different times and the ways in which persons and groups dealt with one another in creating the university. The functionalist perspective would concentrate upon what changes made universities seem to be necessary, what purposes they fulfilled for the society, and what effects universities have upon their students and upon societies. The conflict perspective would concentrate upon which groups and classes benefit from the university and how access to higher education operates to preserve the position of the privileged groups. For some problems, one perspective may be more useful than another. The development of the hospitality pattern, mentioned earlier, is neatly described in terms of the functionalist perspective as a custom which arose to meet a special need at a special time and place. The conflict perspective is not very helpful in understanding the rise and decline of the hospitality pattern, but the rise of labor unions (to advance workers' interests against those of management) is nicely analyzed within the conflict perspective.

There are many other perspectives in sociology—resource theory, systems theory, social learning theory, exchange theory, phenomenology, ethnomethodology, and others—but to inflict all of them upon introductory sociology students might convince them that they were in the wrong course! On some topics, different perspectives are so sharply opposed to each other that they cannot possibly be reconciled. On social class and social inequality, for example, the functionalist and conflict perspectives flatly contradict each other about the sources of inequality and the possibilities of attaining social equality. Conflict theorists emphatically deny much of what functionalists say about inequality, and vice versa (as shown in Chapter 14).

More often, however, the different perspectives are complementary, with one pointing out what another slights or ignores. The different perspectives overlap, and all are used by most sociologists but in different mixtures. Thus, no functionalist denies the reality of class exploitation, and no conflict theorist argues that *all* the interests of rich and poor are opposed (e.g., pure drinking water and clean air are good for both). These are differences in emphasis, and most sociologists would refuse to be classified under any of these labels. Many sociologists, however, have their favorite perspectives, upon which they rely most heavily. But all perspectives are useful and necessary for a complete understanding of society.

SOME STUDY SUGGESTIONS

A common complaint of sociology students is, "I read the book and I know the material, but I can't seem to figure out the tests." Naturally enough, students who have studied are puzzled and frustrated when their test scores do not reflect what they feel they have learned. Why does this happen?

The textbook material in an introductory sociology course is not entirely unfamiliar and reads quite easily. The student can read through a chapter without finding anything that seems hard to understand. At the end, having found nothing very difficult, the student lays the book aside, feeling this assignment is finished.

Because the material *is* often familiar and not difficult to read, a student may have the illusion of having fully understood the assignment but have only a vague idea of the meaning of the concepts presented. Each paragraph has one or more main ideas, together with illustrative material intended to explain and clarify them. For example, turn back to the section on "Social Science and Common Sense" at the beginning of this chapter. This section contains only one major idea: Common sense includes both folk wisdom and folk nonsense, and scientists try to tell us which is which. All the rest is illustration and explanation.

The student should underline and remember the main ideas and concepts, not the illustrative material. After reading a paragraph, it is a useful habit to raise one's eyes and ask, "What must I remember from that paragraph?" If nothing very clear can be recited, the paragraph needs to be studied again. After reading a section, look at the heading again and try another recitation for the complete section. Again, if one cannot give in one's own words a decent summary of the section, it has not really been "studied" enough.

Many students have trouble with tables, graphs, and figures. The secret in understanding them is to read everything around the edges before studying the body of the figure. For example, look at Figure 13-1 on p. 319. First, read the title, "Total Federal, State and Local Government Spending as Percent of GNP" (gross national product). Read the

"Source" credit at the bottom, which is often followed by some explanatory notes. Check the vertical axis showing percentages, and the horizontal axis showing dates. After reading this, study the main body of the figure. What conclusions can you now draw? Most figures are not difficult if one simply takes time enough to study all the edges of the figure first.

Additional study suggestions are given at the opening of the *Study Guide and Source Book to Accompany Horton and Hunt, Sociology* (which is generally available in the bookstores handling this textbook).

SUMMARY

Sociology is the scientific study of human social life. Today science is replacing common sense as a source of dependable knowledge about human behavior. All science is based on *verifiable evidence*. The basic technique of scientific investigation is *observation*. Scientific observation differs from just looking at things in that scientific observation is: (1) *accurate,* seeking to describe what really exists; (2) as *precise* and exact as necessary; (3) *systematic,* in an effort to find all the relevant data; (4) *recorded* in complete detail as quickly as possible; (5) *objective,* in being as free from distortion by vested interest, bias, or wishful thinking as is humanly possible; (6) *conducted by trained observers,* who know what to look for and how to recognize it; (7) *conducted under controlled conditions* which reduce the danger of fraud, self-deception, or mistaken interpretation. The steps in a scientific research project are: (1) define the problem, (2) review the literature, (3) formulate the hypotheses, (4) plan the research design, (5) collect the data, (6) analyze the data, (7) draw conclusions, and (8) replicate the study. Remember that before the conclusions can be accepted as established, *replication,* in which these conclusions are confirmed by repeated research, is needed. While the scientific method proceeds from evidence to conclusion, the popularly used *normative* method starts with a conclusion and hunts for evidence to support it.

Whether the study of our social relationships is a science is often debated. Sociology is a very new discipline, recently emerged from the speculations of nineteenth-century social philosophers and social reformers. To the extent that human social life is studied through scientific methods so that a body of verified knowledge is developed, these studies become social sciences.

Several perspectives are used in sociology. Each views society from a different outlook. The *evolutionary perspective* concentrates upon the sequences through which changing societies pass; the *interactionist perspective* focuses on actual day-to-day communication and behavior of persons and groups; the *functionalist perspective* sees society as an interrelated system in which each group plays a part and each practice helps the system to operate; the *conflict perspective* sees continuous tension and group struggles as the normal condition of society, with stability and value consensus being carefully contrived illusions which protect privileged groups. Each perspective is used, to some degree, by most sociologists, and is needed for a full understanding of society.

GLOSSARY

conflict perspective the view that society is in a continuous state of conflict between groups and classes, and tends toward dissent, tension, and change.

evolutionary perspective the view that different societies show many similarities in their development.

functionalist perspective the view that society is an organized network of cooperating groups tending toward consensus and stability.

hypothesis a tentative, unverified statement of the possible relationship between known facts; a reasonable proposition worthy of scientific testing.

interactionist perspective the view of society that concentrates upon interaction between persons and groups.

normative investigation research which seeks to confirm a conclusion already held.

objectivity the quality of observing and accepting facts as they are, not as one might wish them to be.

replication repetition of studies by other researchers to confirm findings.

science a body of organized, verified knowledge; a set of methods whereby a body of verified knowledge is obtained.

sociology the scientific study of human social life.

variable anything which varies from case to case, such as age, sex, and education among human beings.

verifiable evidence factual observations which other trained observers can see, weigh, count, and check for accuracy.

QUESTIONS AND PROJECTS

1   What is the difference between sociology and plain old-fashioned common sense?

2   Can scientists prove that ghosts and spirits do not exist or that fortune telling and mind reading do not work? Why are scientists so skeptical?

3   Suppose a supervisor says, "I've hired all kinds of workers, and school dropouts don't work out as well as high school graduates." What would be necessary for this statement to be a scientifically justified conclusion?

4   Suppose you were a reporter for the campus paper, writing a news account of a violent confrontation between students and police. Should you try to write it with strict objectivity, or should you "slant" it, using polemical language and omitting certain facts while emphasizing others in order to support the side you felt to be morally right?

5   What proportion of the general statements made in the course of an evening's conversation are based upon informal recollection and what proportion make reference to some systematic, recorded observations? Test your estimate by keeping count of each in a conversational group.

6   Read Sinclair Lewis's novel *Arrowsmith*. What are some of the difficulties Martin had to meet in becoming rigorously scientific?

7   Why do you think a pseudoscience such as astrology, which has repeatedly been shown to have no predictive value, has so large a following, even among well-educated people?

8   Books of unscientific sensationalism, such as Charles Berlitz's *The Bermuda Triangle*, often become bestsellers, while competent debunking books, such as Lawrence Kusche's *The Bermuda Triangle Mystery— Solved* (New York, Warner Books, 1975) sell poorly. Why?

9   Write three statements of some event or issue, one written as a neutral observer, another as a supporter, and the third as an opponent.

10   Formulate some testable hypothesis such as, "Male students collect more parking tickets on campus than female students," or, "Entrance examination scores are not predictive of college graduation." Outline the research design, showing data to be sought and variables to be controlled.

SUGGESTED READINGS

Bell, Colin, and Howard Newby: *Doing Sociological Research*, The Free Press, New York, 1977. Two British sociologists tell what actually happens in social research, including value clashes, government interference, and problems of sampling at a time of racial unrest.

Blume, Stuart S.: *Toward a Political Sociology of Science*, The Free Press, New York, 1974. A discussion of how science is influenced by politics and of how science may be used in making political decisions.

*Chase, Stuart, with Edmund de S. Brunner: *The Proper Study of Mankind; An Inquiry Into the Science of Human Relations*, 2d ed., Harper & Row, Publishers, Inc., New York, 1962. A highly readable little book on the contribution of social science to the solution of human problems.

*Cuff, E. C., and G. C. F. Payne (eds.): *Perspectives in Sociology*, George Allen & Unwin, Ltd., London, 1979. Presents the major perspectives used in sociology. For the advanced student.

*Gardner, Martin: *Science: Good, Bad and Bogus*, Prometheus Books, Buffalo, N.Y., 1981. A readable, entertaining book showing the differences between science and pseudoscience.

Homans, George E.: *The Nature of Social Science*, Harcourt, Brace & World, Inc., New York, 1967. A brief philosophical discussion of what social science is all about.

*Inkeles, Alex: *What is Sociology: An Introduction to the Discipline and the Profession*, Prentice-Hall, Inc., Englewood Cliffs, N.J., 1964. A brief description of what sociology is and what sociologists do.

Reiser, Martin et al.: "An Evaluation of the Use of Psychics in the Investigation of Major Crime," *Journal of Police Science and Administration*, 7:18–25, March 1979. A research study finding that psychics are useless in crime detection.

Wilson, Everett K, and Hanan Selvin: *Why Study Sociology? A Note to Undergraduates*, Wadsworth Publishing Company, Inc., Belmont, Cal., 1980. A brief pamphlet explaining what sociology is and what it is good for.

Following is a series of readable books, some of which are accounts of frauds and hoaxes, and others of which are critical appraisals of cultist ideas and theories:

Milbourne Christopher, *Mediums, Mystics and the Occult*; *L. Sprague DeCamp and Catherine C. DeCamp, *The Ancient Engineers*; *Barrows Dunham, *Man Against Myth*; *Bergen Evans, *The Natural History of Nonsense*; Christopher Evans, *Cults of Unreason*; *Martin Gardner, *Fads and Fallacies in the Name of Science*; *C. E. Hansel, *ESP: A Scientific Evaluation*; Harry Houdini, *Miracle Mongers and Their Methods*; Joseph Jastrow, *Error and Eccentricity in Human Belief*; *Philip J. Klass, *UFOs Explained*; *Lawrence D. Kusche, *The Bermuda Triangle—Solved*; *Curtis D. MacDougall, *Hoaxes*; Norman Moss, *The Pleasures of Deception*; *The Amazing Randi (James A. Randi), *The Magic of Uri Geller*; D. Scott Rogo, *In Search of the Unknown: The Odyssey of a Psychic Investigator*; Robert Silverberg, *Scientists and Scoundrels: A Book of Hoaxes*; *Barry Thiering and Edgar Castel (eds.), *Some Trust in Chariots: Sixteen Views on Erich von Däniken's Chariots of the Gods*; any issue of *The Skeptical Inquirer*, quarterly journal published by the Committee for the Scientific Investigation of Claims of the Paranormal.

* An asterisk before the citation indicates that the title is available in a paperback edition.

2 Fields and Methods of Sociology

As the recent spate of disaster movies such as *Earthquake* and *The Towering Inferno* underscore, we are fascinated with disasters. Social scientists and laymen alike, we always have been. And we have always been fascinated by questions that relate to our functioning in the midst of and in the aftermath of disasters. Do we panic? Run aimlessly? Help each other? Do we have the inner resources to cope with the disaster? Do outside resources (agencies) function adequately on our behalf? Is the cataclysmic event apt to scar us emotionally?

Since 1917, when Samuel H. Prince of Columbia University first applied social science methodology to the study of a mass calamity—a munitions ship explosion in Halifax Harbor, Nova Scotia, a horror that killed 1,600—a substantive body of disaster research that helps answer such questions has been accumulated. Nonetheless, because of problems inherent in disaster research— funding, reaching the impact area quickly, being accepted by the community and more— the picture of how we behave during and after disaster cannot even now be presented in completely satisfying detail.

(*Myron Brenton,* "Studies in the Aftermath," *Human Behavior,* May 1975, p. 56.)

Few scientists study more different things in more different ways than do sociologists. The sociologist may be digging through obscure census reports to see where the American people are moving, or studying a new social movement as a participant observer, or conducting an evaluation study to see whether an action program is working. Almost any kind of social phenomena is a fit subject for sociological research, providing proper scientific procedures are followed. How this is done is the subject of this chapter.

THE FIELD OF SOCIOLOGY

First of all, *forget whatever you have read about sociology in the popular magazines and newspapers*, for much of it is inaccurate. A magazine writer who wishes to make some offhand guesswork sound more impressive may preface it with the phrase, "Sociologists fear that . . .," "Sociologists are alarmed by . . .," or "Sociologists are wringing their hands over . . ." This journalistic device helps a writer to speak authoritatively without knowing very much about the subject. Some papers, such as *The New York Times*, or the *Wall Street Journal*, quote sociologists accurately most of the time. But as a general rule, any undocumented newspaper or magazine statements about what "sociologists think" should be dismissed as unreliable.

Careless use of the term "sociologist" is very common. Magazine and newspaper writers, social workers, labor leaders, government officials, social critics, or anyone else who is interested in social relations may be described as sociologists. This is incorrect. A sociologist is one who has earned advanced degrees or pursued other advanced studies in sociology (not in psychology, theology, social work, or some other field) and is engaged in teaching, research, or other professional work in the field of sociology.

No formal definition of sociology is very satisfactory. Short definitions do not really define; long definitions are cumbersome. Yet a definition of some sort is needed, and sociology is often defined as *the scientific study of human social life*. Human beings behave differently from other animals. They have unique forms of group life; they pursue customs, develop institutions, and create values. Sociology applies scientific methods to the study of these phenomena in the search for scientific knowledge.

Sociology concentrates its study upon the group life of human beings and the product of their group living. The sociologist is especially interested

Sociologists study group life. (*Barbara Pfeffer/Black Star*)

in customs, traditions, and values which emerge from group living, and in the way group living is, in turn, affected by these customs, traditions, and values. Sociology is interested in the way groups interact with one another and in the processes and institutions which they develop. Sociology is subdivided into many specialized fields, of which a partial list includes:

Applied Sociology
Collective Behavior
Community
Comparative Sociology
Crime and Delinquency
Cultural Sociology
Demography
Deviant Behavior
Formal and Complex Organizations
Human Ecology
Industrial Sociology
Law and Society

Leisure, Sports, Recreation, and the Arts
Marriage and the Family
Mathematical Sociology
Medical Sociology
Methodology and Statistics
Military Sociology
Political Sociology

Sociology is interested in the way groups interact with one another.

Race and Ethnic Relations
Rural Sociology
Social Change
Social Control
Social Organization
Social Psychology
Sociological Theory
Sociology of Education
Sociology of Knowledge and Science
Sociology of Occupations and Professions
Sociology of Religion
Sociology of Small Groups
Stratification and Mobility
Urban Sociology

These topics are not the exclusive property of sociology, for no discipline can stake out a field and post "keep out" signs around it. Sociology is only one of the social sciences. Other disciplines share its interest in many topics. For example, its interest in communication and public opinion is shared by psychology and political science; criminology is shared with psychology, political science, law and police science, and so on. Sociology is especially close to psychology and anthropology, and overlaps them so constantly that any firm boundaries would be arbitrary and unrealistic. The more we learn about human behavior, the more we realize that no one field of knowledge can fully explain it.

METHODS AND TECHNIQUES OF SOCIOLOGICAL RESEARCH

The methods of sociological research are basically those outlined in the preceding chapter and used by all scientists. As Karl Pearson has remarked, "The unity of all science consists alone in its method, not in its material. The man who classifies facts of any kind whatever, who sees their mutual relation and describes their sequences, is applying the scientific method and is a man of science" [1900, p. 12].

While scientific methods are basically alike

for all sciences, scientific *techniques* differ, for techniques are the particular ways in which scientific methods are applied to a particular problem. Each science must, therefore, develop a series of techniques which fits the body of material it studies. What are some of the techniques of sociological research?

Cross-sectional and Longitudinal Studies

Every study has some sort of time setting. A study which covers a broad area of observation at a single point in time is called a *cross-sectional* study. For example, Campbell, Converse, and Rodgers's study, *The Quality of*

Sociologists study the behavioral norms of different societies. How many norms are suggested by this picture? (*Ken Heyman*)

American Life [1976], reports interviews with a national sample of 2,700 households, inquiring as to their satisfactions and dissatisfactions. They found that married people are happier than single people, that prosperous people are happier than poor people, and made many other interesting observations.

If the study extends over time, describing a trend or making a series of before-and-after observations, it is called a *longitudinal* study. Thus, Levine and Meyer [1977] studied changes in black and white enrollment in Kansas City public schools between 1960 and 1974. They found that schools with a relatively small black enrollment (under 29 percent) were likely to "remain desegregated, while schools with a higher percentage of black students became almost totally resegregated" as a result of what has come to be known as "white flight."

The national public opinion polls (Gallup, Harris, and others) are cross-sectional studies, but if the same set of questions is repeated at intervals over a period of years, longitudinal comparisons can be drawn.

Longitudinal studies may be either *prospective* or *retrospective*. A retrospective study (often called an *ex post facto* study) works backward in time, using data that are already recorded. For example, Wynder and Evarts [1950] used hospital records of 605 lung cancer victims and found that all but eight were cigarette smokers. When a retrospective study shows strong evidence of a relationship between two facts, the next step often is to see whether a prospective study will confirm the relationship. A prospective study begins with the present and carries observations forward over a period of time. Thus Dorn [1959] and Kahn [1966] followed the health history of 200,000 veterans for eleven years, finding that the pack-a-day-or-more smokers were sixteen times as likely to die from lung cancer as were nonsmokers. Prospective studies take a long time to complete and are often very costly, making them one of the least common types of research study.

Sometimes longitudinal conclusions are drawn from cross-sectional studies. A cross-sectional study may show differences between age groups, and this is often interpreted as evidence of changing attitudes or behavior. For example, numerous studies have shown that young people are more permissive than older people about sex behavior and drug use. Does this mean that values are changing and that the values of today's youth will be everybody's values tomorrow? Or is this a life-cycle change, with the young growing more conservative as they grow older? A cross-sectional study will not tell this.

Longitudinal conclusions from cross-sectional studies are often dead wrong. For example, ever since "intelligence" testing began, cross-sectional comparisons have consistently shown that average IQ seems to peak in early adulthood and declines steadily thereafter. But these surveys were conducted during a period of steadily rising levels of public education. Each thus compared better educated young people with less well educated older people. More recent longitudinal studies measuring IQs of the *same persons* over a period of years report no consistent decline in IQ until old age, with some aspects of "intelligence" improving and others declining with advancing years [Baltes, 1968; Baltes and Schaie, 1974]. Longitudinal conclusions can only be established by longitudinal studies, even though cross-sectional studies may suggest promising hypotheses.

Laboratory and Field Experiments

All sciences use experiments. In the laboratory experiment, materials or people are brought into the laboratory for study. In laboratory experiments with people, people are recruited, assembled, and perhaps paid for engaging in the experiment. Dollard's famous frustration-aggression studies [1939] were conducted by assembling a number of students as experimental subjects, supposedly to study the effects of fatigue upon task performance. These students were subjected to intense frustration through prolonged boredom, nonarrival of promised food and games, and other intentional annoyances, while their aggressive responses were cataloged.

The field experiment takes research out to people instead of bringing people to the research laboratory. A massive field experiment involving vaccination of several million children established the value of the Salk polio vaccine. A continuing series of field experiments are seeking to find effective ways of promoting birth control in underdeveloped countries and among disadvantaged groups in the United States [Berelson, 1966; Ridker, 1976; Singh, 1979].

The concept of any experiment is quite simple: Hold all variables constant except one, cause it to vary, and see what happens.

One of the best ways to control all variables is to use *control groups*. A control group is a group of subjects who are like the experimental group in all respects except the variable(s) which we are studying. As an example, suppose we want to know whether abolishing grades would increase learning or increase loafing. To test this by experiment we would need a *control group* of classes which follow the usual teaching and grading procedures, and an *experimental group* of classes using whatever experimental procedure is being tested. To "hold all other variables constant," the control and experimental groups would need to be alike in students' abilities, subject studied, quality of teaching, students' work load, students' finances, and anything else likely to affect their performance. We would also need a reliable instrument to measure learning outcomes (after reaching agreement upon *what* learning outcomes were important). Then the results of the trial could be objectively determined. If the experimental group shows greater or lesser learning gains than the control group and this difference is confirmed by replication (repetitions of the experiment by other researchers), then significant conclusions can be drawn.

Failure to use suitable control groups may destroy a study's usefulness. For example, two psychologists [Miale and Selzer, 1976] examined the Rorschach tests which were given to sixteen Nazi leaders at the time of the Nuremberg war crimes trials and reported that fifteen of them were "psychopathic" in various degrees. But Miale and Selzer failed to compare the Nazi leaders' tests with Rorschach tests from a control group of leaders from other countries. Thus, even if we assume that the analyses are correct, we do not know whether these researchers have uncovered personality characteristics of *Nazi* leaders, or characteristics of *leaders*. Thus, this study is of limited value.

There are two common ways of setting up experimental and control groups. One is the *matched-pair* technique. For each person in the experimental group, another person similar in all important variables (such as age, religion, education, occupation, or anything important to this research) is found and placed in the control group. Another technique is the *random-assignment* technique, in which statistically random assignments of persons to experimental and control groups are made—such as assigning the first person to the experimental group, the next to the control group, and so on. Suppose we wish to measure the effectiveness of an experimental treatment program for delinquents in a reformatory. Using one technique, we should match each delinquent who received the experimental treatment (experimental group) with another delinquent, matched for other variables thought important, who received only the usual treatment (control group). Using the random-assignment technique, every second (or third, or tenth) delinquent would be assigned to the experimental group upon arrival at the reformatory, with the others becoming the control group. Wherever the researcher is permitted to make assignments in this way, the random-assignment technique is far easier and at least as accurate; but often, when the research situation does not allow this technique, the matched-pair technique may be used.

Experiments in sociology face certain difficulties. An experiment involving thousands of people may be prohibitively expensive. It may take years to complete a prospective study. Our values forbid us to use people in any experiments which may injure them. The scientific world reacts strongly in those infrequent instances where human subjects have been used in a hazardous or harmful manner [J. Katz, 1972; Jones, 1981]. When people are unwilling to cooperate in an experiment, we cannot force them to do so (although we may occasionally trick them into unconscious cooperation). Furthermore, when people realize that they are experimental subjects, they begin to act differently, and the experiment may be spoiled. Almost any kind of experimental or observational study upon people *who know they are being studied* will give some interesting findings which may vanish soon after the study is ended.

Planned experiments upon human subjects are most reliable when these subjects do not know the true object of the experiment. They may be given a rationale, a reasonable explanation of what the experimenter is doing, but this rationale may be a harmless but necessary deception which conceals the true purpose of the experiment. For example, McClelland [1971] wished to study the effects of alcohol upon normal people in a party atmosphere but told the subjects that he was studying the effects of a party atmosphere upon fantasy, and had them write imaginative stories about pictures he showed them at intervals. But as Kelman points out [1966], the use of deception in social research poses the ethical question of distinguishing between harmless deception and intellectual dishonesty and may even produce errors in the outcome (subjects may detect the deception and begin second-guessing the researcher!).

Because of all these limitations, social sci-

ences (excepting psychology) make limited use of planned experiments. We use them wherever practical, but depend more heavily on other techniques.

Observational Studies

Observational studies are like experiments in all respects except one: In an experiment the scientist arranges for something to happen in order to observe what follows, whereas in an observational study the scientist observes something which happens, or has already happened, by itself. Both rely upon systematic observation under controlled conditions in a search for verifiable sequences and relationships. Both are used in all the sciences, but the procedures for using them vary according to the material being studied. The types of studies which follow are not mutually exclusive, for a study may fit into more than one of these several categories.

IMPRESSIONISTIC STUDIES. These are informal descriptive and analytic accounts based on observations which are less fully controlled than in more formal studies. They definitely are *not* a rambling series of anecdotes but are an organized presentation of purposeful observations. Suppose, for example, a sociologist with a special interest in the family visits Russia. To make an impressionistic study, this sociologist would outline in advance the kinds of information to be sought, the kinds of people to seek out and question, the places to visit, printed matter to collect, and other sources of possible information. Then, while traveling, the scholar would be alert for chances to ask questions about family life, visit "typical" families, scan papers and magazines and collect any other information. The scholar returns home with some very definite impressions of Russian family life, but they are not based on a systematic, scientifically controlled investigation—on an orderly search of the published literature, on a scientifically constructed sample of informants, and so on.

Responsible scholars will call this sociologist's judgments impressions, and will not state them as scientifically established conclusions.

No matter how elaborate, carefully planned, and systematically conducted a study may be, if the recorded data consist of the observer's impressions, it is classed as an impressionistic study. Thus, the Lynds [1929, 1937] spent many months in "Middletown" (Muncie, Indiana); they systematically searched newspaper files, interviewed virtually everyone who held a position of authority or was locally said to be important, and participated in community life. They ended up with a large mass of impressions which were highly perceptive and probably accurate, but not easily verifiable. A new "Middletown" series of studies, repeating and elaborating upon the Lynds' methods, is now appearing [Caplow et al., 1982], revealing many changes in Middletown in the intervening half century.

Bias is a major hazard in impressionistic research. Studs Terkel [*Working*, 1972] and LeMasters [*Blue-Collar Aristocrats*, 1976] spent hundreds of hours listening to working people share their ideas and feelings; then from their huge collection of tapes, notes, and recollections they selected a small portion for publication. This method clearly carries the danger that the observer's feelings will color the findings.

Despite this hazard, impressionistic studies are highly useful in social science. They provide many hypotheses and research leads, and suggest many insights which might be overlooked by other methods. The best of the impressionistic studies hold an honored place in sociological literature.

STATISTICAL COMPARATIVE STUDIES. If the information needed has already been written down somewhere, it is sensible to look up the record. (The Levine and Meyer study, cited on p. 28, is an example, since all the data needed were in school records.) Much sociological research consists of looking up recorded statistical facts and comparing and interpreting them. For a simple example, consider the question, "Now that women have greater freedom to lead an interesting and independent life without marriage, are more women remaining single?" While the *reasons* for remaining single may be a complicated question, the *proportion* of women remaining single can easily be derived from census data, which show the proportion of single women dropping from 24.3 percent in 1890 to 11.9 percent in 1960, then rising to 17.0 percent in 1980. (These figures give the percentage of all American women, 14 years old or older, who had never been married, with correction for changes in the age distribution of the population.) Many such questions can be answered quickly by checking data in the annual *Statistical Abstract of the United States*, which summarizes statistics collected by many government and other agencies and should be found in any library. Other questions may require study of more specialized statistical sources, such as the many *Special Reports* issued by the Bureau of the Census.

Many research questions involve a comparison of several kinds of statistical data from several sources. For example, using income data from the U.S. census, Jacobs [1978] computed an "index of economic equality" for each American state. Then, using crime statistics from *Uniform Crime Reports* (published by the U.S. Department of Justice), he computed an "index of imprisonment probability," a ratio between the number of crimes reported to the police and the number of criminals imprisoned for that type of crime. He hypothesized that imprisonment ratios for property crimes (but not for violent crimes) should be higher wherever economic inequality was greater, and found that his data supported these hypotheses.

Sometimes the researcher must go out and collect original data. For example, Budd [1976] wondered whether marriages are affected by having lived together before marriage. Since little has been published on this question, Budd surveyed 151 volunteer couples (54 cohabiting couples, 48 married couples who had cohabited, and 49 married couples who had not cohabited. She found very few differences between the marriages of those who cohabited before marriage and those who had not. (*Tentative* conclusion: premarital cohabitation has little effect upon marriage. Replication studies invited!)

Many people "have no use for statistics." Often they do not like statistics because they do not understand them. Statistics, like shotguns, are dangerous when handled by the ignorant, as is shown in Huff's entertaining little book, *How to Lie with Statistics* [1954]. Those who know the uses and abuses of statistics realize that statistics are nothing more or less than *organized, measured facts*. They are as trustworthy or untrustworthy as is the scientific method of the person who compiles them. To reject statistics is but a way of rejecting facts.

Sociologists make a great many comparative statistical studies. As almost any kind of research is likely to involve statistical organization and comparison of facts at some point or other, the sociologist must be something of a statistician, and citizens who hope to be intelligently aware of the world they live in must know how to interpret statistics, lest they be duped by every clever propagandist in sight.

QUESTIONNAIRE AND INTERVIEW STUDIES. Sometimes the facts we need are not recorded anywhere, and we can find them only by asking people. Thus, Ferree [1976] interviewed 135 married women with elementary school children, and reported that the wives who were full-time homemakers were considerably more "dissatisfied with life" than wives who are employed outside the home. But six large national interview studies of the same question found no consistent relationship between wives' satisfaction with life and whether they were employed outside the

home [Wright, 1978]. Again, we are reminded that a single study seldom proves much until it is confirmed through replication.

Questionnaire and interview studies are systematic ways of asking questions under scientific controls. A questionnaire is filled out by the informant personally; an interview schedule is filled out by a trained interviewer who asks the questions of the informant. Both methods have their pitfalls, which the trained sociologist should be able to avoid. The informants may not understand the question; they may pick an answer even though they do not have any firm opinion on the matter; they may give an "acceptable" answer rather than the real one; or they may be swayed by the way the question is worded.

Even though questionnaire and interview studies have a margin of error, they may still be useful, for they are more reliable than guesswork. Public officials seldom take a position on an issue without first reviewing the public opinion polls, while legislators often delay casting a vote until receiving the latest opinion poll from their districts. Few business executives set a production schedule or plan a sales campaign without first commissioning some "market research."

PARTICIPANT-OBSERVER STUDIES. Some things can be fully understood only by experiencing them. The *participant observer* seeks insight by taking part in whatever is being studied. For example, a participant observer wishing to study labor unions might join one, work at a job, attend union meetings, and possibly become a minor union official. To study a religious sect, one would join it and share in its worship and other activities. Through personal participation and intimate observation, the participant observer may gain insights which no *external* observation would provide.

Some years ago, a white novelist was commissioned by *Ebony* magazine to make a participant-observer study of black life. With his hair trimmed short and his skin darkened

The participant observer seeks insight
by taking part personally.

by a drug, he traveled about the South, where everyone identified him as a black. Although he was a native southerner, he found that the experience of being treated as a black brought many surprising revelations about black life in the United States at that time [Griffin, 1961]. In another participant-observer study, Zablocki visited and lived in 120 rural communes over a ten-year period [Zablocki, 1980].

There are pitfalls in this technique. The participant observer may become so emotionally involved as to lose objectivity and become a dedicated partisan instead of a neutral observer. Or the participant observer may overgeneralize—that is, assume that what is found in the group studied is also true of all other groups. Since the data are largely impressionistic, conclusions are not easily verified. Yet the participant observer is not just ''looking at things,'' but is applying a sophisticated scientific methodology [Bruyn, 1966; Friedrichs and Ludke, 1975] which has given us many insights and suggested many hypotheses for further study.

Is it ethical to pretend to be a loyal member of a group in order to study it? Is such a deception justifiable? It is not easy to say when a deception ceases to be harmless. Perhaps the best answer is that a reputable scientist will be careful not to injure the people being studied.

The *eyewitness account* is an amateur, small-scale participant-observer study. How do people act after a disaster, such as a tornado or an explosion? What happens at a religious revival, a riot, a picket-line disturbance? Rarely is there a visiting sociologist, pencil in hand, ready to record the event. Social scientists often seek eyewitness accounts from persons who were there. A detailed eyewitness account, collected as soon as possible after the event, is a useful source of information. Such accounts must be used with care, for the

A white man (on the right), John Griffin, artificially darkened his skin so he could pass for a black man and make a participant-observer study of black life. (*New American Library*)

eyewitness is usually an untrained observer, who may not be reliable. Many studies have shown the undependability of eyewitness identification and how easily eyewitness reports can be "slanted" by the way the questions are put to the witness [Loftus, 1974, 1979; Buckhout, 1975]. Yet the eyewitness account is priceless source of data for the social scientist.

CASE STUDIES.   The case study is a complete, detailed account of an event, situation, or development. It may be a life history of a person, a complete account of an event, or a detailed study of an organization. Erikson [1976] made a study of the consequences of one disaster, the dam break and flash flood in 1972, in Buffalo Creek, West Virginia, interviewing survivors and reading all the recorded testimony available. The case history of a group—a family, a clique, a union, a religious movement—may suggest some insights into group behavior. An accurate, detailed account of a riot, a panic, an orgy, a disaster, or any social event may have scientific value. An unhappy family, a happy family, a community, an organization—almost any phenomenon can be studied by the case-study technique.

Perhaps the greatest value of the case study is in the suggestion of hypotheses, which can then be tested by other methods. Much of our reliable knowledge about juvenile delinquency, for instance, has developed through the testing of hypotheses which were suggested by early case studies of delinquents [Thomas, 1923; Shaw, 1931]. Much of our present knowledge of personality disorganization stems from hypotheses suggested by a classic collection of case studies in Thomas and Znaniecki's *The Polish Peasant in Europe and America* [1923]. These hypotheses are not often *tested* by the case-study method but by other methods.

A generalization cannot be based upon a single case, for a case can be found to "prove"

almost anything. Generalizations must be based upon a large mass of carefully processed data, and the collection of a great many case studies is expensive. Also it is difficult to "add up" a number of case studies or compute averages or other statistical computations. Therefore we seldom use case studies when seeking to test a hypothesis. But after the hypothesis has been tested and we have arrived at some sound generalizations, a good case study may give a beautiful illustration of these generalizations. For example, there is conclusive evidence that juvenile delinquency is closely associated with unsatisfactory family life [Glueck and Glueck, 1959]. A case study showing how unsatisfactory family life has apparently encouraged delinquency in a particular family makes a vivid illustration of this generalization.

These several kinds of studies often overlap, and a study may fit into more than one classification. For example, Roebuck and Frese [1976] made a study of an after-hours nightclub (serving liquor after legal closing hours). They posed as ordinary patrons while listening and talking with the "night people." Theirs was a participant-observer study (they observed patrons while posing as patrons), an impressionistic study (they collected impressions, not statistics), and a case study (they studied *one* club). The Zablocki study of communes mentioned earlier was a participant-observer study (he lived in communes), a cross-sectional study (120 of them), a longitudinal study (over a ten-year period), a questionnaire study (asking the same questions in each), and a statistical comparative study (he collected factual data on communards and compared them with other groups of people).

EVALUATION RESEARCH.   Almost half the federal government's expenditures are for "human resources," including social action programs such as Head Start, delinquency prevention, drug rehabilitation, job training, and many others. Do they work? Or is the money wasted? May they even do more harm than good?

The use of scientific research procedures to measure the effectiveness of an action program is called *evaluation research* [Suchman, 1967; Abt, 1977; Cook, 1978]. Evaluation research may use any of the kinds of studies described in the preceding pages. Its object is to replace guesswork with knowledge in deciding what programs to continue and how to improve them. (At least in theory, this is the purpose; in practice, the purpose of evaluation research may be to develop proof of the program's "success" so that funding will be continued.)

Evaluation research is not easy, for many variables must be controlled. Often the findings of various evaluation studies are so conflicting that no firm conclusions can be drawn. For example, Nancy St. John [1975] reviewed dozens of studies of the effects of school desegregation on pupil learning and found that the reported effects varied so widely that no clear decision could be rendered. Even when numerous studies do agree, they may be disbelieved or ignored. Studies critical of an agency may be quietly buried, and those whose conclusions conflict with popular beliefs are disregarded. For example, a number of studies have shown that high school driver-training courses have little or no effect upon driver accident rates [Moynihan, 1968; Harmon, 1969; Conley and Smiley, 1976], but it appears that people have made a common-sense judgment that driver training "must work" and simply ignore evidence that it does not.

Despite the difficulties and pitfalls, evaluation research is one of the most important and most rapidly growing areas of sociological research, with new books appearing every year [Guba and Lincoln, 1981; Meyers, 1981; Crane, 1982], along with an *Evaluation Studies Review Annual* and a quarterly journal, *Eval-*

uation Review. While evaluation research is imperfect, the alternative is to rely on hunches and guesswork in designing social action programs.

The Problem of Sampling

In most research, we save time by examining only a sample of an entire *universe*—whatever we are studying, whether it is tomato plants, laboratory animals, college freshmen, or working wives. If the sample is properly selected, it will give an accurate picture of the entire universe under study. But to do this, the sample must be *representative*; that is, all kinds of people (or tomato plants, or whatever) must appear in the sample *in the same proportions* as they appear in the universe being studied. Thus, a representative sample of the student body must contain the same proportion of freshmen, males, blacks, commuters, business majors, and married students as found in the entire student body. The most common way of doing this is to select a *random sample*.

The term, "random," suggests a selection without any system or design, such as choosing anyone who is handy—people passing a particular street corner, or climbing the library steps. But this would be an *uncontrolled sample*, for there are no controls to insure that it will be representative.

A *random sample* is selected so that each person in the universe being studied has an equal chance of being in the sample. We might take every tenth, or fiftieth, or hundredth name in the student directory. Or we might feed all the student numbers into the computer and program it to make a random selection. Every tenth address on the community's mail-delivery routes, every twentieth hospital admission, or every hundredth driver's license would give random samples of local residents, hospital patients, or automobile drivers.

While a random sample is quite representative, a *stratified random sample* is still more perfectly representative. In such a sample, we first determine what percentage of each category of the universe under study would be in the sample and then program the computer to select a random sample of each category. For example, suppose that our university student body is 32 percent freshmen, 49 percent male, 12 percent black, and 45 percent commuters (plus other categories). In a representative sample, each 100 members of the sample should include 32 freshmen, 49 males, 12 blacks, and 45 commuters. The computer is then programmed to make a random selection of 32 freshmen from all the freshmen, 49 males from all the males, and so on.

A *self-selected* sample is composed of volunteers, such as persons who write letters to the editor or to their senator or who mail in magazine questionnaires. It is unknown how these volunteers compare with those who did not volunteer. Is it mainly the "far-outs" or the "squares" who mail in the questionnaires? Thus, *The Hite Report* [Hite, 1976], a sex book pretending to be a research study of women's sex lives, was based upon a *3 percent* return of mailed questionnaires. Ms. Hite's sequel, *The Hite Report on Male Sexuality* [Hite, 1981] did a little better, getting a 6 percent return. With such tiny returns, these books should be viewed as popular entertainment, not as research.

DISAGREEMENTS IN SCIENCE

Since scientists are supposed to follow certain standard procedures in collecting data and arriving at conclusions based upon scientific evidence, unsullied by bias, vanity, or vested interest, why do scientists so often disagree? Sometimes two different scientists, working with the same data, arrive at opposite conclusions. For example, the Jacobs study mentioned earlier [Jacobs, 1978] concluded that more property crimes are committed where economic inequality is greater. But another sociologist, using the same data, found no such relationship as Jacobs claimed [Bailey, 1981]. Each of these scholars claims that the other is using defective methodology [Bailey, 1981; Jacobs, 1981].

Such contests are common in all sciences. Differing sets of data, differing methods of handling data, differing perspectives, and possible errors all add up to many disagreements. Most disagreements are resolved in time, but by then new disagreements have arisen. It would be easier for students if everything were neatly classified as "definitely true" or "definitely false," but the

---

Science separates itself from pseudoscience along a number of dimensions. One of these dimensions is accessibility of the data. Scientific data are consensually validated by open inspection of the recorded observations or through replication of the relevant phenomena. Following publication of major observations it is an accepted practice in science for researchers to allow colleagues who are doing serious work in the same field to have access to their original data. When researchers consistently refuse to allow colleagues such access, something important is being signaled. Of course data may get lost or destroyed or be difficult or costly to retrieve in the form required. Or they may be classified information or have commercial value that a scientist may wish to exploit prior to their general release. However, when none of these considerations is applicable, a refusal to supply a copy of a set of data leads to the unpleasant inference that something is wrong, that the data do not support what is claimed for them, that the data are an embarrassment following an extravagant claim that cannot be substantiated.

(David F. Marks, "Remote Visiting Revisited," *The Skeptical Inquirer*, Vol. VI, No. 4, Summer 1982, p. 19.)

world of scientific knowledge just is not like that. Separating scientific truth from error is a difficult task, but an exciting one!

PURE AND APPLIED SOCIOLOGY

A distinction between pure and applied science is drawn in every scientific field. *Pure science* is a search for knowledge, without primary concern for its practical use. *Applied science* is the search for ways of using scientific knowledge to solve practical problems. A biochemist who seeks to learn how a cell absorbs food or how a cell ages is working as a pure scientist. If this biochemist then tries to find some way to control the aging process, this is applied science. A sociologist making a study of "the social structure of a slum neighborhood" is working as a pure scientist; if this is followed by a study of "how to prevent delinquency in a slum neighborhood," this is applied science. Many people view sociology entirely as an applied science—trying to solve social problems. Properly viewed, it is both a pure and an applied science. For unless a science is constantly searching for more basic knowledge, its "practical applications of knowledge" are not likely to be very practical.

Practical applications of sociological knowledge have become quite common. Some sociologists are employed by corporations, government bureaus, and social agencies, often in evaluation research but sometimes in administration. Sociologists are often consulted by legislative committees in preparing new legislation. While the political clout of opposing interest groups may be the prime determinant of social policy decisions, the policy recommendations of social scientists are a significant factor in the legislative process.

On many social questions, such as the causes and treatment of crime and delinquency, drug and alcohol addiction, sex offenses, the causes and consequences of race discrimination, or the adjustment of the fam-

ily to a changing society, there *is* considerable scientific knowledge within the social sciences. Often this knowledge is rejected by people who prefer to follow their prejudices, but as a nation, we are beginning to apply scientific methods to our thinking about social issues.

Popular Sociology

A great deal of sociological material reaches print through people who are not sociologists. The popular magazines are studded with articles on crime, family life, sex, education, suburbia, social class—practically every sociological topic imaginable. This is popular sociology—treatment of sociological topics, usually by writers without much formal sociological training, and aimed at a popular audience. Popular sociology at its worst is seen in articles like the "sex-and-sin" exposés upon which certain men's magazines dwell so fondly. Such articles are generally descriptively inaccurate, with a total lack of the interpretative analysis which would fit the facts into a relevant social context. At the opposite pole are many writers who do a fairly creditable job of popularizing sociological findings. For example, Stoner and Parke's *All God's Children* [1977], a study of new religious cults, and Davis's *Hometown* [1981] are written by nonsociologists, but the authors are careful, observant, sensitive reporters.

"Pop sociology" often contains inaccuracies and instances of misplaced emphasis, doubtful interpretation, oversimplification, and too-sweeping generalization. Yet it is likely that popular understanding of sociological topics has been greatly increased by such writers.

Why isn't popular sociology written by professional sociologists? For the same reason that popular science is usually written by journalists, rather than by scientists. Popular writing is a special skill which few scientists or professors have mastered. Furthermore, the scientist's passion for accuracy and for a careful qualification of all statements is a positive handicap in popular writing. Unwillingness to oversimplify, to overdramatize, or to indulge in grandly sweeping generalization make the professional's writing more accurate but less exciting. Sociologists write for the scholarly audience while journalists popularize sociology, more or less accurately, for the public.

THE ROLES OF THE SOCIOLOGIST

What is the proper task of the sociologist? Is it merely to observe human action with the calm, detached curiosity of the ecologist who counts the lemmings as they dive into the sea? Or should the sociologist rush into social action? Should the professor of sociology encourage students to develop a detached understanding of social phenomena or inspire them to man the barricades for social reform? What is the proper role for the sociologist in a changing society?

The Sociologist as Research Scientist

Like all scientists, sociologists are concerned with both collecting and using knowledge. They share in these tasks in various ways.

CONDUCTING SCIENTIFIC RESEARCH.   As a scientist, the sociologist's foremost task is to discover and organize knowledge about social life. A number of full-time research sociologists are employed by universities, government agencies, foundations, or corporations, and many sociologists divide their time between teaching and research. Many university sociologists are engaged in "funded" research, with all or part of their salaries and their research expenses paid from research grants made by government agencies, foundations, or corporations. These grants are made to sociologists who submit an acceptable proposal for research on a particular topic. Since little research can be conducted

without research funds, this gives the funding agencies great power to influence the direction of sociological research.

Radical critics of sociology (including some sociologists) claim that, behind a facade of ethical neutrality and objectivity, sociologists have prostituted their research talents to the support of the interests of the funding agencies, and have thus supported militarism, racism, and other forms of oppression [Gouldner, 1962, 1970; Frederichs, 1970, pp. 82–85; any issue of *The Insurgent Sociologist*].

Whether sociological research has been widely corrupted in this manner may be debated [Horton and Bouma, 1971]. What is indisputable is that problems of bias and partisanship are present in all research, and that research findings are often helpful to the interests of some people and damaging to the interests of other people [Becker, 1967]. Even the definition of a research problem may carry an implicit bias. For example if we state a research problem as, "What characteristics of poor people contribute to their poverty?" we imply that the responsibility rests mainly on the poor people themselves; but if we define the problem as, "What social arrangements produce poverty?" then the responsibility is placed upon "society."

Throughout most of the history of sociology, sociologists were often accused of being radical subversives whose research and teaching were a threat to established institutions and vested interests. Many older sociologists today, still bearing the scars of the anticommunist witchhunts of the 1950s, are puzzled and hurt when students and younger sociologists accuse them of having been lackeys of capitalistic oppression all their lives! But the question of the responsibility of the scientist to society is as old as science itself, and will not soon be settled.

CORRECTING POPULAR NONSENSE.   Another task of the sociologist as a scientist is to clear away the intellectual rubbish of misinformation and superstition which clutters so much of our social thinking. Sociologists have helped to bury a great deal of nonsense about heredity, race, class, sex differences, deviation, and nearly every other aspect of behavior. It is due partly to the findings of sociology that today we rarely hear an educated person argue that the white race is innately superior, that women are intellectually inferior to men, that behavior traits are inherited, or that rural people are less "immoral" than urbanites—ideas which nearly every educated person accepted a half century ago. By helping replace superstition and misinformation with accurate knowledge about human behavior, sociologists are perhaps performing their most important function.

MAKING SOCIOLOGICAL PREDICTIONS. Although the track record of sociologists in making social predictions is not impressive, *someone* must make social predictions. Every policy decision is based upon certain assumptions about the present and future state of the society. A legislator who says "We need more severe penalties to curb drug pushing" is predicting that more severe penalties actually will curb the narcotics business without creating even greater problems. Another legislator who says "Legalize marijuana" is making a set of predictions about the consequences of this action. Thus every policy recommendation inevitably implies a set of assumptions and predictions. What sort of predictions do sociologists offer? Here are a few samples, offered without explanation or documentation at this point, as examples of the kind of predictions sociologists can make:

The trend toward employment of women will continue until most women are working for most of their married lives.

Birth rates will fall to approach death rates, or death rates will rise to approach birth rates.

Despite some experimentation with alternatives, the monogamous nuclear family will continue to be the basic family type in the United States.

The present popularity of jeans and casual clothing amoung young people will be followed by a return to high-style clothing.

The recent trend toward early retirement will soon be replaced by efforts to lengthen the work career.

Most social science prediction consists not of predicting specific developments, as the astronomer predicts an eclipse, but of forecasting the general pattern of trends and changes which seem most probable [e.g., Bell, *The Coming of Post-Industrial Society: A Venture in Social Forecasting*, 1973]. All such predictions or forecasts should be offered with a certain humility, for no certainty attends them. Instead, social scientists offer them as the best, most informed guesses available upon which to base our policy decisions and expectations for the future.

The Sociologist as Policy Consultant

Sociological prediction can also help to estimate the probable effects of a social policy. Every social policy decision *is* a prediction. A policy (e.g., federal grants for Head Start) is begun in the hope that it will produce a desired effect (e.g., narrow the educational gap between poorer and more prosperous children). Policies have often failed because they embodied unsound assumptions and predictions. Sociologists can help to predict the effects of a policy, and thus contribute to the selection of policies which achieve the intended purposes. For example:

What effect does dropping out of high school have upon a youth's future earnings? (Little or none, when other factors are equal.)

What would be the effect of intensified law enforcement upon campus marijuana use? (Little or no reduction, with aggravation of other student-police problems.)

Would low birthrates and a small-family norm increase marital happiness? (Yes; there is research evidence that smaller families are better off in every way.)

Would publishing the names of juvenile delinquents help to reduce delinquency? (No; it would more likely increase it).

Would the suppression of obscene literature help to reduce sex crimes and sex immorality? (Our limited evidence suggests that it would not.)

Would legal barriers to abortion strengthen family life? (No; most sociologists believe this would increase illegitimate births, unwanted children, child abuse, and family discord.)

These are a few of the many social policy questions which sociologists could help to settle. One of the greatest services any scholarly group can offer is to show the society what policies are most likely to work in achieving its objectives. This is a service which sociologists are qualified to perform.

The Sociologist as Technician

Some sociologists are engaged in planning and conducting community action programs; advising on public relations, employee relations, problems of morale or of "intergroup relations" within the organization; working on human relations problems of many sorts. Often these sociologists have specialized in social psychology, industrial sociology, urban or rural sociology, or the sociology of complex organizations.

Recently the term *clinical sociologist* has appeared to describe the work of the sociologist as technician [Gardner, 1978]. To some extent, this is a new name for what sociologists have been doing for a long time, but it also includes a considerable broadening of the range of sociologists' efforts to be useful in society.

In such positions the sociologist is working as an applied scientist. He or she has been engaged to use scientific knowledge in pursuing certain values—a harmonious and efficient working force, an attractive public image of the industry, or an effective community action program. This role raises a question of ethics. When a sociologist accepts employment as a technician, pursuing values chosen by an employer, has scientific integrity been compromised? To take an extreme example, there is evidence [Monroe, 1962] that gambling operators engaged social scientists to find out why people do or do not gamble, so that the operators could learn how to attract more customers. (We do not know whether any sociologists were included.) Would this be a form of scientific prostitution?

The radical critics of "establishment sociology" charge that sociologists have "sold out" whenever they serve as technicians or research scholars in any kind of effort to maintain or improve the efficiency of the government, military, capitalistic, or welfare establishments. Thus, not only are sociologists (if any) working in war-related activities condemned, but even sociologists working in programs to improve the health of poor children in Mississippi, to increase agricultural output in Peru, or to teach birth control in village India are sometimes accused of supporting "oppression." This is the classic view of the revolutionist—any attempt to make the present system work better, or to help people find better lives within the system is "oppressive" because it helps to perpetuate the system.

There is no simple answer to the question of what clinical appointments it is proper for the sociologist to accept. Each sociologist's answer will be found partly in the prevailing views of the academic world at that moment and partly in his or her own conscience.

The Sociologist as Teacher

Teaching is the major career of many sociologists. In addition to the concerns and problems of teaching in any field, the problem of value neutrality versus value commitment is a particularly acute question. For example, in a course on "poverty," should the sociologist supervise an objective study of facts, theories, and policies—possibly sympathetic but as objective as possible? Or should the course be designed to produce dedicated advocates of a particular action program? Should the sociologist seek to convert students to conservatism, liberal reformism, or revolutionary activism? For some decades the ethics of university teaching have demanded that the teacher refrain from all conscious "indoctrination," but this question is now under spirited debate.

The Sociologist and Social Action

Scientists seek to discover knowledge. Should scientists also tell the society how this knowledge *should* be used? For example, the geneticists already know something about human heredity, and before very long it may be possible to control the genetic makeup of babies, and "order" babies according to a specifications list. Who should decide what sort of baby should go to whom? The scientists? The parents? The government?

The basic question is whether science—specifically sociology—should be value-free. For example, sociologists know some things about population growth, race relations, urban development, and many other matters involving questions of public policy. Should sociologists become public advocates of birth control programs, legalized abortion, women's liberation, legalized marijuana, racial integration, and many other programs which they may consider socially desirable?

Early sociologists gave an emphatic "yes" to this question. Without an adequate foundation of scientific knowledge, they rushed to support all sorts of public policies they believed wise. Between 1920 and 1940, many sociologists shifted to the view that sociology should be a more nearly "pure" science, discovering knowledge but not attempting to decree how it should be used. They sought

to build sociology on the model of physics or chemistry, as a value-free science. As such, it should be committed to no values except those of free scientific inquiry. Sociologists generally avoided involvement in controversial issues and sought the status of "pure" social scientists.

More recently, this view has been challenged in both physical and social science. The *Bulletin of the Atomic Scientists* carries many articles by scientists urging their fellows to claim a larger role in deciding the uses of nuclear science discoveries. Many sociologists today believe that sociologists should claim a major role in making decisions about public policy and should involve themselves in the major issues of our society [Lindesmith, 1960; Horowitz, 1964; Stein and Vidich, 1964; A. Lee, 1966, 1973, 1978; Becker 1967]. They charge that sociologists have buried themselves in "safe" research topics, leaving the really important questions to nonsociologists—questions such as "How can poverty be reduced?" "How can schools be integrated?" "How can communities be organized for more civilized social living?" "Should the goals and values of American society be altered to promote human welfare?" They feel that not only do sociologists have a duty to say what society *might* do about problems of race conflict, population growth, birth control, drug addiction, divorce, sex deviation, medical care, etc., but that sociologists have a duty to say what our society *should* do about such problems. Books like Shostak's *Putting Sociology to Work* [1974] provide concrete examples of how sociologists are involving themselves in social issues and constructive social action and show what they have learned from these experiences.

Sociology today, in common with all the other social sciences, has some members who insist that, both individually and as an academic discipline, sociologists should openly and publicly support the "radical reconstruction of society" [Szymanski, 1970; Colfax and Roach, 1971; D. Horowitz, 1971; Sternberg,

1977]. This question is receiving much attention in sociological literature [Douglas, 1970; Lee, 1978; Harris, 1980]. Whether sociology should be value-free is an unsettled question, but sociologists are agreed upon the following propositions:

(1) Sociologists should show the relationships between values. In short, sociologists may say, "If *this* is what you want, *here* is what you must do to get it." If stable, enduring marriages are more important than happiness in marriage, then divorce should be made more difficult; if *happy* marriages represent the more important value, then fairly easy divorce should permit the unhappily married to separate and try again. If we wish to arrest urban blight and suburban sprawl, some private property rights will have to be sacrificed. If we wish to clean up polluted rivers, we must be prepared to spend a lot of tax money in doing so. Sociologists may clarify what value sacrifices must be made if we wish to attain certain other values.

(2) A sociologist as an *individual* may properly make value judgments, support causes, and join reform movements, like any other citizen. As a scientist, the sociologist may not know whether television violence is harmful to children, and therefore might not make public recommendations, but as a parent will make a decision according to his or her personal beliefs and values. As a scientist, the sociologist may not be able to say whether gambling or marijuana should be forbidden,

but as a citizen he or she is free to express opinions and support personal value judgments.

Beyond this there is no complete agreement among sociologists concerning what role they should assume. Most sociologists have some firm opinions on what policies society should follow and are in considerable agreement with one another upon many of these policies. Possibly the time will come when the social policies which seem best to most sociologists will also seem best to the rest of the society. As persons who cannot and would not divorce themselves from the society in which they live, most sociologists hope so.

THE STUDY OF SOCIOLOGY

Students are sometimes delighted to find in sociology (or another social science) evidence that some of their parents' fondest beliefs are outmoded superstitions. But when they find evidence that their *own* beliefs are scientifically unfounded, their reaction to this correction may not differ greatly from that of their parents. To separate sense from nonsense is one of the objectives of sociology. Only those who are willing and able to subject their beliefs, assumptions, and practices to objective scientific scrutiny will gain much from the study of any of the social sciences.

The Use of Concepts in Sociology

Every field of study makes the student memorize many words to which the field attaches special meanings. This is not an idle ritual; it is done because precise concepts are necessary. First, *we need carefully expressed concepts to carry on a scientific discussion*. How would you explain machinery to a person who had no concept of "wheel"? How useful to a specialist would a patient's medical history be if her physician had recorded it in the language of the layman? The several dozen sociological concepts which will harass the

As a citizen, the sociologist is perfectly justified in supporting causes.

student in this book are necessary for a clear discussion of social phenomena.

Secondly, *the formulation of concepts leads to increased knowledge*. Some accurate descriptive knowledge must be organized before a concept can be framed. Then the analysis and criticism of this new concept point up the gaps and errors in present knowledge. Use of the concept often calls attention to facts and relationships which may have been overlooked. Years ago while studying migration, Park [1928] framed the concept of the *marginal man* who is on the fringes of two groups or two ways of life while fully belonging to neither. The use of this concept quickly led to the recognition that there were many kinds of marginal persons—the person of mixed racial ancestry, who belongs clearly to neither race; the supervisor, who is not clearly either "management" or "labor"; the ambitious climber, no longer in the lower class yet not securely a middle-class person; and many others. Sound concepts like that of marginality lead to increased knowledge.

Finally, concepts are useful as verbal shorthand. At the hardware store, it is faster to ask for a "wing-nut" than for "one of those funny nuts with little ears on it so it can be tightened by hand." The term "control group" replaces an entire sentence in a research report or discussion. Every discipline develops concepts as time-savers.

Most of the concepts of sociology are expressed in words which also have a popular meaning, just as the term *order* has one meaning in zoology, another at the restaurant table, and still another at a law-and-order political rally. Every science appropriates some common words and makes them into scientific concepts by giving them a specific definition. Sociology is no exception.

Careers in Sociology

A student who becomes interested in a subject may wonder what possibilities it holds for a career. A combination of courses which con-

TABLE 2-1
EMPLOYMENT OF UNDERGRADUATE SOCIOLOGY MAJORS, 1920–1980s*

	TIME OF GRADUATION		
Occupation	1920–1960s	1970s	1980s
Teaching	21.0	9.8	8.3
Planning	12.3	4.1	6.6
Social work	11.4	5.7	0.0
Homemaking	7.0	2.8	3.3
Counseling	6.1	8.2	3.3
Management	5.3	10.6	15.0
Graduate school	4.4	9.8	8.3
Secretarial	3.4	3.7	16.6
Retail trade	2.6	13.1	11.6
Clerical	0.9	9.4	20.0
Other	11.5	9.0	2.2
Retired, unemployed	14.0	3.7	0.0

* Responses of 419 undergraduate sociology majors from Florida State University. Percentages add up to more than 100 because listing includes "first," "present," and "any other" occupations.
Source: Graham C. Kinloch, "Undergraduate Sociology Majors and the Job Market," *The Southern Sociologist*, 14:20–21, Winter 1983.

stitutes an undergraduate major or minor in sociology is not, in itself, preparation for a professional career as a sociologist. Undergraduate majors and minors are useful mainly as background preparation for other careers: (1) In *social work*, the better jobs demand a graduate degree in social work, and a strong undergraduate major in sociology is usually recommended. (2) In *the professions*—medicine, law, engineering—it has been found that undergraduate social science courses are useful. (3) *Secondary schools* present some demand for sociology teachers. (4) *Civil service positions* often include undergraduate sociology among the acceptable educational qualifications for a wide variety of positions in lower and middle brackets. (5) *Sociologists are employed* in small numbers by industry, trade associations, labor unions, foundations, and in fairly large numbers by research organizations, in a wide variety of positions, very often in the administration and conduct of research. (6) *Newly emergent careers* in many sorts of action programs have developed in recent years—local human relations councils, fair employment practices commissions, affirmative action programs, economic opportunity programs, job retraining programs, foreign aid programs, and many others. Changes introduced by the Reagan administration have, for at least the moment, greatly curtailed employment opportunities in these positions, and their long-term future is uncertain.

An M.A. degree is generally sufficient to obtain a teaching position at a junior college or community college, but promotions and university appointments usually require a Ph.D., which is even more necessary for a career in sociology than it is in most of the other sciences. Among those scientists with enough "professional standing in the scientific community" to be listed in the National Register of Scientific and Technical Personnel, in 1970 (the most recent issue available as this is written), a doctor's degree was held by 76 percent of the sociologists, as compared with 66 percent of the psychologists, 42 percent of the economists, 41 percent of the physicists, 36 percent of the chemists; the sociologists were exceeded only by the anthropologists, 90 percent of whom held a doctorate. Of all sociologists, about 84 percent are employed by educational institutions, with the remainder scattered among many employers, mainly government agencies and private foundations. Teaching is the major activity of 58 percent of sociologists, with 22 percent engaged primarily in research, and 16 percent in management and administration, most often management and administration of research (leaving 4 percent in "other" work).

For a quarter century after World War II, the employment outlook for sociologists was excellent. But since 1977, college enrollments have been falling. The Reagan administration cut funds for student loans and aids and eliminated most federal government funding for social science research. As this is written,

the employment outlook for new sociology Ph.D's is not favorable. To imply otherwise would be dishonest. The market for sociologists is highly sensitive to federal government policies, and these can change rapidly. Any student interested in sociology as a career should consult sociology faculty members upon the current employment prospects and should obtain a copy of the booklet *Careers in Sociology* by writing to the American Sociological Association, 1722 N Street, NW, Washington, DC, 20036).

For most students, sociology will not be a career but merely part of their general liberal arts education. Whatever career they enter, they will be members of a society, residents in a community, participants in many groups, and carriers of the culture to the next generation. The study of sociology may aid them to fill with greater insight these varied roles which are their destiny.

SUMMARY

Sociology attempts to study society scientifically. Each social science has its own focus, and sociology's is upon the group life of the human race and the social products of this group life.

The methods of sociological research include *experimental* and *observational* studies, and many studies can be either *cross-sectional studies* or *longitudinal studies* (which may be either *prospective* or *retrospective*).

Observational studies are of several kinds: *impressionistic studies, participant-observer studies, case studies, questionnaire and interview studies, statistical comparative studies,* and *evaluation research studies.* A single study may fit into more than one of these categories (e.g., a longitudinal participant-observer study).

Sociology like all sciences may be either *pure* or *applied. Pure sociology* searches for new knowledge, while *applied sociology* tries to apply sociological knowledge to practical problems. A good deal of more or less accurate sociology is popularized by professional journalists, who are sometimes incorrectly called sociologists.

The sociologist in the professional role of social scientist tends to be a pure scientist devoted to discovering and teaching truth and occasionally making sociological predictions. The sociologist may function as an applied scientist when employed as a technician or consultant, or when in the role of private citizen. Whether sociologists as scientists and teachers should select, recommend, and actively promote those policies which they believe society *should* follow is an unsettled question.

The study of sociology will be successful only if the student is willing to learn about matters which already appear to be familiar. The student must learn some concepts which are needed for a precise scientific discussion. Granted a willingness to engage in serious preparation, the student may find a prospective career in sociology.

GLOSSARY

bias a tendency, usually unconscious, to see facts in a certain way because of one's wishes, interests, or values.
case study a complete, detailed account of an event, situation, or development.
control group a group of subjects who resemble the experimental group in all respects except the variable(s) being studied.
cross-sectional study one which covers a broad range of phenomena at a single point in time.
evaluation research a study measuring the effectiveness of an action program.
experimental group subjects whose responses to various experimental influences are observed.
impressionistic study the systematically collected impressions of a researcher.
longitudinal study one which examines the same body of phenomena over a period of time.
matched-pair technique one which matches each member of an experimental group with a person in the control group who is similar in all respects except the variable(s) being studied.
participant-observer study one in which the researcher becomes an active participant in whatever is being studied.
popular sociology popularizing of sociological findings by nonsociologists in popular media.
prospective study one which follows the same body of phenomena forward through a period of time, beginning with the present.
random-assignment technique one which builds experimental and control groups by assigning members at random to each group.
random sample one in which every person has an equal chance to appear, as when every fifth or tenth, or hundredth name is selected.
representative sample one in which all kinds of people appear in the same proportions as they appear in the total population studied.
retrospective study one which studies a body of phenomena, working backward from the present over a period of time.
self-selected sample one in which members of the sample are included by voluntary action, such as returning a questionnaire or a letter.
stratified random sample one in which a random sample is taken of each of the various categories of people in the universe studied.

QUESTIONS AND PROJECTS

1 How would you explain sociology to an uneducated person with no understanding of academic fields of knowledge? How would you explain it to a well-educated person whose education had included no sociology courses?
2 What is a sociologist? How is the term often misused?
3 What is the difference between a prospective and a retrospective study? Outline a research design of each type to study the relation between college grades and starting salaries after graduation.
4 How do you "control" a variable? In studying the

possible relation between grades and starting salaries, what are some variables that should be controlled? How could they be controlled?

5 Why are experimental studies rather rare in sociology?

6 What precautions are needed in using eyewitness accounts as sources of scientific data?

7 How does the participant-observer technique differ from merely looking at things? Isn't everyone a participant observer?

8 In one study 1,000 questionnaires are mailed and 800 completed questionnaires are returned; in another study 50,000 questionnaires are mailed and 5,000 are returned. Which study will arrive at the more reliable conclusions?

9 What are the pros and cons of defining the sociology teacher's role as including active promotion among students of values, goals, and social policies the teacher believes right?

10 When you are in an informal student "bull session," listen to each statement with these questions in mind: "How scientifically sound is this statement? Is it based upon scientific fact or upon guesswork, folklore, and wishful thinking? Could it be documented with adequate scientific support?" At the conclusion, try to estimate what proportion of the statements could be scientifically substantiated.

11 Discuss the implications of these two wordings of a possible questionnaire item:
   a. Do you favor the taking of unborn human life?
   b. Do you favor compulsory childbirth?

12 Write a brief, impressionistic account of some group or some community you have observed. Then list several of your generalizations about the group and outline a research project for collecting the empirical data which would enable you to test the accuracy of these statements.

13 Many communities made cross-sectional studies in the mid-1970s and found that black children equalled whites in school achievement in the lower grades but fell progressively further behind as grade level advanced. How could these findings be interpreted as: (*a*) evidence of school failure? (*b*) evidence of school improvement?

14 Some years ago, the U.S. Army commissioned a research team to develop a prediction test to tell whether a man would be more effective in the tropics or the arctic. At considerable expense, the team presented a one-question test which was as reliably predictive as a longer test. The question: "Do you prefer hot weather or cold weather?" Was the money wasted?

SUGGESTED READINGS

Adams, Samuel Hopkins: "The Juke Myth," *Saturday Review,* April 2, 1955, pp. 13ff.; reprinted in Edgar A. Schuler et al. (eds.): *Readings in Sociology,* 5th ed., Thomas Y. Crowell Company, New York, 1974, pp. 41–45. An amusing account of the method whereby the author of a famous study arrived at some highly dubious conclusions about heredity and crime.

*Bates, Alan P.: *The Sociological Enterprise,* Houghton Mifflin Company, Boston, 1967. A brief paperback telling what sociologists do and how they become sociologists. Chap. 5, "Training for Careers in Sociology," and Chap. 6, "Careers in Sociology," are especially recommended.

Brenton, Myron: "Studies in the Aftermath," *Human Behavior,* May 1975, pp. 56–61. A short, readable article summarizing several studies of the effects of natural disasters upon the survivors.

Caplow, Theodore, Howard M. Bahr, Bruce A. Chadwick, Reuben Hill, and Margaret Holmes Williamson: *Middletown Families: Fifty Years of Change and Continuity,* The University of Minnesota Press, Minneapolis, 1982. An impressionistic study, updating and elaborating upon the Lynds' studies of Middletown a half century ago.

Dynes, Russell R.: *Organized Behavior in Disaster,* D. C. Heath and Company, Lexington, Mass., 1970. A summary of research on behavior in disaster situations, showing how different research procedures are used.

*Freeman, Howard E., and Clarence C. Sherwood: *Social Research and Social Policy,*

Prentice-Hall, Inc., Englewood Cliffs, N.J., 1970. A brief statement of how social research can be designed to contribute to humane social policy.

Lantz, Herman R.: *People of Coal Town*, Southern Illinois University Press, Carbondale, 1971. A largely impressionistic case study of a community. Gives few statistics and no sweeping generalizations, but presents some hypotheses and interesting sociological description.

Levitan, Sar A.: "Evaluating Social Programs," *Society*, May/June 1977, pp. 66–68. A brief explanation of evaluation research.

Lin, Nan: *Foundations of Social Research*, McGraw-Hill Book Company, New York, 1976. A standard textbook in research methods.

Loftus, Elizabeth: "The Incredible Eyewitness," *Psychology Today*, December 1974, pp. 116–119; or *Eyewitness Testimony*, Harvard University Press, Cambridge, Mass., 1979. Comments upon the undependability of eyewitness identifications.

Roebuck, Julian B., and Wolfgang Frese: *The Rendevous: A Case Study of an After-Hours Club*, The Free Press, New York, 1976. An interesting participant-observer study of the "night people" at play.

*Saunders, William B.: *The Sociologist as Detective: An Introduction to Research Methods*, Praeger Publishers, New York, 1976. A simply written explanation and illustration of the types of social research study.

*Shostak, Arthur B. (ed.): *Putting Sociology to Work: Case Studies in the Application of Sociology to Modern Social Problems*, David McKay Company, Inc., New York, 1974. Shows how sociologists may share in sound action programs.

Statistical Abstract of the United States, published annually by the Bureau of the Census, and *The World Almanac and Book of Facts*, published annually by the Newspaper Enterprise Association. Two useful sources of statistical and factual information on practically any subject, available in any library. Every student should be familiar with them.

* An asterisk before the citation indicates that the title is available in a paperback edition.

Society and the Individual

Many species enter the world fully able to care for themselves. All the behavior they need to find food, grow, and reproduce is already programmed within their genes. Most of them become some other creature's breakfast, but the few survivors go about their business already knowing what they should do and how to do it.

The human animal has no such programming. Without long tender care the human infant dies, for humans have few inborn behavior patterns. Without a society to protect them, all human infants would perish. Without a culture to provide behavior patterns to learn and follow, most humans would die before finding out how to survive.

Part Two explores how humans build societies and develop cultures, and how each person acquires a culture and becomes part of a society. Chapter 3, "The Cultural Context," studies the nature and development of culture. Chapter 4, "Personality and Socialization," shows how personality is shaped through the interaction of heredity, environment, culture, group experience, and unique experience. Chapter 5, "Role and Status," shows how most behavior is organized into a series of roles which people can fill easily only if properly prepared. Chapter 6, "Sexuality and Sex Roles," explores the nature of human sexual behavior and changing sex roles. Chapter 7, "Social Order and Social Control," shows how most people are led to act as they are socially expected to act much—but not all—of the time.

3 The Cultural Context

A Totonac Indian from the va-
nilla-producing lowlands of
Mexico's east coast found it
hard to understand why American tourists wore such gaudy
sport shirts, draped themselves
with such large camera bags,

bought so many useless trink-
ets, and always talked so loud.
"Why are foreigners so queer?"
he exclaimed, as he pointed to
a group of tourists crowding
onto a bus headed for the pyramids just north of Mexico City.

(Eugene A. Nida,
" 'Why Are Foreigners So
Queer?' A Socioanthropological
Approach to Cultural Pluralism,"
*International Bulletin of
Missionary Research*, 5:102,
July 1981.)

What seems ordinary to people from one
society may seem outlandish to those from
another. An act can have different meanings
in different societies. Just as a whale may be
unaware that it floats in seawater, members
of a society are generally unaware that they
are following *belief* and *custom* in their behavior. They seldom wonder *why* they believe
and act as they do. Only by imaginatively
stepping outside one's own body of belief
and custom can one become aware of its
actual nature. From their life experiences
people develop a set of rules and procedures
for meeting their needs. The set of rules and
procedures, together with a supporting set
of ideas and values, is called a *culture*.

A person who is commonly considered
"cultured" can identify operatic arias, read a
French menu, and select the right fork. But
people who are bored by the classics, belch
in public, and speak in four-letter words also
have culture. Like most sociological concepts,
culture is a word with both a popular and a
sociological meaning.

CULTURE AND SOCIETY

The classic definition of culture, framed by
Sir Edward Tylor (1871, vol. 1, p. 1], reads,
"Culture . . . is that complex whole which
includes knowledge, belief, art, morals, law,
custom and any other capabilities and habits
acquired by man as a member of society."
Stated more simply, *culture is everything which
is socially learned and shared by the members of a
society*. The individual receives culture as part
of a social heritage and, in turn, may reshape

the culture and introduce changes which then
become part of the heritage of succeeding
generations.

Culture may be divided into *material* and
nonmaterial culture. Nonmaterial culture consists of the words people use, the ideas,
customs, and beliefs they hold, and the habits
they follow. Material culture consists of man-
ufactured objects such as tools, furniture,
automobiles, buildings, irrigation ditches,
cultivated farms, roads, bridges, and, in fact,
any physical substance which has been
changed and used by people. Such manufac-
tured objects are called *artifacts*. In the game
of baseball, for instance, the gloves, bats,
uniforms, and grandstands are a few elements
of material culture. The nonmaterial culture
would include the rules of the game, the skills
of the players, the concepts of strategy, and
the traditional behavior of players and spectators. The material culture is always the
outgrowth of the nonmaterial culture and is
meaningless without it. If the *game* of baseball
is forgotten, a bat becomes just a stick of
wood. Since the most important part of culture is the *heritage of ideas*, this nonmaterial
culture will be the major emphasis of this
book.

Culture is often confused with society, but
the two words have different meanings.
Whereas a culture is a system of norms and
values, a *society is a relatively independent, self-
perpetuating human group which occupies a territory, shares a culture, and has most of its
associations within this group*.

A *society* is an organization of people whose
associations are with one another. A *culture*
is an organized system of norms and values

which people hold. Thus, the Plains Indians included a number of societies (which we call "tribes"), yet to a considerable extent they shared a similar culture. Adjoining societies may have quite different cultures, as with the United States and Mexico, or they may have quite similar cultures, as with the United States and Canada.

With both concepts—society and culture—the boundaries are indistinct. Most societies have some contact with neighboring societies. Many times in history two societies became so interwoven that they became one. Thus, many societies were absorbed into Roman society. Also, a single society may include groups of people who differ in culture, such as the French-, German-, and Italian-speaking segments of the Swiss population or the French- and English-speaking segments of the Canadian population.

SOCIAL AND CULTURAL DEVELOPMENT

Biological Factors

The recent growth of a discipline known as sociobiology has drawn renewed attention to biological factors in human behavior. Sociobiology is defined by its most prominent advocate [E. Wilson, 1975, p. 4] as "the systematic study of the biological basis of human behavior." We shall look at some ways in which the interaction of biology and culture influence human behavior, starting with the development of human society.

Cultural accumulation at first was very slow. People lived in the open or in caves; they used simple stone tools to skin animals and cut off chunks of meat; for digging edible roots, they probably used pointed sticks. There is some evidence that fire was used, but it is not known whether humans could make fire themselves or simply preserved fires started by lightning. During this period humans became skilled hunters, but there is

TABLE 3-1

IF A MILLION YEARS* OF HUMAN HISTORY WERE COMPRESSED INTO THE LIFETIME OF ONE SEVENTY-YEAR-OLD PERSON

1,000,000 years of history	Compressed into one seventy-year lifetime
1,000,000 years ago	Pithecanthropus erectus is born.
500,000 years ago	Spent half a lifetime learning to make and use crude stone axes and knives.
10,000 years ago	Nine months ago, the last ice age over, left the cave dwellings.
5,000 years ago	About three months ago, began to cast and use metals and built the Pyramids.
2,000 years ago	Seven weeks ago, Christ was born.
200 years ago	Five days ago, crossed the Delaware with Washington.
80 years ago	Yesterday, the airplane was invented.
11–15 years ago	This afternoon, landed on the moon, and in early evening, broke the DNA (genetic) code.
In the year 2000 A.D.	Tonight, celebrates the arrival of the twenty-first century!

*Or several million years, according to some anthropologists.

considerable argument as to whether these early hominids were humans at all. Their cranial capacity was in the range of 425 to 725 cubic centimeters, which would give them a skull measurement similar to that of the ape and far below the 1,000 to 2,000 cubic-centimeters range of today.

An acceleration in cultural development did not take place until the appearance of Neanderthal man about 150,000 years ago, with a cranial capacity similar to that of modern man—averaging about 1,500 cubic centimeters. Humans now had enough brains to build a culture, but basic inventions such as the wheel, the plow, writing, and many others were needed before a complex culture was possible.

SOCIAL EVOLUTION. Biological evolution was one of the exciting ideas of the nineteenth century. While many scholars contributed to evolutionary theory, its most influential sponsor was the naturalist Charles Darwin. After traveling the world and classifying tens of thousands of present life forms and fossil traces of earlier life forms, he developed, in his *Origin of Species* (1859), the theory that the human race had gradually evolved from lower orders of life. This came about through the survival of those biological forms best fitted to survive. The early sociologists wondered if there might be an evolutionary pattern in the development of human culture and social life.

Auguste Comte in his *Positive Philosophy* (1851–1854) wrote of three stages through which he believed human thought inevitably moved: the theological, the metaphysical (or philosophical), and finally the positive (or scientific). Herbert Spencer, a sociological "giant" of the nineteenth century, was enamored of "social Darwinism." He saw social evolution as a set of stages through which all societies moved from the simple to the complex and from the homogeneous to the heterogeneous. Implicit in the thinking of both Comte and Spencer was an optimism which saw the progress of society unfolding in a way that would gradually end misery and increase human happiness.

Wars, depressions, and totalitarian governments dampened this optimism and made the idea of social evolution seem naive. The cultural relativists (defined on page 69) denied that one could speak of a "higher" or "lower" type of culture and claimed that every culture was simply one of many possible ways of coping with the environment. The anthropologists denied that the direction of change is always from the simple to the more complex and pointed out that many primitive tribes had a far more elaborate kinship system and more ritualistic and ceremonial life than do modern societies. Culture historians such as Spengler and Toynbee deny the existence of any upward linear progress. They claim that

---

EVOLUTIONARY CHANGES AS SOCIETY INDUSTRIALIZES

Division of labor becomes more complex.
Bureaucracies grow in size and power.
Birthrates and death rates fall.
Inequality in income decreases.
Formal education increases.
Money and markets become important.
Kinship declines in importance.
Laws binding on all members of the society develop.

Source: Based upon Smelser, 1966, p. 111; Parsons, 1971, p. 5; Lenski and Lenski, 1982, p. 364.

---

societies have moved in cycles in which democracy and dictatorship follow each other with each great civilization eventually destroyed by barbarians.

Ideas, however, are hard to kill. The notion of social evolution,[1] which in the middle of the twentieth century seemed dead indeed, is very much alive today. One of the factors in its revival is the example of developing countries. As they become industrialized, they copy the technology and economic structures and many other features of the Western societies as a part of this "modernization" [Moore, 1963; Levy, 1967; Inkeles and Smith, 1974].

Are there common characteristics which all industrial societies share? Are there common patterns which developing countries must follow as they modernize? All steel mills, for example, must operate in much the same way and cannot shut down for an afternoon siesta. Modern technology brings many common cultural characteristics to any people who embrace modern technology.

[1] In our discussion of social evolution we are heavily indebted to Richard P. Appelbaum, *Theories of Social Change*, Markham Publishing Co., Chicago, 1970.

Geographic Factors

Climate and geography are undoubtedly factors in cultural development. Extremes of climate or topography are serious obstacles to many kinds of cultural development. Great civilizations do not flourish in the frozen Arctic, the torrid desert, the lofty mountain range or the tangled forest. People can live in these areas and may develop ingenious means of coping with natural forces, but such areas have not produced great cities or highly developed civilizations. On the other hand, the earliest great civilizations known to the world developed in the lowlands of great river basins. When one speaks of ancient Egypt, Mesopotamia, or India, one is talking primarily of the river valleys of the Nile, Euphrates, Tigris, and Indus. Only such areas met the requirements for an early civilization: (1) fertile land which could support a dense population, with part of the people free to engage in nonagricultural work, and (2) easy transportation to link together a large area.

Within the geographic extremes, however, it is hard to find any definite relationship. We can find too many examples of similar cultures in different climates and of different cultures in similar climates. For example, the Hopi and the Navajo have lived for centuries in the same area of the American Southwest. The Hopi are agriculturalists living in blocks of adobe apartment houses. The Navajo are sheep-herding nomads living in small, round, domed stick-and-mud houses. Their religion and family systems are very different. Dozens of such examples show that geographic environment sets certain limits but does not dictate any particular type of social life.

Nonhuman Social Organization

Many nonhuman species have an orderly system of social life. Many bird species mate for a lifetime and (in contrast to humans) are absolutely loyal to their mates. Many species of insects, such as ants and bees, have an elaborate pattern of social life, complete with specialized occupations, lines of authority, and detailed distribution of duties and privileges.

The organization of social life in animals above the insect level also shows many similarities to human society. This nonhuman social life may not be entirely determined by instinct. One of the best known instances is the pecking order in chickens [Guhl, 1953]. Establishment of dominance is as much a concern among chickens as among humans. The chicken yard is a highly stratified area in which some hens peck other hens without being pecked in return. Dominance is not granted automatically but is won either by fighting or by a convincing show of force. Once dominance is established, it tends to last for some time, and a hen which has been dominant in one group has an advantage when she moves into another poultry neighborhood. All this certainly sounds a bit similar to the determination of leadership in boys' gangs.

Dominance patterns and territorial defense patterns appear among many species [Ardrey, 1966]. Nonhuman societies show many other similarities to human societies, yet the differences are far more impressive. Among each nonhuman species, social life tends to be uniform and unchanging. Each lion pride acts much like all other lion prides and, apparently, the same as lion prides have acted for ages. Among humans, social life is infinitely variable and continuously changing.

The most important difference between humans and other animals is the degree to which the life of other animals is based on instinct rather than learning. Human beings are notably lacking in those inborn patterns of behavior which we call *instincts* in nonhuman species. Instead, they inherit a set of organic needs, urges, and hungers which we call *drives*, which must be satisfied in some way or other. In their trial-and-error efforts

Some animals form social groups. (© *YLLA; Rapho-Photo Researchers, Inc.*)

to satisfy their urges, humans create culture, with its tremendous variations from society to society. Unable to rely upon instinct, human beings must build culture in order to survive. Culture is a type of substitute for instinct since it gives humans direction and frees them from perpetual trial and error.

LANGUAGE AND SYMBOLIC COMMUNICATIONS. Many animals can exchange feelings through growls, purrs, mating calls, and other sounds. Some animals give off odors or make bodily movements which convey meanings to one another. These sounds and motions are not *language*, for each is largely or entirely an inborn, instinctive response rather than an acquired, symbolic response. We do not know

whether a dog growls or barks because it wants to tell another dog something; perhaps it barks because it feels like barking. As far as we know, no dog has yet developed a barking code (e.g., one short bark for "let's eat," two yips for "after you," etc.). A language is just such a code—*a set of sounds with a particular meaning attached to each sound*. A largely emotional or instinctive set of yips and yells is not a language, even though these sounds do serve to carry some accurate meanings to others of the species. A mother soon learns from her baby's cry whether it is hungry, sick, or angry; but the baby is expressing its emotions, not using language. Only when an *artificial* meaning is attached to each sound, so that the sound becomes a symbol—only then do we have language. The idea of "chair" might be represented by any one of thousands of vocal sounds; when the members of a society agree in dependably recognizing one particular vocal sound as meaning "chair," then a *word* has been added to the language. We limit the term *language* to symbolic communication and exclude the exchange of meanings through instinctive cries and sounds as not being true language.

Some highly popular books and magazine articles have coined the term "body language" for the exchange of meanings through gestures and body postures [Fast, 1970; Scheflen, 1973]. Some meanings probably are exchanged in this way. The question has received some scientific study [Ekman and Friesen, 1974; Henley, 1977; Druckman et al., 1982], but the current popularizations are largely based upon intuition and guesswork not upon scientific research. Furthermore, although "body language" may be a form of communication, it is not true *language*, since language is limited to communication through symbols.

Only human beings use symbols; therefore, only human communication reaches beyond the level of exchanging very simple feelings and intentions. With symbolic communication people can exchange detailed directions, share discoveries, organize elaborate activi-

Only the human race uses symbols.

ties. Without it, they would quickly revert to the caves and thickets.

ANIMAL "CULTURE."   Animals can learn; they can form interacting groups and have a social life; they can even communicate with one another at a very simple level. Some animals use objects as tools. For example, the Galápagos finch selects a suitable twig, pokes it into a crack in the tree bark, and gobbles up insects and spiders which scuttle out. It then saves the twig for the next poke [Smullen, 1978].

Chimpanzees have been taught to recognize a few words in both sign language [Gardner and Gardner, 1969] and plastic symbols [Premack, 1971]. Two chimpanzees which became famous because of their role in these experiments, Washoe and Sarah, can even produce their own messages. As Goodall and others have shown, chimpanzees have a greater capacity to form attachments, feel emotion, and make humanlike responses than people had ever imagined [Scarf, 1973; Goodall, 1978]. Such data lead some scientists to conclude that animals can have a culture [D. Hanson, 1973].

There is no evidence, however, that chimpanzees use anything like language in the wild [Lancaster, 1975; p. 71]. It is doubtful if any nonhumans can understand syntax or form sentences much less teach these skills to one another [Terrace, 1979].

A dog can be trained not to eat until given the signal by its master. But we cannot imagine a hungry dog passing up a juicy morsel because dogs have reached a collective opinion that a particular food, although nutritious, is quite unsuitable for a proper "gentledog." The conclusion of most social scientists is that only humans have a culture.

CULTURE AS A SYSTEM OF NORMS

Since culture includes the ways in which things should be done, we say that culture is

Animals both resemble and differ from humans in behavior.
(*Susan Kuklin/Photo Researchers, Inc.*)

normative, which is another way of saying that it defines standards of conduct. For shaking hands, we extend the right hand; this is proper in our culture. For scratching our heads we may use either hand; our culture has no norm for head scratching.

The term ''norm'' has two possible meanings. A *statistical norm* is a measure of what actually exists; a *cultural norm* is a concept of what is expected to exist. Sometimes the statistical norm is referred to as the ''real'' culture and the cultural norm as the ''ideal'' culture. Often people do not distinguish between the two norms. The famous Kinsey studies sought to find some statistical norms of sexual behavior in the United States. The

effort infuriated many people who confused statistical with cultural norms. A statistical norm is a measure of actual *conduct* with no suggestion of approval or disapproval. A cultural norm is a set of behavior *expectations*, a cultural image of how people are supposed to act. A culture is an elaborate system of such norms—of standardized, expected ways of feeling and acting—which the members of a society generally acknowledge and generally follow. These norms are of several kinds and several degrees of compulsion, as seen in the following classification. Most of these concepts were developed by the early sociologist William Graham Sumner in his *Folkways*, published in 1906.

Folkways

Social life everywhere is full of problems—how to wrest a living from nature, how to divide the fruits of toil or good fortune, how to relate ourselves agreeably to one another, and many others. Human beings seem to have tried every possible way of dealing with such problems. Different societies have found a wide variety of workable patterns. A group may eat once, twice, or several times each day; they may eat while standing, seated in chairs, or squatting on the ground; they may eat together, or each may eat in privacy; they may eat with their fingers or use some kind of utensils; they may start with wine and end with fish, start with fish and end with wine, or reject both. And so it goes for thousands of items of behavior. Each trait is a selection from a number of possibilities, all of which are more or less workable. Through trial and error, sheer accident, or some unknown influence, a group arrives at one of these possibilities, repeats it, and accepts it as the normal way of meeting a particular need. It is passed on to succeeding generations and becomes one of the ways of the folk—hence, a folkway. *Folkways are simply the customary, normal, habitual ways a group does things.* Shaking hands, eating with knives and forks, wearing neckties on some occasions and sport shirts on others, driving on the right-hand side of the street, and eating toast for breakfast are a few of our many American folkways.

New generations absorb folkways partly by deliberate teaching but mainly by observing and taking part in life about them. Children are surrounded by folkways. Since they constantly see these ways of doing things, they come to believe these are the only real ways. Customs of other groups appear as quaint oddities and not as practical, sensible ways of getting things done.

Even the most primitive society will have hundreds of folkways; modern, industrialized societies have thousands. Sorting out the proper folkway becomes so difficult that Emily Post was able to earn a fortune as an interpreter of our folkways, even though her fat volume does not catalog those followed by all Americans but lists only some of the nonoccupational folkways of the urban upper class. Visitors to a foreign country may need an etiquette book, lest they give offense.

Mores

Some folkways are more important than others. If one uses the wrong fork for one's salad, this is not very important, but if, in our society, a woman chooses anyone but her husband to sire her child, many aspects of financial obligation, property inheritance rights, family relationships, and sentimental linkage become disrupted. We therefore recognize two classes of folkways: (1) those which should be followed as a matter of good manners and polite behavior and (2) those which *must* be followed because they are believed essential to group welfare. These ideas of right and wrong which attach to certain folkways are then called *mores.* By *mores* we mean *those strong ideas of right and wrong which require certain acts and forbid others.* (*Mores* is the plural of the Latin word *mos,* but the singular form rarely appears in sociological literature.)

Members of a society normally share a sublime faith that violation of their mores will bring disaster upon them. Outsiders, however, often see that at least some of the group's mores are irrational. They may include food taboos which make cattle, hogs, or horses unfit to eat; modesty taboos which forbid exposure of the face, the ankle, the wrist, the breast, or whatever is considered "immodest"; language taboos which forbid misuse of certain sacred or obscene words; and many others. Such taboos seem very important to their believers but may be entirely unknown in other cultures and may have no necessary connection with group welfare. It is not necessary that the act forbidden by the mores

TOURISTS NEED CULTURAL KNOWLEDGE

Even a friendly grin can go wrong. Americans usually smile when shaking hands, but some German-speaking people find smiles too affectionate for new business acquaintances. So, while you're sizing up a German as a cold fish, he or she may be pegging you as the overly familiar type.

Try to break the ice in Germany with the "Wie geht's?" ("How goes it?") you got from watching war movies, and you'll be twice wrong. The expression is too informal and the question too personal for first encounters.

In Chinese-speaking areas, though, inquiring after a person's health is a proper first greeting, especially for the elderly.

But compliments are tricky in the Orient. You exchange them more readily there than in the U.S., but pay a Chinese-speaking person a compliment and he or she will surely decline it. Disagreeing is merely the way they accept praise. So if an Oriental compliments you, best be modest about it.

You can get into trouble by being too complimentary about objects in a Chinese or Japanese home; your host may feel obliged to give you the item.

The French are also evasive about compliments. They never say "merci" in response to praise, and if you respond to a compliment with "thanks," a French-speaking person could even interpret it as ridicule.

Formality is a must in France. Frenchmen who have worked side by side in an office for decades stick to formal pronouns when addressing each other, unless they also happen to have been school or military buddies.

And while using first names in business encounters is regarded as an American vice in many countries, nowhere is it found more offensive than in France.

Hand gestures are far from international. Italians wave goodbye with palm up and fingers moving back and forth—a beckoning signal to Americans. But when people wave the fingers with the palm down in China, Japan, and other Oriental areas, it's not goodbye—they mean "come here."

People who speak a romance language use more hand gestures than most Americans, but you can go wrong imitating them. For example, if you form a circle with thumb and forefinger, most Europeans will know you mean "it's the best," or "O.K." But in some Latin American countries the same gesture has a vulgar connotation.

The easiest place to have a gesture misunderstood abroad is in someone's home. Bearing gifts is expected in Japan, but can be considered a bribe in the Soviet Union. Portuguese and Brazilians like to bring foreigners home for dinner, but when it's time for you to go, politeness may compel them to insist that you stay. In some countries punctuality is expected; in others the custom is to arrive late. No matter where you go abroad, you can never assume that your best table manners will carry the day. You need a thorough rundown on local etiquette before you visit.

(Reprinted from the December issue of *Business Week* by special permission. © 1977, by McGraw-Hill, New York, 10020).

Within each modern country, etiquette varies among ethnic groups, regions, and social classes. Have you ever made a social blunder because of such differences?

should actually be injurious. If people *believe* that the act is injurious, it is condemned by the mores. Mores are *beliefs* in the rightness or wrongness of acts.

The irrationality of mores should not be exaggerated. Some mores are based upon a very genuine cause-and-effect relationship. For example, random killings would threaten group survival and individual peace of mind; therefore, every known society has condemned the killing of a fellow member of that society (except under certain specified circumstances). All known societies have developed an incest taboo, disapproving of sexual intercourse between close blood relatives, presumably because they found that sexual competition within the family was too disruptive. All mores are ideas which approve certain acts and forbid others in the *belief* that group welfare is being protected. Sometimes these beliefs are groundless, but sometimes they are fully justified.

Mores are not deliberately invented or thought up or worked out because someone decides they would be a good idea. They emerge gradually out of the customary practices of people, largely without conscious choice or intention. Mores arise from a group belief that a particular act seems to be harmful and must be forbidden (or, conversely, that a particular act is so necessary that it must be required). Originally, then, mores were a practical group belief about group welfare. For example, suppose that, through some coincidence, several members of a tribe have nasty accidents after swimming in a certain pool. The tribe comes to believe that there is something dangerous about the pool. When all members of the tribe believe that people should stay away from the pool, the mores have defined this act as wrong. Persons who swim in the pool thereafter are likely to expect misfortune, and others who know of their act will wait to see how they are punished. Thus, any misfortune will be interpreted as a punishment and will reinforce these mores. Before long, their origin is forgotten and people think of a dip in this pool as being wrong *in and of itself* not just because it seems to have been followed by misfortune. In this way, mores, which originate as practical group beliefs about the effects of actions, become transformed into absolutes—into things which are right because they are right and wrong because they are wrong. In other words, *mores become self-validating and self-perpetuating.* They become sacred. To question them is indecent, and to violate them is intolerable. Every society punishes those who violate its mores.

Mores are taught to the young not as a set of practical expedients but as a set of sacred absolutes. They must be internalized. To *internalize* means *to learn or accept something so completely that it becomes an automatic, unthinking part of our responses.* When fully internalized, mores control behavior by making it psychologically very difficult to commit the forbidden act. For example, we do not refrain from eating our children or our enemies because of an intellectual decision that cannibalism is impractical or wasteful but because the idea of cannibalism is so repellent to us that the thought of eating human flesh is sickening. Most of us would be unable to eat human flesh even if we tried to do so. Mores function by making their violation emotionally impossible. In a society with a clearly defined, firmly implanted set of mores, there is very little personal misconduct.

Some people claim that mores are just group opinions and are not the same as "real" right and wrong. They argue for absolute standards of morality, claiming that the nature of the universe makes certain actions definitely wrong and others definitely right, regardless of time, place, or circumstances. This is an important ethical issue but one which usually has meaning only for philosophers and theologians. As far as the behavior of most people is concerned, "mores" is simply another word for "real" right and wrong. For, as Sumner [1906] has observed, mores can make anything right and prevent condemnation of anything. Examples of contrasting definitions of wrong and right by mores are numerous. Some of these moral views seem bizarre indeed to a Western observer: the Kurtachi defecate in public and eat in private; the Balinese expose the breasts and hide the legs; Buganda men must be fully clothed, the women must go naked [Stephens, 1970]. Some Western mores appear equally odd to members of non-Western societies.

Medieval mores made it right for the Church to tolerate prostitution and even share in its income. Most of the Reformation churchmen, both Catholic and Protestant, who ordered the torture and burning of heretics were not cruel or evil but were decent and often kindly men who did what the mores of the time and place required them to do. Mores of our recent past have approved child labor, slavery, and persecution of minorities and have condemned pacifism, woman suffrage, and sex education. At all times and places good people feel pure and righteous when following their mores, whatever they may be.

Institutions

Some clusters of folkways and mores are more important than others; for example, those concerned with forming families and raising children are more important than those concerned with playing football. Organized clusters of folkways and mores dealing with highly important activities are embodied in the *social institutions* of the society. Institutions include behavior norms, values and ideals, and systems of social relationships. For a formal definition we suggest: *An institution is an organized system of social relationships which embodies certain common values and procedures and meets certain basic needs of the society.* In most complex societies there are five "basic" institutions—family life, religion, government, education, and organization of economic activities. In modern societies, science is institutionalized. Beyond these, the concept tapers off into less significant clusters of behavior patterns like those surrounding baseball, hunting, or beekeeping, which are sometimes loosely called institutions but probably should not be included because they are so much less important.

Institutions are among the most formal and compelling of the norms of a society. When the folkways and mores surrounding an important activity become organized into a quite formal, binding system of belief and behavior, an institution has developed. For example, banking, corporate enterprise, investment markets, checking accounts, and collective bargaining are economic institutions which began with simple barter thousands of years ago and passed through many stages of development. An institution thus includes (1) a set of behavior patterns which have become highly standardized; (2) a set of supporting mores, attitudes, and values; and (3) a body of traditions, rituals and ceremonies, symbols and vestments, and other paraphernalia. Social institutions will be treated in detail in later chapters but are introduced here because the concept must be used throughout our discussion.

Laws

While some mores function simply as mores, there is a strong tendency for them to become incorporated into the laws of a society. Many people will obey mores automatically or because they want to do the "right" thing. A few people, however, are tempted to violate mores. These people may be forced to conform by the threat of legal punishment. Thus, the law serves to reinforce the mores. Those who still will not conform are punished, imprisoned, or even executed. Sometimes laws are passed which do not really harmonize with mores, and their enforcement then becomes difficult or even impossible.

One example of this is the Eighteenth Amendment, passed in 1919, which outlawed the manufacture or sale of intoxicating liquor.

Sometimes laws do not harmonize with the mores.

No legislation, for instance,
decreed the end
of corsets for women.

The law was bitterly opposed by a sizeable proportion of the population and was repealed in 1933 when it became obvious that enforcement was impossible. Many people today would say the same is true of laws prohibiting the sale and possession of marijuana. Laws against ethnic discrimination did not reflect everyone's views when they were passed but are defended on the ground that they "educate" and thus promote a change in the mores which leads to an eventual willingness to observe such laws.

Mores do change, and the actions they command in one era, they may forbid in another. The change, however, is seldom conscious and deliberate but is a gradual adaptation to changing circumstances. Sumner referred to this kind of change as *crescive*, a type of natural development little affected by conscious human decisions [Sumner, 1940, pp. 53–55]. No legislature, for instance, decreed the end of corsets for women; they were simply phased out as more relaxed lifestyles made them needless. Similarly, it was not formal changes in the laws but a change of beliefs which finally ended the burning of witches.

This discussion of law as a codified expression of the mores is a functionalist view of law. Conflict sociologists see law as a tool of the powerful in controlling and exploiting the powerless. They see law as a means of legitimizing exploitation, while police and courts enforce the arrangements whereby some maintain their privileges at the expense of the underprivileged [Krisberg, 1975; Quinney, 1977]. Both views are correct. In any complex society, law enforces the mores and also protects and preserves the social system in which there are always some who are more privileged than others.

Values

Mores are ideas about whether acts are right or wrong. *Values are ideas about whether experiences are important or unimportant.* For example, there is no moral debate about whether classical music is right or wrong. But while some people consider hearing Beethoven's Ninth Symphony one of life's great experiences, for others it is a crashing bore. People who highly value physical fitness will exercise regularly and watch their food and drink. Values thus guide a persons' judgments and behavior.

In each society, some values are prized more highly than others. Punctuality, material progress, and competition are major values in American society, while none of these is important to the Hopi Indians. The members of a simple society generally are closely agreed upon a single set of values, while complex societies develop conflicting value systems. For example, is it more important to promote maximum economic development or to protect the environment? Should people develop individuality or be responsive to group opinion? Is change better than stability? Would a return to the "simple life" be a gain or a loss? Value disagreements are endless in complex societies, and values change from time to time. Value shifts also affect the folkways and mores. For example, the value shift toward sexual permissiveness is changing the mores of courtship, legal decisions about "palimony," and patterns of family life.

Meanwhile, the Moral Majority and others are making a determined effort to restore traditional sex and family values.

Value is closely related to price [Mitchell, 1968, p. 218]. Price is the money cost of a good or service, and the price one will pay measures how highly one values one good or service compared to others.

Values are an important part of every culture. An act is considered "legitimate"—that is, morally acceptable—when it is in harmony with accepted values. When our values defined the admirable woman as dutiful, domestic, and dependent, it was "legitimate" to discourage higher education for women; now that we increasingly admire women who are self-reliant, independent, and successful, higher education for women is considered legitimate and necessary.

THE STRUCTURE OF CULTURE

A culture is not simply an accumulation of folkways and mores; it is an *organized system* of behavior. Let us see some of the ways in which culture is organized.

Cultural Traits and Complexes

The smallest unit of culture is called a *trait*. Hoebel's definition [1949, p. 499] is: "A reputedly irreducible unit of learned behavior pattern or material product thereof." Traits of the material culture would include such things as the nail, the screwdriver, the pencil, and the handkerchief. Nonmaterial culture traits would include such actions as shaking hands, driving on the right-hand side of the road, kissing to show affection, or saluting the flag. Each culture includes thousands of traits.

Is the dance a trait? No; it is a collection of traits, including the dance steps, some formula for selecting the performers, and a musical or rhythmic accompaniment. Most important of all, the dance has a meaning—

Material culture consists of any physical substance which has been changed by human intervention.

as a religious ceremonial, a magical rite, a courtship activity, a festive orgy, or something else. All these elements combine to form a *culture complex*, a cluster of related traits. Another cluster of objects, skills, and attitudes forms the surfing complex.[2] Dozens more could be added.

The culture complex is intermediate between the trait and the institution. An institution is a series of complexes centering upon an important activity. Thus, the family includes the dating complex, the engagement-and-wedding complex, the honeymoon complex, the child-care complex, and several others. Some complexes are parts of institutions; others, revolving around less important activities—such as stamp collecting—are simply independent complexes.

Subcultures and Countercultures

Every modern society includes some groups of people who share some complexes which are not shared by the rest of that society. Immigrant groups, for example, develop a blend of the culture of their host nation and of the mother country. The rich have a life-style very different from that of the poor. The

---

[2] The term *complex*, as used in sociology, should not be confused with its use in psychology (e.g., inferiority complex) where the meaning is entirely different.

"adolescent culture" has special styles of behavior, thought, and dress, and a vocabulary which adults can scarcely translate. Each subculture has its private vocabulary which serves to preserve a private world against outsiders. Institutions tend to produce behavior patterns not found outside of the institutional setting, and the expressions "culture of the school" or "culture of the factory" suggest special sets of behavior patterns. Such terms as "army life," "preacher's kid," and "ivory tower" evoke pictures of special cultural settings.

Clusters of patterns such as these, which are *both* related to the general culture of the society and yet distinguishable from it, are called subcultures. The subcultures in our society include occupational, religious, national, regional, social-class, age, sex, and many others. Literature abounds in descriptions of subcultures, ranging from serious studies such as Howell's study of lower-class family life, *Hard Living on Clay Street* [1973], or Liebow's study of black men in *Talley's Corner* [1967], to Clausen's lighthearted description of carnival life in *I Love You Honey, but the Season's Over* [1961], or Birnbach's collection of middle- and upper-class American youth norms in *The Official Preppie Handbook* [1980].

Subcultures are important because each complex society does not have a single, uniform culture; instead it has a common core of traits and complexes plus an assortment of subcultures. Persons live and function mainly within certain of these subcultures. The immigrant may live within the immigrant subculture, and the army wife on a military post may have very little contact with civilians or civilian values. The child passes through several age subcultures and behaves according to their values, often distressing its parents, who apply the values of a different age subculture. Class and ethnic subcultures are discussed in Chapters 14 and 16.

Subcultures which are in active opposition to the dominant culture are called *countercul-*

The individual lives and operates mainly within certain subcultures.

tures. The delinquent gang, for instance, is not a group with no standards or moral values; it has very definite standards and a very compelling set of moral values, but these are quite different from those of conventional middle-class groups. Youths trained in this culture are influenced *against* the dominant cultural norms; hence, they are "countercultural." Similarly, American converts to Asian religious groups often adopt vegetarianism, prolonged meditation, celibacy, and a disdain of material success [Glock and Bellah, 1976, p. 1]. All these practices are quite opposed to the norms of the dominant American culture.

It should be remembered that a counterculture rejects *some, but not all,* of the norms of the dominant culture. Followers of the youth counterculture of the 1960s and 1970s, while rejecting most of the gadgets of a "materialistic" society, generally sought the finest stereo sound systems they could afford. Leading rock musicians, while singing lyrics condemning materialistic society, are highly materialistic in setting and collecting their fees. Street-level dealers in illegal drugs are reported to be torn between their desire to help impoverished followers of the drug subculture and their desire to make a healthy

Dancing is found in most societies. (© Paolo Koch/Photo Researchers, Inc.; Photo Researchers, Inc.; Marc and Evelyne Bernheim/Woodfin Camp & Assoc.; Bill Bernstein/ Black Star)

profit for themselves [Langer, 1977]. Such apparent inconsistencies do not denote insincerity or hypocrisy; they simply show that even the most extreme counterculture is a rejection of only part of the norms of the dominant culture.

Countercultures introduce many social changes. Whether they *cause* the changes, or simply reflect and draw attention to changes already arriving, may be debated [Yinger, 1978, 1982, chap. 14]. In any event, some of the "outrageous" behavior of countercultures today will be among the cultural norms of tomorrow [Leventman, 1981].

Cultural Integration

The culture of the Plains Indians centered upon the buffalo. From its carcass they drew most of their material culture as they used its flesh, hides, tendons, bones, sacs, membranes, and many other parts for one purpose or another. Their religion was mainly directed at ensuring the success of the buffalo hunt. Their status system measured success largely according to a man's hunting skill. Their nomadic way of life was attuned to the buffalo migrations. In other words, the different parts of the culture all fitted together in an interrelated system of practices and values. When the white man killed off the buffalo, the Plains Indian tribes were demoralized because the core of their culture had been destroyed.

Just as a pile of bricks is not a home, a list of traits is not a culture. A culture is an *integrated system* in which each trait fits into the rest of the culture. It is no accident that hunting peoples worship hunting gods, fishing peoples worship sea gods, and agricultural peoples worship sun and rain gods. The different parts of a culture must fit together if conflict and confusion are to be avoided. Conflict theorists would add that beneath the calm surface of an integrated culture may lurk many unrecognized clashes of interest and great injustice and that an integrated culture need not denote a just society.

The Eskimo male from time to time engages in conflicts, often violent ones, and surprising enough, the apparent cause in his sexually lax society is adultery. It is not considered adultery when a husband lends his wife to a friend. Nor is it considered adultery when a husband and wife join other couples in the game known as "putting out the lamp"—during which period of darkness they pick at random a partner of the opposite sex. Adultery exists only when a woman has sexual intercourse without the express approval and prior knowledge of her husband. Since such approval can usually be had for the asking, adultery has a significance other than sexual gratification. It is one man's unspoken challenge to another. And the offended husband must respond to the challenge or else he will live out the rest of his life in shame.

(Peter Falk, *Man's Rise to Civilization*, E. P. Dutton & Co., Inc., New York, 1968, pp. 43–44.)

How does this illustrate cultural relativism?

Cultural Relativism

We cannot possibly understand the actions of other groups if we analyze them in terms

The goodness or badness of a cultural trait depends upon its setting.

of *our* motives and values; we must interpret their behavior in the light of *their* motives, habits, and values if we are to understand them. Consider, for example, the administration of justice in the far North. The Canadian Mounties are occasionally called to go into the Arctic region to apprehend Eskimos who have committed a murder. This action in terms of our culture is a crime, and the individual has violated the mores. In the culture of many Eskimo tribes, however, the killing may have been justified, since their mores demand that a man avenge an assault upon a kinsman [Ruesch, 1977]. This type of revenge is not considered improper but is the only kind of action an honorable man could take. We would condemn the man who takes the law into his own hands and seeks revenge, while they would condemn the man who has so little courage and group loyalty as to allow his kinsman to go unavenged.

Cultural relativism means that the *function and meaning of a trait are relative to its cultural setting*. A trait is neither good nor bad in itself. It is good or bad only with reference to the culture in which it is to function. Fur clothing is good in the Arctic but not in the tropics. Premarital pregnancy is bad in our society, where the mores do not approve it and where there are no entirely comfortable arrangements for the care of illegitimate children; premarital pregnancy is good in a society such as that of the Bontocs of the Philippines, who consider a woman more marriageable when her fertility has been established and who have a set of customs and values which make a secure place for the children. Adolescent girls in the United States are advised that they will improve their marital bargaining power by avoiding pregnancy until marriage. Adolescent girls in New Guinea are given the opposite advice, and in each setting the advice is probably correct. The rugged individualism and peasant thrift of early America would produce great unemployment if they were widely practiced in our present mass-production economy. In some

hunting societies, which occasionally face long periods of hunger, to be fat is good; it has real survival value, and fat people are admired. In our society, to be fat is not only unnecessary but is known to be unhealthful and fat people are not admired.

The concept of cultural relativism does not mean that all customs are equally valuable, nor does it imply that no customs are harmful. Some patterns of behavior may be injurious everywhere, but even such patterns serve some purpose in the culture, and the society will suffer unless a substitute is provided.

Sociologists are sometimes accused of undermining morality with their concept of cultural relativism and their claim that almost "everything's right somewhere." If right and wrong are merely social conventions, say our critics, one might as well do whatever one wishes. This is a total misunderstanding. It is approximately true that "everything's right somewhere"—but not everywhere. The central point in cultural relativism is that in a particular cultural setting, certain traits are right because they work well in that setting, while other traits are wrong because they would clash painfully with parts of that culture. This is but another way of saying that a culture is integrated, and that its various elements must harmonize passably if they are to operate efficiently in serving human needs.

REAL AND IDEAL CULTURE

In most societies some behavior patterns are generally condemned yet widely practiced. In some places these illicit behavior patterns have existed for centuries side by side with the cultural norms which are supposed to outlaw them. Malinowski cites as an example of this type of behavior the Trobriand Islanders, a group whose incest taboos extend to third and fourth cousins.

If you were to inquire into the matter among the Trobrianders you would find that . . . the natives show horror at the idea of violating the rules of exogamy and that they believe that sores, disease and even death might follow clan incest. . . .

[But] from the point of view of the native libertine, *suvasova* (the breach of exogamy) is indeed a specially interesting and spicy form of erotic experience. Most of my informants would not only admit but actually did boast of having committed this offense or that of adultery (*kaylasi*); and I have many concrete, well-attested cases on record. (Bronislaw Malinowski, *Crime and Custom in Savage Society*, Routledge & Kegan Paul, Ltd., London, 1926, pp. 79, 84. Used with permission of Routledge & Kegan Paul, Ltd., and Humanities Press, Inc.)

As in all societies, the Trobrianders have some standardized ways of evading punishment. Malinowski [p. 81] observes, "Magic to undo the consequences of clan incest is perhaps the most definite instance of methodical evasion of law."

This case illustrates the difference between the real and ideal culture. The *ideal culture* includes the formally approved folkways and mores which people are supposed to follow (the cultural norms); the *real culture* consists of those which they actually practice (the statistical norms). For example, Warriner [1958] found that in Kansas, a legally "dry" state at the time of his research, many people drank in private while supporting the "temperance" morality in public. He concluded that the official morality served to prevent a disruptive public controversy, without interfering with their drinking behavior. There are many such divergences between the real and the ideal culture in our society.

A clash between the real and ideal culture patterns is generally avoided by some kind of rationalization which allows people to "eat their cake and have it, too." For example, Lowie [1940, p. 379] describes some Burmese villages which were Buddhist and whose inhabitants were therefore forbidden to kill any living thing, yet the villagers were dependent upon the murderous occupation of fishing. They evaded this contradiction by not literally killing the fish, which "are merely put out on the bank to dry after their long soaking in the river, and if they are foolish enough to die while undergoing the process, it is their own fault." Some such evasions and rationalizations are a part of every culture. In America, for example, many environmental issues are "settled" by passing stern antipollution laws to make the environmentalists happy and then "bending" these laws whenever they seriously inconvenience the polluters. A strict enforcement of highway speed limits might arouse so much argument and hostility among drivers who were only a little over the speed limit as to make the entire system unworkable, so a margin of about 10 miles an hour is generally permitted. Thus, the stated 55-mile-an-hour speed limit (ideal culture) becomes a 65-mile-an-hour limit in practice (real culture).

Practical compromises are universal. In some primitive societies courtship and marriage rituals are so cumbersome and costly that most marriages occur through elopement, which is "indecent." If the couple are unusually awkward, they may be caught and severely beaten, but ordinarily they are able to make good their escape. After a period of penance, they are welcomed back into the social group. Thus the society can maintain a public morality without disrupting a useful practice. Such "adjustments" between real and ideal culture are found in all societies.

ETHNOCENTRISM

There is an Eskimo tribe who call themselves the *Inuit*, which translates as "the real people" [Herbert, 1973, p. 2]. Sumner called this outlook *ethnocentrism*, formally defined as "that view of things in which one's own group is the center of everything and all others are scaled and rated with reference to it" [Sumner, 1906, p. 13]. Stated less formally, ethnocentrism is the habit of each group taking for granted the superiority of its culture. We assume, without thought or argument, that monogamy is better than polygamy, that young people should choose their own mates, and that it is best for the young married couple to live by themselves. Our society is "progressive," while the non-Western world is "backward"; our art is beautiful, whereas that of other societies may be viewed as grotesque; our religion is true; others are pagan superstition.

Ethnocentrism makes our culture into a yardstick with which to measure all other cultures as good or bad, high or low, right or queer in proportion as they resemble ours. It is expressed in such phrases as "chosen people," "progressive," "superior race," "true believers," and by epithets like "foreign devils," "infidels," "heathen," "backward peoples," "barbarians," and "savages." Like the Bostonian who "didn't need to travel because he was already here," we are usually quick to recognize ethnocentrism in others and slow to see it in ourselves.

Most, if not all, groups within a society are ethnocentric. Caplow [1964, p. 213] studied fifty-five sets of six organizations each, including fraternities, churches, insurance companies, colleges, and many others. He found that members overestimated the prestige of

their own organizations eight times as often as they underestimated it. Levine and Campbell [1972] list twenty-three facets of a "universal syndrome of ethnocentrism," that is, ethnocentric responses which they find in all societies. Ethnocentrism is a universal human reaction, found in all known societies, in all groups, and in practically all individuals.

Exposure to the history of minority groups is helping both minorities and the majority to become aware of their ethnocentrism. Consider the following comments on the origin of many discoveries: "Black history has made people aware that white people did not give America such things as the stoplight, the shoe last, heart operations and sugar refining, but that black people did; that John Smith did not develop corn and tobacco, but learned to grow these crops from the Indians." [Brazziel, 1969, p. 349].

Personality and Ethnocentrism

All groups stimulate the growth of ethnocentrism, but not all members of the group are equally ethnocentric. There is some evidence that many people in American society develop a personality which is predisposed to ethnocentrism. How can we explain this? One answer is that some of us are strongly

---

WHICH OF THESE STATEMENTS ARE ETHNOCENTRIC?*

1 Labor productivity is lower in Guatemala than in the United States.
2 Never trust anyone over thirty.
3 Turn off that junk so I can study.
4 I don't like rock music.
5 I don't like classical music.
6 Hard-hat workers are selfish and narrow-minded.
7 Christians are devout; heathens are superstitious.

8 I prefer my religion to all others.
9 Politicians are crooks.
10 Sociologists have the answer to social problems.
11 Orientals are inscrutable.
12 Americans know how to handle business.
13 The United States has the greatest industrial production of any nation.

*Items 1 and 13 are simple statements of fact. Items 4, 5, and 8 state beliefs or preferences without any ethnocentric reflections upon the beliefs or preferences of others. The rest of the items are ethnocentric.

ethnocentric as a defense against our own inadequacies. At one time, it was believed that social science had established a definite link between personality patterns and ethnocentrism. In *The Authoritarian Personality*, Adorno [1950] found that ethnocentric people tended to be less educated, more socially withdrawn, and religiously more orthodox. In this approach, ethnocentrism was defined primarily as intense and uncritical loyalty to an ethnic or national group along with prejudice against other ethnic or national groups. The trouble with this definition is that it excludes some other types of ethnocentrism. If an uncritical loyalty to the views of one's group is to be the test of ethnocentrism, then members of supposedly liberal and educated circles may be just as ethnocentric as those in conservative and uneducated circles. The conservatives may be uncritical of religious orthodoxy and national patriotism and quite sure of the superiority of their own ethnic group. The self-styled liberal may be equally rigid in the opposite direction: sure that the national foreign policy is always wrong, that orthodox religion is mere superstition, and that business people, blue-collar workers, and politicians are invariably either stupid or corrupt [Greeley, 1970; Hoffer, 1969; Lerner, 1969; Lipset and Ladd, 1972].

Ethnocentrism may be appealing because it reaffirms the individual's "belongingness" to the group while it offers comfortingly simple explanations of complex social phenomena. The old, the socially secluded, the less educated, and the politically conservative may be ethnocentric, but the young, the well educated, the widely traveled, the politically "left," and the well-to-do may also be [Ray, 1971; Wilson et al, 1976]. It is debatable whether there is any significant variation, by social background or personality type, in the degree to which people are ethnocentric.

Effects of Ethnocentrism

Is ethnocentrism good or bad for people? First, we should have to decide how to define "good" and "bad," and even then we might find the question very unsettled. Ethnocentrism gets us into many of our muddles, yet it is doubtful whether groups can survive without it.

PROMOTION OF GROUP UNITY, LOYALTY, AND MORALE.   Ethnocentric groups seem to survive better than tolerant groups. Ethnocentrism justifies sacrifice and sanctifies martyrdom. The attitude, "I prefer my customs, although I recognize that, basically, they may be no better than yours," is not the sort of faith for which dedicated believers will march singing to their deaths.

Ethnocentrism reinforces nationalism and patriotism. Without ethnocentrism, a vigorous national consciousness is probably impossible. Nationalism is but another level of group loyalty. Periods of national tension and conflict are always accompanied by intensified ethnocentric propaganda. Perhaps such a campaign is a necessary emotional preparation for the expected sacrifices.

PROTECTION AGAINST CHANGE.   If our culture is already superior, then why tinker with

ETHNOCENTRISM AND AFRICAN PLACE NAMES

Before African rule	After African rule
Dahomey	Benin
Belgian Congo	Zaire
Gold Coast	Ghana
Nyasaland	Malawi
Leopoldville	Kinshasa
Lorenco Marques	Maputo
Bathurst	Banjul
Fort Lamy	Njamea
Southwest Africa	Namibia
Tanganyika	Tanzania
Rhodesia	Zimbabwe

Note: This is a case of ethnocentrism on both sides. Europeans tended to select names which emphasized European influence while Africans reversed the process when they gained power.
Source: Adapted from Larry Heinzerling, "Spirit of Black Nationalism Still Evident in Africa's New Names," *AP*, April 1, 1976.

Ethnocentrism also acts to discourage change.

alien innovations? From the Biblical Hebrews to nineteenth-century Japan, ethnocentrism has been used to discourage the acceptance of alien elements into the culture. Such efforts to prevent culture change are never entirely successful; change came to both the Hebrews and the Japanese. Yet if people share a serene, unquestioning faith in the goodness of their culture—a conviction so completely accepted that no proof is necessary—then change is delayed. In discouraging culture change, ethnocentrism is undiscriminating. It discourages both the changes which would disrupt the culture and the changes which would help it attain its goals.

Since no culture is completely static, every culture must change if it is to survive. Ethnocentrism in India today helps to keep it from turning communist, but India may not remain noncommunist unless it rapidly modernizes its technology and controls its population growth, and these changes are delayed by ethnocentrism. In an age of atom bombs and pushbutton warfare, when the nations must probably either get together or die together, ethnocentrism helps to keep them tied to concepts of national sovereignty. Under some circumstances, then, ethnocentrism promotes cultural stability and group survival; under other circumstances, ethnocentrism dooms the culture to collapse and the group to extinction.

It is ironic that those seeking to promote change often fail because of their ethnocentrism. They dismiss "native" ways as useless and assume that our "modern" technology must be superior. For example, American agricultural development programs have often failed because they tried to transplant American cattle, American crops, and American farm technology into undeveloped countries (see p. 530). Closer home, American sheepmen are still clamoring to resume coyote poisoning, which is environmentally destructive and not even very effective [Zumbo, 1981; Steinhart, 1982]. They ignore a simple method of coyote control followed by the Navajo of Arizona for generations. The Navajo raise dogs with their sheep and do *not* make pets of them. The dogs protect the sheep, cost little, and do no environmental harm [Black, 1981]. Ethnocentric faith in high technology and disdain for "backward" peoples often blinds us to practicality.

XENOCENTRISM

This word means a preference for the foreign. It is the exact opposite of ethnocentrism [Shils, 1972; Wilson et al, 1976]. It is the belief that our own products, styles, or ideas are necessarily inferior to those which originate elsewhere. It is the conviction that the exotic has a special charm which the familiar can never achieve. It is based on the glamor of the strange and faraway and the prestige of distant centers, supposedly removed from the sordid limitations of one's own community.

There are many occasions when people seem happy to pay more for imported goods on the assumption that anything from abroad is better. Are French fashions, German beers, or Japanese electronic wares really superior? Or are people inclined to assume they are superior because of the lure of the foreign label?

What applies to material products is also true of ideas and life-styles. Although the United States was originally hailed as a bastion of freedom challenging the despotisms of Europe, it did not take long for many intellectuals to adopt a xenocentric viewpoint:

No sooner did the ocean crossing become comfortable than the expatriates [Americans leaving their country] began their flight across the Atlantic to the more congenial cultural climate of the old world . . . the criticism of American materialism, . . . once associated with aristocrats, [was] now voiced by intellectuals, "Coca-colization"; that is of pervasive vulgarization of life. The United States was regarded as the source, or at least the prototype, of a culture built upon possession, upon the diffusion of an idolatry for material things; and it was on this account judged harshly. (Oscar Handlin, "Liberal Democracy and the Image of America," *Freedom at Issue*, 43, November/December, 1977, pp. 14–15. Reprinted by permission.)

Those who leave their country to live abroad are not the only ones who reject ethnocentrism. In every society a few persons reject their group or some part of its culture. There are anti-Semitic Jews, blacks who reject black identity, aristocrats who lead revolutions, priests who abandon their faith, and so on. This rejection of one's group or its culture is a form of deviant behavior that will be discussed in Chapter 7.

Is there any rational basis for xenocentrism or is it just a form of shallow snobbery? Revisionist historians who blame America for

---

CULTURE AND BIOLOGY

A survey by the Food and Agriculture Organization of the United Nations (FAO) warned that a growing preference for bottle feeding over breast feeding in urban areas "has a dramatic impact on child malnutrition in low-income groups," because unlike sterile and nutritious mothers' milk, overdiluted or unsanitary formula can promote intestinal disorders and hasten the onset of malnutrition.

(*Agenda*, 1, May 1978, p. 21.)

Are there any other "modern" practices which developing peoples might be wise to ignore?

---

all the world's troubles and radical critics who pounce gleefully upon every imperfection in "Amerika" but are blind to brutality and genocide in Communist and Third World countries may be as irrational as the most ethnocentric flag-waver.

CULTURE AND HUMAN ADJUSTMENT

Is culture a help or a burden to human beings? Some of each. It helps them to solve some problems, gets in their way as they grapple with others, and itself creates still others.

Culture and Biological Adjustment

Culture contains many gadgets which help people in their unremitting battle with nature. Since people suffer in cold and hot weather, they wear clothes and build houses. Nature offers wild fruit, seeds, and berries; people domesticate them and increase their yield. Hands are poor shovels, but bulldozers remake the surface of the earth. Human beings cannot run fast, swim well, or fly at all; yet no other living thing travels so fast as they. Humans are fragile, delicate beings, quick prey to death through heat or cold, thirst or hunger. Through culture they can moisten the desert and dry the swampland, can survive arctic cold and tropic heat, and can even survive a trip through outer space.

While culture helps people adjust to their environment, it also interferes with their biological adjustment in many ways. Every culture offers many examples of patterns harmful to physical well-being. The Hindu belief that people should not kill anything has filled India with stray dogs, scrawny cattle, and all manner of parasites, thus wasting food and spreading diseases. Through culture we have improved our weapons until we can destroy the entire human race. We follow methods of agriculture and land use which destroy the soil and flood the land. We pollute the air,

We congratulate ourselves on our ability to control our physical environment.

foul the streams, and poison our foods. Many of us eat, smoke, and drink more than is good for us. We eat polished rice or white bread which is stripped of vital food elements, while passing up beef, pork, horse meat, snake meat, snails, milk, or whatever valuable source of nourishment is under taboo in our particular society. If we were descended from cats instead of primates, we would be better equipped for the night hours we like to keep. In every culture there are norms that are healthful and others which are injurious.

Culture and Social Adjustment

Some cultural norms seem to interfere with the meeting of basic human needs. During our Great Depression of the 1930s, we recognized that there was something very wrong when adults were idle and children were hungry while work went undone and food rotted in the fields. The norms of the culture may cultivate certain feelings, such as guilt, personal unworthiness, or sexual inhibitions to a degree which any modern psychologist would judge as physically and mentally unhealthy. As seen in Chapter 4 the Dobuans' emphasis upon witchcraft made people fearful, anxious, and distrustful of others. A culture may include no comfortable place for certain categories of persons. Thus, widows

in certain parts of India were expected to perish in their husbands' funeral pyres, while, until recently, most unmarried women in America were more or less welcome members of some relative's household.

Some cultural norms may be elaborated to the point of impracticality. It is said that Marie Antoinette was unable to get a glass of cold water; court etiquette required it to pass through so many hands that it was always tepid by the time it reached her. Rivers [1922] tells how on Torres Island in Melanesia, canoe building was surrounded with such an elaborate set of magical rites and taboos that only a small group of hereditary canoe builders dared to try to build one. Others were familiar with the manual skills for canoe building, but since they lacked the secret magic, it was unthinkable that they should build the craft. Therefore, when the hereditary canoe-builder families died out, the Torres Islanders went without canoes despite their desperate need for them. Thus in almost any culture, one can find norms which seem useless or harmful.

If this deliberate frustration seems stupid to the reader, let him or her try to explain why the United States and the Soviet Union continue building nuclear warheads when they already have enough to incinerate the entire world several times over or why we have unemployment when there is much useful work waiting to be done?

SUMMARY

Culture is everything which is socially learned and shared by a human society. *Material culture* is made up of artifacts people make. *Nonmaterial culture* comprises the behavior patterns, norms, values, and social relationships of a human group. A *society* is a relatively independent, self-perpetuating human group which occupies a particular territory and has most associations within this group.

Culture accumulated slowly in prehistoric

times; rapidly in recent centuries. *Sociobiology* studies the biological factor in human behavior and social development. Evolutionary theories of social development were once popular and are enjoying a revival today. Animal societies are based largely upon instinct; human societies largely upon culture.

Folkways are the customs of a society. *Mores* are the ideas of right and wrong which become attached to some kinds of behavior. Mores may become sanctified by religion and strengthened by being made into *laws*. *Values* are ideas about whether experiences are important or unimportant.

Institutions are major clusters of folkways and mores which center on an important human need.

A *trait* is the simplest unit of culture; related traits are grouped into *culture complexes*. A *subculture* is the behavior and value system of a group which is a part of the society, but which has certain unique cultural patterns. A *counterculture* is a subculture which is not merely different from but sharply opposed to the dominant values of the society.

A culture is an *integrated* system of behavior with its supporting ideas and values. In a highly integrated culture all elements fit harmoniously together.

Cultural relativism describes the fact that the function and meaning of a culture trait depend upon the culture in which it operates. Traits are judged "good" or "bad" according to whether they work efficiently within their own culture.

Every society has an *ideal culture*, including the patterns which are supposed to be practiced, and a *real culture*, including illicit behavior which is formally condemned but widely practiced. Clashes between the two are evaded by rationalization. In some cases, illicit patterns are ways of getting necessary tasks done and thus, even though the mores do not approve the illicit actions, may actually contribute to cultural stability.

All societies and groups assume the superiority of their own culture; this reaction is called *ethnocentrism*. The ideas and customs about which people are ethnocentric vary from society to society, but all known societies, and all groups within a society, display ethnocentrism.

Culture both aids and hinders human adjustment. It enables people to survive in an inhospitable physical environment, although in many respects it sustains habits which are physically injurious. We could not live without culture; sometimes it is not easy to live with it.

GLOSSARY

counterculture subculture not merely different from but in opposition to the conventional and approved culture of the society; e.g., the drug subculture.
cultural relativism concept that the function, meaning, and "desirability" of a trait depend upon its cultural setting.
culture everything which is socially learned and shared by members of a society.
drive hereditary urge which

temporarily disappears when it has been satisfied.
ethnocentrism tendency of each group to take for granted the superiority of its own culture.
evolution the theory that present forms of life have developed from earlier, simpler forms.
folkways customary, normal, habitual behavior characteristic of the members of the group.
hominoids any of the species of early humans and/or their ancestors.

instinct an inborn behavior pattern characteristic of all members of a species.
institution an organized cluster of folkways and mores centered around a major human activity; organized system of social relationships which embodies certain common values and procedures and meets certain basic needs of society.
internalize to learn something so thoroughly that it becomes an automatic, unthinking part of our responses.
mores strong ideas of right

and wrong which require certain actions and forbid others.

Neanderthal race of prehistoric people who lived between 60,000 and 300,000 years ago.

norm a standard of behavior. A statistical norm is a measure of actual conduct; a cultural norm states the expected behavior of the culture.

social Darwinism the belief that social arrangements developed gradually on the basis of a competitive struggle in which the best adapted humans and social forms survived.

society a relatively independent, self-perpetuating human group which occupies a particular territory, shares a culture, and has most activities within this group.

sociobiology the systematic study of the biological basis of human behavior.

subculture a cluster of behavior patterns related to the general culture of a society and yet distinguishable from it; behavior patterns of a distinct group within the general society.

symbol anything which represents something beyond itself; such as a word, a gesture, or a flag.

values ideas about whether experiences are important or unimportant.

xenocentrism a preference for foreign ideas or products.

QUESTIONS AND PROJECTS

1 Does social development lead to uniformity? If not, what limits does it place on variation?

2 What are the limits which genetic inheritance places on social policy?

3 Should society prevent reproduction of those who have the potential capacity of transmitting hereditary defects? Defend your answer.

4 Assume it may become possible to control the genetic makeup of babies, "ordering" whatever combination of characteristics we desire. What conflicts would this create?

5 Which would give greater understanding of Roman culture—studying the ruins, sculpture, and public works that have been excavated or studying the records of the nonmaterial culture preserved in literature, letters, and legal documents? Why?

6 How do you differentiate between society and culture?

7 What is meant by the statement that, when firmly established, mores operate automatically? Does this happen in our society?

8 In what respects are your values similar to those of your parents? In what respects do they differ? How do you explain these differences?

9 Apply your knowledge of the integration of culture in evaluating the proposal that our society should return to the "simple life."

10 Select an occupational group and describe the *special* behavior typical of that occupation.

11 Cheating in college is sometimes defended on the ground that it is necessary if a student is to reach the goal of graduation. Is this position defensible in terms of cultural relativism? Why or why not?

12 Are there any respects in which real campus subculture differs from ideal campus subculture?

13 Is ethnocentrism the opposite of cultural relativism? Explain.

14 In what ways does ethnocentrism aid in national survival in the modern world? In what ways does it jeopardize national survival?

15 Can one have opinions and preferences without being ethnocentric? Make a list of several ethnocentric expressions of opinion or judgment. Now make a list of several nonethnocentric statements of opinion or judgment.

16 Read the article by Frankel listed in the readings. Are the dangers he lists in securing greater control of human heredity serious? What effect would control of heredity have on social evolution?

17 Read D. Ramsey and D. Kirk, "Lessons From Japan," *Newsweek*, 96:61–62, September 8, 1980. Would the type of labor policies followed by Japanese industrialists be feasible in the United States? Why or why not?

18 Read either "Are Those Apes Really Talking?" *Time*, 115:50–57, March 10, 1980, or C. R. Thompson and R. N. Church, "Explanations of the Language of a Chimpanzee," *Science*, 208:86–88, January 2, 1981.

Report on similarities and differences in communication between chimpanzees and humans.

SUGGESTED READINGS

Arens, W., and Susan P. Montague: *The American Dimension: Cultural Myths and Social Realities*, Alfred Publishing Company, New York, 1976. Basic themes in American life as exemplified in the culture, such as soap opera as a clue to American kinship patterns, football as an example of coordination through division of labor, and poker as an illustration of the myth that one can gain wealth through individual effort!

*Barash, David P.: *Sociobiology and Behavior*, Elsevier Publishing Company, Inc., New York, 1977. A brief, readable book dealing primarily with behavior in animals, but also including some speculation on a possible human "biogram."

Clark, Matt, and Maria Gosnell: "The New Gene Doctors," *Newsweek*, 96:120–123, May 18, 1981. A brief and readable article on the social implications of developments in genetic research.

Ellis, Lee: "The Decline and Fall of Sociology, 1975–2000," *The American Sociologist* 12:56–65, May 1977. A quasi-satirical article which predicts that sociology is soon to be sup-

planted by sociobiology, with rejoinders by Barash, Homans, Kunkel, Lenski, Mazur, and Van den Berghe.

*Etzioni, Amitai: *Genetic Fix*, The Macmillan Company, New York, 1973. Sociological analysis of issues involved in "genetic counseling."

Frankel, Charles: "The Specter of Eugenics," *Commentary*, 57:25–33, March 1974. A philosopher looks at the promise and danger of producing human types on demand by altering the genes.

Jencks, Christopher: "Heredity, Environment and Public Policy Reconsidered," *American Sociological Review*, 45:723–736, October 1980. Develops the idea that the effects of heredity depend on the interaction of the inherited trait with the environmental situation.

Langer, John: "Drug Entrepreneurs and Dealing Culture," *Social Problems*, 24:377–386, February 1977. Describes the conflict between the drug dealer as business entrepreneur and as participant in a counterculture.

Linton, Ralph: *The Study of Man: An Introduction*, Appleton-Century-Crofts, Inc., New York, 1936. A classic analysis of the role of culture in human affairs. Chaps. 5, 6, 20, and 25 are especially recommended.

McGehee, Charles L.: "Spiritual Values and Sociology: When We Have Debunked Everything, What Then?" *American Sociologist*, 17:40–46, February

1982. Argues the importance of values as a vital part of the culture.

Miner, Horace: "Body Ritual among the Nacirema," *American Anthropologist*, 58:503–507, June 1956; The Bobbs-Merrill Company, Inc., Indianapolis, reprint S-185. An anthropologist describes quaint customs and odd values of a well-known modern culture which the student may recognize.

Podhoretz, Norman: "The New Inquisitors," *Commentary*, 55:7–8, April 1973. A brief analysis of the development and enforcement of ethnocentric attitudes among liberal intellectuals on college campuses.

*Reed, John Shelton: *The Enduring South: Subcultural Persistence in Mass Society*, Heath Lexington Books, Lexington, Mass., 1972. A brief and lively sketch of the factors which make for the persistence of a distinctive subculture in the American South.

Stine, Gerald James: *Biosocial Genetics: Human Heredity and Social Issues*, The Macmillan Company, New York, 1977. A primer for those interested in the social impact of genetic engineering.

Westhues, Kenneth: *Society's Shadow: Studies in the Sociology of Countercultures*, McGraw-Hill Ryerson Ltd., Toronto, 1972. A readable description of countercultures from the perspective of the sociology of religion.

* An asterisk before the citation indicates that the title is available in a paperback edition.

4 Personality and Socialization

The little girl skipped away, her fat curls bouncing in the sun, and sang in a clear high voice: "Sticks and stones will break my bones but names will never hurt me. When I die, you will cry for all the names you called me."

And Francie did cry. Not for all the names called but because she was lonesome and nobody wanted to play with her. The rougher children found Francie too quiet and the better behaved ones seemed to shun her. Dimly, Francie felt that it wasn't all her fault. It had something to do with Aunt Sissy who came to the house so often, the way Sissy looked and the way the men in the neighborhood looked after Sissy when she passed. It had something to do with the way papa couldn't walk straight sometimes and walked sideways down the street when he came home. It had something to do with the way neighbor women asked her questions about papa and mama and Sissy. Their wheedling offhand questions did not deceive Francie. Had not mama warned her: "Don't let the neighbors pick on you."

So in the warm summer days the lonesome child sat on her stoop and pretended disdain for the group of children playing on the sidewalk. Francie played with imaginary companions and made believe that they were better than real children. But all the while her heart beat in rhythm to the poignant sadness of the song the children sang while walking around in a ring with hands joined. . . .

(Reprinted by permission from Betty Smith, *A Tree Grows in Brooklyn*, Harper & Row, Publishers, Inc., New York, 1943, pp. 83–84.)

The above passage is from an autobiographical novel which tells of the life of a slum child who grew up to become quite different from most of her schoolmates. A thoughtful reading of this perceptive novel will illustrate, possibly better than any textbook, how each person develops a unique personality through a process we call socialization.

THE MEANING OF PERSONALITY

When we hear someone say that "Marge has a lot of personality," this tells us that Marge is a colorful and interesting person. But the term personality is incorrectly used, because one's personality includes *all* of one's behavior characteristics. Used correctly, one person does not have *more* personality than another; one has a *different* personality than another. A useful definition is offered by Yinger [1965, p. 141], who says: "Personality is the totality of behavior of an individual with a given tendency system interacting with a sequence of situations."

The phrase, "a given tendency system," indicates that each person has characteristic ways of acting, and acts much the same day after day. When we remark, "Isn't that just like Ruth," we recognize that Ruth has a behavior "tendency system" that is quite characteristic of her. The phrase, "interacting with a sequence of situations," indicates that behavior is a joint product of a person's behavior tendencies and the behavior situations that person meets. To understand personality, we need to know how behavior tendency systems develop through the interaction of the biological organism with various kinds of social and cultural experience.

FACTORS IN THE DEVELOPMENT OF PERSONALITY

The factors in personality development include: (1) biological inheritance, (2) physical environment, (3) culture, (4) group experience, and (5) unique experience.

Biological Inheritance and Personality

A brick house cannot be built of stone or bamboo; but from a pile of bricks, a great variety of houses can be built. Biological inheritance provides the raw materials of

> Every man is in certain respects
>
> Like all other men
> Like some other men
> Like no other man
>
> (Clyde Kluckhohn and Henry A. Murray (eds.), *Personality in Nature, Society, and Culture,* Alfred A. Knopf, Inc., New York, 1953, p. 53.)
>
> Which of the "factors in the development of personality" is linked with each of the three statements above?

personality, and these raw materials can be shaped in many different ways.

All normal, healthy human beings have certain biological similarities, such as two hands, five senses, sex glands, and a complex brain. These biological similarities help explain some of the similarities in the personality and behavior of all people.

Every person's biological inheritance is also *unique,* meaning that no other person (except an identical twin) has exactly the same inherited physical characteristics. Not long ago most people believed each person's personality was little more than the unfolding of that person's biological inheritance. Such personality traits as perseverance, ambition, honesty, criminality, sex deviation, and most other traits were believed to arise from inherited predispositions. Few believe this today. Instead, it is now recognized that all personality characteristics are shaped by experience. In fact, some claim that individual differences in ability, achievement, and behavior are almost entirely environmental, and that individual differences in biological inheritance are not very important [e.g., Whimby, 1975].

This is the nature-nurture controversy which has been raging for centuries. Interest in the biological basis for individual differences in intelligence and behavior is currently rising. Studies of identical twins are a favorite re-

search approach. One study of 2,500 high school twins concludes that "about half the variation among people in a broad spectrum of psychological traits [within our society] is due to differences among people in genetic characteristics," while the other half is due to environment [Nichols, 1977]. The most extensive twin study ever made was by the Medicogenetical Institute of Moscow, which separated a thousand sets of identical twins at infancy, placing them in controlled environments for two years' observation. The findings strongly supported a hereditary basis for many characteristics, including intelligence differences. This conclusion displeased Stalin, who abolished the institute and executed its director [Hardin, 1959, p. 235].

As the fate of this scholar shows, the question of heredity versus environment is not simply a scientific question but is also a political issue. Thus, Marxists and others who promote the goal of equality of rewards are annoyed by evidence that people differ in native abilities. Conservatives joyously seize upon evidence of unequal native abilities and cite this to justify unequal rewards. But individual differences in biological inheritance are real, regardless of whether this fact makes one happy or unhappy.

For some traits, biological inheritance is more important than for others. A number of studies have shown, for example, that the IQ of adopted children more closely resembles the IQ of their natural parents than of their adoptive parents; and within a particular family, the natural children follow the IQ of the parents far more closely than do the adopted children [Skodak and Skeels, 1949; Munsinger, 1975; Horn, 1976a; Scarr and Weinberg, 1976; Juel-Nielson, 1980]. But, while individual differences in IQ seem to be more highly determined by heredity than by environment, many other differences are almost entirely environmental. One recent study found evidence for heritability strong for sociability, compulsiveness, and social ease, but found heritability to be unimportant for lead-

Studies of adopted children offer one kind of evidence in the nature-nurture controversy. (*Erika Stone/Peter Arnold, Inc.*)

ership, impulse control, attitudes, and interests [Horn, 1976*b*]. Two recent studies concluded that childhood temperament, specifically timidity, is rooted in biological inheritance [Herbert, 1982a]. Thus we may conclude that biological inheritance is important for some personality traits and less important for others. In no case can the respective influence of heredity and environment be precisely measured, but most scientists agree that whether one's inherited potentials are fully developed is strongly affected by one's social experience.

BIOLOGICAL MATURATION AND PERSONALITY. No 2-year-old can learn to read, because (among other reasons) the eye muscles are not fully enough developed. No 10-year-old can very well understand the feelings of two adults in love. Some kinds of learning are possible only after a certain level of maturation has been reached. For example, Kagan after long systematic observation of small children, concluded that the child cannot develop a sense of "self-awareness" and does not use the term "I" until the age of 17 to 22 months [Kagan, 1981, pp, 47–75]. Below this age, the central nervous system is too immature to handle this concept.

SOCIAL AND CULTURAL DEFINITIONS OF PHYSICAL CHARACTERISTICS. Millions of people believe that fat people are jolly, that people with high foreheads are intelligent, that redheads are hot-tempered, and that people with large jaws are forceful. Many such folk beliefs have been proved untrue when tested empirically, but occasionally a valid association is found. For example, one researcher [Bar, 1977] compared a sample of redheads with a control group with various hair color, and reported that redheads actually *are* more often hot-tempered and aggressive. He suggests a genetic link between this physical characteristic (red hair) and these personality traits (hot tempers, aggressiveness). But even if his statistical associations are confirmed by replication studies, has a *genetic* link been proven?

There is another possible explanation. Each physical characteristic is *socially and culturally defined* in every society. For example, fat girls are admired in Dahomey. A physical characteristic can make one a beautiful person in one society and an ugly duckling in another. Therefore, *a particular physical characteristic becomes a factor in personality development according to how it is defined and treated in one's society and by one's reference groups.* If redheads are expected to have hot tempers and are excused for their temper tantrums, it should not be surprising if they develop hot tempers. As indicated earlier, people respond to the behavior expectations of others, and tend to become whatever other people expect them to become.

It is always possible, of course, that there really is a genetic link between a particular physical trait and a behavior trait. In most cases, however, any statistical association is probably due to social and cultural reaction to the physical trait. The most useful test is that of *universality*. If, for example, lantern-jawed people were found to be highly aggressive in *all* societies, then we would suspect a genetic basis. But if this association were found in only a few societies, then we would suspect that the lantern-jawed individual developed aggressiveness in response to social expectations. To conclude, it is seldom the physical trait itself but the social expectations it arouses which produce certain behavior traits.

Physical Environment and Personality

Some of our earliest manuscripts are attempts to explain human behavior in terms of climate and geography. Sorokin [1928, chap. 3] summarizes the theories of hundreds of writers, from Confucius, Aristotle, and Hippocrates down to the modern geographer Ellsworth Huntington, who have claimed that group differences in behavior are due mainly to differences in climate, topography, and resources. Such theories fit beautifully into an ethnocentric framework, for geography provides a respectable, apparently objective explanation of our national virtues and other peoples' vices.

As shown in Chapter 3, physical environment is a minor factor in cultural evolution. It is even less important in personality development. Practically any kind of personality can be found in every kind of climate.

True, the physical environment has *some* influence upon personality. The Athabascans developed a set of dominant personality traits which enabled them to survive in a harsh subarctic climate [Boyer, 1974]. The Australian bushmen had a desperate struggle to stay alive, while it took the Samoans only a few minutes a day to gather more food than they could eat. Some regions even today can support only a very thinly scattered population, and density of population has some effects upon personality. The Ik (pronounced "eek") of Uganda are slowly starving, following the loss of their traditional hunting lands, and, according to Turnbull [1973], they have become one of the most selfish, grasping peoples on earth, totally lacking in kindness, helpfulness, or compassion, even seizing food from the mouths of their children in the battle to survive. The Quolla of Peru are described by Trotter [1973] as the most violent people on earth, and he attributes this to hypoglycemia arising from dietary deficiencies. Obviously, physical environment has some influence upon personality and behavior. But of the five factors discussed in this chapter, physical environment is least often important—far less often than culture, group experience, or unique experience.

Culture and Personality

Some experience is common to all cultures. Everywhere infants are nursed or fed by older persons, live in groups, learn to communicate through language, experience punishments and rewards of some kind, and have some other experiences common to the entire human species. It is also true that each society gives to virtually all its members certain experiences which many other societies do not offer. From the social experience common to virtually all members of a given society, there emerges a characteristic personality configuration typical of many members of that society. DuBois [1944, pp. 3–5] has called this the "modal personality" (taken from the statistical term, "mode," referring to that value which appears most frequently in a series). How the modal personality may vary between two different cultures is seen in the following contrast. (Most of these observations were made several decades ago, before these cultures had been so greatly changed by contact with outsiders.)

THE ANXIOUS DOBUAN. [Fortune, 1932; Benedict, 1934, chap. 5] The Dobuan child in Melanesia might think twice about coming into this world if it had any choice in the matter. It enters a family where the only member who is likely to care much about it is its uncle, its mother's brother, to whom it is heir. Its father, who is interested in his own sister's children, usually resents it, for its father must wait until it is weaned before resuming sexual relations with its mother. Often it is also unwanted by its mother, and abortion is common. Little warmth or affection awaits the child in Dobu.

The Dobuan child soon learns that it lives in a world ruled by magic. Nothing happens from natural causes; all phenomena are con-

trolled by witchcraft and sorcery. Illness, accident, and death are evidence that witchcraft has been used against one, and call for vengeance from one's kinsmen. Nightmares are interpreted as witchcraft episodes in which the spirit of the sleeper has narrow escapes from hostile spirits. All legendary heroes and villains are still alive as active supernaturals, capable of helping or harming people. Crops grow only if one's long hours of magical chants are successful in enticing the yams away from another's garden. Even sexual desire does not arise except in response to another's love magic, which guides one's steps to him or her, while one's own love magic accounts for one's successes.

Ill will and treachery are virtues in Dobu, and fear dominates Dobuan life. Every Dobuan lives in constant fear of being poisoned. Food is watchfully guarded while in preparation, and there are few persons indeed with whom a Dobuan will eat. The Dobuan couple spend alternate years in the villages of wife and husband, so that one of them is always a distrusted and humiliated outsider who lives in daily expectation of poisoning or other injury. At any moment each village shelters visiting spouses from many different villages, and none of these visitors can trust either their village hosts or one another. In fact, no one can be fully trusted; men are nervous over their wives' possible witchcraft and fear their mothers-in-law.

To the Dobuans, all success must be secured at the expense of someone else, just as all misfortune is caused by others' malevolent magic. Effective magic is the key to success, and success is measured by accomplishments in theft and seduction. Adultery is virtually universal, and the successful adulterer, like the successful thief, is much admired.

On the surface, social relations in Dobu are cordial and polite although dour and humorless. There is very little quarreling, for to give offense or to make an enemy is dangerous. But friends are also dangerous; a show of friendship may be a prelude to a poisoning or to the collection of materials (hair, fingernails) useful for sorcery.

What kind of personality develops in such a cultural setting? Dobuans are hostile, suspicious, distrustful, jealous, secretive, and deceitful. These are rational reactions, for the Dobuans live in a world filled with evil, surrounded by enemies, witches, and sorcerers. Eventually they are certain to be destroyed. Meanwhile they seek to protect themselves by their own magic, but never can they know any sense of comfortable security. A bad nightmare may keep them in bed for days. If measured by Western concepts of mental hygiene, all Dobuans would be paranoid to a degree calling for psychotherapy. But simply to call them paranoid would be incorrect, for their fears are justified and not irrational; the dangers they face are genuine not imaginary. A true paranoid person *imagines* that other people are threatening injury, but in Dobu other people really *are* out to get you! Thus the culture shapes a personality pattern which is normal *and useful* for the culture.

THE COOPERATIVE ZUNI [Cushing, 1882; Stevenson, 1901; Benedict, 1934, chap. 4; Bunzell, 1938; Kluckhohn and Strodtbeck, 1938; Vogt and Albert, 1966; Crampton, 1977]. The Zuñi of New Mexico are a placid people in an emotionally undisturbed world. The child is warmly welcomed, treated with tender fondness, and receives a great deal of loving attention. Responsibility for child care is diffuse; a child will be helped or corrected by any adult present. Faced with a united front of adults, children rarely misbehave, and may be scolded but are very rarely punished. Shame is a most important control and is most often aroused by embarrassment in the presence of others. It is the opinions of others, more than conscience, which controls behavior among the Zuñi.

Fighting and aggressive behavior are se-verely disapproved and Zuñi are taught to control their tempers at an early age. Overt quarreling is almost unknown. For example, one wife became weary of her husband's many amours. "So," she said, "I didn't wash his clothes. Then he knew that I knew that everyone knew, and he stopped going with that girl." [Benedict, 1934, p. 108]. Without a word, the issue was settled.

Zuñi values stress harmony, cooperativeness, and absence of competitiveness, aggressiveness, or acquisitiveness. Immoderation of any form is scorned, and alcohol used to be rejected because it encouraged immoderate behavior. (This control has weakened, and alcoholism is now a problem.) Property is valued for direct use but not for prestige or power. While Zuñi do not lack ambition, they gain power through their knowledge of the rituals, songs, and fetishes. A "poor" man is not one without property but one without ceremonial resources and connections.

Ceremonialism saturates every aspect of Zuñi life. While surrounded by supernatural powers, these are seen as usually helpful beings who like people to be happy. Witchcraft is present and is seen as the primary cause of death and other troubles. Witch trials are brutal and can be followed by execution, but are more commonly followed by humiliation and ostracism. The most dreadful of rumors is to be suspected of being a witch. Any peculiar or aggressive behavior may arouse such suspicions, while conspicuous conduct or wealth may attract the attention and arouse the jealousy of witches. Yet Zuñi life is not dominated by witchcraft as among the Dobuans. Worship is a dominant activity. Priestly magic centers upon weather control, human fertility, and healing ceremonies. Success comes from an exact following of the rituals, giving a sense of security and of control over the environment.

Cooperation, moderation, and lack of individualism are carried into all Zuñi behavior. Personal possessions are unimportant and are readily lent to others. The members of the matrilineal household work together as a group, and the crops are stored in a common storehouse. One works for the good of the group not for personal glory.

Leadership roles are seldom sought but must be forced upon one. Issues and disagreements are normally settled not by appeal to authority, by power display, or by confrontational debate but by long, patient discussion. A simple majority decision does not settle a matter comfortably; consensus is necessary and unanimous agreement is desired.

The normal personality among the Zuñi stands in stark contrast to that of the Dobuans. Where the Dobuan is suspicious and distrustful, the Zuñi is confident and trusting; where the Dobuan is apprehensive and insecure, the Zuñi is secure and serene. The typical Zuñi has a yielding disposition and is generous, polite, and cooperative. The Zuñi are unthinkingly and habitually conformist, for to be noticeably different is something which makes the individual and the group very uneasy. Apparently this serves to control behavior without the sense of sin and the guilt complexes found in many societies, including our own.

As the two foregoing sketches illustrate, personality differs strikingly from society to society. *Each society develops one or more basic personality types which fit the culture.* The Dobuans do not consciously or intentionally train their children to be hostile and suspicious; yet the atmosphere of constant treachery and fear has this result. Each culture, simply by being what it is, shapes personality to fit the culture. Let us consider some aspects of the culture which affect the process of personality development.

NORMS OF THE CULTURE. From the moment of birth, the child is treated in ways which shape the personality. Each culture provides a set of general influences, which vary endlessly from society to society. As Linton writes,

In some [societies] infants are given the breast whenever they cry for it. In others they are fed on a regular schedule. In some they will be nursed by any woman who happens to be at hand, in others only by their mothers. In some the process of nursing is a leisurely one, accompanied by many caresses and a maximum of sensuous enjoyment for both mother and child. In others it is hurried and perfunctory, the mother regarding it as an interruption of her regular activities and urging the child to finish as rapidly as possible. Some groups wean infants at an early age: others continue nursing for years. . . .

Turning to the more direct effects of culture patterns upon the developing individual, we have an almost infinite range of variations in the degree to which he is consciously trained, discipline or the lack of it and responsibilities imposed upon him. Society may take the child in hand almost from infancy and deliberately train him for his adult status, or it may permit him to run wild until the age of puberty. He may receive corporal punishment for even the smallest offense or never be punished at all. As a child he may have a claim upon the time and attention of all adults with whom he comes in contact or, conversely, all adults may have a claim upon his services. He may be put to work and treated as a responsible contributing member of the family group almost from the moment that he is able to walk and have it constantly impressed upon him that life is real and earnest. Thus in some Madagascar tribes children not only begin to work at an incredibly early age but also enjoy full property rights. I frequently bargained with a child of six for some object which I needed for my collection; although its parents might advise, they would not interfere. On the other hand, the children in a Marquesan village do not work and accept no responsibility. They form a distinct and closely integrated social unit which has few dealings with adults. The boys and girls below the age of puberty are constantly together and often do not go home even to eat or sleep. They go off on all-day expeditions, for which no parental permission is required, catch fish and raid plantations for food, and spend the night in any house they happen to be near at sunset.

The way the child is treated shapes the personality. (*Leonard Freed/Magnum*)

Examples of such cultural differences in the treatment of children could be multiplied indefinitely. The important point is that every culture exerts a series of general influences upon the individuals who grow up under it. These influences differ from one culture to another, but they provide a common denominator of experience for all persons belonging to a given society. (Ralph Linton, *The Study of Man,* © 1936, renewed 1964. Reprinted by permission of Prentice-Hall, Inc., Englewood Cliffs, N.J.)

Some of the American literature on psychoanalysis and child development, drawing heavily upon the theories of Freud, has attached great importance to specific child-training practices. Breast feeding, gradual weaning, demand-feeding schedules, and a relaxed induction to bowel and bladder training have often been recommended, with the opposite practices being blamed for all sorts of personality difficulties. These recommendations are generally unsupported by any carefully controlled comparative studies, although dramatic case histories may be cited in illustration. One serious effort [Sewell, 1952] to test these recommendations made a comparison of American children who had received differing training practices. This study found that no measureable adult personality differences were associated with any particular child-training practices.

Studies of personality development in other cultures have likewise failed to substantiate Freudian theories of the results of specific child-training practices [Eggan, 1943; Dai, 1957]. Apparently, it is the total atmosphere, and not the specific practice, which is important in personality development. Whether a child is breast-fed or bottle-fed is unimportant; what is important is whether this feeding is a tender, affectionate moment in a warmly secure world, or a hurried, casual incident in an impersonal, unfeeling, unresponding environment.

Subcultures and Personality   The picture of a modal personality for each society holds fairly true for the simple society with a well-integrated culture. But in a complex society with a number of subcultures, the picture changes. Are there personality differences between the Yankee and the Deep Southerner? Does the sharecropper think and feel as does the urban professional? In a complex society there may be as many modal personalities as there are subcultures.

The United States has many subcultures—racial, religious, ethnic, regional, social-class, perhaps even occupational. The boundary lines are indistinct, and some subcultures are more important than others. For example, the Catholic and Protestant subcultures probably affect less of a member's life than the Jewish subculture, and still less than the Amish subculture. Yet subcultures are real, and we have some justification for speaking of the "urban middle-class personality" or of the "typical salesperson." Of course, we must not exaggerate; it is likely that personality similarites within our culture greatly outnumber personality differences between subcultures, and there are personality differences within each subculture. But the physician,

the minister, the carnival worker, and the migrant fruit picker show some predictable personality differences from one another. Therefore we cannot describe the normal American personality without first naming the subculture we have in mind.

Individual Deviation from Modal Personality
In even the most conformist of societies there is some individuality in personality. The modal personality merely represents a series of personality traits which are most common among the members of a group, even though comparatively few of them may have developed every one of the traits in the series. Wallace [1952a] used Rorschach tests on a sample of Tuscarora Indians and concluded that only 37 percent of them showed all twenty-one of the modal personality traits which had been established as characteristic of the Tuscarora. Other similar studies [Wallace, 1952b; Kaplan, 1954] show that while a modal personality type characteristic of a society exists, it is not a uniform mold into which all members are perfectly cast. Likewise, in discussing the "typical" personality of nations, tribes, social classes, of occupational, regional, or other social groups, we must remember that the typical or modal personality consists of a series of personality traits, a *great many* of which are shared by *most* members of that group. Each society and social group allows a certain amount of individual deviation from the modal personality. When this deviation extends beyond what the group or society considers "normal," then that person is considered to be a "deviant." Such deviation will be considered in some detail in Chapter 7.

SOCIALIZATION AND THE SELF

The infant enters this world as a selfish little organism preoccupied with its physical needs. It soon becomes a human being, with a set of attitudes and values, likes and dislikes, goals and purposes, patterns of response, and a deep, abiding concept of the sort of person it is. Every person gets these through a process we call *socialization*—the learning process which turns him or her from an animal into a person with a human personality. Put more formally, socialization is *the process whereby one internalizes the norms of the groups among whom one lives so that a unique "self" emerges.*

Group Experience and Personality

At the start of life there is no self. There is a physical organism but no sense of person. Soon the infant feels out the limits of its body, learning where its body ends and other things begin. The child begins to recognize people and tell them apart. At first, any man is a "daddy" and any woman a "mummy," but eventually the child moves from names which distinguish a status to specific names which identify individuals, including itself. At about the age of 18 months to 2 years, the child begins to use "I," which is a clear sign of a definite self-awareness—a sign that the child is becoming aware of being a distinct human being [Cooley, 1908; Bain, 1936; Kagan, 1981]. With physical maturation and the accumulation of social experiences, the child forms an image of the kind of person he or she is—an image of self. One ingenious way of trying to get some impression of a person's self-image is the "Twenty Questions Test" [Kuhn and McPartland, 1954], in which the informant is asked to write twenty answers, exactly as they come to mind, to the question, "Who am I?" One's formation of the self-image is perhaps the most important single process in personality development.

SOCIAL ISOLATES.

Seven hundred years ago, Frederick II, Holy Roman Emperor, conducted an experiment to determine what language children would grow up to speak if they had never heard a single spoken word. Would they speak Hebrew—then thought to be the oldest tongue—or Greek, or Latin, or the language of their parents? He instructed foster mothers and nurses to feed and bathe the children but under no circumstances to speak or prattle to them. The experiment failed, for every one of the children died. [Cass Canfield, undated promotional letter, Planned Parenthood Federation.]

Whether this anecdote is historically true is not known, but it does point attention to social experience as a necessity for human growth. Personality development is not simply an automatic unfolding of inborn potentials, as is shown by social isolates. Several times each year the newspapers report instances of neglected children who have been chained or locked away from the normal family group. They are always found to be retarded and generally antisocial or unsocial. Without group experience human personality does not develop. The most dramatic reports are those of so-called feral children, separated from their families and supposedly raised by animals [Singh and Zingg, 1942; Krout, 1942, pp. 106–114]. Social scientists doubt that a child would live for long in the care of animals. They suspect that so-called feral children are simply socially isolated and neglected children who had been either lost or abandoned by their parents and then discovered by others some time thereafter [Ogburn, 1959].

It is doubtful that allegedly feral children are examples of animal nurture. It does seem evident, however, that children who suffer extreme emotional rejection and are severely deprived of normal loving care fail to develop the personality we usually consider human. This conclusion is consistent with the findings of a number of experiments in which animals which normally live in groups were raised in isolation from their normal groups. Harlow and Harlow, [1961] raised monkeys in isolation from all contact with other monkeys, with only a heated terry-cloth-covered wire framework as a substitute "mother," from which they received their bottle and to which

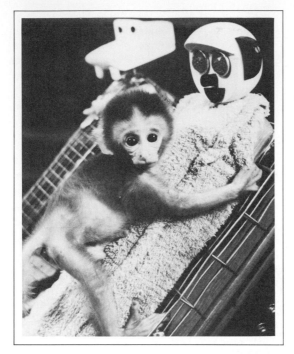

How many of the needs of the infant monkey could this substitute "mother" fulfill? (*Harry Harlow/Wisconsin Primate Laboratory*)

they clung when frightened. As infants they seemed satisfied with this substitute "mother," but as adults they were almost entirely asocial. Many were apathetic and withdrawn; others were hostile and aggressive. None showed the social group behavior of normal adult monkeys. Apparently the substitute mother met the infant's need for affection and security but was unable to carry the monkey through any further stages of psychosocial development. Some did not even mate as adults. Those who eventually became mothers were neglectful and abusive, showing none of the normal "mothering" behavior [Harlow, 1975; Greenberg, 1977; Prescott, 1979]. Monkeys apparently need to receive mother love as infants in order to express it as adults.

Other animal experiments show similar failures of isolated animals to develop the adult behavior normal for their species [Krout, 1942, pp. 102–105]. Of course, monkeys are

not human beings, and we should be careful about drawing inferences from behavior parallels. But it is interesting to note that Harlow's account of the effects of maternal deprivation in monkeys correspond so closely with observations of the effects of maternal deprivation in humans [Spitz, 1965]. It appears that both monkeys and humans need intimate group experience if they are to develop into normal adults.

REFERENCE GROUPS.   Throughout one's life certain groups are important as models for one's ideas and conduct norms. Such groups are called *reference groups.* At first, the family group is the most important, since it is the only group most infants have when they are most impressionable. All authorities agree that the basic personality characteristics of the individual are formed in these first years within the family [White, 1975; Shaffer and Dunn, 1982]. Somewhat later, the *peer group*— other persons of the same age and status— becomes important as a reference group. A child's failure to gain social acceptance in its peer group is often followed by a lifelong pattern of social rejection and social failure. Unless one has had a fair measure of child and adolescent peer group acceptance, it is difficult if not impossible for one to develop an adult self-image as a competent and worthwhile person. For this reason, perceptive

Reference groups are important models.

teachers and counselors devote much effort to helping wallflowers raise their acceptance level in the peer group [Oden, 1976].

Many studies have shown that by the middle teens the peer group has become an extremely important reference group, and possibly the *most* important influence upon attitudes, goals, and conduct norms [e.g., Otto, 1977; Hoge and Petrillo, 1978; Youniss, 1980]. The teenager's disgusted retort, "Oh, *Mother!*" neatly epitomizes the frequent clash between parent norms and peer norms, in which parent norms are often the loser.

As we mature, a succession of reference groups emerges and fades. The high school crowd dissolves, and students go to college, where they judge their academic performance against that of their classmates [Bassis, 1977]. Workers' images of their competence may be more dependent upon their perceptions of how they are seen by fellow workers than upon their perceptions of how they are seen by supervisors, meaning that fellow workers are a more important reference group than are supervisors. From hundreds of possible reference groups a few become important for each person, and from these groups' evaluations the person's self-image is continuously formed and reformed.

MULTIPLE GROUPS AND SOCIALIZATION. All complex societies have many groups and

Group acceptance and rejection affect personality development. (*Ed Lettau/Photo Researchers, Inc.*)

subcultures with differing and sometimes opposing standards. One is presented with models of behavior which are rewarded at one time and punished at another, or approved by some groups and condemned by others. Thus the boy learns that he should be "tough" and able to "stand up for his rights," yet at the same time he should be orderly, considerate, and respectful. Some caution the young girl to remain chaste, while others urge her to be "emancipated." In a society in which each person moves in a number of groups with differing standards and values, each person must work out some way of dealing with these opposing pressures. People may deal with this problem by compartmentalizing their lives, developing a different "self" for each group in which they move. Or they may select a favorite reference group to conform to and have their real life within, rejecting other groups, as in the case below:

> "Thirteen arrests." The judge shook his head over my file. "Gang fightings, shootings, burglary, stealing a car. . . . I don't know what to make of you. Your parents are hardworking, religious people in pretty good circumstances. Your IQ is extraordinarily high. Why do you do these things?"

> I shrugged. What a dumb question. Every boy I knew did these things. Maybe I just did more of them and better. ("A Gang Leader's Redemption," *Life*, Apr. 28, 1958, pp. 69ff.)

This boy had adopted the standards of a delinquent peer group rather than those of his family. Research studies [Warner and Lunt, 1941, p. 351; Rosen, 1955; Cary, 1974] have usually emphasized the power of the peer group to cultivate behavior patterns contrary to those of the family. Not all youths, however, are as firmly wedded to peer group standards, and not all peer groups are as much in conflict with family or society. Most youths find their principal extrafamily group allegiance in athletic teams, church youth

groups, neighborhood clubs, or youth cliques in harmony with most of the standards of conventional adult society. A great deal has been written in recent years about the "youth revolt" and the "generation gap." Yet careful surveys show that while there is a strong urge for change among today's young people, they are in fundamental agreement with their parents on basic values more often than they are in disagreement [Yankelovich, 1972; Erskine, 1973; Wright, 1975; Lubeck and Bengtson, 1977; Martin, 1982].

Why do some youths select peer groups which generally support adult values while others choose peer groups at war with adult society? The choice seems to be related to self-image. Habitual delinquents are usually those who see themselves as unloved, unworthy, unable, unaccepted, unappreciated; they join with other such deprived youths in a delinquent peer group which reinforces and sanctions their resentful, aggressive behavior. Law-abiding youths see themselves as loved, worthy, able, accepted, appreciated; they join with others like themselves in a conforming peer group which reinforces socially approved behavior. Truly, seeing is behaving. How we see ourselves is how we behave.

Unique Experience and Personality

Why is it that children raised in the same family are so different from one another, even though they have had the same experiences? The point is that they have *not* had the same experiences; they have had social experiences which are similar in some respects and different in others. Each child enters a different family unit. One is the firstborn, and is the only child until the arrival of the second, who then has an older brother or sister to fight with. Parents change and do not treat all their children exactly alike. The children enter different peer groups, may have different teachers, and survive different incidents. Identical twins have identical heredity and (unless separated) come much closer to having the

Each person's experience is unique, exactly duplicated by that of no one else. (*Erika Stone/ Peter Arnold, Inc.*)

same experiences. They enter a family together, often have the same peer groups, and are treated more nearly alike by other people; yet even twins do not share *all* incidents and experiences. *Each person's experience is unique in that nobody else's perfectly duplicates it.* An inventory of the daily experiences of several children in the same family will reveal many differences. So each child (excepting identical twins) has a unique biological inheritance, exactly duplicated by no one, and a unique set of life experiences, exactly duplicated by no one.

Furthermore, *experiences do not simply add up; they integrate.* Personality is not built by piling one incident upon another like a brick wall. The meaning and impact of an experience depends upon other experiences which have preceded it. When a popular girl is stood up by her date, this is not the same experience for her as it is for the wallflower. Psychoanalysts claim that certain incidents in one's experience are crucial because they color one's reaction to later experience. "Psychological" movies and novels often imply that psychoanalysis consists of probing into one's unconscious and dredging up *the* traumatic experience which caused all the trouble. This is a gross oversimplification. No boy develops a neurosis because his father destroyed a favorite toy when he was 3 years old. But it is possible that such a traumatic episode might become the first of a series of mutual rejection experiences and thus color the meaning of a great many later experiences. This means that each person's experience is an infinitely complicated network of millions of incidents, each gaining its meaning and impact from all those which have preceded it. Small wonder that personality is complex!

Still another factor appears in the selection of roles to play within the family. Children imitate each other a great deal, but they also strive for separate identities. Younger children often reject those activities which their older siblings already do well and seek recognition through other activities. Parents may unwittingly aid this selection process. Mother may say, "Susie is mama's little helper, but I guess Annie is going to be a tomboy," whereupon Susie starts clearing the table while Annie turns a few handsprings. Sometimes a child in a well-behaved family selects the "bad boy" role, and scowls impressively while his parents describe their problem to visitors. In large families a child may be hard pressed to find a role not already annexed by an older sibling. Thus, in these and many other respects each person's life experience is unique—unique in that nobody else has had exactly this set of experiences, and unique in that nobody else has the same background of experience upon which each new incident will impinge and from which it will draw its meaning.

THEORIES OF PERSONALITY DEVELOPMENT

Several scholars have advanced some interesting theories of personality development. None is "proved" by the kind of empirical evidence or research experiments which establish, for example, that germs cause disease or that self-confidence improves performance. Each is a provocative theory which explains a complicated matter in a believable way.

Cooley and the Looking-glass Self

Just how does a person arrive at a notion of the kind of person he or she is? This concept of self is developed through a gradual and complicated process which continues throughout life. The concept is an image that one builds only with the help of others. Suppose a girl is told by her parents and relatives how pretty she looks. If this is repeated often enough, consistently enough, and by enough different people, she eventually comes to feel and act like a beautiful person. There is convincing research evidence that beautiful people actually *are* treated more indulgently and are seen as more intelligent, altruistic, and admirable than other people [Berscheid and Walster, 1974; Wilson and Nias, 1976; Cash and Salzbach, 1978; Murphy, 1981]. The beautiful people often appear to be more poised and self-assured than ugly ducklings, for they are judged and treated differently [Schwebbe and Schwebbe, 1982]. But even a pretty girl will never really believe that she is pretty if, beginning early in life, her parents act disappointed and apologetic over her and treat her as unattractive. *A person's self-image need bear no relation to the objective facts.* A very ordinary child whose efforts are appreciated and rewarded will develop a feeling of acceptance and self-confidence, while a truly brilliant child whose efforts are frequently defined as failures may become obsessed with feelings of incompetence, and its abilities can be practically paralyzed. It is through the responses of others that a child decides whether it is intelligent or stupid, attractive or homely, lovable or unlovable, righteous or sinful, worthy or worthless. A recent guidebook [Samuels, 1977] tells in detail how a child should be treated if it is to develop a confident self-image.

This "self" which is discovered through the reactions of others has been labeled the "look-

Self-image is based upon the reaction of others. (*Sybil Shackman/Monkmeyer*)

ing-glass self" by Cooley [1902, pp. 102–103], who carefully analyzed this aspect of self-discovery. He may, perhaps, have been inspired by the words in Thackeray's *Vanity Fair:* "The world is a looking glass and gives back to every man the reflection of his own face. Frown on it and it will in turn look sourly upon you; laugh at it and with it, and it is a jolly, kind companion."

There are three steps in the process of building the looking-glass self: (1) our perception of how we look to others, (2) our perception of their judgment of how we look, and (3) our feelings about these judgments. Thus, we are constantly revising our perception of how we look. Suppose that whenever you enter a room and approach a small knot of people, they promptly stop talking and melt away. Would this experience, repeated many times, affect your feelings about yourself? Of if whenever you appear, a conversational group quickly forms around you, how does this attention affect your self-feelings? Wallflowers are people who came to believe early in life that they could not make conversation. How did this happen?

Just as the picture in the mirror gives an image of the physical self, so the perception of the reactions of others gives an image of the social self. We "know," for instance, that we are talented in some respects and less talented in others. The knowledge came to us from the reactions of other persons. The little child whose first crude artistic efforts are sharply criticized soon concludes that it lacks artistic talent, while the child whose efforts win praise from parents comes to believe in its abilities. As the child matures, others will also give a reaction which may differ from that of its parents, for the social looking glass is one which is constantly before us.

We note that it is the *perception* of the judgments of others which is the active factor in the self-image forming process. We may misjudge the reactions of others. It may be that the compliment which we take at face value is mere flattery; a scolding may have been caused by the boss's headache rather than by our own errors. Thus the looking glass image which we perceive may easily differ from the image others have actually formed of us. Several research efforts have sought empirical evidence of the correlation between a person's *perception* of the judgments of others and the *actual* judgments they have made of the person. These studies find considerable variation between the individual's perception of how others picture him or her and the picture they actually hold.

Calvin and Holtzman [1953] found that individuals vary considerably in their ability to perceive accurately the judgments of others about them, and that the less well-adjusted person was less accurate in these perceptions. Another experiment, by Miyamoto and Dornbusch [1956], found that a subject's self-conception is closer to his perception of a group's impression of him, than to the actual impression of him which they reported, as is shown in Table 4-1.

In this study of ten groups totaling 195 male subjects, the "perception of group response" is each subject's estimate of how the other members of the group rate him according to four characteristics—intelligence, self-confidence, physical attractiveness, and likeableness. The "actual group response" is the rating actually assigned to him by the others in the group. In most of these groups (of fraternity members and classmates who knew each other well) the subjects' self-conceptions were closer to their perceived response than to the actual response of the group to them. Clearly, it is our perception of the judgments of others

TABLE 4-1

SELF-CONCEPTION AS RELATED TO PERCEIVED AND ACTUAL
GROUP RESPONSE

Characteristic	Number of groups in which subjects' self-conceptions were closer to their perceptions of group response	Number of groups in which subjects' self-conceptions were closer to actual group response
Intelligence	8	2
Self-confidence	9	0 (1 tie)
Physical attractiveness	10	0
Likeableness	7	3

Note: This experiment shows that in most cases the subjects' self-image was closer to how they *believed* others viewed them (left column) than to how others *really* viewed them (right column). This supports the idea that it is our *perception* of the feelings of others toward us, and not their true feelings, which shapes our self-concept.
Source: S. Frank Miyamoto and Sanford M. Dornbusch, "A Test of Interactionist Hypothesis of Self-Conception," *American Journal of Sociology*, 61:399–403, March 1956.

Have you ever realized that you had misjudged the impression you made upon others?

and not their actual judgments which shapes our self-image, and these perceptions are sometimes inaccurate.

Mead and the "Generalized Other"

The process of internalizing the attitudes of others has been aptly described by George Herbert Mead [1934, part 3, pp. 140–141] who developed the concept of the *generalized other*. This generalized other is a composite of the expectations one believes others hold toward one. When one says, "Everyone expects me to . . .", one is using the concept of the generalized other.

Awareness of the generalized other is developed through the processes of role taking and role playing. *Role taking* is an attempt to act out the behavior that would be expected of a person who actually held the role one is "taking." In children's play, there is much role taking, as they "play house" ("You be the mama and I'll be the papa and you be the little baby"), play cops and robbers, or play with dolls. *Role playing* is acting out the behavior of a role one actually holds (as when the boy and girl *become* father and mother), whereas in role taking one only pretends to hold the role.

Mead sees a three-stage process through which one learns to play adult roles. First, there is a preparatory stage (1 to 3 years) in which the child imitates adult behavior without any real understanding (as when the little girl cuddles her doll, then uses it as a club to strike her brother). Next comes the play stage (3 to 4-years) when children have some understanding of the behavior but switch roles erratically. One moment the boy is a builder, piling blocks upon one another, and a moment later he knocks them apart, or at one moment he is a policeman and a momemt later an astronaut. Finally comes the game state (4 to 5 years and beyond) where the role behavior becomes consistent and pur-

poseful and the child has the ability to sense the role of the other players. To play baseball, each player must understand his or her own role as well as the role of all the other players. Thus, through child play one develops an ability to see one's own behavior in its relation to others and to sense the reaction of other persons involved. Some attempts to test Mead's theories experimentally have generally been supportive. For example, Rubin and Maioni [1975] found a positive correlation between small children's participation in dramatic play and their ability to take the view of others.

It is through this awareness of others' roles, feelings, and values that the generalized other takes form in our minds. It is thus a composite of the roles which other people play and of the expectations they have toward us. It can roughly be equated with the expectations of the community, or at least of those segments of the community in which one moves. By repeatedly "taking the role of the generalized other," one develops a concept of the self—of the kind of person one is.

A failure to develop this ability to adopt another's point of view (to take the role of another) seems to cripple personality development. Chandler [1970] tested a group of delinquent boys and found them to be several years retarded in their role-taking abilities. After several weeks of an "actor's workshop" in which each boy took all the roles in succession (aggressor, victim, arresting officer, judge), the boys gained several years in their role-taking skills. This supports Mead's theory that role taking is an essential learning process in socialization.

Other authorities have added the concept of the *significant other*. The significant other is the person whose approval we desire and whose direction we accept. As Woelfel and Haller [1971, p. 75] define the concept, "significant others are those persons who exercise major influence over the attitudes of individuals." Significant others may be influential because of the roles they fill (parents, teachers) or because one has selected this significant other as important (popular celebrities, best friends, favorite relative, boyfriend or girlfriend). They are important to us, and therefore their ideas and values tend to become our ideas and values.

Freud and the Antisocial Self

Both Cooley and Mead were interactionists, who saw personality as shaped through our social interaction with others. Both assumed a basic harmony between self and society. To Cooley, the "separate individual" was an abstract idea which had no existence apart from society, just as "society" has no meaning apart from individuals. The "socialized self" is shaped by society, and society is an organization of the persons it socializes. Thus self and society were two aspects of the same thing.

Freud saw self and society in basic conflict not harmony. He saw the self as a product of the ways in which basic human motives and impulses are denied and repressed by society. Freud believed that the rational portion of human motivation was like the visible part of an iceberg, with the larger part of human motivation resting in the unseen, unconscious forces which powerfully affect human conduct. He divided the self into three parts: the id, the superego, and the ego. The *id* is the pool of instinctive and unsocialized desires and impulses, selfish and antisocial; the *superego* is the complex of social ideals and values which one has internalized and which form the conscience; the *ego* is the conscious and rational part of the self which oversees the superego's restraint of the id. Thus, the ego is the control center, the superego is the police officer, and the id is the seething cauldron of selfish, destructive desires. Since society restricts the expression of aggression, sexual desire, and other impulses, the id is continually at war with the superego. The id is usually repressed, but at times it breaks through in open defiance of the superego, creating a burden of guilt that is difficult for the self to carry. At other times the forces of the id find expression in disguised forms which enable the ego to be unaware of the real underlying reasons for its actions, as when a parent relieves hostility by beating the child, believing that this is "for its own good." Thus Freud finds that the self and society are often opponents and not merely different aspects of the same thing.

Freud's theories have inspired bitter controversies, rival "schools," and numerous interpretations and revisions. His concepts represent ways of looking at personality rather than actual entities which can be verified through specific experiments. There is no simple empirical test which can be used to determine whether the superego, ego, and id are the best possible concepts to use in describing the component parts of the human personality. Attempts at empirical testing have failed to confirm many of Freud's theories, while offering some support for others [Fisher and Greenberg, 1977]. Most social scientists today agree that Freud was probably right in his claim that human motives are largely unconscious and beyond rational control and do not always harmonize with the needs of an orderly society.

While Cooley and Mead describe the development of the self in somewhat different terms, their theories complement rather than oppose each other. Both contradict Freud in that they see self and society as two aspects of the same reality, while Freud sees self and society in eternal conflict. But all see the self as a social product, shaped and molded by the society.

Erikson and the Eight Stages of Life

Erik Erikson is a German-born scholar who has lived in the United States since 1933. He never completed any college degree, yet he rose to hold professorships at California and Harvard. Trained in Freudian psychoanalysis,

TABLE 4-2
ERIKSON'S EIGHT STAGES OF LIFE

Age	Identity crisis to be resolved	Basic virtue to be developed
Infancy	Trust vs. mistrust	Hope
Early childhood (2–3)	Autonomy vs. shame and doubt	Will
Play stage (4–5)	Initiative vs. guilt	Purpose
School stage (6–11)	Industry vs. inferiority	Competence
Adolescence (12–18)	Identity vs. role confusion	Fidelity
Young adulthood (19–35)	Intimacy vs. isolation	Love
Middle adulthood (36–50)	Generativity vs. stagnation	Care
Old age (51+)	Integrity vs. despair	Wisdom

Source: Erik Erikson, *Childhood and Society*, W. W. Norton & Company, Inc., New York, 1963, and *Youth and Crisis*, W. W. Norton & Company, Inc., New York, 1968.

How do these stages of Erikson's compare with your recollections of your own development?

he moved beyond Freud to develop a theory of life-cycle socialization through eight stages marked by *identity crises*. These are turning points in development when one must move in one of two general directions.

These stages, shown in Table 4-2, begin in infancy, when the infant learns either trust or mistrust. If its mother (or mother substitute) is consistently affectionate and loving and attentive to the infant's physical needs, the infant forms feelings of security and trust. If the mother is inattentive, cold, rejecting, or abusive, or even inconsistent, the infant becomes insecure and distrustful.

During the second stage, "autonomy versus doubt and shame," children learn to walk, talk, use their hands, and do many other things. They begin to establish autonomy; that is, they begin to make choices of their own, to express their will, to form and pursue wishes. If encouraged in this, they develop a sense of autonomy, a sense of themselves as capable persons. If thwarted in this stage, Erikson believes they develop doubt about

themselves and feelings of shame in their relations with others.

In each of the following six stages, there is a similar identity crisis in which certain learnings are necessary for a healthy personality. In stage three, one resolves the oedipal conflict and begins developing a moral sense. In stage four, the child's world broadens, technical skills are learned and feelings of competence enlarged. These first four stages correspond to Freud's four stages of childhood psychosexual development—oral, anal, genital, and latent. In stage five, the adolescent develops a sense of personal identity through interaction with others. In stage six, the young adult develops lasting love relationships with the opposite sex. In the middle years of stage seven, one makes one's contribution to one's family and to society. In the last stage, one comes to terms with the end of life, either in dignity or in despair. For each of the stages, there is a companion *basic virtue* which develops through the successful passing of that crisis. If the learnings appropriate to one stage are missed, it may be possible but difficult to acquire them later in life [Erikson, 1963, 1968; Roazen, 1976].

Erikson's theories have been highly influential. He popularized the term identity crisis, which is often misused to mean any period of doubt or confusion. Whether each learning is centered in its appropriate stage may be argued. Is the "identity versus role confusion" crisis centered in adolescence, or does it arise at other times? Is "wisdom" a unique virtue of the aged? Like all theories of development, Erikson's are difficult to prove or to disprove.

Piaget and Developmental Learning

Jean Piaget, trained as a biologist, achieved recognition as a child psychologist studying the development of intelligence. He spent thousands of hours observing children at play and questioning them about their actions and feelings. He did not develop a comprehensive theory of socialization but concentrated on how children learn to talk, to think, to reason, and eventually to form moral judgments.

Piaget believes that children think differently from adults and that humans are biologically programmed to move toward rational, logical thought through a predictable series of developmental stages. By "developmental" stages, we mean that the learnings of one stage are necessary to move on to the next stage. Just as the small child must learn to walk before it can learn to run, it must learn obedience to external rules before it can develop self-control based on moral values. The small child can learn literal rules ("Wash you hands before eating!" "Don't pull kitty's tail!") but cannot grasp the purposes behind them. "Bad" is measured by effect not by intent; thus, to break another's toy intentionally is no worse than to break it accidentally.

At about 7 or 8, the child begins to see rules as based on practicality, mutual respect, and justice. Thus the child gradually replaces a morality based on obedience to external

authority and fear or punishment with self-control based on cooperation and mutual consideration. Not all complete these learnings, some remaining at a childlike level of moral behavior throughout their lives [Piaget, 1932, 1951, 1965; Piaget and Inhelder, 1969]. Many, but not all, of Piaget's hypotheses have been confirmed by the research studies they stimulated [Kohlberg, 1964, p. 399], and he is today one of the most frequently cited child psychologists. There are other "life-stage" systems [Sheehy, 1976; Hareven, 1978; Levinson, 1979], but they focus more upon role transitions than upon socialization.

IMPORTANCE OF SELF-IMAGE

As already hinted, personal self-image is a highly active factor in behavior. There is a great deal of research showing the importance of self-image. In Campbell's *The Sense of Well-Being in America*, he found that of all factors related to "satisfaction with life," one's feelings of "satisfaction with self" ranked highest, with "standard of living" second and "satisfaction with family life" third [Campbell, 1981, p. 48]. The famous study *Equality of Educational Opportunity* [Coleman, 1966, pp. 319–325] found that the most important personality characteristic associated with school learning was the child's self-concept and sense of control over its environment—that is, the child's feeling that its efforts would make a difference. Effective teaching in school, plant, or army rests upon building the learner's self-confidence [Leviton, 1975]. Conversely, the lack of a satisfactory self-image nearly always cripples learning or task performance. Studies of some years ago, for example, showed that black school children had lower self-esteem than white children, and this was believed to be a factor in black children's poorer school performance. Recent studies, however, no longer find lower levels of self-esteem among black children [Greenberg, 1972; Beglis and Sheikh, 1974; Hilbary, 1975]. This may be one reason why the learning gap between black and white children has narrowed significantly during the past decade [Burton and Jones, 1982].

An unsatisfactory self-image often leads to unpleasant, antisocial, or delinquent behavior [Schwartz and Tangri, 1965; Kaplan, 1975, 1977]. In fact, a great deal of behavior, ranging from mildly annoying habits such as bragging and "know-it-all" arrogance to serious neuroses and delinquencies can be viewed as desperate attempts to repair an intolerable image of self as incompetent, unworthy, or unimportant. The ultimate response to feelings of unworthiness is suicide [Kaplan and Pokorny, 1976]. Truly, the image of self lies at the core of behavior.

SUMMARY

Personality is one's total behavior tendency system. Our *heredity* gives us a set of needs and potentialities which other factors may channel and develop. Our *physical environment* is relatively unimportant in personality development. Our *culture* provides certain fairly uniform experiences for all members of our society. Our group experience develops personality similarities within groups and differences between groups; the unique experience of each person shapes his or her individuality.

The normal personality differs dramatically from society to society, as is shown by the suspicious, treacherous, insecure Dobuan and the amiable, secure, cooperative Zuñi. Each society develops a normal personality, produced by the total experience of a person raised in the society. Such cultural influences include norms of the culture, ideal personality types presented as models, and many other kinds of experience. All these influences tend to develop a *modal personality* type for that society.

More complex societies may have a number of subcultures, each developing its characteristic personality and reducing the overall uniformity of personality within the culture. Even in simpler societies there is no complete uniformity in personality; only a minority of the members share all the traits of the modal personality. In complex societies variation in personality is still greater.

Socialization requires group experience, with *social isolates* failing to develop a normal human personality. Socialization is heavily centered upon development of the concept of *self*. Cooley saw a person forming his or her image of the self—the *looking-glass self*—in the "looking glass" of other peoples' reactions to him or her, and the person's feelings about those reactions. *Reference groups* are groups whose standards we apply to ourselves and whose approval we desire. *Peer groups* are groups of our own age and status, and are highly important reference groups, especially in childhood and adolescence. Mead emphasized *role taking* in children's play as the learning process whereby one becomes aware of the feelings of others. Through applying the standards of the *generalized other* to one's own actions, one develops an image of self. Freud saw the self as composed of unsocialized inborn impulses (the *id*) restrained by a socially acquired conscience (the *superego*) while the conscious or rational part of the self (the *ego*) seeks to keep a balance between id and superego. Cooley and Mead viewed self and society as two aspects of the same thing, whereas Freud viewed the self as basically antisocial, with most personality difficulties arising from the clash between impulses of the self and restraints of society.

Erikson saw personality development as a lifelong process. People pass through eight successive *identity crises*, in each of which a constructive or an ineffective set of learnings takes place and an appropriate *basic virtue* should be acquired. Piaget advanced a developmental model of how the child replaces obedience to authoritarian rules with a mature morality based on mutual consideration.

In a complex culture with many kinds of groups, one may have difficulty in developing a satisfactory self-image and an integrated system of behavior. One may resolve this problem by compartmentalizing one's life and acting differently in each group or by conforming to one group while, if possible, ignoring any others whose standards conflict with those of that one group. Failure to do either may bring confusion and maladjustment. While there are common elements in the experience of all people and even more in the experience of people within a particular society, each person is still unique.

GLOSSARY

ego, superego, and id Freudian concepts. The *id* is the instinctive, antisocial, selfish desires and impulses of the individual. The *superego* is the social ideals and values which one has internalized and which form the conscience. The *ego* is the conscious and rational part of the self which oversees the restraint of the id by the superego.

feral children children supposedly reared apart from human society and therefore unsocialized.

generalized other the totality of values and standards of one's community or one's social group, whose judgments one applies to one's own behavior in forming one's concept of self.

identity crisis for Erikson, one of eight major turning points in life when important directions in personality development are taken. Popularly used for any period of uncertainty.

looking-glass self perception of the self that one forms by interpreting the reactions of other people to oneself.

modal personality a personality configuration typical of most members of a group or society.

peer group a group of one's "equals," usually similar persons with whom one habitually associates.

personality the totality of behavior of an individual with a given tendency system interacting with a sequence of situations.

reference group any group accepted as model or guide for one's judgments or actions.

self a person's awareness of, and attitudes toward, one's own person.

social isolates organisms lacking normal social contacts with other members of their species.

socialization process by which one internalizes the norms of that person's groups so that a unique self emerges.

unique experience the total experience of a person, which no other person exactly duplicates.

QUESTIONS AND PROJECTS

1 How do we know that personality is not simply the maturing and unfolding of inherited tendencies?

2 What might be some possible differences in social life and human personality if human infants were normally born (and nursed) in litters instead of one at a time?

3 In what way is the question of heredity and environment a political issue?

4 It has been said that a person raised in one culture may learn to act like people in an adopted culture but will never to able to think and feel like a person of the adopted culture. Do you agree?

5 Suppose the Dobuans were visited by a man who persistently acted in a straightforward, trusting, confident manner. Tell why you believe they would or would not:
   a. Admire him
   b. Copy him
   c. Fear him
   d. Pity him

6 If culture develops similarities in personality within a society, how do we explain personality differences within a society? Are such personality differences greater within a simple or a complex society? Why?

7 How would you explain the fact that groups which have a major socializing influence upon one person may leave another person in the same vicinity unaffected?

8 Comment on this statement: "What I really am is more important to me than what other people think of me."

9 Why are some beautiful and talented people so unsure of themselves?

10 How is the self a social product?

11 How do games contribute

to the development of the self?

12 Do you feel that Freud and Cooley are in basic disagreement on the nature of the self? Explain.

13 How can children in the same family develop such strikingly different personality traits?

14 Explain how a number of types of annoying people—braggart, bully, gossip, Casanova—may be seeking to repair an unsatisfactory self-image.

15 For slavery to be profitable, it was necessary for slaves to *feel* inferior and *feel* fit only to be slaves. How were slaves in the United States made to feel inferior? Why has the self-image of black people in the United States been changing?

16 When the Shell Oil Company planned an office building in Japan, the Japanese objected to the private offices which American executives cherish. They don't like to work alone. What does this show about culture and personality?

17 Can you recall a specific "looking-glass" incident in your experience? Write it up, describing your actions, others' reactions, your perception of their reactions, and your feelings about that perception. How do you think this incident affected you?

18 Write an account of a typical day in your life, listing all the standardizing cultural influences which you have experienced along with nearly every other American, and state how you suspect each has helped to shape your personality.

19 Prepare an analysis of the behavior of "Yank," the fireman in Eugene O'Neill's *The Hairy Ape*. Is his behavior consistent with what this chapter outlines about others and the concept of self?

SUGGESTED READINGS

* Benedict, Ruth: *Patterns of Culture*, Houghton Mifflin Company, Boston, 1961 (1st ed., 1934). Shows how each integrated culture develops a behavior and personality which is normal and useful for that society.

* Elkin, Frederick, and Gerald Handel: *The Child and Society: The Process of Socialization*, Random House, Inc., New York, 1976. A simply written description of the socialization process.

Eysenck, Hans J.: *The Biological Basis of Personality*, Charles C Thomas, Publisher, Springfield, Ill., 1971. A comprehensive summation of the evidence on the biological basis of personality.

Farber, Susan: "The Telltale Behavior of Twins," *Psychology Today*, 15:58 ff. January 1981. A brief article on the similarities among twins raised separately.

*Goffman, Erving: *Presentation of Self in Everyday Life*, Social Science Research Center, University of Edinburgh, 1956; Anchor Books paperback, Doubleday & Company, Inc., Garden City, N.Y., 1959. A detailed picture of how the self emerges through everyday experiences.

Grinker, Roy R.: "The Poor Rich," *Psychology Today*, 11:74–81, October 1977. An account of how personality problems of the rich develop from their unusual socialization as children.

Kuhn, Manford: "Self-attitudes by Age, Sex, and Professional Training." *Sociological Quarterly*, 1:39–55, January 1960; The Bobbs-Merrill Company, Inc., Indianapolis, reprint S 156. Exploration of self-attitudes by members of different social categories through use of the Twenty Questions Test.

*Rose, Peter I. (ed.): *Socialization and the Life Cycle*, St. Martin's Press, Inc., New York, 1979. A collection of articles on the socialization process at different ages and in different groups.

* Spiro, Melford: *Children of the Kibbutz*, Harvard University Press, Cambridge, Mass., 1958, 1965, 1975. A study of socialization in the agricultural communes of Israel.

Wilson, Glenn, and David Nias: "Beauty Can't Be Beat," *Psychology Today*, 10:97–99, September 1976. A popular article showing how the beautiful people get treated by others.

* An asterisk before the citation indicates that the title is available in a paperback edition.

5 Role and Status

All the world's a stage,
And all the men and women
merely players.
. . . .
And one man in his time plays
many parts,
His acts being seven ages. At
first the infant,

Mewling and puking in the
nurse's arms.
. . . .
Last scene of all
. . . .
Is second childishness and
mere oblivion . . .
(William Shakespeare,
As You Like It, act 2, scene 7.)

Deeply embedded in the nature
of talk are the fundamentals of
theatricality.
(Erving Goffman,
Forms of Talk, University of
Pennsylvania Press,
Philadelphia, 1981, p. 2.)

Shakespeare's classic description of the world as a stage emphasizes the changes in role and status which come with age. These are important and inescapable, but others, such as those accompanying various occupations, are equally significant. Goffman points out that conversation itself is a form of theater.

Status is usually defined as the *rank or position of a person in a group, or of a group in relation to other groups.* (In fact, some sociologists prefer to use the term *position* instead of *status*). *Role* is *the behavior expected of one who holds a particular status.* Each person may hold a number of statuses and be expected to fill roles appropriate to them. In a sense, *status* and *role* are two aspects of the same phenomenon. A status is a set of privileges and duties; a role is the acting out of this set of duties and privileges.

The norms of the culture are learned mainly through learning roles. While a few norms apply to all members of a society, most norms vary according to the statuses we fill, for what is correct for one status is wrong for another. *Socialization, the process of learning enough of the folkways and mores to become a part of the society,* is largely a process of learning role behavior.

SOCIALIZATION THROUGH ROLE AND STATUS

Each person must learn to fill roles as child, student, probably husband or wife, parent,

employee, organization member or officer, member of a particular race and social class, citizen, resident of a community, and many others. Role learning involves at least two aspects: (1) We must learn to perform the duties and claim the privileges of the role, and (2) we must acquire the attitudes, feelings, and expectations appropriate to the role. Of these two aspects the latter is the more important. Almost anyone (male or female) can fairly quickly learn how to feed, bathe, and diaper a baby; what one does not learn quickly are the attitudes and sentiments which make baby care a satisfying and rewarding activity. One cannot fill a role happily and successfully without having been socialized to accept that role as worthwhile, satisfying, and appropriate.

Role training for most of the important roles begins early in childhood as one starts to form attitudes toward those roles and statuses. Most of the role training is painless and unconscious. Children "play house," play with the toys given them, watch and help mother and father, hear and read stories, listen to family talk, and share in family life. From all this experience they gradually form a picture of how men and women act and of how husbands and wives treat each other.

Social Roles and Personality

The little boy who takes the role of the father while playing house is aware that he must think and act in a different manner than when

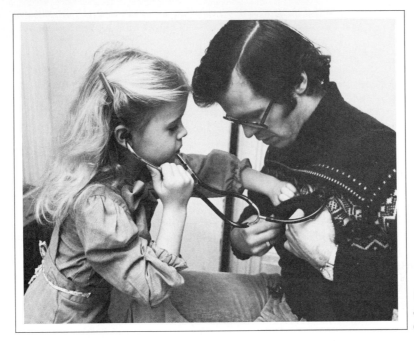

Role training begins early. (*Suzanne Szasz/Photo Researchers, Inc.*)

he is simply playing his own role, that of child. At first he may have little understanding of the reasons underlying a father's actions, but this understanding grows and his "pretend" roles will help prepare him for the time when he actually becomes a father. At a more mature level "pretend" role taking has been a helpful aid in assisting people to understand reactions of others in a diagnostic and therapeutic technique known as *psychodrama*, developed by Moreno [1940] and others. A husband, for example, may take the role of the wife while she takes his role as they reenact some recent discussion or conflict in an unrehearsed dialogue. As each tries to take the part of the other, voicing the other's complaints and defenses, each may gain greater insight into the other's feelings and reactions.

The concept of role implies a set of expectations. We expect to act in certain ways, and we expect other people to act in certain ways. Whether a new role is pretend or genuine, one must analyze one's own behavior and the behavior of others. The self does not remain unchanged after this kind of experience. The married woman is in a different status than the single woman. Her role is different, and in some ways she will be a different person.

Occupational roles also produce personality changes, so that there are "reciprocal effects of man on job and job on man" [Kohn and Schooler, 1973]. In a famous role-taking experiment, Zimbardo [1973] set up a mock prison complete with a simulated cell block, uniformed guards, and the usual prison routines. Student volunteers were randomly divided into "prisoners" and "guards," while the "guards" were instructed to invent their own means of control. The "prisoners" quickly become rebellious and sullen while the "guards" became brutal and abusive to a degree which surprised and alarmed those supervising the experiment. The experiment was suspended because the "prisoners" suffered uncontrollable rages, crying fits, and other symptoms resembling those of schizophrenia, and the supervisors feared some might suffer serious mental or physical injury [Craig Haney et al., 1973].

While this experiment is artificial in that all the participants realized it was temporary playacting, it nonetheless is significant. If playacting roles can have so great an effect upon behavior, how much greater must be the effect of genuine role playing upon behavior. It is likely that persons with certain personality characteristics are attracted to occupational roles which call for those characteristics, while those roles in turn tend to develop and reinforce the personality characteristics the role requires.

Role Sets

The term *role set* is used to indicate that a status may have not just a single role but a number of associated roles which fit together [Merton, 1957a, p. 369]. A wife, for example, is also a daughter, a relative, a neighbor, a citizen, a sex partner; probably a mother, a hostess, a cook and housekeeper, and a worker; and possibly a churchgoer, PTA member, union member, employer, or civic personage. Thus her role set involves a constellation of related roles, some of which may require drastically different types of adjustment. It is not uncommon for people to fail to operate equally well in all items of their role set. The charming office receptionist may be a poor bookkeeper; the attentive father may be a wretched lover; the eloquent preacher may be a poor administrator. Successful role performance often requires competence in a

A role set. How many roles are being filled? (*Erika Stone/Peter Arnold, Inc.*)

number of related behaviors. Meanwhile, one may fill several different role sets at the same time. A person may be a business manager, a parent, a church officer, a reservist in the National Guard, and a prominent civic leader. This multiplicity of roles may make for some role strain but not necessarily so, and it may also increase one's overall fulfillment and life satisfaction [Sieber, 1974].

Role Behavior

While a *role* is the behavior *expected* of one in a particular status, *role behavior* is the *actual* behavior of one who plays a role. Actual role behavior may vary from expected behavior for a number of reasons. One may not see the role the same way others see it, one's personality characteristics affect how one feels about the role, and not all persons filling a role are equally committed to it as it may conflict with other roles. All these factors combine in such a way that no two individuals play a given role in exactly the same way. Not all soldiers are brave, not all priests are saintly, not all professors are scholarly. There is enough diversity in role behavior to give variety to human life. Yet there is enough uniformity and predictability in role behavior to carry on an orderly social life.

Uniforms, badges, titles, and rituals are aids in role behavior. They lead others to expect and perceive the behavior called for by the role and encourage the actor to act in accord with role expectations. For example, in an experiment an instructor delivered identical lectures to two class sections, wearing a clerical collar in one and ordinary clothing in the other. He was perceived by students as more "morally committed" when wearing the clerical collar [Coursey, 1973]. Another experiment showed that people are more obedient to a uniformed guard than to a man in a business suit [Bickman, 1974]. Both the patient and the physician feel more comfortable if the physician conducts an intimate

physical examination while wearing a white coat in a sterile office than if he or she conducts the examination wearing bathing garb at poolside. The appropriate uniforms, badges, titles, equipment, and setting are all aids to role performance.

While much role behavior is the unconscious playing of roles to which one has been socialized, some role behavior is a highly conscious, studied effort to project a desired image of the self. The concept of *dramatic role presentation* refers to a conscious effort to play a role in a way which will create a desired impression among others. Conduct is regulated not only by role needs but also by what the audience expects. Few of us will ever be movie stars, but everyone is an actor with a wide variety of audiences. The children in the home, the neighbors, the office force, other students in a school—all these and many others form audiences. As Goffman [1959, 1967, 1981] has noted, we put on a presentation of ourselves when the audience is present, acting out roles so that we give a calculated picture of the self. The debutante making a grand entrance at a party, the officer controlling traffic, the sales executive making a pitch, the parent lecturing a child, the tough guy on the playground, the student assuming a pose of studious attentiveness—everyone at some time and place is an actor seeking to impress an audience. When our success at creating a desirable impression is threatened, we may resort to a face-saving device in self-protection [Berk, 1977]. Persons of both sexes and all ages sometimes lay claim to fictitious sexual adventures in order to give a more "sophisticated" image of themselves. Business suits creep out of hiding and haircuts shorten when corporate recruiters visit the campus. Even among groups where "naturalness" and lack of affectation are prized, the frayed blue denims and bare feet are no less a studied presentation of self than are the Brooks Brothers suits in the executive dining room.

ASCRIBED AND ACHIEVED STATUS AND ROLE

Statuses and roles are of two sorts: those ascribed to us by our society, irrespective of individual qualities or efforts, and those we achieve through our own efforts [Linton, 1936, chap. 8].

To illustrate the difference: Princess is an *ascribed* status. One does not become a princess through ability or choice or effort. One is born a princess and will remain a princess whether one is stupid or brilliant, ugly or beautiful, obstreperous or gracious [Young and Mack, 1959, p. 160]. But prime minister, fire fighter, student, and husband and wife are all *achieved* statuses. One becomes these things through one's own choices and actions. Child and adult are ascribed statuses. The child is treated as a child and the adult is treated as an adult regardless of their choices or wishes. "Old" is also an ascribed status. If one survives, one becomes old regardless of one's wishes. Some resist the status in ways which others consider "childish," yet "old" they become, for there are no ways to choose or reject an ascribed status.

Ascribed Status and Role

If a society is to function efficiently, people must perform a vast number of daily chores willingly and competently. The simplest way to ensure their performance is to parcel most of the routine work of the society into a series of *ascribed* roles and to socialize people to accept and fill their ascribed roles. Since role training must therefore begin early in childhood, ascribed roles must be assigned according to some criterion which can be known in advance. Sex and age are universally used as a basis of role ascription; race, nationality, social class, and religion are also used in many societies.

ASCRIPTION BY SEX. Although role training may be largely unconscious, it is no less real.

As a noted American educator has remarked, "Adults ask little boys what they want to be when they grow up. They ask little girls where they got that pretty dress." No wonder that by adolescence boys were concerned about careers while girls were preoccupied with getting married. This is no accident, since a major part of the socialization process consists of learning the proper activities of men and women. The little girl played with dolls, helped mother in the housework, and was rewarded for being a "little lady," while learning that "tomboy" activities, though possibly tolerated, were not really "ladylike." The boy found out that dolls were for girls and that no worse fate could befall him than to be a "sissy." Many years of differential training, if consistent, will bring boys and girls to maturity with great differences in their responses, feelings, and preferences.

Every society handles many tasks by making them part of a sex role. Yet most of the sex-linked tasks can be performed equally well by either men or women, provided they are socialized to accept the tasks as proper for them. Thus, in Pakistan men are household servants; in the Philippines, pharmacists are usually women, while men are preferred as secretaries; in the Marquesas, baby tending, cooking, and housekeeping are proper male tasks, while women spend much of their time primping; in many parts of the world much of the heavy agricultural labor is performed by women.

Masculine and feminine roles are subject to infinite variation, yet every society has had an approved pair of sex roles which people were expected to fill. Individuals may be permitted to bypass some parts of the pattern at times, but they risk alienation from the society unless they can identify themselves with the role expected of their sex. Some societies have a recognized status and role for those who do not absorb the expected sex identities. For example, the *nadle* among the Navajo and the *berdache* among the Plains

Most sex-linked tasks can be performed well by either sex. (*Carl Frank/Photo
Researchers, Inc.*)

Indians are recognized gender statuses which
differ from both male and female sex statuses
[Hill, 1935; Lurie, 1953; Voorhies, 1973;
Forgey, 1975]. But in most societies no comfortable status is open to those whose sex-
role behavior falls outside those societies'
approved alternatives. Homosexuality (discussed in Chapter 6) is a status and role which
is fiercely debated in our society.

Many considerations which presumably
underlie our ascribed sex roles are themselves
changing today. The assumption of vast innate sex differences in intellect and aptitude
has been discredited. Greater dependability
and availability of contraception and abortion
has weakened the rationale for a double
standard of sexual behavior. Declining family
size means that women spend less time in
childbearing and child care. The shift from
human to machine power means that greater
masculine physical strength becomes less important. The growing concern for equal rights
in recent years has led many women to
become aware of the vast inequalities they
have endured. For all these reasons many
women today are in full revolt against sex-
role ascription.

ASCRIPTION BY AGE.   In no society are children, adults, and the aged treated alike. Age

roles vary greatly among societies. American children spend their childhood in pampered play while Navajo children tend sheep and do weaving at an early age; the aged in prerevolutionary China were honored authority figures within the family as long as they lived, while the American aged most often retire in age-segregated households. Persons whose behavior is inappropriate for their age status are either laughed at or resented. The teenager who claims adult privileges is irritating, while the mature person who acts like a teenager is ridiculed. "Act your age" is a common rebuke.

Although age-status ascription is universal, it is changing. Within recent years, American voting age has been reduced to 18, drinking ages in many states have been lowered to 18 or 19 (although in some states the drinking age has been restored to 21), and colleges have abandoned their *in loco parentis* supervision of college students. Status of the aged is also changing in American society.

Status of the Aged Old age, in many primitive or traditional societies, is highly honored, perhaps because, in such a society, the old are closest to the source of hallowed tradition. Thus in pre-Communist China, the grandmother was the reigning female in the multiple-family home and the grandfather was a patriarch whose whim was close to law. In agricultural societies, it was practical for old persons to shift gradually to less strenuous work as their strength waned, but they were still respected for their wisdom and were provided with security and companionship within a three- or four-generational household. Most people worked, as much as they were able, until entirely incapacitated and then usually died quite quickly. "Retirement" was practically unknown.

The industrial revolution removed most of the aged from a landowning income base and offered few jobs to persons of declining energy. Most of the aged were dependent upon children or charity. Rapid social change made useless the "wisdom" of the aged, who might be loved but were seldom consulted or respected and were simply marking time until death [Atchley, 1980; Harris and Cole, 1980].

As shown in Table 5-1, this is changing. The proportion of the aged has increased, partly because of lower birthrates (reducing the proportion of young people) and partly because of lower death rates among the aged since about 1950. Private pensions and Social Security have made fewer of the aged dependent on children or charity. Aged-based retirement has ended work for many who are still healthy and vigorous. For the first time in history, retirement (before total exhaustion)

TABLE 5-1
CHANGING STATUS OF AGED IN WESTERN SOCIETIES

Preindustrial	Early industrial	Late industrial
High birthrates; high death rates; few aged	High birthrates; falling death rates among young; few aged	Falling birthrates; falling death rates among aged after 1950; rapid increase of aged
Farm-based income; family-based security	Income from employment; abrupt cutoff when unable to work	Substantial retirement income
Gradual-retirement; work adjusted to age and strength	Abrupt retirement through incapacity	Age-based retirement; more options
3- to 4-generational family normal	3- to 4-generational family less common	3- to 4- generational family rare; retirement communities growing
Social activity in family	Isolated from social activity	Age-segregated social activities
Honorific status	Denigrated status	Growing political power
Influential as library of wisdom	Reduced influence, wisdom ignored	Wisdom ignored; political power recognized

has become a reality for most people. Increased numbers have brought greater political power, offsetting the modern tendency to simply ignore the aged. The new disciplines of geriatrics and gerontology study the aging process and the problems of the aged. Although many of the aged are still lonely or poor or both, the status of the aged has become far more comfortable in recent decades.

ASCRIPTION BY MERIT.   We may today have developed a form of quasi ascription through our trend toward *meritocracy*. A meritocracy is *a social system in which status is assigned according to merit*, and today, merit is most commonly measured by scores on standardized tests which control access to educational programs and occupational roles.

If one assumes that these scores are reasonably stable for an individual, then the result is a kind of caste system in which test scores, largely dependent upon heredity and early environment, may shape one's entire life. This means that a new type of ascribed status has developed, not directly dependent upon the status of one's ancestors but perhaps almost as rigid.

THE REVOLT AGAINST ASCRIPTION.   All kinds of status ascription are under attack throughout much of the world. Tests claiming to measure intelligence or aptitudes are criticized and efforts are made to limit their use. "Racial discrimination" is another term for status ascription by race. Racial and ethnic groups are rebelling against subordinate status ascription. There is no universal surge toward racial equality, for in some parts of the world, racial and ethnic persecutions have been rising. But in many areas, racial and ethnic minorities are militantly demanding an end to status ascription by race and are finding many supporters among the general population. Differences in class status are under sharp attack as undemocratic and oppressive. Ascription by age and sex is a topic of equally bitter debate.

. . . revolt against sex-role ascription

In conclusion, role ascription offers a simple way of dividing the work of society, and it facilitates early and successful role preparation. But role ascription is successful only when most people wholeheartedly accept their ascribed roles. Vast numbers of people are today questioning or rejecting them. While it seems doubtful to sociologists that all status and role ascription will cease, changes in ascription will continue.

Achieved Status and Role

A social position which is secured through individual choice and competition is known as an *achieved status*. Just as each person occupies a number of ascribed statuses, assigned without regard to individual ability or preference, so one occupies a number of achieved statuses which are secured through one's own ability, performance, and possibly good or ill fortune.

In traditional societies most statuses are ascribed, with occupation and general social standing determined at birth. Industrialized societies have a greater range of occupations, require greater mobility of labor, and allow greater scope to change status through individual effort. The society stressing achieved status will gain in flexibility and in ability to place people in occupations best suited to their talents. The price it pays for these advantages is seen in the insecurity of those unable to "find themselves" and in the strain of constant adjustment to new roles. Achieved status requires people to make choices, not only of occupation but also of friends, organizations, schools, and place of residence. Further, it leads people into roles which were not foreseen or desired by their parents. In the traditional society, where statuses and roles are ascribed, people are trained from childhood and guided through life by rules of conduct which they have carefully learned in preparation for roles they are destined to play. In a changing society where they are free to experiment, people meet situations far removed from the parental way of life and may have to feel their way awkwardly into unfamiliar roles.

Ascribed and achieved statuses are basically different; yet they interact with each other and may overlap. Thus it is easier for one with the ascribed status of male to reach the achieved status of President of the United States than it is for one with the ascribed status of female. General social standing in the community (social-class status) is partly ascribed, reflecting the status of one's parents, and partly achieved through one's own accomplishments. At many points the boundaries between achieved and ascribed status are indistinct; yet the concepts are useful.

PSYCHIC COSTS OF ACHIEVED STATUS. The ideal of the society which permits most statuses to be achieved is to place people according to their abilities. To some extent this effort enables the highly talented to move upward, but it also destroys the alibi of the failures. In a society where most statuses are ascribed, individuals are not expected to improve their lot. Those who receive low rewards and little prestige feel no guilt or shame. They are taught that their role and status are right and proper. They can take pride in their accomplishments without any need to compare them with those of persons in other statuses. They are freed from the sense of insecurity, the nagging of ambition, or the sting of failure. Socialization is eased when people are not expected to change their status; they have only to accept and learn their ascribed social roles. Shoemakers can feel contented and fulfilled by being good shoemakers, without feeling that they have failed because they have not become rich merchants. By being good shoemakers they are fulfilling the hopes and expectations of their parents, their spouses, and themselves.

It is more difficult to rationalize one's low status if hereditary barriers are removed and positions are supposedly open to all on the basis of ability. If positions are filled on competitive examinations and if adequate schooling is free to everybody, then the reason for low status must be indolence or incompetence, and this is not a comfortable admission. The low-caste person in India could blame his or her status on the inexorable laws of the universe; the American university student who fails to graduate has no such handy excuse.

The losers often charge that their merit is unrecognized and that supervisors use merit designation as a mask for favoritism. Devices such as seniority rules, group quotas, veteran preference, and similar techniques perform a double function. They limit favoritism, but they also slow the advance of those who might move ahead more rapidly on a strictly merit basis.

Defenders of capitalist society claim that most statuses are open to achievement through individual effort and ability. Critics of capitalist society (including most conflict sociologists) charge that opportunity for achievement is far from equal. They allege that the "free" schools, the ability and aptitude tests, and the selection and promotion process are all rigged to favor the "ins" over the "outs," the children of the prosperous over the children of the poor, and the whites over the minorities. Thus, they charge, the "achieved" statuses are, to a considerable degree, really ascribed according to one's sex, class, and race [Katz, 1971; Greer, 1972; Collins, 1975, pp. 449–450; Bowles and Gintis, 1976].

Extended discussion of these charges is found in Chapter 16, "Social Mobility." The degree to which these charges are correct is a matter of debate. To whatever extent statuses are equally open to achievement, task assignment through achieved statuses makes the maximum provision for attainment of roles on the basis of individual ability. It provides a high degree of choice and flexibility at the cost of psychic insecurity for the individual who cannot compete successfully. In essence the achieved status probably represents both the most efficient use of the human potential and the greatest threat to the individual's peace of mind.

Status Inconsistency

Each person holds several different statuses at the same time, and these statuses may not carry the same rank. The deposed prince who runs a restaurant, the new college graduate who works as a waitress, and the world-famous statesman's son who is successful at nothing are examples. The term *status inconsistency* is used when *one of a person's statuses is incompatible with his or her other statuses* (the terms *status discrepancy* and *status incongruity* are also sometimes used). Status inconsistency means that one's several statuses do not go together in the expected manner.

Age, sex, and class are three kinds of statuses which may be inconsistently combined. The young soldier may be old enough to drive a tank but not old enough to buy a beer. Old men who pursue young women are disapproved; old women who seek young lovers are ridiculed; old men who announce the birth of a child are met with a ribald cynicism.

Status inconsistency is also present when one is not generally recognized to hold a status which one feels to be deserved, such as the new-rich who are scorned by the blue bloods, or the immigrant physician who must

Status inconsistency

work as a hospital orderly until gaining certification.

Status inconsistency produces confusion. Should one talk baseball or baby-sitting with the liberated male who keeps house while his wife runs a bulldozer? When a woman executive's male secretary answers the phone, callers may assume they have the wrong number.

Persons suffering status inconsistency may respond by identifying with the higher-ranked status and by seeking to avoid or deny the lower-ranked status, as with the new-rich who cultivate upper-class manners or immigrants who "Americanize" their names. Or they may identify with the lower of their statuses, as in the case of the successful and prosperous black who, instead of seeking acceptance among rich whites, becomes a militant leader of poor black people. Awareness of status inconsistency generally produces a behavior response of some kind [Lenski, 1954; Mitchell, 1964; Treiman, 1966; Broom and Jones, 1970; House and Harkins, 1975; Hornung, 1977; Wilson and Cooper, 1979].

Role Personality and True Personality

If role preparation were entirely adequate, each person would develop a personality which perfectly harmonized with his or her role demands. But imperfections in preparation, plus unpredictability of future role demands, make it certain that many people will develop a personality which differs considerably from the *pattern of personality traits which the role requires*—the *role personality*. For ascribed roles and statuses, the divergence may be small enough so that little clash will occur between role personality and true personality. Thus, most children give up the pattern of crying and throwing tantrums as they grow up, and very few men wish to wear women's clothing.

For achieved roles and statuses, which often are not selected until after one's adult personality has already been formed, considerable divergence between role and true personalities is fairly common. For instance, in the role of salesperson one needs to be friendly, extroverted, and perceptive of the reactions of others. Suppose one's true personality is shy, withdrawn, contemplative, and insensitive to the reactions of others. Such a person is unlikely to become a salesperson or to succeed as one. If the person does succeed, it is done by masking the true personality with an outward show of friendliness and a deliberately cultivated attentiveness to the clues to others' reactions. This role playing is not easy to accomplish successfully and may entail a good deal of emotional strain. If the role playing is done successfully over a long period of time, however, the true personality may gradually be modified to come closer to the role personality. Eleanor Roosevelt was a rather shy young woman and a hesitant and reluctant public speaker. In her role as wife to a politically ambitious but physically handicapped husband, she forced herself into vigorous political activity and became an eloquent speaker. Apparently she found the role a rewarding one, for long after her husband's death she accepted a diplomatic appointment, remained a tireless world traveler and public speaker, and became one of the most remarkable women of her age. On the other hand, the wives of many men prominent in public life have rejected the role of politician's wife and divorced their husbands.

It is likely that a good deal of success and failure in achieved roles is explained by the degree to which the true personality coincides with the required role personality. Personnel management today uses job analyses, psychological tests, depth interviews, and other devices in an effort to fit people into jobs where there will be little clash between true and role personalities.

ROLE STRAIN

It would be ideal if each person could fill all roles in a role set with equal ease, but few people are able to do this. *Role strain* refers to the *difficulty people have in meeting their role obligations*. Role strain may arise through inadequate role preparation, role transitional difficulties, role conflicts, or role failure.

Inadequate Role Preparation

The small child playing house or helping with the dishes, the teenager who baby-sits, the high school student with a part-time job—all these are experiencing a *continuity in socialization* by learning skills and attitudes at one period of life which they can use at another. By continuity in socialization we simply mean that experiences at each life stage are an effective preparation for the next stage. An example of how continuity in the socialization process provides a smooth transition into the adult role is seen in the child-training practices of the Cheyenne Indians, as described by Benedict.

> The essential point of such training is that the child is from infancy continuously conditioned to responsible social participation while at the same time the tasks that are expected of it are adapted to its capacity. . . . At birth the little boy was presented with a toy bow, and from the time he could run about serviceable bows

suited to his stature were specially made for him by the man of the family. Animals and birds were taught him in a graded series beginning with those most easily taken, and as he brought in his first of each species his family duly made a feast of it, accepting his contribution as gravely as the buffalo his father brought. When he finally killed a buffalo, it was only the final step of his childhood conditioning, not a new adult role with which his childhood experience had been at variance. (Ruth Benedict, "Continuities and Discontinuites in Cultural Conditioning," *Psychiatry*, 1:161–167, May, 1938.)

Such an easy transition from one status to the next is by no means universal. Our culture is characterized by built-in *discontinuities,* which make the socialization experience in one age period of little use in the next. In frontier America, boys and girls learned their adult roles by simply observing and taking part in whatever was going on around them—clearing land, planting crops, caring for babies, and so on.

Today there is less opportunity for such continuity. Most adult work is performed away from home, where children cannot watch and share it. Many households offer only a poor opportunity for a child to learn the skills, attitudes, and emotional rewards of housekeeping and parenthood. Children and teenagers have few important tasks in most households, and much of the child's play activity is not closely related to adult tasks and responsibilities.

Another imperfection in our socialization process is that moral training of boys and girls introduces them mainly to *formal* rules of social behavior rather than to informal modifications of these rules which operate in the adult world. In other words, they are taught the ideal, not the real culture. The result is that young people become cynical as they find that the textbook maxims do not work out. The politician does not appear as a public servant who negotiates a livable adjustment between bitter opponents but as one who compromises on sacred principles;

the business executive looks like a greedy manipulator rather than an individual struggling to find a place in the market; the minister is apparently not one who mediates the ways of God to humanity but a huckster who fails to live up to the ideals the church proclaims. Thus, many young people graduate from a naïve idealism directly into a naïve cynicism without ever reaching an appreciation of the services of those who work out livable compromises with the unsolved problems of society.

Some gap between the formal expressions of mores and actual adjustments of social life is probably found in all societies. And in all societies, "maturity" involves coming to terms with these inconsistencies in some sort of livable compromise.

Such discontinuities are also favored by rapid social change, since parents cannot possibly anticipate the type of world their children will face. Thus, parents in Sri Lanka in the 1930s often raised their children as Christians because Christianity was the religion of the enlightened and the powerful. Today, these children find Christianity a handicap now that Buddhism has become identified with resurgent nationalism in a newly independent country. Similarly, the American farmer may carefully train his children in the attitudes and techniques appropriate to farming, although it is a predictable certainty that many of these children are headed for urban life and work.

Current sex-role changes also create problems in role preparation. Should dolls be given to little girls, little boys, or to both? Should little girls be socialized to view motherhood and homemaking as their primary fulfillment or socialized to believe that such a commitment is a waste of their potential? Should boys be socialized to view the "provider" task as their primary duty or to accept an equal willingness to sacrifice career advancement while sharing equally in household and child care duties?

Such examples could be multiplied endlessly. They show how it is impossible to prepare young people for the roles they will play as adults in a changing society. Since adult roles cannot be accurately predicted, socialization and education can be adequate only if they prepare the child to fill a wide variety of roles. Memorization and rote learning in schools have been replaced, in theory, by efforts to develop abilities in "problem solving" and "adjustment," but how successfully may be debated. Yet the rapidity of change and the uncertainty of future role ascriptions make flexibility and adaptability necessary conditions for survival.

Role Transitional Difficulties

In many societies there are role transitions—especially in ascribed age roles—which are structured in such a way as to be inevitably difficult. This is because of discontinuities in role preparation—because the learning experiences of one age status do not provide the attitudes and values needed to fill the next role one is expected to assume.

In most primitive societies the adolescent period is not marked by any unusual stress. At any given age in most primitive societies individuals have a clearly defined status and role; they, and everyone else, know exactly what their duties and privileges are. Our society has no clearly defined age statuses, except for the relatively minor legal maturity at 21, which adding still greater confusion, is now sometimes only 18. Our American youth and their parents have no standardized set of duties and privileges to guide them. Parents are uncertain about just how much "maturity" to concede to teenagers, and they bicker endlessly about their choice of companions, the hours they keep, their use of money, the use of the car, and how much adult freedom they should have. Coleman, a distinguished educational sociologist, suggests that in American society, prolonged schooling tends to isolate youth from adults and to shift socialization to the peer group;

this, he believes, perpetuates the irresponsibilities of childhood and fails to prepare youth for adult roles [Coleman, 1974].

In most primitive societies adolescents enter a period of training which ends in an elaborate ceremony, in which they may endure ordeals or submit to circumcision, tattooing, or scarification. Such ceremonies, called "rites of passage," establish their status and announce that they are now ready to assume adult responsibilities, and their successful role performance is almost guaranteed. Our closest equivalents are found in such events as confirmation, getting a driver's license, holding a full-time job, graduating from high school or college, and getting married. Yet we lack any systematic preparation, or any general agreement upon the age, achievement, or type of ceremony which clearly establishes transition into adult status.

Among the Plains Indians warriors were trained from childhood to be aggressive, hostile, and uncompromising; then upon moving from warrior to "old man" status, they were expected to be placid peacemakers. This called for an abrupt reversal in personality, and few could make the transition gracefully. An equally painful transition is demanded in our society. To be successful in the active adult role, one must develop independence and self-reliance, must learn to find satisfaction in useful work and in being adviser and protector of the young. As an aged person, one is expected to become dependent and submissive, able to respect oneself with no useful work to do, and must learn to keep advice to oneself while being ignored or patronized by the young. Is it any wonder that some old people sicken and die soon after retirement, while many others become bored and fretful? The rapidly developing field of *geriatrics* indicates a serious concern with this problem. But as long as youth suggests activity, adventure, and romance, while age symbolizes uselessness and irrelevance, growing old will continue to be a painful experience [George, 1980].

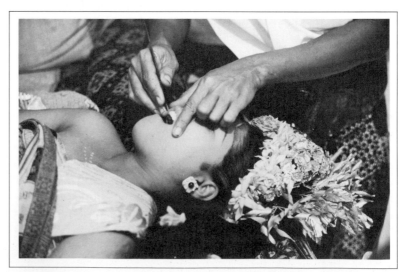

Rites of passage: car keys in the United States, teeth filing in Bali, ritual beating in Nigeria. (*Mimi Forsyth/Monkmeyer; Ken Heyman; Marilyn Silverstone/ Magnum*)

Role transitions often are also made more difficult through the necessity of *role relinquishment*. To accept a new role, one often must relinquish an old one, along with whatever rewards it carried. The "swinging" single who marries, the alcoholic who must resume responsibilities when he or she goes "on the wagon," and the business owner who must surrender power and authority to a successor—these are a few examples of difficult role relinquishment. Just as the Plains Indians found it difficult to relinquish the warrior role, many parents find it difficult to relinquish control over their children. Efforts to "rehabilitate" prostitutes generally fail because "the life" is more exciting than any

"straight" jobs which these women can hold. To succeed in "straight" jobs, ghetto youth must forget their street skills and surrender much personal worth and dignity, as these are measured in the world of ghetto street life. Thus, an unwillingness to relinquish the rewards of a current role may prevent the full acceptance of a new role.

RESOCIALIZATION AS ROLE PREPARATION. Sometimes people must make role transitions which call for so much unlearning and relearning that the process is called *resocialization*, such as when one enters prison, military service, a monastery, or convent. While a convent may resocialize novitiates more gently than a marine basic training camp, the objective and the process are the same: Isolate recruits from family, friends, and civilian life; strip them of their present self-identities; imbue them with a sense of their personal unworthiness; then rebuild a new identity appropriate to the role. *Brainwashing* as used by the Chinese Communists is another name for resocialization. In prisoner of war camps the Chinese operated in Korea, American prisoners were isolated, humiliated, starved, exhausted, subjected to endless questioning and prolonged fatigue, and sometimes tortured. Some prisoners eventually began to repeat, apparently sincerely, the things the Chinese wanted them to say [Somit, 1968]. The kidnappers of Patricia Hearst used brutal brainwashing techniques to reshape her orientation [Hearst, 1982]. Somewhat similar (though less brutal) procedures have been used by many agencies attempting resocialization, such as Synanon (a drug therapy group), the Unification Church of the Rev. Sun Myong Moon, Alcoholics Anonymous, and others.

Resocialization is most effective when it proceeds within a "total institution," such as a prison, military post, or religious commune, where the entire experience of the subject is controlled. While such resocialization dramatically changes a person's role behavior, it is doubtful that there is much change in true personality. Unless one remains within a setting where resocialization can be reinforced continuously, the subject usually reverts to the former self. Thus, brainwashed prisoners recanted their "confessions" soon after their release, ex-marines are not noticeably different from other people after they return to civilian life [Schreiber, 1979], the revival convert who does not unite with a religious group soon "backslides" into sin, and members of Alcoholics Anonymous are encouraged to continue attending meetings for reinforcement of their resolve to remain sober. Resocialization requires frequent reinforcement if it is to endure [SanGiovanni, 1978].

Role Conflicts

There are at least two kinds of role conflicts: conflict between roles and conflict within a single role. (1) Two or more roles (either independent roles or parts of a role set) may impose conflicting obligations upon a person. The employed wife finds that the demands of her job may conflict with home duties; the married student must reconcile student role demands with duties as husband or wife; the police officer must sometimes choose between duty and arresting a friend. Or, (2) within a single role there may be a structured (built-in) conflict. The military chaplain, preaching a gospel of love, must sustain men in their readiness to kill, a role conflict which many chaplains find disturbing [Burchard, 1963; Zahn, 1969]. Among younger Catholic clergy, conflict between vows of celibacy and desire for marriage is the greatest source of role strain [Schoenherr and Greeley, 1974]. The "company doctor" in any industry with health hazards had better not find that many workers' illnesses are due to unhealthful working conditions or there will soon be a new company doctor.

In many occupational roles, ranging from mechanic to physician, there is a built-in "conflict of interest" in that the obligation to be honest with the customer or patient may conflict with the desire to make money, so that a number of needless repairs to car or body may be made. Very few roles are completely free from structured role conflicts.

There are several common processes which reduce role strain and protect the self from guilt. These include *rationalization, compartmentalization*, and *adjudication*. The first two are not conscious, intentional protective devices; if they were, they would not "work." Only when people are not aware of them will these processes operate successfully.

Rationalization is a defense process whereby one redefines a painful situation in terms which are socially and personally acceptable. The classic illustration is that of the man who comes to feel he is fortunate that he didn't marry that girl who rejected him, or even comes to believe that it was really *he* who rejected her! Rationalization conceals the reality of role conflict, preventing awareness that any conflict exists. Thus, our belief in democracy and our denial of equality to women and to black people caused few anxieties as long as we believed women and blacks were on the intellectual level of children. "All men are created equal," but slaves were not *men*, they were *property*. The Catholic doctrine (which Luther and Calvin also followed) of "just" and "unjust" wars makes it possible for Christians on both sides to commit mass murder with a clear conscience. The angry parent thrashes a disobedient child "for its own good." Through rationalization, the situation is defined in such a way that there is no role conflict and therefore no role strain.

Compartmentalization reduces role strain by fencing one's roles off into separate parts of one's life so that one responds to only one set of role demands at a time. It has been noted that many cruel Nazi concentration camp guards and executioners were kindly, affectionate husbands and fathers. Their work and family roles were entirely separated. The business executive who conspires to violate

He develops a wardrobe of role personalities.

the antitrust laws in the afternoon and speaks eloquently at a citizen's law-and-order meeting in the evening is not necessarily aware of the hypocrisy but is merely switching roles. Within each role are found the pressures and justifications which make the expected role behavior seem necessary and good. Uniforms, judicial robes, surgical gowns, and professional titles are aids in insulating roles from one another. Many people cannot "relax" (that is, cannot step fully outside a role) until they are "out of uniform."

If one is successfully socialized, one develops a wardrobe of role personalities and slips into one or another as the situation demands. At the office, a woman may treat men with a brisk, formal efficiency; yet with husband or lover she may be tender, responsive and "feminine." This process of switching role personalities creates the possibility of emotional strain whenever it is not entirely clear which of several sets of attitudes and guidelines should apply to a particular behavior situation. Many an employer, faced with the necessity of laying off employees, finds it painful to ignore their human needs and treat them impersonally as "cost factors in production." The dishonesties, deceptions, and exploitations that are a part of many occupational roles are inconsistent with the usual moral and religious training. For persons who are not fully successful in fencing their behavior off into compartments, these cultural contradictions become mental conflicts within the individual. Some psychiatrists hold that such culture conflicts, and the mental conflicts they produce, are major causes of personality disorder.

Cultural conflicts and inconsistencies are probably found in every culture. In well-integrated cultures, these inconsistencies are so well rationalized, compartmentalized, and fenced off from one another that the individual does not sense them at all. Thus, many primitives who treated one another with great tenderness were ruthlessly cruel to outsiders; their humanitarian mores applied only to tribal fellows, while outsiders were considered and treated like any other animals of the forest. By contrast, our belief in a universal God of all humanity makes it harder for us to bomb our enemies with a clear conscience (but we generally manage to, somehow). *Cultural contradictions and multiple roles are upsetting only when they subject the individual to conflicting pressures in a situation that demands a single action.* For example, should a girl be a "good girl" according to her mother's or her boyfriend's definition? Should a mother encourage her daughter to remain chaste or encourage her to use the pill? Suppose an employee is ordered to do something dishonest or immoral. Should the employee do as told and protect the family meal ticket or risk dismissal by following his or her conscience? When torn between the irrational demands of an aging, senile parent and one's duty to spouse and children, what should one do? For many such role conflicts, there is no satisfactory compromise. When role strain becomes unendurable, neurotic or psychotic behavior may follow.

Adjudication differs from the protective devices just discussed in being conscious and intentional. It is a formal procedure for turning over to a third party a difficult decision on a possible role conflict, thereby relieving the individual of responsibility or guilt. Much of the work of professional associations and the codes of ethics which they develop is devoted to the solution of role conflicts. Cynics may argue that such professional associations usually operate to defend the interests of the profession. In many codes of ethics, clauses protecting competing members from one another greatly outnumber the statements protecting the clients or customers. Yet members of professions have been barred from the profession for violating the expected role behavior, and the need to justify action before one's peers does place some limitations upon behavior. In any event, a decision on proper role behavior by the professional association or labor union means that the in-

dividual is relieved of the duty of making his or her own decision.

Role Failure

Role failure is painful, with physical or mental illness a common result. In Latin American societies, a folk illness called *susto* is reported to be common among people whose role performance is inadequate [O'Nell, 1975]. In a stable, well-integrated society with a high proportion of ascribed roles, most of these roles will be filled successfully because people will have been prepared for them since earliest childhood. Most roles can be filled successfully by nearly any person who has been adequately prepared. But in a rapidly changing and less well integrated society such as ours, where we cannot predict all adult roles in advance and where discontinuities limit role preparation, a good deal of role failure is inevitable. Some persons fail in their roles as adults, never developing adult responsibility and self-control but continuing to act "childish" at all ages. Every society ascribes how "men" and "women" should act, but not all of us act as we are expected to act. Some are sex-role failures, such as the woman who hates men so fiercely she cannot work comfortably beside them, or the man who fears women so greatly he cannot leave the protection of his mother.

Even more persons fail in some of their achieved roles. Some fail to achieve the role they seek—the desired degree, long-sought admission to graduate school, the occupation of one's ambitions, the artistic calling one cannot resist, the passionate response of a desired lover. Various surveys have shown that roughly one-half of American teenagers aspire to a professional career, but since there is room in the professions for only about one in six workers, most of these teenagers will be disappointed. And many who achieve the role they crave will fail to fill it successfully. Many husbands and wives either fail to choose suitable marital partners or fail in their married roles. The result is either divorce or a lifetime of frustration. Many parents fail to socialize their children successfully. Only a few in any occupation or profession can be spectacularly successful, because for each manager there must be many subordinates. Those who seek the highest levels of excellence in a particular role are usually frustrated. Role failures of many kinds and degrees keep swelling the ranks of unhappy, frustrated people.

THE FINAL STATUS: DEATH

All societies ascribe a status to the dead and a role to the survivors. In most societies the dead are not really "gone," for their spirits remain. Occasionally these spirits are viewed as benevolent, but more often they are feared as dangerous or evil.

All societies developed norms for treating the dead. The Tasmanians buried hurriedly, avoided the burial places, feared the dead, and never even mentioned their names [Murdock, 1949, p. 10], while the Tanala revered their dead, treating them as though they were "away" not "dead" and inviting them to all the ceremonials of the living [Linton, 1936, p. 454]. The Eskimo buried their dead quickly but followed burial with prolonged mourning; the Samoans, after a frenzy of lamentation at the moment of death, then followed the burial with a prolonged party, with feasting, games, and songs [Murdock, 1949, pp. 214, 78].

Such ceremonials, however much they may vary from society to society, have the same basic function in all societies: to comfort the bereaved, to reintegrate surviving friends and relatives into an active social life, and in many societies to protect against the malevolence of the spirits of the dead. Some critics have branded American funeral ceremonies as an obscene extravagance and a monument to the cunning greed of morticians [Mitford, 1963]. Such critiques overlook the important function of funeral ceremonies in helping the

bereaved to accept the reality of death, to ease feelings of guilt, and to resume an active existence [Pincus, 1974; Pine, 1976; Vernon, 1978]. Funerals are the last of the "rites of passage" [van Gennep, 1960] and they are regarded as especially important. The Irish wake, a time when people gathered in the house of the deceased to drink and socialize as they mourned the dead, was an effective form of social therapy. Preparations for the wake kept the family busy; lamentation and weeping provided emotional release, as did the drinking; and visits by friends and neighbors reaffirmed their place in a social network [Kane, 1968]. By contrast, the conventional middle-class American funeral gives friends and relatives little chance to socialize or to find emotional catharsis through an unrestrained expression of grief.

Funeral ceremonies offer the last chance for a display of wealth which will show the importance of the deceased and his or her family. Burial in a pauper's grave is the final disgrace, while an elaborate casket and tomb reveal the affection and the status of the survivors. To some extent, it seems true that the less prosperity the individual has had in life, the more important it is to make an impressive exit. One survey found, in fact, that funeral expenses were practically identical for those of high and low income [Salomone, 1968, p. 56].

Whether funeral rites are a meaningless ceremony or a helpful therapeutic process probably depends as much on the attitudes with which death is approached as it does on the nature of the ceremony. Some see American society as a youth-oriented society which resists old age and is unprepared for death. For some people, the acceptance of death is based on a religious faith that life goes on and the grave is a new beginning rather than an end. Too many, however, have not found any rationale which prepares them for acceptance of death, either for themselves or their friends and relatives, so that the last act of life is seen as empty and meaningless

Funeral rites: white is the color of mourning in Vietnam; a funeral procession in New Guinea; a Jewish ceremony in the United States. (*Marc Riboud/Magnum; Magnum; © Eugene Gordon, 1982/Photo Researchers, Inc.*).

[Strauss, Glasser, and Quint, 1968; McCarthy, 1980].

The definition of death is changing. Now that heroic medical procedures can keep some life processes operating after brain function has ended, the issue of how long to preserve human bodies has arisen. The ending of brain function is the accepted medical test of death, but there is no generally accepted legal definition of death. Thus, the question of when to pull the plug on life-sustaining machines is morally disturbing and legally hazardous. The patient's "right to die" is another unsettled question. Several states have laws allowing a hopelessly ill patient to reject medical treatment and die with dignity. The burn center at the Los Angeles County, California, medical center allows hopeless burn patients to choose whether to have maximum medical treatment or to die quietly and more quickly with only pain-controlling medication. Most of them choose to die quickly [Imbus and

Zawacki, 1977]. Whether there is a "right to suicide" is being seriously debated by doctors, theologians, and the public [Portwood, 1978].

The traditional charade in which everyone pretends not to know that the patient is dying is today being replaced by realism and candor. Counseling services and group therapy assist both terminal patients and their families in accepting death [Goleman, 1976; Hotchkiss, 1978; Brim, 1979]. Kübler-Ross [1975] states that terminal patients typically pass through five stages in the process of coming to terms with death: denial, anger, bargaining, depression, and final acceptance. Her analysis has been challenged by empirical research [Kastenbaum, 1976, p. 45] but continues to be influential.

The new interest in helping the terminally ill to face death has brought charges that hospitals are too often concerned only with healing and do not help those who are dying [Noyes and Clancy, 1977]. This has led to development of the hospice movement which centers attention on the patient who is not going to be cured. The effort is to make the patient as comfortable as possible while increasing social contacts with friends and relatives. Most are home-care programs, although sometimes special wards are provided. Pain relief is emphasized, with no costly efforts to prolong life [*Wall Street Journal,* May 13, 1982].

Like any social innovation, the hospice movement encounters some opposition [Rossman, 1977], yet it will probably endure as it restores the historic place of friends and relatives in this last stage of life.

SUMMARY

Socialization takes place largely through learning roles. *Social status* is a position in society with consequent privileges and duties; a *role* is the behavior expected of one who occupies a particular status. Even in a single status, people are confronted with a related cluster of roles in what is known as a *role set.* One may assume several role sets at the same time, taking a multiplicity of roles which gives potential both for strain and for fulfillment. *Role behavior* is the actual behavior of one who plays a role, and it is affected by *dramatic role presentation,* in which the individual acts in a deliberate effort to present a desired image to the spectators.

Roles and statuses are of two sorts: those which are *ascribed* to persons according to age, sex, class, race, or some other inherited characteristic and those which are *achieved* through personal choice or effort. Achieved statuses are often gained at a substantial psychic cost, since the efforts and frustrations may be intense. A *meritocracy* is a form of quasi ascription, in which a status is open to achievement, but largely inherited characteristics give some persons great advantages in the competition.

A sweeping revolt against ascription seeks to reduce or end ascription of nearly all sorts. Whether role ascription can or should be ended is a matter of debate.

When a person's several statuses are inconsistent with one another, this is called *status inconsistency. Role personality* refers to the complex of personality characteristics appropriate for a particular role. Role and personality interact, with individual personality characteristics affecting role choice and role behavior, while the experience of playing a role, in turn, affects the personality.

Role strain refers to the difficulty of meeting role obligations. *Inadequate role preparation* may leave one poorly equipped, mainly in attitudes and values, to appreciate and enjoy a role. Many *role transitions* are difficult, usually because of *discontinuities in socialization,* or because the necessary *role relinquishments* demand that some current satisfactions be sacrificed. Some role transitions require so much role relearning that the term *resocialization* is used.

Role conflicts arise from conflicting duties within a single role or from conflicting demands imposed by different roles. Role conflicts can be managed by *rationalization,* in which the situation is redefined in the mind of the actor so that the person is aware of no conflict; by *compartmentalization,* which enables one to operate within a single role at a time; and by *adjudication,* in which a third party makes the decision. *Role failure* is quite common, especially in a changing society.

Dying is the final role, and death is the final status, which all societies recognize with ceremonies to aid the bereaved in accepting death and resuming life. The death status in America is changing through attitudes of growing acceptance and candor. The hospice movement is an attempt to ease the death process.

GLOSSARY

achieved role or status a role or status attained by individual choice, effort, action, or accomplishment.

ascribed role or status a role or status assigned according to hereditary traits without regard to individual preference, ability, or performance.

compartmentalization isolating roles from one another so that one is unaware of role conflicts.

discontinuity in socialization experiences at one life stage which do not aid or may even hinder transition into a later status.

dramatic role presentation a conscious effort to play a role in a manner which will create a desired impression upon others.

meritocracy a social system in which status is assigned according to individual merit.

rationalization redefining a painful situation in terms which are personally and socially acceptable.

resocialization the unlearning and relearning needed for a major role transition.

rite of passage any ritual which marks movement from one status to another, such as ceremonies attending birth, puberty, marriage, or death.

role expected behavior of one who holds a certain status.

role behavior the actual behavior of one who fills a role.

role conflict contradictory demands within a role; competing demands of two different roles.

role personality a pattern of personality traits a particular role requires.

role relinquishment giving up one role in order to accept another.

role set a cluster of associated roles that together form a social status.

role strain difficulty in meeting one's role obligations.

role transition change from one role to another.

status position of an individual in a group, or of a group in relation to other groups.

status inconsistency some disparity between one's several statuses.

QUESTIONS AND PROJECTS

1 Are *role* and *status* two separate concepts or two aspects of the same phenomenon? Explain.

2 What is the function of children's play in socialization?

3 Why is finding a suitable role and status more difficult for the aged in late industrial societies than in preindustrial societies? Analyze the situation of contemporary aged in terms of continuities and discontinuities in socialization.

4 Why do the aged have mixed attitudes on early retirement? What are the pros and cons of age-segregated communities?

5 Describe the shift from the status and role of a high school student to that of college student and the shift from civilian to soldier in terms of cultural continuities and discontinuities in socialization.

6 In role preparation for most adult roles, which is more important: the attitudes and values which make that role acceptable or the knowledge and skills necessary to fill the role? Illustrate for the homemaker, schoolteacher, army officer, and research scientist, and for old-age roles.

7 Is there any conflict between your roles as college student and as son or daughter? If you are a married student, a third (and possibly a fourth) role is added. What possible role conflicts are added?

8 What social costs accompany an emphasis upon achieved status? Ascribed status?

9 In what respects is your present role as college student preparing you for later roles? In what respects is your present role experience irrelevant or even dysfunctional?

10 Are there any respects in which you are already assuming role personalities which differ from your true personality? Are you aware of any stresses which this acting a part produces?

11 What are the pros and cons of a meritocracy as compared with alternative methods of status ascription or achievement?

12 Describe some situation you know about in which a person has been under pressure to fill two or more conflicting roles. How did he or she resolve the conflict? Would you say the

resolution was successful or unsuccessful?

13 Which role transition requires the greater degree of resocialization: from civilian to soldier or from soldier back to civilian?

14 Who would face the greater role transition problems: the soldier who, after twenty years of service, returns to civilian life or the priest who, after twenty years in the priesthood, leaves and marries?

15 Why are we changing our traditional view that a patient should be kept alive as long as possible?

SUGGESTED READINGS

Abbott, Andrew: "Status and Status Strain in the Professions," *American Journal of Sociology*, 86:819–835, January 1981. An analysis of role strain coming from conflict between popular and professional classifications of role and status.

Bell, Marilyn J.: "Attitudes Toward the Female Role: Life Experiences and Problems Recounted by Older Women," *Sociological Spectrum*, 1:21–38, January/March 1981. An empirical study of the problems of older women.

Berk, Bernard: "Face-Saving at the Singles Dance," *Social Problems*, 24:530–544, June 1977. Describes how people save face when they are unsuccessful in attracting dance partners.

Bryan, James H.: "Apprenticeships in Prostitution," *Social Problems*, 12:287–297, Winter 1965; also, Barbara Sherman Heyl, "The Madam as Teacher: The Training of House Prostitutes," *Social Problems*, 24:545–555, June 1977. Two articles describing the role preparation and training of prostitutes.

Cockerham, William C.: "Self-Selection and Career Orientation Among Enlisted U.S. Army Paratroopers," *Journal of Political and Military Sociology*, 6:249–259, Fall 1978. Relation of career concept to role performance of paratroopers.

*Goffman, Erving: *Forms of Talk*, University of Pennsylvania Press, Philadelphia, 1981. An analysis of speech and body language as role playing.

Harris, Diana K and William E. Cole: *Sociology of Aging*. Houghton Mifflin Company, Boston, 1980. A standard gerontology textbook.

Ostrander, Susan A.: "Upper-Class Women: The Feminine Side of Privilege," *Qualitative Sociology*, 3:23–44, Spring 1980. Status and role of affluent women often seen as the beneficiaries of the past sysem of gender rewards and duties.

Palmer, C. Eddie: "Dog Catchers: A Descriptive Study," *Qualitative Sociology*, 1:79–107, May 1978. Work duties and role performance of a seldom mentioned occupation.

*Simpson, Ida Harper, et al.: *From Student to Nurse*, Cambridge University Press, New York, 1979. A description of how the novice internalizes the role of nurse.

Snyder, Mark: "The Many Me's of the Self-Monitor," *Psychology Today*, 13:32–40, March 1980. How people become the role they play and the consequences for personality.

Vernon, Glenn: *The Sociology of Death: An Analysis of Death Related Behavior*, The Ronald Press Company, New York, 1970, 1978. A standard work on the sociology of death.

Walters, Vivienne: "Company Doctors' Perceptions of and Responses to Conflicting Pressures from Labor and Management," *Social Problems*, 30:1–12, October 1982. A research study of role conflict.

Zimbardo, Philip, et al.: "A Pirandellian Prison," *The New York Times Magazine*, April 8, 1973, pp. 38 ff.; also, Craig Haney, Curtis Banks, and Philip Zimbardo, "Interpersonal Dynamics in a Simulated Prison," *International Journal of Criminology and Penology*, 1:69–97, February 1973. Report of a famous experiment in which "guards" and "prisoners" in a mock prison played their roles all too enthusiastically.

6 Sexuality and Sex Roles

Wanda: Did you see here that two sociologists have just proved that men interrupt women all the time? They—
Ralph: Who says?
Wanda: Candace West of Florida State and Don Zimmerman of the University of California at Santa Barbara. They taped a bunch of private conversations, and guess what they found. When two men or two women are talking, interruptions are about equal. But when a man talks to a woman, he makes 96% of the interruptions. They think it's a dominance trick men aren't even aware of. But—
Ralph: These people have nothing better to do than eavesdrop on interruptions?
Wanda: —but women make "retrievals" about one-third of the time. You know, they pick up where they left off after the man—
Ralph: Surely not all men are like that, Wanda.
Wanda: —cuts in on what they were saying. Doesn't that—
Ralph: Speaking as a staunch supporter of feminism, I deplore it, Wanda.
Wanda: (sigh) I know, dear.

(*Time*, September 25, 1978, p. 82. Reprinted by permission from *Time, The Weekly Newsmagazine*; copyright Time, Inc., 1978.)

Chicago Police Department statistics for 1976 show that, for the first time, more women than men killed their spouses in Chicago.

(*Chicago Sun-Times*, September 7, 1977, p. 24.)

In a changing world, one thing remains constant. The sexes continue to find each other troublesome and irresistible. Most men live with women, and most women live with men, most of the time, in nearly all known societies.

The sex drive is a predisposition (apparently biological) to seek sexual and sex-related response from one or more others, usually of the opposite sex. It awakens in early teens and remains powerful throughout life. The intensity of interest in sexuality is suggested in a survey of *Psychology Today* readers, asked to rate a series of jokes for "funniness." The sex jokes were rated "very funny" over twice as often as the nearest other category, with older adults being the most enthusiastic consumers of sex humor [Hassett and Houlihan, 1979]. Evidence of the power of sexuality is everywhere. Few novels or movies can be successful if they lack the element of "love interest." Sexual attraction, and sometimes eroticism, are prominent in the art, music, and literature of most complex cultures. Kingdoms, fortunes, careers, and reputations have been thrown away in hopes of consummating a love; friends, family, and honor have been sacrificed; quarrels between or over lovers are a common prelude to murder. Perhaps even more convincing evidence of the power of the sex drive is provided by the host of men and women who labor patiently at humdrum tasks to make happier lives for their loved ones. Some scholars have attributed practically *all* human effort—from wartime heroics through earning a paycheck to washing clothes—to the desire to impress and possess one (or more) of the opposite sex, but such speculation cannot be tested. Different drives cannot be measured comparatively, yet the power of the sex drive is doubted by virtually no one.

There is some debate over whether this sex drive is innate or learned. Some scholars [e.g., Simon and Gagnon, 1977] question whether there is an inborn sex drive, claiming that our impulse to seek sex partners and use our sex organs is a product of social learning. However, because the sex drive is universal, arising in most members of all human societies, most scholars assume that the human sex drive is a biological inheritance.

SEXUAL FOUNDATIONS OF HUMAN SOCIAL LIFE

The sex drive is one of the building blocks for human social life. While no inborn drive compels humans to act in any particular way, each drive consists of a set of recurrent tension

The sex drive is one of the
building blocks for social life. (©
*Stephen Shames/Woodfin Camp
& Assoc.*).

states which impels people to *some kind of
activity* to relieve the tension. A drive cannot
be ignored and will not "go away." Some
ways of relieving tension will be found, will
be repeated by many people, and will become
part of the culture. What are some features
of the human sex drive which have affected
our patterns of social life?

Continuous Sexuality

Sexuality includes all the feelings and behavior
linked to sex through either biology or social

learning. The female of most species is sexually active only during a seasonal estrous
period, when she emits a chemical called a
pheromone which powerfully attracts and sexually excites males of that species. At other
times the female is unreceptive, and without
the pheromone, males are unstimulated. In
many species the mating season is the only
time when males and females associate. The
human species shares with the anthropoids
the biological fact of *continuous sexuality*,
meaning that the female may be sexually
active at any time. The human female passes

through no biological cycles of sexual acceptance and rejection. She emits no pheromones (as far as we know), and the male needs none.

There are some species whose males and females associate continuously while mating only seasonally. Continuous sexuality, therefore, is not necessary for continuous association, but it is a guarantee that the sexes will associate continuously. This makes continuous sexuality a part of the biological basis for human social life.

Variety and Continuity

The twin human desires for sexual continuity and sexual variety are another part of the biological basis for human social life. Some species mate for life and are strictly faithful to their mates; others are promiscuous, with the female mating with any (or all) males available. Humans apparently wish to do both. In all human societies most sexual intercourse of most adults is between persons who are regular sex partners. Persons who enjoy sex experience together wish to repeat it with each other. In most societies, most of these regular sex partnerships become institutionalized in a socially recognized relationship, usually either marriage or concubinage. But this desire for sexual continuity is complicated by an opposing desire for sexual variety.

Twin desires for continuity and variety

Many societies insist upon marital fidelity and punish adultery most severely (stoning is a fairly common punishment), yet adultery is well known in all societies. In some societies adultery is practically universal, as among the Todas of India, whose language lacks any word for adultery.[1] Thus, tolerance of adultery is one way of dealing with the desire for sexual variety. Prostitution is known in all complex societies and in many of the simpler ones, including virtually all which try to restrict sexual intercourse to a single partner. The church in medieval Europe approved of prostitution as a regretful but necessary concession to man's sexual nature.[2] Still other responses to the desire for sexual variety include polygamy, concubinage, the mistress system, and divorce. Even those whose extramarital sexual adventures are limited to erotic daydreams and wistful longings attest to the desire for sexual variety.

Pliability of the Sex Drive

In most species the sexual behavior of all healthy adult males is very much alike, and that of all healthy adult females is very much alike. True, some learning may be involved. In the wild state the "social" animals (those who normally live in groups, such as lions, monkeys, and wolves) can learn mating procedures through imitation. When socially deprived, like Harlow's monkeys who had only a cloth-covered wire frame as a substitute "mother," many did not mate at all, and many who did mate then killed, abused, or neglected their children [Harlow, 1961, 1975]. Sheltered house dogs, raised without watching other dogs mate, often must be helped

---

[1] This chapter's references to the sexual norms of various societies are taken from George P. Murdock, *Our Primitive Contemporaries,* The Macmillan Company, New York, 1949; and from Clellan S. Ford and Frank A. Beach, *Patterns of Sexual Behavior,* Harper & Row, Publishers, Inc., New York, 1951. Although quite old, these sources are used because no recent studies comparing the sexual patterns of many societies have been published.
[2] Interestingly enough, these medieval theologians made no such assumptions about woman's sexual nature, but they did saddle women with most of the blame, since they were the carriers of sexual temptation which led men into sin.

in their first mating. But in all solitary species, among which the males abandon the females after the mating period (cats, bears, porcupines, and many others), the young cannot learn to mate through imitation. If sexual behavior depended upon social learning, these species would be extinct. Thus, among most nonhuman species, sexual behavior is instinctive, is not greatly affected by learning, and is highly uniform within each species.

In stark contrast, the striking feature of human sexuality is its variability. All human drives are subject to cultural conditioning, and the sex drive spectacularly so. While we assume that an inborn drive makes men and women powerfully attracted to each other, the manner of expressing this attraction shows great variation in every detail. Every aspect of human sexual feeling and behavior is culturally patterned and varies from society to society, from time to time within a society, and from group to group within complex societies. In virtually all sorts of sexual matters, such as who appears sexually desirable (slender if a Dobuan, plump if a Chiricahua), who makes the overtures (girls in Bali, boys among the Mbundu), how sex play by preadolescent children is viewed (with approval among the Chewa, with censure among the Cuna), the view of sexual foreplay (expected as among the Ponape, who may prolong foreplay for hours, or absent as among the Lepcha), where intercourse is proper (in the house as among the Pukapukans, or in the bush as among the Witotos), what positions are customary (male above as among the Trobrianders, side by side as among the Masai, sitting as among the Palau), how the female should act (passive as among the Chiricahua, or aggressive and vigorous as among the Hopi)—in all these and other respects, we find great variety. What we do sexually and how we feel about it is culturally patterned. Thus, the Trobriand mother, learning that her daughter is joined in bed by a boy each night, is pleased that her daughter is developing nicely, but would be horrified to hear that her daughter and a boy were eating together—feelings quite the reverse of those of the traditional American mother. Sex behavior neatly illustrates the generalization that practically everything is right someplace and practically nothing is right everywhere. As Ford and Beach observe:

> Choroti women spit in their lover's face during coitus, and the Apinaye woman may bite off bits of her partner's eyebrows, noisily spitting them to one side. Ponapean men usually tug at the woman's eyebrows, occasionally yanking out tufts of hair. Trukese women customarily poke a finger into the man's ear when they are highly aroused. Women of many societies bite the skin of the partner's neck, shoulder, or chest when sexual excitement is at its height. The red marks left on the skin may be a subject of jest; the Toda greet any person who is so marked with the quip, "You have been bitten by a tiger." (Clellan S. Ford and Frank A. Beach, *Patterns of Sexual Behavior*, Torchbooks, Harper & Row, Publishers, Inc., New York, 1951, p. 56.)

This list of interesting sexual practices could be extended for many pages. While this might be entertaining, it would be redundant. The examples given above are sufficient to make the point that *human sexual feelings and behavior are culturally patterned*. Where sex is concerned, almost everything one can imagine is "right" someplace, is practiced with a clear conscience and a serene sense of moral propriety by those socialized to view it so. And practically everything is "wrong" someplace. The practice of homosexuality illustrates this generalization.

HOMOSEXUALITY. The term *homosexual* is applied both to persons who have a strong preference for sex partners of the same sex and to those who, regardless of sex preference, engage in sex relations with persons of the same sex. A capacity to respond sexually to both sexes is present among humans and many other species [Ford, 1980]. Nonhuman primates often engage in homosexual behav-

Sexuality and Sex Roles

A preference for intimate sexual response from one of the same sex. (*Cary Wolinsky/Stock, Boston*)

ior [Mitchell, 1981, p. 47]. Animals of many species will occasionally attempt to mount another member of the same sex. Such mountings rarely include penetration or orgasm, although some sexual arousal of the partner is not uncommon. Such animal homosexuality is often (but not always) associated with immaturity, absence of a heterosexual partner, overcrowding, or some other unusual circumstance. Animal homosexuality is clearly "natural" in that it appears with some frequency among a number of species. Yet there is no animal species in which homosexuality is the predominant or customary form of adult sex behavior, and we have no reports of individual animals that are exclusively homosexual.

Homosexuality appears, at least occasionally, in all or nearly all human societies. Homosexuality is either absent, rare, or secret in about one-third of the societies studied by Ford and Beach. In about two-thirds, some form of homosexual behavior is considered acceptable and normal for at least some categories of people or stages of life. A number of societies include institutionalized homosexual roles, as among the Koniag, who socialize some male children from infancy to fill female roles. Among the Siwans of Africa, all men and boys are expected to engage in anal intercourse and are viewed as peculiar if they do not do so. Female homosexuality is either less common or less carefully noticed but is also known in many societies.

With homosexual as with heterosexual behavior, it is approximately correct that "everything is right somewhere and nothing is right everywhere." Unlike other animals, there are some humans who are exclusively or predominantly homosexual. Kinsey's studies [1948, 1953] have clearly established that for American males homosexuality-heterosexuality is a continuum, not a pair of distinct categories. In other words, while some are exclusively homosexual and some are exclusively heterosexual, many are some intermixture of homosexual and heterosexual feelings and behavior. One may be 10 percent homosexual and 90 percent heterosexual in inclination, another may be 50:50, another 60:40, and yet another be 90 percent homosexual and 10 percent heterosexual. Kinsey reported in 1948 that over one-third of American males had experienced at least one homosexual orgasm, while he estimated that about 4 percent of the males and 2 percent of the females were exclusively homosexual.

Kinsey's percentages, however, report sexual behavior, not sexual preference. Some persons have sex relations, at least occasionally, with partners of the same sex because of availability and convenience rather than preference. Such relations are more or less common in prisons, isolated military posts, remote construction camps, and other places where heterosexual partners are not easily available. Some men who really prefer female sex partners may drop into "tearooms" (certain public men's rooms known for homosexual encounters) where a quick orgasm is available without the cost, time, or obligations involved in finding a female partner [Humphreys, 1970, 1975]. Whether such persons should be labeled "homosexual" is debatable, and we will here limit use of the term to those who are homosexual in preference.

Just as the degree of homosexual activity varies among individuals, so does degree of involvement in the homosexual subculture. Some share openly and deeply in the homosexual subculture, having most of their social relationships with other homosexuals. Some are "closet homosexuals," concealing their homosexual activity and often sharing a household with a spouse and children. Others show every intermediate level of involvement in the "gay community."

Homosexuals are very much like heterosexuals in everything except sexual preference. A number of studies have found no other personality traits that distinguish homosexuals from heterosexuals [Hooker, 1969]. Apart from difficulties arising from the social treatment of homosexuals, personality maladjustments are no more common among homosexuals than among heterosexuals [Clark, 1975; Oberstone and Sukoneck, 1975].

What causes homosexuality? The mental illness theory sees homosexuals as victims of sex-role confusion. According to much psychiatric opinion, the male homosexual is most often a product of a dominating but seductive mother and a cold, remote father [Bieber, 1962, p. 172; Saghir and Robins, 1973, ch. 8; Hart and Richardson, 1981, pp. 28–35]. But the most comprehensive research study of homosexuals yet published, comparing large samples of homosexuals and heterosexuals, found no significant differences in family backgrounds, parental types, or relationships with parents [Bell et al., 1981]. This research team, failing to find any explanations in the social experience of homosexuals, concluded with a strong suspicion that homosexuality may be biological or organic in origin. This suspicion is reinforced by many homosexual autobiographies in which people tell how they discovered a sex preference during childhood or adolescence which they resisted but were unable to change and eventually came to accept [Williams, 1977]. Several studies have found significant differences between the hormone levels of homosexuals and heterosexuals [Bell et al., 1981, p. 2–3]. But if homosexuality were simply biological, we would expect it to be equally common at all times and places, and this is untrue.

The social-learning theory holds that one learns homosexual behavior through the same reward-punishment system that shapes most social learning. According to this theory, if most childhood and adolescent interaction with the opposite sex is pleasant and rewarding, one becomes a heterosexual; if these experiences are uncomfortable and anxiety-laden and if attempts at heterosexual intercourse are unsatisfying, one may become a homosexual. But the punishments for homosexuality have been so severe in our society that one wonders how, if the social learning theory were correct, there could be *any* homosexuals at all. We also note that the increased social acceptance of homosexuals in recent years has apparently not increased the number of homosexuals, as might be expected if homosexuality were a learned sex role [Mitchell, 1981, p. 56]. Most homosexuals had heterosexual parents, and most children of homosexual parents are themselves heterosexual [Green, 1978]. There is no convincing evidence that having a homosexual parent, uncle, teacher, or neighbor increases the likelihood of a child's becoming a homosexual.

Punishment and discrimination against homosexuals is often defended as necessary to prevent homosexuals from seducing young people into homosexuality. How realistic is this fear? We can see here, once again, that theory is important, for our answer depends upon which theory of homosexuality is accepted. If homosexuality is a biological predisposition which homosexuals do not choose and are powerless to change, then seduction into homosexuality is unlikely, making punishment of homosexuals needless, useless, and cruel. If homosexuality is a personality defect arising from unsatisfactory parent role models in childhood, seduction by homosexuals is again unlikely and punishment is again needless and useless. If homosexuality is a product of reward-punishment social learning, then seduction is possible and punishments might discourage homosexuality, and a rational argument can be made for excluding homosexuals from jobs where one is a role model, such as teaching or the ministry. And there is also the question of values: Is homosexuality an abomination which should be repressed or is it an alternative life-style which people should be free to choose and follow without penalty? Until all these questions of theory and values are settled, a rational set of social policies concerning homosexuality is difficult to agree upon.

To summarize, the sex drive is a powerful drive which is involved, in some way, in much of our activity. This drive, and the variety of behaviors through which it is expressed, must somehow be incorporated into the social structure of each society. Almost every possible sexual arrangement is found in some society or other. Each of many kinds of sexual arrangements will "work" to people's satisfaction, provided that it harmonizes with the other social arrangements of the society. (Remember the concepts of cultural integration and cultural relativism!)

SEX DIFFERENCES

In most of the higher species, males and females behave differently in some respects. With no culture to explain them, these sex differences must be rooted in biology. This suggests (but does not prove) that male-female behavior differences among humans may also be biologically based. The human sexes are visibly different in some physical characteristics. Do they also differ in behavior capacities and natural inclinations? Are any such differences great enough that culture must in some way reflect them?

To some degree, the answer is yes. Work-role ascription in simple societies was highly affected by physical sex differences. Men considerably exceed women in average upper-body strength. Although women do a lot of moderately heavy physical labor in many societies, tasks calling for bursts of great strength or speed, such as hunting, fighting, tree clearing, or heavy lifting, are nearly always done by men. The almost continuous childbearing and nursing in most societies has generally limited women's work to that which could be combined with baby care—work which was repetitive, interruptible, and calling for no great physical strength. This had the effect of assigning most of the adventurous and exciting work to men (possibly the earliest "fringe benefit") and most of the drudgery to women. Yet there are enough exceptions, such as males cooking in Samoa or baby tending in the Marquesas, to show that functional practicality was not the only determinant of gender work roles.

In modern societies physical strength and

CHANGING
CONCEPTIONS OF
SEXUALITY

Traditional-Romantic Ideology	Modern-Naturalistic Ideology
Gender roles should be distinct and interdependent, with the male gender role as dominant.	Gender roles should be similar for males and females and should promote equalitarian participation in the society.
Body-centered sexuality is to be avoided by females.	Body-centered sexuality is of less worth than person-centered sexuality, but it still has positive value for both genders.
Sexuality is a very powerful emotion and one that should be particularly feared by females.	One's sexual emotions are strong but are manageable by both males and females in the same way as are other basic emotions.
The major goal of sexuality is heterosexual coitus, and that is where the man's focus should be placed.	The major goals of sexuality are physical pleasure and psychological intimacy in a variety of sexual acts, and this is so for both genders.
Love redeems sexuality from its guilt, particularly for females.	A wide range of sexuality should be accepted without guilt by both genders provided it does not involve force or fraud.

Source: Ira L. Reiss, "Some Observations on Ideology and Sexuality in America," *Journal of Marriage and the Family*, 43:271–283, May 1981.

Which of these more closely fits your beliefs? On a 1 (traditional) to 10 (modern) scale, where would you place yourself?

---

reproductive function are less important factors in work-role ascription. Even the physical differences are shrinking. In many fields of athletic competition, women are catching up with men. The gap between men's and women's records in all events which both enter has narrowed by an average of one-third between 1934 and 1973 [Lips, 1978, p. 184], and women are expected to surpass men soon in some events [Douglas and Metler, 1977].

What are the facts about those sex or gender differences[3] which affect achievement poten-

tial? Maccoby and Jacklin [1974, pp. 349–355] reviewed all the available research on sex differences among Americans. They concluded that: (1) Research clearly establishes boys' greater aggressiveness, boys' greater mathematical and visual-spatial abilities [see also Benbow and Stanley, 1980], and girls' greater verbal ability. (2) Research establishes no significant sex differences in sociability, suggestibility, self-esteem, rote or repetitive learnings, higher cognitive learnings, analytic ability, achievement motivation, responsiveness to auditory or visual stimuli, and responsiveness to heredity or to environment. (3) Research is inconclusive or contradictory on sex differences in tactile sensitivity, fear, timidity, anxiety, activity levels, competitive-

---

[3] The terms "sex" and "gender" are often used interchangeably, although some scholars define sex as the biological part and gender as the socially learned part of sexuality [Baxter and Lansing, 1980, p. 4; Oakley, 1981, p. 41].

In many countries, nearly all menial tasks are done by women. (*Luis Villota/Photo Research-ers, Inc.*)

ness, dominance, compliance, and nurturant behavior.

For even the real differences shown above, we still have the question: Are they inherited or learned differences? No known society treats boys and girls alike. No known society offers identical male and female adult models for children to copy. If there is any chance that boys and girls could have learned certain different behaviors, we question whether they are biologically based. Furthermore, any behavior characteristic rooted in heredity will appear in *all* human societies. Most sex differences in behavior fail this test. From this we suspect that most sex differences in behavior are learned not inherited.

But how about those sex differences which might be biological? If males surpass females in mathematical and visual-spatial abilities, isn't it reasonable to favor men for engineers and airline pilots? First, we are not certain that these ability differences *are* biological. They may be, but this has not been proved. Second, all sex differences (except in reproductive apparatus) are *average* differences. Most of these average differences are not very great, with a great deal of overlapping. Thus, while boys' math scores average higher than girls' scores, *all* of the upper third of the girls

score higher than *all* of the lower three-fifths of the boys. If math scores are to be used as admission tickets, should not the scores themselves be used rather than using gender, which is only slightly associated with math scores?

What does all this mean? Simply that (aside from physical strength and reproduction) most sex differences are social products, not biological building blocks. With few exceptions, sex roles can be whatever a society makes them. At present, it is unclear what our society wishes them to be. The traditional sex roles of American society are under fierce attack and are changing with a speed which is gratifying to some and upsetting to others.

CHANGING SEX ROLES

Women's roles have shown great change throughout history. If we define women's status as "high" when women have considerable independence, power, and choice, then women's status has varied greatly in time—fairly high in ancient Egypt, low in early Greece and in the early Roman republic, higher in the later Roman empire, and low again in the Christian era after the fall of

TABLE 6-1
A CROSS-CULTURAL STUDY OF SEX STEREOTYPES*

Male-associated items

Active (23)	Dominant (25)	Opportunistic (20)
Adventurous (25)	Egotistical (21)	Progressive (23)
Aggressive (24)	Energetic (22)	Rational (20)
Ambitious (22)	Enterprising (24)	Realistic (20)
Arrogant (20)	Forceful (25)	Reckless (20)
Assertive (20)	Hardheaded (21)	Robust (24)
Autocratic (24)	Hardhearted (21)	Rude (23)
Clear-thinking (21)	Humorous (19)	Self-confident (21)
Coarse (21)	Independent (25)	Serious (20)
Courageous (23)	Initiative (21)	Severe (23)
Cruel (21)	Inventive (22)	Stern (24)
Daring (24)	Lazy (21)	Stolid (20)
Determined (21)	Logical (22)	Unemotional (23)
Disorderly (21)	Loud (21)	Wise (23)
	Masculine (25)	

Female-associated items

Affected (20)	Emotional (23)	Sexy (22)
Affectionate (24)	Fearful (23)	Softhearted (23)
Attractive (23)	Feminine (24)	Submissive (25)
Charming (20)	Gentle (21)	Superstitious (25)
Curious (21)	Mild (21)	Talkative (20)
Dependent (23)	Sensitive (24)	Weak (23)
Dreamy (24)	Sentimental (25)	

*Items associated with males or with females in at least 20 of 25 countries (number of
countries shown in parenthesis)
Source. John E. Williams and Deborah L. Best: *Measuring Sex Stereotypes: A Thirty-Nation
Study*, Sage Publications, Beverly Hills, CA, 1982, p. 77.

How many of the above items are properly descriptive of males and of
females in American society?

Rome [Leslie, 1982, chap. 6]. What causes the status of women to change?

Factors in Sex-Role Change

DECLINING SEXIST BELIEFS. The traditional sex-role ascription in American society assumed a series of innate sex differences in abilities and limitations which are no longer believed by educated persons. It was handy to attribute one's discriminatory practices to the will of God or of nature, but this no longer works very well. It is widely recognized that "normal" sex roles are normal for only a specific time and place [Peal, 1975]. Thus, the intellectual foundation for the subordinate roles of women has been demolished.

CHANGING WORK ROLES. The importance attributed to the work one does has always been closely related to one's status and power. In ancient societies where priests seemed to have the greatest control over what happened to people, priests had the highest status; today physicians may be said to have taken their place.

In hunting societies where men caught the food and women generally prepared it, the man's success in hunting determined whether the group ate or starved. In food-gathering societies (collecting eggs, nuts, berries, grains,

SEX DIFFERENCES

Throughout human societies, men are more likely than women to:

Compete intensely with others of their own sex for sex partners.

Desire more than one spouse (polygyny).

Feel sexual jealousy.

Be sexually aroused by visual sex stimuli.

Be attracted sexually by youth and beauty.

Desire sexual variety.

View sex as a service given their sex by the opposite sex.

(According to Don Symons, "Eros and Alley Oop," *Psychology Today*, 14:52–61, February 1981.)

How many of these generalizations fit you?

fruits, herbs) and under hoe agriculture, women's direct contribution to food supply increased, and women's power also increased [Whyte, 1978, p. 67]. In colonial America the shortage of women and the needs of frontier life gave women a considerably higher status than in Europe at that time.

Industrialization, both in nineteenth-century America and in the developing countries today, lowered the status of women [Inglitzin and Ross, 1976]. In peasant societies, women shared with men in primary production (growing food, weaving cloth), while industrialization made men the primary breadwinners and women the helpers. But during the later stages of industrialization and in the postindustrial society,[4] family size shrinks and more wives become employed outside

[4] The term *postindustrial* refers to a society in which production has become so efficient that only a minority of workers are employed in production (growing food, operating mines and factories) while the majority of workers are engaged in "services" (teaching, trade, clerical, etc.).

the home. In the postindustrial society, muscle grows steadily less important as a job requirement, and husbands find it impractical to keep their wives "barefoot and pregnant." Although husbands may appreciate their wives' paychecks, their control is less complete than it was when husbands earned the entire cash income themselves. Blood and Wolfe [1960] developed a "resource theory of family power," based upon data showing that the wife's power within the family tends to vary according to how closely her paycheck matches (or exceeds) her husband's. While women have been very slow to gain power equal to their economic contribution, the economic base for male dominance is steadily eroding.

Some Contrary Evidence The foregoing paragraphs follow the functionalist perspective. They stress the importance of women's work as a determinant of women's status. Yet the experience of recent decades does not fully support this analysis. The proportion of all women who are in the labor force nearly doubled between 1940 and 1980 (from 27 to 51 percent), yet the income gap between employed men and women increased during most of this period. Annual earnings of full-time, year-round female workers fell from 64 percent of male earnings in 1955 to 60 percent in 1979. Some of this decline may be attributed to the very rapid growth of the female labor force. As compared with the male labor force, the female labor force became overloaded with beginning workers at entry-level earnings [Lloyd and Niemi, 1979, p. 74]. But even when seniority is held constant, women still fall far behind men in average earnings. Why?

There are several explanations. Among "full-time" workers, women average about 1½ fewer hours per week than men [Lloyd and Niemi, 1979, p. 57]. In the highly paid careers, the crucial years in which one either gains or fails to gain career momentum is the decade from 25 to 35—precisely the decade when women are most likely to take time out for children [Thurow, 1981]. Only about 10 percent of women workers are unionized, compared with 26 percent for men, and highly unionized occupations usually pay more than nonunionized occupations.

The greatest single reason, however, is that women workers, especially older women, are heavily concentrated in jobs which are traditionally low-paid. All "female" jobs are and have been poorly paid compared with "male" jobs that are comparable in training and skill demanded. The present earnings gap is greatest with the older women workers who are the most heavily concentrated in low-paid "female" jobs [Lloyd and Niemi, 1979, p. 59].

Today the principle of "equal pay for equal work" is firmly established in law, although sometimes evaded in practice. More important, it applies only when men and women do the same kind of work. Jobs of equal difficulty and jobs demanding equal training or skill may be differently paid if the work itself is different. For example, the city of San Jose made a study of 225 city government jobs, rating each on a point scale for know-how required, problem-solving responsibility, accountability, and working conditions [Bunzel, 1982, p. 80]. A typical comparison: senior telephone operator, 175 points (female-dominated), $15,210; senior water technician, 172 points (male-dominated), $21,710. A National Academy of Sciences study in 1981 concluded that less than half the 40 percent difference in men's and women's average earnings were due to men's greater skills and experience [Lubin, 1982a].

These and many other studies show that even when occupation, training, seniority, and productivity are equal, pay scales usually are not equal [Suter and Miller, 1973; Treiman and Terrell, 1975; Featherman and Hauser, 1976; Lloyd and Niemi, 1979, p. 74]. A final bit of evidence: A questionnaire sent to 170 persons who had sex-change operations (transsexuals) found that "each person who changed from female to male earned more after the change" [Fisk, 1982].

Examples of inequality could cover many more pages, yet there are some improvements. For young women who work as many hours as young men, earnings are now almost equal [Scanzoni, 1978, p. 169]. Some unions are now replacing "equal pay for equal work" with "equal pay for comparable worth" as a goal [Lubin, 1982a]. Unless there is a strong backlash against women's rights, average earnings should soon reflect current changes in women's work roles.

There are a few places where women are favored. Private pension plans pay equal monthly pensions to men and women with equal work histories and contributions, but since women (on the average) live longer, they collect more pension dollars per dollar of contributions than men collect. The Social Security system treats men and women workers exactly alike, yet women collect more in benefits than men for two reasons: They live to collect benefits for an average of four more years, and the system returns to low-paid workers far more benefits per dollar contributed than to high-paid workers. Thus women make 28 percent of the contributions but receive 54 percent of the benefits [Stiglin, 1981]. Women also pay lower life insurance premiums. One life insurance actuary reports that "a representative working woman will pay between $5,600 and $3,300 less during her lifetime for coverage than the equivalent working man" [Auger, 1982]. Yet on balance, women are far more often the victims than the beneficiaries of sex inequality. It may be true that in the long run functional roles determine sex statuses, but this force takes a long time to operate. In the short run, the conflict perspective may suggest more effective techniques for changing sex roles. The present feminist effort to change sex roles through organized action is clearly based upon the conflict model of social change.

ORGANIZED ACTION. The "old" feminism of

Susan Rakstang, a 32-year-old mother of two and an architect, concedes that life would be more pleasant for her family if she didn't have a job.

"Who doesn't like to come home to a home-cooked dinner? We all do. But we all can't. So we all pitch in," she says. "I'm a healthy, strong human being. For me, not to work would be just as frustrating as for any man."

Charlene Sisco, a 36-year-old medical secretary, hates working outside her home. Struggling to balance her duties to her six-year-old son and her job, she hopes one day she can afford to quit. Women were better off when they stayed home "rather than competing with men," she says. Now, "my whole life is a time clock."

The women differ on many issues. Mrs. Rakstang, who works primarily because she likes to, supports feminist goals to the extent of contributing to some women's organizations. Mrs. Sisco, who works because she must, believes the feminist movement has done more harm than good, and she is pleased about the imminent demise of the Equal Rights Amendment for lack of ratification.

(Sue Shellenbarger, *Wall Street Journal*, June 29, 1982, p. 1.)
Reprinted by permission of *The Wall Street Journal*, © Dow Jones & Company, Inc., 1982. All rights reserved.

With which of these women do you most closely identify?

the nineteenth century eventually gained voting rights but not much else. The "new" feminism is an expression of the general spirit of protest which developed in the 1960s. The leaders of the New Left (the radical student movement of the 1960s) were overwhelmingly sexist, despite their radicalism on other issues. They treated "women's issues" as trivial details which would be cleared up by socialist revolution. Meanwhile they treated women as sex objects and servants who did the grubby work while the men planned strategy and pondered great ideas [Gottleib, 1971; Deckard, 1979, pp. 349–352]. But the students who shared in activist protest movements nearly always held equalitarian sex-role attitudes [Orcutt, 1975]. The National Organization for Women (NOW) was formed in 1966 with Betty Friedan, author of the influential book, *The Feminine Mystique* [1963], as its first president. It called for "a sex-role revolution for men and women which will restructure all our institutions: child rearing, education, marriage, the family, medicine, work, politics, the economy, religion, psychological theories, human sexuality, morality, and the very

evolution of the race." [Friedan, 1973]. A few more radical splinter groups, such as SCUM (Society for Cutting Up Men) and WITCH (Women's International Conspiracy from Hell) [Morgan, 1970, pp. 514–519, 538–553], attracted a flurry of headline interest, but their main contribution may have been to establish the radical boundaries of the movement and make other feminist organizations look more conservative.

There have been very few membership studies of feminist organizations, and these report activist members to be largely young, white, educated, middle or upper class, and tending to be atheistic or agnostic in religion and liberal to radical in politics and sex mores [Carden, 1974; Dempewolff, 1974]. While this description may fit activist members of the feminist movement, it probably does not fit many of the millions of less radical women who lend some degree of support to the movement. As with all social movements, the feminist movement embraces a variety of personalities and viewpoints.

The new feminism has pursued three principal strategies: (1) a legal attack on all forms of formal sex discrimination, (2) an attack on traditional sex-role socialization, and (3) an attack on sexist institutional practices.

The Legal Attack on Sex Discrimination   In rapid succession a number of laws and executive orders have outlawed virtually all forms of formal sex discrimination. The Equal Pay Act of 1963 requires equal pay for equal work. The Civil Rights Act of 1964 outlaws discrimination on the basis of sex as well as race, color, and religion. Executive Orders 11246 and 11375 bar discrimination by federal suppliers and contractors, and add machinery for enforcement. The Education Amendments of 1972 forbid schools and colleges receiving federal funds to practice sex discrimination in admissions, curriculum, or staff. The Equal Credit Opportunity Act of 1974 bars discrimination on the basis of sex or marital status in credit transactions. These and other laws, together with a number of landmark court decisions, have clearly established the illegality of sex discrimination in recruiting, training, hiring, promotion, and rates of pay. A number of employers have been ordered by courts to pay millions of dollars to women as compensation for past discrimination. While sex discrimination certainly is not ended, the easily demonstrable forms of sex discrimination (in hiring and in equal pay for equal work) have become so troublesome and costly that most large employers have discontinued them.

After a half century of refusal Congress finally passed the Equal Rights Amendment (ERA) in 1972. This states that "equality under the law shall not be denied or abridged by the United States or by any state on account of sex." Although thirty states quickly ratified it, enthusiasm cooled and it died for lack of ratification in 1982.

Why did the ERA fail to gain ratification? Public opinion polls consistently showed the ERA with solid majority support (two to one

in 1981). It was endorsed by the presidential candidates and party platforms of both major parties in 1972 and 1976. But Mr. Reagan and the Republican platform failed to endorse the ERA in 1980, a sign that support was weakening.

Social movements typically have an active life of only a decade or two. They arouse interest, generate momentum, reach a peak of influence, and then wane (see Chapter 19). After a while people seem to tire of a movement, and public interest turns to other topics. But the effort to pass the ERA is not dead. Feminist leaders announced in 1982 that they were digging in for the long haul to elect sympathetic legislators [*MS*, Aug. 1982, p. 11], a standard technique of political action groups.

Affirmative Action Programs   Affirmative action programs are now required of all employers covered by the Civil Rights Act of 1964 and all recipients of federal funds (which includes virtually all schools, colleges, and universities). It is not enough for these employers, contractors, or school systems to show that they are not discriminating *against* women or minorities. They must show a positive, actively implemented program to locate, recruit, train, hire, and promote women (or minority members) and must set hiring "goals." These goals—which some call "quotas"—led to charges of "reverse discrimination." In the early 1970s, for example, many advertisements for college faculty positions specified "women only." Such advertisements soon ended, but rumors of favoritism persisted. The present picture is mixed: discrimination in favor of women in some places and discrimination against women in some others.

Federal government pressure for affirmative action has declined markedly during the Reagan administration [Lubin, 1982*b*]. A *Wall Street Journal* news story in June 1982 told

BUSINESS VOTES 'YES' ON WOMEN AS EXECUTIVES . . .

Q. *Here are a series of statements about women in the workplace. Do you agree or disagree?*

	PERCENT	
	Agree	Disagree
A. Contributions of women executives in the company are more positive than negative	94%	2%
Women executives are performing on the job as well as or better than expected	86	5
Quite a number of women use sex and guile to get ahead	7	87
Some men now can't get ahead in certain jobs because they are being saved for women	8	89

. . . BUT STILL FINDS IT HARD TO ACCEPT THEM AS BOSSES

Q. *Do you agree or disagree with these statements?*

	PERCENT	
	Agree	Disagree
A. It has been harder to promote women to high-level positions than we thought it would be	41%	52%
Men don't like to take orders from women	41	49
Women don't like to take orders from other women	39	45

Source: Business Week, June 28, 1982, p. 10. Data compiled by Louis Harris & Associates Inc.

Are there any of these items on which you would vote with the minority?

---

how corporation executives were staging seminars for middle managers and personnel officers to remind them that, despite Reagan administration disinterest in enforcement, the antidiscrimination laws were still in effect and that failure to follow them could bring multimillion-dollar lawsuits against their corporations [Greenberger, 1982]. As this is written, it is unclear whether affirmative action is dead or just resting.

The Attack on Sex-Role Socialization Masculinity and *femininity* refer to the differing feelings and behavior expected of males and females at a particular time and place and are largely a product of sex-role socialization. Such socialization has been accomplished in many ways, many of which are unintended and unconscious [Travis and Offir, 1977; Pogrebin, 1980]. In American society boys have been rewarded for being aggressive, competitive, and career-oriented; girls have been rewarded for being gentle, "ladylike," and domestic. Men have been trained to direct and command; women have been trained to obey and serve and to get their way through coquetry and manipulation. When frustrated, men have been expected to shout and women to cry. Men were praised while women were scolded for showing a fierce dedication to career success at the expense of other values. Men were rated according to their career advancement ("He is a prominent lawyer in Washington"), while women were evaluated by their domestic skills ("She has a very successful husband, a lovely home, and three perfectly darling children"). Thus men were rated by their accomplishments, while women were rated by the accomplishments of the men to whom they were attached. In hundreds of different ways, the sexes have been socialized to feel differently about themselves and to act differently. [Chappell, 1978; Stockard and Johnson, 1980].

There is ample evidence that sex-role stereotypes are very much alive today [Gilbert et al., 1978]. In almost every work activity men are judged to be more competent than women. In many experiments alternate male and female names or pictures have been attached to some piece of work to be evaluated by a team of referees—a literary essay, an analysis of a management problem, a legal brief. Until very recently all such experiments found that a majority of the referees, *both male and female,* evaluated a work more highly when it was attributed to a male author [Pheterson et al., 1971]. A number of studies show that when women are successful, it is likely to be attributed to either luck or great effort, while men's success is more often attributed to ability [Deaux and Enswiller, 1974; Levine, 1982]. Men are still judged as generally more competent, even in many "women's" occupations, for the most prestigious fashion designers, hair stylists, interior decorators, and chefs are usually men.

No legislation can achieve genuine sex equality unless there are changes in the ways men and women feel about themselves and each other. For this reason feminists are attacking the sex-role socialization which pro-

Most sex differences in personality are produced by sex-role socialization. (*Laimute E. Druskis/Editorial Photocolor Archives*)

duces these sex stereotypes [Sprung, 1976]. They object to anything which reflects and perpetuates sex-role stereotypes—giving toy trucks and tools only to boys and dolls and tea sets only to girls; TV shows which cast men in dominant roles and women in supporting, domestic, or comic roles; and magazine ads depicting the sexes in only traditional work roles. Feminists launched a spirited attack on "sexist" textbooks, in which little girls cower and whimper while little boys are heroically protective, and where men and boys appear in adventurous work roles and women only in housewife roles or "feminine" occupations. They object to sexist vocabulary and the use of the terms "man," "mankind," "he," "him," and "his" to refer to human beings in general [Nilson et al., 1977]. Feminists ask that these generic masculine terms be replaced by neuter or evenly balanced terms, and that sex-role stereotypes be deleted. In this effort feminists were quickly and easily successful. Textbook publishers soon sent detailed instruction manuals to their authors, while editors thoughtfully edited out sexist usages authors overlooked.

Changing sex-role stereotypes is not easy. In one school experiment, a six-week crash program attempted to show children how both sexes could profit from nonstereotyped roles. The program used all the "right" teaching aids and materials. At the end, the girls showed the desired attitude changes but the boys had become more rigid in their acceptance of stereotyped roles [Guttentag and Bray, 1976]. Yet there is evidence of substantial shifts toward more equalitarian attitudes in children [Duncan and Duncan, 1978; Duncan, 1980]. A number of guidebooks on nonsexist socialization have appeared [Sprung, 1976; Pogrebin, 1980]. When today's children become adults, they will probably show more flexible gender roles than their parents.

The Attack on Sexist Institutional Practices
Two recently published books illustrate two different approaches to the question, "Why

do so few women become corporate executives?" One, Henning and Jardim's *The Managerial Woman* [1977], written in a pop psychology style, assumes that executive promotion is now equally open to women and concludes that women's own behavior is responsible for their lack of success. While this may be true in some cases, this superficial treatment overlooks the many traditional and structural barriers to women's executive career. Although condemned by serious scholars as misleading and pernicious [Patterson and Loseke, 1978; Rubin, 1978], this book sold very well, as is often true of books which tell people what they like to hear in a way which sounds authoritative. Rosabeth Moss Kanter's *Men and Women of the Corporation* [1977], which gives a balanced analysis of the processes of female executive mobility, reveals the many subtle ways in which the traditional structure and operation of the corporation has discouraged female executive promotion. Although highly praised by reviewers as a major contribution to our knowledge of sex mobility [Patterson and Loseke, 1978; Rubin, 1978], it sold poorly in the mass market.

Our institutions are saturated with sexism,

Both men and women admit that there is still a network of social contacts that only grudgingly admits women. "I was not invited to a dinner party which included all the men working on a matter in which I was involved," says a woman partner in a Washington firm who asked that her name not be used. "I was told afterward that it was because my husband would be uncomfortable being relegated to a place with the wives while we talked business."

(*The New York Times Magazine*, November 22, 1981, p. 98.)

Should we "save" people from possible embarrassment, or allow them to decide for themselves?

often so deeply buried and so heavily encrusted with tradition as to be unnoticed. Institutional titles are often sexist, from "freshman" to "master's degree" and from "workman" to "chairman." Most personnel policies have been based upon the assumption that men's career interests are primary and enduring, while women's career interests are temporary and secondary to their other interests. The "old-boy network" of personal acquaintance and friendship is most important in locating vacancies and gaining recommendations in education, business, and the professions. This network has usually bypassed women [Walum, 1977, p. 160]. It is only recently that women have been hired for executive-track positions or been sent to conventions and training seminars. Over one-third of the masters of business administration candidates are now women, but the Business Roundtable, the most prominent organization of business executives, has yet to accept its first female member [*Time*, April 19, 1982, p. 65]. And, although female executives in the $50,000-plus bracket are becoming far more common than some years ago, they are disproportionately in "public relations," where they have high visibility but little power [*Business Week*, May 8, 1978, p. 122].

In still more subtle ways a male bias pervades institutional practices. Women making a complaint seem to be more likely than men to receive a series of irrelevancies and evasions known as the "cooling out treatment." Business and professional societies (and until recently, academic meetings) usually arrange innocuous diversions to occupy the members' wives while the men do something important. When a woman answers the phone in an executive office, she is assumed to be a secretary; a man answering is assumed to be an executive. In blue-collar jobs, male resentment and "hassling" is a problem, while the lack of women's toilets and locker rooms is a handy excuse for rejecting women.

The idea that women are unfitted by nature for most traditional male jobs is no longer

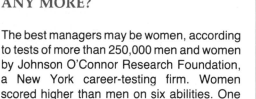

CAN'T WE TRUST ANY OF OUR BIASES ANY MORE?

The best managers may be women, according to tests of more than 250,000 men and women by Johnson O'Connor Research Foundation, a New York career-testing firm. Women scored higher than men on six abilities. One aptitude, grasping the abstract, is key for successful management, the firm says.

(*Wall Street Journal*, July 6, 1982, p. 1.)

Do you believe this? On what basis—evidence or preference—do you accept or reject it?

held by most educated people. In no traditional male occupation which women have entered—from business management to truck driving—is there clear evidence that women

FIGURE 6-1 Female construction workers in the United States. (*Source: U.S. Department of Labor, Bureau of Labor Statistics, 1982.*)

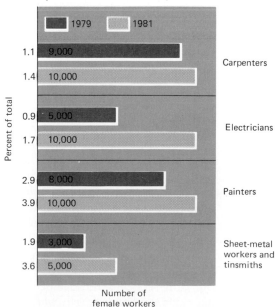

> This [logging] is a male society. Few women apply for work requiring such great upper-body strength, and those who do confront a relentless macho atmosphere. At one camp men chose lots to sit next to a woman choker setter on the crummy so they could harass her on the way home; she quit. A logging supervisor says, "The idea that a woman could possibly do what they do—well, it just kills them."
>
> (William E. Blundell, "Natural Enemies: To Loggers, the Woods Are Dark and Deep—But Far from Lovely," *Wall Street Journal*, Dec. 8, 1981, p. 16.
>
> Is this outrageous? Or does it "serve her right"? Does your answer reveal anything about yourself?

have not generally performed well. For example, a national survey of senior medical students reports that nearly all accepted women as fully competent, but nearly one-half rejected the idea of women in leadership positions in medicine [Scanlon et al., 1982]. Even as coal miners and loggers, women perform adequately but face unequal treatment and severe hazing from resentful male workers [Blundell, 1981; Hymowitz, 1981]. Women are still a long way from acceptance as equals.

MARXIST ANALYSIS OF SEXISM

Marxist ideology views sex inequality as an aspect of class exploitation and asserts that sexism cannot be ended without a socialist revolution [Ostrander, 1973; Reiter, 1975; Syzmanski, 1976; Eisenstein, 1977]. But the early Marxist revolutionists viewed women's rights as trivialities which should not divert them from the serious business of revolution. They were always hostile to the feminist movement, before and after the Russian Revolution [Clements, 1979; Farnsworth, 1980; Porter, 1980]. More recently, the Soviet Union's first feminist magazine, *The Women and Russia*,

ended its short and troubled life with the arrest and exile of its editors in 1980 [*Time*, Aug. 4, 1980, p. 41].

The Russian Revolution did bring women some kinds of legal equality, especially, in rights to education, property, marriage, and divorce. Women entered practically every occupation and now form a major fraction of the professions and the bureaucracy [Deckard, 1979, pp. 223–246]. But many writers have taken too uncritically the official claims of sex equality. This writer, in his travels through several Communist European countries, has noted how nearly all menial tasks visible to tourists are done by women. You can practically depend on it that the person driving the tractor will be male while the person wielding the hoe will be female.

For the vast majority of Russian women, the gift of the Russian Revolution was a double work load. Men's roles were virtually unchanged, while an outside job was added to women's home responsibilities. Women still do the housework and most of the shopping, a very time-consuming task in the Soviet Union [Gordon and Klapov, 1975, pp. 73–76]. Practically all women in the Soviet Union hold jobs, and most of them hold menial jobs [Sacks, 1976, 1977]. The male/female income gap is reported to be about the same as the United States. [Lapidus, 1978]. A Polish sociologist (now in the United States) concludes that "available statistical data do not give evidence that women's situations in capitalistic and socialistic countries are substantially different" [Horoszowski, 1971, p. 180]. The Marxist rhetoric of sex equality, whatever its intent, had the effect of "freeing" women to fill *two* jobs. It is possible that increasing the labor force, instead of achieving sex equality, may have been the primary goal of Communist policy in the Soviet Union and its satellite states [Sacks, 1976].

It should be noted that many Marxist scholars today do not view the Soviet Union and its satellites as truly Marxist societies but as traitors to Marxism. Thus they may sharply criticize the Soviet Union and argue that nothing that happens in the Soviet Union or its satellites tells anything about the truth or error of Marxist doctrine.

How about other Marxist societies? We know little about the status of women in the People's Republic of China. The more brutal mistreatments such as female infanticide, sale into prostitution, and foot binding began to disappear after China became a republic in 1912. The Communist victories in 1949 increased the rights of women, such as equal rights to divorce (not equally easy but equally difficult to get) and equal rights in marriage. It brought greatly increased employment of women but no substantial change in sex roles or the division of labor [Weitz, 1977, pp. 211–218]. It is reported that virtually all women work, with grandmothers often retiring in their early fifties to help with child care while mothers work. Day-care nurseries are said to reduce working mothers' workload [Kessen, 1975, pp. 36–37], but no detailed work-time studies are available. Men still hold practically all the top positions. Women supposedly get equal pay for equal work, but nearly all are in the low-paid jobs [Deckard, 1979, pp. 246–254]. Because we have few reports, which cannot easily be verified, we cannot be certain about women's status in China.

It is clear that socialist revolution carries no guarantee of sex equality. The Marxist theory that sex equality and economic equality must go together is flatly contradicted by the experience of two of the world's most successful examples of economic equality. The Hutterites, comprising a number of religious agricultural communities, provide perhaps the world's most perfect example of complete economic equality, yet they are one of the most completely male-dominated societies in history [Hostettler, 1974]. The Israeli kibbutz sought to establish complete economic and sexual equality in their agricultural communes. While achieving economic equality quite successfully, the trend in recent years is *away from* sex equality, replacing an originally equalitarian system with increasing sex-

role differentiation [Mednick, 1975; Tiger and Shepher, 1975; Gerson, 1978; Spiro, 1979].

It would appear then that Marxist societies have enlarged women's rights in some important respects but with few gains in occupational status, income, or power. The Marxist theory of a necessary linkage between sex equality and economic equality may eventually prove to be correct, but this is not yet evident.

FUTURE SEX ROLES

The current trend in modern nations is clearly toward greater sex equality, but what form of sex equality? Alice Rossi [1970, pp. 173–186] suggests three theoretical sex-equality models: (1) a pluralist model in which sex roles are different but equal, with men and women holding different work roles which are equally rewarded and prestigious; (2) an assimilationist model in which women are absorbed equally into all levels of the existing occupational and political system; and (3) an androgynous model in which sex-role ascription is ended, with men and women filling occupational and household roles which are practically identical. The pluralist model is probably impractical, for in no society in history have all kinds of work been equally prestigious or rewarded. This model would need to go beyond "equal pay for equal work," which would leave most women in low-paying jobs. It would require "equal pay for comparable worth," with an evaluation of the "worth" of every kind of job [Bunzel, 1982]. This is a complicated calculation and has not even been applied to pay scales *within* the sexes. Opinion is divided upon the other two models, with most feminists apparently favoring the androgynous model.

Androgyny: Possible or Desirable?

IS ANDROGYNY POSSIBLE? Androgynous persons can engage comfortably in both masculine and feminine behaviors, with both sexes very much alike in personality and behavior. Aggressiveness, independence, self-reliance, and career ambitions would be equally shared by men and women, while such traditionally "feminine" traits as dependence upon others, sensitivity, gentleness, and submissiveness to others would also be equally shared by men and women. Is this a realistic hope?

It is debatable whether any human society has ever been androgynous, and many attempts to establish androgynous arrangements have failed. Some scholars believe that male dominance is rooted in hormone differences between the sexes and is therefore inevitable [Goldberg, 1973; Van den Berge, 1975]. Others claim that male dominance may be universal throughout human societies but is not inevitable [Walum, 1977, pp. 143–145]. Still others question the universality of male dominance. They note that male dominance certainly is not found in many nonhuman species [Katchadourian, 1979, p. 70; George, 1979]. In many human societies, men dominate some decisions and activities while women dominate others, while a few societies come very close to being unisex [Whyte, 1978; Sanday, 1981]. The anthropologist Marvin Harris states, "Male supremacy is on the way out. It was just a phase in the evolution of culture." [Harris, 1975]. One scholar argues that the human male's natural inclinations

are androgynous and that "masculinity" is a grotesque distortion of man's true nature, but he presents no substantial evidence to support this claim [Pleck, 1981]. It is clear that no final answer can be given unless some society succeeds in achieving androgynous sex roles and maintaining them over a number of generations.

IS ANDROGYNY DESIRABLE? A number of research studies conclude that androgynous persons are more competent, flexible, and adaptable, have higher self-esteem, and are generally happier and better adjusted then men who are "masculine" or women who are "feminine" in personality [Bem, 1975a, 1975b, 1976; Spence and Helmreich, 1978; Orlofsky and Windle, 1978; Heilbrun, 1981, p. 89]. Yet these studies are not very consistent with one another [Lips, 1978, pp. 138–143], and some studies contest the conclusion that androgynous persons are superior [Burger and Jacobson, 1979]. Crosby and Nyquist [1980] note that four different scales are in use to measure androgyny and report that several studies show that over one-third of those classed as androgynous on one scale would not be androgynous as measured by another. We might conclude that the available research clearly shows that the traditional "masculine" and "feminine" personalities are not linked to mental health, effective functioning, or personal happiness, but the su-

A NOTE OF DISSENT . . .

The prevailing orthodoxy runs along these lines: that sex differences are trivial or superficial, in both degree and effect; that they exist only because of social conditioning; that this conditioning is designed to insure male hegemony; and that the ideal personality is androgynous. Because there is very little evidence to support any of these beliefs, the case is often made not

by argument but by intimidation. To question these ideas is to risk jeers and hissing when the issues are discussed in public and a torrent of abusive letters when they are debated in print.

(Joseph Adelson, summarizing Robert May, *Sex and Fantasy: Patterns of Male and Female Development*, W. W. Norton & Company, Inc., New York, 1980, in *The New York Times Book Review*, March 9, 1980, p. 3. Reproduced by permission of the New York Times Company.)

Do you think this is an accurate statement?

periority of the androgynous personality has not been established either.

In a three-generational study of over 200 families, Troll found no relationship between women's happiness and their level of achievement or entrance into nontraditional work roles but found that "happy women seem to remain just as happy whether they are competing in the traditionally masculine workplace or pursuing the more traditional role of housewife." [Troll, 1982, p. 43]. Another study, reviewing five National Opinion Research Center surveys during the 1970s, concluded that "women with traditional sex-role attitudes are in fact more satisfied with their lives than women with non-traditional attitudes" [Alapach, 1982, p. 281]. Research on happiness levels of working and nonworking wives is mixed, and we do not yet have sufficient evidence to say whether the nontraditional work roles and the changed gender roles which women are today entering will increase the sum total of their contentment with life.

Would androgynous gender roles be beneficial to men? Some scholars claim that husbands, wives, and children would *all* gain through equal involvement of both parents in housework, child care, occupations, and community activities [Bruck, 1977]. A number of semipopular books (nearly all written by men) pursue the "male liberation" theme [Farrell, 1975; David and Brannon, 1976; H. Goldberg, 1976; Amńeus, 1979; Kranowitz, 1981]. They say that sex equality would relieve males of many pressures (to project machismo, to assert their "manhood," always to win) and would bring them increased emotional satisfactions (a true sense of joyous sharing, greater intimacy, a newfound ability to feel and to care, a closer relationship to children, greater occupational flexibility). Yet there are other men who fear that equal rights would be the destruction of civilization [Doyle, 1970; Reyburn, 1972; Gilder, 1973].

As stated earlier, gender roles can be whatever we agree to make them (without necessarily destroying civilization). Whether an-

drogynous roles will bring greater fulfillment cannot be predicted with any certainty. What is certain is that sex equality and androgyny will be hollow promises without an equal sharing of housework and child care. Without these, "equality" for women may be more exploitation than liberation.

Future Trends

What is the future of gender-role change in American society? Scanzoni [1978, p. 156] expects the trend toward sex equality to continue, and most other sociologists would probably agree.

It is interesting to note that, a century ago, the goal of reformers, socialists, and utopians was to "liberate" married women from work outside the home so they could give full time to house and children [Drucker, 1981]. Thus the "reform" of one century may become the "oppression" of the next. A century from now, will the present be recalled as a milepost on the road to progress or as a misguided experiment? None can be sure, but this writer is of the opinion (repeat, *opinion*) that the drive for sex equality will survive and continue.

SUMMARY

The human sex drive is notable for (1) *continuous sexuality*, which ensures the continuous association of the sexes; (2) the *desire for continuity*, which makes for enduring sexual partnerships; (3) the *desire for variety*, which conflicts with the desire for continuity; and (4) remarkable *pliability*, with sex interest channeled through whatever patterns a society has established as "normal." Homosexuality illustrates both the possibility of channeling the sex drive and the difficulty of doing so with complete success.

Human sex differences, except for purely physical differences, are due largely to different socialization. Sex roles are changing as a result of (1) discrediting of sexist beliefs, (2)

work-role changes brought by industrialization and urbanization, and (3) organized action. Most forms of sex discrimination in the United States have been outlawed but have not disappeared. *Affirmative action* programs seek to implement existing legislation, while the drive for the Equal Rights Amendment seeks to complete the legal barriers to sex discrimination. Feminists also organize to combat sex-role socialization and sexist institutional practices.

Marxists perceive sexism as a form of class exploitation, with sex equality unattainable without economic equality. Evidence for this theory is unconvincing, although Marxist societies have been substantially reducing sex discrimination.

Whether androgynous sex roles are possible or desirable is sharply debated but not yet known.

GLOSSARY

androgyny having both masculine and feminine personality characteristics in the same person, with neither set dominant.
gender often used interchangeably with *sex*, although some scholars distinguish between sex and gender, with sex being the biological part and gender the socially learned part of sexuality and sex roles.
homosexual a term applied both to persons with a strong preference for sex partners of the same sex and to persons who, regardless of preference, engage in sex relations with persons of the same sex.
masculinity/femininity feeling and acting in the ways expected of males and females at a particular time and place.
sex a biological quality distinguishing male from female (or, rarely, some intermixture of both).
sex drive a predisposition, probably biological, for humans to seek sexual and sex-related response from one or more others, usually of the opposite sex; this is greatly directed and expanded by social learning to include many nongenital feelings and behaviors.

sexism/sexist beliefs in or policies of male superiority or sex inequality; uncritical acceptance of sex-role stereotypes.
sex-role/gender-role the expected behavior of males and females at a particular time and place.
sexual identity/gender identity one's awareness and acceptance of being male or female.
sexuality all the feelings and behaviors linked to sex through either biology or social learning.

QUESTIONS AND PROJECTS

1   What is a drive? How does it differ from a wish?
2   In what respects is the sex drive like all other basic human drives?
3   How does the human sex drive differ from that of most other animals?
4   Since "practically everything is right someplace," should not people be free to do whatever they wish sexually?
5   What difference does it make whether we view homosexuality as a biological characteristic or a socially learned role?
6   Are sex differences a cause or result of sex-role differentiation?
7   Under what circumstances do you think traditional patterns of male dominance might be restored?
8   What evidence is there that sex-role socialization in the United States is changing?
9   What is meant by the statement that "normal" sex roles are normal for only a specific time and place?
10   Why does women's status decline during the early stages of industrialism, then rise later?
11   The "old" feminism of the nineteenth century struggled for decades and accomplished very little, while the "new" feminism has made substantial gains more quickly and relatively easily. Why?
12   What are some of the ways in which sex-linked personality characteristics are cultivated in men and women?
13   When both partners work, what difficulties are created if one career is considered

primary and the other subordinate? What difficulties arise if both are considered equally important?

14 What evidence is there for and against the Marxist theory that sex equality and economic equality are inseparable?

15 Which of Rossi's three models of sex equality do you prefer? Why?

16 Organize your answers to the questions "Is androgyny possible?" "Is androgyny desirable?" To what extent are your answers based on research evidence, and to what extent upon your biases?

17 What reasons are there to believe that the drive for sex equality will continue or that it is entering a long period of failure and inactivity?

18 Ask each class member to state his or her role expectations for self and future living partner, covering a prepared list of specifics (such as career primacy, household tasks, child care, etc.). Compile and compare group averages for males and females. Then match individual male and female statements at random and calculate the degree of agreement.

SUGGESTED READINGS

Campbell, Angus, et al.: *The Quality of Life: Perceptions, Evaluations, and Satisfactions,* Russell Sage Foundation, New York, 1976. Chapter 12, "The Situation of Women," gives research data on the satisfactions and discontents of women.

Carden, Maren Lockwood: *The New Feminist Movement,* Russell Sage Foundation, New York, 1974. History and analysis of the Women's Liberation Movement.

* Ford, Clellan S., and Frank A. Beach: *Patterns of Sexual Behavior,* Harper & Row, Publishers, Inc.; New York, 1951. Description and comparison of the sex practices of many simple societies.

* Goldberg, Stephen: *The Inevitability of Patriarchy,* William Morrow & Company, Inc., New York, 1973. A sociologist's argument that male domination arises from biological differences.

Horoszowski, Pawell: "Women's Status in Socialistic and Capitalistic Countries," *International Journal of Marriage and the Family,* 1:1–18, March 1971, and 1:160–180, April 1971.

* Kanter, Rosabeth Moss: *Men and Women of the Corporation,* Basic Books, Inc., Publishers, New York, 1977. A mature analysis of the process of feminine executive mobility.

Maccoby, Eleanor Emmons and Carol Nagy Jacklin: *The Psychology of Sex Differences,* Stanford University Press, Stanford, Cal., 1974. A comprehensive review of the origin and extent of sex differences.

* Montagu, Ashley: *The Natural Superiority of Women,* Collier Books, The Macmillan Company, New York, 1974, and Wallace Reyburn: *The Inferior Sex,* Prentice-Hall, Inc., Englewood Cliffs, N.J., 1972. Two opposing views of the superior sex.

Peal, Ethel: " 'Normal' Sex Roles: An Historical Analysis," *Family Process,* 14:389–409, September 1975. Shows how sex roles are "normal" for only a given time and place.

* Sprung, Barbara (ed.): *Perspectives on Non-Sexist Early Childhood Education,* Teachers College Press, New York, 1976. A book of readings showing how children might be socialized for more nearly androgynous sex roles.

* Stockard, Jean and Miriam M. Johnson: *Sex Roles: Sex Inequality and Sex Role Development,* Prentice-Hall, Inc., Englewood Cliffs, N.J., 1980.

* Tavris, Carol and Carole Offir: *The Longest War: Sex Differences in Perspective,* Harcourt Brace Jovanovich, New York, 1977. An analysis of sex-role socialization and the struggle for sex equality.

* Walum, Laurel Richardson: *The Dynamics of Sex and Gender: A Sociological Perspective,* Rand McNally College Publishing Co., Chicago, 1977.

* An asterisk before the citation indicates that the title is available in a paperback edition.

7 Social Order and Social Control

The Hawaiians had long obeyed some of the *Kanawai* [laws]. They had always honored fathers and mothers, and their days had been long upon the land. They had utterly abolished idols before the Longnecks came.

Theft they had dealt with in a way that had served well enough, though it could scarcely have been pleasing to Jehovah. In the old days if a man took something from one below him in the social scale, it was not stealing; for that which was taken had in reality belonged by virtue of rank to the taker. And if a commoner made off with the calabash or the weapon of a superior, the injured man could go to the thief's house and take back his possession, along with anything else he saw that he wanted.

But when the *haoles* [whites] came with their bean pots and silver spoons, their monkey wrenches and linen towels, their sawed lumber and their keen edged axes, this method no longer served. Complaints from foreigners rang unceasingly in the governor's ears. White men did not want to go poking into native huts to find their lost articles. They wanted Boki to haul up the thief and arrange for restitution and punishment.

Gradually the enlightened chiefs saw what they must do. Some of them put their men in irons for proven theft or set them free only to work and pay for what they had stolen. The boy prince Kauikeaouli, when his beloved *kahu* was found accessory to a theft, consented quickly to the man's dismissal. "My *kahu* must go," he declared, "or by and by the foreigners will think that I myself am guilty."

The *haoles* applauded such measures. Here was a Commandment they liked to see enforced.

Then there was the Commandment forbidding murder in a few short words. Once, if a native killed in sudden anger, it was proper for the victim's relatives to avenge the deed, unless the murderer took shelter in a place of refuge. If the guilty man were of equal rank with the victim's avenger, there might be an appeal to the king or the governor or to the chief of the district. The aggrieved one and the accused would then sit cross-legged in the judge's yard and each would eloquently argue his case till the magistrate made his decision.

But these customs failed when Honolulu swarmed with hot-headed sailors, and brown and white alike drank rum and got *huhu* [drunk]. Again, as with theft, the traders wanted stern laws, strictly enforced, so that the riffraff of all nations would think twice before bashing their fellows on the head. They told the chiefs to build a lofty engine of death which would string up a murderer by the neck and leave him hanging limp from a rope's end—a potent reminder to the living to restrain themselves

(Reprinted by permission of Dodd, Mead & Company from *Grapes of Canaan*, by Albertine Loomis, pp. 227–229. © 1951 by Albertine Loomis.)

The decay of the traditional system of law and order when outsiders brought social changes and new problems to Hawaii could be duplicated in many other lands. Changes in a society demand changes in its ways of maintaining social order. When the Hawaiian chiefs shifted from their traditional customs to the jails and gallows suggested by the traders, they were seeking to adjust the techniques of social control to a changed situation—a problem in every modern society.

The study of *social control*—the means through which people are led to fill their roles as expected—begins with the study of the social order within which people interact. Consider, for example, the orderly arrangements which underlie the bustling confusion of a great city. Tens of thousands of people take their places and perform their tasks with no apparent direction. Thousands of vehicles butt their way through clogged canyons, missing by inches but seldom actually colliding. Thousands of kinds of merchandise arrive at the expected places in the expected amounts at the expected times. Ten thousand people whom one never sees will labor on this day so that meals will be ready when needed, drinking fountains will flow, drains

When social controls fail: looting in New York during a power blackout in 1977.
(*United Press International*)

will carry off wastes, bulbs will blink and glow, traffic will part to let one pass, and other needs will be met. A hundred people may serve one within an hour, perhaps without a word to any of them.

This is what is meant by *social order*—a system of people, relationships, and customs operating smoothly to accomplish the work of a society. Unless people know what they may expect from one another, not much will get done. No society, even the simplest, can operate unless the behavior of most people can be predicted most of the time. Unless we can depend upon police officers to protect us, workers to go to work on schedule, and motorists to stay on the right side of the road most of the time, there can be no social order. The orderliness of a society rests upon a network of roles according to which each person accepts certain duties toward others and claims certain rights from others. An orderly society can operate only as long as most people fulfill most of their duties toward others and are able to claim most of their rights from others.

How is this network of reciprocal rights and duties kept in force? Sociologists use the term *social control* to describe *all the means and processes whereby a group or a society secures its members' conformity to its expectations.*

SOCIAL CONTROL

How does a group or society cause its members to behave in the expected manner?

Social Control Through Socialization

Fromm [1944] has remarked that if a society is to function efficiently, "its members must acquire the kind of character which makes them *want* to act in the way they *have* to act as members of society. . . . They have to *desire* to do what objectively is necessary for them to do.''

People are controlled mainly by being socialized so that they fill their roles in the expected manner through habit and preference. We suspect that very few people actually *enjoy* paying taxes, washing dishes, or getting up for a midnight baby-feeding, yet most people do those things when expected. As we stated in an earlier chapter, the crucial part of one's role preparation is the learning of attitudes and wishes which make the role attractive. Most role failures come not because one is unable to perform the role's tasks but because one is trapped in a role one does not really want or enjoy.

Socialization shapes our customs, our wishes, and our habits. Habit and custom are great time-savers. They relieve us of the need for countless decisions. If we had to decide whether and how to perform each act—when to arise, whether and how to wash, shave, dress, and so on—few students would get to class at all! The members of a society are schooled in the same customs and tend to develop much the same set of habits. Thus habit and custom are great standardizers of behavior within a group. If all members of a society share similar socialization experiences, they will voluntarily and unthinkingly act in very much the same ways. They will conform to social expectations without any conscious awareness that they are "conforming," or any serious thought of doing otherwise. The desire of two people to get married arises from motives less academic than a wish

Social control operates by socializing people to *want to do* what is expected of them. (*Alice Kandell/Photo Researchers, Inc.*)

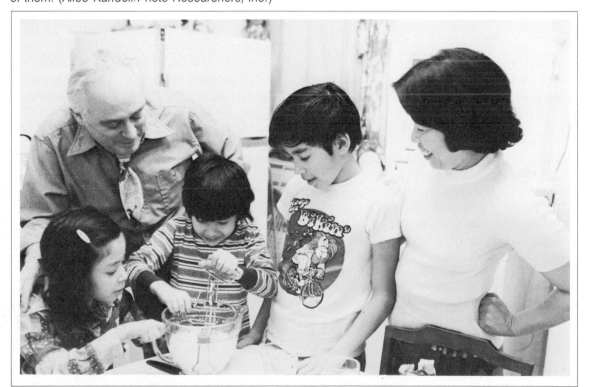

to "conform to the nuclear monogamous family pattern," yet such conformity is the result.

Through socialization, one internalizes the norms, values, and taboos of one's society. We repeat that to internalize them means to make them part of one's automatic, unthinking responses. People who fully internalize the mores will obey them even when nobody is looking, because the idea of violating them is unlikely to occur to people who have fully internalized them. If seriously tempted, conscience may arise to prevent a violation. This is what happens, most of the time, in a society with a stable, integrated culture and a consensus upon values. As we shall see, few if any modern societies fit this model at all perfectly.

Social Control Through Social Pressure

In a novel by Sinclair Lewis, George F. Babbitt, a small-town realtor, somehow strays into "radical" notions about government and politics. Soon his business declines, his friends begin to avoid him, and he grows uncomfortably aware that he is becoming an outsider. Lewis describes how Babbitt's associates apply these subtle pressures until, with a sigh of relief, Babbitt scurries back into a comfortable conformity [Lewis, 1922, chaps. 32, 33]. In all human societies, and even in many nonhuman species, this tendency to conform to group pressure and example is evident. Nineteenth-century explorer David Thompson was impressed by the reckless, headlong flight of wild horses, and when his dull, placid packhorse escaped to join the wild horses, it amazed him to see how quickly it assumed their wild temperament, "with nostrils distended, mane flying, and tail straight out" [Ryden, 1971, p. 106].

Lapiere [1954] sees social control as primarily a process growing out of the individual's need for group acceptance. He claims that groups are most influential when they are small and intimate, when we expect to remain in the groups for a long time, and when we have frequent contacts with them. All authorities agree that our need for acceptance within intimate groups is a most powerful lever for the use of group pressure toward group norms.

One experiences this group pressure as a continuous and largely unconscious process. Its operation is illustrated by the life of one of the author's acquaintances. He spent most of his working life as a small farmer in central Michigan; like most of his neighbors, he thought conservatively, voted Republican, and scolded labor unions. During World War II he moved to Detroit and worked in a war plant, joined a union, became a union officer, and voted Democratic. After the war, he retired to a small central Michigan village where he again thought conservatively, voted Republican, and scolded labor unions. He explained these about-faces by claiming that the parties and the unions had changed. He did not realize that it was *he* who had changed. Like most of us, he soon came to share the views of his group associates. This tendency to conform to group attitudes is so compelling that the Catholic church in France found it necessary to abandon its worker-priest program. This was an effort to stem the drift of French workers toward communism by sending out priests who would take ordinary jobs and work beside the workers, meanwhile leading them back to the church. After a ten-year trial, when it became evident that the workers were converting the priests to the Marxian view of the class struggle, the program was curtailed [Brady, 1954].

Social psychologists [Sherif, 1935; Bovard, 1951] have made a number of classic experiments which show how a person tends to bring personal expressions in line with those of the group. The method in such experiments usually consists of asking the members for individual estimates, attitudes, or observations on a topic, then informing them of the group norm, and finally asking for a new expression from each member. Many of the informants modify their second expression in the direction of the group norm. In a series of ingenious experiments, Asch [1951], Tuddenham [1961], and others have shown that many people will even alter an observation which they *know* to be correct rather than oppose the group. Each subject in these experiments was surrounded by a group which, by secret prearrangement, made factual observations that the subject *knew* to be wrong; yet one-third of these subjects accepted the wrong observation when opposed by a unanimous group opinion to the contrary. Schachter [1951] has also shown experimentally how the member who sharply deviates from group norms in opinion is rejected by the group. These and many other experiments have proved the reality of group pressures so convincingly that no recent replications have seemed necessary.

We often notice that a new member of a group is more carefully conformist and more fiercely loyal than the old members. Religious converts often show a zeal which puts lifelong members to shame. An experiment by Dittes and Kelly [1956] helps to explain this. They found that among members who equally value their membership in a group, those who feel *least accepted* are the most rigidly conformist to a group's norms. Meticulous conformity is a tool for gaining acceptance and status within a group, while rejection is the price of nonconformity.

It is probable that no other structure even approaches the tremendous controlling power of the group over the individual. Any parent who has tried to counter a teenager's argument, *"All* the kids are wearing them!" is fully aware of the controlling power of the group.

INFORMAL PRIMARY-GROUP CONTROLS. Groups are of two kinds, primary and secondary; these concepts will be analyzed in detail in a later chapter. For our present discussion it is sufficient to note that primary groups are small, intimate, informal groups, such as the family, clique, or play group, while secondary groups are impersonal, formal, and utilitarian groups, such as a labor union, trade association, church congregation, or student body.

Within primary groups, control is informal, spontaneous, and unplanned. The members of the group react to the actions of each member. When a member irritates or annoys the others, they may show their disapproval through ridicule, laughter, criticism, or even ostracism. When a member's behavior is acceptable, a secure and comfortable "belonging" is the usual reward. Many novelists have used the subplot in which a character violates the norms of the group in some way, is disciplined by group disapproval, and must earn group acceptance through penitence and renewed conformity (like Sinclair Lewis's Babbitt).

In most primitive societies, where virtually all groups were primary groups, there was very little serious misconduct. Each person was born into certain kinship groups—for example, a family, a clan, and a tribe. One could not move on to another tribe or clan, for a person divorced from kinship ties had no social existence—that is, no one was obligated to regard and treat him or her as a human being. One who wanted to survive *had* to get along with the groups in which one was enmeshed. Since there was little privacy and no escape, the penalty of serious nonconformity was an intolerable existence. For example, the polar Eskimo institutionalized ridicule and laughter as a social control. The person who violated cultural norms was mercilessly ridiculed. Lowie describes the use of scorn and ridicule by a number of American Indian peoples:

When a Fox Indian boy in Illinois was taught not to steal and never to abuse his wife, his elder did not hold up to him any tangible punishment here or hereafter nor any abstract rule of morality. The clinching argument was, "The people will say many things about you, although you may not know it."

Within primary groups, control is informal, spontaneous, and unplanned.
(*J. Berndt/Stock, Boston*)

Gossiping sometimes took special forms of ridicule. An Alaskan youth thus reports his experience: "If you do not marry within your village, they joke about you—they joke so much that it makes it disagreeable." The Crow sang songs in mockery of a miser, a bully, or a man who should take back a divorced wife—the acme of disgrace. Certain kinsmen had the privilege of publicly criticizing a man for breaches of etiquette and ethics, and there was nothing he would fear more than to be thus pilloried. This system was developed by the Blackfoot along slightly different lines. "For mild persistent misconduct, a method of formal discipline is sometimes practiced. When the offender has failed to take hints and suggestions, the head men may take formal notice and decide to resort to discipline. Some evening when all are in their tipis, a head man will call out to a neighbor

asking if he has observed the conduct of Mr. A. This starts a general conversation between the many tipis, in which all the grotesque and hideous features of Mr. A.'s acts are held up to general ridicule, amid shrieks of laughter, the grilling continuing until far into the night. The mortification of the victim is extreme and usually drives him into a temporary exile or, as formerly, upon the warpath to do desperate deeds."

A primitive man sacrifices half his property lest he be dubbed a miser; he yields his favorite wife if jealousy is against the code; he risks life itself, if that is the way to gain the honor of a public eulogy. That is why savages of the same tribe are not forever cutting one another's throats or ravishing available women, even if they lack written constitutions, jails, a police force, and revealed religion. (From *Are We Civilized?* by

Robert H. Lowie, copyright, 1929, by Harcourt, Brace and World, Inc.; © 1957, by Robert H. Lowie. Reprinted by permission of the publisher.)

In many authenticated instances where primitives have violated important norms, they have committed suicide because they could not endure the penalty of group disapproval [Malinowski, 1926, pp. 94–99]. In such a group setting, the penalty for serious nonconformity is so unbearable that serious nonconformity is rare. Likewise in complex cultures, wherever persons are trapped in primary-group settings which they cannot easily escape, as in a prison cell or a military unit, this great controlling power of the primary group comes into operation.

In many societies, the group is held responsible for the acts of any of its members. For example, if a Tlingit Indian of the American Northwest murdered a member of another clan, his own clan had to provide for execution a person equal in social status to the murdered victim, while the actual murderer was punished by living with the knowledge that he had caused the execution of a clansman. In the army, one dirty rifle or messy locker may deprive an entire platoon of its weekend pass. Such forms of collective punishment may seem unjust, *but they work!* A soldier whose indolence has once caused his platoon to lose its weekend pass is unlikely to repeat the error—or to be permitted to forget it!

A great deal of "leadership" and "authority" rests upon the skillful manipulation of the group as a control device. Successful teachers, for example, often use the class to maintain discipline; they manipulate the situation so that the child who misbehaves will look ridiculous before the class. But if they allow a situation to develop wherein the misbehaving child appears to the class as a hero or matryr, this control is lost.

Normal people everywhere need and seek approval of others, especially of primary-group associates upon whom they depend for intimate human response. English workers sometimes punish another worker who has violated group norms by "sending him to Coventry." This means that workers will not speak, answer, or look at the person, and will act as though the other worker weren't there at all. The victim usually either does penance or quits the job. Thousands of novels, dramas, and operas have elaborated this theme. Most people will give almost anything, even their lives if necessary, to retain this approval and the comforting feeling of belonging to the group most important to them. It is the overwhelming need for group acceptance and approval that makes the primary group the most powerful controlling agency in the world.

SECONDARY-GROUP CONTROLS. As we shift from primary- to secondary-group situations, we also shift from informal to more formal social controls. Secondary groups are generally larger, more impersonal, and specialized in purpose. We do not use them to meet our need for intimate human response but to help us to get certain jobs done. If a secondary group does not meet our needs, we can generally withdraw with no great anguish, for our emotional lives are not deeply involved. To maintain our status in the secondary group is desirable but not a desperate emotional necessity as it is in the primary group. True, it is possible in our society for people to change their primary groups—leave their families, divorce their mates, find new friends—but this is painful. The secondary group is generally a less compelling control agency than the primary group.

The secondary group is still an effective control. Some of the informal controls still operate in the secondary group. No normal person wants to appear ridiculous at the union meeting, the church worship service, or the chamber of commerce banquet. Such informal controls as ridicule, laughter, gossip, and ostracism operate in secondary-group settings, but generally with a reduced impact. Meanwhile, other more formal controls are characteristic of secondary groups—parliamentary rules of order, official regulations and standardized procedures, propaganda, public relations and "human engineering," promotions and titles, rewards and prizes, formal penalties and punishments, and still others.

These formal controls of the secondary group are most effective when reinforced by a primary group. A prize or decoration is more sweet when an admiring family and an applauding clique of close friends can watch the presentation ceremony. Within the large, impersonal secondary group may be many very closely integrated primary groups, such as squads within an army or work crews within a corporation. These primary groups can either reinforce or undermine the formal secondary-group controls and greatly affect the performance of the secondary group. Much of the human engineering approach in industry is an effort to use these primary groups to reinforce the controls and the objectives of the corporation.

LANGUAGE AS A CONTROL. Language is a way of describing reality, and changes in language may change the way people see reality. This is what symbolic interactionists mean by "the social construction of reality." A redefinition which ascribes new meanings to familiar words may promote a redefinition of attitudes and relationships. For example, recent use of the term, "welfare rights" has had some success in changing the image of "welfare" from a charity (which the poor gratefully accept in whatever amount offered) to a "right" (for which recipients may legitimately negotiate, bargain, and battle). After all, a "right" is simply a claim which other people will recognize and grant. Revolutionary and terrorist groups may call themselves an "army" and assume military titles ("field marshal," "chief of staff"). A field marshal over a ten-person "army" may be absurd, but if the media can be persuaded to use these terms, it lends an air of legitimacy to the group, making it more acceptable to the society at large. Sometimes groups use language for the opposite effect. An *argot* is a *special language of a subculture.* It includes

---

A SAMPLE OF SKID ROW ARGOT

bull   a police officer or railroad detective

carrying the banner   walking all night for lack of a place to stay

earbeating   the long sermon at a mission service

flop   a men's cubicle hotel or a room in a flophouse

meat truck   picks up the bodies of skid row men who die

mission stiff   one who gets food, lodging, and clothes from missions

nosedive   coming forward to accept Christ in a mission service

pink lady   drink made from alcohol obtained by squeezing Sterno through a handkerchief

snipe   a used cigarette butt

spider   the last alcohol in a bottle

starter   the first coin one gets toward enough for a bottle

tank   jail

went south   going to buy a bottle for someone else and disappearing with the money

Source: Adapted from William McSheehy, *Skid Row*, Schenkman Publishing Company, Cambridge, Mass., 1979, pp. 95–99.

Are you familiar with any subculture for which you could prepare a sample of argot?

specially coined words as well as ordinary words with a special meaning attached. For example, Howard [1974, p. 44] reports that in the ghetto (at that particular moment), to be called "all bad" meant that one had dash, verve, and style, while "bad motherf—" was a compliment. An argot serves important functions of social control. It promotes communication within the group, since each term is freighted with meaning which only group members can understand. Argot also excludes outsiders; to enter the group, one must "speak the language." Learning the argot thus not only strengthens the tie between the individual and the group, it also cuts down communication with the world outside. No individuals are entirely cut off from contacts outside the subculture, but as Bernstein [1966] observes, the argot serves to maximize social barriers between the group and the rest of society. It thus operates to maintain what sociologists call "boundary maintenance."

COMMUNIST SOCIAL CONTROL. Formal social control in Western democracies rests heavily upon written laws, trials to determine guilt, and punishment "according to law." Social control in the People's Republic of China (PRC) rests so little upon written laws that it is debatable whether they even have a legal system [Pepinsky, 1976, p. 82]. Although the PRC uses continuous indoctrination, total control of the communications media, and harsh punishments when necessary, primary reliance is upon group pressure.

Americans who wish to escape group pressure can disappear for a fresh start elsewhere. This is almost unthinkable in the PRC, where no one can be anonymous. The Chinese change jobs, residence, and associates far less often than Americans and can rarely do so without official approval [Pepinsky, 1976, pp. 92–93]. Every person is assigned to a *danwei*, a small study group, through school, office, block, or commune. This is the basic building block of Chinese society. Most necessities (ration cards, travel permits, job changes, housing assignments, health clinic appoint-

ments, marriage or divorce permits) come to one through the *danwei*. A detailed dossier on every member is kept by the *danwei*, including information on one's class background for three generations.

In most urban areas each block or small area has a street committee of unpaid committee members who keep close watch on those assigned to it. This street committee functions as a social service agency, making job and housing recommendations, health clinic referrals, and keeping informed on the needs of the members. The street committee is also a surveillance agency, reporting suspicions and infractions to the police. The street committee also decides which couples in the neighborhood may have another child and on occasion may order a woman to have an abortion [Butterfield, 1982].

Every person (except small children) *must* regularly share in a study group of about six to twelve persons. Every member must take part, with no escape into silence. Problems are discussed, practical solutions developed, and "holdouts" are pressed, more or less gently, to agree. Party directives are discussed, and the behavior of each member is reviewed. Failure to engage in self-criticism, acknowledging one's errors and promising improvement, brings persistent efforts at persuasion, followed by more grim penalties if necessary. The main effectiveness, however, depends upon group manipulation of guilt and shame. Thus the Chinese Communists have organized and institutionalized the behavior modification techniques of behaviorist psychology [Pepinsky, 1976, pp. 96–99; LaMott, 1977].

Chinese social control is undeniably effective—possibly the most effective of any society in history. What Americans view as basic human freedoms are entirely absent in the PRC, but simply to call it repressive is superficial. Social control in the PRC is both very kind and very cruel. No one is neglected. A child or wife who is persistently abused, a person who is ill and untended, or one who is perplexed by a problem of any sort is far more assured of sympathetic attention and assistance than in the United States. A child who persistently misbehaves or a parent who neglects or abuses a child is soon faced by a united front of disapproval from everyone he or she knows. Few can resist this for long. But control can be harsh. One is conceded no right to any idea, wish, or goal which is not in harmony with the public good, as officially defined. One who resists may expect punishments ranging from group disapproval through denial of job and housing to the ultimate punishment—confinement in a "reeducation center" until one relents or dies.

Social control in other Communist societies is similar to the PRC pattern in making use of social pressure, but it is somewhat less complete, and greater use is made of courts and legal punishments. As in all societies, when social pressures fail, force is the ultimate control.

Social Control Through Force

Many primitive societies succeed in controlling the behavior of individuals through the mores, reinforced by the informal controls of the primary group, so that no formal laws or punishments are necessary. But with larger populations and more complex cultures, formal governments, laws, and punishments are developed.

When the individual does not wish to follow the regulations, the group tries to compel him or her to do so. In large groups, however, the individual is too anonymous for informal group pressures to be brought to bear. Furthermore, in larger societies with complex cultures, some subcultures that conflict with the culture of the majority are likely to develop. The "moral consensus"—the nearly complete agreement on what is right and wrong—which we usually find in a small

Nonconformity is disapproved of in all societies. (*Constantine Manos/Magnum*)

society with a stable culture is seldom found in larger societies with changing cultures. In such societies the person who rejects the majority norms may find emotional support from a group of other persons who think and act as he or she does. (A few of the many current examples might include the Amish community, the hippie commune, or the homosexual subculture.) So conventional society sometimes uses force—in the form of laws and formal punishments—to compel a required minimum of conformity. This force is not always successful but is used in every complex society.

Situational Determinants of Behavior

When people see some behavior they do not like, they often attribute it to evil human nature, wicked impulse, weak character, or some other *individual* cause. What separates the sociologist from others here is the sociologist's habit of looking for *social* factors in the causation of behavior. True, when one individual or a few people change in character or behavior, the explanations may be purely individual. But when any *large number* of people change their character or behavior in the same direction, the probable cause is some change in social and cultural influences upon behavior. A major part of social control consists of efforts to manipulate the behavior situation, for most people will respond with the kind of behavior the situation encourages. This is true to a far greater degree than most people recognize.

One's behavior in a particular situation is usually a result of the needs, pressures, and temptations of that situation. There is ample evidence that many people who would not cheat a blind newspaper vendor will cheat the supermarket if they get a chance to do so; a little cheating on one's income tax is apparently engaged in by practically everybody; soldiers who did not rob their neighbors

back home "liberated" many articles from the enemy population; people do things as part of a mob which they would never do as individuals. War atrocities are committed by all armies, including American armies [Taylor, 1970]. Whether a surrendering enemy is shot or taken prisoner depends more upon circumstances at the moment of surrender than upon the character of the capturing troops [Draper, 1945]. Kinsey's data show that most civilian husbands are faithful to their wives, at least most of the time; but it appears that most overseas military personnel, during long separations from their wives, seized almost any attractive opportunity for infidelity.

Labor union officials believe in labor unions—except for their own employees! So when staff employees of the large unions seek to organize and bargain collectively with their bosses, these union official-bosses seem to react just like any other employers, even crossing picket lines when their office workers go on strike. [*Business Week*, March 21, 1971, p. 31]. And when union staff workers go on strike, they act just like any other workers on strike; thus in Michigan, several local chapters of the Michigan Education Association were unable to get the aid of MEA staff negotiators in bargaining with their local school boards because the MEA staff was on strike against the MEA [Cote, 1977]. Finally, when union membership and dues fall off, unions lay off staff members just as business corporations do [*Wall Street Journal*, Feb. 23, 1982, p. 1]. Argyris [1967] reports that, "As a sociological experiment, two Detroit ministers went to work on an assembly line and soon found themselves cheating on quality, lying to their foremen and swearing at the machines." Their new work situation carried pressures and frustrations to which they responded like any other workers. Illustrations of how the total behavior situation affects behavior outcome could be multiplied almost without end. Many are found in Chapter 19, "Collective Behavior and Social Movements."

People tend to obey an authority figure; therefore, guards are dressed in impressive uniforms [Beckman, 1974]. In a widely criticized experiment, Milgram [1974] found that in a university laboratory setting, volunteer research subjects would obey a scientist's orders, even when they believed that their obedience was inflicting excruciating pain upon other subjects involved in the experiment. The atrocities of warfare, often in obedience to orders, become understandable as we study the way the total behavior situation affects behavior.

True, the internalized norms and other personality characteristics one brings to a situation are a factor in one's behavior; sometimes they are the determining factor. A few people are honest in *all* situations; some husbands and wives will be faithful despite *any* temptation. But more often than our folklore admits, a situation promotes a characteristic kind of behavior among most of the participants. For example, county fairs are attended mainly by local people, often as family groups, in decently appointed and policed fairgrounds, with people divided into many small groups and crowds. Behavior in this situation is generally orderly. Rock music festivals are attended mainly by young people with no local ties or family responsibilities, with ready drug availability, and a focal interest and a hypnotic beat to unify them into an active crowd. Little wonder that rowdy behavior, petty vandalism, and angry confrontations with local residents often develop.

Violence at sports events has become a growing problem, leading to actual cancellation of some sports events for fear of expected violence [Clary, 1977]. Yet this violence is not randomly distributed. It is more likely at night games (after fans have had more time to booze it up) and is more likely after than before the game, leading one pair of sociologists to suggest that the time to play the *Star-Spangled Banner* is *after* the game [Bryan and Horton, 1978].

There are many other practical applications of this form of social control. For example, if we wish to discourage littering, sermons on littering are less effective than strategically placed litter barrels; but if these are allowed to overflow and are not emptied regularly, the control effect is destroyed [Finnie, 1974]. Many old-time slums, with their busy street life and their well-populated doorsteps, had less crime than the modern high-rise housing

---

Bridgestone gives its employees lifetime jobs as well as all the typical Japanese trimmings. Two-thirds of the 3,700 workers . . . live onsite in company apartments for which they pay about $30 a year. The average wage is $12,545 a year.

The company also provides tennis courts, baseball and soccer fields, a gymnasium, a kindergarten, a hospital and even a subsidized wedding ceremony-room—no small perquisite in Japan, where wedding prices can be exorbitant.

In return, the company gets employee loyalty, in ways little and big. The employee cafeteria works on the honor system. There isn't any cashier. Employees simply throw what they owe in a box as they walk out the door, taking what change they're entitled to from the box. Bridgestone says the cafeteria has never been shorted.

The last strike at Bridgestone was in 1947. Employees eagerly participate in new ways to improve the quality of Bridgestone's products while cutting the cost and time needed to make them. "As long as we don't have layoffs, the union is active in helping us increase productivity," says Motozo Mazutani, a manager at the Kodira plant.

Would these management policies work in the United States? Can this employee behavior be explained in terms of group pressure? In terms of situational determinants of behavior?

Manipulating the behavior situation . . . (*Ed Lettau/Photo Researchers, Inc.*)

projects which replaced them, whose empty sidewalks and corridors actually invited crime [Jacobs, 1961]. Architectural design is now being reconsidered in view of the discovery that design affects crime rates [Jeffery, 1971, 1977; Wise, 1982]. Thus, the deliberate manipulation of situational determinants of behavior is one of the principal means of social control.

SELF-FULFILLING PROPHESIES.   A self-fulfilling prophesy is one in which the prophesy starts a chain of events which make it come true [Merton, 1957a, chap. 11]. For example, if I point at a girl in class and say, "You are going to blush! Watch her blush, everybody!" she is almost certain to blush brightly. The classic example is the bank run. If it is reported that a certain bank is likely to fail, this may start a bank run which guarantees that it will fail.

Self-fulfilling prophesies are fairly common in social behavior. The prophesy that "there will be violence in the streets if . . ." has often been followed by violence. The self-fulfilling prophesy has been a handy weapon of demagogues. It enables them to encourage a particular development while piously bewailing it.

SOCIAL DEVIATION

No system of social control works perfectly. Some persons fail to behave as expected in all known societies, although nonconformity varies greatly in form and frequency between societies [Edgerton, 1976] But there are some common features of deviation in all societies.

Characteristics of Deviation

DEVIATION IS DEFINITIONAL.   No act is deviant of itself; it becomes deviant when it is *defined* as deviant. As Becker notes [1963, p. 9], "Deviance is not a quality of the act the person commits, but rather a consequence of the application by others of rules and sanctions to an offender. The deviant is one to whom that label has successfully been applied; deviant behavior is behavior of persons so labeled." *Deviation* is, then, *any behavior defined as a violation of the norms of a group or society.*

APPROVED AND DISAPPROVED DEVIATION. Both Florence Nightingale and Jack the Ripper were deviants. Some deviants—the genius, the saint, the hero—may be honored and revered (usually after they are dead, and no longer a nuisance). Sociologists have given little study to the approved forms of deviation. For all practical purposes, the sociological study of deviation is the study of disapproved deviation. Much deviant behavior is forbidden by law. To a major degree, the study of deviant behavior is the study of criminal behavior.

RELATIVE AND ABSOLUTE DEVIATION.   Most people in modern societies are neither completely conformist nor completely deviant. A completely deviant person would have a hard time staying alive. Even the more spectacular deviants, such as pyromaniacs, revolutionists, or hermits, are generally fairly conventional in some of their activities. And nearly all "normal" people are occasionally deviant. Kinsey [1948, pp. 392, 576] has shown how over half our adults could be imprisoned for using techniques of lovemaking which were (and still are) forbidden by the laws of most states. A number of studies have shown that

most people have committed a number of major crimes for which they could be prosecuted if all laws were fully enforced [Porterfield, 1946; Wallerstein and Wyle, 1947; Gold, 1970]. It is clear that nearly everyone in our society is deviant to some degree; but some are more frequently and broadly deviant than others, and some conceal their deviant actions more fully than others. To some extent the deviant is one who does openly what others do secretly.

DEVIATION FROM REAL OR IDEAL CULTURE? Since the real and ideal cultures often diverge, as mentioned in Chapter 3, conformity to one may be deviation from the other. For example, the ideal culture includes the cultural norm of obedience to all laws, yet practically no one obeys all laws.

Where important values are involved in the

Transvestites are one kind of deviant.
(*David Hurn/Magnum*)

divergence between what people say (ideal culture) and what they do (real culture), this becomes an important distinction. In each discussion of deviation where this distinction in important, the normative base—real or ideal culture—should be either implied or expressly stated. For example, in any discussion of premarital intercourse or of certain sex "crimes" which are widely practiced by married couples, the normative base should be specified.

NORMS OF EVASION.   Whenever the mores or laws forbid something that many people strongly wish to do, *norms of evasion* are likely to appear. These are *the patterns through which people indulge their wishes without openly challenging the mores.* For example, Roebuck and Spray [1967] show how the cocktail lounge functions to facilitate discreet sexual affairs between high-status married men and unattached young women. More common norms of evasion in our society would include driving a few miles over the speed limit, truckers' systematic violation of weight limits, and a little cheating on one's income tax.

The fact that a particular norm is often violated does not create a norm of evasion. It is only when there is a *pattern* of violation which is *recognized and sanctioned by one's group* that we have a norm of evasion. Patronizing a bootlegger became a norm of evasion when it became a standard, group-approved way of getting forbidden alcoholic beverages. In becoming group-sanctioned, the evasion loses its moral censure. Among some groups, success in "fixing" traffic tickets or in seducing women will earn one the admiration of others. Norms of evasion thus are a semi-institutionalized form of deviant behavior.

Sometimes a pattern of deviation is neither sufficiently accepted to be a norm of evasion nor sufficiently condemned to be routinely suppressed. In such situations, the toleration of such deviation may operate as a form of social control. Prostitutes and gamblers may be permitted to operate as long as they pro-

vide information to the police. In most prisons, influential prisoners who can ensure a quiet and orderly cell block are permitted to commit minor rule infractions [Strange and McCory, 1974]. Thus, tolerance of some deviation, with the implied threat of withdrawing this privilege and actually enforcing the rules, functions to maintain social control.

DEVIATION IS ADAPTIVE.   Deviation is both a threat and a protection to social stability. On the one hand, a society can operate efficiently only if there is order and predictability in social life. We must *know*, within reasonable limits, what behavior to expect from others, what they expect of us, and what kind of society our children should be socialized to live in. Deviant behavior threatens this order and predictability. If too many people fail to behave as expected, the culture becomes disorganized and social order collapses. Economic activity may be disrupted, and shortages may appear. The mores lose their compelling power, and the society's core of common values shrinks. Individuals feel insecure and confused in a society whose norms have become undependable. Only when most people conform to well-established norms most of the time can a society function efficiently. Revolutionists, once they have destroyed the old system of social control, promptly seek to create a new one which is often more restrictive than the one they have overthrown.

On the other hand, *deviant behavior is one way of adapting a culture to social change* [Coser, 1962; Sagarin, 1977]. No society today can possibly remain static for long. Even the most isolated of the world's societies faces sweeping social changes within the next generation. The population explosion, technological change, and the passing of tribal or folk cultures are requiring many peoples to learn new norms, while changing technology continues to demand adaptations from more advanced peoples. But new norms are seldom produced by deliberative assemblies of people who solemnly pronounce the old norms outworn and call for new ones. While the grave deliberations of congresses, religious councils, and professional associations may speed or slow down the new norms, their pronouncements more often serve to legitimize new norms which are well on the way to general acceptance. New norms emerge from the daily behavior of individuals responding in similar ways to the impact of new social circumstances (functionalist view) or from the success of some groups in imposing new rules upon other groups (conflict view). The deviant behavior of a few persons may be the beginnings of a new norm. As more and more people join in the deviant behavior and as organized groups begin to promote and justify the deviant behavior, it ceases to be deviant and a new norm is established.

The emergence of new norms is neatly illustrated in the decline of the patriarchal family. In an agrarian society where all the family worked together under the father's watchful eye, it was easy to maintain male dominance. But changing technology moved the father's job to the shop or office, where he could no longer keep his eye on things; changing technology also began drawing the wife into jobs where she worked apart from her husband and earned her own paycheck. The husband was no longer in a strategic position to assert his male authority, and, bit by bit, it weakened. In the nineteenth century, the relatively independent, equalitarian woman with a mind or her own and a habit of firmly voicing it was a deviant; today she is commonplace, and the women's movement is calling for additional changes of gender status. Functionalist theory emphasizes the changes in work role and strategic situation which paved the way for the new norms; conflict theorists emphasize the organized political action needed to gain legal recognition of the new norms.

Deviant behavior thus often represents tomorrow's adaptations in their beginnings. Without any deviant behavior, it would be

The deviant behavior of one generation may become the norm of the text.

difficult to adapt a culture to changing needs and circumstances. A changing society therefore needs deviant behavior if it is to operate efficiently. The question of *how much* deviation and *what kinds* of deviation a society should tolerate is a perpetual puzzle. It is easy now for most people to agree that the eighteenth-century republicans and the nineteenth-century suffragists were socially useful deviants, while the utopians were harmless and (according to many) the anarchists were socially destructive. But which of today's deviants will prove tomorrow to have been today's trail blazers—the nudists, hippies, gays, pacifists, marijuana users, commune members, free-lovers, one-worlders, or who? It is difficult to say.

Not all forms of deviation will fit the above analysis. The behavior of the assassin, the child molester, or the alcoholic rarely contributes to the forging of a useful new social norm. At any particular moment, deviant behavior takes many forms, only a very few of which will become tomorrow's norms. Much deviation is entirely destructive in its personal and social consequences. But *some* deviation is socially useful, as is indicated above. To separate the socially harmful from the socially useful deviations requires an ability to predict the social norms that tomorrow's society will require.

Theories of Deviation

No matter how efficient the social control, some people become deviant. Why?

BIOLOGICAL THEORY.   Some people are *unable* to conform because of biological defect. Those with severe physical or mental handicap cannot possibly fulfill all the usual behavior expectations. But deviation through biological inability to conform is not very common and appears to be a minor factor in the kinds of deviation which draw strong social disapproval. The idea that certain body types are predisposed to certain kinds of behavior is almost as old as human history. A number of scholars, including Lombroso [1912], Kretschmer [1925], Hooton [1939], von Hentig [1947], and Sheldon [1949] have made studies claiming to find that certain body types are more prone to deviant behavior than others. The most elaborate theory is that of Sheldon, who identifies three basic body types: endomorph (round, soft, fat); mesomorph (muscular, athletic); and ectomorph (thin, bony). For each type, Sheldon describes an elaborate series of personality traits and behavior tendencies. For example, he finds that delinquents and alcoholics are generally mesomorphs. He attributes neurosis largely to one's effort to be different from what one's body type predisposes one to be.

Physical-type theories appear occasionally as "scientific" articles in popular magazines and Sunday papers. They have become quite popular, possibly because they seem to offer a simple, scientific way of classifying people and predicting or explaining their behavior. Social scientists, however, are quite skeptical of the body-type theories [Clinard and Meier, 1979, p. 31]. Although these theories are supported by impressive empirical evidence, critics have noted serious errors in method which cast doubts upon their findings. For example, the process of classifying subjects into the several body types included no adequate methodological safeguards against un-

conscious bias: consequently, a borderline subject may have been placed in whatever body-type class he or she "belonged" in order to support the theory. The subject groups used in most of these studies were composed of institutionalized delinquents, who are not properly representative of all types of delinquents. Furthermore, the control groups of "normal" people were collected so unsystematically that it is doubtful whether they were a representative cross section of people.

A recent example of biological theory is the double-Y-chromosomes proposal. About one of each thousand males inherits an extra Y chromosome. Such males have been claimed to be abnormally susceptible to criminal or antisocial behavior [Montague, 1968; Fox, 1971]. But replication studies have failed to confirm any association between double Y chromosomes and deviant behavior [Pfuhl, 1979, p. 43; Liska, 1981, p. 9]. So another biological theory is rejected as unsubstantiated.

Most nineteenth-century scholars attribute most deviant behavior to biological causes, while most modern scholars attribute relatively little deviation to biological causes. Some scholars claim that recent research supports a larger causal role for biological factors than is generally conceded [Edgerton, 1976, chap. 6]. Certain chemicals and drugs can produce dramatic behavior changes. Hirschi claims that intelligence, as measured by IQ, has a significant causal effect upon juvenile delinquency (even after controlling for race and class) [1977]. Other scholars dismiss biological factors as relatively unimportant in deviation [Liska, 1981]. It remains an unsettled question.

PSYCHOLOGICAL THEORY.   To whatever extent mental defect and mental illness are organically caused, the psychological theories overlap with the biological theories.

There is no doubt that mental illness and personality maladjustment are associated with some kinds of deviant behavior. This *has* to be true since deviant behavior is often used as a symptom in diagnosing mental illness. One is diagnosed as mentally ill because of one's deviant behavior, and then this deviant behavior is attributed to the mental illness. It goes like this:

"He is deviant because he is mentally ill."
"What makes you think he is mentally ill?"
"His deviant behavior."

Deviant behavior is not the only symptom used in diagnosing mental illness. It is probably true that some deviation is caused by mental illness. It is also true that mental illness or serious personality maladjustment is not much more common among deviants than among other people [Pfuhl, 1979, p. 48]. Thus, psychological theories are not very helpful in explaining deviant behavior.

SOCIALIZATION THEORY.   Socialization theory begins with the functionalist assumption that there is a common core of norms and values shared by most of a society's members. Of course, the image of a perfectly integrated culture whose norms and values are shared by *all* members of a society is just a *model*, a starting point for analysis. Socialization theorists recognize that this model imperfectly fits American society but consider it a useful reference point for beginning analysis.

Socialization theory maintains that social behavior, both deviant and conforming, is controlled mainly by internalized norms and values. Deviation is attributed to some disruption of the process of internalizing and expressing those values in one's behavior.

Cultural Transmission Theory   This version of socialization theory notes that people usually internalize the values of those with whom they associate comfortably. How, then, does one internalize the values which produce deviant behavior?

Deviant Subcultures   If most of one's associates are deviants, one will probably become de-

viant. The term, *delinquency area*, was developed by Shaw and McKay [Shaw, 1930, 1931; Shaw, McKay and McDonald, 1938; Shaw and McKay, 1942]. They claimed that in the deteriorated and disorganized slums of the cities, delinquent behavior was a *normal* behavior pattern. In such an area, youths learn deviant values and behaviors which become *fixated* in their personalities. (Today, we would say *internalized*.)

Differential Association   Sutherland noted that criminal behavior is found in all regions and classes not just in slums. He proposed a *differential association* theory that criminal behavior is learned through contact with criminal patterns which are present, are acceptable, and are rewarded in one's physical and social environment. A person "engages in criminal behavior if, and only if, the weight of the favorable definitions exceeds the weight of the unfavorable definitions." [Sutherland, 1949, p. 234].

While Sutherland focused on criminal behavior, his theory fits all deviant behavior. A person becomes deviant if the deviant patterns are more common, or more commonly rewarded, in the social world in which the person moves (that is, among the significant others whose approval is desired.) Thus deviants learn deviant behavior in the same way conformists learn conforming behavior.

ANOMIE THEORY.   The concept of *anomie* was developed by Durkheim [1897]. The term translates roughly as "normlessness." It describes a society which has many conflicting sets of norms and values. No one set is strongly enough held and widely enough accepted to be very binding. The anomic society lacks consistent guidelines for people to learn; the anomic person has internalized no clear guidelines to follow.

Merton [1938] theorized that anomie also develops from the disharmony between cultural goals and the institutionalized means of attaining them. He notes that while our society encourages *all* its members to aspire to wealth and social position, our approved ways of reaching these goals enable only a few to succeed. True, an exceptional poor boy or girl reaches wealth and fame, and these exceptions keep alive the myth of equal opportunity. The youth of average abilities and no special opportunities or "connections" has very little chance of becoming rich and famous. Many who see little real chance of succeeding by following the rules may then violate them. As Merton concludes:

> It is only when a system of cultural values extols, virtually above all else, certain common success goals for the population at large while the social structure rigorously restricts or completely closes access to approved modes of reaching these goals for a considerable part of the same population, that deviant behavior ensues on a large scale. . . .

> The moral mandate to achieve success thus exerts pressure to succeed, by fair means if possible and by foul means if necessary. (Robert K. Merton, "Social Structure and Anomie," in his *Social Theory and Social Structure*, The Free Press, New York, 1957, chap. 3, pp. 146, 169.)

Deviance becomes widespread, then, when many people turn from approved to disapproved means of seeking success. But there are several responses to the goals-means choices which Merton outlines [1957a, pp. 140–157], as shown in Table 7-1. (1) *Conformity* is an acceptance of both the conventional goals and the conventional, institutionalized means of seeking them. (2) *Innovation* is an attempt to attain conventional goals through unconventional means (including illicit or criminal means). (3) *Ritualism* preserves the institutionalized means, which have become ends in themselves, as goals are largely ignored or forgotten. The rituals, ceremonies, and routines are followed, but the original meanings or functions have become lost. (4) *Retreatism* abandons both conventional goals and the institutionalized means for attaining them, as illustrated by most of the advanced

TABLE 7-1
MERTON'S TYPOLOGY OF INDIVIDUAL ADAPTATIONS

Modes of adaptation	Culture goals	Institutionalized means
I. Conformity	+	+
II. Innovation	+	−
III. Ritualism	−	+
IV. Retreatism	−	−
V. Rebellion	±	±

Note: This table presents five ways in which people may respond to a society's system of goals and to its standardized means of attaining them. In this table + signifies "acceptance," − signifies "rejection," and ± signifies "rejection of prevailing values and substitution of new values."
Source: Robert K. Merton, *Social Theory and Social Structure,* The Free Press, New York, 1957, p. 140.

Which of these "modes of adaptation" most nearly fits you?

alcoholics, drug addicts, hippies, skid-row habitués, hermits, and other dropouts. (5) *Rebellion* involves a retreat from the conventional goals and means, with an attempt to institutionalize a new system of goals and means. Revolutionists are an illustration.

Merton's theory nicely fits many deviants, especially the poor and disadvantaged. But deviation also appears among the well-born and successful. The radical activism among college students in the 1960s could hardly be attributed to "lack of opportunity" for conventional success. Merton's analysis also does not explain white-collar crime or sex deviations. It is ingenious but incomplete.

McClosky and Schaar [1965] suggest that normlessness may be simply one aspect of a negative and distrustful outlook on life and society. They present evidence that anomie appears not only among Merton's frustrated failures but also among the highly successful. They find that persons who score high on anomic scales also show high scores for hostility, anxiety, pessimism, authoritarianism, political cynicism, and other symptoms of alienation.

The concept of *alienation* is more inclusive than anomie. Although definitions vary, most sociologists follow Seeman's definition, which includes the components of *powerlessness, meaninglessness, normlessness, isolation,* and *self-estrangement* [Seeman, 1969; Johnson, 1973, p. 16; Geyer, 1980, pp. 16–29]. The alienated person not only has no fully internalized system of binding norms but also feels like a powerless, helpless victim of a heedlessly impersonal social system in which he or she has no real place. The alienated person has few group affiliations or institutional loyalties. Alienation is therefore an almost total emotional separation from one's society.

Marxist scholars stress the concept of alienation, holding that capitalist society inevitably alienates its workers and even its intellectuals because of its isolation of workers from control over work policies, work conditions, or managerial decisions [Blauner, 1964; Kon, 1969; Anderson, 1974]. Such alienation weakens the binding power of traditional norms and controls, and thus encourages deviant behavior. Marxist analysts see increasing alienation as a symptom of the approaching end for capitalism. Whether alienation is actually increasing is difficult to know, for we have no clear historical baselines for comparison.

SOCIETAL REACTION THEORY. This theory, also called *labeling theory,* begins with the fact that deviation is created by the *definition* of an act as deviant. We cannot have rule breakers without rule makers. Societal reaction theory stresses the manufacture of deviation through the *labeling process.* By labeling an act as deviant, we set in motion a chain of events which tend to push the person into greater deviation and, finally, into a deviant life organization. Thus the act of labeling begins a self-fulfilling prophesy.

The concepts of primary and secondary deviation, proposed by Lemert [1951, pp. 75–76; 1967], help to show how people may become confirmed deviants. *Primary deviation* is the deviant behavior of one who is conformist in the rest of one's life organization. The deviant behavior is so trivial, or so generally tolerated, or so successfully concealed

that one is not publicly identified as deviant, nor does one consider oneself a deviant but as a "decent person" who has a little secret or eccentricity. Lemert writes that "the deviations remain primary . . . as long as they are rationalized or otherwise dealt with as functions of a socially acceptable role" (1951, p. 75). *Secondary deviation* is that which follows one's public identification as a deviant. Sometimes the discovery of a single deviant act (of rape, incest, homosexuality, burglary, drug use), or even a false accusation, may be enough to label one as a deviant (rapist, dope fiend, etc.). This labeling process [Lemert, 1951, p. 77; Becker, 1963, chap. 1; Schur, 1971; Pfuhl, 1979, chap. 6] is highly important, for it may be the point of no return on the road to a deviant life organization. One engaging in primary deviation can still maintain a conventional set of roles and statuses and can still share the normal conformity-reinforcing group pressures and associations. But being labeled a "deviant" tends to isolate one from these conformity-reinforcing influences. Persons so labeled may be dismissed from their jobs or barred from their professions, ostracized by conventional people, and possibly imprisoned and forever branded as "criminal." They are almost forced into association with other deviants by their exclusion from conventional society. As one becomes dependent upon deviant associations and begins to use deviation as a defense against the conventional society which has branded one, the deviation becomes the central focus of one's life reorganization.

For a number of authors, this societal reaction theory describes how a deviant act often triggers a chain of events which deepen and confirm a pattern of deviation. Chambliss illustrates with the example of a small group of boys who, labeled as "bad boys," actually became the bad boys they were accused of being:

The community responded to the Roughnecks as boys in trouble, and the boys agreed with that perception. Their pattern of deviancy was reinforced, and breaking away from it became increasingly unlikely. Once the boys acquired an image of themselves as deviants, they selected new friends who affirmed that self-image. As that self-conception became more firmly intrenched, they also became willing to try new and more extreme deviancies. With their growing alienation came freer expression of disrespect and hostility for representatives of the legitimate society. This disrespect increased the community's negativism, perpetuating the entire process of committment to deviance.

When it is time to leave adolescence . . . [it is likely that the Roughnecks'] noticeable deviance will have been so reinforced by police and community that their lives will be effectively channeled into careers consistent with the adolescent background. (William J. Chambliss, "The Saints and the Roughnecks," in James M. Henslin (ed.), *Deviant Life-Styles*, Transaction Books, New Brunswick, N.J., 1977, pp. 303–304. Published by permission of Transaction, Inc., from *Society*, vol. 11, no. 1. Copyright 1973 © by Transaction, Inc.)

To labeling theorists, much of the responsibility for juvenile delinquency arises from the clumsy efforts of police, courts, and caseworkers who unwittingly teach youths to think of themselves as delinquents and to act as delinquents [Ageton and Elliott, 1974; Kasselbaum, 1974, p. 67]. This sounds plausible, but is it true? As Matza observes, this progression is not an inexorable process; that is, the deviant is not helplessly swept down a chute from which there is no escape [1969]. Instead, the deviant *has a choice*. At many points in the process of becoming delinquent, the person elects to continue.

Labeling theorists claims that many "mentally ill" people are only mildly eccentric until they are labeled as "mentally ill." Then people start treating them differently. Income and work status usually suffer as one is dismissed or passed over for promotion [Link, 1982]. Efforts to reject the "illness" label are seen by others as additional "symptoms" of mental illness. Any efforts of the "patient" to act as a normal person may be resisted, while the

Some cultural conflicts can encourage mental conflicts.

patient is rewarded for sinking into a helpless, dependent passivity. In a famous experiment, Rosenhan and several colleagues arranged to be admitted to a psychiatric hospital labeled as schizophrenics. The staff treated them as schizophrenics and ignored the fact that they behaved perfectly normally. From this Rosenhan concluded that the patients' label, not their behavior, determined their treatment by the staff [Rosenhan, 1973]. Thus the "manufacture of madness" creates mental illness where there may be nothing more than annoying or mildly eccentric behavior [Scheff, 1966; Szasz, 1970]. But replication studies have failed to support Rosenhan's thesis [Lindsay, 1982], and the "manufacture of madness" thesis is not well substantiated.

Research studies testing labeling theory are conflicting and inconclusive [Mahoney, 1974; Gove, 1975, 1980]. Most primary groups resist expelling the deviant member and seek to bring the person back to conformity [Orcutt, 1973]. Empirical evidence shows that under some conditions labeling encourages additional deviation, while under some other conditions labeling encourages a return to conformity [Tittle, 1975, 1980; Horowitz and Wasserman, 1979]. For example, some police officials believe that publishing names of persons arrested for drunken driving does act to reduce and not to increase drunken driving [Garino, 1982], but this has not been tested.

St. Louis—Posting bond used to be the main worry of motorists arrested for drunken driving here.

No more. "Quite frequently, when they're arrested, their primary concern is, 'Is my name going to be in the paper?'" says traffic safety Sgt. Richard Swatek.

That's because the *St. Louis Globe-Democrat*, since late last year, has been publishing a daily list of drunk-driving suspects in its area, stretching to such small towns as Glen Carbon, Ill.

"Everybody looks at it," says Sgt. Swatek. "It's like a gossip column."

"I'm sure publishing the names does a lot of good," says Sgt. Donald Hasseldick, director of a St. Louis County program aimed at drunken driving. "No one wants his name associated with a criminal offense."

How would you design a research project to test whether this program works?

In summary, it appears that labeling sometimes increases and sometimes reduces further deviation, but labeling theory offers no explanation of which effect labeling will have or of why a person commits that first act of deviation.

CONFLICT THEORY.

Cultural Conflict Theory. When there are a number of subcultures (ethnic, religious, national, regional, class) in a society, this reduces the degree of value consensus. The clashing norms of differing subcultures create a condition of anomic normlessness. The norms of the dominant culture become written into law, making criminals of those sharing a divergent subculture. The culture of the lower class is in conflict with dominant norms, which are mostly middle-class norms. Thus lower-class persons, merely by living out the cultural norms they have learned, come into conflict with the conventional morality, as outlined in a classic article by Miller some years ago [1958].

The cultural conflict theory provides a reasonable explanation for some kinds of deviation among some groups, such as among second-generation immigrants or mistreated racial minorities, but it offers little insight into deviation among the well-born and powerful.

Class Conflict Theory. Class conflict theorists reject the consensus model of a stable, integrated society whose members are in basic agreement upon values. They consider that conflict of values, not consensus upon values, is the basic reality of modern Western societies. They view "consensus upon values" as a myth which is artfully cultivated by the powerful for their own benefit, as it makes *their* values seem to be the values of everybody.

Class conflict theorists attribute deviation not to the different cultural norms of different social classes but to their different *interests.* Marx argued that capitalist societies develop laws and institutions which protect the interests of the propertied classes and make criminals of all who challenge their privilege. Conflict criminologists follow Marx in seeing crime as a product of class exploitation. Laws are passed to protect the existing capitalist order. Most crime is property crime, and most police work is property protection. Deviation will continue as long as class inequalities and class exploitation continue [Chambliss and Mankoff, 1976; Quinney, 1980].

Some points of conflict theory are untestable. How, for example, does one prove whether our "consensus" upon private property rights is a genuine consensus or a piece of clever propagandizing by the powerful?

Whether all should have equal incomes or some should get more than others is a moral question not a scientific question. Such questions can never be settled by any empirical evidence.

Conflict theories of deviation are plausible. But if true, then crime and other deviation should vary with the degree of class inequality and exploitation. Evidence on this is inconclusive. Some studies find a relationship between crime and economic inequality or unemployment [Jacobs, 1978], while others find no such relationship [Berger, 1974, pp. 66–70; Spector, 1975; Bailey, 1981]. According to conflict theory, Japan should have a high crime rate, with its urbanization, rapid social change, capitalist economy, and great inequality. Yet Japan has one of the lowest crime rates in the world [Bayley, 1976; Japan Society, 1977]. Switzerland is another capitalist, materialistic country with great inequality but a very low crime rate [Clinard, 1978]. Recorded crime in England declined sharply during the 19th century although inequality and exploitation continued unabated, and then, contrary to conflict theory, crime increased greatly in the 20th century even though inequality and exploitation were declining [Davies, 1983].

The class conflict theory fits lower-class and minority crimes better than upper-class crimes, fits property crimes better than crimes against individuals, and has no clear explanation for some kinds of deviation. It is a plausible explanation for some kinds of deviation, but is not well substantiated by empirical evidence.

CONTROL THEORY. The control theorists accept the model of a society whose consensual values can be identified. They assume that there *is* a normative system from which to deviate. Control theorists assume that most people conform to the dominant values because of both inner and outer controls. The inner controls are the internalized norms and values one learns (control theorists share this view with socialization theorists). The outer controls are the social rewards for conformity and the penalties for deviation which one receives.

Control theory emphasizes the bond which ties the individual to conventional society. Hirschi [1969] sees four components in this bond: belief, attachment, commitment, and involvement. *Belief* refers to the internalized values; the stronger the belief, the lower the likelihood of deviation. *Commitment* is related to how great are the rewards which one gets from conformity. *Attachment* is one's responsiveness to the opinions of others, the extent to which one is sensitive to the approval of conforming persons. *Involvement* refers to one's activities in community institutions such as church, school, and local organizations. The higher one ranks on each of these items, the lower the probabilities of deviation. As Friday and Hage [1976, p. 347] observe, "When adolescents have meaningful kin, community, educational, and work role relationships, they become socialized to the dominant norms."

Deterrence is among the external controls. After being ignored for decades, deterrence theory is again popular among criminologists. It assumes that people act rationally enough of the time to make systematic punishment a useful control. There have been a great many deterrence studies in recent years. While they do not completely agree, they generally conclude that many deviant acts can be deterred if they carry a high probability of punishment [Silverman, 1976; Tittle, 1980].

Control theory is supported by studies conducted over many years showing an association between deviation and the lack of effective bonds to the major institutions [Short and Strodtbeck, 1965; Akers, 1973; Conger, 1976]. But which is cause and which is effect? Are the conformists' strong ties to conventional institutions the *cause* of the conformity, or are they just a symptom of conformity? Do their bonds to home, church, school, and job cause them to be conformist, or are they drawn to these institutions because they are already conformists? We are not certain. Perhaps both are true.

IMPORTANCE OF DEVIATION THEORY. Our theories of deviation are not very satisfactory. There are many theories, each quite plausible and each supported by a good deal of research evidence. But for every theory either the evidence is inconsistent and mixed, or it applies to only some kinds of deviation or to some sets of circumstances. Thus no theory offers a good explanation for deviation of all kinds. Such a theory may be impossible. In medicine, we have no single theory to explain "illness," for illness is of many kinds and has many causes. Deviation, too, is of many kinds and may have many causes.

A general theory of deviation may never be developed, but theory building is not just a parlor sport for scholars. Theory is important, for our social control efforts stem from our social control theory. If we accept biological theory, we look to genetics and medicine for answers; if we accept class conflict theory, we seek to reduce class inequality; if we accept deterrence theory, we increase our efforts to detect and punish deviants; if we accept control theory, we make efforts to bind people more tightly to the basic institutions of society. The search for valid theory is difficult and frustrating but most necessary.

FREEDOM AND ORDER

Defining certain acts as deviant is a way of reinforcing conventional norms. Nearly a century ago Durkheim [1893] stated that scandalous behavior unites the community in support of conventional norms. Erikson [1966] claims that deviance clarifies the norms; when certain acts are defined as deviant, this shows people "how far they can go." No known society has allowed complete freedom to "do your own thing." All communes which have

The punishment of deviants is very real in every society.

attempted to grant such license have failed. The only enduring communes have operated under the rule of a charismatic leader or under a system of their own rules and procedures [Roberts, 1971, chap. 11]. All societies and all groups punish deviants with punishments ranging from nonacceptance and ridicule to every imaginable form of torture, mutilation, imprisonment, and death. Often the punishment has more the flavor of vindictive revenge than of intended control.

The deviants sometimes accept punishment with stoical calm, as did the early Christians, and sometimes they protest bitterly over their persecution and oppression, as did the hippies and radical leftists of the 1960s. The "persecution" theme is a useful promotional tactic which organizers have used for centuries. But although often exaggerated and sometimes provoked, persecution of deviants is very real in every society.

Can freedom and order be reconciled? Without social order, people can do nothing with reasonable assurance of safety and comfort. Yet the process of maintaining social order may destroy freedom. One can also have extended discussions on the meaning of freedom (*Whose* freedom to do *what*, for example).

We are caught in an inescapable dilemma. Complete freedom for all to do as they wish brings chaos and destroys the freedom for anyone to live in safety. Yet most measures of social control reduce the individual's freedom of choice and action. Also, too harsh measures of control may provoke disorder, destroying the order they are intended to preserve. How to strike the most comfortable balance between freedom and order is a question which will never be resolved to everyone's satisfaction.

SUMMARY

Social order prevails when the ordinary activities of a people go on predictably and comfortably. In simple societies, *socialization* maintains social order by preparing people to want to act as they are expected to act, and *social pressure* rewards people with acceptance and approval when they act as expected. In more complex societies, *force* is also necessary to maintain order. In many situations, behavior is greatly controlled by the needs and pressures of the situation—*the situational determinants of behavior.*

Deviation is any violation of the rules of behavior. An act is not deviant until defined as deviant. While there are both approved and disapproved forms of deviation for each society, it is the disapproved deviation that draws the interest of sociologists.

Deviation is relative, in that most people are sometimes deviant and no one is entirely deviant. *Norms of evasion* are recognized modes of rule breaking. Deviation is sometimes *adaptive*, serving as a way of changing the norms of a society.

There are many theories of deviation. *Biological theory*, holding biological factors responsible for most deviation, is no longer widely held. *Psychological theory*, giving psychological maladjustments as causes of deviation is much less widely accepted today than formerly. *Socialization theory* attributes deviation to some failure to internalize the dominant norms and values. Failure may be due to socialization within a deviant subculture. Through *differential association*, one is more often exposed to favorable than to critical evaluations of deviation. *Anomie theory* states that complex societies tend to become normless, providing no clear guidelines for people to learn and follow.

Societal reaction theory, or labeling theory, focuses on rule makers as well as rule breakers. The labeling of one as deviant often starts changes in one's social treatment and associations, pushing one from occasional, or *primary deviation*, into *secondary deviation*, in which one's life-style is organized around the deviation.

Conflict theory of deviation takes two forms: *cultural conflict theory* sees deviation arising from the clash of the norms of different subcultures: *class conflict theory* sees deviation arising from the clashing interests of different social classes. *Control theory* attributes deviation to a lack of close, binding ties to the society's basic institutions—family, church, school, work. Control theory sees both internalized norms and systematic punishments as useful controls.

Each theory has some supporting evidence, but no theory explains all kinds of deviation. Theory is important, since control policy is based on theory.

GLOSSARY

alienation an emotional separation from a society or group, combining feelings of normlessness, meaninglessness, powerlessness, social isolation, and self-estrangement.

anomie condition of a society with no single, consistent set of norms and values for people to internalize and follow.

argot special language terms of a subculture.

cultural deviant one who deviates in behavior from the norms of the culture.

deviant subculture a subculture whose norms are in opposition to those of the dominant culture.

deviation behavior which is defined as a violation of the norms of a group or a society.

deviation, primary deviant behavior of a person who is conformist in the rest of his or her life.

deviation, secondary deviant behavior which follows from public identification as a deviant.

labeling identifying one as a deviant, often followed by a change in one's treatment by others.

norms of evasion recognized and sanctioned patterns through which people indulge their wishes without openly challenging the mores of a society.

self-fulfilling prophesy a prediction which starts a chain of events making the prediction come true.

social control all the means and processes whereby a group or a society secures its members' conformity to its expectations.

social order a system of people, relationships, and customs operating smoothly to accomplish the work of a society.

QUESTIONS
AND PROJECTS

1 How does social order depend upon predictablity of behavior?

2 Some ancient societies required many human sacrifices. Why did victims consent to die quietly instead of revolting?

3 Evaluate this statement: "Only weaklings follow the herd. A person with true strength of character will do what is right without being swayed by the group."

4 In the factory a "rate buster" is a worker on piecework who produces and earns so much that management may revise the piece rate downward. How do other workers treat this person? Is he or she anything like a "course spoiler" in college, who works so hard in a course that the professor begins to expect more from the other students?

5 What do you think of the Tlingit practice of holding the entire group morally responsible for the acts of each member? Does the practice make for effective social control? How widely could we follow it? Is it consistent with our ethos? Does our society have the kind of group structure in which such a practice is workable?

6 In George Orwell's *1984* (Harcourt Brace Jovanovich, Inc., New York, 1949), he imagined a society in which everyone was totally controlled. Has this happened?

7 Under what circumstances will practically all students cheat? When will very few students cheat? How does this contrast in attitude illustrate situational determinants of behavior?

8 In a hippie commune, where each member is "free," what group controls might operate?

9 Why do "backward" or primitive societies have less crime and fewer violations of the mores than "progressive" societies like ours?

10 Under what circumstances might publishing the names of deviants (*a*) discourage repeated deviation or (*b*) encourage the drift into secondary deviation?

11 How does the concept of secondary deviation help one interpret the disorganization of the life of drug addicts?

12 Labeling theorists seem to imply that the problem of deviation could be solved by simply not labeling deviants. Would this be practical for any kinds of deviation? Impractical for any kinds?

13 How would you interpret the high crime rate in the ghetto in terms of Merton's theory of cultural goals and institutionalized means? In terms of the Marxist alienation theory?

14 Discuss these propositions:

(*a*) Norms of evasion are a threat to social stability. (*b*) Norms of evasion are a protection to the stability of a society.

15 What difference does it make which theory of deviation we accept?

16 Read one of the disaster studies such as William Form, et al., *Community in Disaster*, Harper & Row, Publishers, Inc., New York, 1958; Harry E. Moore, *Tornados over Texas*, University of Texas Press, Austin, 1958; or Allen H. Barton, *Communities in Disaster*, Doubleday & Company, Inc., Garden City, N.Y., 1969. Show how social order breaks down and then is restored.

SUGGESTED READINGS

* Becker, Howard S.: *Outsiders: Studies in the Sociology of Deviance*, The Free Press, New York, 1963, 1966. A concise description of how people become deviant, applied particularly to marijuana users and dance musicians.

Brown, Paula: "Changes in Ojibwa Social Control," *American Anthropologist*, 54:57–70, January 1954. Tells how loss of traditional controls and lack of effective replacements left the Ojibwa with an unsolved problem of social control.

Bryan, James: "Apprenticeships in Prostitution," *Social Problems*, 12:287–297, Winter 1965. Shows how call girls become socialized into the call girl role.

Clinard, Marshall B. and Robert F. Meier: *Sociology of Deviant Behavior*, Holt, Rinehart and Winston, Inc., New York, 1979. A comprehensive textbook on deviation.

* Davis, Nanette J.: *Sociological Constructions of Deviance: Perspectives and Issues in the Field*, Wm. C. Brown Company Publishers, Dubuque, Iowa, 1975, 1980. A systematic outline of deviance and control theory.

* Farrell, Ronald A. and Victoria L. Swigert: *Deviance and Social Control*, Scott, Foresman and Company, Glenview, Ill., 1982. A concise outline with interesting short readings on deviance and control.

Goode, Erich: *Deviant Behavior: An Interactionist Approach*, Prentice-Hall, Inc., Englewood Cliffs, N.J., 1978. A recent textbook on deviance.

Henslin, James M. (ed.): *Deviant Life-Styles*, Transaction Books, New Brunswick, N.J., 1977. A readable collection describing a variety of deviant life-styles.

* Kephart, William M.: *Extraordinary Groups: The Sociology of Unconventional Life-Styles*, St. Martin's Press, Inc., New York, 1976. Describes a number of deviant communities, ranging from the Amish to modern communes.

Miller, Gale: *Odd Jobs: The World of Deviant Work*, Prentice-Hall, Inc., Englewood Cliffs, N.J., 1978. Interesting descriptions of deviant careers—confidence men, safecrackers, fortune-tellers, strippers, and others.

* McCaghy, Charles H., James K. Skipper, Jr., and Mark Lifton: *In Their Own Behalf: Voices from the Margin*, Appleton Century Crofts, New York, 1974. A wide variety of deviants tell their own stories.

* Matza, David: *Becoming Deviant*, Prentice-Hall, Inc., Englewood Cliffs, N.J., 1969. Argues that the deviant is not helpless but has a choice at various points in the process of becoming deviant.

* Suran, Bernard G.: *Oddballs: The Social Maverick and the Dynamics of Individuality*, Nelson-Hall Publishes, Chicago, 1978. Illustrates the author's thesis that the oddballs are the real innovators, by examining the lives of several nonconformists from Moses to Lenny Bruce.

*An asterisk before the citation indicates that the title is availiable in a paperback edition.

PART THREE

Social Organization

In William Golding's popular novel *Lord of the Flies,* a plane crash strands a number of boys on a remote, unpopulated island. Groups soon begin to form, leaders emerge, rules and procedures develop. They begin to form a society, although a brutal and terrifying one.

This is what is meant by *social organization.* A society is more than a number of people occupying a space, just as an automobile is more than a heap of auto parts. Used as a noun, social organization is the way the members of a society are divided into groups and the enduring arrangements they develop. Used as a verb, social organization is the *process* of forming groups and developing those enduring patterns of association and behavior which we call *social institutions.*

Chapter 8, "Groups and Associations," describes the kinds of groups people form and how these groups affect the behavior of their members. Chapter 9, "Social Institutions," tells how the more important norms of a culture and the important relationships of a society are organized in enduring working systems. Chapter 10, "The Family," examines what is often viewed as the most basic of all social institutions. Chapter 11, "Religious Institutions," studies humanity's efforts to come to terms with supernatural forces and ultimate values. Chapter 12, "Education, Science, and Technology," describes how knowledge is organized and transmitted, especially in modern societies. Chapter 13, "Political-Economic Institutions," studies how the production and distribution of goods and services is organized and controlled.

8 Groups and Associations

In extreme cases, the loss of one's social ties can kill. . . . When the tribe decides to punish one of its members for breaking a taboo, a witch doctor points a magic bone at him and recites some incantations which place him under a spell of death. "The man who discovers that he is being 'boned' is a pitiable sight," wrote an explorer in Australia, as quoted by the Harvard physiologist Walter Cannon. "He sways backwards and falls to the ground . . . he writhes as if in mortal agony and, covering his face with his hands, begins to moan. After a while he becomes very composed and crawls to his wurley [hut]. From this time onward he sickens and frets . . . his death is only a matter of a comparatively short time."

In Cannon's view, the primary fact in the victim's disintegration is the withdrawal of tribal support. Once the bone is pointed, his fellow tribesmen give him up for dead—and in his isolation, he has no alternative but to die. His heart becomes exhausted by overstimulation, his blood pressure drops calamitously, and his vital functions cease. Much the same appears to happen to some old people in this country when they are consigned to dismal nursing homes or back wards of hospitals, abandoned by the rest of the members of their "tribe."

(Maya Pines, *Psychology Today*, 14:43–44, December 1980.)

For most members of all known societies, the total withdrawal of all group relations would be a sentence of death. What is the "group," and what makes it so important?

While "group" is one of the most important concepts in sociology, there is disagreement upon its definition. Such confusion is not because sociologists can't make up their minds! Confusion persists because most concepts in sociology are not invented and then put into use; instead, most sociological terms are familiar words which sociologists use with special meanings. Some terms continue to be used with more than one meaning, because to invent an entirely new set of several words to cover the several meanings would be even more confusing.

Consequently, there are several meanings of "group" in the sociological literature. In one usage the term denotes *any physical collection of people* (e.g., "a group of people were waiting . . ."). In this usage, a group shares nothing except physical closeness. Many sociologists would call such a collection of people an *aggregation* or a *collectivity*.

A second meaning is that of *a number of people who share some common characteristic*. Thus, males, college graduates, physicians, old people, millionaires, commuters, and cigarette smokers would each be a group. *Category* would be a more satisfactory term, but sociologists often use "group" where "category" would be more precise.

Another usage defines a group as *a number of people who share some organized patterns of recurrent interaction*. This would exclude all casual, momentary meetings of people, such as the lineup at a ticket window. This definition would include the family, the friendship clique, organizations like a club or church organization—any kind of collective contact between people who repeatedly interact according to some pattern of actions and relationships.

Another usage (which your authors prefer) is *any number of people who share consciousness of membership together and of interaction*. By this definition, two persons waiting for a bus would not be a group but would become a group if they started a conversation, a fight, or any other interaction. A number of people waiting at a stop light would be an *aggregation* or a *collectivity*, not a group, unless something—a street orator, an accident, a suicide—caught their attention and held their interest, converting them into an *audience*, which is one kind of group (see Chapter 19). A busload of passengers would not ordinarily be a group, because they have no consciousness of interaction with each other. It is possible that interaction may develop and groups may form in the course of the trip. When children begin to play together, or boy meets girl, or business executives discover a common interest in the stock market or the baseball game, groups begin to develop—transient and fleeting though they be.

The essence of the social group is not physical closeness but a consciousness of interaction. A stimulus incident may change an aggregation into a group. For example, let a bus driver announce that he is stopping for a beer, and the aggregation of passengers promptly becomes a group, sharing their annoyance and protesting this delay. This consciousness of interaction is necessary for them to be a group, while mere physical presence is not necessary at all. Many groups meet rarely if at all but interact by telephone, letters, bulletins, and magazines. The term *group* covers many kinds of human interaction.

GROUP AND INDIVIDUAL

As shown in Chapter 4, it is through group experience that human beings become distinctively *human*. We enter the world as animals with extraordinary learning capacities (and, according to most religions, with a soul). It is through group experience that we internalize the norms of our culture, and come to share values, goals, sentiments, and most of what sets us apart from the other animals.

Is it true, as is sometimes said, that the group is no more than the sum total of its members? Does the following quotation answer that question?

The tendency to form into groups is found in many species. (*Elliot Erwitt/ Magnum*)

Take each of us alone, a man apart from the Cheyenne people who remember the same things and wish for the same things. Take each one of us that way, and you have nothing but a man who cannot respect himself because he is a failure in the white man's way. A man who does not respect himself cannot make a good future. There is no strength in his spirit. Now take all of us together as Cheyenne people. Then our names are not the names of failures. They are the names of great and generous hunters who fed the people, fighters who died for freedom just as white men's heroes died, holy men who filled us with the power of God. Take us together that way and there is a drink for every man in the cup of self-respect, and we will have the strength of spirit to decide what to do and to do it. We will do good things as a tribe that is growing and changing that we cannot do as individual men cut off from their forefathers. (From an introduction to a Northern Cheyenne land consolidation program, quoted in *Indian Affairs*, Newsletter of the Association on American Indian Affairs, Inc., no. 37, New York, June, 1960.)

This statement shows how a person's feelings and behavior are affected by group membership. Whether one is a coward or a hero may be more greatly determined by group ties than by any individual characteristics, as is shown by sociological studies of military groups.

During the Korean war a few American soldiers who were prisoners of war agreed to cooperate with the enemy and propagandized against the American cause. Physical hardship, poor food, limited medical attention, and inadequate shelter played a part in weakening their resistance, but these conditions were not considered sufficiently severe to account for their behavior. There was some torture and often the threat of torture but this affected only a few of the prisoners. The Chinese used something more powerful than physical force—*the systematic attack upon group ties*, described by Biderman [1960] and Schein [1960]. Just as "dying is easy for anyone left

alone in a concentration camp,"[1] death came easily to prisoners of war who were isolated from their fellows.

The Chinese used such techniques as solitary confinement, isolation of small groups of prisoners, and frequent shifting of personnel to hamper formation of cohesive groups. More important, they also sought to divide prisoners in their attitude to each other and to cut them off from any feeling of effective links with the homeland. Casual information gathered in interviews was used to convince prisoners that all the others were informers and that they might as well give in, too. If a prisoner resisted what he thought were improper demands from the Chinese, the whole unit was denied food or a chance to sleep until the objector had been forced to come round by his own buddies.

By contrast with the Korean war, the Vietnam war produced proportionately fewer examples of "incorrect" behavior among American POWs.

This change is usually attributed to a new system of training instituted after the Korean war which stressed that, above all else, a POW must keep in communication with other POWs and obey the senior American officer at all times. He was no longer a lonely and abandoned individual but part of a functioning group. It wasn't easy to do, since the North Vietnamese frequently moved prisoners, seldom kept them in large groups, and tried to restrict communication.

The role of communication and group ties in sustaining morale among American POWs is especially striking, since American public opinion was sharply divided about the war in Vietnam. The North Vietnamese constantly reminded the POWs of this antiwar feeling but apparently with little effect on POW attitude or behavior.

In this respect behavior of American POWs

[1] An anonymous concentration-camp survivor, quoted in *Life*, Aug. 18, 1958, p. 90.

in Vietnam is similar to the way the German army survived years of unbroken defeats in World War II. During the war the Allies nursed the hope that "psychological warfare" could undermine the German soldier's faith in his cause and his loyalty to his government and thus impair his fighting morale. Postwar studies [Shils and Janowitz, 1948] have shown that this approach was not very effective. It was rooted in the unsound theory that the soldier is sustained mainly by loyalty to his country and faith in the rightness of its cause, whereas postwar investigations found that *he is sustained mainly by his unity with, and loyalty to, the small military units to which he is attached.* As long as the soldier's immediate group— the primary group which we shall analyze within a few pages—remained integrated, he continued to resist. Even those who were critical of their "cause" remained effective soldiers because of their group loyalties. Among the comparatively few German deserters, their failure to have become fully absorbed into the primary-group life of the army was far more important than any political or ideological doubts. Long after their cause was clearly lost, most German units of all sizes continued to resist until their supplies were exhausted or they were physically overwhelmed.

American military leaders fully recognize the difference between an aggregation and a group. After each of our recent wars (World War II, Korea, Vietnam) they commissioned social scientists to find out why some units performed so much better than others. Each time they received the same reply: Given adequate training, equipment, and supplies, performance differences were due mainly to the sense of unity and cohesion within differing units. A unit with a continuous stream of replacements cannot be a top outfit. No matter how well qualified as individual soldiers, the replacements are not worth much until they become real members of the group. Our military leaders are now trying to reduce transfers and would like to keep the same

persons together in a company for an entire three-year tour of duty [Webbe, 1980]. In such ways, scientific knowledge about how groups operate is being put to practical use.

Is it only in warfare that the individual develops a sacrificial loyalty and a heroic courage? By no means. We cite research on military groups (even though some may find this displeasing) because they have been more intensively studied than most other kinds of groups, and from this study we have learned something about groups of all kinds. We see how the group is a vital social reality, with profound effect upon the behavior of individuals in all social situations.

Knowledge about group behavior can be applied to any kind of group. For example, the success of Japanese industry is attributed, in part, to its success in cultivating group loyalties. Where American workers and managers typically glare at one another across a gulf of suspicion and distrust, Japanese workers and managers are partners in a joint effort to improve quality and cut costs [Ouchi, 1981; Pascale and Athos, 1981]. American managers have often tried to promote worker loyalty to "the company" but have had little success. Workers have generally perceived this as a manipulative trick not as a genuine sharing.

To put this in terms of sociological theory, Japanese industry is organized along the functionalist assumption that workers, managers, and stockholders share a common interest in the success of the enterprise. Management (at least in the larger corporations) provides lifetime job security, along with many social and recreational services. Workers are intensely loyal to the company, sing the company song daily in many companies, and join in frequent meetings to seek ways to increase productivity or improve quality. American industrial relations are structured along the conflict theory assumption of conflicting interests of workers and management. It is assumed that management will try to squeeze as much work from labor as possible with as little pay as necessary and that labor will seek as much pay as it can get for as little work as necessary. Wages and working conditions are negotiated through a power contest called "collective bargaining," with contractually specified "fringe benefits" instead of company "paternalism." Functionalist theory assumes that workers tend, in the long run, to get about what they are worth; conflict theory assumes that wages are determined by workers' effective use of bargaining power. Thus it makes a great deal of difference in group relations whether functionalist or conflict theory is followed.

SOME KINDS OF GROUPS

In-groups and Out-groups

There are some groups to which I belong—my family, my church, my clique, my profession, my race, my sex, my nation—any group which I precede with the pronoun, "my." These are *in-groups*, because I feel I belong to them. There are other groups to which I do not belong—other families, cliques, occupations, races, nationalities, religions, the other sex—these are *out-groups*, for I am outside them.

The least advanced primitive societies live in small, isolated bands which are usually clans of kinsfolk. It was kinship which located one's in-group and out-group, and when two strangers met, the first thing they had to do was establish the relationship. If kinship could be established, then they were friends—both members of the in-group. If no relationship could be established, then in many societies they were enemies and acted accordingly.

In modern society, people belong to so many groups that a number of their in-group and out-group relationships may overlap. Members of the senior class treat freshmen as an out-group most of the time, but in the stadium both unite as an in-group cheering for the same team. Similarly, those who have an in-group relationship as members of the same church may be in different political parties; members who work together in the PTA may find that they are no longer in the same in-group when someone plans a party at the country club.

Exclusion from an in-group can be a brutal process. Most primitive societies treated outsiders as part of the animal kingdom; many had no separate words for "enemy" and "stranger," showing that they made no distinction. Not too different was the attitude of the Nazis, who excluded the Jews from the human race. Rudolf Hoess, who commanded the Auschwitz concentration camp in which 700,000 Jews were put to death, characterized this slaughter as "the removal of racial-biological foreign bodies."[2]

In-groups and out-groups are important, then, because they affect behavior. From fellow members of an in-group we expect rec-

> ## EXCLUSION FROM A GROUP CAN BE BRUTAL
>
> In a work so dangerous [logging], it is vital to cull the unfit and the incompatible. A streak of meanness often is the first sign that a man is on the way out. . . . The victim may have his lunch destroyed or his clothes set fire; then another man may invite him behind a tree for a faceful of knuckles. Finally the hook tender—the boss union logger—may simply say, "Go on down the road. We don't want to see you anymore".
>
> (William E. Blundell, "Natural Enemies: To Loggers, the Woods Are Dark and Deep—But Far from Lovely," *Wall Street Journal*, Dec. 8, 1981, p. 16.)
>
> Can one be an effective and successful worker if one fails to gain acceptance into the work group?

[2] See Rudolf Hoess, *Commandant of Auschwitz*, tr. by Constantine Fitzgibbon, The World Publishing Company, Cleveland, 1960, in which Hoess tells with nostalgic pride how efficiently he organized this operation; reviewed in *Time*, Mar. 28, 1960, p. 110.

ognition, loyalty, and helpfulness. From out-groups our expectation varies with the kind of out-group. From some out-groups we expect hostility; from others, a more or less friendly competition; from still others, indifference. From the sex out-group we may expect neither hostility nor indifference; yet in our behavior a difference undeniably remains. The 12-year-old boy who shuns girls grows up to become a romantic lover and spends most of his life in matrimony. Yet when men and women meet on social occasions they tend to split into one-sex groups, perhaps because each sex is bored by many of the conversational interests of the other. The clique is one kind of in-group. Thus our behavior is affected by the particular kind of in-group or out-group which is involved.

SOCIAL DISTANCE.   We are not equally involved in all our in-groups. One might, for example, be a passionate Democrat and a rather indifferent Rotarian. Nor do we feel equally distant from all our out-groups. A loyal Democrat will feel far closer to the Republicans than to the Communists. Bogardus [1958, 1959] and others [Westie, 1959] have developed the concept *social distance* to measure the *degree of closeness or acceptance we feel* toward other groups. While most often used with reference to racial groups, social distance refers to closeness between groups of all kinds (see Table 8-1).

Social distance is measured either by direct observation of people interacting, or more often by questionnaires in which people are asked what kind of people they would accept in particular relationships. In these questionnaires, a number of groups may be listed and the informants asked to check whether they would accept a member of each group as a neighbor, as a fellow worker, as a marriage partner, and so on through a series of relationships.

A social-distance test, administered to white students in the United States in 1972, showed a low (favorable to medium or neutral) social-distance score for all groups. A similar test administered to South African whites about the same time indicated a high rate of social distance. The South African social distance was great not only between white and black but also between white South Africans and recent European immigrants to that country [Lever, 1972; Brown, 1973]. Thus, while in-groups and out-groups are found in all societies, feelings of social distance are greater in some societies than in others.

The social-distance questionnaires may not accurately measure what people actually would do if a member of another group sought to become a friend or neighbor. The social-distance scale is only an attempt to measure one's feeling of unwillingness to associate equally with a group. What a person will actually do in a situation also depends upon the circumstances of the situation (situational determinants of behavior), which will be illustrated at some length in the chapter on race and ethnic relations.

REFERENCE GROUPS.   There are groups which are important to us as models even though we may not be a part of the group. The opinions of "high society" may be important to the social climber who has not yet made the social register. At times the in-group and the reference group may be the same, as when the teenager gives more weight to the opinions of the gang than to those of his or her teachers. Sometimes an out-group is a reference group: American Indians used war paint to impress their enemies, and each sex dresses to impress the other sex. A reference group is any group to which we *refer* when making judgments—any group whose value judgments become our value judgments. You will recall the concepts of the reference group and the looking-glass self, and how the young child is interested in the reactions of everyone with whom it is in contact, while the more mature person selects particular groups whose approval—or disapproval—is especially desired.

Social distance is sometimes visible . . . and sometimes enforced by law. (*Bob Adelman/Magnum; Georg Gerster/Photo Researchers, Inc.*)

TABLE 8-1

AVERAGE SOCIAL DISTANCE FELT TOWARD VARIOUS DEVIANT GROUPS*

Groups (in order of increasing intolerance)	Mean social distance (Range 1 to 7)
Intellectuals	2.0
Ex-mental patients	2.9
Atheists	3.4
Ex-convicts	3.5
Gamblers	3.6
Beatniks	3.9
Alcoholics	4.0
Adulterers	4.1
Political radicals	4.3
Marijuana smokers	4.9
Prostitutes	5.0
Lesbians	5.2
Homosexuals	5.3

*Responses of a representative public sample. (Social distance is a measure of acceptance or rejection. A score of 1.0 would show little or no social distance, while a score of 7.0 would show great social distance.)
Source: J. L. Simmons, *Deviants*, Glendessary Press, Berkeley, Calif., 1969, p. 33.

Would any of these groups be rated differently today?

STEREOTYPES. A *stereotype* is *a group-shared image of another group or category of people* Stereotypes can be positive (the kindly, dedicated family doctor), negative (the unprincipled, opportunistic politician), or mixed (the dedicated, fussy, sexless old-maid teacher). Stereotypes are applied indiscriminately to all members of the stereotyped group, without allowance for individual differences. Stereotypes are never entirely untrue, for they must bear *some* resemblance to the characteristics of the persons stereotyped or they would not be recognized. But stereotypes are always distorted, in that they exaggerate and universalize *some* of the characteristics of *some* of the members of the stereotyped group.

Just how stereotypes begin is not known. Once the stereotype has become a part of the culture, it is maintained by *selective perception* (noting only the confirming incidents or cases and failing to note or remember the exceptions), *selective interpretation* (interpreting observations in terms of the stereotype: e.g., Jews are "pushy" while gentiles are "ambitious"), *selective identification* ("they look like school teachers . . ."), and *selective exception* "he really doesn't act at all Jewish"). All these processes involve a reminder of the stereotype, so that even exceptions and incorrect identifications serve to feed and sustain the stereotype.

Stereotypes are nonetheless constantly changing. The dowdy old-maid teacher is so rare today that this particular stereotype is virtually dead. A stereotype generally dies when confirming illustrations can no longer be found.

Stereotypes and Humor Out-groups are often shown in stereotyped ways which emphasize their imperfections. This prevents us from seeing them as individual human beings with the normal assortment of virtues and vices. Stereotypes thus enable us to apply a double standard under which we assume the best of our own group and the worst of others.

Stereotypes form the basis of ethnic humor. Some years ago comedians used many ethnic stereotypes (thrifty Scots, money-grubbing Jews, quarrelsome Irish, dumb Swedes). Sometimes white Americans would be made up as blacks in minstrel shows in order to present the lazy, unreliable, yet somewhat cunning behavior attributed to blacks. At other times dialect shows emphasized the inability of immigrants to speak proper English.

Today, ethnic humor has changed but not disappeared. It is now acceptable to present stereotypes of the majority group, while minority comedians may use negative stereotypes to illustrate attitudes which are now obsolete. On television, Archie Bunker exaggerated the stereotype of the conservative, white, blue-collar worker, while Maude on another TV show presented a stereotyped image of the white liberal determined to treat the maid as a companion whether she wished it or not. Several predominantly black pro-

One negative sterotype, the belief that feminists are unattractive, has been tested by research. At the University of Connecticut, 30 women were asked their attitude about the women's movement. They divided about half and half, with some supporters and some opponents. Photographs of the women were taken and then shown to a group of students who showed a high measure of agreement when ranking them for attractiveness. The more attractive and the less attractive women were equally distributed among the feminists and the anti-feminists. When another group of students were shown the photographs and asked to pick the supporters and opponents of the women's movement, the ster-

eotype prevailed. Invariably, the less attractive were identified as feminists. The interesting thing is that the students' own attitudes did not influence their acceptance or rejection of the stereotype. As the report concludes—"Apparently, even feminists buy the idea that beauties are not feminists and feminists aren't beauties."

(Phillip A. Goldberg and Marc Gottesdiener, "Another Put-Down of Women? Perceived Attractiveness as a Function of Support for the Feminist Movement," *Journal of Personality and Social Psychology,* 32:113–115, July 1975.)

How do you suppose the unflattering stereotype of the feminist arose?

grams used stereotypes as a put-down in confrontations between their characters. At one time stereotypes in drama and story were accepted as true portraits. Today they are funny because they are regarded as burlesque rather than truth.

Stereotypes are important because people treat members of other groups in terms of the stereotyped views they hold of that group. They interact, at least initially, with the stereotype rather than with the true person. This results in many individual injustices, since only some persons in a group fully fit the stereotype.

Significance of Stereotypes Stereotypes are standard weapons of political debate. Political victories often hinge upon hanging an unflattering stereotype upon one's opponent. The stereotype of the feminist as a grim, humorless, sexless man-hater surely helped to defeat the Equal Rights Amendment. Much political strategy centers upon promoting positive (our side) or negative (their side) stereotypes.

Stereotypes also affect the behavior of those who are stereotyped. A flattering stereotype is copied, while an unflattering stereotype is sometimes avoided but not always. Treatment

in terms of the stereotype may encourage people to become more like the stereotype even when it is an unflattering one. We recall from the study of socialization and the looking-glass self in Chapter 4 how people tend to become what others think them to be. When women were generally assumed to have no interests in or talent for anything but the homemaker role and the opportunity-reward system rewarded them for being good homemakers but punished them if they sought anything else, it is not surprising that most women did not seriously *want* anything else. Thus the stereotype operates as a self-fulfilling prophesy, molding feelings and behavior in the direction of the stereotype.

Primary and Secondary Groups

Primary groups are those in which we come to know other people intimately as individual personalities. We do this through social contacts that are *informal, intimate, personal,* and *total* in that they involve many parts of the person's life experience. In the primary group, such as family, clique, or set of close friends, the social relationships tend to be relaxed. The members are interested in one another as persons. They confide hopes and fears,

Primary groups are small, intimate, personal, and relationship-oriented. (*Nancy Hays/ Monkmeyer*)

share experiences, gossip agreeably, and fill the need for intimate human companionship. Primary groups must be small if all members are to know another intimately, while secondary groups can be of any size. In the *secondary group* the social contacts are *formal, impersonal, segmental,* and *utilitarian.* One is not concerned with the other person as a person but as a functionary who is filling a role. Personal qualities are not important; performance—only that part, or segment, of the total personality involved in playing a role—is important. The secondary group might be a labor union or a trade association, a country club, or a PTA, or it might be two persons bargaining briefly over a store counter. In any case the group exists to serve a specific, limited purpose involving only a segment of the personalities of the members.

The terms "primary" and "secondary" thus describe a type of relationship and do not imply that one is more important than the other. The primary group may do some work, but it is judged by the quality of its human relationships rather than by its efficiency in getting work done. The secondary group may be congenial, but its principal purpose is to get work done.

One does not consider a home "good" just because the house is clean. Primary groups are not judged so much by their "efficiency" in performing some task as by the emotional satisfactions they bring to their members. Thus, the quartet of ladies who meet for bridge Tuesday afternoons may play a pretty sloppy bridge game but share a lot of pleasant, relaxed conversation. Tournament and duplicate bridge players are more like secondary groups. Here, virtual or total strangers meet and play to win. A "good partner" is a skillful player who wastes no time on distracting small talk. The major goal is a winning score (and master points chalked up), not sociability. A good lunch-table clique is one that has fun; a good labor union is one that protects its members' interests. Primary groups are judged by the satisfying human response they supply; secondary groups are judged by their ability to perform a task or achieve a goal. In brief, *primary groups are relationship-oriented*, whereas *secondary groups are goal-oriented.*

Primary and secondary groups are important because feelings and behavior are different. It is in the primary group that personality is formed. In the primary group one finds intimacy, sympathy, and a comfortable sharing of many interests and activities. In the secondary group one finds an effective tool for achieving certain purposes, but often at the price of suppressing one's true feelings. For example, the salesperson must be cheerful and polite, even with a splitting headache and when the customer is a boor. The con-

cepts are useful because they describe important differences in behavior.

TASK GROUPS. Some groups are neither clearly primary nor secondary but are intermediate, with some features of each. *Task groups* (or task-oriented groups) are *small groups formed to do some task or set of tasks* [Nixon, 1979, p. 18]. They include work teams, committees, and panels of many sorts. Some scholars consider the task group to be the most common form of group in our society [Fisher, 1980, p. 3].

Task groups resemble primary groups in being small, for only small groups are efficient work units. This is why large labor forces are broken down into small work teams. Task groups also resemble primary groups in that interaction is typically face-to-face and informal. But the task-group contacts are impersonal, segmental, and utilitarian. Members

A task group is a small work group, not clearly either primary or secondary in nature. (*Sybil Shelton/Monkmeyer*)

are not much interested in one another as persons and are not concerned with the entire person but just with work performance in the task group.

GEMEINSCHAFT AND GESELLSCHAFT. Somewhat similar to the concept of primary and secondary groups are the concepts of *Gemeinschaft* and *Gesellschaft*, developed by the German sociologist Ferdinand Tönnies [1887, tr. 1957]. These two terms translate roughly as "community" and "society." The gemeinschaft is a social system in which most relationships are personal or traditional, and often both. A good example is the feudal manor, a small community held together by a combination of personal relationships and status obligations. Although great inequality existed, the lord of the manor was personally known to his subjects, while their duties to him were balanced by his obligation for their welfare. When money was used, economic transactions were governed by the concepts of a just price; more often the people involved simply carried out a network of customary obligations to one another. Written documents were scarce, formal contracts unknown, bargaining rare, and behavior of all types operated in traditional ways that were known and accepted by all the community. Children had little hope of raising their position in life and equally little fear of falling beneath parental status. Except for occasional feast days, life was monotonous; but loneliness was rare in a community of lifelong neighbors.

In the gesellschaft, the society of tradition is replaced with the society of contract. In this society neither personal attachment nor traditional rights and duties are important. The relationships between people are determined by bargaining and defined in written agreements. Relatives are often separated because people move about and live among strangers. Commonly accepted codes of behavior are largely replaced by rational—or

"cold-blooded"—calculation of profit and loss. The gesellschaft flourishes in the modern metropolitan city. Some of the contrasting characteristics of gemeinschaft and gesellschaft relationships are summarized in this comparison:

Gemeinschaft relationships	Gesellschaft relationships
Personal	Impersonal
Informal	Formal, contractual
Traditional	Utilitarian
Sentimental	Realistic, "hard-boiled"
General	Specialized

Thus in the gemeinschaft, primary-group relationships were dominant, while in the gesellschaft, secondary-group relationships gained in importance.

THE SECONDARY-GROUP TREND

Our sentiments and emotional ties are centered in primary groups, but the modern trend toward a gesellschaft society based on secondary groups has been irresistible. The small principalities of feudal Europe have given way to national states, and the intimate association of master and worker in the guild workshop has yielded to the giant corporation employing thousands of people. Population has moved from the country to towns and cities, and a lifetime in one home has become a rarity as about one American family in five moves each year.

An industrialized urban society attacks the primary group in at least two ways. First, it increases the relative proportion of secondary-group contacts, as one activity after another is withdrawn from the primary group and assumed as a secondary-group function. Second, the primary-group associations which remain are at the mercy of secondary-group needs. Changes in industry may move the wage earner about, disrupting local associations. A prolonged economic depression, the result of a maladjustment of secondary relationships, may deprive parents of earning power and substitute the relief administrator as a symbol of authority. Military needs may take one out of the family and to the other side of the world. The worker's family must adjust itself to whatever working hours the corporation finds most profitable. Negotiations between the union and the corporation may result in work changes which break up informal primary groups formed on the job. The "little red schoolhouse" where a small group of children and a teacher formed an intimate primary group lasting for years is succeeded by the consolidated school, drawing hundreds of children from a large area and shifting them about from class to class and teacher to teacher. Scores of similar examples show how many primary groupings have become transient and changing units, swept along by the heedlessly changing needs of a gesellschaft society.

Contributions of the Gesellschaft

While the trend to secondary-group relationships in the gesellschaft has brought sacrifices, it has also brought benefits. Most obvious is the efficiency of large-scale impersonal organizations in which sentiment surrenders to practicality. The huge gains in material comfort and in life expectancy in the modern world would be impossible without the rise of goal-directed secondary organizations in which the paternal squire has been replaced by the efficiency expert and the production manager.

Nor has the rise of the gesellschaft and the accompanying division of labor had only material advantages. These changes have opened channels of opportunity and specializations of function which, while they fragment society, also open a greater chance to develop individual talents. Much has been written about how modern societies are "oppressive" and "alienating"; yet earlier societies offered

far fewer choices and opportunities for self-fulfillment. The contrast between the thousands of occupations in the metropolis and the handful of pursuits in the rural village shows how a society dominated by secondary groups opens the way for specialized careers.

The secondary group also has a tendency to impose patterns of conformity on its members. In this way it offers a counterbalance to the prejudices or vested interests of the immediate locality. Since its boundaries extend beyond the primary group, it forces people to assume a broader perspective. This difference in attitudes may be seen in the tendency of religious organizations, operating on a national or international scale, to promote viewpoints which may be unpopular in local congregations. A case in point is the decision of the national Protestant Episcopal church to ordain women—a step vigorously opposed by many parishes [Seabury, 1978, p. 40].

To put this in "academese": Large national organizations tend to be *universalistic*—that is, guided by national viewpoints, interests, and values; local groups and organizations tend to be *particularistic*—that is, guided by local viewpoints, interests, and values. Sometimes the universalistic guidelines bring more humane social policy, as in the case of the voting rights which blacks in some parts of the country gained largely because of pressure from other parts of the country. And sometimes universalistic guidelines bring oppression and inhumanity, as in the massacre of the Jews in Germany or the "liquidation of the kulaks" (small landowner-farmers who resisted collectivization in the Soviet Union). The present struggle of the Amish in the United States to maintain their own schools taught by noncertified Amish teachers is an example of the clash between universalistic and particularistic values.

Persistence of Primary Groups

The secondary group has not replaced the primary group. In fact, the two major primary

199

Groups and Associations

Second-Best Wishes: For $25, a Chicago firm will remember you with a card on your birthday, Christmas, and eight other holidays of your choice. The Personalized Services Group says its "personalized greetings let you know someone cares and is thinking about you,"—even if it's only you.

(*Moneysworth*, December 1981, p. 2.)

Why would there be a market for such a service? Who would be likely to use it?

groups, the clique and the family, appear to be more essential than ever. The clique is a small group of intimates with strong in-group feelings based on common sentiments and interests. It may develop in almost any group situation. Nearly every secondary group shelters a large number of cliques which provide personal intimacy within a large impersonal organization.

Despite a high divorce rate and some experimentation with communal living, most of the world's population still live in families and probably always will. Furthermore, today's family is steadily becoming less directed toward work-related goals and more concerned with human relationships. Yesterday's family was primarily a work crew, sometimes a brutally repressive one; today's family is primarily a companionship group and a perfect example of primary-group persistence. Primary groups persist in a secondary-group-dominated world because of the human need for intimate, sympathetic association.

Extensive research literature shows the human need for affection and intimate response. Loneliness, isolation, and the breaking of treasured human relationships are among our prime causes of illness and death [Lynch, 1977]. A nine-year longitudinal study of 7,000 adults finds that people with a strong "social network" of friends and relatives are less than half as likely to die in a given year as persons with no such network [Berkman, 1980]. Even having a pet is associated with longevity, although whether the relationship is causative or selective in not known [Curtis, 1982]. (That is, people with pets may live longer because pets improve their emotional lives [causative relationship], or it may be that the healthy people are more likely to want and keep pets [selective relationship]).

Most people cannot function well unless they belong to a small group of people who really care what happens to them. When a factory moves, workers often accept unemployment rather than relocate, even when relocation costs are paid for them. Ferman [1977] states that ". . . blue collar families rely heavily on a 'network' of neighbors and relatives for friendship and exchange of services. To pick up and move," he says, "they may have the same job instability in the new place, but they're not going to have the same network to fall back on." Whenever people are ripped from family and friends and thrust into large, impersonal, anonymous groups, as in a college dormitory or an army camp, they feel such great need for primary groups that they promptly form them.

Primary Groups Within Secondary Groups

If we classified groups according to the extent to which they show primary- or secondary-group traits, the result would be a listing of secondary groups such as the army, the corporation, and the national state, and a list of primary groups such as the family, the clique, and the gang. Proceeding in this fashion, we should then contrast the impersonal goal-oriented nature of the large organization with the personal, relationship-oriented focus of smaller intimate groups. Such a separation is often assumed when we attempt to analyze the efficiency of large organizations. If we are interested in the productivity of industrial labor, we might study the goals, techniques, and rewards of the factory and then look at

There are primary groups within secondary groups. (*Sybil Shelton/Monkmeyer*)

the character and training of the individuals who make up the labor force.

The fallacy of this approach is that it overlooks the extent to which every large organization is a network of small primary groups. A person is not simply a unit in an organization chart designed by top management; he or she is also a member of a smaller informal group with its own structure and its own system of statuses and roles which define the behavior of its members. In the factory the worker finds a place in a group of peers with its own leadership, from which the supervisor is usually excluded. The supervisor is part of "management" and therefore cannot be part of a worker in-group. Since workers need the approval and support of the clique more than the approval of their

supervisors, they meet the demands of management only when these demands harmonize with their in-group needs and attitudes.

The influence of the primary group is one reason why incentive pay plans giving the worker a bonus for greater output have frequently been ineffective. The logic of such plans is that many workers will work harder if paid in proportion to the work they do. The major defect in such plans is that they would destroy the unity of primary groups. Rather than a number of equals cooperating together, the work gang would become a number of competing individuals each striving to outdo the others. Aside from the strain of continuous competition, this situation threatens the workers' social relationships. As a defense, factory cliques develop a norm

Primary groups persist in a world
dominated by secondary-groups.

that provide intimacy and personal response in an otherwise impersonal situation. While these and other primary groups are often destroyed or modified by the impact of secondary groups, the primary groups in turn exert a major influence on the secondary group. Primary groups may resist the goal-directed efforts of secondary organizations; or they may tie the organization together, helping members to cooperate in their work tasks.

GROUP DYNAMICS

For a long time sociologists were busy trying to convince a skeptical world that the group was real and not simply a collection of people. Only after World War II did sociologists (and scholars from psychology, communications, and management) begin the serious study of small groups [Bales, 1950; Homans, 1950; Bavelas, 1962]. *Group dynamics* is the *scientific study of the interaction within small groups.* For example, Bales developed a method for studying the interaction within a small problem-solving group. The group was observed through one-way glass and each person's statements were recorded for "interaction process analysis" under one of twelve categories such as: Shows solidarity, raises others' status, gives help, reward; Agrees, shows passive acceptance, understands, concurs, complies; Asks for opinion, evaluation, analysis, expression of feeling; Shows antagonism, deflates others' status, defends or asserts self. When statements or responses were entered on a chart, a profile of each person's interaction could be plotted, patterns of leadership or resistance could be documented, and a composite profile of the entire group's behavior could be shown. A three-stage sequence of stages could be recognized in the problem-solving process: (1) Orientation stage: members ask and give information; (2) Evaluation stage: members assess information, share opinions; (3) Control stage: members suggest solutions, reach conclusion. This was

of a "fair day's work." The worker who attempts to ignore this norm is the butt of ridicule, ostracism, and possible violence. Management may employ time-and-motion-study experts to decide a "reasonable" output, but new norms cannot be effective unless they are also accepted by the worker primary groups [Davis, 1972, pp. 488–490].

While the primary group in the secondary setting can be an obstacle, it can also be a positive aid in the accomplishment of organizational goals [Dunphy, 1972, pp. 23–25]. At times primary groups may even violate the rules of the larger secondary organization in order to get things done. If the formal rules are not always workable in all situations, primary worker groups simply trim some corners—that is, break a few rules—in order to get the work out. For example, air traffic controllers, who direct plane landings and takeoffs, routinely "shave" the specified minimum distance between planes when the weather is good. An exact following of the rules would cause long delays and stack-ups, thereby increasing inconvenience and danger.

Just as we cannot realistically consider the individual apart from society, so we cannot understand secondary and primary groups completely except in relation to each other. In modern society, many of the former functions of primary groups have been assumed by large, impersonal, goal-directed secondary groups. Each of these secondary groups, however, creates a new network of primary groups one of the first efforts to observe systematically a group in action and to plot or diagram its behavior [Bales, 1950; Bales and Strodtbeck, 1951].

In another set of experiments, Bavelas [1962] arranged groups of five persons in different patterns, such as the circle, the chain, the Y, and the wheel, as shown in Figure 8-1. In the circle everyone had an equal chance to communicate with everyone else; in the other patterns the person at the center had maximum communication and the others were restricted. Morale and leadership turned out to be closely related to centrality of position. Member satisfaction with the situation was greatest in the circle, where no one person emerged as a leader. In the wheel, where the one in the center became the leader, production was greater but group satisfaction less. As an offset to its lower production, the circle

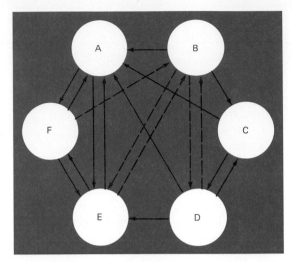

FIGURE 8-2 A sociogram showing the structure of a small group. The circled letters identify group members; solid lines and arrows show the direction of positive attraction or liking; broken lines and arrows show the direction of dislike; lack of any line connecting circles shows neutral feeling.

Which member is probably the most influential? Which seems likely to be expelled from the group?

FIGURE 8-1 Position affects communication networks. Each circle represents a person, and spokes represent communication channels. (*Source: Based on Alex Bavelas, ''Communication Patterns in Task-Oriented Groups,'' in Dorwin Cartwright and Alvin F. Zander (eds.),* Group Dynamics, *Harper & Row, Publishers, Inc., New York, 1962, p. 670.*)

Which person is located so as to be best informed and most influential?

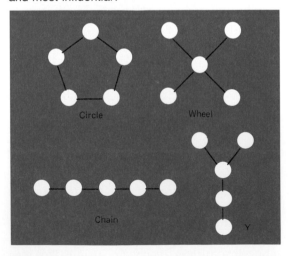

was found to adapt more quickly to new tasks than the other patterns.

All groups have structure. This is the network of relationships and communication patterns among group members. For example, some members are well-liked, others are barely tolerated. The *sociogram*, developed by Moreno [1951] and others, is a picture of the structure of a group, as shown in Figure 8-2. *Sociometry* is the specialty of social psychology that studies, measures, and diagrams social relationships in small groups.

A constant stream of textbooks and research studies in group dynamics now appears under such titles as *Interaction in Small Groups* [Crosbie, 1975], *The Process of Group Communication* [Appelbaum et al., 1979], *Small Group Decision Making* [Fisher, 1980], and *The Small Group* [Nixon, 1980]. Organizations of all sorts, from the military services to the YMCA, are seeking ways to make their operations more effective. We lack space here to review the insights found through small-group research, but they are many and useful. For example, we have known for years that large lecture sections in college are as effective in teaching factual material as small sections, but that small sections generate more intellectual excitement and stimulate more student thinking [Bloom, 1954, pp. 37–38]. Small-group research helps us to know how to make work more effective and less frustrating.

VOLUNTARY ASSOCIATIONS

It has been said that if a planeload of Americans knew they were about to crash, they would appoint a landing committee. De Tocqueville a century and a half ago remarked upon the American habit of forming associations:

> Americans of all ages, all conditions, and all dispositions constantly form associations. They have not only commercial and manufacturing companies, in which all take part, but associations of a thousand other kinds, religious, moral, serious, futile, general or restricted, enormous or diminutive. The Americans make associations to give entertainments, to found seminaries, to build inns, to construct churches, to diffuse books, to send missionaries to the antipodes; in this manner they found hospitals, prisons, and schools. If it is proposed to inculcate some truth or to foster some feeling by the encouragement of a great example, they form a society. Wherever at the head of some new undertaking you see the government in France, or a man of rank in England, in the United States you will be sure to find an association. (Alexis de Tocqueville, *Democracy in America*, II, 106, J. P. Mayer and Max Lerner (eds.), Harper & Row, Publishers, Inc., New York, 1966.)

Voluntary associations are any kind of formal organization in which membership is voluntary. For many people, voluntary associations occupy a good share of their free time.

Structural Features

Most voluntary associations—church organizations, PTA, recreational clubs, neighborhood associations, and others—have volunteer officers, a minimum constitution (if anyone can find it), and bylaws or procedures which are highly "flexible" and sometimes forgotten or ignored, In such organizations, the informal aspects greatly overshadow the "formal organization" aspects, as the association operates vaguely and loosely according to *Robert's Rules of Order*.

Where membership is fairly small, with a general consensus upon simple goals, such informal operation is highly efficient. It helps people do things with a minimum of bureaucratic fuss. Where membership is large or geographically scattered, and when goals or policies are controversial, a more formal and rigid organization develops. A large association with a scattered membership, such as the National Rifle Association or Rotary International, must have a bureaucracy with a paid professional staff that conducts routines and an elected board of directors that determines policies. In practice, however, the function of the board of directors is generally to approve the policies which the professional staff has developed and "sold" to the board. While the membership theoretically controls the organization, actual control is by a small clique of officers and professionals. This tendency for all large groups and organizations to fall under the control of a small clique of active members has been called by Robert Michels [1949] the "iron law of oligarchy." (The term "oligarchy" means "rule by the few.")

Functions of Voluntary Associations

Voluntary associations come in three main types: personal interest, social service, and political action. They serve the following functions:

OUTLET FOR PERSONAL INTERESTS. When one wishes to pursue an interest which most other people do not share, the usual answer is the voluntary association. Those who enjoy golf can form a golf club, since taxpayers may decline to finance adult playgrounds. When birth control was too controversial for governments to support, individuals could establish voluntary planned-parenthood associations. A variety of voluntary associations thus provide a type of "cultural pluralism," in which varied interests can be supported within the same society. The voluntary association enables a minority of people to pursue their goals without being held back by an indifferent or hostile majority.

TESTING GROUND FOR SOCIAL PROGRAMS. The voluntary association can develop a program and so demonstrate its value that it is ultimately taken over by the church, the school, or the state. The Sunday school began as an individual project by Robert Raikes, then was promoted through the London Sunday School Society, and is now an organic part of most Protestant churches. Planned-parenthood programs are today supported, in part, by federal grants. Most welfare functions of the modern state were born in voluntary associations which saw a social need, pioneered a program, and educated the public to the point where government was expected to assume responsibility.

STRUCTURE FOR CONTINUING SERVICE PROGRAMS. When the social services pioneered by voluntary associations become subsidized by or assumed by government, these services generally become more generously financed and more widely available to people. They also tend to discourage voluntary services, replacing them with service programs that are bureaucratic, impersonal, inflexible, elaborately regulated, and enormously more expensive [Glazer, 1983]. Yet voluntary associations continue to provide some social services indefinitely—Salvation Army shelters for homeless men, disaster relief from the Red Cross, food kitchens operated by churches, and many other services from the "service clubs" (Rotary, Kiwanis, Lions) and United Fund agencies. No other country approaches the United States in its range of voluntary service programs.

CHANNEL FOR POLITICAL ACTION. The voluntary association enables the private citizen to share in making major social decisions. Political-action groups, ranging from Naders Raiders to Moral Majority, and from the League of Women's Voters to the National Right to Life Committee have been channels for individuals to share in the democratic process.

Participation in Voluntary Associations

Although voluntary associations provide a means for individuals to increase their social power by banding together, this is more true of some types of people than of others. The middle and upper classes are more likely than the lower classes to enter voluntary associations. Smith and Freedman [1972, p. 154] summarize the situation as follows: "All of the work on the topic points to a single direction. Low socio-economic status . . . is highly correlated with low rates of participation and even lower rates of leadership position in organizations."

An exception appears in the case of black-white participation in the United States. In spite of the much larger lower-class proportion of the black population, blacks are more active in voluntary associations than whites [Williams et al., 1973]. Mexican-Americans, by contrast, tend to have a lower rate of participation, although they show some recent evidence of increasing participation [Kutner, 1976].

In the 1960s the "War on Poverty" sought to stimulate organization of poor people in voluntary associations. The effort was not very successful, as most of the poor never became involved [Moynihan, 1969]. Among those who did participate, the "least poor" were most represented and black participation was greater than white [Curtis and Zurcher, 1971]. Yet poor people *can* be mobilized for effective social action under some circumstances, as described in Piven and Cloward's *Poor Peoples' Movements: Why They Succeed; How They Fail* [1977].

Most voluntary associations are class-limited, meaning that most members of an association come from about the same class level. There are few if any welfare clients in the golf club, or wealthy business owners in the Ku Klux Klan. Both rich and poor belong to churches but generally not to the same churches.

One voluntary association which crosses class lines is the volunteer fire department. These departments are the only local defense against fires in many small communities and may also give emergency medical and ambulance service. Members are unpaid, and they often share in organizing social events for fund raising. A variety of skills, both mechanical and organizational, are needed to operate a volunteer fire department. This draws persons from a considerable range of class backgrounds [Jacobs, 1976]. But in most voluntary associations, as in most friendship groups, members usually come from similar class levels [Fischer, 1977, p. 77].

Volunteer fire departments often cross class lines. (© *Marjorie Pickens, 1983*)

Therapeutic Self-Help Groups

Many people face problems which seem beyond their ability to handle. Have you ever tried to lose weight, stop smoking, change drinking habits, or make some other behavior change? Have you ever needed to face the aftermath of mental illness, or the loss of a loved one, or accept a disfigurement? If so, you can appreciate the circumstances which lead people to join with others who have similar problems and to gain help from the group in making an adjustment.

As early as 1936 Dale Carnegie realized that many people who wished to speak effectively could not learn to do so by themselves. He organized "classes" which were really groups which supported and encouraged shy and timid people to speak more fluently in public. The most prominent noncommercial therapeutic group, Alcoholics Anonymous (AA), has operated only since 1935. No one knows how many different types of self-help groups exist, but a 1963 listing showed 263 such organizations [Jackson, 1963]. The number has probably increased since then as many other self-help groups have followed the AA model. Persons sharing a particular problem—an alcoholic spouse, a mentally ill family member, a weight problem, a habit of child abuse, a physical handicap, a handicapped child, or one of many others—assemble to discuss their problem and gain group support in accepting and dealing with it [Katz and Bender, 1976].

One of the main techniques is the use of group pressure to reward each gain toward the behavior goal. An example is the procedure of Take Off Pounds Sensibly (TOPS):

> At the beginning of the agenda, each member must be weighed by an official Weight Recorder. Weights are recorded on Weight Charts and losses or gains for the week are computed. Members weighing less than they did at the previous meeting are designated "Tops" and are decorated with a cardboard heart specifying the amount of weight lost. Members whose weight has remained constant are labeled "Turtles." Members whose weight has increased become "Pigs" and have to wear a pig-shaped label or bib (Hans Toch, *The Social Psychology of Social Movements,* The Bobbs-Merrill Company, Inc., Indianapolis, 1965, p. 73).

Therapeutic self-help groups transform people from helpless victims into persons more capable of controlling their lives. Such groups end one's isolation and offer the consoling knowledge that others face similar problems successfully. The person is not a lonely victim of character weakness or special

---

Why do tribal societies cling to their traditional folk healing rituals even while using modern scientific medicine?

Consider what happens at a *yebachai,* the healing dance used for serious illness by the Navajo of northern Arizona. The patient's relatives and close friends gather from miles around. Night and day without interruption for several days, relays of dancers shuffle in a circle and keep up a singsong chant. The patient drifts in and out of slumber with the hypnotic cadence of the ancient chant as a constant reminder of the emotional support of loved ones, gathered to devote several days to helping him or her get well. For all this, the antiseptic hospital room, with its parade of impersonal technicians and its trickle of ill-at-ease visitors, is simply no match.

The achievements of modern scientific medicine are truly impressive. What they lack is the strong group support given by the folk healing practices of many simple societies. We know that much human illness is psychosomatic, rooted at least in part in emotional stress. Many simple societies have far more effective psychosomatic medicine than we moderns, for they retain group support as a healing therapy.

(Freely adapted from Lyle Saunders, *Cultural Differences and Medical Care,* Russell Sage Foundation, New York, 1954.)

misfortune ending in hopeless disaster; instead, the person is one among many whom the group can help.

SUMMARY

Both strength and weakness grow from the manner in which a person is integrated into a network of groups. A fundamental distinction is that between *out-groups* and *in-groups*—a distinction which has been measured by the use of the concept of *social distance*. *Reference groups* are those which we accept as models and as guides for our judgments and actions. *Stereotypes* are distorted impressions of the characteristics of out groups which have become widely accepted in a society. Emotional conditioning is largely the result of *primary-group* contacts, but modern societies are increasingly affected by the growth of *secondary-group* relationships. While many groups may be easily characterized as either primary or secondary, the two types of influence interact, each affecting the other. Task groups are intermediate, showing some characteristics of primary groups and of secondary groups.

Since the industrial revolution, the trend has been from the traditional *gemeinschaft* toward the *gesellschaft*. This has meant a loss of intimacy and security, which has been countered to some extent by the growth of new primary groups within a secondary-group setting.

Group dynamics studies the interaction within groups and the processes of problem solving and decision making to gain understanding and to solve organizational problems.

Voluntary associations, which are especially numerous in the United States, provide people with an outlet for individual interests, a testing ground for social action programs, a structure for continuing social services, and a channel for political action. Active involvement in voluntary associations is more likely with the middle class than with the lower class, although in the United States blacks seem to be more organizationally committed than whites. *Therapeutic groups* of many kinds may bring support and possibly understanding to troubled people. The noncommercial therapeutic groups uniting people with a common problem (such as AA) have been highly effective with many people.

GLOSSARY

category a number of people sharing some common characteristics.

clique a small group, of intimates with strong in-group feelings based on shared sentiments and interests.

collectivity a physical collection of people.

contractual relating to a formal listing of joint privileges and duties, as distinct from traditional informal assignments.

gemeinschaft a society in which most relationships are either personal or traditional.

gesellschaft a society based on contractual rather than traditional relationships.

group any number of persons sharing a consciousness of membership and of interaction; often used interchangeably with aggregation, collectivity, or category.

group dynamics the scientific study of interaction within small groups.

primary group small group in which people come to know one another intimately as individual personalities; distinct from the impersonal, formal, utilitarian secondary group.

reference group any group accepted as model or guide for our judgments and actions.

secondary group group in which contacts are impersonal, segmental, and utilitarian, as distinct from the small, intimate, highly personal primary group.

social distance degree of closeness to, or acceptance of, members of other groups.

sociogram a graph showing relationships within a group.

sociometry a method of studying, measuring, and diagraming social relationships in small groups.

stereotype a group-shared image of another group or category of people.
voluntary association formal organization directed toward some definite function which one enters voluntarily rather than by ascription.

QUESTIONS AND PROJECTS

1 Why do sociologists have so many different definitions for the term *group?*

2 Comment on this statement: "A group is made up of individuals; and the characteristics of a group are the sum of the characteristics of its members."

3 Is courage an individual character trait or a response to group influences?

4 What differences are found in the in-group–out-group distinction in primitive and modern societies?

5 Why are primary and secondary groups important? In-groups and out-groups?

6 To what extent would you expect social distance to be related to geographic distance?

7 Why was the morale of most American POWs in Vietnam able to survive both the hardships of capture and propaganda stressing the divided nature of American public opinion about the conflict?

8 Is there a sociological explanation of how decent, clean-cut American young men could have been guilty of atrocities in Vietnam?

9 When one notices a person who does not fit the stereotype commonly applied to him or her, does this observation undermine or reinforce the stereotype? Why?

10 Since all groups are different, what is the point of intensive study of a small group?

11 Why is it that only small groups are efficient work units and that large work forces must be divided into small groups to be efficient?

12 What is meant by the statement, "This relationship between A and B may be either causative or selective"?

13 Can you think of any conflicts between groups who are roughly equal in wealth and power?

14 Suppose we wish to change the behavior of a group of people. Which is more likely to be successful: (1) work directly with individuals to change their behavior and thereby to change the group; (2) change the situation or operation of the group, on the assumption that this will affect the behavior of the individuals in the group.

15 Do extracurricular activities on campus resemble voluntary associations in the larger community? Are they a valuable part of the school or simply a waste of time?

16 If you live outside a major city, there is probably a volunteer fire department in your vicinity. Visit the

chief and find out what you can about the regular occupations of the volunteers. Do they represent the kind of community cross section described in the article by Jacobs?

SUGGESTED READINGS

Becker, Tamar: "Black Africans and Black Americans on an American Campus: The African View," *Sociology and Social Research,* 57:168 181, January 1973. A discussion of tension between two groups with a common physical appearance but different cultural backgrounds.

Fisher, B. Aubrey: *Small Group Decision Making: Communication and the Group Process,* McGraw-Hill Book Company, Inc., New York, 1980. A textbook in group communication and decision making.

Gibbard, Graham S., John J. Hartman, and Richard D. Mann (eds.): *Analysis of Groups,* Jossey-Bass, San Francisco, 1974. A series of articles on various aspects of the intensive group experience: T-groups, therapy groups, and encounter groups.

*Gordon, Suzanne: *Loneliness in America,* Simon & Schuster, Inc., New York, 1976. A profile of loneliness from the misunderstood child to the solitary aged person; discusses attempts to combat loneliness; the Singles Business, the Encounter Business, and the Magic Business (EST).

Hunt, Chester L. and Luis La-car: "Social Distance and American Policy," *Sociology and Social Research*, 57:495–509, July 1973. Describes social distance in the Philippines, where Americans are still one of the most accepted groups.

Jacobs, Alan H.: "Volunteer Fireman: Altruism in Action," in W. Arens and Susan P. Montague (eds.), *The American Dimension: Cultural Myths and Social Realities*, Alfred Publishing Company, New York, 1976, pp. 194–205. A discussion of the volunteer fire department as a type of voluntary organization which enlists members of all social classes.

Jacobs, James B.: "Street Gangs Behind Bars," *Social Problems*, 21:395–409, 1974. An analysis of the results when imprisonment of a large number of gang members enabled them to take over the informal group structure of a prison.

Katz, Alfred H. and Eugene I. Bender: *The Strength in Us: Self-Help Groups in the Modern World*, New Viewpoints, a division of Franklin Watts, New York, 1976. A scholarly but popularly written book describing self-help groups both in the United States and in other countries.

Nixon, Howard L., II: *The Small Group*, Prentice-Hall, Inc., Englewood Cliffs, N.J., 1979. A textbook on the sociology of small groups.

Ross, Jack: *An Assembly of Good Fellows: Voluntary Associations in History*, Greenwood Press, Westport, Conn., 1976. A description of the role of voluntary organizations from primitive bands to clubs in nineteenth-century England.

*Smith, Constance and Anne Freedman: *Voluntary Associations: Perspectives on the Literature*, Harvard University Press, Cambridge, Mass., 1972. A comprehensive and readable summary of research on all aspects of voluntary associations.

Tolley, Howard: "Common Cause and Campaign Financing: Reform Liberals 'Open Up' the System," *Intellect*, 106:122–125, October 1977. How a voluntary association changed U.S. election campaign practices.

* An asterisk before the citation indicates that the title is available in a paperback edition.

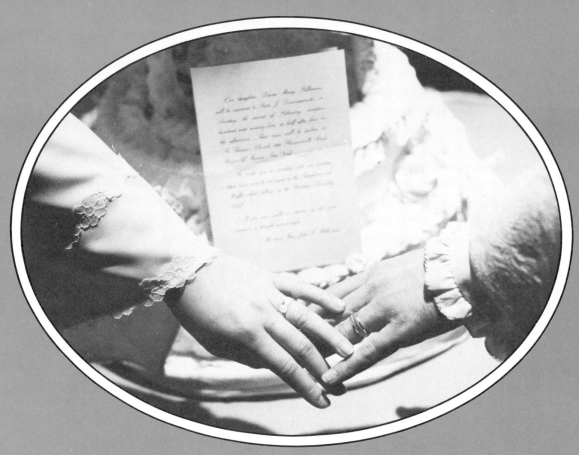

9 Social Institutions

Duels of honor were private encounters about real or imagined slights or insults. The practice, considerably facilitated by the fashion of wearing a sword as part of everyday dress [of gentlemen], seems to have spread over the rest of Europe from Italy from the end of the 15th century. Italy, in any case, was the great center of professional swordsmanship, and as the duel of honor became prevalent, the nobility of Europe flocked to Milan to learn the secret strokes that fencing-masters had to teach. Men would fight on the slightest pretext and often, at first, without witnesses, but as this secrecy came to be abused (e.g., by ambushes), it soon became usual for duelists to be accompanied by friends or seconds. Later these seconds would also fight, to prove themselves worthy of their friends.

(Reprinted by permission from Encyclopedia Britannica, 14th edition, © by Encyclopaedia Britannica, Inc.,

Dueling was an institutionalized way for gentlemen of the fifteenth to eighteenth centuries to settle differences. A cluster of procedures (norms) had developed which transformed undignified brawls into highly ritualized combat, with specialized roles (principals, seconds, attendants), a set of rules and penalties, and a supporting ideology which was generally accepted by society. Alexander Hamilton had only two choices when challenged by Aaron Burr: accept the challenge or retire from public life in disgrace. However, dueling was already losing public approval in the United States and elsewhere. Only a few decades later, Abraham Lincoln was able to laugh off a dueling challenge by announcing his choice of weapons—a peck of small potatoes at twenty paces!

THE INSTITUTIONAL CONCEPT

What is an institution? The sociological concept is different from the common usage. An institution is not a building; it is not a group of people; it is not an organization. An *institution* is *a system of norms to achieve some goal or activity that people feel is important*, or, more formally, *an organized cluster of folkways and mores centered around a major human activity.* Institutions are structured processes through which people carry on their activities.

Institutions and Associations

Institutions do not have members; they have followers. This is a subtle but important distinction. Let us illustrate: A *religion* is not a group of people; a religion is a system of ideas, beliefs, practices, and relationships. A *church* is an association of people who accept the beliefs and follow the practices of a particular religion. Unless there are believers to follow it, a religion dies. The religion is not the people; it is a system of beliefs and practices.

Most students have no difficulty distinguishing the *game* of football from the football *team.* The game is a set of rules and practices, together with supporting values and sentiments. The game cannot be played without players, but the players are not the game; they are the association of persons who play the game.

This, then, is the distinction between institution and association. Our banking institutions are our standardized ways of handling certain financial transactions; bankers are people who conduct those transactions; a bank is an organized group of bankers (together with clerks, typists, tellers, etc.). The student need only remember that *the institution is always the organized system of ideas and behavior; the association is the organized group of people engaging in the behavior.*

Each institution has its cluster of associa-

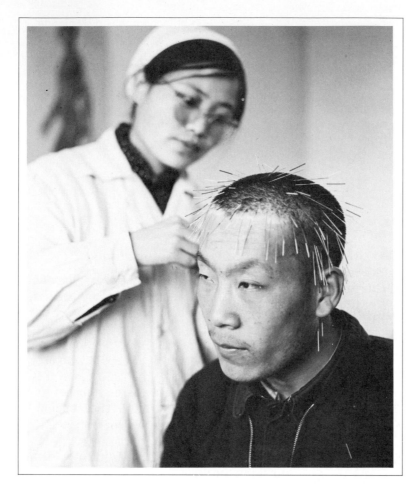

A society's health institutions consist of whatever procedures are accepted, routinized, and trusted. Here, a Chinese patient receives acupuncture, and a Tanzanian native doctor tells a woman the sex of her unborn child by examining the wings of a chicken. (*Paolo Koch/Rapho-Photo Researchers, Inc.; Tom Pix/Peter Arnold, Inc.*)

tions through which people practice the norms of that institution. The church has its organized local congregations, Sunday schools, clubs, and groups of many kinds, carrying out the work of the church; the school has its PTA, alumni association, and athletic association; the state has its political organizations, voters' leagues, taxpayers' associations, and organized pressure groups. Institutions and associations are very much interrelated, yet the concepts are distinct and should not be confused. Religion is a social institution; the First Methodist Church on Main Street is an association. The corporation is a social institution; the First National Bank and the Ford Motor Company are associations. Edu-

cation is a social institution; Harvard University and the PTA are associations. In general conversation, a person may be referred to as an "institution" (e.g., "Coach Brown really became an institution at old Siwash"). This is a popular and not a sociological use of the term.

An *institution is an organized system of social relationships which embodies certain common values and procedures and meets certain basic needs of the society.* In this definition, "common values" refers to shared ideas and goals, the "common procedures" are the standardized behavior patterns followed, and the "system of relationships" is the network of roles and statuses through which people carry out this

behavior. Thus, the family includes a set of common values (about love, children, family life), a set of common procedures (child care, family routines), and a network of roles and statuses (husband, wife, grandparents, baby, teenaged child, fiancé) which form the system of social relationships through which family life is carried out.

Five important basic institutions in complex societies are the familial, religious, governmental, economic, and educational institutions. In modern societies the values and procedures of science are so important and so highly standardized that we add "scientific institutions" to the list. The activities involved in social work or medical care have become

so definitely patterned that we also might speak of either of these systems of behavior as institutions. In referring to the Middle Ages one could speak of chivalry and knighthood as aspects of the institution of feudalism.

THE DEVELOPMENT OF INSTITUTIONS

The Process of Institutionalization

Institutions emerge as the largely unplanned products of social living. People grope for practical ways of meeting their needs; they find some workable patterns which harden through repetition into standardized customs. As time passes, these patterns acquire a body of supporting folklore which justifies and sanctions them. The custom of "dating" developed as a means of mate selection. Banks gradually developed as the need for storing, transferring, borrowing, and lending money gave rise to a series of standardized ways of doing these things.

From time to time, people might gather to codify and give legal endorsement to these practices as they continued to develop and change. In such manner, institutions arise.

Institutionalization consists of the establishment of definite norms which assign status positions and role functions for behavior. A norm is a group expectation of behavior. Institutionalization involves replacement of spontaneous or experimental behavior with behavior which is expected, patterned, regular, and predictable.

A tavern brawl is noninstitutionalized behavior; a professional boxing match is institutionalized. A set of social relationships has become institutionalized when (1) a regular system of statuses and roles has been developed, and (2) the system of status and role expectations has been generally accepted in the society. Dating in American society meets both these qualifications. A rather clearly defined set of courtship roles emerged, in

Many parents accept, somewhat unhappily, live-in boy or girl friends.

which the duties and privileges of each party are defined (he asks, she accepts, he pays, etc.) and safeguarded with some limitations or restraints intended to prevent complications; thus, dating became part of our marriage and family institutions. In recent years formal dating has declined in favor of less formal boy-girl companionship; this simply shows that institutions change.

When we say that dating became institutionalized, we mean that it was generally accepted in the society as a necessary part of growing up and finding marriage partners. Many societies have also institutionalized premarital sexual intercourse, making it a normal and expected part of the activities leading to marriage. Although premarital intercourse is common in American society, it has not been institutionalized. Present trends, which include providing contraceptives and abortions to the unmarried and allowing nonmarital cohabitation in dormitories may be leading to the institutionalization of premarital intercourse. Today, many parents accept, somewhat unhappily, the fact that their unmarried children have live-in boyfriends or girlfriends, but nonmarital cohabitation will not be institutionalized unless (or until) Mother sends her daughter off to college with the fond hope that she will find a nice boy to sleep with.

This has been a functionalist analysis of institutionalization. We have said that people grope for ways of meeting their needs and that ways which seem to work out well are repeated, standardized, and eventually institutionalized. Conflict theorists doubt that the institutionalization process is this undirected and automatic. They claim that the prosperous and powerful are able to guide the institutionalization process along lines beneficial to themselves. Thus, the corporation became an economic institution more rapidly than labor unions did because corporations were beneficial to investors.

The extent to which the institutionalization process is undirected or consciously controlled is one of the continuing unsettled questions in sociology.

Individual Roles in Institutional Behavior

Not all roles are institutionalized. The "bad boy" role and the "model child" role in the family are noninstitutionalized roles, while son and daughter are institutionalized roles. An institutionalized role is a set of behavior expectations that limit one's free choices. All judges act a good deal alike when on the bench, however much they differ at other times. Every Methodist minister and every Catholic priest finds duties and privileges that are quite precisely defined by the institutional role; to deviate from the expected role in any way is hazardous. Even presidents and kings, apparently so powerful, have very limited freedom of action. When Edward VIII insisted on marrying a divorced woman, he was forced to abdicate the throne of England. When Richard Nixon attempted to conceal a scandal, he was forced to resign as American President.

Institutionalized role behavior is guided by role expectations not by personal preferences. Noticing that a banker friend is most generous and amiable at the Rotary Club, a bankrupt loan applicant is surprised to find that this same banker is firmly ungenerous with the depositors' money. Many an employee who is promoted to a supervisory role tries to remain a comrade with the old work crew; this rarely succeeds, for the new role inevitably alters the relationship to the old buddies whom one now bosses.

It is true that individual personality differences do affect institutional behavior to some degree. One supervisor is grouchy and another is cheerful; one professor is stimulating and another is dull. But the range of individual variation is limited and is greatly overshadowed by role requirements. Conflicts that arise within an association are sometimes due to clashes of personality but more often to the clash of institutional roles. The supervisor and the inspector clash because the supervisor must keep production going while the inspector keeps finding defects to correct. The salesperson is frustrated when the credit manager refuses to extend more credit to a slow-paying customer. University deans *must* rule against a great many of the proposals advanced by students or faculty members. Once promoted to a deanship, the extremely popular faculty member soon becomes known as just another autocratic administrator. Institutionalized roles often require one to take actions which infuriate others.

INSTITUTIONAL TRAITS

Cultural Symbols

People have developed symbols which serve as a shorthand reminder of the institution. The citizen is reminded of allegiance to government by the flag; to religion by a crucifix, crescent, or Star of David; to the family by a wedding ring; to education by the school colors or animal totem (mascot); and to the system of economic controls by brand names and trademarks. Music also has symbolic meanings. National anthems, school songs, religious hymns, and singing commercials all use the art of melody to strengthen institutional ties. Buildings may become institutional symbols, so that it is hard to think of home

All institutions must adapt to a changing society.

without a house, religion without a church edifice, education without a school building, or government without the presidential mansion or king's palace.

Codes of Behavior

The people involved in institutional behavior must be prepared to carry out their appropriate roles. These roles are often expressed in formal codes, such as the oath of allegiance to the country, the marriage vows, the medical profession's oath of Hippocrates, and the codes of ethics of several other groups.

A formal code of behavior, however impressive, is no guarantee of proper role performance. Husbands and wives may prove unfaithful to marital vows, citizens who fervently repeat the pledge of allegiance may evade their taxes, and church members who have sworn fidelity to their religious creed may lapse into indifference. If the behavior code is fully learned and often reinforced, it may be observed; if not, and if there are no swift and sure punishments for violation, the code may be quietly ignored.

A formal code is only a part of the total behavior that makes up an institutional role.

TABLE 9-1
A PARTIAL LIST OF THE TRAITS OF MAJOR AMERICAN SOCIAL INSTITUTIONS

Family	Religion	Government	Business	Education
Attitudes and behavior patterns				
Affection	Reverence	Loyalty	Efficiency	Love of knowledge
Loyalty	Loyalty	Obedience	Thrift	Class attendance
Responsibility	Worship	Subordination	Shrewdness	Studying
Respect	Generosity	Cooperation	Profit making	"Cramming"
Symbolic culture traits				
Marriage ring	Cross	Flag	Trademark	School colors
Wedding veil	Ikon	Seal	Patent sign	Mascot
Coat of arms	Shrine	Mascot	Slogan	School song
"Our song"	Hymn	Anthem	Singing commercial	Seal
Utilitarian culture traits				
House	Church building	Public buildings	Shop, factory	Classrooms
Apartment	Church equipment	Public works	Store, office	Library
Furnishings	Literature	Armament	Office equipment	Stadium
Car	Liturgical supplies	Blanks and forms	Blanks and forms	Books
Code of oral or written specifications				
Marriage license	Creed	Charter	Contracts	Accreditation
Will	Church law	Constitution	Licenses	Rules
Genealogy	Sacred books	Treaties	Franchises	Curricula
Marriage law	Taboos	Laws	Articles of incorporation	Grades
Ideologies				
Romantic love	Thomism	Nationalism	Laissez faire	Academic freedom
Open family	Liberalism	States' rights	Managerial responsibility	Progressive education
Familism	Fundamentalism	Democracy	Free enterprise	Three "r's"
Individualism	Moral majority	Republicanism	Rights of labor	Classicism

Note: This outline, almost a half century old, is reproduced with very little change. Does this suggest anything about social institutions?
Source: Adapted from table "Nucleated Social Institutions" in F. Stuart Chapin, *Contemporary American Institutions*, Harper & Row, Publishers, Inc., New York, 1935, p. 16.

Even modern business makes use of tradition, ritual, and sentiment.

Much of the behavior in any role—parent, soldier, priest, professor, politician—consists of an elaborate body of informal traditions, expectations, and routines which one absorbs only through long observation of and/or experience in the role. Children who have never lived in a happy family are likely to have difficulty in successfully filling the roles of

parent and husband or wife. Like roles of all kinds, institutional roles can be filled most successfully by those who have internalized the proper role attitudes and behavior.

Ideologies

An ideology may be loosely defined as *a system of ideas which sanction a set of norms.* The norms define how people are expected to act; the ideology explains *why* they should act that way and why they sometimes fail to act as they should. A more imposing definition reads: "Ideologies may be defined as any set of ideas that explain or legitimate social arrangements, structures of power, or ways of life in terms of the goals, interests, or social position of the groups or collectivities in which they appear." [Newman, 1973, p. 52].

The ideology of an institution includes both the central beliefs of the institution and a

A manifest function of education is to transmit cultural values. (*Sybil Shelton/Monkmeyer*)

rational justification for the application of institutional norms to the problems of life.

The simpler cultures may not have developed elaborate ideologies surrounding institutional behavior. An outsider's question, "Why?" might be met with puzzlement rather than with an elaborate explanation. The more complex cultures generally include elaborate institutional ideologies. Each of the more highly developed religions, for example, has a highly developed set of beliefs about such topics as the nature and origin of the universe, its supernatural beings and forces, and about the purpose and destiny of human beings. Each modern political system is supported by an elaborate system of ideology which justifies institutional norms and interprets current events. Juvenile delinquency, for example, is very differently explained in capitalist and communist societies, while Hindu and Christian religions have very different images of "progress."

INSTITUTIONAL FUNCTIONS

Society is so complex and interrelated that it is impossible to foresee all consequences of an action. Institutions have *manifest* functions, which are the professed objectives of the institution, and *latent* functions, which are unintended and may be unrecognized, or, if recognized, regarded as by-products [Merton, 1957*b*].

Manifest Functions

These are functions which people assume and expect the institution to fulfill. Families should care for children. Economic institutions should produce and distribute goods and direct the flow of capital where it is needed. Schools should educate the young. Manifest functions are obvious, admitted, and generally applauded.

Latent Functions

These are unintended, unforeseen consequences of institutions. Our economic institutions not only produce and distribute goods, they also sometimes promote technological change and philanthropy and sometimes promote unemployment and inequality.

Educational institutions not only educate youth, they also provide mass entertainment and keep the young out of the labor market and, according to some conflict theorists, protect the children of the rich from having to compete with the children of the poor. Government welfare programs not only help the poor, they also provide jobs for middle-class personnel. Scientific research not only increases knowledge, it also makes obsolescent many ways of doing things.

Latent functions of an institution may (1) support the manifest function, (2) be irrelevant, or (3) may even undermine manifest functions. The latent functions of religious institutions in the United States include offering recreational activities and courtship opportunities to young people. Most church leaders agree that these activities help churches pursue their manifest function of promoting religious faith and practice. (In fact, some would argue that these activities have become manifest functions.) By contrast, it is doubtful that the sports spectacles staged by schools and colleges have much effect upon the manifest function of promoting education; instead, they are largely irrelevant to this manifest function. There are also instances where latent functions undermine manifest functions. For instance, the manifest function of civil service regulations is to secure a competent, dedicated staff of public employees to make government more efficient. The latent function of civil service is to establish an entrenched bureaucracy which may protect incompetent employees and frustrate the programs of elected officials. The manifest function of the regulation of drugs by the government is to protect consumers against injurious substances; a latent function is to delay the introduction of new, lifesaving drugs. The manifest function of Western health institutions has been to reduce illness, premature death, and human misery; the latent function has been to promote a population explosion and massive famine in the underdeveloped countries. There are, therefore, many instances in which latent functions might more accurately be termed "latent dysfunctions," since they tend to undermine the institution or to impede attainment of its manifest functions.

INTERRELATIONSHIP OF INSTITUTIONS

No institution exists in a vacuum. Each is affected by the rest of the culture. Acts within each institution affect the others.

Consider the case of the family. In most simple societies, the family (or possibly the clan, which is an extended family) is the only social institution. Work is organized by family units, children are trained by family members, control is exercised by the family, worship is generally by family groups. No other social structure may be needed in a simple society.

With increasing cultural complexity, situations develop which are not easily handled by the family. Trade with other tribes eventually brings specialized traders, who conduct trade as individuals not as family representatives. Work skills become more specialized, with what economists call "division of labor." This means that many people are working all day as specialized individual workers not as part of a family work team. Eventually, the organization and supervision of much work activity moves outside the family into shop or office with a foreman, rather than a family member, giving the orders.

Within the past century, the shift from farm to nonfarm work has reduced the father's authority, reduced family size as children became an expense rather than an asset, and encouraged away-from-home employment of women. The night shift forces millions of workers to change their family-life routines. The watch-and-help system of job training on the farm is replaced by formal educational institutions.

Thus changes in one institution force changes in others. The urban family is a less satisfactory haven for the aged than the family farm used to be; the state responds with Social Security. As workers drift from farm to factory and from gemeinschaft to gesellschaft relations, the church revises its language, its procedures, and, perhaps, its doctrines, in an effort to remain "relevant" to the needs of an urbanized, industrial society. New scientific discoveries bring growth to some industries and decline to others, while prompting new regulations by government. In such a variety of ways, each institution interacts with other institutions and is affected by them.

Institutions often demand uncomfortable sacrifices from their followers. Many religions require painful hardships and self-denials; the military demands unquestioning obedience and separation from loved ones; corporate private enterprise demands that needless workers be fired and that unprofitable businesses go bankrupt. Coser [1974] has applied the term, "greedy institutions" to those which impose restrictive demands upon one's other institutional activities.

Goffman [1961] has coined the term, "total institutions" for those which isolate one from the rest of society. Examples would include the prison, the mental hospital, the monastery and some other religious orders, the military academy and, to some extent, the military services. (We note that Goffman is speaking of *the* prison, as a system of institutionalized

Total institutions separate one from the rest of society. Both Buddhist monks and military recruits have their heads shaved as part of the initiation ritual. (*Horace Bristol/Photo Researchers, Inc.; Hiroji Kubota/Magnum Photos.*)

norms, relationships, and values. He is not speaking of *a* prison, which is an association of persons involved in this system of norms, relationships, and values.)

Marxist scholars see the interrelationship of institutions as mostly a one-way street where the economic institutions dominate the others. The way in which productive wealth is owned and controlled dictates the form of all other institutions—according to Marxist thought. Thus the feudal system of ownership and control created one kind of society, while the capitalist system created another.

In Marxist thought, this system of ownership and control of "the means of production" ultimately shapes all the cultural norms and values. The family takes the form that fits the mode of production. The state, police, laws, and courts all maintain the economic system and protect the property rights of those who have property rights. The school (where there are schools) prepares people for their assigned slots in the system—the poor and powerless to labor and the wealthy and powerful to control. The church intones prayers in praise of the whole business. Thus the economic institutions are the dominant institutions with all the others taking the form that harmonizes with the economic institutions.

Non-Marxist scholars see the economic institutions as less than all-powerful. For example, the German sociologist, Max Weber, in *The Protestant Ethic and The Spirit of Capitalism* [1904] argues that the capitalist system flourished most when combined with the values of Calvinist Protestantism. Where Marx argued that economic change stimulated religious change, Weber argued that religious change stimulated economic change.

Most scholars agree that in modern societies, the economic institutions may be more influential than any of the others. But it is also true that other institutions influence economic institutions. The family has an influence over economic practices. For example, growing concern for family values in recent years has led middle-level corporate executives to resist the frequent relocations which top management desires. Some scholars believe that it is science and technology not the "ownership and control of the means of production" that is the dominant force in modern social change (as discussed in Chapter 20).

Institutional Autonomy

Those who fill leadership roles in each institution jealously guard its territory (while often invading that of other institutions). Business interests resist government controls while seeking government favors and subsidies. Religious leaders defend "freedom of religion" while trying to get religious education into the schools. Educators seek a continuous expansion of educational programs while uneasily defending "academic freedom." A religion-based social movement is now asking the state to compel the schools, if they teach evolution, also to teach "creation science." Scientists and educators are debating whether to ignore this movement or to wage battle against "creation science" on the grounds that it is not real science, but just an attempt to get religion into the schools. The battle for institutional autonomy is unending.

INTELLECTUALS AND BUREAUCRATS

Role of the Intellectual

Social institutions are the objects of constant comment by the intellectuals in all complex societies. Even governments may flourish or fall as intellectuals support or undermine them [Brym, 1980, p. 11]. An intellectual is one who, regardless of education or occupation, is devoted to the analysis of ideas. The intellectual's power is indirect. Intellectuals are seldom "in control" of anything (except possibly the universities), but they are influential, since their writings affect the thinking of those who are in authority [Kadushin, 1974].

Intellectuals are often found in "wordy" occupations such as religion, teaching, journalism, and law. However, many persons in these occupations are not really "intellectuals," since they are not seriously concerned with examining ideas but operate in a routine fashion; and some persons in less verbal fields may develop intellectual interests. An example would be Eric Hoffer [1951; 1969; 1976], a longshoreman who became a well-known social commentator. What makes one an intellectual is not occupation or education but attitude toward ideas: ". . . he lives for ideas—which means he has a sense of dedication to the life of the mind which is very much like a religious commitment" [Hofstadter, 1964, p. 27]. Of course, no one is an intellectual all the time. Even Einstein ate, slept, and played the violin for relaxation. An *intellectual is one whose major work is with ideas.*

Ideas are important parts of institutions. Those who work seriously with ideas are both helpful and dangerous to existing institutions. Intellectuals can explain current events in ways which fulfill the claims of existing institutions. Communist intellectuals, for instance, have the task of showing how all recent history really fulfills the predictions of Marx and Lenin, even when this task requires a spectacular distortion of the facts. China's 1966 campaign to destroy the influence of the intellectuals reflected Mao Zedong's fear that intellectuals were wavering in their support of the revolutionary regime [Bloodworth, 1966].

The intellectual cannot be fully trusted, because the ability to defend the ideology includes the ability to reveal its defects. The intellectual may even develop a rival ideology. It is the intellectuals who promote revolutions and lead the attack upon revered institutions. Conversely, it is the intellectuals who are called upon to defend institutions under attack. The difficulties of the intellectual come when institutional loyalty clashes with devotion to truth as the intellectual perceives it.

Sometimes the intellectual is alternately praised and condemned as were Plato, Galileo, Luther, Trotsky, and many others. In his youth, Milovan Djilas interpreted communism as the main hope for social justice. His writings were praised and he became Vice-President of Yugoslavia. Later, he wrote a book describing communism as a new form of human exploitation [1957]; its publication resulted in his being imprisoned by the same authorities who had praised his previous works. The treatment of dissident intellectuals varies according to the nature of the government. As used today, "totalitarian" is almost a synonym for "Communist," although in the 1930s, it also applied to Nazi Germany and Fascist Italy and Spain. Totalitarian governments seek to control all important aspects of the culture, even such things as art, music, and clothing styles. Totalitarians force intellectuals in all institutions, with the partial exception of church leaders, to follow the party line. Dissenters are exiled, imprisoned, or executed.

Authoritarian regimes will tolerate no threat to their rule, but they do not seek to control the entire culture. An intellectual who becomes the leader of a dissident group will be ruthlessly silenced, but an occasional critic who attracts no great following may be tolerated as evidence that the regime is really not as dictatorial as its opponents charge.

In democratic countries, intellectuals usually suffer little from government pressure but may be victimized by the intolerance of other scholars, the timidity of administrators, or censorship by newspaper editors and TV programmers who do not share their views. In earlier years, business interests sometimes sought to silence the critics of capitalism. In recent decades, pressure also came from leftist groups who scolded intellectuals who failed to support radical ideals. But only in the democracies can dissenting intellectuals operate without fear of active persecution. Some, ranging from rightist Ayn Rand [1961, 1979] to leftist Herbert Marcuse [1964, 1972] have become wealthy and famous.

Role of the Bureaucrat

With the single exception of the family, elaborate bureaucracies surround all major institutions. Most institutional behavior is now conducted by associations. Religious worship (in most Western religions) is centered in organized churches; education has schools with teaching staffs, school boards, and education associations; economic behavior is run by corporations, unions, and trade associations; government has a bewildering array of bureaus, offices, and departments. Institutions are *not* bureaucracies, yet it is impossible to study much institutional behavior without studying the bureaucracies which administer so much of it.

A *bureaucracy* is a *pyramid of personnel who conduct rationally the work of a large organization.* Thompson [1977, pp. 13–17], drawing mainly on the work of Max Weber [1904], presents the principal characteristics of bureaucracy as (1) *specialization,* to assign each task to an expert, (2) *merit appointment and job tenure,* to ensure competent personnel; (3) *formalistic impersonality,* to see that a set of formal procedures is carried out impartially; and (4) *a chain of command,* to define each person's authority and responsibility.

When people first tackled projects too complicated for family or clan to organize, bureaucrats first appeared. Some feel that perhaps the ancient irrigation and flood-control projects first gave rise to the need for a disciplined and organized division of labor [Wittfogel, 1957]. Bureaucrats are never very popular. Many people regard themselves, rightly or wrongly, as productive workers and look with suspicion upon the bureaucrat who "does no real work" but just organizes and records the work of others.

Bureaucracy inevitably develops in all large organizations—all government departments, churches, universities, voluntary associations, and private business concerns. Suppose, for example, a business concern has an office force of three persons. They can divide the work casually and informally, and each

The individual who can discern the real pattern of power will find adjustment easy.

can get from the supply closet whatever office supplies are needed. Suppose the office force grows to 3,000. Now an orderly division of work and authority is necessary to get work done; a set of formal policies is needed to keep supplies in order, along with a system of inventory control and requisitions to keep supplies in stock and to prevent pilferage. Bureaucracy thus has at least three roots: the needs for efficiency, for uniformity, and for prevention of corruption.

BUREAUPATHOLOGY.   Although bureaucratic organization performs needed services, it also tends to develop certain types of problems. Sometimes labeled "bureaupathology" [Thompson, 1977, pp. 153], these problems include excessive routinization, aloofness and invidious status, "grade creep" [Samuelson, 1976], and undue assumption of policy-making authority [Cooper, 1981, p. 139].

Excessive routinization leads to "buck passing," in which officials handle a request by simply referring it to some higher authority so that it is hard to know who, if anyone, is really making a decision. This practice leads to charges that the office is bound up in "red tape" and more concerned with official forms than with meeting human needs. The problem of invidious status arises when bureaucrats exalt their own importance in comparison to those they are supposed to serve. This is especially galling when the bureaucrat gives

Bureaucracies tend to accumulate rules
and procedures.

distasteful news to the citizen who is nominally the bureaucrat's employer. For example, when the tax assessor says taxes must be raised or when the claims officer denies an application for unemployment compensation, citizens are annoyed. Negative decisions are difficult to accept under any circumstances and are much more distasteful when given by one who appears pompous and self-righteous.

"Grade creep" does not refer to academic marks (although it might also apply!) but to the classification of jobs and pay in which grade one is low-paid, grade two, a little higher, and so on. Samuelson [1976] points out that there is constant pressure to shift jobs to higher and higher classifications. Thus the typist becomes a stenographer; the stenographer, a private secretary; the secretary, an administrative assistant; and the administrative assistant, a bureau chief. Since the pressure of employees for a higher classification is constant and the governmental or corporate personnel office exerts little pressure for economy, this upward pressure is hard to resist.

Finally, it is charged that governmental bureaucracies do not restrict themselves to administration but become involved in policy making which should be done by the legislature or the executive. The charge is that bureaucratic officials either distort the acts of the legislature or make rules which exceed legislative authorizations. Such charges formed a major part of Ronald Reagan's presidential campaign in 1980. His efforts to cut back on bureaucratic authority apparently had some success, since the new regulations in 1981 were 25 percent fewer than in the previous year [Pauly, et al., 1982]. However, the legislature cannot spell out the rules to be applied in each of thousands of different situations. This is done by the bureaucracy. This creates endless argument over whether a particular bureaucratic decision is undermining, fulfilling, or exceeding a legislative policy. A new administration may use bureaucratic rulings to overturn the policies and nullify the legislation of an earlier administration. An extreme example is the effort of Secretary of the Interior James Watt to change conservation policies to permit oil drilling on federal wilderness areas. This so incensed the Congress that it passed a resolution against Watt's ruling [*Congressional Quarterly Weekly Report*, August 14, 1982.]

ADJUSTING TO BUREAUCRACY. Bureaucracies tend to accumulate rules and procedures. Many bureaucracies become so entangled in red tape that their daily work can be accomplished only by violating or evading some of the rules. Employees can stage a limited form of strike—a "work slowdown"—by simply abandoning their shortcuts and following the rule book.

The difficulties of bureaucratic organization lead to attempts both to improve it and to revolt against it. The formal study of administration is an attempt to make bureaucracy an efficient instrument for meeting organizational needs. Training programs for business persons, educators, public officials, and the clergy all stress courses in "administration" (a more popular term for bureaucratic procedures). Since bureaucracy is both a necessity and an annoyance, efforts to improve bureaucracy are as continuous, and perhaps as effective, as crusades against sin.

Discontent with bureaucratic rule appears

In the summer of 1956, we were in one of the early tourist groups to visit war-torn Yugoslavia. We were at a border crossing, leaving Yugoslavia for Italy.

At that time, there was little for tourists to buy in Yugoslavia, and I had more local currency than could be taken from the country. There was no currency exchange at the border and no place to spend it. I did not want to be arrested for currency violation. Several times I offered the money to the customs official; he waved me away, pretending not to understand. I sat in the bus, bills in hand, ready for surrender. At last, all papers stamped, the official smiled and waved us on.

Then I realized what had happened. The rule against taking local currency from the country was intended to control large money movements not to catch a visitor with a few too many *dinars*. The official could not exchange my *dinars*, and to confiscate them would be poor public relations. He was trying not to see them, and I was making it hard for him.

Both in bureaucracies and elsewhere, deviations are often handled by not seeing them. The office manager who overlooks a fifteen-minute coffee break stretched to twenty minutes; the professor who suspects a student of cheating but shrinks from the sticky business of proving it; the mother who would rather not know everything her daughter and boyfriend are doing—all are dealing with possible deviations by not seeing them.

This has a corollary. If one really wants to do something slightly, but not seriously, against the rules—don't ask! Just do it! If asked, the official must either refuse or openly condone a violation. If not asked, the official will probably ignore it. (A personal experience of this writer.)

among members or clients of all kinds of formal organizations. The established churches are often threatened by irregular clergy or by competing religious sects and cults. The elaborately organized business may be undercut by a smaller competitor which can change direction faster.

Schools face taxpayers' revolts due in part to a feeling of helplessness of the average citizen in dealing with educational administration. Labor-union leaders often find their control jeopardized by wildcat strikes in which the rank and file take action that official union leaders would rather suppress.

Various kinds of "direct action" seek to force modification in bureaucratic action and have brought a type of voluntary group action which is noisy, abrasive, and intolerant of bureaucratic delay:

. . . parents roll baby carriages into the streets to keep bulldozers from cutting new highways through their neighborhoods . . . professional women strike and march for women's rights . . . penitentiary inmates go on hunger strikes. White collar professionals and managers join in boycotts against gun manufacturers and non-union lettuce farmers . . . suburban housewives march against escalating meat prices. Blue collar workers demonstrate against busing their children across town. (Theodore Levitt, *The Third Sector: New Tactics for a Responsive Society*, Amacom, New York, 1973, pp. 73–74.)

Whether or not they work, such tactics produce an "adversary society" [Levitt, 1973, p. 72] which exacts a high price in loss of trust and in disorder. A different tactic is the attempt to work within the bureaucracy through the ombudsman.

The Ombudsman This office was developed in Sweden in 1913 [Gellhorn, 1967, p. 194] and has been adopted by corporations, governments, and universities in many countries as an orderly way of securing redress against a bureaucracy. The ombudsman usually has the power to investigate complaints and can often compel a reversal of an official decision. While the ombudsman may be a real protector of the humble citizen, there are latent effects of the office which are a bit different in character. For instance, supervisors may be less concerned with correcting alleged injustices themselves in the belief that the ombudsman can take care of any trouble. Also, the fear of being called to account for any kind of irregularity may make officials even more bureaucratic and inflexible in the effort to prove that they have followed all regulations to the letter.

Whatever the ultimate effect of the growing acceptance of the ombudsman, there is no doubt that the office is one of many efforts to make bureaucracy humane and efficient.

There is no easy answer to the problems of bureaucratic abuse. The uniform and impersonal character of bureaucracies is the basis for their usefulness; yet these same qualities sometimes make bureaucracies unresponsive to human needs.

The Incentive Alternative Some problems may be better handled by incentives than by regulation. For instance, consider the case of branch managers of corporations. One corporation will devise a rule book for branch management and will have frequent inspections to see that the rules are followed. Another will hire the best managers it can find and allow them to make their own decisions as long as profits are satisfactory. The second corporation may have more success.

Similar procedures may be followed in the effort to reduce industrial accidents. One method is to attempt to analyze every possible source of danger and write a manual of rules designed to prevent accidents. Since such rules are a bother, there must be frequent inspections to see that the rules are followed. This is typical bureaucratic procedure. An alternate procedure is to offer reward or punishment for results but leave the methods up to the individuals involved. Incentives are now used in the case of Workers' Compensation, where the fees paid by the company are based, in part, upon its accident rate. Incentives cannot replace rules and regulations everywhere, but they are less bother-

some and perhaps more effective than regulations wherever practical.

Despite their imperfections, bureaucracies provide necessary services fairly efficiently. For instance, interviews with a sample of people using government agencies reported a quite high level of satisfaction with the treatment they received, ranging from 58 percent satisfied with medical and hospital care to 88 percent satisfied with the way their retirement problems were handled by Social Security [Kahn et al., 1975, pp. 66–69].

Governmental, educational, religious, and business activities could not be carried on without a bureaucracy and, apparently, many people are satisfied with the results.

CONFIDENCE IN INSTITUTIONS

Functionalists assume that a healthy society will show strong support for the society's social institutions—a consensus upon existing

TABLE 9-2
PUBLIC CONFIDENCE IN 10 KEY INSTITUTIONS
(Percent saying "great deal" or "quite a lot")

Institution	1980	1979	1977	1975	1973
The church or organized religion	66%	65%	64%	68%	66%
Banks and banking	60	60	*	*	*
The military	52	54	57	58	*
The public schools	51	53	54	*	58
The U.S. Supreme Court	47	45	46	49	44
Newspapers	42	51	*	*	39
Organized labor	35	36	39	38	30
Congress	34	34	40	40	42
Television	33	38	*	*	37
Big business	29	32	33	34	26

*Not asked.
Source: Religion in America, 1981, the Gallup Organization, Inc. and the Princeton Religion Research Center, Inc., Princeton, N.J., p. 45.

During this period, has public confidence in key institutions risen, fallen, or shown no clear trend?

A U.S. District Court judge in Salt Lake City withdrew judgments for a case he first tried in 1956 and ordered the case, *Bulloch et al. vs. The United States,* retried. The reason, explained Judge A. Sherman Christensen in his August 4 opinion, is because the plaintiffs unveiled evidence at a trial in May demonstrating how the government had "perpetrated a fraud upon the court" during the 1956 proceedings.

At issue was whether Utah sheep ranchers were entitled to government compensation for the deaths of 4,390 sheep. The suit charged that the sheep had been poisoned by fallout from nuclear weapons detonated at the Nevada Test Site.

The ranchers' attorney pieced together evidence documenting how the AEC [Atomic Energy Commission] had deliberately misled the court in 1956.

(J. Raloff, *Science News,* 122:100, Aug. 14, 1982.)

What does it do to "confidence in American institutions" when people learn that their government has lied to them?

"The government" includes thousands of departments, agencies, offices, bureaus, and commissions. If, each year, only one in each thousand tells lies to the public, a new exposé of government dishonesty would appear every month or so. How deeply should a single instance affect our "faith in American institutions"?

institutions. Conflict theorists feel that such a "consensus" may conceal grave injustices and may serve to lend moral approval to exploitative practices. For better or worse, consensus upon institutions is a sign of cultural stability while a low level of "confidence in existing institutions" is a symptom of approaching change.

As shown in Table 9-2, the American people's confidence in American institutions fluctuates. The level of confidence may be taken as a crude measure of general contentment. It is not known just how low the levels of confidence can fall without bringing major changes, perhaps revolutionary changes. And whether such changes would be "corrective" or "disruptive" depends upon one's own perspective.

SUMMARY

A *social institution* is an organization of norms for doing something people feel is important. Institutions develop gradually from the social life of a people. When certain important activities have become standardized, routinized, expected, and approved, this behavior has been *institutionalized.* An *institutionalized role* is one which has been standardized, approved, and expected, and is normally filled in a quite predictable manner, regardless of the person filling it. Each institution includes a cluster of *institutional traits* (codes of behavior, attitudes, values, symbols, rituals, ideologies), *manifest functions* (those functions which it is intended to perform), and *latent functions* (those results which are unintended and unplanned).

Leaders of institutionally related associations (schools, churches, businesses, etc.) normally seek some degree of *institutional autonomy,* or independence from other institutions. Institutions are also *interrelated,* so that changes in one institution affect the others in a continuous cause-and-effect relationship.

Intellectuals are people whose major work is with ideas. Their power is one of influence, since their work may affect the thinking of those who are in authority. Intellectuals can attack or defend the institutions of their society.

Bureaucracy is an administrative personnel which is specialized, appointed on merit, impersonal, and directed by a chain of command. While much criticized and ridiculed, bureaucracy is necessary and inevitable in all large organizations. It arises from the needs for efficiency, uniformity, and prevention of corruption.

Reactions to bureaucracy include efforts to improve it through analysis and training and to restrict bureaucratic authority. Some organizations have used ombudsmen to provide their members with relief from discriminatory treatment by officials. Alternatives to bureaucracy rely on giving rewards for reaching goals without requiring the following of detailed regulations.

Confidence in American institutions fluctuates, and a low level of public confidence may bring institutional change.

GLOSSARY

autonomy self-government; freedom from outside direction.
association organized group of people pursuing some common interest.
bureaucracy a pyramid of officials who conduct rationally the work of a large organization.
ideology system of ideas which sanction a set of norms.
institution an organized cluster of folkways and mores centered around a major human acitivty; an organized system of social relationships which embodies certain common values and procedures and meets certain basic needs of society.
intellectual one whose work is dealing mainly with ideas.
latent functions unintended effects of a policy, program, institution, or association.
manifest functions intended purposes of a policy, program, institution, or association.
ombudsman (ombudsperson) an official empowered to investigate and sometimes adjust complaints against officials.

QUESTIONS AND PROJECTS

1 What are five basic social institutions found in all complex societies? How does an institution differ from an association?

2 What is meant by the process of institutionalization? Is art an institution? Recreation? The United Nations? Marriage? Football? The Roman Catholic Church?

3 Emerson made the statement, "An institution is the lengthened shadow of one man." As the terms are defined in this book, was he talking about institutions or associations?

4 Does your school have an ombudsman? Ask to see the annual report of that office. If this is not available, ask permission to look over some of the cases handled. Decide what principles were used in handling cases. What is the effect of this process on faculty and student morale? On academic standards?

5 Why does dissatisfaction with bureaucracy arise? What is the major obstacle in eliminating bureaucratic features which cause resentment?

6 Do you feel that premarital sexual relationships have been institutionalized on your campus? Why or why not?

7 Should students marry while in college? Should women members of the armed forces be discharged if they are pregnant? Justify your answer in each case.

8 Woody Hayes, popular and highly successful football coach of Ohio State University, was fired after losing his temper and attacking a member of an opposing team. What does this incident illustrate about the nature of institutionalized roles?

9 Read "Blacks vs. The White House," in *Newsweek*, 99:24–25, Jan. 25, 1982. Write a report explaining both the rationale for the withdrawal of regulation by the Internal Revenue Service and the reason why people active in civil rights organizations objected. What does this article indicate about the problems involved in the use of bureaucratic power?

10 Read "The Functions of Sacerdotal Celibacy," pp. 150–162, in *Greedy Institutions*, by Coser (listed in Suggested Readings). Do you think abolition of the requirement of priestly celibacy would strengthen or weaken the Roman Catho-

lic Church? Defend your answer.

SUGGESTED READINGS

Albrecht, Milton C.: "Art as a Social Institution," *American Sociological Review*, 33:383–390, June 1968. Presents art as a social institution, but one which does not follow exactly the format for other institutions.

*Brym, Robert J.: *Intellectuals and Politics*, George Allen & Unwin, Ltd., London, 1980. A brief and perceptive discussion of the relation between intellectuals and political power.

*Coser, Lewis A.: *Greedy Institutions: Patterns of Undivided Commitment*, The Free Press, New York, 1974. Some institutions and some associations demand the complete dedication of people involved. Ex

amples include the eunuchs who performed tasks for rulers, activists in the Communist party, the Catholic priesthood, the domestic servants, or housewives who subordinate all nonhousehold interests. A readable book revealing total institutional commitment.

Gordon, Laura Kramer: "Bureaucratic Competence and Success in Dealing with Public Bureaucracies," *Social Problems*, 23:197–208, December 1975. A study of welfare agencies showing how middle-class clients were most successful in getting what they wanted.

Graham, George P.: "Catholics, Divorce and Annulment," *USA Today*, 107:47–49, January 1979. Shows how intellectuals promoted institutional change.

Pryce-Jones, David P.: "The Bête Noire of France's Left," *The New York Times Magazine*, Dec. 11, 1977, pp. 55ff. How

Jean-Francois Revel and other intellectuals are beginning to deny any agreement between intellectuals and Marxism.

Snyder, Eldon E. and Elmer A. Spreitzer: *Social Aspects of Sport*, Prentice-Hall, Inc., Englewood Cliffs, N.J., 1983. A sociology of sport with a major emphasis on the relations of sport to the major social institutions.

*Thompson, Victor A.: *Modern Organization*, University of Alabama Press, 1977. Particularly valuable for its treatment of bureaupathology.

Zucker, Lynne G.: "The Role of Institutionalization in Cultural Persistence," *American Sociological Review*, 42:726–743, October 1977. A research report showing how cultural traits tend to persist longer when they are institutionalized.

10 The Family

It happened one morning when Johnny [an American ex-GI] came to work and found Maggi, Kim Sing, Povenaaa, and three other men rolling dice. Teuru [Johnny's native girlfriend] stood nearby, watching the game with interest, advising Maggi, "You better try harder! You need three more sixes!"

"What's the game?" Johnny asked.

"Dice," Teuru said.

"I can see that. What's it about?"

Teuru blushed and looked away, so Johnny asked Povenaaa. "Don't bother me now," the excited man cried. Suddenly there were shouts of triumph and Maggi swore the Chinaman had cheated, but Kim Sing grinned happily and picked up the dice.

"The damned Chinaman gets the baby," Povenaaa spat.

"Gets what?" Johnny asked.

"The baby."

"Whose baby?"

"Teuru's."

"I didn't know Teuru had a baby."

"She doesn't . . . yet."

"You mean . . . my baby?" Johnny fell back with his mouth gaping. Then he yelled. "Hey! What's this about my baby?"

"He won it," Maggi said disconsolately.

Grabbing Teuru the American cried, "What are they talking about?"

"When it's born," Teuru said. "All the people in Raiatea would like to have it. So we rolled dice."

"But it's your own baby!" he stormed.

"Sure," she said. "But I can't keep it. I'm not married."

"Your own flesh and blood!"

"What's he mean?" Teuru asked Maggi.

Johnny Roe looked beseechingly at the fat woman and asked, "Would you give away your own baby? Would you give away Major?"

The crowd in the vanilla shed burst into laughter and Johnny demanded to know the joke.

"It's Major!" Povenaaa roared, punching Johnny in the ribs. "Major's not her baby. She's Hedy's."

"You mean that Hedy. . . ."

"Of course," Maggi explained. "Hedy had to go to Tahiti for a good time before settling down. So she gave me Major."

Johnny Roe had heard enough. He stormed off and bought two bottles of gin, and when Teuru found him he had returned to his Montparnasse days except that now he blubbered, "Our baby! You raffled

off our baby with a pair of dice!"

He kept this up for a whole day and Teuru became afraid that it was the start of another epic binge, so she broke the gin bottles and said, "All girls give away their first babies. How else could they get married?"

Johnny sat upright, suddenly sobered, "What do you mean, married?"

"What man in Raiatea would want a girl who couldn't have babies?"

"You mean . . . the men don't care?"

"Very much! Since people find I'm to have a baby, several men who never noticed me before have asked when you were going away."

"What happens then?" Johnny asked suspiciously.

"Then I get married."

Johnny fell back on his pillow and moaned, "It's indecent. By God, it's indecent."

Family patterns vary greatly from society to society, yet there are few cultural patterns about which people are as highly ethnocentric as their family patterns. If the family is so important, why have we been unable to find and agree upon some ideal pattern of family life which best serves human needs everywhere?

As mentioned before, in the most primitive societies the family is the only social institution (or possibly the clan, which is an extended kinship group that is, in some societies, more important than the immediate family). Among the Polar Eskimos, there were no other institutions—no chiefs or formal laws, no priests or medicine men, no specialized occupations. Within the family all the business of living was fulfilled. Some primitive societies institutionalized some things that we would not consider a part of family life. For example, some primitives developed an institutionalized pattern of trading with neighboring peoples with whom they were not at all friendly. One people would leave some trade goods at a certain spot where they would soon be picked up by the other people, who would leave their trade goods in exchange. But this required no special functionaries or officials, no special institutional structure. Thus the most primitive societies had no physical or social needs which called for any institutional structure beyond the family.

As a culture grows more complex, its institutional structures become more elaborate. The family is an adequate structure for handling the economic production and consumption of primitive hunters and farmers. But what happens when they develop extensive trade with neighboring or distant tribes? Before long the group includes traders, shippers, and other specialists whose work is no longer a part of the family life of the society. Later, specialized artisans begin to produce trade goods, giving rise to further occupational differentiation. Economic institutions exist whenever economic functions are performed in routine ways by specialists, operating outside their family roles and functions.

In the most primitive societies, order is maintained with no formal laws, police, or courts. The only authority known in many simple societies is family authority; that is, certain family members have certain authority over others. With increasing tribal size and growing cultural complexity, more formal political organization is needed. Family heads are joined into tribal councils, tribes combine into confederations, and bureaucracies begin to develop. Warfare, in both primitive and modern societies, is a powerful stimulus to political organization, for only through political organization can an aroused rabble become an effective army. In like manner, religious and educational institutions develop as professional functionaries, following standardized procedures, withdraw from the family certain activities which are too complicated for the family to handle well.

The family, then, is the basic social institution from which other institutions have grown as increasing cultural complexity made them necessary. A study of the family will tell us something about it and about institutions in general.

STRUCTURE OF THE FAMILY

Like all institutions, the family is a system of accepted norms and procedures for getting some important jobs done. Defining the family is not easy, as the term is used in so many ways. A family may be: (1) a group with common ancestors; (2) a kinship group united by blood or marriage; (3) a married couple with or without children; (4) an unmarried couple with children; (5) one person with children. Members of a commune may call themselves a family but are generally unable to occupy a house in an area zoned for "single-family residence." If several students seek to rent and share a house in such an area, they discover that the legal definition of a family is important.

The childless unmarried couple living in "nonmarital cohabitation" is not recognized as a family by the U.S. Bureau of the Census, but it recently set up a new category for "persons of opposite sex sharing living quarters," abbreviated to *posselq* (rhymes with "jostle you").

"If you like me and I like you,
Come and be my posselq."

The U.S. Bureau of the Census defines a family as "two or more persons related by blood, marriage, or adoption and residing together in a household." Common practice, however, is to include as a family any of the five categories listed above. Sociologists find the census definition unsatisfactory because it excludes the *extended family*, which is the basic social institution in so many societies. A more sociological definition of the *family* might be *a kinship grouping which provides for the rearing of children and for certain other human needs*. If a society is to survive, people must find some workable and dependable ways of pairing off, conceiving and raising children, meeting economic needs, caring for the ill and aged, and carrying out certain other functions. These family functions vary considerably from society to society, while the family forms vary even more greatly. In fact, if one were to list every possible way of organizing family life, a search of anthropological literature would probably reveal that each form of organization was the accepted pattern in at least one society. With only a few exceptions, where family patterns are concerned, everything is right someplace.

Composition of the Family Group

When we speak of the family, we ordinarily think of a husband and wife, their children, and occasionally an extra relative. Since this family is based upon the marital or "conjugal" relationship, it has been called the conjugal family. Today, however, it is most often referred to as the *nuclear family*. The *consanguine family* is based not upon the conjugal relationship of husband and wife but upon the blood relationship of a number of kinspersons. The consanguine family is an extended clan of blood relatives together with their mates and children. The term *extended family* is often used to refer to the nuclear family plus any other kin with whom important relationships are maintained. While Americans use the extended family for family reunions and other ceremonial purposes, most of the routine family functions proceed on a nuclear family basis.

Our folklore warns against in-laws and urges the couple to set up a household of its own. This is known as *neolocal marriage*, as distinct from *patrilocal marriage*, where the married couple lives with the husband's family, and from *matrilocal marriage*, where the couple lives with the wife's family. Our laws require a husband to maintain his wife in a home apart from other relatives if she insists. Our laws require parents to support their own minor children but impose only slight obligation to care for their parents and no obligation to care for brothers and sisters, cousins, uncles and aunts, nephews and nieces, or other relatives.

The consanguine family has a very different atmosphere. Whereas the conjugal family has a married couple at its core, surrounded by a fringe of blood relatives, the consanguine family has a group of brothers and sisters at its core, surrounded by a fringe of husbands and wives. In most instances of the consanguine family, a married person remains primarily attached to his or her parental family and remains a semioutsider in the spouse's family. This has important consequences. One's principal responsibilities are toward the family into which one was born, not the family into which one has married. Thus, a woman may depend not upon her husband but upon her brothers for protection and help in raising her children. Her husband does not escape, however, for he is saddled with his sister's children. [For classic descriptions of the consanguine family, see Linton, 1936, chap. 10: Murdock, 1949, chap. 3.]

Where family patterns are concerned, almost everything is right someplace.

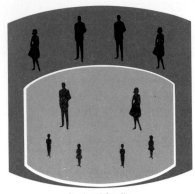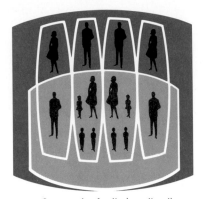

Conjugal family
The basic family unit consists of husband and wife and their children with a fringe of relatives.

Consanguine family (matrilocal)
The basic family unit consists of a group of sisters and brothers, and the sisters' children, with a fringe of spouses. (In the less common patrilocal form, it is the children of the brothers who complete the family.)

FIGURE 10-1   Conjugal and consanguine family types.

In such a family, affection and responsibility are widely diffused among a fairly large group of people. Children are the joint responsibility of the entire family, and a child develops a relationship with its aunts very like that with its mother. It is surrounded by many adults, any of whom may momentarily act as parents toward it. This type of family tends to turn out personalities with less individuality than ours, since each child has more nearly the same socialization experience. Such a family protects the individual against misfortune. If a child's mother dies or is neglectful, good substitutes are at hand. The consanguine family offers little opportunity for individuality and little danger of loneliness or neglect.

Obviously the consanguine family is not practical everywhere. Where both the family of birth and the family of marriage are in the same village, it is easy to be with one's mate while fulfilling obligations to one's parental family. If they are in different villages, strain is imposed. In a highly mobile, individualized, specialized society like ours, the consanguine family would be unworkable. But

for the Tanala of Madagascar, whose farm work required a cooperative team of a half dozen or more adult males, the consanguine family was ideal [Linton, 1936, chap. 12].

Marriage

There are few societies in which it is usual for a couple quietly to pair off and start "playing house." While this is fairly common in America today, it is not the fully approved and expected (and therefore not the institutionalized) arrangement. Marriage is *the approved social pattern whereby two or more persons establish a family.* It involves not only the right to conceive and rear children (who are sometimes conceived as an institutionalized preliminary to marriage) but also a host of other obligations and privileges affecting a good many people.

The real meaning of marriage is the acceptance of a new status, with a new set of privileges and obligations, and the recognition of this new status by others. Wedding ceremonies and rituals are merely ways of publicizing and dramatizing this change of status. Homosexual couples in our society would like to be married and recognized as a family. At present, this is legally impossible in any of the United States. A legal marriage legitimizes a social status and creates a set of legally recognized rights and duties. A homosexual "marriage" creates no new status which others are obliged to recognize, nor are any legally enforcible rights and duties created. Only new laws could do this (and the first faint beginnings of such legal changes are now being made [*Time,* 118:74, Dec. 13, 1982]).

In matters of marriage our ethnocentrism is conspicuous. To us it is monstrous that parents should arrange and compel the marriage of two persons who may never even have met. How do they know whether they will love each other? Why are not their wishes consulted? Our reaction illustrates the usual error of ethnocentrism—assuming that people with another culture will think and feel as we would think and feel if transplanted into their situation. It overlooks the fact that most people wish and feel only what their society trains them to wish and feel. We think of marriage as a romantic adventure with a person we have come to love. The girl in classical China, about to enter an arranged marriage with a stranger, eagerly anticipated her marriage as a desirable status and a fulfilling association with a man who had been wisely chosen by her parents. Each society has viewed the other with an ethnocentric pity; we pitied their young people for their lack of freedom; they pitied our young people for their lack of parental assistance. In neither case did the young people themselves feel any need for pity. Today, of course, the Chinese family has changed greatly in the People's Republic [Yang, 1959; Huang, 1961; Kessen, 1975, chap. 3; Leslie, 1982, pp. 111–113].

ENDOGAMY AND EXOGAMY. Every society limits choice in marriage by requiring that one choose a mate *outside* some specified

group. This is called *exogamy.* In our society the prohibition applies only to close blood relatives; one may not marry a brother or sister, first cousin, or certain other close relatives. Many societies extend the circle of prohibited kin to forbid marriage within the clan, the village, or sometimes even the tribe.

Most societies also require that mates be chosen *within* some specified group. This is called *endogamy.* Clan, village, and tribal endogamy are quite common among primitive societies. In our society, racial endogamy was required by law in many states until the U.S. Supreme Court held all such laws unconstitutional in 1967, but custom and social pressure continue to discourage racial intermarriage throughout our society. With varying degrees of pressure we also encourage religious endogamy and class endogamy in our country.

Every society practices both exogamy and endogamy as it specifies the limits of group closeness (exogamy) and the limits of group distance (endogamy) within which mates must be found. Sometimes between these two limits there is little room for hunting! The Aranda of Central Australia have a complicated marital pattern known to anthropologists as an "eight-class system with exogamy and indirect patrilineal descent." To skip the detailed explanations, this means that a man can marry only a woman from a particular group within the proper subsection of the opposite half of his tribe [Murdock, 1936, pp. 27–30]. In a number of societies, a formula such as this makes an actual choice unnecessary, for only one person may be in the permissible category for a boy or girl to marry. If there is none at all, then the couple who are supposed to become parents-in-law normally adopt a marriageable boy or girl from another family with a surplus. After all, an institution is a structure for meeting human needs, and it usually does so in one fashion or another.

MARITAL CHOICE. The process of arranging a marriage shows a fascinating range of possi-

A majority of the world's societies allow polygamy. (© *Tony Howarth/Daily Telegraph Magazine, 1980; Woodfin Camp & Assoc.*)

bilities. As shown above, some societies follow a formula whereby the children of certain socially designated kinsfolk marry each other, so that the individual choices may be unnecessary. Where actual choices are necessary, they may be made in many ways. The couples can do their own choosing, sometimes with parental guidance or parental veto. The parents can arrange the marriage, with or without considering the couple's wishes. A wife may be purchased, or perhaps a complicated series of gifts are exchanged between families. Wife capture is not unknown. Each of these patterns is the standard way of arranging marriages in some of the world's societies. All of them work—within the society in which they exist—and are supported by the surrounding values and practices of the culture. Wife capture worked very well for the Tasmanians,

who practiced village exogamy and were not greatly concerned over the differences between one woman and all the others. For our society, it would be less practical. This illustrates the concept of cultural relativism—a pattern which works well in one cultural setting might work badly in another. As Peters shows [1971], parental engagement of 3-year-old girls to teenaged boys works out very well for the Shirishana of Brazil, while any attempt to impose the Western concepts of marriage would undermine Shirishana stability and invite chaos.

MONOGAMY AND POLYGAMY. To all properly ethnocentric Americans, there is only one decent and civilized form of marriage—*monogamy*—one man to one woman (at a time). Yet a majority of the world's societies have practiced *polygamy*, allowing a plurality of mates. There are three theoretical forms of polygamy. One is *group marriage*, in which several men and several women are all in a marriage relationship with one another. While this is an intriguing theoretical possibility, there is no authentic instance of a society in which group marriage has been fully institutionalized, with the possible exception, at one time, of the Marquesans [Murdock, 1949, p. 24]. A very rare form is *polyandry*, where several husbands share a single wife. The Todas of Southern India provide one of our few examples. Here, as in most other cases, polyandry was fraternal, meaning that when a woman married a man, she automatically became wife to all his brothers, and they all lived together with little jealousy or discord. Toda polyandry becomes understandable when one learns that they lived in a harsh environment where food was scarce and female infanticide was used to limit population size [Murdock, 1936, pp. 120–121; Queen et al., 1974, chap. 2]. Only where some situation has created a shortage of women is polyandry likely to be found [Unni, 1958]. But the scattered handful of societies which practice polyandry serve to show how a practice which seems to us to be contrary to human nature can still be the accepted and preferred pattern for people who are socialized to expect it. The usual form of polygamy is *polygyny*—a plurality of wives, not usually sisters and generally acquired at different times during one's life.

Mention of polygyny will arouse a predictably ethnocentric response from most Americans. They conjure up images of female degradation and helpless enslavement and rise to impressive heights of moral indignation at such heathen brutishness. The facts are otherwise. It would be difficult to show that women have generally had a more satisfactory status in monogamous than in polygamous societies. Even in polygynous societies, most of the marriages were monogamous. It is generally only the more successful and powerful men who could af-

ford or attract more than one wife. In many polygynous societies, the second wife filled the status function of the second Cadillac in our society. Far from feeling resentful, the first wife often urged her husband to take more wives, over whom she generally reigned as queen bee. Polygyny in operation took many forms in different societies, all of them far removed from the imagination of the normal ethnocentric American. Polygyny is today declining in most of the developing countries but is still common in the more remote tribal areas.

DIVORCE. What is to be done when a married couple can't live comfortably together? Although most societies make some provision for divorce, some make it very difficult or perhaps give the privilege of divorce only to the men. Some make divorce very simple. Among the Hopi, divorce is rather rare but very uncomplicated. The husband merely packs up and leaves, or in his absence his wife tells him to get lost by pitching his things outside the door.

The social and family structure of many societies makes divorce a fairly painless and harmless operation. In many societies where there is no great emphasis upon romantic love and no intense individual love attachments, divorce entails no great heartbreak. Where the consanguine family surrounds the child with a protective clan of kin and designates the mother's brother as the responsible male in a child's life, the loss of a child's biological father is hardly noticed. The meaning of divorce depends upon how it relates to other aspects of the institution of the family. In our society, with its strong accent upon individual love attachments within an isolated nuclear family unit, a divorce may complete the collapse of the emotional world for both child and adult.

Variations in Family Structure

We could extend the list of "odd" family patterns indefinitely. Some societies, like ours, encourage an informal camaraderie between brother and sister; among others, such as the Nama Hottentots, brother and sister are expected to treat each other with great formality and respect, may not address each other directly, or even be alone together. Such *avoidances* are found in many societies. Mother-in-law avoidance is very common; the Crow husband may not look at or speak to his mother-in-law or even use a word which appears in her name. In many societies avoidance taboos demand extreme decorum toward certain relatives, while *privileged relationships* permit special familiarities with certain other relatives. Thus, the Crow, who must act with great decorum toward his sister, mother-in-law, son-in-law, and his wife's brother's wife, is socially expected to show great familiarity toward his sister-in-law, joke with her, and engage in various immodesties. Among the Nama Hottentots, brother-sister incest is the worst of all offenses, but cross-cousins[1] enjoy a "joking relationship" which includes loose talk, horseplay, and sexual intimacy. All this is merely to say that the family includes a varying number of people whose relationship to one another is very different in different societies.

Is there any sense in all this, or is the family an irrational jumble of odd notions and historical accidents? Two things we should remember. First, many different patterns will "work," as long as all members of the society accept them. Wife purchase, wife capture, or wives-for-the asking—any one of these patterns works out acceptably, provided the people view it as the proper way to stake out a mate. Thousands of societies have been in existence at some time or other. It is not suprising that most of the possible ways of organizing human relationships have been tried out sometime, somewhere. Many of them have survived, showing that people are highly adaptable animals, capable of being

[1] Cross-cousins are the children of a brother and sister with their respective mates; where the related parents are of the same sex, as in the case of two brothers or two sisters, the cousins are called parallel cousins.

trained to find their satisfactions in a remarkable variety of ways.

Second, we invoke the concept of cultural relativism and repeat that how a custom works depends upon how it relates to the rest of its cultural setting. Where wife purchase exists, the transaction is not merely a way of arranging marriages but is also a central feature of the entire economic and social system. The consanguine family exists in certain societies because it is an efficient *economic* unit in such societies and not just because it is nice to have the family together. Societies which are today becoming industrialized and commercialized are also replacing the consanguine with the nuclear family, which better meets the needs of a mobile, individualized society. As we stated in an earlier chapter, institutions are interrelated.

FUNCTIONS OF THE FAMILY

The family in any society is an institutional structure which develops through a society's efforts to get certain tasks done. What are the tasks commonly performed through the family?

The Sexual Regulation Function

The family is the principal institution through which societies organize and regulate the satisfaction of sexual desires. Most societies provide some other sexual outlets. With varying degrees of indulgence, each society also tolerates some sex behavior in violation of its norms. In other words, there is in all societies some deviation of the real culture from the ideal culture in sexual behavior. Most societies have some norms of evasion which define how to conduct disapproved sex activities discreetly (e.g., the American "business trip"). But all societies expect that most sexual intercourse will occur between persons whom their norms define as legitimately accessible to each other. These norms sometimes allow for considerable sexual variety; yet no society is entirely promiscuous. In every society there are mores which forbid certain persons access to one another. What may look to us like promiscuity is more likely to be a complicated system of sexual permissions and taboos which we do not fully understand.

A clear majority of the world's societies have allowed young persons to experiment with sexual intercourse before marrying [Murdock, 1949, 1950]. Many societies think the idea of virgin marriage is absurd. Yet in such societies this premarital sex experience is viewed as preparation for marriage not as recreation. Sometimes its principal purpose is to determine fertility; a girl who conceives is ready to marry. Most of these societies have not merely *allowed* premarital sex behavior; they have *institutionalized* it. They have defined it as a proper and useful activity and have developed a supporting set of institutional arrangements which make it safe and harmless. Since there is full social approval, there is no fear, shame, or disgrace. The family structure and living arrangements in such societies are generally of a sort where one more baby is no special inconvenience or burden. Premarital sex experience can be a useful and harmless preliminary for marriage in a society which has institutionalized it. Ours has not, but possibly may do so.

The Reproductive Function

Every society depends primarily upon the family for the business of producing children. Other arrangements are theoretically possible, and most societies arrange to accept children produced outside a marriage relationship. But no society has established a set of norms for providing children except as part of a family.

The Socialization Function

All societies depend primarily upon the family for the socialization of children into adults who can function successfully in that society. Thinkers from Plato to Huxley [1932, 1958]

have speculated about other arrangements, and dozens of experiments in communal child rearing have been attempted and abandoned. After the Russian Revolution, the Soviet Union experimented with removing children from families to raise them in special child-care facilities, hoping to free their mothers for labor and to rear the children more "scientifically." But Russia never practiced this idea very widely, soon gave it up, and then did everything possible to strengthen the family [Alt and Alt, 1959; Chao, 1977]. In the Soviet Union and China today, school and family cooperate closely to socialize children for conformity, obedience, and altruism [Bronfenbrenner, 1970; Kessen, 1975; Che, 1979; Stacey, 1979; Von Frank, 1979]. In modern Israel, children in the kibbutz (cooperative farm) are raised in communal cottages and cared for by nursery workers while the other women work elsewhere in the kibbutz. Parents are normally with their children for a couple of hours a day and all day on Saturday. This communal rearing seems to work very successfully in the kibbutz [Bettelheim, 1964, 1969; Leon, 1970], although some critics disagree [Spiro, 1958]. Yet only a few of the Israeli children ever lived in the kibbutz, and the proportion is declining as the founders pass away and the youth find the kibbutz dull. To paraphrase an American ballad, "How you gonna keep 'em on the kibbutz, after they've seen Tel Aviv?" In Israel today, the family is reclaiming functions from the kibbutz [Talmon, 1972; Mednick, 1975; Tiger and Shepher, 1975; Gerson, 1978] and the family survives as the standard institution for looking after children.

The family is the child's first primary group, and this is where its personality development begins. By the time the child is old enough to enter primary groupings outside the family, the basic foundations of its personality are already firmly laid. The kind of person it will be is already profoundly influenced. For example, Mantell [1974] compared the early family backgrounds of a sample of Green Berets (an elite volunteer unit in the Vietnam war, noted for its ruthlessness) with a matched sample of war resisters, finding many significant differences. The Green Berets came from parents who were typically authoritarian, conventionally religious, insensitive, not affectionately demonstrative, supervisory rather than companionable with children, and demanding of unquestioning obedience; resisters' parents were the opposite in nearly every characteristic.

One of the many ways in which the family socializes the child is through providing models for the child to copy. The boy learns to be a man, a husband, and a father mainly through having lived in a family headed by a man, a husband, and a father. Some socialization difficulties are encountered where such a model is missing and the boy must rely upon the secondhand models he sees in other families or among other relatives. There is no fully satisfactory substitute for a mother and a father, although they need not be the biological parents.

The importance of the family in the socialization process becomes clear when its impact is compared with that of other influences. For example, Mayeske [1973] studied the roles of racial-ethnic group, social class, and quality of school attended as causes of different rates of learning in children. He found that none of these was nearly as important as the presence or absence of a family atmosphere which encouraged learning aspirations and study habits. A recent study by Mercy and Steelman [1982] concludes that the main reason for social-class differences in children's intellectual attainments is the different family atmosphere at different social-class levels. Numerous such studies have established the family as the primary determinant of child socialization.

SOCIALIZATION IN THE MULTIPROBLEM FAMILY. A "multiproblem family" is one with a depressing assortment of problems and inadequacies. It is usually poverty-stricken and conflict-ridden, is often fatherless, and is beset by other problems such as unemploy-ment and irregular work habits, alcoholism, drug addiction, illegitimacy, dependency, delinquency, and physical and mental illness. Such families fail to fulfill *any* of the family functions adequately and thus socialize their children to continue the pattern of inadequacy and dependency. Malnutrition permanently blights their physical and intellectual growth and contributes to their school failure [Birch and Gussow, 1970]. Every slum, rural or urban, white or black, throngs with the "drifters"—children of disorganized lower-class families—who are deprived of love and affection, alienated from society, purposeless, and hopeless.

The Affectional Function

Whatever else people need, they need intimate human response. Psychiatric opinion holds that probably the greatest single cause of emotional difficulties, behavior problems, and even of physical illness, is *lack of love*, that is, lack of a warm, affectionate relationship with a small circle of intimate associates [Fromm, 1956; Schindler, 1954, chap. 10; Hayanagi, 1968]. A mountain of data shows that the serious delinquent is typically a child whom nobody cares very much about. Infants who receive good basic physical care but who are not cuddled, fondled, and loved are likely to develop a condition medically known as *marasmus* (from a Greek word meaning "wasting away"). They lose weight, fret and whimper listlessly, and sometimes die [Ribble, 1943, chap. 1; Evans, 1972; Mussen et al., 1974, pp. 216–223]. A classic study many years ago showed how children in the sterilized but impersonal atmosphere of hospitals or foundling homes will suffer in emotional development and often show startlingly high rates of illness and death [Spitz, 1945]. Lack of affection actually damages an infant's ability to survive.

The evidence is overwhelming that our need for companionship and intimate, affectionate human response is vitally important to us. Indeed, this is probably our strongest

WHAT SHOULD WE GIVE OUR CHILDREN?

Are we offering things as parent substitutes? Are we offering presents instead of presence? Are we giving things because we are reluctant to give time, or self, or heart? Are we bribing our children, making deals, buying their affection? ("All a kid needs are love and securities.") Are we asking them to accept tokens of our love in lieu of the real thing? Like Pavlov's dog, the child has become conditioned to respond to the ringing of the doorbell with visions of goodies: "Whatja bring me?" We have developed the strange phenomenon of the "expectant child," for whom every event calls for a present. The world owes him a giving. We have reached the point in our lives where the salesman no longer asks, "What does he need?" but "What doesn't he have?"

(Sam Levinson, *Everything But Money*, Simon & Schuster, New York, 1966, p. 192. Copyright © 1951, 1952, 1953, 1955, 1956, 1958, 1959, 1961, 1966 by Sam Levinson. Reprinted by permission of Simon & Schuster, a division of Gulf & Western.)

Do you think that when a child becomes "spoiled" (inconsiderate, self-centered, greedy), it is because of what the child has been *given* or because of what the child has been *denied*?

social need—far more necessary than, for example, sex. Many celibates are leading happy, healthy, and useful lives, but a person who has never been loved is seldom happy, healthy, or useful.

Most societies rely almost entirely upon the

Socialization through intimate family interaction. (© *Jim Anderson/Woodfin Camp & Assoc.*)

family for affectionate response. The companionship need is filled partly by the family and partly by other groupings. Many primitive societies had organizations and clubs somewhat like modern lodges and fraternities, filling much the same functions. Yet even these were often organized on a kinship basis and were, therefore, an extension of the family.

The Status Definition Function

In entering a family, one inherits a string of statuses. One is ascribed several statuses within the family—age, sex, birth order, and others. The family also serves as a basis for ascribing several social statuses—as, for example, a white, urban, middle-class Catholic. In any society with a class system, the class status of a child's family largely determines the opportunities and rewards open to it and the expectations through which others may inspire or discourage it. Class status can be changed through some combination of luck and personal efforts, as is described in Chapter 15, "Social Mobility." But each child *starts out* with the class status of its family, and this has great effects upon one's achievement and rewards. The assignment to a class may seem unfair; yet it is inevitable. The family cannot avoid preparing the child for a class status similar to its own, for the very process of living and growing up in such a family is preparation for its class status. The child normally absorbs from its family a set of interests, values, and life habits which make it easy to continue in the class status of its family, difficult to achieve a higher class status, and painful to accept a lower class status.

The Protective Function

In all societies the family offers some degree of physical, economic, and psychological protection to its members. In many societies any attack upon a person is an attack upon that person's entire family, with all members bound to defend the family member or to revenge the injury. In many societies guilt and shame are equally shared by all family members. In most primitive societies the family is an extended food-sharing unit which starves or fattens together; as long as one's relatives have food, one has no fear of hunger. And in many primitive societies, as in ours, few persons outside one's family care very deeply what happens to one.

The Economic Function

As stated earlier, the family is the basic economic unit in most primitive societies. Its members work together as a team and share jointly in their produce. In some societies the clan is the basic unit for working and sharing, but more often it is the family. This situation, however, is now changing.

THE AMERICAN FAMILY TODAY

The family is a prime example of the interrelatedness of institutions, for changes in the family mirror changes in the other institutions with which it dovetails. For example, in most hunting societies men are clearly dominant over women, who make inferior hunters because of their limited strength and frequent childbearing. But as the economic base shifts from the hunt to the garden, women's role in the family grows somewhat more influential, for women can and do perform most of the hoe agriculture. As the plow replaces the hoe, male dominance again tends to grow, for plowing generally calls for the greater strength of the male. Thus there is some relation between one's power within the family and the nature of one's economic contribution. Other examples of interrelatedness will follow.

Number of native white women aged
15–44 giving birth (per thousand)

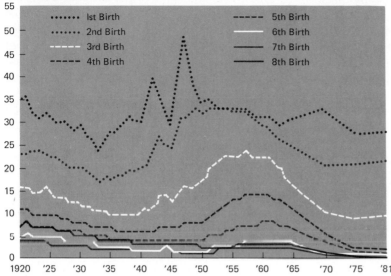

FIGURE 10-2 Family size in the United States since 1920. (*Source: U.S. Department of Health, Education, and Welfare,* Vital Statistics of the United States, *1964, vol. 1,* Natality, pp. 1–11; and Statistical Abstract of the United States, *1981, p. 59.*)

Changing Family Structure

FAMILY SIZE HAS DECREASED. It is no secret that the twelve-child families of the last century are rare today. The birthrate in the Western world began falling about a century ago. It reached a low during the Great Depression of the 1930s, when in the United States it fell to 16.6 births per thousand in 1933, rose to 26.6 in 1947, and fell to 14.7 by 1976, rising to 16.2 in 1980. Today's "smaller family," however, does not mean that all families are proportionately smaller. As Figure 10-2 shows, small families are about as common as they were a half century ago, but very large families are increasingly rare.

The Women's Liberation Movement has encouraged women to view childbearing as an option not as a duty. The proportion of couples who choose to remain childless has increased [Veevers, 1980], and more women are delaying parenthood, with about one-

third having their first child at 25 or older [Wilkie, 1981].

Why has overall family size declined in the Western world? Contraceptive devices have provided the means but not the motive. Contraceptives are not the cause of smaller families any more than ropes are the cause of suicides. The motives for desiring smaller families carry us into many other aspects of the culture. The shift from an illiterate agricultural society to a literate, specialized, industrialized society has changed children from an economic asset into an expensive burden. Shifts in patterns of recreation, in aspirations for education and social mobility, and changing concepts of individual rights have all united to curb indiscriminate childbearing. At present, the traditional idea that raising a large family is a noble service to society is rapidly being replaced by the idea that bearing many children is an act of irresponsible self-indulgence. Thus, changing technology, changing economics, and changing values are all involved in the change in family size.

SINGLE-PARENT FAMILIES HAVE INCREASED. Throughout most of Western history, children remained in the custody of the father in those few families broken by separation rather than by death. Within the past century the idea that children of separated parents "belonged" with the mother gained an acceptance that was seldom questioned. Today this assumption is questioned by no fewer than 650,000 fathers who care for their children themselves (but still only 12 out of each 1,000 households). Several studies seem to show that fathers can successfully raise children by themselves, even though it presents some special problems [Orthner et al., 1976; Dresden, 1976; G. Collins, 1979].

While the proportion of all households composed of a married couple with children

present fell by one-fourth between 1970 and 1981 (from 40.3 to 30.3 percent; see Table 10-1), those headed by females increased 65 percent, to one in nine families. Those families headed by a never-married female increased 356 percent between 1970 and 1981, to a total of over 1 million. Of all families *with children,* one-parent families increased from 11 percent in 1971 to 21 percent in 1981. At a given moment, 20 percent of today's children are living in a single-parent household, while today's child has a 50:50 chance of living in a single-parent household at sometime before the age of 18 [above figures from U.S. Bureau of the Census, 1982*a*].

Whether the single-parent family is necessarily damaging to children can be debated. Blechman [1982] observes that if socioeconomic status, education, and other variables are controlled so that number of parents is the only variable being measured, then few differences in child development can be shown. But is it realistic to isolate single parenthood from the circumstances which so often accompany it? Most single-parent families are poor, and three-fourths of them are on welfare [Segalman and Basu, 1977]. A major part of their low income and poor education is a *result* of their being single parents (or teen-aged parents). A longitudinal study of women who divorced and did not remarry found that they suffered an average income decline of 50 percent [Duncan and Morgan, 1982]. Among householders under 25 years of age, the female-headed household averages only one-third of the income of the couple-household, and for householders 25 to 44 years of age, the female-headed household still has only 42 percent of the couple-household income [U.S. Bureau of the Census, 1980*a*]. If the same women were members of two-parent households, a great many of them would not be poor. But most of them *are* poor, and their stress levels are high. Single-parent mothers are the greatest consumers of mental-health services, while their children's rate of use of mental-health services is four times that of

TABLE 10-1
COMPOSITION OF U.S. HOUSEHOLDS, 1970 AND 1981

Type of household	1970	1981
Family households:		
Married couple, no children under 18	30.3%	29.6%
Married couple with children under 18	40.3	30.3
One parent with children under 18	5.0	7.6
Other (e.g., extended)	5.6	5.7
Total	81.2	73.2
Nonfamily households*:		
Persons living alone	17.1	23.0
Other	1.7	3.8
Total	18.8	26.8

*Maintained by a person or persons who do not share their quarters with any relatives.
Sources: U.S. Bureau of the Census, *Current Population Reports: Household and Family Characteristics,* March 1981, ser. P-20, no. 371, March 1982, p. 2.

In which of the above categories has the greatest *number* of people had a change of status? In which category has there been the greatest *proportionate* change?

In socialization two parents are generally better than one. (*Erika Stone/Peter Arnold, Inc.*)

children from two-parent families [Guttentag, 1980]. Some part of these difficulties can be attributed directly or indirectly to the single-parent status.

It is also clear that a single-parent family *can* be a healthy environment for children. A support network of helpful relatives or friends can make a great difference [McLanahan et al., 1981]. The character of the parent is clearly more important than the form of the family [Marotz-Baden et al., 1979]. One responsible, loving parent may be better for children than two quarrelsome, abusive parents locked in endless conflict. But it is difficult to argue that two responsible, loving parents are not better than one.

UNMARRIED PARENTHOOD HAS INCREASED. Since 1950, the illegitimacy rate has multiplied more than four times, from 4.0 to 17.1 percent of all births. For each thousand unmarried white women aged 15 to 16, births increased from 13.8 in 1970 to 15.1 in 1981, while falling from 95.5 in 1970 to 85.3 in 1981 for black women. Nearly one-third of the babies born to white teenagers are born out of wedlock, and over three-fourths of those born to black teenagers are born out of wedlock [Statistical Abstract, 1981, p. 95]. Over one-half of all black babies in the nation are born out of wedlock [*Time*, 116:67, Nov. 9, 1981]. In some areas the figure is much higher—77 percent in central Harlem [*The New York Times*, Nov.

8, 1981, p. 20]. A survey of all New York City children born out of wedlock in the 1960s and 1970s found three-fourths of them living on welfare in 1975 [Auletta, 1982]. What are the prospects for children born into a neighborhood where most of the children are illegitimate and are living on welfare in single-parent households? What are their chances for ever sharing the "American dream"?

A generation ago nine out of ten illegitimate babies were placed for adoption; today more than nine in ten of them are kept by their mothers. This often condemns the mother to a life of economic deprivation and the baby to a life of emotional deprivation [Furstenberg, 1976; Fosberg, 1977]. One wonders about the ultimate social consequences of having a significant part of the next generation raised by unmarried adolescents whom we do not consider mature enough to sign a contract, drive a car, cast a vote, or buy a drink.

Some people oppose sex education in schools and teenage contraception and pregnancy services lest they arouse sexual curiosity and stimulate premarital sexual intercourse. What research evidence we have suggests otherwise. There is some evidence that sex education reduces teenage sex activity and that

---

The girl who has an illegitimate child at the age of 16 suddenly has 90 percent of her life's script written for her. She will probably drop out of school, even if someone else in her family helps to take care of the baby; she will probably not be able to find a steady job that pays enough to provide for herself and her child; she may feel impelled to marry someone she might not otherwise have chosen. Her life choices are few, and most of them are bad. Had she been able to delay the first child, her prospects might have been quite different.

(Arthur Campbell, "The Role of Family Planning in the Reduction of Poverty," *Journal of Marriage and the Family,* 30:236, May 1968.)

---

premarital childbirth is reduced by the availability of contraception and abortion services [Moore and Caldwell, 1981]. Within three years after a pregnancy clinic began operating in two St. Paul high schools, the student pregnancy rate fell by 40 percent [Edwards, 1980]. During the past decade the percentage of sexually active teenagers has increased greatly, the use of contraception by teenagers has doubled, and the premarital pregnancy rate has declined [Villadsen, 1982]. As this is written, however, it appears that family-planning services and abortion services may be reduced. If this happens, an increase in premarital pregnancies, illegitimacies, and unwanted children can be predicted.

SINGLE-PERSON HOUSEHOLDS HAVE INCREASED. It was historically difficult for a person to live comfortably alone. Only by joining a family or by setting up a household complete with servant staff could one live in comfort. Today the physical accommodations are more favorable—furnished apartments and maid service, wash-and-wear clothes, laundromats, and catering services of many kinds make it easier for the singles.

Historically, women lived with parents or relatives until married. Any younger woman who wished to live alone was suspected of evil intentions. Today one's own apartment and set of wheels have become almost symbols of passage into adult status. Single-person households have increased from 4.7 percent of all households in 1950 to 23 percent in 1981, with 50 percent of the females and 69 percent of the males between 20 and 24 being single [U.S. Bureau of the Census, 1982*b*]. A number of books have been written in praise of the single life-style [e.g., Adams, *Single Blessedness,* 1976]. While opinions on single "blessedness" may vary, the increase in single-person households is a highly significant change in American family patterns [Stein, 1981]. For example, the single person is more vulnerable to many of life's hazards (such as illness or unemployment) and more susceptible to deviation than are people living in families [Davis and Strong, 1977].

NONMARITAL COHABITATION HAS INCREASED. In frontier America, where churches and government offices were few and distant, common-law marriage was common and respectable. Although there was no marriage license or ceremony, these couples *invited and accepted* a public recognition of themselves as husband and wife. Such common-law marriages were entirely legal and binding, provided an acceptance and recognition of them as husband and wife could be shown. This, however, created uncertainties and invited abuses. As the frontier passed, most states withdrew recognition of common-law marriages as legal and binding.

There have always been some unmarried couples who lived together openly as "lovers" rather than as husband and wife. Except in sophisticated, "arty" circles, they were generally condemned as scandalous and immoral. Today, however, nonmarital cohabitation without any commitment to marry has become quite common. Between 1970 and 1981, nonmarital cohabitation multiplied by 3½ times, to include 3.6 million persons [U.S. Bureau of the Census, 1982b, p. 5], although married-couple households outnumber non-married-couple households about 30 to 1.

Nonmarital cohabitation in Sweden, which

Couples used to marry and set up housekeeping. But now . . .
(*Mimi Forsyth/Monkmeyer*)

was fairly common but viewed as deviant until about 1965, is reported as fully institutionalized by 1975 [Trost, 1979, p. 186]. A longitudinal study of 111 cohabiting Swedish couples found that after 3½ years, 22 were separated, 25 had married, and 51 were still cohabiting [Trost, 1979, p., 173]. Nonmarital cohabitation has become quite common in the United States, with varying degrees of acceptance by parents and others. Whether it will ever become institutionalized is an open question.

For most cohabiting couples, nonmarital cohabitation seems just another stage of the courtship process, without any firm commitment to marry [Macklin, 1978, p. 233]. Macklin estimated in 1976 that about one-fourth of all American college students had cohabited, another one-half would do so if an acceptable partner appeared, and one-fourth would not do so [Macklin, 1978, p. 213]. While most cohabiting couples have made no firm commitment to marry, most do marry or else they separate within a few years. Very few plan or will choose nonmarital cohabitation as a permanent life-style [Macklin, 1978, p. 234]. In a *Good Housekeeping* poll [March, 1978, p. 88] one-half the cohabiting informants had married their partner, and another one-fourth were still cohabiting. Thus, cohabitation has become a fairly common preliminary to marriage, a point easily confirmed by noting the addresses of marriage license applicants as printed in the newspaper.

One study of cohabiting persons' scores on the Minnesota Multiphasic Personality Inventory found that cohabiting college students, as compared with other students, tended to be somewhat more irreligious, nonconformist, immature, impulsive, manipulative, selfish, outgoing, friendly, fun-loving, and creative [Catlin et al., 1976]. But the more common nonmarital cohabitation becomes, the more closely will such couples approach a representative cross section of their age group.

If has often been suggested that some form of "trial" marriage would prevent a lot of mismatches and unhappy marriages. There is no convincing evidence that nonmarital cohabitation does this. Research studies quite consistently show that nonmarital cohabitation is remarkably like conventional marriage in its problems and adjustments and that nonmarital cohabitation has scarcely any measurable effects upon the marriages of those who marry [Blaine, et al., 1975; Stafford, 1977; Macklin, 1978, pp. 215–228; Jacques and Chason, 1979; Risman and Hill, 1981]. We may conclude that nonmarital cohabitation has become a widely accepted preliminary to marriage but is having very little effect upon marriage and the family.

THE QUIET REVOLUTION IN WOMEN'S EMPLOYMENT. Perhaps the greatest change of all has been the increase in "working wives." Women workers today form over two-fifths of our labor force. About 61 percent of all married women (aged 20 to 45) living with their husbands are in the labor force, and over nine out of ten married women work for some part of their married lives. The labor force now includes 56 percent of all women with children under 6 years old, and 70 percent of all women with children between 6 and 18 years old. [*Statistical Abstract*, 1981, pp. 386, 388]. Married women with children are now more likely to be employed than married women without children (explained, perhaps, by the fact that many of the "married women without children" are of retirement age). From these data, the "normal" life pattern of the American woman emerges. Typically, she begins working before marriage, works until her children arrive, when she *may* take off a few years but, if so, returns before long. Obviously, it has become normal for the American wife to work for a major part of her lifetime.

Historically, a woman who worked was living evidence that she had no husband able and willing to support her. A survey of 140 married women workers in 1908 found that only 6 husbands held jobs above the grade

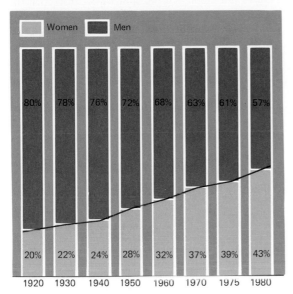

FIGURE 10-3 Composition of the labor force, United States, 1920–1980. (*Source: U.S. Department of Labor, Bureau of Labor Statistics.*)

of unskilled laborer [Bureau of Labor Statistics, 1908, pp. 163–164]. The working wife, once a lower-class phenomenon, is now common among the prosperous middle classes. There is no reason to believe that this trend will be reversed. The "American standard of living" now requires two incomes. In the words of one middle-class couple, "You can make do with one income, but you get accustomed to a style of living where you spend more quickly, and it becomes almost a necessity to have a double salary." [*Time*, 110:57, Aug. 21, 1978]. As the "normal" standard of living increasingly becomes insupportable on a single income, the pressure upon the nonworking wife to get a job is difficult to resist. Most of the readers of this textbook will be either working wives or the husbands of working wives for a major part of their married lives.

This quiet revolution has affected the household division of labor. The work time of housewives has *not* been reduced by laborsaving devices; today's wives spend *more* time on housework than those of a half

century ago [Hall and Schroeder, 1970; Vanek, 1974, p. 231]. The time once spent in hand-washing clothes and home-canning is now spent in putting in order a daily avalanche of toys, books, magazines, and hobby gear, chauffeuring children, attending the PTA, and doing other tasks which grandmother did not do.

Obviously, when the wife works, *something has to give.* Some of the housekeeping niceties may be sacrificed, and some tasks may be commercialized (sending out the laundry, buying prepared foods), but the working wife still works longer than the housewife by an average of about ten hours a week. A study of time-use in twelve European and American countries [Converse, 1972] found that this ten-hour figure held true within a very small variation for all the twelve countries studied. Husbands and children, on the average, assume only a modest share of household tasks when wives work. No matter whether the husband works long or short hours, he still does very little housework [Clark, Nye, and Gecas, 1978; Hoffreth and Moore, 1979]. One study concludes that, as compared with husbands of nonworking wives, husbands of working wives spend about four more hours a week on household chores [Bohen and Viveros-Long, 1981, p. 134], while another study credits them with less than two hours per week of additional household chores [Pleck, 1979]. Husbands of working wives do give considerable help with child care [Scanzoni, 1978, p. 77], and a recent survey of male college students reported three-fourths saying that they expected to spend as much time as their wives in bringing up children [Katz, 1978]. It will be interesting to see whether their performance matches their promise. Most of the male readers of this book have discovered, or will discover, whether their masculinity will dissolve in dishwater.

THE DUAL-CAREER FAMILY IS BECOMING COMMON. For some years, many wives have worked, but few have had careers. Most

TABLE 10-2
COLLEGE UNDERGRADUATE WOMEN'S
PLANS FOR CAREER AND FAMILY WHILE
CHILDREN ARE PRESCHOOL AGE*

Career plans	Number	Percent
Yes, full-time career	19	9.6
Yes, part-time career	68	34.3
No career	74	37.4
Conditional (depends upon finances, husband, job)	9	4.5
Not applicable (plan no career or plan no children)	23	11.6
No answer; don't know	5	2.5

Expected division of time between career and family	Number	Percent
Most to career, little to family	0	0.0
Much to career, some to family	7	3.5
Equal to career and family	105	53.0
Some to career, much to family	60	30.3
Little to career, most to family	13	6.6
Other: plan no career, plan no children, conditional, no answer	13	6.6

Source: Adapted from Esther R. Greenglass and Reva Devins, "Sex Roles, Factors Related to Marriage and Career Plans of Unmarried Women," *Sex Roles*, 8:57–71, 1982.
*Based upon responses of 198 unmarried women undergraduate college students at York University, Toronto.

Do these data suggest that today's college-educated women are no longer family-oriented?

working wives viewed their jobs as temporary, supplemental or supportive, and subordinate to their husband's careers. Whether these working wives are happier than full-time housewives is uncertain. Several studies [e.g., Nye, 1963; Ferree, 1976; Booth, 1979] conclude that working wives are more satisfied with their lives than housewives. But the National Commission on Working Women reports that "the average woman worker is a lonely person in a dead-end job, seething with frustration over her lot" [*Business Week,* Feb. 5, 1979, p. 28]. Six national surveys by the University of Michigan and the National Opinion Research Center find no consistent relationship between wives' working and their life satisfaction [Wright, 1978; Campbell, 1980, p. 137]. There is some evidence that the

happiest category of women are those with husband, children, and a job to which they are only moderately committed [Campbell, 1975; Shaver and Friedman, 1976]. Most of these women were socialized when sex-role expectations were more traditional. Where today's young women will find their greater life satisfaction may be changing. As shown in Table 10-2 over half the college women who gave a definite answer to the question plan to have a career.

A growing number of young women today are asserting their equal right to a *career*, not just a *job.* Unlike a job, a career implies a major, long-term commitment to a sequence of positions carrying increasing responsibility and expertise. Many women today expect that any necessary sacrifices of career goals to family life should be joint and equal, not unequally imposed upon the wife. A couple who try seriously to apply this formula will find that many adjustments must be made [Holmstrom, 1973; Rapoport and Rapoport, 1976; Hopkins and White, 1977; Heckman et al., 1977; Pepitone-Rockwell, 1980]. These range from who stays home when Junior is ill to what happens when a career move beneficial to one career would damage the other career. The greater one's career success, the greater becomes the likelihood that one must move to continue advancing [Duncan and Perucci, 1976]. It is clear that a man or woman who values career success above all other values should marry only a spouse who is willing to sacrifice career ambitions to family values [Fowlkes, 1981]. Either one or both must make some career sacrifices or irreconcilable conflicts are predictable.

One study found that a majority of the dual-career couples were either childless or past child-rearing age [Ramey, 1977]. Where there are children, the major responsibility for child care usually falls upon the wife [Johnson and Johnson, 1977]. Dual-career couples with children usually employ domestic help, leading critics to charge that this creates a class of women who must do house-

CAREER PROSPECTS OF THE HOUSEHUSBAND

Mr. Demers is one of many American men who have foresaken the 9-to-5 world of business to rear their infants and toddlers [for three years, while his wife finished medical school]—only to face the harsh consequences of that choice when the children are older: Finding someone willing to hire a former male homemaker is next to impossible.

"The hurdles men face returning to the job market are about three times greater" than those faced by women, says Charles Arons, president and chief executive officer of Casco Industries, a Los Angeles-based employment and recruiting firm. Mr. Arons says he sees a steadily increasing number of men with tales of woe similar to Mr. Demers's. That's understandable, he says, because "there isn't a male I know of in an executive position who would accept raising kids as a legitimate excuse for not working for three years."

What causes this situation? Will it change?

work and child care so that other women can have a more privileged life-style [Hunt and Hunt, 1977]. Some dual-career couples resolve the job-transfer dilemma by commuting, but this sort of part-time marriage is often a prelude to divorce [Gallese, 1978]. Dual careers are clearly difficult to operate within the nuclear family in a specialized, mobile society.

THE STATUS OF DIVORCE HAS CHANGED. Divorce is the object of much agonized dismay by Americans who cannot accept divorce as an integral part of the modern American family system. Divorce is not necessarily a symptom of moral decay or social instability. The average Anamatian peasant married three times and usually had some outside love affairs, without producing any dire consequences [Freilich and Coser, 1972]. To invoke again the concept of cultural relativism, whether divorce is a disruptive crisis or a useful adjustment depends upon the culture.

Why has divorce increased so greatly? We do not know whether marital unhappiness has increased, since we have no reliable measures of marital unhappiness in earlier times. What we *do* know is:

1 The decline of a set of uniform sex-role expectations increases the likelihood that a husband and wife may disagree about their rights and duties.

2 The increasing specialization, individuation, and mobility of modern life, together with our rapid rate of social change, make it less likely that a couple will share the same tastes and values for a lifetime.

3 Women's economic dependence upon men has decreased. Unhappy wives in earlier generations were virtually helpless, whereas today's unhappy wife has some alternatives: work, if she is able; welfare, if she is not [Udry, 1981].

4 Divorce has become socially acceptable, with divorcees no longer branded as moral lepers or social outcasts.

5 Divorce feeds upon itself as an increasing fraction of people have parents, relatives, or friends who are divorced. Research shows that one's readiness to divorce is more highly correlated with one's social contacts with divorced persons than with one's level of marital unhappiness [Greenberg and Nay, 1982]. Close contacts with divorced persons transform divorce from a remote nightmare into a rational alternative.

6 No-fault divorce laws have made divorce less costly and complicated.

To sum, up, marital unhappiness may or

THE NEW EXTENDED FAMILY

In about one in five American families with two or more children living in the household, at least one of these children is from an earlier relationship. This new extended family is the confused tangle of relationships created by divorce and remarriage. Suppose Arthur and Adrienne get a divorce, with Arthur keeping their sons, Billy and Bobby, while Adrienne keeps Carole and Charlene. Arthur marries Darlene, who brings along her daughters, Eileen and Elizabeth, while her ex-husband Daniel, who has custody of their sons, Frank and Frederick, marries Gloria, who has custody of her two children, Harold and Howard. Adrienne marries Ivan, who kept his two sons, Joseph and Jacob, when he divorced Kathryn, who kept their daughters, Lenore and Louise. Thus Billy and Bobby live with their father and stepmother, along with Eileen and Elizabeth, and are periodically visited by Carole and Charlene and Frank and Frederick, while they periodically visit their mother and their sisters, Carole and Charlene, where they also see Ivan and his sons, Joseph and Jacob, and possibly his daughters, Lenore and Louise. If all family members are still living, each child now has eight grandparents, four parents, and eight brothers and sisters, plus any new half-brothers or -sisters who may arrive someday.

(Inspired by Michael Norman, "The New Extended Family," *The New York Times Magazine,* Nov. 23, 1980, pp. 26ff.)

An institutionalized role, such as father or grandparent, carries recognized guidelines for behavior. Explain the confusions in the new, extended family due to the absence of institutionalized roles.

---

may not have increased, but readiness to use divorce as an answer has multiplied enormously. The most recent projections are that about 38 percent of first marriages of women now aged 25 to 29 will end in divorce, that 75 percent of divorcees will remarry, and that 45 percent of the remarried will divorce again [Glick and Norton, 1979].

A society can get a very low divorce rate in at least five ways. First, it can deemphasize love. In many societies marriage is a working partnership but not a romantic adventure as well. If less is expected of marriage, more marriages will be "successful." Second, it can separate love from marriage. A number of societies have a series of men's clubs for companionship, and allow men wide freedom to prowl in search of sex adventure. Here again, less is demanded of the marriage. Third, the society can socialize its members to be so much alike in personality and expectation that practically all marriages will work out successfully. The stable, well-integrated society generally succeeds in accomplishing this leveling; our society does not. Fourth,

familism may be so encompassing that divorce is intolerable. In other words, so many of one's necessities, privileges, and satisfactions may be connected to the marital and family ties that to sever the marital tie is to cancel nearly all the claims and privileges which make life tolerable. This was approximately true in early America, where divorce was legally simple but not very practical. Finally, divorce can be legally forbidden, or made so difficult that most unhappily married couples are unable or unwilling to seek di-

They differ more and more greatly in personality and expectation.

vorce as a solution. Our society has actually done none of these things. It socializes people so that they differ more and more greatly in personality and expectation, gives them values which lead them to expect a great deal of marriage and to demand a high level of love satisfaction in marriage, and provides no approved outlet for their frustrated marital needs when they fail. All this makes a fairly high rate of marital failure and divorce an inescapable part of our modern social structure.

Changing Family Functions

Structure and function are two aspects of the same thing. Changes in one are both cause and effect of changes in the other. What changes in function accompany changes in family structure?

THE ECONOMIC FUNCTIONS HAVE GREATLY DECLINED. A century ago the American family was a unit of economic production, united by shared work on the farm. Today only one of thirty-five families is a farm family; and even the farm family is not the self-sufficient unit of the past. Except on the farm, the family is no longer a basic unit of economic production; this has shifted to the shop, the factory, the office. The family is no longer united by shared work, for its members work separately. Instead, the family is a unit of economic *consumption*, united by companionship, affection, and recreation.

THE SEXUAL REGULATION FUNCTIONS HAVE DIMINISHED. Although most sexual intercourse is still marital, the proportion has probably fallen below the 90 percent figure claimed by Kinsey in 1948 [p. 588]. Research studies show no great change in premarital sexual behavior between 1948 and 1965, but after 1965 females began catching up (or down?) to the male figure of about four out of five being sexually experienced before marriage [Zelnik and Kantner, 1978]. A research

study finds well over 90 percent of college students approving of sexual intercourse among persons who are engaged, in love, or with "strong affection," while over two-thirds even approve of intercourse among those who are "not particularly affectionate" [Perlman, 1974]. Many other studies [Schmidt and Sigursch, 1972; Hunt, 1974; Yankelovich, 1977; Zelnik and Kantner, 1978] point to the same conclusion: virgin marriage has become relatively uncommon and may virtually disappear in the near future. Whether this is a "sexual revolution" as some scholars proclaim [Skolnik, 1973, pp. 410–413] or whether it is only another of many historical swings between permissiveness and restrictiveness [Hindus, 1971; Shorter, 1971] is not yet apparent.

THE REPRODUCTIVE FUNCTION HAS DECLINED IN IMPORTANCE. True, birthrates are much lower than a century ago, but if one considers only the size of the *surviving* family, then the family reproductive function is not so greatly changed. A few centuries ago one-half to three-fourths of the children died in infancy or childhood; today over 96 percent reach adulthood. Today's average American family of slightly under three surviving children is not far from what it has been through most of Western history. The birthrate in the United States (when adjusted for age distribution) has been falling, but future changes cannot be predicted. A further decline in family size, aside from its ecological implications, may be expected to increase family harmony. There is solid research evidence that the smaller families are less stressful, more comfortable, and "most satisfactory to spouses, parents, and children" [Nye et al., 1970], and are happier and better adjusted [Hurley and Palonen, 1967; Schooler, 1972; Glenn and McLanahan, 1982]. Even when other variables (such as income, education, and occupation) are controlled, children in smaller families are more healthy, creative, and intelligent [Lieberman, 1970]. But if small families are good

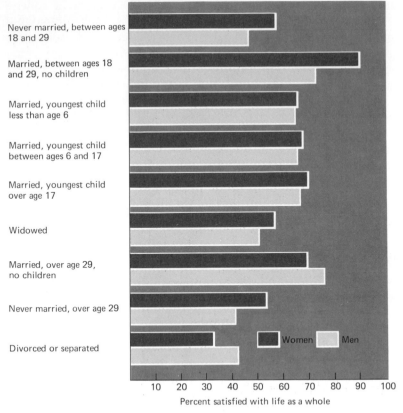

Never married, between ages
18 and 29

Married, between ages 18
and 29, no children

Married, youngest child
less than age 6

Married, youngest child
between ages 6 and 17

Married, youngest child
over age 17

Widowed

Married, over age 29,
no children

Never married, over age 29

Divorced or separated

Women Men

10 20 30 40 50 60 70 80 90 100

Percent satisfied with life as a whole

FIGURE 10-4   Life satisfaction of women and men at stages of the
life cycle. (*Source: Published by the Institute of Social Research, 1976,
University of Michigan; reprinted by permission of the* ISR Newsletter.)

Are the associations causative or selective? Are the married people
happier *because* they are married (causative), or are the happy, well-
adjusted people more likely to get and stay married (selective)? May
both be true?

for children, having no children seems to be
good for adults. As shown in Figure 10-4, the
happiest adult categories were those with no
children at all. Marriage, but not parenthood,
is associated with superior contentment
[Campbell, 1975].

THE SOCIALIZATION FUNCTION GROWS MORE
IMPORTANT. The family remains the principal
socializing agency, although the school and

the peer groups unquestionably fill important
socializing functions. Other social agencies
are occasionally called in for guidance. The
major change has been in our *attention* to the
socialization function. An earlier generation
knew little about "personality development";
today nearly every literate parent knows about
Dr. Spock [1945, 1957, 1974, 1977.] We know
something today of the role of emotional
development in school progress, career suc-

cess, physical well-being, and practically all other aspects of the good life. Our great-grandparents worried about smallpox and cholera; we worry about sibling jealousies and peer-group adjustment.

How has the quiet revolution affected the socialization function? Does the child suffer when mother takes a job? There have been several dozen studies of this question [reviewed by Stoltz, 1960; Herzog, 1960; Nye and Hoffman, 1963; Schooler, 1972]. The earlier studies failed to control for such variables as social class or family composition. As a result, the working-mother sample had a higher proportion of poor, uneducated slum dwellers, widows, and divorcées than the nonworking-mother sample. Such poorly controlled studies seemed to show that children suffered when mother worked. Later studies compared children of working mothers with children of *otherwise comparable* nonworking mothers. Although not entirely conclusive, these studies do not show any general tendency for children to suffer when the mother is employed. Although the evidence is somewhat mixed, it appears that *whether* the mother works is not very important, while the *kind* of mother she is and the kind of home she and the father provide are the more important variables [Hoffman, 1963]. The question appears to have been settled, for it has attracted very little research interest in recent years.

At the very time that the socialization function is growing more important, the changing structure of the family—increasing divorce, illegitimacy, and single-parent and dual career families—would appear to make it more difficult for the family to perform its socialization function. Time will tell whether this fear is well-founded.

THE AFFECTIONAL AND COMPANIONSHIP FUNCTIONS GROW IN IMPORTANCE. The primary community, the small group of neigh-

The companionship function grows in importance. (*Mimi Forsyth/Monkmeyer*)

bors who knew one another well and had much in common, has disappeared from the lives of most Americans. Urbanization and specialization have destroyed it. In an increasingly heedless, impersonal, and ruthless world, the immediate family becomes the bulwark of emotional support. Only within the family can one hope to find enduring sympathy when troubled, or an unjealous joy at one's success. For both sexes and all races and at all ages, the single, the widowed, the divorced, and the separated show lower levels of happiness and higher death rates for all the leading causes of death. It is literally true that the lonely die sooner.

The importance of the affectional and com-

In a research study of wives of recently retired husbands, most wives reported positive aspects arising from their spouses' retirement. Particularly mentioned were time available to do what one wants, increased companionship, flexibilty of schedule, and husband doing more household chores. Most respondents also reported negative aspects to their husbands' retirement, including financial problems, not enough for husband to do, and too much togetherness. The wives suggested that husbands should keep busy and that wives should continue their preretirement activities. The most constant correlate of wives' satisfaction in the early years of retirement was the participation of husbands in household tasks.

Adapted from Elizabeth A. Hill and Lorraine T. Dorfman, "Reaction of Housewives to the Retirement of Their Husbands," *Family Relations*, 31:195–200, April 1982.

Do you suppose that husbands' household help is a causative or a selective factor in wives' greater satisfaction?

panionship functions are further magnified by the expansion of the *postparental period*. In earlier generations relatively few parents lived very long beyond the maturing of their children. In 1870, as shown in Table 10-3, fewer than half the American fathers and mothers were still living when their youngest child married. By 1960, this median length of the postparental period had grown from nothing at all to sixteen years for women and fourteen years for men, and was still lengthening. A fairly long postparental period, as a *normal* rather than an exceptional life stage, is a very recent development. The bucolic literature about loving grandparents and great-grandparents gives little hint of how rare they really were. The modern appearance of the postparental stage of the life cycle means that most couples now reach that point where there is no urgent necessity for them to remain together—unless shared affection and companionship make it seem worthwhile.

THE STATUS DEFINITION FUNCTION CONTINUES. Many families continue to prepare children to retain the class status of the family; others seek to prepare their children for social mobility. They do this mainly by trying to give children the kind of ambitions, attitudes, and habits which prompt them to struggle for a higher class status and to fill it successfully. This is called *anticipatory socialization*, for it is an effort to socialize children for a class status which it is hoped they will someday achieve. At best, this effort is only partly successful. The child may acquire the ambitions and work habits which prompt it to struggle successfully for upward mobility, but no family can fully succeed in socializing a child for a way or life not practiced by that family.

THE PROTECTIVE FUNCTIONS HAVE DECLINED. The traditional family in Western society performed most of the functions of organized social work today—nursed the sick, gave haven to the handicapped, and shelter to the aged. Today, we have a medical technology which only specialists and hospitals can handle. Today's urban household is an impractical place in which to care for some kinds of handicapped people. Family care of the aged was a practical arrangement when the aging couple stayed on the farm, joined by a married child and mate. The parents could retire gradually, shifting to less strenuous tasks but remaining useful and appreciated. This pattern is available today to only a tiny minority, and many elderly couples feel—and are—useless and unappreciated in the homes of their children. Our rapid rate of social change and social mobility also means that many tensions may develop when three generations live under one roof. So for a variety of reasons—most of which have nothing to do with selfishness or personal responsibility—many of the protective functions of the traditional family have been shifted to other institutions.

TABLE 10-3
THE NEW POSTPARENTAL STAGE IN THE AMERICAN FAMILY

		MEDIAN AGE			
	At marriage	At birth of last child	At marriage of last child	At death of spouse	Number of postparental years
Female					
1890	22	32	55	53	−2*
1960	20	26	47	63	16
1980	22	27	48	66	18
Male					
1890	26	36	59	57	−2*
1960	23	28	49	63	14
1980	23	29	51	68	17

*The 1890 couple had no postparental stage at all, since at least one of them was usually dead before the marriage of their last child. Today the postparental stage averages about seventeen or eighteen years.
Source: Adapted and updated from Gerald R. Leslie, *The Family in Social Context*, 3d ed., Oxford University Press, New York, 1976, p. 272.

What other social changes are produced by this new postparental stage?

Family Violence

There is nothing new about violence within the family, but only recently has it been "discovered" as a social problem [Pfohl, 1977]. The first national survey of family violence was made in 1975 by Straus, Gelles, and Steinmetz, [1980]. As they say, "The marriage license is a hitting license." As shown in Table 10-4, in a single year about one in nine American husbands and wives commit at least one act of violence against their mates, with a median frequency of two or three violent acts during a year. Interestingly enough, wives "beat" husbands slightly more often than husbands "beat" wives, but serious injury is far more often inflicted by the husbands (or lovers) [Steinmetz, 1977; Gelles, 1979, p. 139]. Violence in self-defense is also more common among wives, and this helps explain the surprisingly high violence index among women [Gelles, 1979, p. 139].

Husband/wife and parent/child violence is found at all class levels but is far more common in the lower classes [Pelton, 1978]. The violent husband is most often poor, uneducated, either unemployed or stuck in a low-paid–low-status job, and is the son of a violent father [Straus, Gelles, and Steinmetz, 1980, pp. 145–150]. The child-abusing parent most often shows the same characteristics. Most were abused children themselves, are young and immature, hold unrealistic expectations for their children's behavior, and react violently when children disappoint them [Thorman, 1980, pp. 24–25]. The most likely victims are unwanted children [Freeman, 1979, p. 28; Straus, Gelles, and Steinmetz, 1980, p. 234] or children who are sickly, fretful, and difficult to handle [Thorman, 1980, p. 19].

The most recently "discovered" form of family violence is parent or elder abuse. This topic is so new that, while the 1981–1982 issue of *Books in Print* lists more than 125 books on

TABLE 10-4
VIOLENCE RATES PER HUNDRED
MARRIAGES, 1975

Violence item	INCIDENT RATE FOR VIOLENCE BY:	
	H	W
Wife-beating and husband-beating (N to R)	3.8	4.6
Overall violence index (K to R)	12.1	11.6
K. Threw something at spouse	2.8	5.2
L. Pushed, grabbed, shoved spouse	10.7	8.3
M. Slapped spouse	5.1	4.6
N. Kicked, bit, or hit with fist	2.4	3.1
O. Hit or tried to hit with something	2.2	3.0
P. Beat up spouse	1.1	0.6
Q. Threatened with a knife or gun	0.4	0.6
R. Used a knife or gun	0.3	0.2

Source: Reproduced by permission from Murray A. Straus and Gerald T. Hotaling (eds.), *The Social Causes of Husband-Wife Violence,* The University of Minnesota Press, Minneapolis, 1980, p. 28.

This table shows *frequency* but not *seriousness* of spouse attacks. What are the research problems in defining and measuring seriousness of spouse violence?

family violence, not one is devoted to parent abuse. Aged parents are particularly vulnerable to violence from their children or grandchildren, and preliminary studies suggest that it is far more common than is generally recognized [Peek, 1982]. As research proceeds, it will be interesting to see whether family violence is three-generational, with abused children growing up to become abusive parents, and, still later, to become abused grandparents.

Family violence is unlikely to disappear. As long as many children are socialized in an atmosphere of family violence, and as adults must cope with poverty, unemployment, un-

wanted children, and a dead-end, hopeless existence, there will be a lot of family violence [Gelles, 1972, pp. 185–189].

INTERRELATIONSHIPS WITH OTHER INSTITUTIONS

No institution is more closely intertwined with other institutions than the family. For example, the form of the family is related to the economy. The slash-and-burn agriculture of the Tanala required a work team of several strong men, making the consanguine family an efficient work unit [Linton, 1936, chap. 20]. One family historian attributes the rise of the modern nuclear family to the development of market capitalism [Shorter, 1975, chap. 7]. We note that as developing countries move into industrialization, the nuclear fam-

---

WHERE DOES CHILD ABUSE BEGIN?

Violence and the threat of violence are the messages which people grow up with. It is not surprising that children who experience harsh punishment at home are the most ardent supporters of capital punishment. At the bottom of the tangled web of violence is the truism that violence does indeed beget violence. Each generation of children brought up on violence is another generation of potential child, wife, and yes, husband beaters. Accept violence as an inevitable part of raising children and [you] accept the consequences of a violent society. Reject violence as a normal part of family life and you begin to see that it is possible to raise a healthy, happy, and well-behaved generation which does not see the fist as the solution.

(Richard J. Gelles, *Family Violence*, Sage Publications, Beverly Hills, Cal., 1979, p. 144.)

Should we attempt to reduce family violence? Or should we accept violence as a part of life?

ily is replacing the consanguine or extended family because it is better adapted to specialization, mobility, and individualism than the extended family [Goode, 1963; Zelditch, 1964, p. 496; Fernandez, 1977, p. 158].

As noted by Keniston [1977], the family is expected to take up the slack in our other institutions. If the business cycle turns downward, the family tightens its belt. Instead of working hours being adjusted to the convenience of the family, the family must adjust to whatever working hours the economy demands. Family size falls as changing technology transforms children from an economic asset to an economic burden. The influence of religion on the family can be great, as shown by the Mormons and the Amish, whose birthrates are among the highest and divorce rates among the lowest in the country.

The direction of institutional interrelationships is highly one-sided. Other institutions affect the family far more than the family affects other institutions. For example, the increase of working mothers makes it rational for either corporations or government to provide extensive day-care facilities, as both have done in many western nations but not in the United States. Yet there is some response to family change by other institutions. The schools are asked to assume tasks the family can no longer do very well. The welfare institutions arose because the modern family could no longer discharge its protective functions efficiently. On balance, however, changes in other institutions produced by the family are outnumbered by changes imposed upon the family by other institutions.

THE FUTURE OF THE FAMILY

If one looks at the divorce rate and dwells on the gloomy strictures of the marriage critics, it is easy to wonder whether the family has a future. But there is firm evidence that marriage and the family are not dying. The one-divorce-to-two-marriages ratio is mis-

leading, since it implies that half the people get divorced, which is untrue. At current marriage and divorce rates, demographers estimate that fewer than two persons in five who marry will become divorced (37 or 38 percent), some of them to be divorced several times, while more than three-fifths of first marriages will last until death [Glick and Norton, 1979; Leslie, 1982, p. 555]. And most divorced people remarry, showing that it is not *marriage* which they reject, just their former partners.

Table 10-5 shows how very few of a national sample of married people were seriously dissatisfied at the moment of survey (although for many, it is a second or third marriage with which they are "satisfied"). While many become dissatisfied with a particular partner, few regard marriage as a trap. The idea that most marriages are wretched is a myth, possibly kept alive by marital failures who find comfort in the idea that everyone else is as miserable as they are.

While a few sociologists doubt that the family has a future [Keller, 1971], most sociologists disagree. It is noteworthy that in the Israeli kibbutz, after more than a generation of successful communal living, including a deliberate effort to abolish the family as a functional unit, the recent trend has been toward increasing the functional significance of the family [Shepher, 1969; Talmon, 1972; Mednick, 1975; Gerson, 1970]. All evidence thus indicates that the family, however often its death may be listed in the obituaries, is nonetheless here to stay [Bane, 1978]. It is even suggested by some scholars that the family is assuming *greater* importance in modern society. The inadequacy of work as a source of major life satisfactions for working-class people and the loss of the primary community as a source of roots and identity leave the family as the greatest source of emotional satisfaction [Kornblum, 1974].

The really important question is not "Will the family endure?" but, "How will it change?" Some believe that the computer revolution

TABLE 10-5

MARRIAGE—A TRAP OR A HAVEN? RESPONSES OF SAMPLE OF MARRIEDS

"Have you ever wished you had married someone else?"

	Yes, often, percent	Sometimes	Once in a while	Hardly ever	Never	Total, percent	N
Women	1	5	6	18	70	100	763
Men	*	4	7	18	72	100	684

"Has the thought of getting a divorce ever crossed your mind?"

	Yes, often, percent	Sometimes	Once in a while	Hardly ever	Never	Total, percent	N
Women	1	4	8	23	64	100	763
Men	1	3	5	20	71	100	685

"All things considered, how satisfied are you with your marriage? Which number comes closest to how satisfied or dissatisfied you feel?"

	Completely dissatisfied, percent					Completely satisfied, percent			
	1	2	3	4	5	6	7		
Women	1	1	3	9	8	23	56	100	763
Men	0	*	1	6	6	27	60	100	685

Source: Angus Campbell, Philip E. Converse, and Willard L. Rodgers, *The Quality of American Life: Perceptions, Evaluations, and Satisfactions,* Russell Sage Foundation, New York, 1976, p. 324.
*Indicates less than 1 percent.

Although this table shows that most married people are pretty well satisfied, we know that more than one in three marriages ends in divorce. How can both figures be true?

will transform the family, with a greatly increased fraction of all work, shopping, play, and everything else going on at home before the computer terminal [Frederick, 1983, p. 21]. "Productivity climbs when computers allow employees to work at home," reports the *Wall Street Journal* (May 3, 1983, p. 1), but workers miss their primary group contacts with coworkers. It is too early to predict the effects of the computer revolution upon the home.

One family historian believes that the nuclear family is crumbling and will be replaced by the "free-floating" couple, less tied to children, close friends, or neighbors than in the past [Shorter, 1975, p. 280]. In contrast to this, two major family theorists have predicted that the next few decades may see a return to a more highly structured, traditional, and less permissive family than that of today [Vincent, 1972; Zimmerman, 1972]. In fact, a rapidly growing movement called Toughlove is encouraging parents to be firm and strict in enforcing rules within the family [Leo, 1981]. A prominent sociologist [Etzioni, 1982] claims that the nuclear family will survive because "no complex society has ever survived without a nuclear family." There is little doubt that the family will survive, but the directions of family change cannot confidently be predicted.

SUMMARY

The family is the basic social institution. It varies greatly in form. The Western family is normally *conjugal,* composed of husband, wife, and children. But in many societies the family unit is *consanguine,* a much larger group of blood relatives with a fringe of spouses. All societies practice *endogamy,* requiring selection of mates within some specified groups, as well as *exogamy,* requiring that one go outside certain groups for selection. Although most marriages are *monogamous,* many societies permit *polgamy,* generally *polygyny,* wherein it is the husband who has more than one mate at a time. Most societies provide for divorce, with wide variance in grounds and procedures. The fascinating variety of family forms shows how basic human needs can be satisfactorily met under a great variety of institutional arrangements. In all societies the family performs certain functions—regulates sex relations, provides for reproduction, socializes children, offers affection and companionship, defines status, protects its members, and serves as a working and sharing team.

The present American family is in the midst of sweeping changes. It is smaller than a century ago. Single-parent families, unmarried parenthood, single-person households, nonmarital cohabitation, and dual-career families have all increased. Divorce appears to

have stabilized at a high level. Family violence has been "discovered" as a social problem.

The sex regulatory, reproductive, and status definition functions of the family have probably been the least affected by recent social changes. In economic function, the production activities of the family have been largely absorbed by separate economic institutions, leaving the family mainly a unit of economic consumption. The protective functions have been largely shifted to other institutions. The socialization and affectional functions have been largely shifted to other institutions. The socialization and affectional functions of the family have gained greatly in relative importance, both because of changes in other institutions and because of our increased knowledge about our personal and social needs.

No institution is more closely interrelated with other institutions than the family, but the direction of the interrelationships is highly one-sided. Other institutions affect the family far more than the family affects other institutions.

The survival of the family is in little doubt, but the directions of future family change cannot be predicted with any certainty.

GLOSSARY

conjugal family family consisting of a married couple and their children.

consanguine family family consisting of a group of married sisters and their children, or a group of married brothers and their children as its core, with a fringe of spouses and other relatives.

endogamy practice of choosing mates within some specified group.

exogamy practice of choosing mates outside some specified group.

extended family the nuclear family plus any other kin with whom important relationships are maintained.

family a kinship grouping which provides for the rearing of children and for certain other human needs.

marriage the approved social pattern whereby two or more persons establish a family.

matrilocal marriage the married couple live with the wife's family.

monogamy a form of marriage permitting only one mate (at a time).

neolocal marriage the married couple set up a household apart from other relatives.

nuclear family also called the *conjugal family;* a married couple and their children.

patrilocal marriage the married couple live with the husband's family.

polyandry a form of polygamy in which a wife is shared by two or more husbands.

polygamy a plurality of mates.

polygyny a form of polygamy in which a husband has two or more wives.

QUESTIONS
AND PROJECTS

1   Why is the family found in all societies? Would it be possible, with modern technology, to dispense with the family?

2   Why do American parents today play only a limited role in guiding the courtship choices of their children? Would it be desirable for them to play a larger role in determining marriage choices?

3   In a society such as the Trobriand, where a man has no special duties or particular affection for his own children, how can he possibly take a truly "fatherly" concern for his sister's children?

4   We use the term "uncle" for the brothers of our father or mother. Among the Todas the term "father" includes not only one's father but all of one's uncles. What is the importance of such variation in terminology? Some societies have no word for "illegitimate." What does the omission mean?

5   How does the family structure within a particular society illustrate concepts of cultural integration and cultural relativism?

6   What are some personality traits that make for conflict between marriage partners? Would these traits also create trouble in a commune, group marriage, or nonmarital cohabitation?

7   The text states that there is almost one divorce to each two marriages but that more than three out of five persons remain married to their first mates until separated by death. How can both be true?

8   Why is family violence most common in the lower classes?

9   Do you believe that a law requiring that parents be notified before their minor children may be given contraceptives would reduce teenage sex or just increase teenage pregnancies? Why?

10 How do recent and current changes in the family illustrate the interrelationship of institutions?

11 Defend each of these positions: (1) "Divorce is a necessary and useful institution for a society like ours." (2) "Divorce is cause and evidence of family breakdown and should be made more difficult."

12 Discuss these two propositions (1) "The proper socialization of the child requires the intimate, continuous, affectionate supervision that only a full-time mother can give." (2) "An uninterrupted mother-child contact encourages an excessive dependence; the child develops most healthfully when cared for by several warmly responsive adults."

13 Discuss these two propositions: (1) "The American family is badly disorganized by the sweeping social changes of the past century." (2) "The American family is reorganizing itself to meet changing human needs in a changing society."

14 Read John P. Marquand's *H. M. Pulham, Esq.*, Little, Brown and Company, Boston, 1941. How does the Pulham family prepare Harry for his sex role and class status and generally socialize him to act in the expected manner?

15 Read Hans Ruesch's novel about Eskimo life, *Top of the World*, Harper & Row, Publishers, Inc., New York, 1950; Pocket Books, Inc.,1951. Evaluate the Eskimo family as an institutional structure for meeting the needs of people in a particular environment.

SUGGESTED
READINGS

Bane, Mary Jo: *Here to Stay: American Families in the Twentieth Century*, Basic Books, Inc., Publishers, New York, 1978. A readable little book containing many policy recommendations for maintaining the family.

Blaine, Graham B., Jr., et al.: "Does Living Together Before Marriage Make for a Better Marriage?" *Medical Aspects of Human Sexuality*, 9:32–39, January 1975. Several scholars offer answers (or nonanswers) to the question stated in the title.

Clayton, Richard R., and Harwin L. Voss: "Shacking Up: Cohabitation in the 1970's," *Journal of Marriage and the Family*, 39:273–283, May 1977. A descriptive study and analysis of nonmarital cohabitation.

Davis, Alan G., and Philip M. Strong: "Working Without a

Net: The Bachelor as a Social Problem," *Sociological Review*, 25:109–120, February 1977. A discussion of the losses and vulnerabilities of bachelor life.

Doten, Dana: *The Art of Bundling*, Holt, Rinehart and Winston, Inc., New York, 1938. An entertaining account of the rise and fall of a quaint American custom, showing how it related to other institutions of that period.

Finkelhor, David, Richard J. Gelles, Gerald T. Hotaling, and Murray A. Straus (eds.): *The Dark Side of Families: Current Family Violence Research*, Sage Publications, Beverly Hills, Cal., 1983. A collection of readable research.

Folsom, Joseph K.: *The Family*, John Wiley & Sons, Inc., New York, 1934, 1943, chap. 1, "The Family Pattern." An interesting parallel-column comparison of American and Trobriand family patterns.

Fosberg, Lacey: "The Make-Believe World of Teen-Aged Maternity," *The New York Times Magazine*, Aug. 7, 1977, pp. 29ff. A popular presentation of the problems and consequences of teenaged motherhood.

Freedman, Jonathan L.: "Love + Marriage = Happiness (Still)," *Public Opinion*, 1:49–53, November/December 1978. A brief article summarizing a number of recent studies, all showing how much happier and healthier the marrieds are than the singles.

Furstenberg, Frank F., Jr.: *Unplanned Parenthood: The Social Consequences of Teen-Age Childbearing*, The Free Press, New York, 1976. A research study of what happened to teenage parents and their children.

Hunt, Janet G. and Larry L. Hunt: "Dilemmas and Contradictions of Status: The Case of the Dual-Career Family," *Social Problems*, 24:402–416, April 1977. A brief article suggesting that dual careers are incompatible with the nuclear family.

Journal of Social Issues, 35, no. 4, 1979. Presents a series of research articles on the effects of divorce on children.

*Kephart, William M.: *Extraordinary Groups: The Sociology of Unconventional Life-Styles*, St. Martin's Press, Inc., New York, 1982. A noted sociologist offers a readable analysis of a variety of communal groups, ranging from the Hutterites to modern communes.

*Levitan, Sar A. and Richard S. Belous, *What's Happening to the American Family?* The Johns Hopkins Press, Baltimore, 1981. A readable description of family change.

Macklin, Eleanor D.: "Review of Research on Nonmarital Cohabitation in the United States," in Bernard I. Murstein (ed.): *Exploring Intimate Lifestyles*, Springer Publishing Co., Inc., New York, 1978, pp. 196–243. A summary of research.

Pepitone-Rockwell, Fran (ed.): *Dual-Career Couples*, Sage Publications, Beverly Hills, Cal., 1980. A collection on dual-career marriages.

*Queen, Stuart A., Robert W. Habenstein, and John B. Adams: *The Family in Various Cultures*, 4th ed., J. B. Lippincott Company, Philadelphia, 1974. Readable descriptions of the family in a dozen different societies.

Schlesinger, Benjamin: *The One-Parent Family: Perspectives and Annotated Bibliography*, University of Toronto Press, Toronto, 1978. A concise description of one-parent families.

*Stein, Peter J., (ed.): *Single Life: Unmarried Adults in Social Context*, St. Martin's Press, Inc., New York, 1981. A collection on singles in American society.

Straus, Murray A., Richard J. Gelles, and Suzanne K. Steinmetz: *Behind Closed Doors: Violence in the American Family*, Anchor Books, Doubleday & Company, Inc., Garden City, N.Y., 1980. Readable description and analysis of family violence.

Wolock, Isabel and Bernard Horowitz: "Child Maltreatment and Maternal Deprivation among AFDC Recipients," *Social Service Review*, 53:175–182, June 1979. Research report finding correlation between family hardship and child abuse.

*An asterisk before the citation indicates that the title is available in a paperback edition.

11 Religious Institutions

SINGAPORE—The government is ordering schools to replace civics and current affairs lessons with compulsory religion classes to save this prosperous island republic from becoming "a nation of thieves."

The "religious knowledge" class for 12- and 13-year-olds will teach Christianity, Islam, Buddhism or Hinduism.

Those without a religion of their own or who do not wish to concentrate on a specific faith will have to do a general study of world religions.

Under the plan, Bible and Buddhist studies would be taught in English and Chinese. Hindu classes would be in English only and Islamic studies would be offered only in Malay.

Goh Keng Swee, deputy prime minister and education minister, said the idea of using religion lessons to improve public morality originated when he was in charge of Singapore's army.

Wallets and watches disappeared if left unattended in army camps for more than 10 seconds, he said.

"So one day, I told the prime minister that the schools are turning out a nation of thieves and that something must be done about this in our education system. He said that they start learning how to steal while in school."

(*Associated Press*, Feb. 18, 1982.)

Religious institutions are a society's important systems of religious beliefs and practices which are standardized and formulated and which are widely shared and viewed as necessary and true. Religious associations are the organized groups of people who share the beliefs and follow the practices of a religion. In Western societies, religion is highly organized into churches with congregational worship, but many societies have religion without religious associations or organizations. The Zuñi Indians are deeply religious, spending as much as half their waking hours in religious ceremonials and activities, yet they have no churches we would recognize as such [Farb, 1968, chap. 6]. Religion takes many forms and directions.

There are many definitions of religion. One sociologist defines it as "a system of beliefs and practices by which a group of people interprets and responds to what they feel is supernatural and sacred" [Johnstone, 1975, p. 20]. This definition is very useful for sociological analysis, since it emphasizes the social and corporate nature of religion and distinguishes religion from secular movements which may also be concerned with important values.

RELIGION AND SOCIETY

The faith of the Singapore government in the effect of religious instruction in the schools, recorded in the chapter epigraph, is shared by many people. All major religions stress such basic virtues as honesty and consideration for others. These are necessary for the orderly conduct of human society, and religion may help people take such ideas seriously.

Whether religious ideals can really be instilled by the schools may be open to question. It is also hard to prove whether or not religion really does produce moral behavior. Many research efforts have attempted to test the effects of professed religious beliefs and church activities upon personal behavior. Bouma reviewed dozens of such studies, finding little evidence that religion had much effect on behavior in American society [1970], and L. Jung's more recent research also found the evidence inconclusive [1980]. It is possible, however, that a religious presence in American society has some effect upon the cultural ethos, thus affecting the behavior of both the religious and the irreligious. This is at least a reasonable assumption [Eastland, 1981].

Religion includes ways of relating to supernatural beings and forces. (*Bonnie Freer/Photo Researchers, Inc.*)

Religion is concerned with more than moral behavior. Religion offers people a world view and provides answers for puzzling questions. It encourages one to rise above selfish interests and involve oneself with the needs of others. Good conduct may grow out of such a world view, but the religious response goes far beyond the following of conventional behavior norms.

Sociologists are interested in the interaction of religion and society. As in all cases of interaction, this is a two-way affair, and sometimes it is difficult to determine the boundary between the religious and nonreligious. Thus, our notions of justice and our form of family life have been influenced by the teachings of Judeo-Christian religion. On the other hand, our religion has also been influenced by the political and economic life of our society. (As stated earlier, institutions are interrelated.) The sociologist does not seek to judge the

truth of the beliefs of any religion; the sociologist *does* seek to discover the social effects of various beliefs and to find tendencies for certain types of religious beliefs and practices to develop under certain social conditions.

Those who seek to understand the nature of society seem impelled to explain the role of religion whether or not they call themselves "religious." Some regard religion as a major influence, others look on it as outdated or even harmful; but regardless of the judgment, it is too important to be ignored.

Religion as an Evolutionary Stage

Auguste Comte, often regarded as the "father" of sociology, advocated the secular view of religion as an evolutionary stage. This is, briefly, the idea that religion was once important but that it has been made obsolete by modern developments. The *sacred*, which is the domain of religion, has been replaced by the *secular*, or that which is removed from the supernatural. Religious belief systems have been displaced by scientific knowledge, while the healing, educational, and social service work of the church has been taken over either by government or by nonreligious private groups. Comte [1855] wrote of the three stages of human thought: the theological (religious), the metaphysical (philosophical), and the scientific (positive). The last stage was the only valid one for Comte, and if religion survived at all, it would only be as a "religion of humanity" based upon science. "Sin" is selfishness, and "salvation" is attained by freeing oneself from selfishness, while "immortality" consists of being remembered for one's loving service to humanity. Modern religious *humanism* is heavily indebted to Comte for its ideas.

There is no doubt that scientific thinking has greatly affected traditional religious belief systems and that many of the functions of religious institutions have been shifted elsewhere. Whether this means the end of religion or merely illustrates institutional change is a subject of debate.

Religion as the Unifying Force of Society

Émile Durkheim, an early French sociologist, spent years studying the religious practices of Australian aborigines and South Seas islanders. In *The Elementary Forms of Religious Life* [1912] he concluded that the main purpose of religion in primitive societies was to help people make contact not with God but with one another. The religious rituals helped people to develop a sense of community as they shared the experiences of marriage, birth, and death and celebrated the planting and harvest seasons and the winter solstice and the vernal equinox. This united the group, leaving none to face life alone. They were thus worshipping society not God or gods.

In a country of many different faiths and denominations, religion cannot easily unite the entire society, but it can unite each religious group in a mutual support system. Meanwhile, the unifying effects of religion upon society may be fulfilled by what Bellah [1974, 1975, 1980] and others have called "civil religion." The concept of civil religion in America is that, even though the United States does not have a state church, there is still a definite religious influence in national life. Despite many different churches, separated by many differences, the American civil religion has common elements stressed by all major churches.

Civil religion is a body of religious beliefs which are widely held throughout the society. They have a supernatural basis and are promoted by most churches. Civil religion supports government actions when they are in harmony with beliefs of civil religion. Conversely, civil religion condemns government actions which conflict with civil religious principles.

The expression of a civil religion predates the founding of the republic. It can be seen in the prayers of the early Puritan settlers as they asked God's blessing on their venture into a new land and is expressed in the statements of many American statesmen. In the *Declaration of Independence*, we read that it is based on "the laws of nature and of nature's God" and also that "men are endowed by their *creator* with certain inalienable rights." Not only is religion regarded as the foundation of proper governmental action, but religious values are seen as sustaining the moral conduct required of citizens in a democratic state. Some of the early American statesmen were undoubtedly influenced deeply by religious convictions, while others were convinced atheists or agnostics who wished to free the young nation from all religious control.

While some authorities find frequent traces of civil religion [Wimberly, 1976], others see little evidence that it is a potent factor in political life. [Thomas and Flippen, 1972]. A

MARXISM AS WORLD RELIGION

The anti-Christ, that human embodiment of the devil responsible for all evil in the world, is the bourgeoisie. The state of sin is capitalism, which heightens the alienation of man and leads him astray from a proper relationship with his omnipotent and all-knowing God, technology. The major prophets are Marx and Engels and their writings, especially *Capital,* constitute the Bible. The saints are later Marxists, especially Lenin, Stalin and Mao (though the various sects debate the authenticity of one or another of them). The Christ figure is the proletariat and the Holy Spirit is revolutionary consciousness. With the aid of technology's progressive work, the Christ-proletariat will eventually bring about the millenium of socialism, setting the stage for the final, triumphant transition to the state of ultimate grace, communism.

Such is the dominant theology of the modern world, born in the nineteenth century and bearing all the marks of the Christian culture that prevailed when it was conceived.

John Boli, "Marxism as World Religion," *Social Problems,* 28:510–511, June 1981; (From "Comments on Christopher K. Chase-Dunn, " 'Socialist States in the Capitalist World-Economy,' " *Social Problems,* 27:509–531, June 1980).

Do you think Marxists enjoy having Marxism called a religion?

recent survey found that the ideas in civil religion are shared by a majority of the members of all major Christian churches, although not by a majority of Jews and other non-Christians [Wimberly and Christenson, 1981]. It seems that there are, indeed, strands of thinking based on a religious foundation which influence American governmental ideas and practices, but such religious underpinnings are not very specific and are often countered by strictly secular viewpoints.

Religion as the "Opiate of the People"

The view of Karl Marx is based on his basic premise that the economic forces are dominant in society and everything else is secondary. Religion is seen as "false consciousness" [Wood, 1981, pp. 12–15], since it deals with what is either trivial or nonexistent and really reflects the economic interests of the dominant social class. Religion is the "opiate of the people" because it offers them a "pie in the sky" to divert them from the class struggle and prolong their exploitation. Thus all communist governments have been hostile to religion. Some scholars, however, would argue that Marxism is a competing religion.

Religion as a Dynamic Force

The view of religion as a sort of shadow institution which merely reflects the power and interests of the dominant classes was challenged by the German sociologist, Max Weber. Weber [1864–1930] examined the rise of capitalism and felt that it was favored by the attitudes stressed by ascetic Protestantism. Thus, rather than religion being without real influence, it actually helped to formulate the direction of economic change. Weber's ideas are dealt with in more detail later, in the discussion of the latent effects of religion.

STRUCTURES OF RELIGIOUS ASSOCIATIONS

Each major religion affects society through the cultural ethos—the dominant values—which it fosters, but it also affects society through the religious associations it stimulates.

In many simple societies religion is institutionalized but unorganized. This is to say the society has religious institutions—systems of belief and practice which are standardized, formalized, and viewed by virtually all the society's members as necessary and important. But very simple societies generally have no religious organizations. Religious practices and rituals are conducted often by family members but with no organized system of bishops, priests, etc. Many simple societies have a recognized religious specialist in the village, usually called a "medicine man" by Europeans, but no organizational structure. The Christian religion is highly organized, with the main forms being the ecclesia, cult, sect, and denomination.

Ecclesia

The *ecclesia* (or church type) is a state church of which virtually all members of a society are at least nominal members. It accepts state support and sanctions the basic cultural practices of the society. The Church of England in Great Britain and the Lutheran churches in the Scandinavian countries are somewhat vestigial forms of the state church, or ecclesia. In a much more vigorous form it can be seen in Roman Catholicism in Spain and Italy; in Islamism in Saudi Arabia, and in Buddhism in Tibet before the communist regime.

Cult and Sect

The *cult* and the *sect* are at opposite poles from the ecclesia. Both are generally small and usually challenge existing social and religious values. The *cult* may claim links with traditional religion, but its major claim is to a new religious emphasis [Stark and Bainbridge, 1979]. The Unification Church of the Rev. Sun Myung Moon (the "Moonies") combines some of the usual Christian beliefs with some features of Oriental religion in a novel fashion [Kodera, 1981]. The cult may claim that it will transform the society, as the

TABLE 11-1
RELIGIONS—PAST, PRESENT, AND FUTURE (Members in Millions and as a Percent of World Population)

Religion	1900	Percent*	1980	Percent	2000	Percent
Christian	558	34.4	1,433	32.8	2,020	32.3
Roman Catholic	272	16.8	809	18.5	1,169	18.7
Protestant and Anglican	153	9.4	345	7.9	440	7.0
Eastern Orthodox	121	7.5	124	2.8	153	2.4
Other Christian	12	.7	155	3.6	258	4.1
Nonreligious and atheist	3	.2	911	20.8	1,334	21.3
Muslim	200	12.4	723	16.5	1,201	19.2
Hindu	203	12.5	583	13.3	859	13.7
Buddhist	127	7.8	274	6.3	359	5.7
Tribal and shamanist	118	7.3	103	2.4	110	1.8
Chinese folk religion	380	23.5	198	4.5	158	2.5
"New religions"	6	.4	96	2.2	138	2.2
Jewish	12	.8	17	.4	20	.3
Other†	13	.8	36	.8	61	1.0
World population	1,620		4,374		6,260	

*Does not equal 100%, because of rounding off.
†Includes Confucian, Sikh, Shinto, Baha'i, Jain, Spiritist, and Parsi.
Source: World Christian Encyclopedia, Oxford University Press, New York, 1982, p. 6.

Which of these categories has shown the greatest change between 1900 and 1980? Which religion has shown the greatest proportional growth?

Religious needs remain constant, while forms of religious expression change.
(*Doug Wilson/Black Star*)

Unification Church claims, or it may look inward and stress ecstatic personal religious experience. It may also stress a particular concern, such as faith healing, and not attempt to deal with all aspects of life.

While the cult claims to offer new insights which the traditional churches have overlooked, the *sect* offers a return to original truths which other churches are accused of having abandoned. The Amish, for example, try to live as they believe the early Christians lived in the days of the New Testament. The sect is concerned about all aspects of life and insists that its members follow its doctrines without deviation. Its mores may differ greatly from those of the general society. It may be pacifist in a warlike state, collectivist in an individualized economy, or austere in an affluent society. However, the sect makes no serious attempt to sway the general society and asks only to be ignored. It sometimes secures toleration because it is regarded as too small to be threatening. For instance, a

government which would not tolerate widespread pacifist attitudes can ignore a few Quakers or Mennonites. If a sect grows in members and makes its peace with the general society, it then becomes a denomination.

Denomination

The fourth category, the *denomination*, is a large group but one with less than a majority of the nation's citizens. Like the sect, it is concerned with all aspects of life and behavior. It is usually supported by private gifts rather than government subsidy. Since it is still a minority, it does not feel as much pressure to accept all majority social norms as does the ecclesia. Thus, at least until recently, Methodists deviated from the majority in their criticism of drinking and gambling, and Catholics differed in their opposition to divorce and birth control. On the other hand, the denomination is too large to prevent deviation among its members, and their behavior tends to follow general social practices. Yet the denomination attempts to influence the behavior of both its own members and the general society. The idea of separation of church and state is accepted in theory but often violated in practice.

Classification of a religious group as ecclesia, cult, sect, or denomination does not imply any value judgment concerning its validity or prestige. Rather, the classification reflects a difference in emphasis and in pattern of relationship to the general society. There are no churches, however, which are "pure" types, and the classification is a continuum with degrees of difference rather than a dichotomy with absolute contrasts [Stark and Bainbridge, 1979]. Since no single church claims a majority of Americans, it is probably correct to say that the United States does not have an ecclesia and that all the larger groups are denominations.

MANIFEST AND LATENT FUNCTIONS OF RELIGION

All institutions have both manifest and latent functions, and religious institutions are no exception.

Manifest Functions

Functions of religion cluster about three types of concerns: a pattern of beliefs called *doctrines*, which define the nature of the relationship of human beings to one another and to God; *rituals* which symbolize these doctrines and remind people of them; and a series of *behavior norms* consistent with the doctrines. The work of explaining and defending the doctrines, carrying out the rituals, and reinforcing the desired behavior norms leads to a complex pattern of worship, teaching, evangelism, exhortation, and philanthropic works requiring considerable investment of money and personnel.

In some societies, the manifest functions

of religion include actually controlling the state, as in Iran, where the Shah was replaced by a theocracy controlled by Muslim ayatollahs.

Latent Functions

Few people will object to the manifest functions of religion, but some of the latent functions of the churches bring consequences which often surprise even the faithful. At the same time, they may stimulate either approval or opposition from those who do not consider themselves very religious.

Churches are a setting for sociability as well as worship. Church youth groups provide an opportunity to practice leadership skills and a setting for courtship and mate selection. Churches decorate the community with buildings that are sometimes beautiful and inspirational; they stimulate art and music; they provide concerts and festivals. (Some would include these as manifest functions of some religions.) Churches help newcomers to become acquainted, help people "social climb." One of their manifest functions is to unite the community in human brotherhood; a latent function is to help divide the community by race and class. While preaching that "all people are equal before God," churches

The sociability functions of the church

provide a setting for conspicuous display of wealth by members attired in their Sunday best.

INTERRELATIONSHIP WITH OTHER INSTITUTIONS

Religion and the Family

The interrelationship between religion and the family has received only a limited amount of study from sociologists. A sample of twelve recent "marriage and the family" textbooks (those which were conveniently available on your author's bookshelf) devoted an average of 1½ pages to "religion," mostly to mixed marriages. Yet religious beliefs, practices, and values are an important factor in family life. The conversion of the Roman Empire to Christianity greatly reduced divorce, adultery, fornication, and homosexuality; returned women from a not greatly subordinate to a thoroughly subordinate status; and cultivated a pervasive and enduring identification of sex with unworthiness and sin [Leslie, 1982, chap. 6]. Recent changes in family practices and values (smaller families, use of contraception and abortion, greater sex equality, increased tolerance for divorce, extramarital sex experience, nonmarital cohabitation) have more often been resisted or reluctantly accepted by the churches than actively supported by them. Personal acceptance of such changes has been more rapid among the relatively nonreligious than among the devoutly religious persons. Religion is clearly a factor in family life, but one which it is difficult to isolate and measure.

Religion and the Economy

Does religion have any effect upon practical business matters? Business actions may sometimes appear to be entirely godless and amoral; yet religion *does* have an effect upon the economy. Religious beliefs affect work habits, patterns of consumption, and the acceptance or rejection of new products and practices.

THE PROTESTANT ETHIC.   One of the most influential theories about the interrelationship between religion and the economy is stated in Weber's *The Protestant Ethic and the Spirit of Capitalism* [1904]. Weber noted that the Protestant leaders of the Reformation did not intend to erect the spiritual foundations for a capitalistic society and often denounced capitalistic trends in their day. Yet the industrial revolution and the growth of large-scale business concerns was much more rapid in predominantly Protestant than in largely Catholic areas, and in mixed areas Protestants were much the more active in business development. This circumstance helps explain the economic depression in France which followed the expulsion of the Huguenots in the late seventeenth century. The phrase "as rich as a Huguenot" became a popular stereotype, and expulsion of these Protestants slowed down French industry while acceler-

---

Mr. [Osamu] Tezuka agrees with a view that is common among psychologists in Japan, that the Buddhist religion plays a role in the degree to which robots [in factories] have entered the Japanese psyche. "Unlike Christian Occidentals," he said, "Japanese don't make a distinction between man, the superior creature and the world about him. Everything is fused together and we accept robots easily along with the wide world about us, the insects, the rocks—it's all one. We have none of the doubting attitude toward robots as pseudo-humans that you find in the West. So here you find no resistance, simply quiet acceptance."

Henry Scott Stokes, "Japan's Love Affair with the Robot," *The New York Times Magazine,* Jan. 10, 1982, p. 75.

How does this illustrate the interrelationship of institutions?

ating business development in countries where Huguenots settled as refugees [Bierstedt, 1974, p. 558].

The Protestant ethic made religious virtues of individualism, frugal living, thrift, and the glorification of work—practices which obviously favored the accumulation of wealth. These practices are usually attributed to the Protestant emphasis on individual responsibility rather than churchly sacraments, to the interpretation of worldy success as a sign of godly favor, and to the reaction against the symbols of wealth, which had been accumulated by the traditional church. None of these Protestant practices originated in a deliberate desire to encourage commerce, and perhaps for that reason their effect was all the more potent. While most social scientists accept Weber's Protestant ethic theory as a plausible hypothesis, some disagree [Fanfani, 1955, and Samuelson, 1961].

Whatever may have been the case in earlier years, the Protestant ethic is no longer the monopoly of any religious group. Protestants have been influenced by a "consumer's ethic" emphasizing installment buying, leisure, recreation, and luxury consumption. Catholics and others have perhaps come closer to the Protestant ethic as they see that a disciplined life pays off in material rewards [Hunt and Hunt, 1975, p. 600].

Evidence suggests that no one religious group today can claim a clear edge in the possession of an ethical system which leads to economic success [Bouma, 1973]. A recent study of the effect of ethno-religious background on the early career [Stryker, 1981] does find that both educational and career entry levels are influenced by religio-ethnic background, although less than by social class factors. This influence does not follow a strict Protestant-Catholic split; Jews rank higher than either. Apparently, even though the earlier Catholic and Protestant attitudes have changed, the attitudes cultivated by religious groups may still have some effect on worldly achievement.

Religion and Government

Religion and government are interrelated in many ways. For example, political party support in the United States is associated with religious preference. In the 1982 Congressional elections, Democratic candidates were supported by 47 percent of the Protestant voters, by 60 percent of the Catholics, and by 75 percent of the Jews [*Public Opinion*, 5:36, December/January 1983]. No candidate for high elective office admits to being an atheist or agnostic, and all three presidential candidates in 1980 claimed to be "born again" Christians. The percent of Americans believing that "religion is gaining influence" upon American life has fluctuated widely in recent years, from 36 percent in 1965, to 15 percent in 1970, to 45 percent in 1976, to 39 percent in 1978 (*Public Opinion*. 3:35, December/January, 1980).

Religious leaders often seem to have little power as compared with government leaders. This attitude was expressed in blunt fashion by the late Soviet dictator, Iosef Stalin. When advised that the Pope had criticized some of his policies, he replied: "How many army divisions does *he* have?" [Sulzberger, 1958].

There are times, however, when religious leaders have effectively humbled monarchs. One may cite the incident when Henry II of England walked barefoot to the tomb of Thomas à Becket to submit to the discipline of the priests of Canterbury Cathedral [Durant, 1950, p. 761]. The Shah of Iran was a nearly absolute monarch with a lavishly equipped modern army. The Muslim leader, the Ayatollah Khomeini, had no arms or money and lived as an exile in Paris. However, his calls to Muslims to revolt against a ruler who allegedly had violated their religion were so effective that the Shah fled and his government fell. Evidently, army divisions are not the only source of power.

State-church conflict is a persistent part of social life. There are perennial issues such as the legitimacy of surgical operations, blood

Institutional functions change. Government has assumed many services once performed by family or church. (*Hugh Rogers/Monkmeyer Press Photo Service*)

transfusions, or immunizations on which groups such as Jehovah's Witnesses or Christian Scientists may take issue with health authorities. Amish parents may object to sending their children to high school, and sometimes a pacifist sect or pacifist members of denominations may come under state censure because of their opposition to a military draft. At other times, there is a feeling that the state should intervene to protect members of a closely controlled cult from harmful actions by cult leaders.

These issues often arise but usually involve only small groups of people. Other issues affecting more people involve the efforts of Roman Catholics and some other churches to secure support for their schools or to block the state from sanctioning or providing abortions. Similarly, the mainline Protestant churches sometimes seek to block legalization of gambling.

Critics of this kind of church activity accuse churches of trying to force minority moral values upon the majority. These critics say a church has every right to persuade its own members to follow its code of conduct but should not seek to impose its standards on nonmembers. The church view is that such issues as state support of religious education or the restriction of abortion are not views peculiar to a few churches but standards of right which should apply to all. Views such as these are usually rejected by members of most other churches. Such efforts have some power because many holding these views are "single-issue voters," while opponents are generally concerned about a number of issues and will not support or oppose a candidate on the basis of only one issue. Since elections are often decided by small margins, a few single-issue voters may have influence out of proportion to their number. However, representations by official church leaders on these matters are often undercut by dissension among their members. For instance, the fact that most American Catholics accept contraception [Greeley, 1982, p. 129] has largely nullified the effect of Papal condemnation.

In the late 1970s, an effort to influence government by conservative churchmen took the name of the Moral Majority. It has made vigorous efforts to influence governmental action on such topics as abortion, sex education, pornography, and the teaching of "creationism" in high schools. The Moral Majority leaders do not see themselves as introducing something new but as bringing American society back to the morality of an earlier day. In many ways, it is indeed possible to see the Moral Majority as a resistance movement trying to block, or at least influence, the direction of social change. It meets opposition, but it also strikes a responsive chord with many who are worried about the erosion of authority and the effect of permissive moral standards on youthful character [Yankelovich, 1981]. Similarly, governmental leaders in several Muslim countries are under pressure from Islamic fundamentalists. They accuse the government leaders of having deserted the pure Islamic moral codes for the allegedly degenerate customs of infidels in the West [Bolling, 1980].

Religion and Social Action

Conservatives are persons who may be willing to make minor adjustments, but they are convinced that the basic structures of society are sound. They may accept and even support "reform," but revolution is rejected as likely to bring more harm than benefit. Radicals are not interested in the reform of the social system. Rather, they view the existing system as being so bad that it must be changed completely. They see revolution as necessary surgery whose benefits are great enough to justify the cost.

Both conservatives and radicals can find support in the Bible and in the historic statements of religious bodies. Since conservatives and radicals seem at opposition poles, how can they each claim religious support? This is a very complicated topic about which many large volumes have been written—Troeltsch's book on the subject [1931] is probably the classic example.

The conservative perspective holds that religion should promote personal salvation. Religion should develop a spirit of love, unselfishness, and faith which can survive social difficulties. Religion should not seek to change the world but to change individuals into dedicated believers.

While the conservatives profess a lack of interest in politics, they may become involved (as in the case of the Moral Majority) when governments accept changes which are thought to threaten religious principles.

The radical perspective holds that God calls people to build the Kingdom of God here on earth, a society in which love and justice reign. People seldom agree on the nature of an ideal society, and the attempt to establish one tends to produce radical and even revolutionary attitudes.

Communists are radical critics of capitalist society who often criticize religion as the handmaiden of oppression. Yet some clergy have been accused of holding communist views and of promoting communist causes. The Roman Catholic Church in South America was long known as a conservative supporter of the existing society, but in recent years, priests in South America and elsewhere, influenced by the theology of "Christian liberation" [Bucher, 1977; Riding, 1979; Hunt, 1982], have become sharp critics of the status quo.

Issues vary from time to time. In the 1960s, a concern for racial justice gave way to agitation against the Vietnam war. Currently, concern over possible nuclear war has led some church people, including a number not usually considered radical, to demonstrate against the prevailing nuclear policy [Novak, 1982]. Regardless of the issues, some church people will follow a "social gospel" while others concentrate upon individual salvation.

While there are both radical and conservative clergy, there is frequently a divergence between religious leaders and lay members. The "social gospel" and radical social action usually get more support among the clergy than among the membership [Hadden, 1969; Hoge and Carroll, 1973, p. 181]. The clergy who proclaim that vital religious concerns are involved in social issues may be seen by the laity as simply "talking politics" and straying away from really "religious" topics.

RELIGION AND SOCIAL STRATIFICATION

Possibly churches are better attended in the United States than in Europe because religion in the United States is linked with a precarious ethnicity. European countries generally have only one or two churches, and these are supported by state funds. European churches are a part of the national life and tradition, but they are so much taken for granted that the individual feels little obligation to support them and is little concerned about the link between religion and the rest of life. In the United States there are many churches, each linked to a certain segment of society. Thus, one way people reaffirm their identity is by affiliation with a church composed primarily of "people like us." If the church perishes, an aspect of their identity has disappeared, and since there is no state support, the church will die unless it is supported by voluntary efforts of its members. Under these circumstances church nonsupport is often seen as being a traitor to one's group.

Who are the "people like us?" Usually, they are people who share a common group background and a common economic status. Gordon refers to this combination of traits as *ethclass* [1978, p. 134], meaning a *group identity based on both ethnicity and social class.*

Ethnicity and Religious Stratification

One way to look at the United States is to compare the Anglo-Saxon core group with all others. American culture has been based so much on the English model that usually members of this group think they have no distinct ethnic status but are merely "American." However, they are a distinct kind of ethnic American, and usually they are more likely to worship in churches with members from a background similar to theirs.

Those outside the Anglo-Saxon core group are aware of a distinct ethnic identity, and this is also expressed in their churches. Immigrants to America were told that religion was the one activity which could legitimately escape Americanization or Anglo conformity, as it was sometimes called [Cole and Cole, 1954, pp. 135–140]. Since there was no official American church, people could join the church of their choice, and if they wished to import a church from their ancestral home, this was entirely proper.

Thus, we not only have Lutherans, but Swedish Lutherans, Danish Lutherans, Norwegian Lutherans; among Catholics there are parishes known as Polish Catholic, Mexican Catholic, French Catholic, German Catholic, Italian Catholic, and Irish Catholic—to name only a few. Blacks found that the church was, for many years, the one institution they could control and call their own. Blacks were primarily Methodists and Baptists, but they worshipped in black denominations entirely separate from white churches. Judaism is a religion in which most worshippers are ethnically Jewish. Even though there are many nonreligious Jews, it is hard to think of the concept of Jewishness without also thinking of the Jewish religion. Similarly, there were not only Orthodox churches but Greek, Russian, and Serbian Orthodox churches. Buddhist temples serve as social and cultural centers for many Japanese-Americans, and the mosque keeps ancestral memories alive for Americans of Arab ancestry. This is only a partial list, for there are few, if any, Americans for whom there is no church identified with their ethnic background.

In 1976, the rejection of a black applicant for membership in the church attended by President Carter (who opposed the decision) drew attention to racially separate churches. Although such racial segregation was once common in American churches, most churches today are formally open to all people and the charge of imposed segregation is usually unwarranted. Instead, segregation of ethnics today is usually self-segregation. The predominantly black churches are the largest organizations in the United States controlled by blacks. Few blacks would like to see this sphere of black leadership dismantled for the sake of ethclass integration into predominantly white churches.

In many cases the church and the individual show the effect of both "Americanization" and the persistence of a distinct ethnic tradition. When immigrants first came to America, they established a church in which the service and the building were like those in the old country. The priest was a fellow ethnic, and the language of worship was their native tongue. Sometimes there was also a bilingual school with teachers of their own nationality and a mixed use of English and the native language.

The church, though, was not simply a foreign survival—it was also a bridge between the new country and the old. The church offered some of the ancestral culture, but it also afforded contact between the newly arrived immigrant and those at least partially acculturated to American ways. This type of cultural bridge may have done as much to Americanize the immigrants as to conserve their original culture. A study of Mexican-Americans, for instance, finds that those in parochial schools became more familiar with the Anglo culture than those attending public schools [Lampe, 1975]. Recent Oriental immigrants, including refugees from Vietnam, brought along their ethnic churches. Like earlier immigrant churches, they serve as a bridge between the old society and the new

society [Yoon, 1981; McIntosh and Alston, 1981].

Ethclass Status Changes

What happens when a person's idea of ethclass status changes? What happens when one moves up or down the economic ladder or when one becomes more anxious to be recognized as a "real" American than a transplanted ethnic?

One adjustment is that the individual shifts to a church composed of people who share the status he or she has acquired (or hopes to acquire). The Jew may become a Unitarian, the member of a storefront church may become a Baptist or Methodist, while the Baptist or Methodist may become a Presbyterian, Congregationalist, or Episcopalian.

Another alternative is to drop out of church. If our family church no longer fits our sense of ethclass identity, then religion may seem irrelevant and meaningless—a reminder of associations that we would rather forget. America has many people without any religious involvement. Nonreligious groups and activities may serve the ethclass function as satisfactorily as did the church. American churches have been strengthened because they have served to foster an ethclass identity, but when that identity changes, the church may lose a major source of its strength. Why should one attend a Swedish Lutheran church when no longer concerned about Swedish ethnicity? The person may shift to another church or may get along without any church involvement at all.

The ethnic church may keep its members by shifting from an ethnic to a unique theological emphasis. Then people do not stay with the church because of its ethnic reminders but because it alone has the truth. If other churches have "sold out" to a liberal, modernizing world view, then their church is the one which has the true faith [Yinger, 1963, p. 97].

Probably the more frequent adjustment is that as the ethclass status of its members

The uniting of spiritual faith with national pride was strengthened when a Polish cardinal was installed as Pope John Paul II. (*Wide World Photos*)

changes, the church also changes. A classic example of this trend are the Methodists, once a lower-class group known as the "shouting Methodists," attending highly emotional services in austere, barnlike buildings. As the members moved up to middle-class status, the Methodist Church changed to sober, dignified services in neo-Gothic buildings [Currie, 1968, p. 140]. The nationality-linked church which once had services far different from most American churches will Americanize its services, perhaps, for example, switching to the English language. It then becomes an association with ethnic connections but still compatible with American culture. The American Buddhist temples are striking examples. Like Christian churches, some of these temples have pastors and regular Sunday services, although these are totally unknown in Buddhism as practiced in Japan!

Differentiation within a denomination also

accommodates ethclass differences. The upper-class Catholic usually lives in a wealthier parish in which ethnic connections have become weakened. Assimilated and wealthier Jews leave the Orthodox synagogues in the inner city for the Reform or Conservative Jewish temples in the suburbs. Protestant congregations in university towns develop a style of worship and preaching more formal and intellectual than that in churches serving mainly factory workers. Every church regards itself as embodying universalistic truths which apply to all people, but every church must appeal to those who make up its particular ethclass membership.

Similar ethnoreligious links can be found in other countries. Catholicism in Poland owes much of its strength to its association with Polish nationalism. Through the centuries, when the nation was carved up among other countries and there was no Polish state, the "faith of our fathers," found in the Roman Catholic Church, carried both a religious and a patriotic implication. Now that Soviet armies garrisoned in the country limit the Poles' freedom of action, their Catholicism serves as a reminder that they are different from their Russian conquerors. The very fact that the Russian Communists are atheists who denounce Catholicism and try to hinder its operation testifies to its legitimacy as a symbol of still undaunted nationalism. When the Pole worships in a church, he or she is, at one time, both worshipping God and asserting that the Russian armies have not yet killed the Polish spirit. This combination of spiritual faith and national pride was greatly strengthened when a Polish cardinal was installed as Pope John Paul II.

CONTEMPORARY TRENDS IN RELIGION .

Conflict and Ecumenicity

Human social life has tendencies which both develop boundaries between groups and tear these boundaries down to form wider associations. In religion, this process is seen in the fractionalizing of religion by building boundaries through denominationalism and in the moderating of these boundaries through ecumenicism.

RELIGIOUS RIVALRY. While religion usually praises the virtues of peace, it has often divided people into warring camps. On occasion, groups identified by religion, such as the Catholics and Protestants in Northern Ireland or the Christians and Muslims in Lebanon, carry on savage warfare. This warfare is usually not directly concerned with religious doctrines but is simply a power struggle among groups who carry religious labels.

On the other hand, there have been, and still are, many instances in which differences in belief and ritual are the occasion for competition, argument, political conflict, family disagreement, and even physical violence. At the very least, people learn that their own church carries truth and other churches are tainted by falsehood, a belief which creates in-groups and out-groups between which mutual understanding is difficult.

Such religious rivalry seems to be carried to an extreme in the United States, which has no official church and in which over 200 sects and denominations seek the loyalty of an often shifting membership. Changes in religious beliefs and practices still cause people to produce new denominations. Recent examples are the Association of Evangelical Lutheran Churches, consisting of certain churches which previously were of the Missouri Synod (Lutheran), and the Anglican Catholic Church, established by Episcopalians who objected to that church's ordination of women.

Such rivalry does not necessarily weaken organized religion. The variety of religious groups means that every social group can find a religious association in which it feels at home. Further, competition between churches presumably makes their members and pastors more alert and active, producing a net increase in total religious effort.

There are drawbacks to such religious rivalry. These drawbacks may be classed as both practical and ideological. On the practical side, such division means that religious influence is fragmented rather than unified. In a time when antireligious elements are vigorous in their criticism, the churches speak with so many voices that many cannot decide what is the religious viewpoint. There are also difficulties on an ideological basis. While each church has an ideology justifying its existence, all churches find it scandalous that so many different and competing voices should each proclaim that it has the true faith [Johnstone, 1975, p. 266]. Further, the passage of time has softened some of the views to the point where church members may neither know nor care about the points of difference. Finally, religious people seek reconciliation and understanding and are disturbed when religiously based conflict produces discord and prejudice.

THE ECUMENICAL MOVEMENT.   One reaction to the problems of religious rivalry has been the development of an ecumenical movement. "Ecumenical" means universal, and this implies an emphasis on matters which unite rather than on those which divide. One form of ecumenicism is sharing divergent and common viewpoints in conferences which seek to enlarge mutual understanding. Another is in "comity" agreements indicating which denomination will establish a congregation in a particular place. There are also organizations cutting across denominational lines. In earlier years, these included Christian Endeavor (a youth group), the American Peace Society, the American Anti-Slavery Society, the American Sunday School Association, and many others. A number of interdenominational groups carry on social service activities in urban areas. Ecumenical concerns also led to the formation of councils of churches at the local, state, national, and world levels.

The Conference on Church Union seeks to assist Protestant denominations to unite [Lyles, 1981]. In 1982 three Lutheran bodies agreed to unite [Mann, 1982], and in 1983 the two major Presbyterian churches (separated into northern and southern halves by the Civil War) agreed to reunite [*Newsweek*, 101:72, June 20, 1983].

Enthusiasm for ecumenicity has waxed and waned and run into some difficult problems. One of these is that although the ecumenical movement began in Europe and North America and has its main numerical and financial support there, the World Council of Churches is now dominated by churches based in the developing areas of Africa, South America, and Asia. These non-Western churches often support "liberation theology" of vigorous anti-Western nationalism [Herzog, 1981] which, to American or European churches, seems quite the opposite of a message of reconciliation. An ecumenical organization such as

---

SECULAR LOSSES

What is the least stable religious background in the United States? The secular home! Analysis of merged national samples from the annual General Social Surveys finds that of Americans who described the religions of their parents as "None," less than 40 percent remained without a religious affiliation. Thus while the many religious groups in the nation typically retain 70 percent or more of their born-members, the majority of those who are raised without religions convert . . . as witnessed by the national data, irreligiousness seems very hard to transmit from parent to child.

Rodney Stark, "Must All Religions Be Supernatural?" in Bryan Wilson (ed.), *The Social Impact of New Religious Movements*, The Rose of Sharon Press, Inc., New York, 1981, p. 166.

Why is it apparently easier for parents to transmit religion to their children than it is to transmit irreligion?

the World Council of Churches strives to be as inclusive as possible, yet success in this compounds its problems. The more inclusive the organization, the more divergent the beliefs included and the more likely it is that one or more groups will feel that they have been overwhelmed by hostile interests. Every concession to bring in additional groups is likely to strain the tolerance of the present members.

In spite of obstacles, ecumenical interest persists and the movement is even venturing into new fields. It received a big boost when the Second Vatican Council sanctioned Catholic participation in ecumenical activities and also sought to alleviate Christian-Jewish tensions. There have been efforts to extend ecumenicity to non-Christians and even to atheists! Ecumenical conferences have discovered common ground between such ancient enemies as Christians and Muslims [O'Shaughnessy, 1974]. There have been dialogues between Communists and Christians [Mayrl, 1978]. At a major 1982 conference in Lima, Peru, clergy from the Roman Catholic, Eastern Orthodox, and Protestant churches reached a "convergence" upon many doctrinal issues [Cornell, 1982]. Such conferences do not create unanimity, but they enlarge the areas of agreement among different churches.

Persistence of Religious Institutions

To most intellectuals in the early twentieth century, it seemed that the future of organized religion depended on whether or not it could make its peace with science. Some felt it was inevitable that scientific skepticism would make religious beliefs irrelevant, if not completely untenable. The churches pinned their hopes for survival on one or the other of two sharply differing strategies. Some thought that secularism could be halted by steadfast adherence to traditional religion. Others hoped that the scientific challenge to religion could be outflanked by an accommodating modernist approach which accepted scientific discovery and denied that there was any conflict between religious truth and a rational view of the universe.

The effort to harmonize scientific and religious thinking includes most of the so-called mainline churches. This category includes the Roman Catholic Church, the larger and more liberal Protestant denominations, and Conservative and Reform Judaism. In addition to reconciling their beliefs with scientific discoveries, the mainline churches have also sought to adjust to the changing life-styles of recent years. For instance, Protestants are less likely now than formerly to hear sermons against

CATHOLIC ANNULMENTS HIT RECORD

Divorced Catholics in the United States are receiving annulments in record numbers, the result of streamlined procedures for dissolving a marriage by a church trying to end the estrangement of thousands of its members.

No longer is it necessary to prove such charges as homosexuality, insanity, deceit or bigamy, to have a marriage declared null in the eyes of the Roman Catholic Church.

To receive an annulment today, a divorced Catholic must show that at the time of the wedding, he or she lacked judgment or maturity or suffered from an emotional or psychological disability.

Last year, church figures said, there were an estimated 77 annulments in the United States for every one in 1968. Americans get 70 percent of all annulments granted by the Roman Catholic Church.

Ann Blackman, *Associated Press*, Jan. 12, 1982.

Is this an example of institutional adaptation to social change?

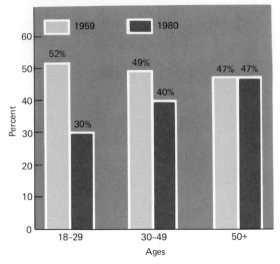

FIGURE 11-1 Church attendance in the United States. Percent attending a religious service in preceding week, 1959 and 1980. (*Source: Adapted from* The Gallup Poll–Public Opinion, 1959–1971, *Random House, Inc., New York, 1972, p. 1585, and* Religion in America, *The Gallup Organization, Inc. and The Princeton Religion Research Center, Inc., Princeton, N.J., 1982.*)

It appears that youth attendance has declined while attendance among the middle-aged has stabilized. Does this mean that young people have become less religious?

"Demon Rum," while the liberalization of Catholic rules on annulments represents a major concession to the temptation to end unsatisfactory marriages through divorce.

Rather than disappearing, the mainline churches grew substantially during the 1950s and early 1960s, but since then, they have lost membership while the fundamentalist and evangelistic churches and the exotic religious sects and cults have grown [Kelley, 1978]. Evidence is mixed as to whether religion in general has gained or lost influence in Western societies in the twentieth century. In most parts of Europe, attendance at religious services has declined steadily since 1900. In Sweden, for example, only about 4 or 5 percent of the people attend services on

an average Sunday and only about 15 percent attend "occasionally" [Tomasson, 1971, p. 112].

Religion in the United States has fared somewhat better than in Europe. Membership increased substantially to a peak of about 64 percent in 1962 and has held at about 61 percent since 1975 [*Yearbook of American and Canadian Churches,* various dates]. Weekly attendance figures are more difficult to measure. The 1982 *Yearbook of American and Canadian Churches* reports attendance figures of 40 to 42 percent since 1971; a Gallup poll reports them as varying between 30 and 52 percent over the 1959 to 1980 period (see Figure 11-1). As for religious belief, a Gallup poll in December 1980 reported 71 percent of Americans believing in "a Heaven where people who have led good lives are eternally rewarded," with 66 percent expecting to go there.

One of the major religious developments of the twentieth century is the "electronic church." Radio and television evangelism has developed charismatic "media stars" with huge audiences and multimillion-dollar budgets. They are feared by established churches as competitors, draining away their funds and members [Mariani, 1979; Hadden and Swann, 1981]. It is hard to tell whether this really happens very much or whether the electronic church draws mainly those who otherwise would attend no church at all.

THE APPEAL OF THE CULTS. Cults are found in all religions and are usually short-lived. (Some groups, such as Synanon or Scientology have no supernatural basis, yet they operate as cults.) Cults may call for a complete attack on existing values, and their members are often fanatically loyal, although they often leave for another cult after a few years.

Cults are thought to emerge in a rootless society in a time of rapid social change and, significantly enough, have flourished especially in California. They seem to thrive best

283

*Religious
Institutions*

No other cult has come to the awful end of the Peoples Temple, but intensity of commitment is typical of cults. (*United Press International*)

where mainline churches are the weakest [Stark and Bainbridge, 1981].

Cults emphasize devotion to a magnetic and charismatic leader. The intensity of allegiance to a cult leader was demonstrated in grisly fashion when over 900 members of the Peoples Temple committed suicide (or succumbed to mass murder) at the prompting of their leader, the Rev. Jim Jones [Richardson, 1980]. No other cult has come to the awful end of the Peoples Temple, but the intensity of commitment is often so strong that cultist activity may be the equivalent of the escape from self-consciousness found in hallucinogenic drugs.

Cults have different traditions and teachings, but they all fill the same function. They offer introspection and self-discovery together with the warm embrace of a supportive group. They stress purity of emotion rather than scientific, logical, or even traditional reasoning. In a confusing world, they offer certainty; in an impersonal society, they provide companionship; in a materialistic world, they challenge people to deny concern for personal possessions.

Cults occasionally attempt to change social institutions, but more often they simply encourage people to withdraw from society. Parents are often distressed when children apparently lose all ambition or family loyalty and follow some cultist leader. It seems like the ancient story of the Pied Piper of Hamlin, whose siren tunes lured the village children away from their homes. Parents have kidnapped teenagers to get them away from a cult so that a critical outsider can "deprogram" them and show them the error of cultish ways [Sage, 1976]. Hard questions of civil liberty then arise [Robbins and Anthony, 1978]. Has the cult member been deprived of freedom when placed under strict communal regulations and "brainwashed" by a constant stream of one-sided propaganda? Or are young people deprived of their liberty when parents kidnap or trick them from the cult and force them to listen to criticism of their newfound way to salvation? Deprogramming success is often temporary [Shupe and Bromley, 1980, chap. 6]. It may be compared with programs to "dry out" alcoholics or drug addicts. It may be possible to make a temporary "cure," but unless there is a major change in the way the person views his or her life situation, the habit is likely to reoccur. Deprogramming is a form of high-pressure resocialization. As pointed out earlier, resocialization is effective only when reinforced at frequent intervals. Unless the deprogramming of a cultist is reinforced by daily life experiences which he or she finds satisfying, a return to the cult is likely. Similarly, it is possible to bring logical arguments against cultist beliefs, but they are likely to be retained in some form as long as they meet strong personality needs.

Cults come and go, and their membership is hard to estimate, perhaps a million and a half in the United States. Usually the cultist experience is a transient one, as members linger a few months or years and then move on to different experiences. But the total activity and membership of cults seem to be increasing. As one authority says, "The cult phenomenon is very much alive and well although individual cults . . . may flower today and wither tomorrow" [Johnstone, 1975, p. 129].

THE MAINLINE CHURCHES. A *mainline church* is a *religious denomination which seeks to harmonize religious and scientific viewpoints*. Mainline churches are still influential and still attract the bulk of believing worshippers, but they have difficulty in capturing the rather free-floating type of religious interest now apparent throughout the world. They are caught by conflicting demands which are difficult to satisfy. They seek to keep the mystery of religion while accepting scientific viewpoints and insist on individual freedom while asking for responsible behavior. Their acceptance of science disturbs those attracted by the occult, while their insistence on the spiritual nature of ultimate reality offends the skeptics. Similarly, their belief in individual freedom frustrates those seeking authoritarian guidance, while their demand for responsible behavior alienates those who wish "to do their own thing" without concern for societal standards. Thus, the mainline churches seek a synthesis between mysticism and rationalism and between freedom and responsibility. Whether this can be done or whether a more generally satisfying religious experience will be provided by other types of religion remains to be seen.

THE FUTURE OF RELIGION. Every human society has developed religious belief systems. Even in avowedly atheistic societies, such as the communist states, secular belief systems and practices develop which strongly resemble religions.

The survival of religion as a human experience is as certain as any prediction a sociologist can make. The question is not whether religion will survive but what forms and directions it will take. One theologian expects that the mainline liberal churches will continue to lose members, that the financial problems of churches will increase, and that the conservative evangelical churches will have "growing pains" [McKinney, 1981]. Others question whether organized religion will be as influential in the future as in the past [Swatos, 1981; Johnson, 1982].

No organizations in the modern world have a record of longevity which equals that of the major churches, and it may well be, as Greeley [1969] argued some time ago, that churches will play much the same role in the future as they have in the past. Religious questions are a perennial part of life, and some institutionalized means of meeting religious needs will probably be a permanent part of human society. However, the persistence of religious needs does not guarantee that the churches which seek to meet these needs in the future will resemble those we know today.

SUMMARY

The sociology of religion is the study of the mutual interaction of religious and other social institutions. *Religion* is often defined as people's organized response to the supernatural, although several movements which deny or ignore supernatural concerns have belief and ritual systems which resemble those based on the supernatural.

Analyses of the social role of religion include the secular viewpoint of Comte, the integrative emphasis of Durkheim and Bellah, the conflict approach of Marx, and Weber's treatment of the dynamic power of the Protestant ethic.

Civil religion refers to a system of widely held religious beliefs, not expressed completely by any one denomination, and alleged to be a major influence in American political life.

The classification of churches into *cults,*

sects, denominations, and *ecclesias* indicates different methods of relating to the society. The sect seeks to impose a rigid pattern of ideal conduct on its members but seeks toleration rather than change from the larger society. The cult may seek to transform society but more often concentrates upon creating satisfying group experience. The denomination is a major religious group which hopes that a separation of church and state will enable it to be influential even though not dominant. The ecclesia is a church claiming to be the spiritual expression of the total society.

The manifest functions of religion are found in its expressed objectives of reaching people and persuading them to observe religious rituals, share religious beliefs, support the churches, and carry on religiously sanctioned activities. Latent functions are usually unrecognized; they may diverge from or even oppose the manifest objectives professed by the churches. Latent functions include providing sociability, aiding upward social mobility, encouraging several kinds of social stratification, and promoting a set of economic values (capitalist or otherwise).

Conflict often occurs between church and state. Sometimes conflict comes over ethical issues such as abortion or military service. At other times there is conflict over function, as when the state takes over social services and handicaps efforts of the churches to engage in these activities. The Moral Majority is a movement seeking to restore older values in American society.

Churches may favor either *conservative* or *radical* tendencies in the total society. *Fundamentalist* theology and emphasis upon personal salvation tend toward conservatism, while a *social gospel* often favors more radical political action.

Social stratification is expressed in churches, and this is especially obvious in the multidenominational system in the United States. Even though all churches try to reach the total population, each tends to attract a particular ethclass group. The fact that religious activity is one way to express ethnicity may have contributed to the strength of American churches.

Religious differences have sometimes led to conflict, but currently an *ecumenical* movement is seeking cooperation (and sometimes organic union), reconciliation, and understanding. Ecumenicity is a persistent movement which has extended beyond Christian churches to consider other religions and even the Marxists.

Religion adjusts to changing life-styles. This can be seen in the changes in *mainline churches* and in the flourishing of cults.

Church attendance and membership peaked in the 1960s. Since then, the mainline churches have declined slightly, while the conservative churches and exotic groups have grown.

The rise of scientific secularism has not destroyed religion as some feared. Instead, people's need for reassurance and meaning has endured, and interest in religion now appears to be at a high level. While religious forms may change, religion survives. There are human needs which only religion can fill, and there is little reason to believe religion will not endure.

GLOSSARY

charismatic expression highly emotional religious expression, including speaking with tongues (glossolalia).

civil religion religious beliefs that are widely held throughout the society.

conservative one who may accept minor reforms but who believes the existing social system is essentially sound.

cult a small religious group which stresses ecstatic religious experience and ignores most other concerns.

denomination fairly large religious group usually supported by private gifts and therefore not as pressured as the ecclesia to accept all majority social norms.

ecclesia a church of which virtually all members of a society are at least nominal members; receives state support and supports most cultural norms.

ecumenical universal.

ethclass a group sharing the same class position and ethnic background.

fundamentalists those who stress the importance of religious beliefs they regard as "fundamental." These include the virgin birth of Christ, the physical resurrection, and the accuracy of the Scriptures in every detail.

liberal one who accepts the social system as basically sound but feels extensive modifications may be required. In religion, a religious person who rejects many fundamentalist beliefs.

mainline church a religious denomination which seeks to harmonize religious and scientific viewpoints, including (in the U.S.) Catholics, Presbyterians, Methodists, Disciples of Christ, American Baptists, Episcopalians, United Church of Christ, and Reform and Conservative Judaism.

religious institutions systems of belief and practice which are standardized, formalized, and viewed by virtually all society's members as necessary and true.

sect a small religious group

seeking to return to a strict observance of earlier religious values and doctrines.

secular society a society ruled by rational or scientific rather than religious values.

secularization movement from a sacred to a rationalistic, utilitarian, experimental viewpoint.

social gospel the belief that religion has a major concern with social justice.

QUESTIONS AND PROJECTS

1 Why in a highly scientific society is religion still alive and well? What persisting human needs explain the persistence of religious institutions?

2 Is it possible that a church could be an ecclesia in one country and a denomination in another? Can you think of an example?

3 Why is it that, unlike in Europe, the denomination

rather than the ecclesia is the dominant form of religious organization in the United States?

4 Why is it that most cults don't last very long? Why do cult members tend to switch from cult to cult?

5 The Socialist Workers Party in the United States, a small group with no hope of winning a major election, is bitterly critical of other parties that have missed the true path of Marxian socialism and is very proud of its own steadfast devotion to basic principles. What type of religious group does it resemble? What kind of motivation keeps parties of this type alive?

6 Is it unrealistic for church leaders to hope that rich and poor, who do little else together, can worship together?

7 There have been many religious wars in history. Were religious differences the real cause, or were economic and political power contests the real cause?

8 How has ethnicity encouraged denominationalism in the United States?

9 Debate these propositions: (1) Religious values and doctrines powerfully influence the changes which take place in society. (2) Religious doctrines and values are largely a reflection of changes already taking place in a society.

10 Visit the services of any two churches in contrasting parts of town. Record your impressions of the ethclass distribution of each congregation. What features, if any, of the ritual, sermon, or building seem to be related to the congregations' ethclass composition?

11 Read the articles "The Hare Krishna in San Francisco" by Gregory Johnson and "The Christian World Liberation Front" by Donald Heinz in Charles Y. Glock and Robert Bellah (eds.), *The New Religious Consciousness* [1976]. Note the differences and similarities you find in the two groups. What do you see as the attractions and drawbacks of each for recruiting youth?

12 Make a comparison of the Communist party and the Christian churches as religious associations. Consult either Paul Hollander, *Soviet and American Society*, University of Chicago Press, Chicago, 1978, pp. 190–197; or Waldemar Gurian, "Totalitarianism as a Political Religion" in Carl J. Friedrich (ed), *Totalitarianism*, Universal Library, New York, 1954, pp. 119–129. For each, identify its sacred writing, saints and martyrs, absolute truths, symbols, codes of behavior, manifest and latent functions, claims upon members, and recent examples of disorganization.

13 The conservative churches with a rigid theology seem to be growing more rapidly than liberal churches which seek an accommodation between religion and science. How would you explain this?

Berger, Peter: "Halting the Trend Toward Secularism," *Intellect*, 106:274–275, January 1978. A discussion of efforts to discourage church social activism through denial of tax exemption.

Bolling, Landrum R.: "Islamic Fundamentalism on the Move," *Saturday Evening Post*, 252:52–57, September 1980. Discusses tension between Islamic fundamentalists and government leaders in Muslim countries.

Eastland, Terry: "In Defense of Religious America," *Commentary*, 71:39–45, June 1981. Discussion of the contribution of religious values in moral guidance.

Foss, Daniel A. and Ralph W. Larkin: "The Roar of the Lemming: Youth, Postmovement Groups and the Life Construction Crisis," *Sociological Inquiry*, 49:264–285, nos. 2–3, 1979. The appeal of cults to youth disillusioned by the failure of the antiestablishment youth movements of the 1960s and 1970s.

Jung, L. Shannon: *Identity and Community: A Social Introduction to Religion*, John Knox Press, Atlanta, 1980. A brief and readable exposition of the major issues in the sociology of religion.

Kelley, Dean M.: "Why Conservative Churches Are Still Growing," *Journal for the Scientific Study of Religion*, 17:165–172, June 1978. Kelley updates and defends the view expressed in a book with the same name as the

288

Social Organization

article. For a different point of view, see Gary D. Bouma: "The Real Reason One Conservative Church Grew," *Review of Religious Research*, 20:127–137, Spring 1979. Bouma attributes growth in the Christian Reformed Church to fertility and immigration rather than to its doctrinal appeal.

Mayrl, William W.: "The Christian-Marxian Encounter: From Dialogue to Detente," *Sociological Analysis*, 39:84–89, Spring 1978. A brief discussion of the effort to extend ecumenicity to discussions between Christians and Communists.

Seabury, Paul: "Trendier Than Thou," *Harper's Magazine*, 257:39–52, October 1978. Current trends toward expressivism and social action in the Protestant Episcopal Church.

Stark, Rodney and William Sims Bainbridge: "Secularization and Cult Formation in the Jazz Age," *Journal for the Scientific Study of Religion*, 20:360–373, December 1981. A study of the decline of mainline churches and the growth of cults.

"Varieties of Religious Experience," *Society*, 15:16–83, May/June 1978. A variety of articles, including such topics as cults, brainwashing, fundamentalist conversions, civil religion, the "Moonies," and Jewish orthodoxy.

Wilson, John: *Religion in American Society: The Effective Presence*, Prentice-Hall, Inc., Englewood Cliffs, N.J., 1978. A sociology of religion with an excellent chapter, "Religion, Ethnicity and Race."

Wimberly, Ronald C. and James A. Christenson: "Civil Religion and Other Religious Identities," *Sociological Analysis*, 42:91–100, Summer 1981. An analysis of civil religion and its support in various religious groups.

Yankelovich, Daniel: "The Hidden Appeal of the Moral Majority," *Psychology Today*, 15:23–25, November 1981. Argues that the Moral Majority draws support from those worried by permissive morality among youth.

12 Education, Science, and Technology

In the barrage of rhetoric about problems in education, we sometimes lose sight of the fact that our schools are vibrantly alive and operating successfully in cities and towns across the nation. . . . Many of the problems of the schools—violence, crime, drug and alcohol abuse, teen-age pregnancy—are really problems of society in general. There are other problems, however, with regard to which concerned efforts by different levels of government are bringing out substantial improvement in American education.

For instance, we are educating the handicapped children of this country more effectively today than in the past. We are making giant strides in our struggle to overcome the damaging legacies of discrimination on the basis of race, national origin and sex. We are making inroads in achieving equal opportunity for those disadvantaged by poverty.

Shirley Mount Hufstedler, Secretary of Education in the Carter Administration.

Students are definitely not prepared the way they used to be. Their inability doesn't have to do with their intelligence or capabilities; it has to do with the opportunities and the preparation they have had, and with their motivation.

I so often feel defeated because of the apathy of both students and parents. You see the students sit there day in, day out and never do an assignment, never participate in class or else they don't come to class at all . . . I will send out failure slips to notify parents well in advance of card-marking that their child is failing and that I would like to talk with them about it. At the last conference time, I sent out over 75 of these slips. Three parents responded.

Kids have a lot to contend with, I know. But some days I feel like a fighter who's on the ropes. It's tough to speak to a child in the hallway about something and have obscenities thrown at you. So you arrive at the stance: I'm not going to do or say anything, I cannot take the risk.

(Glenna Norton, High School Teacher, Detroit, Michigan) Reprinted from Mary Long, "The Crisis in Our Schools," *Family Weekly*, October 19, 1980, pp. 4–6. © 1980; 1515 Broadway, New York, N. Y. 10036.

These two views of American schools are both correct. In recent decades, school expenditures increased greatly, experimental programs multiplied, dropout rates fell, and efforts to make school effective for all parts of the population increased dramatically. Salaries of teachers went up twice as much as earnings in general during the 1960s [Moynihan, 1972]. Yet problems multiplied. Complaints of violent and disruptive conduct and learning failures abound. The retrenchment in the early 1980s in educational expenditures is partly explained by disillusionment with previous efforts. School expenditures are being trimmed, while teachers' salaries are falling behind the cost of living. This situation is not unique to the United States but is worldwide [Simmons and Alexander, 1978, p. 353]. Why does education have both such tremendous achievements and such enormous problems?

The sociologist looks for explanations of education's problems and achievements in the system of social relations in which the schools operate. So let us begin by asking how schools developed.

DEVELOPMENT OF EDUCATIONAL INSTITUTIONS

Primitive and very ancient societies had no educational institutions. Children learned what they needed to know by watching whatever was going on and helping wherever practical. It took no school to teach an Indian boy how to hunt. A boy's father (or in some societies, his uncle) would give him instruction in hunting, and these lessons were the nearest thing to "educational institutions" that could be found in a simple society. Such instruction was not an educational institution; it was simply a part of a man's family duties.

Schools appeared when cultures became too complex for all needed learning to be handled easily within the family. As empires grew, they needed tax gatherers and record keepers, and this called for the training of scribes. Developing religions often required that a great many legends, chants, and rituals be memorized. Whether scribes or priests were the first schoolboys is not known. We can imagine that a man with a son or nephew to train might agree to take another nephew and perhaps a friend's son or nephew to teach at the same time. We can imagine that this "class" grew over the generations, with the "teacher" now giving full time to instruction. At this point, with full-time specialists as teachers and formal classes of students, operating apart from the family and viewed as the necessary and proper way to train these boys, we can say that educational institutions arrived.

This functional analysis, attributing the growth of educational institutions to changing labor needs, is rejected by conflict theorists as an oversimplification. They claim that factors other than labor needs may be even more important as causes of increased education.

In all advanced countries, many people get far more education than their work requires [Berg, 1969; Illich, 1971]. Higher education fills status needs for those who wish to feel superior and excludes from competition for the choice positions all those who cannot get the educational credentials, thus preventing the upward mobility of the lower classes [R. Collins, 1979]. Education helps maintain boundaries for ethnic and class subcultures, keeping out those who are improperly mannered [Collins, 1975, pp. 86–87]. Even universal literacy, everywhere accepted as a worthy goal, may have been, in fact, more ornament than necessity [Graff, 1979].

The reasons for the growth of educational institutions probably include all of the factors mentioned above. To determine the relative importance of each is impossible. Whatever they are, they seem to be operating everywhere.

STRUCTURE OF AMERICAN EDUCATIONAL INSTITUTIONS

Formal Schools

Our primary educational institution is the formal school, from kindergarten to graduate school. Our general belief has been that "more is better." The proportion of people attending some kind of school has grown steadily, while the school career has been lengthened from both ends. Kindergartens are still growing, with 96 percent of all 5-year-olds attending in 1980. Six out of seven Americans between ages 25 and 29 had completed high school by 1980, while almost half of those between 30 and 34 had attended college, and over one-fourth had been graduated.

While the public school dominates American education, private (most often Catholic) schools enrolled 12 percent of elementary school and 10 percent of secondary school pupils, while private colleges enrolled 21 percent of all college students in 1980. During

Our primary educational institution is the formal school, from
kindergarten to graduate school.
(© *Michal Heron/Woodfin Camp
& Assoc.*)

recent years, the private-school share declined somewhat at elementary and secondary levels. The number of students attending
private colleges has held constant, but the
proportion of college students in private colleges has dropped from 33 percent in 1965 to
21 percent in 1980.

The 1970s saw an increase in schools conducted by Protestant fundamentalist groups,
usually called Christian schools. They enroll
only about 1 percent of the total students in
precollege education, but their enrollment
grew from 140,000 in 1971 to 450,000 in 1979.
They are open to all races, but they attract
few black students, and one of their major
effects has been to provide an escape from
integration. However, they also appeal on
the grounds of strict discipline, Christian
teaching, and higher academic standards
[Pierce, 1981].

The question of whether private schools
are superior to public schools has been debated for generations. One careful study of
Catholic private schools some years ago could
not substantiate either the special virtues or
the special disabilities often claimed [Greeley
and Rossi, 1966]. A more recent comparison,

covering over 1,000 public and private schools,
concluded that pupils learned more in the
private schools, even after allowing for differences in family background [Coleman, 1981;
Coleman, Hoffer, and Kilgore, 1982]. It attributed this to better discipline and more
demanding academic standards in the private
schools. One unmeasured factor, however,
is the private schools' right to exclude the
student who is disruptive or whose parents
are uncooperative.

THE COMMUNITY COLLEGE MOVEMENT. One
of the most significant trends in higher education has been the growing proportion of
students attending community colleges. The
number of two-year colleges, mostly community colleges, more than doubled between
1960 and 1980 (from 521 to 1,274). They offer
low-cost higher education in or near the
students' home communities. Many take two-
year courses preparing for technical or semi-
professional careers of many kinds—dental
technician, practical nurse, computer pro-
grammer, legal secretary, and many more.
Others take an inexpensive two years at a
community college and transfer to a four-year

college to complete a degree. People already in an occupation enroll in one or more courses to upgrade their skills.

Functionalists see community colleges as a practical response to society's need for more trained workers and to students' need for inexpensive higher education. Some conflict scholars see the community college as a device to preserve inequality by diverting less advantaged youth into a dead end; to "cool them out" so they settle for low-level careers and never compete for admission to professional schools [Alba and Lavin, 1981]. Thus, whether the community college is a mobility ladder or a mobility barrier can be argued.

Other Institutionalized Education

Some schools cater to special educational interests.

CORRESPONDENCE SCHOOLS. Correspondence schools and correspondence courses offered by accredited colleges and universities make many courses available to part-time and physically isolated students.

TRADE SCHOOLS. Trade schools of many kinds offer specialized skills training. Barber and beauty schools, business schools, electronics schools, and many others offer skills training without the "ornamental" subjects. They range from excellent to execrable. Many offer good technical training and placement services at modest cost. Some are mediocre, giving indifferent training, often without regard to the job opportunities in the field. A few are rackets, arousing high hopes with glowing promises, collecting fat fees, and then "cooling out" the student with indifference and inattention. The best test is the proportion of enrollees who complete training and find employment in the field. Any school that will not produce a list of employed graduates should be distrusted.

APPRENTICESHIP. Apprenticeship may be the oldest educational institution, for it probably preceded formal schools. Some skills are more easily learned in the work place than in the classroom. Apprenticeship is the standard route for most skilled trades. Apprenticeship is common only where high levels of skill require extended training. Unions generally control apprenticeship, and the common rule requiring that an applicant be sponsored by two union members tends to exclude all who are not sons, relatives, or close friends of union members. Efforts to open the skilled trades to minorities and women have found it necessary to bypass or breach the apprenticeship rules, and this has been difficult. Conflict analysis beautifully fits the struggle over apprenticeship rules and union admission.

INDUSTRY EDUCATIONAL PROGRAMS. Educational programs are operated by many large corporations and are aimed at training their own employees. The focus is heavily vocational, but a few include enough of the arts, social sciences, and humanities to give their future executives a "well-rounded" college education.

Noninstitutionalized Education

Much education is informal and even unconscious. Children learn a great deal in the home, on the playground, and in the streets. Often this cancels out much that they should be learning in school. Possibly, television is the greatest noninstitutionalized educator. By age 18, an American youth will have spent more time watching TV than attending school [Mayer, 1983]. Television offers fare that makes homework dull by comparison. There are some serious programs, such as *Sesame Street*, designed to educate children. But most children's broadcasting is cartoons. Under the Reagan Administration's "deregulation" program, the Federal Communications Commis-

Television is possibly the greatest noninstitutionalized educator. What do children learn from television? (© *Vivienne/Photo Researchers, Inc.*)

sion ceased pressing networks to carry non-cartoon children's programs, and by 1983 they had practically disappeared from commercial televison [Mayer, 1983].

A diet of frothy, sensational television fare does little to whet the appetite for reading, writing, and arithmetic. At the very least, it takes a real effort to turn to one's studies in a world which offers instant pleasure at the "on" switch.

Other mass media—newspapers, books, magazines, comic books, movies—also make their contributions, positive or negative, to the child's learning. For some children, church

ONE VIEW OF TELEVISION AS EDUCATOR

The most noticeable effect . . . is the creation of a new kind of audience—they cannot be called listeners. Reared with a lifetime of commercial messages that regularly bombard their concentration and redirect their train of thought, students have developed eight-to-12 minute attention spans. Without a "station break," they fidget restlessly, rustle papers, scrape chairs. Many confess to a feeling of discomfort during a full-length feature movie. Teachers have always made provisions for the short attention span of the slow learner and the less mature student; now they must plan rapidly paced activities for even the bright.

Another characteristic . . . is the phenomenon of "turning off." The 10,000 hours of conditioning has created viewers who can screen out background noise. It is this ability that encourages students to attempt homework while watching *Starsky and Hutch.* It is this same ability that allows a pupil to turn off any classroom activity that is prolonged or difficult or just dull.

Teachers are confronted with the frustration of presenting a lesson to an audience wrapped in absolute silence and discovering that no one is listening. No one can repeat what has just been said; only a handful are even aware of the general topic. The students turn off instruction as effectively as they tune out a commercial.

Susan Feinberg, "The Classroom Is No Longer Prime Time," *Today's Education,* 66:74–75, September 1977.

Do you agree with this critique?

is an influence, but when church and school are combined, well over half the child's learning time will be spent with mass media "educators" who are not primarily concerned with learning outcomes.

Contest Versus Sponsored Educational Mobility

One aspect of the educational institutions of every society is the set of assumptions about who needs education and how much. The proportion of youth going on to college varies tremendously between societies, as shown in Table 12-1, and now ranges from roughly 50 percent of all college-age youth in the United States to about 1 percent in the People's Republic of China [*Science News*, 120;119, Feb. 21, 1981]. One set of assumptions underlying educational needs may be contrasted under the terms, *contest mobility* and *sponsored mobility* [R. Collins, 1979, pp. 91–92].

The set of ideas termed sponsored mobility starts with the assumption that most people belong in the social class into which they are born unless they have exceptional abilities. Such unusual ability may be noticed by someone—a rich relative, a philanthropic person, a school official, a government dignitary—who will open the doors necessary to approve this person for advanced education.

Classification into one of two or more tracks begins quite early, after the first several grades are completed. Students are separated into those who go on to high school and those who enter the labor market with no more than some added vocational training. High school and university are reserved for those who are entitled to them on the basis of social position, plus a few who have attracted a sponsor through their unusual ability. The number of occupational vacancies to fill determines the number admitted to professional programs. This severely limits the choices open to most young people. It also produces few failures. Most people who enter a program will complete it and find a position for which they have prepared. It is also an eco-

295

Education, Science, and Technology

TABLE 12-1

PERCENTAGE OF PEOPLE 35–44 YEARS OLD WHO HAD COMPLETED HIGH SCHOOL (SECONDARY SCHOOL) OR COLLEGE IN FOUR COUNTRIES IN 1979

Country	Percent High School Graduates	Percent College Graduates
Brazil	11.3	1.9
France	17.0	8.8
Canada	61.2	16.8
United States	77.1	19.6

Source: Based on data in *The United Nations Demographic Yearbook*, 1980, pp. 715, 726, 738, and *The World Almanac, A Book of Facts*, Newspaper Enterprise Association, New York, 1982, p. 92.

France is now tied with the United States (for tenth place) in per capita gross national product. Obviously, education is only one factor in a nation's productivity. What might some other factors be?

nomical system, for there are few dropouts or overeducated "unemployables."

Contest mobility assumes that everyone should have a chance to compete, and no special sponsorship is necessary. High school is open to everyone, although some students may drop out. All high school graduates may continue their studies, since some colleges will admit even those who have not had the college-preparatory courses. With contest mobility, there are no sharp divisions or termination points. For most curricula, the student does not require a special sponsor (or classification) and is usually eligible for admission. Some colleges have admission standards which exclude lower-ranking students, but some other college will usually take them. Many students are never graduated, and there is a high rate of failure or withdrawal. Contest mobility creates a social obligation to provide high school and college facilities for a large part of the population, many of whom never enter the occupation for which they began preparation.

Like other distinctions between concepts,

the distinction between contest and sponsored mobility is not absolute. American schools come closer to the contest mobility model; European schools come closer to the sponsored mobility model. Communist countries generally claim to ignore "social position" in sorting out students, but otherwise tend to follow the sponsored mobility model. Third World countries show every possible variation or combination. In every society, some decisions must be made about who will enroll in advanced education.

THE SCHOOL AS A SOCIAL SYSTEM

"No man is an island" said John Donne, a seventeenth century poet and clergyman. Sociologists say the same thing when they say that each person is a part of a social system. The school does not consist only of administrators, teachers, and students whose individual traits are simply added together. Rather, the school is a social system in which an established series of relationships determines what happens. Particular traits of individuals are less important than patterns of interaction. Whether the principal is jolly or sober, good-looking or ugly, intelligent or mediocre, a principal is still a principal and must act as principals are expected to act. The same is true of teachers, students, janitors, secretaries, and everyone else involved, regardless of their personal characteristics. Personal traits of individuals affect their ability to play roles in the system but do not determine the roles themselves. We learn little about the school by studying the personalities of individuals but a great deal by studying the expectations which people in different roles have toward one another.

Interaction in the School

Systemic interaction in the school system may be viewed from at least three different perspectives: (1) the relation between insiders and outsiders, (2) the relation between different kinds of insiders, and (3) the relation between insiders in the same positions.

The person most obviously involved in relationships outside the system is the superintendent of schools. This is the person held responsible for operating the kind of school the public (or more exactly, different and often conflicting parts of the public) demands. At the same time, the superintendent is regarded by those within the system as their protector against unreasonable or unprofessional demands by outsiders and as the person who achieves harmony among various groups within the school. This triple task is by no means easy, and this is why superintendents often move on after only a few years with a particular school system.

Superintendents are not, however, the only ones who interact with outsiders. Students find that parents have pretty definite expectations about how they ought to conduct themselves inside the school. In fact, parental expectations and home background have a great influence on student achievement [Johnson and Bachman, 1973]. Teachers and principals are also citizens of the total community. They bring into school the attitudes they have formed in association with neighbors, friends, churches, political parties, and various interest groups. Even school custodians are affected by community interaction and sometimes are regarded by the public as more reliable reporters of school news than teachers and administrators, who may be biased by their professional role and training [Rafky, 1972].

Built-in conflicts in school relationships are numerous. The custodian's responsibility for cleanliness clashes with the public's desire for maximum use of the school building even after classes are ended. The professional freedom of the teachers conflicts with the superintendent's need for an orderly sequence of instruction from class to class and grade to grade. The principal's desire to try new methods is resisted by teacher and student hostility to change and by the system's need to present a solid front to the community. One of the most difficult conflicts today is between the superintendent's desire for instructional excellence within the budget and the demands of the teachers' union for job security and higher salaries.

The social system of the school may be viewed as a number of persons filling various roles, cooperating with one another in pursuit of common goals. It can also be viewed as a number of groups in conflict with one another in pursuit of incompatible goals. Both views are correct. The students want to have fun and get good grades; the teachers want to survive and get more pay. A good many teachers are seriously concerned about student learning; some parents are concerned; the rest do not want to be bothered. The superintendent tries to keep the whole business from falling apart, and it is not uncommon for the principal to face pressures from everyone.

Student Status Systems

Within the school, there is a status system which resembles the social-class system of adult society (discussed in Chapter 14). Just as there are upper and lower classes in adult society, there are upper and lower classes in the school. Membership is largely according to the students' family class background. Most schools cover a considerable range of class backgrounds among students. By junior high school, students have sorted themselves into cliques, with the members of each clique having much the same class origin.

One of the most intensive studies of class factors in schooling was made several decades ago by Hollingshead [1949]. He found that those in the lowest class (of five levels) did not participate in school activities—parties, dances, athletics, clubs, plays—and rarely studied seriously. More recent research [Oakes, 1982] elaborates this picture and shows that attitudes developed in school by lower-class children are consistent with the acceptance of lower-class status in adult life. Although lower-class students expressed as much ap-

preciation and liking for school as students from more affluent families, they more often reported a feeling of being "left out" and more frequently revealed a negative self-image and doubts about their abilities. There was little evidence of any discrimination by teachers, but the whole school experience seemed to confirm these students' acceptance of limited aspirations.

This study was based on the comparison of *tracks* (groupings of students of supposedly comparable ability) in junior and senior high schools. While lower-class students were more likely to be found in the lower tracks, this was not true of all of them. A considerable minority of students from lower-class homes do make the upper tracks. For these students, the school experience is much different than for other lower-class students. Thus, even though the school seems to duplicate the class system of the larger society, it may also be the means by which some students gain upward mobility.

There is also an achievement status system in the school which overlaps the class status system. In a study of this system, top rank among boys was held by the star athletes and top female status was held by their girlfriends; other activities (drama, music) were second, with academic distinction a poor third [Horton, 1967]. This study does not measure any changes from the increased attention to the girls' athletic program in recent years. Whether female athletes will gain equal status with male athletes is not yet clear.

Student Cliques

The clique is a small group of close friends, usually of similar rank in the school status system. It is a primary group united by shared interests and friendship. Each classroom usually has two or more cliques and some dyads (two-person groups) and isolates. A single student leader occasionally unites an entire class in support for or opposition to some cause or to the teacher, but this is unusual. Students govern their behavior in large part

The student clique is a small group of close friends, usually of similar rank in the school status system. How do cliques affect what one learns at school? (*Sybil Shelton/Peter Arnold, Inc.*)

by their desire to be in the good graces of a clique, since no worse fate can befall the student (or anyone for that matter) than not to "belong."

Sociometric research (see Figure 12-1) can identify the relationships between students. They are asked such questions as whom they consider good friends or to whom they would turn for advice. A few students, known sociometrically as "stars," will be chosen by many and are obvious leaders. Those choosing a particular leader and being chosen by only one or two themselves are "followers," while those who are chosen by no one are "isolates." The work of the teacher may be significantly handicapped if he or she tries to upset leader-follower relationships or gives too much attention to some cliques while ignoring others. It is therefore important that the teacher identify the cliques in a class. Sociometric research is only one of the methods used by sociologists in studying schools, but it is one which has made a major contribution to understanding the social factors involved in classroom learning.

FIGURE 12-1   The social structure of a classroom. The connecting lines show two persons, each of whom claims the other as a "best friend." In this classroom, there are cliques of five, four, three, and two members; three persons with a "best-friend" relationship to one clique member; three persons whose "best friends" include a member of another clique; and three isolates with no "best friends."

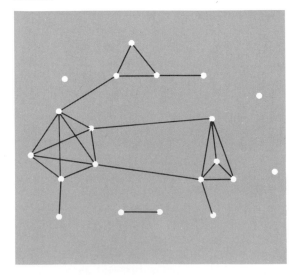

MANIFEST FUNCTIONS OF EDUCATION

The two most important manifest functions of education are to prepare people to make a living and to help people reach their potential for personal fulfillment and social contribution. The two functions are related but not identical. It is difficult to be a well-rounded person unless one can earn a living, and, conversely, an employee may be more valuable with an education which includes more than vocational skills. Yet a good general education does not always produce marketable skills, and narrowly focused vocational education may leave one ignorant of the cultural understanding needed for successful living. Thus, one of the perennial issues in education is the relative concern devoted to general or cultural as opposed to strictly vocational instruction.

Most occupations require basic literacy, while many also demand specialized training. The cybernetics revolution with computer-controlled machines and robots is cutting the demand for unskilled labor and also eliminating some of the traditional craft positions. The market for professionals, semiprofessionals, and technicians is expanding.

The other manifest functions of education are numerous: preserving the culture by passing it on from one generation to the next; encouraging democratic participation by teaching verbal skills and developing the person's ability to think rationally and independently; enriching life by enabling students to expand their intellectual and aesthetic horizons; improving personal adjustment through personal counseling and such courses as applied psychology, sex education, family living, drug abuse; improving the health of the nation's youth through physical exercise and courses in hygiene; producing patriotic citizens through lessons illustrating the country's glory; promoting racial integration; providing public entertainment (athletic events, school band, drama); and finally, "building character." Some of these manifest functions may not be fulfilled, but they are nonetheless *intended* functions of the educational system. In fact, the manifest functions of the school have multiplied so much that we often assume that education can solve all the problems of society.

LATENT FUNCTIONS OF EDUCATION

Creation of Adolescence

One latent function of education has been the creation of adolescence and the prolonging of immaturity. Extended education postpones the child's assumption of adult roles. It delays entrance into the labor market (with the notable exception of farm labor), which some parents applaud, while others resist. Higher education prolongs dependency still further, as even students with part-time jobs usually need some parental assistance. The extreme example of prolonged dependency is the perennial student, accumulating credits (or "incompletes") and sometimes degrees while living on loans, grants, scholarships, assistantships, and odd jobs but never finishing and entering competition for a permanent position.

Weakening of Parental Control

Parental authority over the child is diminished by the school. Parental values may be challenged or even ridiculed as quaint and old-fashioned. Schools often promote student behavior and use teaching materials which challenge parents' moral standards. Schools provide group support to children in rejecting parental standards. In many ways, parental control over children is reduced by the school.

Preserving the Class System

The educational establishment accepts the hierarchy of occupational roles and statuses, for this is necessary to prepare students to fill them. Meanwhile, students are being socialized to accept and fit into this system of statuses and roles. It is no secret that the university departments most closely tied to vocational preparation, such as business, agriculture, and engineering are typically the most politically conservative; those least closely tied to occupation, such as the humanities and social sciences, are the least conservative [Ladd and Lipset, 1978]. Some conflict theorists believe that educational institutions are framed with the *intent* of preserving the class system unchanged [Collins, 1975, p. 450]. Others call it simply a latent consequence of occupational training. Whether educational institutions actually encourage or block individual mobility up and down the class ladder is uncertain, but it will be discussed in Chapter 15.

A Haven for Dissent

Whether this is a manifest or latent function of educational institutions can be argued. Universities deal with ideas. Any serious discussion of ideas is certain, sooner or later, to lead to dissent. Since universities in the past were rather small, isolated enclaves of scholars and young gentlemen and not closely connected to the seats of political power and important practical decisions, a good deal of dissent was generally tolerated as "harmless." Student dissent was viewed rather indulgently, since students generally grew more "sensible" (i.e., conformist) as they matured.

University students in Asia, Africa, and South America have a long history of political activism. Student strikes were common, and university administrations and even governments were sometimes overthrown. Faculty also were politically active and, as intellectuals, were expected to be critics of the existing system. Even after national independence had been achieved in former colonial countries, universities continued to be centers of antigovernment activity, much to the annoyance of the new nationalist governments [Silcock, 1964].

American college students have traditionally been socially conformist and politically inactive. This changed in the 1960s as a wave of student activism swept over the Western world. Universities are no longer small and isolated from the mainstream of society. Students have few vested interests to lose or employers to antagonize and can afford to toy with radical ideas. Marxist ideologies, anticolonialism (anticapitalist colonialism but not anticommunist colonialism), civil rights, and the unpopular Vietnam war were major issues [Johnson and Feinberg, 1980].

During the 1970s, the wave of campus activism subsided. The Vietnam war ended, the civil rights movement gained some victories and then lost momentum, university administrators made many concessions to students, and employment anxieties spread among students. Whether the high degree of campus dissent will ever recur is uncertain, but at this writing, the campus is calm.

INTERRELATIONSHIP WITH OTHER INSTITUTIONS

Education and the Family

Most of what schools do has been taken over from the family. Why? Because as a changing society called for increasing amounts and kinds of learning, families became inefficient places to provide them. Within American experience, basic education—reading, writing, and arithmetic—first left the family for the school. Next, came vocational education. Finally, came a variety of social learnings, ranging from music appreciation to sex education. The school has become the dumping ground for everything society felt the family no longer did well.

And have schools affected the family? Yes, in many ways. Schools often criticize parents and develop programs which intrude upon family routines and schedules. It has been a "two-way street."

Education and Religion

Throughout most of Western history, education and religion have been intertwined. The training of priests was one of the earliest reasons for developing schools. Most of our earlier schools and universities were operated by churches. Public schools and colleges are largely a product of the past century. There are many European countries in which education is still largely church-operated.

Since both church and school teach values, they often come into conflict. One solution is for the church to control the schools, as in many Catholic countries. A second solution is secular public schools, divorced from all church control, as in Mexico. Although Mexico is 96 percent Catholic, secular public schools were mandated in Mexico's new constitution in 1917. A third solution is the dual school system, allowing private church schools as well as secular public schools. This is most common in countries with multiple religious faiths as in the United States. Wherever there is a dual school system, there are continuous efforts by at least some church leaders to influence public school teaching and to gain public support for church schools.

TAX SUPPORT FOR CHURCH SCHOOLS. For many years, leaders of some churches (mostly Catholic) have sought tax support for church schools. The usual suggestion is for tax credits to parents of parochial school pupils or for a *voucher* system giving parents of all students a voucher which can be "cashed" at any school, public or private. Proponents of tax credits argue that parents of parochial school students should not be expected to pay for two school systems. Proponents of the voucher system argue that competition would produce better schools. Opponents of both argue that to fragment education into many competing systems would be inefficient and divisive. A slender majority of the public opposes tax support for private schools [*Public Opinion*, 5:39, June/July 1982], and its enactment is in doubt.

SCHOOL PRAYERS. Supreme Court decisions since 1962 forbid any prayers (except silent prayers) in public schools. A constitutional amendment authorizing prayers in public schools has the support of many conservative church leaders, while many other church leaders are opposed [*Time*, 118:39, Aug. 9, 1982]. Supporters are outraged at "banning God from the schools" and claim that school prayers would help cultivate religious sentiment and public morality. Objectors (especially Jews and other non-Christian groups) claim that their children would be isolated and humiliated by exposure to school prayers in an alien faith. Many church leaders and most behavior scientists doubt that an innocuous school prayer, watered down to offend no one, would have much effect in any direction.

The practical significance of school prayers may be trivial, but their symbolic significance is great. For persons distressed by secularism and permissiveness in modern life, the school prayer offers a chance to "do something" about social trends they deplore. Polls show public support for a school-prayer amendment at about three to one [*Public Opinion*, 5:40, June/July 1982].

EVOLUTION AND BOOK CENSORSHIP. One sign of the current resurgence of religious conservatism is the drive to require that "creation science" be taught wherever evolution is taught in public schools. This issue, too, has symbolic meaning in the struggle of religious conservatism against secularism and religious liberalism. "Creation science" supporters, while not entirely agreed upon a single version of creation, are agreed that human beings and other forms of life were created instantaneously by God without any intervening evolutionary stages. Opponents have two main objections: (1) that the content of school courses of study should be selected by scientists and teachers not by legislators and (2) that "creation science" is not science, just religion misnamed as science. "Creation science" followers reject the compromise of "theistic evolution," which holds that God began and directed the evolutionary process. Thus, the student must choose between science and religion. One wonders which choice most students will make. One state law requiring the teaching of "creation science" has been held unconstitutional [Siegal, 1981], but the issue is far from settled.

Schools also face an intensified effort to remove certain books from school libraries and reading lists [Warner, 1981]. Most often the books are claimed to be "dirty," although, sometimes, the charge is that they are sexist or racist. The books attacked include both what is considered "trash" and some of the most famous and esteemed works of literature. Here, again, should students' reading material be selected by scientists and educators or by parents and self-appointed censors?

Education and the Politicoeconomic Institutions

In earlier societies, education was not closely tied to the politicoeconomic institutions. In large empires, some education was needed for scribes, tax collectors, and other officials, but that was about all. In medieval Europe, only the church was closely connected to the school. Books were so expensive that only the affluent could own them. Aside from some poor boys who became priests, only the sons of the elite attended the universities. "Dangerous" (i.e., other than religious) ideas were no threat, for those who were able to toy with them were so tightly locked into the system of privilege that they would be unlikely to challenge it. Higher education was not very important to the state or the economic system and was generally allowed to play out its harmless games undisturbed.

All this is changed. Aside from religious censorship, systematic efforts to censor or suppress some ideas began when printing presses could distribute them widely among the people. Education everywhere today is cultivated, used, feared, and to a large extent controlled by the politicoeconomic institutions.

Educational Autonomy

Academic freedom and academic tenure represent attempts to protect the independence of educators.

ACADEMIC FREEDOM. The ideology of academic freedom means (1) that schools are to be run by educators with limited interference from others and (2) that scholars and professors can conduct research, can publish, and can teach without fear of reprisal even if the results of their research or teaching should prove unpopular.

For the educator, academic freedom protects the search for truth wherever it might lead. For the society, it gives some assurance that students and the public will receive what actually is the truth as the professor understands it, rather than something the professor is forced to say because of fear or pressure.

Scholars and professors have often come under fire when their teachings or writings offended someone. In Hitler's Germany, Nazi students ran professors off the campus if they failed to endorse Nazi ideas. Academic freedom can help protect teachers from such pressures.

ACADEMIC TENURE. Academic tenure protects a teacher from summary dismissal either because of the teacher's ideas or simply because of favoritism by principals and superintendents. Teachers and professors may be dismissed "for cause," after orderly dismissal procedures, although this is rare and there is some justice to the claim that tenure protects mediocrity. Since tenure makes dismissals difficult, it is often attacked by those who would like to silence those who do not share their views. During the 1950s, attacks on tenure came from extreme conservatives who wished to banish "radicals" from the campus. Today, attacks occasionally come from leftists who want to banish the "conservatives" who resist having the university promote the radical reconstruction of society [Kagan, 1982].

Tenure and seniority have recently been strained by staff reductions. Many colleges and public schools have had to reduce staff because of enrollment decline or budget cuts. Minorities and females were disproportionately hired in recent years to correct past discrimination. If staff cuts now follow seniority rules (last hired, first fired), this will result in the disproportionate layoff of minorities and women, erasing affirmative action gains of recent years. Seniority rights and minority rights are in conflict in this situation, and there is no easy solution.

FEDERAL INTERVENTION. The autonomy of educational institutions in recent years has been reduced by federal intervention. The federal dollars which are so welcome have provided leverage for imposing federal standards and regulations. Antidiscrimination legislation brought additional controls. The Department of Health, Education, and Welfare issued "guidelines" on the hiring and promotion of minorities and on sex discrimination in employment, curriculum, and school activities (especially school athletics). Special education for the handicapped, bilingual instruction, and other special programs have been federally mandated. In some communities, federal courts have assumed direction of the schools, giving orders to school boards about which schools they may close, how district boundaries may be drawn, how much busing they must do, and what race and sex quotas they must meet. In one remarkable instance, Brigham Young University, a Mormon church-related university which accepts no federal funds, had to negotiate with federal

The autonomy of educational institutions
has been reduced by
federal intervention.

officials for permission to continue its practice of housing off-campus male and female students in separate rooming houses [*The New York Times*, June 11, 1978, p. 51]. Whether federal intervention has been proper or improper is not the issue we raise at this point. We cite this as an example of reduced autonomy of one institution under the increased influence of another.

AMERICAN EDUCATION: SUCCESS OR FAILURE?

Few nations of the world compare with the United States in educational expenditures or in average years of schooling completed. Is our great effort a success?

The Decline of Learning

Comparisons between nations are difficult but not impossible. The International Association for the Evaluation of Educational Achievement published twelve volumes of comparative-achievement test findings between 1967 and 1977. The evidence clearly shows that American students did not work as hard or learn as much as students in other developed countries [Lerner, 1982]. Measures

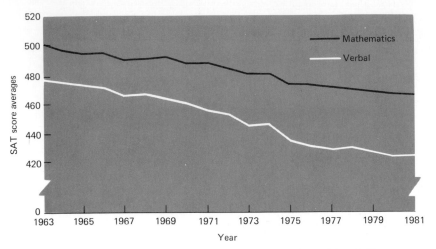

FIGURE 12-2 The SAT score decline. (*Source:* Data from The College Board. Chart by Peter H. Stafford, *Chronicle of Higher Education,* Vol 23, No. 6, October 7, 1981, p. 1. Reproduced by permission of *The Chronicle of Higher Education*)

of changes in learning of American students over time are equally disquieting. By every measure we can quantify, average student learning in the United States has declined in recent years, as shown in Figure 12-2. Even after making allowance for imperfect testing, we cannot avoid the conclusion that students are learning less than those of a generation ago.

What explains this decline? Partly it is due to decreased selectivity of schools. In 1950, half of the 25- to 29-year-old age group had been graduated from high school; in 1980, this figure had risen to 85 percent. Marginal students, who used to drop out, now remain in school and dilute the ability levels. The College Board holds the changing composition of the student body to be responsible for three-fourths of the drop in Scholastic Aptitude Test (SAT) scores between 1963 and 1970 but for only one-fourth of the drop since 1970 [College Board, 1977]. What accounts for the rest of the decline?

DISTRACTING INFLUENCES. The baleful influence of television on school learning has already been mentioned. The possession of

a car offers the temptation of "cruising" and other diversions and often requires a part-time job for its support, crowding out homework. The popular habit of having television or radio providing background noise during homework is probably a distraction. Many other diversions compete for student attention.

School activities apparently are *not* an unfavorable influence. Research finds that the students making higher scores are also the students who participate in high school activities such as debate, music, drama, journalism, or athletics [College Board, 1977, p. 39]. Those who share in extracurricular activities are also less likely to become delinquent [Landers and Landers, 1978].

DILUTION OF OBJECTIVES. When schools whose students learn well are compared with schools whose students learn poorly, certain differences are striking, even after allowance is made for differences in student family and class backgrounds. The distinctive features of schools with high levels of learning are: (1) order and discipline, so that students and teachers can concentrate upon learning rather

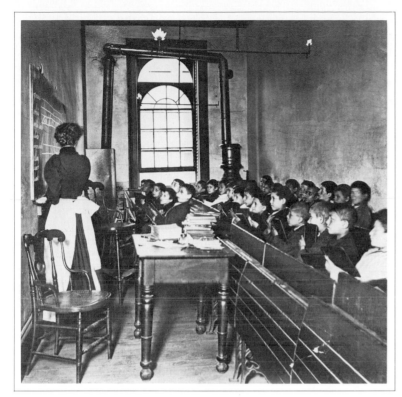

Learning is possible with mini-
mum facilities. (*Constance
Stuart/Black Star; Jacob Riis/
The Bettmann Archive, Inc.*)

than survival; (2) a school atmosphere which emphasizes learning and rewards achievement; and (3) parental support of school efforts to maintain discipline and demand achievement [Coleman, et al., 1966; Coleman, 1981]. Beyond a decent minimum, such variables as excellence of school facilities, advanced degrees of school staff, and per-pupil school expenditures are not very important. While some recent innovations such as Head Start appear to have been successful [Rule, 1982], most of the expensive educational experiments of the 1960s and 1970s proved to have little effect [Armbruster, 1977; Horton and Leslie, 1981, pp. 258–259]. Present school trends are toward discipline, homework, emphasis upon academic achievement, and greater freedom for school administrators to pursue strong school policies without external interference [McPartland and McDell, 1982].

Social-Class Differences in Learning

In the studies cited above, the variable of student class background was controlled so school effectiveness could be isolated and measured. When predicting either individual learning achievement or average achievement for a school, the quality of the school is less important than the family and class background of the students. Year after year, in every study and in every country, children from the lower class learn far less, are more often absent, and drop out earlier than middle- or upper-class children [Jencks, 1972; Clifton, 1981].

Even in countries which claim to give preference to working-class children, unequal learning rates persist [Banks and Finlayson, 1973, p. 178]. In the Soviet Union, Premier Khrushchev increased the proportion of university students from worker and peasant homes. This system was abandoned when it appeared to have lowered academic standards, increased dropouts, and graduated many poorly prepared specialists [Dobson, 1977, p. 314]. Only in some underdeveloped countries is school quality more important than student background [Heyneman and Loxley, 1982]. In these countries, the "poor" schools lack even the minimum facilities and staff needed for decent learning. But everywhere, the picture is the same—most of the low achievers are from working-class families, and most of the high achievers are from middle- or upper-class families [Burstein, Fischer, and Miller, 1980].

Why do lower-class children learn less well? It is possible that lower-class persons average lower in native abilities. This has been debated for generations without any clear decision. Even if we could agree in defining "native ability," we have no measure of native ability which is widely accepted as reliable.

Most educators are agreed that the lower achievement of lower-class pupils is due, at least in considerable part, to home influences which school policies are unlikely to change [Jencks, 1972, p. 53]. Lower-class families are larger, and parents must divide their attention among more claimants. Middle-class parents more often are educated themselves and more often are actively interested in their children's academic progress. Middle-class homes have more books and magazines and quiet space

---

WHAT MAKES A GOOD SCHOOL?

What the study contains is a rather stunning documentation of the practices found in good schools, whether they are public or private . . . good schools have an orderly climate, disciplinary policies that students and administrators believe to be fair and effective, high enrollment in academic courses, regular assignment of home work, and lower incidence of student absenteeism, class cutting and other misbehavior.

Diane Ravitch, "What Makes a Good School?" *Society*, 19:10, January/February 1982.

How many of the characteristics of a good school can teachers and administrators create by themselves, and how many require the active cooperation of parents?

for study. Perhaps most important of all, middle-class children live in a social world with a great many successful people who have gained career success after doing well in school. Having a good school record is a vital part of the typical success model for middle-class children.

Differences in social class background give a boost to middle-class children and a handicap to lower-class children. This is discussed in detail in Chapter 14, "Social Class," (pp. 354–355). For the moment, we simply note that there are large differences in the ease with which children from different classes respond to school opportunities.

Can class differences in learning be reduced? Hauser and Featherman claim that class differences in learning *have* been reduced in recent years [1975, pp. 20–21]. There are a number of inner-city schools whose children are mostly black and poor which show high levels of academic performance [Sowell, 1976a]. It is clear that an orderly school with safe halls and toilets, a dedicated teaching staff with a commitment to learning, and parents who demand and reward good study habits can achieve creditable levels of learning, even if the children are poor and facilities are drab.

MOBILITY LADDER OR BARRIER? It has long been a cherished faith that our schools give everyone a chance to climb the social ladder. A number of revisionist critics, following conflict theory, have challenged this. They argue that the function of American education has been not to aid but to *block* the upward mobility of the immigrant, the black, and the poor. Schools perpetuated inequality by socializing children to stay in the class in which they were born and by steering children into the courses and the schools which would prepare them to do so [Greer, 1972; Carnoy, 1975; Bowles and Gintis, 1976; Apple, 1979; Oakes, 1982]. If their intent was to block upward mobility, the schools have failed. Studies of social mobility show that there has been a good deal of mobility (see Chapter 15). Some detailed factual studies show that turn-of-the-century schools *did* operate as a

mobility ladder for immigrant youth [Kessner, 1977]. Other antirevisionists claim that the "bastion-of-privilege" argument is factually untrue [Ravitch, 1978; Rehberg and Rosenthal, 1978]. The question of whether our schools have been a ladder or a barrier to social mobility continues to be debated with no answer clearly established.

THE LIMITS OF CREDENTIALISM. Many training programs require applicants to pass an admission test. Many careers are forever closed to those who cannot pass the proper tests and collect the necessary diplomas—as shown in Figure 12-3.

Conflict theorists charge that many credentials requirements go far beyond anything needed to ensure competence. Admission tests often screen out those who lack the middle-class niceties of language, manners, and ornamental learning. They protect the "ins" from the competition of the "outs," maintaining inequality and privilege.

Considerable research supports these charges. Credentials and admission test scores have been shown to be poor predictors of job performance [Berg, 1969; Blank, 1972]. Educational qualifications have often been raised with no evidence that job performance will improve. Often it does not, for job performance and job satisfaction are often lower for people who are overeducated for their jobs [Quinn and de Mandilovitch, 1975].

The Equal Employment Opportunity Act requires that admission tests and degree requirements must be demonstrably related to job performance. Many tests have been revised to remove irrelevant questions. Credentialism is not ending, but those demanding credentials must be able to show that they really screen out the incompetent, not the disadvantaged [White and Francis, 1976].

SCIENCE AND TECHNOLOGY AS INSTITUTIONS

A scant century or two ago, science was the private hobby of wealthy gentlemen of lei-

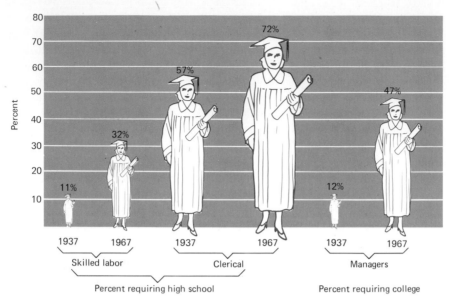

FIGURE 12-3 Increasing rate of credentialism. Percent of employers requiring high school or college diploma for various occupational categories. (*Source: Based on estimates in Randall Collins,* The Credential Society, *Academic Press, Inc., New York, 1979, p. 5.*)

Higher education is increasingly required for the better jobs. Is it always essential, or just for certain positions?

sure. Science was of so little practical importance that throughout the Napoleonic Wars, scientists traveled freely between France and England to share their harmless conversations.

Today, science is institutionalized. This means that it is recognized as highly important. It is standardized; scientists throughout the civilized world follow the same basic methods and procedures, for there is no capitalist or communist or Christian or atheist way to conduct a scientific experiment or to program a computer.

Science is the systematic quest for verifiable knowledge and dependable, orderly sequences, following certain rules and procedures as outlined in Chapter 1. *Technology* is the use of scientific discoveries to solve practical problems. Scientific investigation continuously turns up new findings through methods which have been thoroughly institutionalized. Scientists in governmental,

industrial, or university laboratories work in predictable ways to bring about unpredictable discoveries. Whenever a major breakthrough occurs in either pure or applied science, industrial research and development (R&D) engineers apply this knowledge to the development of improved gadgets or more effective techniques of production. Interaction of other social institutions with science and technology is the most powerful influence of our time. Since this influence works both ways, let us first look at how other institutions influence science and technology.

The pursuit of science and the application of technology are subject to stimulus, restraint, and direction from government, business, religion, and education. Government may prop up outworn practices or may stimulate science and research. Government is today the largest source of research funding. Government may encourage new technology by tax laws favoring purchase of new equipment. Business supports research and introduces new products. Religion may oppose science as a threat to faith or may encourage research as, in the words of the early English scientist Robert Boyle, "laudable attempts to discover the True Nature of the Works of God" [Merton, 1973, p. 234]. Education may simply pass on existing knowledge, or it may train students in the attitudes and methods of scientific inquiry.

Science and technology have irresistible effects on other institutions. Business concerns face bankruptcy unless they use the latest technology, governments find that technical change has altered the problems which they face, religion must adapt its teachings to meet new scientific interpretations, and education seeks to prepare students for scientific and technical developments.

The desire for autonomy among scientists is at least as strong as among the clergy, educators, or business executives, and may be even more effective. One example of this is found in the presence of prominent scientists among dissidents in the Soviet Union. A modern society must foster scientific inquiry, and to do this, it must allow some freedom to its scientists. Even in as totalitarian a state as the Soviet Union, it is impossible to place scientists completely under the rule of government leaders! [Sakharov, 1975].

The Irresistibility of Science and Technology

In one sense, science and technology cannot be stopped once set in motion. Of course, we *could* forbid new scientific and technological research, but this would soon put us in the backwaters of history. All science is interrelated and interdependent, and discoveries in one field open new vistas in others.

Marx may have been wrong in making the economic institutions dominant over all the others. It may be that science and technology have greater effect upon our social relationships than any other institution. Henry Ford's assembly line probably had more effect on labor relations than all the programs of the United Automobile Workers. By inventing the cotton gin and making large cotton plantations profitable, inventors did more to spread slavery than all the politicians. A century later, the mechanical cotton picker destroyed the plantation system the cotton gin had created.

We hear persistent reports that some American corporation has bought up and suppressed some marvelous new invention which threatens its profits. Persons who believe this do not know much about either business or technology. There are no real secrets in science or technology. Anything that scientists and engineers in one corporation or one country can do, the scientists and engineers of any advanced country can duplicate, given a little time and a lot of money. Any highly profitable invention which a corporation bought and tried to suppress would soon be marketed by a competitor (who would steal it if necessary; patent infringement lawsuits are very common). Can anyone seriously imagine that Exxon, for example, would be permitted to suppress a marvelously efficient new motor which would save the United States some $50 billion or so of imported oil each year? Can anyone imagine the Soviet Union failing to use this new motor in their tanks and ships just because patent infringement is not polite? If they could not invent it themselves, someone else surely would. The findings of science are never secret for long.

It is fashionable to conclude a discussion of science and technology with the Frankenstein motif—that is, that humans have created a force they cannot stop or control. Is this humanity-at-the-mercy-of-machine idea correct?

Although the "computer-gone-berserk" is a popular theme of science fiction writers, it is a fiction. Computers have no independent mind; they do only what human programmers tell them to do. It is true that once a new technology is accepted, its latent con-

Science and technology can be the servants and not the masters of society only if we can agree upon their use. How could computers be used as instruments of oppression? (© *Nancy J. Pierce/Photo Researchers, Inc.*)

sequences may be unavoidable. Automobiles pollute, mass production promotes uniformity, and the temptation to use available technology is often irresistible. Repeatedly, a new weapon (the crossbow, the pistol, the cannon, the submarine, the machine gun, poison gas, the atomic bomb) was at first believed to be too terrible to be used—yet it was. Are we to be helpless victims of technology?

This depends upon our values. Automobiles are so convenient that it seems we shall not surrender them until all the fuel is gone; yet Freon-loaded aerosol spray cans, which might damage the ozone layer, were surrendered quite readily. We still use aerosol cans, but without the Freon. It is true that anything useful will be used, but people can decide how it is used.

The question—can people control technology?—has a clear answer. It is yes—but only if there are other values which seem more precious. When people make reckless use of technology, science gets the blame. During the decade of the 1970s, there was a spectacular arousal of environmental concerns. As this is written, the national administration seems to favor development over conservation, but this is probably a temporary digression. Polls clearly show that a majority of the people are willing to sacrifice some comforts and conveniences in order to preserve the environment [Ladd, 1982]. Reckless use of

technology has been challenged, and some gains have been made in harnessing technology to the protection of the environment. Thus, science and technology can be the servants and not the masters if only we can agree upon their use.

As this is written, the scientific establishment is not entirely healthy. The fraction of students entering scientific careers is falling; government and university funding for scientific research is shrinking; about half our scientists and engineers are in weapons research, which provides little of human benefit; and political control of scientific and technological research is increasing [Laubach, 1980]. The autonomy of science diminishes as the domination of government grows. Popular skepticism of science is shown in popular acceptance of unscientific fads such as laetrile [Peterson and Markle, 1979]. Nonscientific cults and fads of many sorts are thriving (see *The Skeptical Inquirer*, any issue).

Those who really understand science have always been in the minority. Science may even go into temporary eclipse in one region, as in Hitler's Germany in the 1930s or in the People's Republic of China in the 1950s, but barring the worldwide destruction of civilization in a nuclear holocaust—which is not at all impossible—science and technology will continue to promote both innovation and change.

SUMMARY

Educational institutions developed as a systematic way to provide what could not be learned easily within the family. The United States has a dual public/private school sytem with a far higher enrollment in higher education than most other countries. Institutionalized education includes schools of many kinds plus the apprenticeship system. A lot of noninstitutionalized education takes place, for better or worse, in homes, on streets, and through the mass media, especially television. *Contest education* in the United States provides for relatively easy admission with expectation of many failures or dropouts. *Sponsored education* in many countries limits admission to higher educational programs, with the expectation that nearly all will be graduated.

The school is a social system with its own network of roles, statuses, and relationships, some of which can be shown on a *sociogram*. Education has a number of manifest functions, the principal of which are to help people attain their potential and to prepare them for occupational roles. Latent functions include prolonging immaturity, weakening parental control, preserving or changing the class system, and providing some shelter for dissent.

Educational institutions affect and are affected by all other institutions and are in a constant struggle for autonomy from them. Current issues between education and religion include tax support for parochial schools, school prayers, the teaching of evolution, and book censorship. Devices for protecting educational autonomy include *academic freedom* and *academic tenure*.

The achievement level of students in America compares poorly with that of students in some other nations and has fallen in recent decades, due, apparently, to decreased selectivity of schools, distracting influences, and dilution of objectives. Present trends are toward strong discipline and demands for higher levels of academic effort.

Large social-class differences in learning are found in the schools of all countries. Differences in study goals and habits appear to be the main cause in the developed countries.

Science and *technology* have become major institutions in modern times. Scientific and technological advances carry latent consequences which sometimes are difficult, if not impossible, to control. Science and technology *can* be directed at human welfare rather than human destruction. Whether or not they *will* be is undetermined.

GLOSSARY

academic freedom the freedom of scholars and teachers to search for and teach the truth as they perceive it.
contest education relatively open admission to higher education with expectation of many failures or dropouts.
science a body of organized, verified knowledge which has been secured through scientific investigation; a method of study whereby a body of verified knowledge is discovered.

sociogram a diagram showing attractions and rejections among a small group of persons.
sociometry method of studying and diagramming social relationships and making sociograms.
sponsored education restrictive admission to advanced education with the expectation that nearly all will be graduated.
technology the use of scientific discoveries to solve practical problems.

tenure the right to remain in a position unless removed because of shortage of funds, incompetence, or misconduct.
tracking grouping students according to ability.

QUESTIONS AND PROJECTS

1 Schools the world over show a good deal of similarity. Why?
2 Has the apprenticeship

system operated as a mobility ladder or a mobility barrier in the United States?

3 Discuss these two propositions: (1) The community college has increased the proportion of American youth who complete a college degree. (2) The community college has "cooled out" and sidetracked many youth who otherwise would have completed a college degree.

4 Think back on your own experience in elementary school. Were you a leader, follower, or social isolate? What cliques existed among students in the classroom? How did they affect the learning process?

5 Would a sociometric survey help the elementary teacher to be more effective? Why or why not? Would this reasoning also apply to a teacher with a college class?

6 It has been suggested that the communications revolution might replace schools with a video computer terminal in each home, where the students do their studying. Do you think this will ever happen? Would anything be lost?

7 Are there any reasons why a person who is anxious to promote radical social change should defend the academic freedom of faculty who oppose radical social change? And vice versa?

8 How do you account for the fact that scientists have been prominent among the Soviet dissidents? Why is it hard for a totalitarian state to make scientists conform to the official views?

9 Why should an increase in school enrollment diminish academic achievement? What other factors may also be influential?

10 What are the things which parents can do (or fail to do) to help their children learn better at school?

11 Is it inevitable that the schools in any society will promote mainly the values and interests of the powerful? Do you know of any exceptions?

12 In what ways is the advance of science a threat to human security? Can people control the use of scientific discoveries? Why or why not?

13 Read the article by Susan Feinberg in the Suggested Readings. Does her impression of the impact of television agree with yours? How should the schools try to deal with television-generated attitudes toward study?

14 Read and compare Edward C. Banfield, *The Unheavenly City Revisited*, pp. 148–178, and Colin Greer, *The Great School Legend*, pp. 130–157. Which discussion of social class and education do you find more convincing?

15 Read the article by Rafky in the Suggested Readings and comment on whether or not it seems realistic in view of your own experience with school custodians. How do you explain the tendency of people in the community to give more weight to the reports of custodians than of school administrators?

SUGGESTED READINGS

Alba, Richard D. and David E. Lavin: "Community Colleges and Tracking in Higher Education," *Sociology of Education*, 54:223–237, October 1981. Finds few differences in dropout rates of students in two- and four-year colleges.

Boorstin, Daniel J.: "Political Revolutions and Revolutions in Science and Technology," in *The Republic of Technology*, Harper & Row, Publishers, Inc., New York, 1978, pp. 22–30. An eloquent statement of the influence of institutionalized science and technology on the rest of society.

*Bowles, Samuel and Herbert Gintis: *Schooling in Capitalist America: Educational Reforms and the Contradictions of Economic Life*, Basic Books, Inc., Publishers, New York, 1976. A radical critique of American education, which is viewed as a device to perpetuate economic inequality.

Collins, Randall: *The Credential Society: A Historical Sociology of Education and Stratification*, Academic Press, Inc., New York, 1979. Attributes the rise of credentialism to a struggle for power and status between Anglo-Saxon Protestants and other groups in American society.

Feinberg, Susan: "The Classroom Is No Longer Prime Time," *Today's Education*, 66:78–79, September 1977. A teacher tells how television has affected the study habits and classroom attitudes of her students.

*Jencks, Christopher, et al.: *Inequality: A Reassessment of the Effect of Family and Schooling in America*, Basic Books, Inc., Publishers, New York, 1972. A critique of the belief that educational reform will produce increased achievement by lower-class students.

Johnson, Norris R. and William E. Feinberg: "Youth Protest in the 60s: An Introduction," *Sociological Focus,* 13:173–178, August 1980. Introduces a special issue filled with articles on campus protest.

Koszuch, Joyce A. and Howard H. Garrison: "A Sociology of Social Problems Approach to the Literature on the Decline in Academic Achievement," *Sociological Spectrum,* 1:115–136, December 1980. An analysis of sociological viewpoints and research related to academic achievement.

Laubach, Gerald D.: "Growing Criticism of Science Impedes Progress," *USA Today,* 109:51–53, July 1980. An eval-uation of recent criticism of science.

Lerner, Barbara: "American Education: How Are We Doing?" *The Public Interest,* 69:59–82, Fall 1982; and Ralph W. Tyler: "The U.S. Versus the World: A Comparison of Educational Performance," *Phi Delta Kappan,* 62:307–310, January 1981. Two differing evaluations of student learning in the United States and other nations.

*Merton, Robert K.: *The Sociology of Science*, The University of Chicago Press, Chicago, 1973. A collection of Merton's papers devoted to the institutionalization of science.

Parelius, Ann Parker and Robert J. Parelius: *The Sociology of Education*, Prentice-Hall, Inc., Englewood Cliffs, N.J., 1978. A textbook which sets forth a "consensus" and a "conflict" view of education.

Peterson, James C. and Gerald Markle: "Politics and Science in the Laetrile Controversy," *Social Studies of Science,* 9:139–166, May, 1979. A case study of political conflict over a scientific issue.

Rafky, David M.: "Blue Collar Power: The Social Impact of Urban School Custodians," *Urban Education,* 6:349–372, January, 1972. A description of ways in which school custodians in smaller towns sometimes exercise power far greater than their position would suggest.

Zeigler, Harmon, Harvey J. Tucker, and L. A. Wilson, II: "School Boards and Community Power: The Irony of Professionalism," *Intellect,* 105:90–93, September/October 1976. Discussion of how schools moved from the control of lay boards to that of professional educators and then, in some respects, to federal bureaucrats.

*An asterisk before the citation indicates that the title is available in a paperback edition.

13 Political-Economic Institutions

An economist can never fix an economy the way a mechanic can fix a car. No matter whether he assures you that the economy will run faster and farther and more smoothly after his repairs than before, there are always human costs as well as human benefits involved. Changes in the economic machinery never lift everyone evenly, like boats on an incoming tide. Usually economic remedies spread their effects unevenly, making the rich richer and the poor poorer, or vice versa; helping the Sun Belt grow faster than the Frost Belt or the other way around; boosting one interest and leaning against another.

And so the *real* challenge—the challenge below the economics of inflation and unemployment, government spending and taxing, international competition and the energy crunch—is political. It is to find resolutions to difficulties that will be acceptable to the people who *are* the economic machinery.

> Robert L. Heilbroner and
> Lester C. Thurow:
> *Five Economic Challenges*,
> Prentice-Hall, Inc.,
> Englewood Cliffs, N.J., 1981,
> p. x.

As the above quotation points out, there is no such thing as "pure" economics or "pure" political science. Every governmental action has economic effects, and every economic problem has political implications. Governmental and economic institutions are so closely intertwined that it seems most practical to look at them together.

DEVELOPMENT OF POLITICAL-ECONOMIC INSTITUTIONS

When humans lived by gathering nuts and herbs, there was little need for either trade or government. The extended family was sufficient to organize their activities. Each society developed institutionalized ways of meeting needs for food, clothing, housing, and whatever else it needed. Food sharing, for example, was an institutionalized practice in many simple societies, especially if they hunted large game. Every household in the village had a recognized *right* to a share of the kill made by anyone in the village [Farb, 1968, p. 43]. This was an institutionalized right. Thus economic institutions emerged from people's trial-and-error efforts to meet their needs (functional analysis), or sometimes, economic institutions emerged from the success of one group in imposing duties or obligations upon another group (conflict analysis).

Trade developed when people wanted something their neighbors produced; gradually the process of exchange became standardized, orderly, and predictable—therefore, institutionalized. Economic institutions emerged as people developed orderly routines for exchanging goods, assigning work tasks, and recognizing claims upon one another. The domestication of animals, the establishment of settled agriculture with claims to land, and the eventual development of industries all led to development of economic and governmental systems.

Just how governments developed is lost to history. We learn from anthropologists that the simplest societies had no government. Some, such as the Polar Eskimo, did not even have recognized "family heads," although some respected persons might have more influence than others [Murdock, 1936, p. 210]. The growth of political authority apparently paralleled the growth of cultural complexity— from family head to tribal council to chief. Yet many simple societies had no chiefs except, perhaps, temporary leaders of a raiding party.

The word "civilized" implies a system of civil law in place of (or in addition to) traditional authority, administered by certain designated officers. Civil government became necessary when the ancient river-valley civilizations arose along the Nile, the Tigris-Euphrates, the Ganges, and elsewhere. Irrigated agriculture, with its system of ditches and control gates, required protection from marauders as well as protection of land rights and other property. Trade and economic development created the need for government.

Feudalism was a set of economic and political institutions which developed in a number of places as an intermediate stage between tribal societies and the national state. It was based upon a set of reciprocal rights and duties. The lord, in his castle with his retinue of knights, provided security, protecting the vassal's person, property, and right to use a piece of land. The vassal gave service and loyalty ("fealty") to the lord. Feudalism was thus a way of organizing life and work at a particular moment in history. It passed when increasing trade, growth of towns, and development of the centralized national state made feudalism an obstacle rather than a

WHERE SHARING IS INSTITUTIONALIZED

When one Eskimo gives to another in his band, he is usually giving to a relative or to a partner. An exchange among those in close relationship is not a gift, and that is why the receiver does not offer thanks. An Eskimo praises a hunter for the way he hurled the harpoon but not for the way he shared the meat from the seal the harpoon killed. Sharing is a kinsman's due, and it is not in the category of a gift. The Arctic explorer Peter Freuchen once made the mistake of thanking an Eskimo hunter, with whom he had been living, for some meat. Freuchen's bad manners were promptly corrected: "You must not thank for your meat; it is your right to get parts. In this country, nobody wishes to be dependent upon others . . . With gifts you make slaves just as with whips you make dogs!"

An important thing about exchange in the life of the Eskimo is that he alternates between feast and famine. One Eskimo hunter may be successful in killing seal after seal while another hunter is having a long streak of bad luck. Anyone who has been molded by a capitalistic culture knows what he might well do in similar circumstances—if he were the fortunate hunter and the others were in need. He would jack up prices. Such a thing could never happen in Eskimo society—not because an Eskimo is innately nobler than you or I, but because an Eskimo knows that despite his plenty today, assuredly he will be in want tomorrow. He knows also that the best place for him to store his surplus is in someone else's stomach, because sooner or later he will want his gift repaid. Pure selfishness has given the Eskimo a reputation for generosity and earned him the good opinion of missionaries and of all others who hunger and thirst after proof of the innate goodness of man.

From *Man's Rise to Civilization as Shown by the Indians of North America from Primeval Times to the Coming of the Industrial State* by Peter Farb. Copyright © 1968 by Peter Farb. Reprinted by permission of the publisher, E. P. Dutton, Inc.

Would institutionalized sharing work as well in a town of a thousand as in a band of perhaps fifty? In a city of a million?

useful institution. Conflicts of interest arose between kings and provincial nobility, between the towns and the feudal estates, and between the church and both the kings and the provincial nobility. Interestingly enough, the rise and fall of feudalism neatly fits the functionalist perspective (institutions arise because they are functionally useful and pass when they cease to be useful) but also fits the conflict perspective (institutions arise because they serve the interests of the powerful and fall when new interest groups appear to contest them).

Almost from their beginnings, governments have been involved in economic affairs. The Bible tells how Egypt's pharaoh, responding to Joseph's interpretation of his dream, collected and stored grain during seven bountiful years to carry the country through seven years of famine [Gen. 41:14–57] (and also transferred most of the land from peasant to state ownership). Rome had state-operated mines throughout the empire, requiring a constant stream of slaves and convicts for their operation (since the working life of the miner was about four years). The economic regulations of Emperor Diocletian in the third century are still cited as examples of detailed government direction of the economy. The medieval guilds regulated entry to the crafts, while the towns tried to prevent their craftsmen from ever leaving town. The mercantilist system of the seventeenth and eighteenth centuries assumed that it was the responsibility of the state to control and direct all economic activity, and modern capitalism is, in part, a reaction against mercantilism.

In the past century, the economic activities of governments have expanded enormously. With economic development comes division of labor. We now have 12,000 occupations listed in the *Dictionary of Occupational Titles* [Cain and Treiman, 1981]. Specialization creates different groups with competing interests—farmers versus middlemen versus consumers, for example—and government mediates the conflicts between them. Thus,

The market is an economic institution in most societies. Does this picture show institutionalized or noninstitutionalized behavior? (*Peter Buckley/Photo Researchers, Inc.*)

economic development spurs the growth of government.

Warfare also feeds the growth of government. A disciplined army can defeat an unorganized horde many times its size. All warfare demands organization. Modern warfare demands the organization and coordination of masses of personnel and mountains of supplies of a thousand different kinds.

In modern societies, the social service function has become a powerful source of governmental growth. About a century ago, Western governments began providing services directly to their citizens, and today, a wide range of health, education, and welfare services are provided by most governments. For all these reasons, government at all levels absorbs about one-third of America's gross national product and still more in some other countries (see Figure 13-1).

Political-economic institutions are more than standardized ways of doing things. As with all institutions, they also include supporting ideas, sentiments, traditions, and values. Canoe building among the Polynesians, the walrus hunt among the Eskimos, rice planting in the wet rice culture of Southeast Asia, the ground-breaking ceremony for the new government building, and the christening of a new aircraft carrier—all these involve ascribed roles, traditions, and elaborate rituals. These rituals solidify the cooperation of humans and bring the blessing of God or the gods on the undertaking. Modern governments are supported by a panoply of flag-waving, martial music, and impressive buildings. Even modern business makes use of tradition, ritual, and sentiment. The singing commercial, stories of charismatic business leaders, gifts to charity and public services, the recognition banquet for retiring employees—all these seek to give the business system the appearance of a warm-blooded collection of human beings rather than simply a cold economic machine.

POLITICAL-ECONOMIC INSTITUTIONAL PATTERNS

Three different types of modern governmental-economic systems have emerged, each of which organizes economic activity differently.

Mixed Economies

No completely "capitalist" societies exist today. The so-called capitalist societies are "mixed" societies in which private property, private enterprise, and the profit system are combined with considerable government intervention and direction. In the allegedly capitalist society of the United States and the allegedly socialist society of Sweden, the relation between government and the economy is similar in kind and differs somewhat in degree. In either case, the larger part of the society's economic activity is carried on by business which seeks to make profits. In each country, however, government operates some enterprises. Government control of the supply of money and credit greatly influences economic activity in each country, while variations in government expenditures also affect the level of business. Finally, both countries operate as welfare states, providing a large

The medieval guilds regulated entry into the crafts. In how many ways does the place pictured here differ from a modern printing plant? (*The Metropolitan Museum of Art, Harris Brisbane Dick Fund, 1953*)

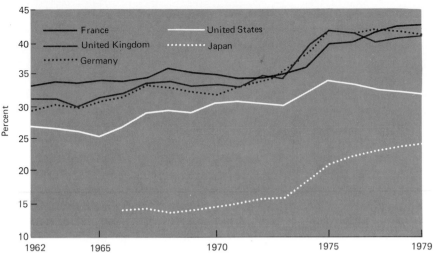

FIGURE 13-1 Total federal, state, and local government spending as percent of GNP. (*Source: From The Conference Board,* Economic Road Maps, *nos. 1022–1023, March 1982. By permission of The Conference Board, 845 Third Avenue, New York, N.Y. 10022.*)

How does the growth of government spending in the United States compare with that in other advanced countries?

number of services such as housing, education, medical care, and a minimum income.

Communist Societies

The term "democratic" is used in communist societies to describe a system in which people have no effective means of control but in which a one-party dictatorship claims to rule in their behalf. Overall coordination of the economy, including the level of prices and wages and the kind of goods produced, is determined by central planning agencies. Agriculture is often organized in collective farms, which usually draw bitter opposition from the farmers [Hunt, 1977]. In China, disillusionment with collective farming has led to the growth of private markets and more individual responsibility and reward for cultivation [Domes, 1982]. The Soviet Union, one of the world's major food exporters before the revolution, has never fed itself since the revolution; only through imports from capitalist countries can the population survive [Barnett, 1982].

In recent years, some communist countries in Europe have reverted to a partially capitalist model, where each industry makes more of its own business decisions and is expected to make a "profit" in its operations. These profits are retained by the government to be used as the government thinks best [Brand, 1981; Wren, 1982]. Yugoslavia is the communist country which allows the individual enterprise the greatest degree of independence in operation. While the communist countries have been reverting to a capitalist model of trade, the so-called capitalist countries have been shifting toward government and worker ownership of capital. In some Western European countries, governments are the major stockholders of many corporations, while the investments of the Rockefellers and Kennedys in the United States are dwarfed by those of union pension funds [Drucker, 1976].

Although there are variations between countries, some type of communist system operates in the Soviet Union, the satellite Eastern European countries, Cambodia, Laos, Vietnam, China, and Cuba.

Communism has become the way some underdeveloped countries try to modernize and industrialize themselves [Ebenstein and Fogelman, 1980, p. 113]. Communism typically gains support in poor countries with an archaic social system, great inequality, and a tiny upper class which clings to privilege but often does little to advance economic growth or to reduce poverty. An authoritarian government ruthlessly suppresses movements for democratic reform, whose leadership is systematically murdered or exiled. To the suffering masses, communism may seem to be the only alternative to more of the same misery [Kiernan, 1972; LaFeber, 1982; Pastor, 1982]. An artful propaganda is supplemented by terrorist activities often financed and sponsored by communist nations. Thus, ideological campaigns win support from intellectuals, while guerrilla terrorism handicaps the operation of the government and may convince the undecided that communism is the irresistible "wave of the future."

It is, however, debatable whether communism offers the most rapid route of economic improvement for underdeveloped countries. Most of the recently independent nations have rejected the communist pattern in favor of a mixed economy. A few of these nations, such as Singapore, South Korea, and Taiwan, have had rapid economic growth and rapidly rising prosperity with a mixed economic system which is more capitalist than collectivist.

Fascist Societies

A fascist society is ruled by a one-party dictatorship organized by a charismatic leader. The people have practically no voice in governmental affairs and find their satisfaction in the glorious strength of the nation. Military power and conquest were major features of Hitler's Germany and Mussolini's Italy, but Franco's Spain and Perón's Argentina operated without military expansionism. In 1982, a neofascist Argentine government invaded the sparsely settled, British-populated Falkland Islands. The invasion came shortly after large-scale demonstrations against the Argentine government and apparently was designed to persuade citizens to "rally around the flag" and forget domestic woes. It illustrates the sociological principle that a group can be unified, at least temporarily, by conflict with an outside enemy.

In fascist countries, private ownership of business is tolerated but with limited freedom and detailed state direction. Welfare benefits are provided by the state and are as high as the stage of industrial development and the needs of the military will allow. All private interests are subordinated to the state. Labor unions become agencies for imposing state policy upon workers, while churches are either forced to support the regime or find their activities severely restricted. Fascism develops in countries with a relatively advanced economy and some democratic experience. Such countries may "turn fascist" when they have been unable to reconcile their social tensions or to solve their social problems democratically [Ebenstein and Fogelman, 1980, p. 113].

Communists and Fascists have each pictured the other as the enemy of human freedom. They have each claimed that the only way to stop the wicked deeds of the other was to put themselves in power, but they look more and more alike, and some scholars begin to speak of a communist-fascist convergence [Fischer-Galati, 1981].

Politicoeconomic Systems of Developing Countries

At the time of this writing, 1983, no countries had governments which exactly fitted the fascist model, but there are a number of dictatorships with many similarities, mostly in developing countries. These are one-party states ruled either by an army general or by a politician with military support. Rather than a strident nationalism, their basis for support

HOW IMPORTANT IS GOVERNMENT?

In the typical less developed country the state dominates much, particularly all the pathways to modernization. Bureaucracies are incompetent and often corrupt and the middle-class—the sector that brought about the transformation in the West that all now fervently desire—is small, weak and beset by regulation. . . .

Tremendous new demands are being put on governments now barely able to cope. With greater competition for every good in society, ethnic and national rivalries are becoming sharper;

terrorism, insurrections and wars are more frequent. And because we have concentrated so long on the relation between people and food, we are hardly aware of important underlying causes of this deepening crisis; the weakness or absence of an innovative middle-class and the correlative dominance of grossly inefficient and corrupt governments.

William Peterson, "The Social Roots of Hunger and Overpopulation," *The Public Interest,* Summer 1982, pp. 37, 52.

Is it possible to develop a modern industrial society without efficient government and a strong middle class?

---

is a claim that they avoid the conflict, corruption, and inefficiency of democratic governments and are better able to lead their nations in economic development. These countries follow their own version of the "mixed economy." They usually provide welfare services for government employees and urban factory workers at the expense of a poor rural population which remains outside the welfare system. Heavy taxes and cumbersome regulations make it difficult for any large-scale business entrepreneurs to operate unless they are political favorites. Many enterprises are government-operated or perhaps personally owned by the dictator and his or her many relatives. These enterprises usually operate inefficiently and only exist because they are subsidized by the rest of the economy. Other local capitalists who survive in spite of obstacles are under constant pressure, especially if they are members of minority ethnic groups. However, governments are impressed with the capital resources and technical skills of foreign corporations and try to attract them through promises of privileges far greater than those allowed native business people.

Most of the countries which have gained their independence since World War II have this type of regime. Even India, which has been the largest exception to this trend, had

such a government for a brief period when martial law was proclaimed by Mrs. Gandhi, then prime minister. Sometimes the dictator justifies his or her rule as a temporary expedient which is laying the basis for an eventual democratic regime. Nigeria did move from a military dictatorship to parliamentary rule, and President Marcos of the Philippines officially ended martial law. Also, Mrs. Ghandi of India was voted out of office after a brief period of dictatorship and was only reelected later when she promised to abide by democratic procedures. Whether these steps are a trend back to democratic government or minor fluctuations remains to be seen.

Fascism, Communism, and Mixed Economies Compared

All three of these governmental-economic systems attempt to increase productivity. The mixed economies permit more individual initiative, while communism and fascism limit individual freedom sharply and depend upon centralized government agencies for planning economic goals and activities. Insofar as they are industrialized, they tend to reduce the extremes of wealth and poverty.

Yet in all three types of societies, inequalities in income persist. In the communist society, inequalities in income stem from unequal wage and salary scales which allow a professional or managerial person to earn several times as much as a common laborer and from "fringe" benefits such as villas, cars, and special luxury shops available only to the communist elite. In the fascist society and in the mixed economy, property ownership and inheritance lead to great differences in income. The greatest inequalities are probably found in the less-developed countries, whose wealthy live even more lavishly than the American wealthy, but whose poor live at a level which makes American welfare clients look rich by comparison.

International trade blunts the differences between different political-economic systems [Wallerstein, 1974, 1979; Chase-Dunn, 1980]. All modern nations need many imports, which must be paid for by exports. Capital is borrowed and lent on an international market. Thus, changes in the world economy over which a single state has little control may be even more significant than the type of political-economic system in a state.

MANIFEST AND LATENT FUNCTIONS

Manifest Functions

The manifest functions of all three systems—communist, fascist, and mixed economy—are to maintain order, achieve consensus, and maximize economic production. No society is completely successful in any of these functions. The totalitarian communist or fascist societies seem most successful in maintaining order, at least temporarily, while the mixed economies have the best record in allowing political liberty, and they have also achieved higher levels of economic production [Barnett, 1982]. Various American studies find per-worker productivity in the Soviet Union about half that in the United States [Schmemann, 1982].

Latent Functions

An analysis of the three types of societies indicates much similarity in their latent functions. One latent function of all modern governmental-economic institutions is the destruction of traditional culture. Customary forms of land tenure, religious belief, family organization, residential location, and many other established patterns of social life undergo change as industrialism develops. Social mobility is encouraged, one consequence of which is increased anomie and alienation.

Another latent function is the acceleration of ecological deterioration. Unless expensive and complicated precautions are taken, every increase in production leads to an increase in environmental destruction. Sometimes capitalists are blamed for this on the grounds that they are unwilling to let anything interfere with profits. However, the communist societies, without any capitalists except the state, have the same problem. Basically, the difficulty is that under any system, environmental protection costs money [Orleans and Suttmeier, 1970; Goldman, 1972; Houck, 1980].

Pollution also costs money. A recent calculation put the cost of compliance with the Clean Air Act of 1977 at $17 billion as contrasted to money benefits of $21.4 billion [Wolcott and Rose, 1982], aside from health and scenic benefits. However, the cost-benefit ratio is not always this favorable, and costs may be immediate while benefits may be delayed. Also, one group may bear the cost while others gain the benefits. Neither communists nor capitalists find it easy to carry pollution-reducing policies into effect.

POLITICOECONOMIC CONFLICT AND COOPERATION

Much of the argument over whether human society is primarily cooperative or competitive in nature focuses on governmental and economic activity. The functionalists see a system where the division of labor causes each to cooperate with others and thereby increase the wealth of all. They see government as a device to coordinate a united effort to get those things judged important by consensus (agreement) of the community. The conflict theorist sees this consensus as artificial rather than real and views both government and economic activity as battlegrounds on which individuals and groups contend with each other for a privileged position.

Consensus is (sometimes) attained through the process of negotiation, argument, and compromise that we call politics. One noted political scientist has defined politics as the study of "who gets what, when and how" [Lasswell, 1958] The justification for this statement is that government affects the income of people in unequal ways. Expenditures always involve both taxes and benefits. Taxes usually weigh more heavily on some than on others. Laws usually make it easier for some people to make money and more difficult for others. Thus, politics is a constant battle of groups and individuals to gain benefits and avoid losses. Sometimes the battle is waged through elections and legislative processes, and sometimes it involves the force of police and armies. In any event, the conflict is real and often brutal.

Conflict, however, is not the whole story. The common good is a reality. The maintenance of order, the construction of roads, provisions for public health, and the support of schools (to name only a few) benefit the entire community and not just the few who sell goods or services as a result. The element of mutual benefit is also present in economic activity. Capital and labor, meaning the owners of industry and the employees, are often in bitter conflict over wages and benefits, yet capital and labor also work together. Without capital to provide equipment, labor would not be productive, and without a labor force, the owners of capital could not operate. Sometimes capital and labor are hard to define. Is a retired steelworker, whose pension is de-pendent on the money paid into his pension fund by corporate dividends, a laborer or a capitalist?

Democratic elections and legislative compromises offer an arena for both conflict and cooperation. Conflict can be expressed through the effort to secure legislation favorable to a particular group. Cooperation is seen in the willingness to abide by the results of elections and legislative actions and by a willingness to compromise which allows measures essential to the whole society to be carried out, even though some groups feel their needs have not been fully met.

Welfare and Conflict

Oddly enough, the welfare obligations assumed by governments in recent years, which bring benefits to so many, have increased conflict. The reason for this is that people's wants are endless, while government resources are limited. Demands have a tendency to rise far more rapidly than the national income rises, but if a government tries to limit expenditures, it risks being overthrown. This is especially true in developing countries in which the "revolution of rising expectations" is likely to make any government seem incapable of meeting its citizens' demands.

The expansion of the welfare state may be ending. Several Western societies have elected governments pledged to cut taxes and trim the welfare state. Even Sweden has vacillated—in 1976, throwing out the party which had introduced the welfare state, then restoring it in 1982 [*Associated Press*, Sept. 20, 1982]. Prediction is risky, but while welfare services probably will not be greatly reduced, they may not be expanded.

Inflationary Trends

What can governments do when confronted with demands which outrun their resources? To meet the demands is impossible; to reject them may result in defeat at the next election or even a violent revolutionary overthrow. The answer is repression or inflation or both. One reason why most developing countries turn toward some type of dictatorship is simply to stifle citizen demands. If the government does not have to face elections and the army protects it from revolutionary violence, it may be able to resist indefinitely the demands that it provide its people a higher standard of living immediately not in some remote future. If nationalistic propaganda can identify a foreign adversary or a minority group within the nation which can serve as a scapegoat and be blamed for economic difficulties, then the government's position is even stronger.

Inflation is worldwide, although communist countries often conceal it by holding the posted price and letting the shelves empty out; meanwhile, goods or services in short supply can be purchased only by making extra "undercover" payments [Simis, 1982]. While inflation has many causes, the main one is that inflation is a way of avoiding hard economic decisions. Governments, faced with demands which cannot be met by tax revenues, print more money (usually by a rather complicated and indirect process). The result is that many people have more money, while the amount of goods and services for sale remains unchanged, so the prices float upward.

Inflation reduces the impulse to save, since money in the future will be worth less than money today. It makes any kind of public or private economic planning difficult and threatens the security of everyone. The greatest victims of inflation are probably the poor, who spend most of their income for necessities which usually show the largest price increases [Heilbroner and Thurow, 1981, p. 25].

No one defends inflation, yet nearly everyone promotes it. Nearly all of us feel underpaid and cry for higher paychecks. Nearly all with something to sell want higher prices. The inevitability of inflation was neatly illustrated by a television documentary on the social security system. *Every* person interviewed felt that social security benefits were too low; *every* person interviewed felt that his or her social security taxes were too high. Everyone wanted to pay less and get more. The inescapable result is higher government deficits, more printing-press money and more inflation.

Doesn't anyone want to control spending? Yes! Everyone wants to cut government spending, provided someone else's ox is gored. Urban consumers want to cut farm price supports, farmers want to cut urban grants, pacifists want to cut defense costs, and so it goes. Everyone has a favorite program to expand—teachers want higher educational grants, environmentalists want more environmental protection, the energy-poor Northeast wants energy subsidies, and the arid Southwest wants more dams. President Reagan, perhaps the most fervent cost cutter of the century, sponsored the largest peacetime increase in defense costs in U.S. history. Legislators, anxious to offend no one, try to give something to everyone, so the budget edges upward. One wonders whether it is possible for a democratic government to control expenses or whether the inherent pressures toward increase are unmanageable.

The Underground Economy

One reaction to inflation and high taxation is the growth of the so-called underground economy, variously estimated at up to $500 billion a year in the United States [MacAvoy, 1982]. In every industrialized country, including the Soviet Union [Horoszowski, 1980; Simis, 1981] much of the economic activity is unreported and thus escapes government regulation and taxation. In Italy, for instance, it is estimated that 70 percent of government employees hold second jobs on which they pay no income taxes.

Typical forms of underground economy include self-employed workers, ranging from cleaning women to professionals, who take

Fast learners. (*Paul Sequeira/
Photo Researchers, Inc.*)

all or part payment in cash with no bills, no
checks, no records; independent business
operators who operate part of their business
on a basis of "strictly cash, no records";
"moonlighting" workers whose second job is
reported neither by them nor by their employers, saving money for both; barter arrangements in which workers trade services
with no money exchanged, as when the
mechanic services the physician's car in return
for medical services. Barter clubs arrange for
exchange of unpaid services, including indirect exchanges, as when a member gives
services to A and gets credit points in the
"bank" with which to pay for free services
from B. Such barter clubs are held illegal by
the Internal Revenue Service but still operate.
The higher the tax rates and the more burdensome the government regulations, the
greater are the temptations of tax evasion and
underground activity ["Tax Dodging—It's a
Worldwide Phenomenon," *U.S. News & World
Report*, 92:37–38, March 8, 1982.]

IDEOLOGY AND THE BUSINESS-GOVERNMENT RELATIONSHIP

Ideologies often develop to define the relationship of institutions to each other. This is

an inevitable part of the function of ideologies,
which have been described as "beliefs that
also carry implications for how people ought
to behave and how society ought to be organized" [Smelser, 1976, p. 51].

Major Economic Theorists

We will consider four thinkers who have
made influential contributions to ideologies
concerning the relation of economic activity
and government. They are Adam Smith, Karl
Marx, John Maynard Keynes, and Milton
Friedman.[1]

ADAM SMITH AND "FREE ENTERPRISE."   Adam
Smith (1723–1790), the economist who wrote
The Wealth of Nations, reasoned that the strongest government was one in a country in which
business prospered. He also felt that economic decisions were best made by individuals responding to the market rather than by

---

[1] The theories of these men have been considered in many books
and are far more complicated than is apparent in this presentation. Our aim has been to indicate their major impact on public
policy, rather than to present definitive treatment of their intellectual content. Although our treatment differs in several ways,
we are indebted to Neil Smelser, *The Sociology of Economic Life*,
Prentice-Hall, Inc., Englewood Cliffs, N.J., 1976, pp. 6–13, for
an interpretation of Smith, Marx, and Keynes and to Milton
Friedman, *Free to Choose: A Personal Statement*, Avon Book Division, The Hearst Corporation, New York, 1981.

government agencies. This theory kept government out of most business decisions and allowed modern industrialism to develop. Smith felt that government had no need to be concerned about wages or prices, since competition would set these at levels best for the total society. If wages in a business were too low, this would discourage workers from seeking jobs and eventually wages would have to be raised. If they were too high, too many applicants would show up, employers could then cut wages, and the excess job applicants would move to other employers. The same would be true of prices; if too high, the seller is left with unsold merchandise and must cut prices. The movement of prices and wages would thus constitute an "invisible hand" which would direct both capital and labor into those economic activities which were most profitable for them and for society as a whole. Government intervention would be not only unnecessary but positively harmful, since it would interfere with rational economic decisions. These ideas form the basis for the system of *capitalism* (or "free enterprise," as it is often called).

KARL MARX AND COMMUNISM.   Karl Marx (1818–1883) looked at economic activity as a conflict theorist. He felt workers wanted wages high and capitalists wanted them low. This created an inevitable antagonism in which one or the other was bound to lose. The capitalists appeared more powerful because of their wealth and influence; but the workers, far more numerous, were bound to triumph in the end. Then they would end the conflict by eliminating the private ownership of capital—hence the name *communism,* implying common ownership by society. A number of nations now profess to operate according to the ideas of Marx, although their policies vary considerably and depart from Marx's ideas at many points.

While the Soviet Union, the oldest Marxist country, has had some accomplishments, the relatively slow pace of its economic development and its brutally oppressive government make this example of communism so unattractive that many modern Marxists deny that it is Marxist. However, the Marxist view of the governmental-economic relationship as mainly the focus of conflict continues to be influential. Many critics look at any change in governmental-economic relationships from the standpoint of their alleged effect on either workers or capitalists. It is usually assumed that if a proposal seems good for capitalists, it is bad for workers. Marxists would say that capital should come from income withheld by government enterprises not from private savings.

Most of the industrialized countries are closer to Adam Smith than to Karl Marx. There are, however, two chief departures from Smith's teaching: the growth of a welfare state and the attempt to use government to ensure prosperity. The welfare state provides people with an alternative when they are stranded by the market economy. Likewise, business leaders interrupt their ritualistic objections to government interference long enough to ask for subsidies and protection against competition. While these trends have had an effect in keeping government expenditures high, they are probably less important than the ideas of Keynes.

JOHN MAYNARD KEYNES AND "FINE TUNING." John Maynard Keynes (1883–1946) would be classified as more of a functionalist than as a conflict theorist. He saw society as a whole in which all groups prospered or suffered together. He felt society suffered because business seemed to move in alternate cycles of prosperity and depression. In prosperity, business saw the chance for good profits and expanded rapidly. The expansion was usually overdone, and then profits fell; operations were then cut back, and unemployment rose. Keynes thought this could be corrected by increasing government expenditures in time of depression and cutting back in times of prosperity. Government expenditures were justified to keep economic activities stable. Deficit spending in a depression when private investment dropped would sustain economic activity and keep people employed. Conversely, a drop in government expenditures during prosperity would allow more activity to be carried on by private business. Governments could borrow money during a depression and pay back the loans with money received from higher taxes in a period of prosperity.

Keynesian thinking was quite influential in the period from 1930 to 1975 and was often used to justify government policies. For a time, Keynesian policies appeared to solve the question of the relation of government and business in capitalist societies and depressions did indeed become less severe. It was all a matter of "fine tuning" of government taxes, financial policies, borrowing, and expenditures in ways appropriate for each stage of the business cycle. But difficulties arose. Increased government expenditures did not always counteract the effects of a business depression as easily as expected, and they seemed to lead to inflation [Roberts, 1978]. The Keynesian remedy was attractive but not always workable [Feldstein, 1981].

A major criticism of Keynesian policy is that there is *always* a demand for more government expenditure. To increase government expenditures during a depression is popular, but to cut back on expenditures during prosperity and pay off government debt is difficult. Legislators cannot resist demands to spend money when it is available. This imperfect following of Keynesian policy leads to ever-increasing government debt and unending inflation.

MILTON FRIEDMAN AND "THE RULE OF THE MARKET." Milton Friedman (1912–   ) is the leading exponent of what has become known as the "Chicago school," which finds that our departure from the teachings of Adam Smith is a major cause of economic troubles. Friedman has faith in the ability of the market to provide what people really want rather than what officials think is good for them. Communism, governmental planning, and Keyne-

sian-inspired deficit spending are all anathema to him. In the first place, they do not work, and secondly, they represent a lessening rather than an expansion of human freedom. He is friendly to tax limitation such as California's Proposition 13 and believes that any procedure has merit if it will decrease taxation and thus limit the expansion of government.

Keynes saw the government control of money and the banking system as a way to maintain purchasing power which had been weakened by a depression. Friedman is a "monetarist" who holds that the tendency to increase the supply of money and credit faster than the supply of goods inevitably leads to inflation.

Friedman thinks that many social welfare measures are devices to give bureaucrats control of the poorer part of the populace. If a welfare minimum is needed, he advocates a negative income tax under which people earning less than an amount considered necessary for health and comfort would receive money direct from the government.

Friedman's theories are so contrary to most current trends that it is difficult for any government to follow them, and even he counsels a gradual shift from a welfare state to a market economy. He is probably at his best in his criticism of collectivist policies which have failed to work as predicted. He has been a major influence in current thought and has paved the way for the current "supply-side" economists who insist that government intervention has often tilted things in the wrong direction. Friedman sees a free market (capitalism) as being essential for a democratic society. Capitalism not only liberates economic energies, but it also limits the likelihood of heavy-handed government dictation.

Ideological Change

Ideologies rise and fall in popularity. For many years capitalism and democracy have come under attack by intellectuals such as Marcuse [1969], who were often repelled by the profit motive and, although not Communists, were attracted by the alleged equality of life under communist rule. In recent years the pendulum has swung back, and it is now the socialist-communist planned society which is under attack. What once was regarded as a perfect society is now seen as a straightjacket which represses both intellectual freedom and the kind of economic initiative which promotes prosperity.

Although the Soviet Union seems likely to survive beyond the expiration date of 1984 predicted by one of its intellectuals [Amalrik, 1969], it hardly stands as a socioeconomic success story. It has only been able to keep its satellite East European nations in line by the use of force, and refugees from communist countries continue to "vote with their feet" [Wrong, 1976, p. 6]. In France, Revel and other intellectuals point to a capitalist America as the hope of the world and communism as its downfall [Pryce-Jones, 1977]. In the United States, scholars such as Kristol, Moynihan, and others, as well as Friedman, argue that the "rule of the market" may be kinder to human rights than a massive welfare state in which the government decides all questions [Podhoretz, 1981]. George Gilder [1981] denies that capitalism is characterized by self-ishness and describes it as centered in faith and reciprocal giving. After a long eclipse, conservative philosophies are again respectable.

It is probably in the underdeveloped countries where the greatest uncertainty about economic policies is found. Many Third World governments, while not slavishly Marxist, follow many socialist and Marxist ideas in operating their economies. The results are not inspiring. Most of their economies teeter on the edge of bankruptcy, kept alive by transfusions of money from Western banks (which will probably never be repaid). Although socialist policies have failed to produce abundance, conditions in most of these countries are not favorable to the emergence of democratic capitalism.

It is possible that Third World countries may yet turn to communism. On the other hand, they often see themselves as oppressed by both communist and capitalist countries and seek to avoid policies which make them a complete vassal of either camp.

POWER AND GOVERNMENT

Definitions of power vary, usually denoting an ability to control the actions of others, even against their will. With respect to government, power refers to the ability of individuals or groups to control the decision-making process.

Organizational Power

The struggle for power is often a contest between organizations. A variety of political action committees (PACs) raise funds to fight reelection of legislators they dislike. The AFL-CIO calls for a higher minimum wage, and the National Chamber of Commerce assails high wages as the cause of inflation. The National Organization for Women battles the Moral Majority over voluntary abortion. The struggle for power is mainly between highly organized groups. When a lobbyist seeks to influence a legislator, the legislator's prime question is, "How many votes does the lobbyist represent?" If individuals are powerful, it is usually because of the organized groups they represent.

The Power Elite

Some years ago a prominent sociologist, C. Wright Mills [1956], developed the idea that American governmental and economic activity was controlled by elite groups of executives who moved back and forth between governmental, academic, financial, and industrial positions. Mills viewed the corporation as either the base from which the executive elite originate or the goal toward which they are moving. He felt that their power meant that society becomes dominated by men primarily committed to a view of life expressed by a prominent executive in the immortal words, "What's good for General Motors is good for the country."[2] Mills made a strong case for the theory that executives who have had similar training, association, and outlook are often found in decision-making positions. There is no doubt that a professional managerial class has developed in the United States. But many social scientists argue that the case for a ruling elite with a virtual monopoly of social power has not been proved [Rossi, 1956; Reissman, 1956; Dahl, 1958; Bell, 1958; Lowry, 1965, pp. xviii–xix; Miller, 1970, pp. 202, 275 276].

IS THERE A CONSPIRATORIAL POWER ELITE?
There are at least three fairly well defined views on this question. The pluralists reject the idea that there is any one cohesive group controlling American life [Dahl, 1961, 1976, pp. 59–61; Rose, 1967; Von der Muhll, 1977; Polsby, 1980]. Following the lead of Merton [1949b], they see power as *polymorphic* (literally, "having many forms"), with "different persons exercising decision making powers for each separate issue" [Ferrell et al., 1973]. Thus, a variety of different groups compete and share power. None of these groups always wins, and major social decisions are the result of compromise, competing influences, and the force of circumstances.

The two other schools of thought see American social decision making dominated by cohesive quasi-conspiratorial groups but differ about who these groups are. The right-wingers [Smoot, 1962; Schlafly, 1964; McBirnie, 1968; Efron, 1975; Buchanan, 1975; Kirkpatrick, 1979] believe the power elite is comprised of radical intellectuals who have infiltrated the government, the schools, and the communications media. By their control

[2] C. Wright Mills, *The Power Elite*, Oxford University Press, Fair Lawn, N.J., 1956, p. 168. For the context of Charles Wilson's statement, see "Conflict of Interest," *Time*, Jan. 16, 1953, p. 70.

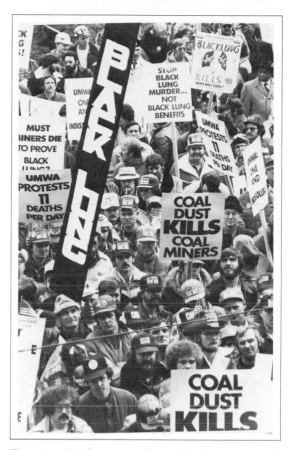

The struggle for power is mainly between well-organized groups. Is this a spontaneous or an organized protest? (*United Press International*)

of the press, radio, and television, they determine the information which reaches the people. Likewise, by occupying key government posts, they make the decisions which sell out American individualism to a leftist internationalism. It is "they" who are responsible for ever-increasing welfare payments and for the court decisions increasing the rights of alleged criminals versus the police.

In recent years the term "new class," which the Yugoslavian writer Djilas gave to the communist bureaucrats, has been applied to journalists, television commentators, and some educators by conservative critics. The new-class label is based on the belief that those in the communications media tend to share a style of life, common economic interests, and a common point of view. This point of view is said to be scornful of such traditional values as familism, nationalism, and free enterprise [Phillips, 1977; Bennett and Delattre, 1978; Berger, 1981].

Some leftists critics [Anderson, 1974; Domhoff, 1970, 1978, 1980] are equally sure that a core of top-level academics, generals, government officials, and corporation executives dominate the society on behalf of big business. It is "they" who maintain an unequal distribution of income and intentionally preserve poverty in order to protect privilege [Gans, 1972]; it is "they" who keep the country at war or on the brink of war to profit the "military-industrial complex."

One recent study compared the "business elite" (a sample of executives of large corporations) with the "media elite" (a sample of top journalists and television news commentators). This study concluded that "each group rates the other as the most influential group in America; moreover, each wants to reduce substantially the power of the other and to take its place as the most influential group" [Rothman and Lichter, 1982, p. 118].

Almost any governmental action will be denounced by someone as the act of an elitist conspiracy. This conspiratorial elite (leftist or rightist, depending upon who is name-calling) is so sly and deceitful that it sometimes accepts a measure which seems to be against its own interests. Thus, according to leftists, the welfare system is supported by the rich as a device for "regulating the poor" and preserving the capitalist system [Piven and Cloward, 1971]. Any given act of government can be interpreted by either the leftist or the rightist critics to prove that the United States is dominated by a power elite.

Can the power elite and pluralist views of power be reconciled? First, while there are few, if any, "conspiracies" and while most important maneuvers are conducted in the open, there is group action. Citizens with

common interests do meet, talk together, and plan strategy. Sometimes they get the changes they desire. More often, they encounter opposition and must make compromises. Second, some people are experts in the management of organizations or in creating a public image. Whether born poor or rich, such people are soon affluent. They tend to join with people like themselves in both formal and informal association and often come to think very much alike. Finally, while many people spend their careers in a single occupation, there is some movement of personnel between institutions. This is most marked in civil government, since many officials have had earlier careers in industry, education, or the military.

One scholar [Whitt, 1979] rejects the pluralist-elitist argument as irrelevant, since both views are partly true but inadequate. He proposes a *class-dialectic model* in which the state normally serves the interests of the dominant class, but this dominant class is sometimes disunited within itself and may be successfully challenged by organized competing class interests. The question of who really runs the government has no simple answer.

Power of Unorganized Masses

In the days of feudalism, government was a monopoly of the nobility and the ordinary person had no direct voice at all. Nevertheless, government usually operated as expected. This was because noble and commoner shared a set of institutionalized ideas about how things should be done. The noble might make the formal government decisions, but he made them on the basis of traditional beliefs accepted by all in the society.

In the modern era of rapid change, tradition has little weight and governments can take actions which violate long-standing traditions. The ordinary citizen has the right to vote but has little understanding of government or contact with its leaders. Is the citizen a helpless pawn pushed about by governmental forces beyond individual control?

Individually, the masses may be powerless. But collectively, no! The unorganized masses can exert a decisive power.

POWER OF MASS MARKETS. In the democratic society the masses exert influence through their choices of what goods to buy, what papers to read, what television programs to watch, and so on. This power is not unlimited, for the consumer can be manipulated, as motivation research has demonstrated [Packard, 1957; Dichter, 1971]. But in a competitive market economy such as ours, consumer preferences are rarely disregarded for very long. Courting the consumers' favor may produce a gaudy vulgarity in product design and shoddy escapism in television programs, but it unquestionably attests to the power of the mass market.

MASS VETO POWER THROUGH NONCOOPERATION. Some decisions can become effective only through mass cooperation. Public health programs, mass-immunization campaigns, and voluntary blood banks are successful only if a great many people cooperate. The American civil-defense effort has limped through decades of monumental public indifference. Government makes selling marijuana a criminal offense but has little success in reducing the supply. Wherever a decision cannot be effective without mass cooperation, the veto power of the masses must be considered.

Direct Political Power of Masses

In a democracy the ultimate power of the masses rests in their franchise to "throw the rascals out." Sometimes, it is true, this power is empty because both candidates hold the same values and serve the same interests. But whenever there is widespread mass discontent with the way things are going in a

democracy, some party or candidate will appeal to this discontent, focus it on certain issues, and propose changes. The recent "tax revolt" is an example, as voters in ten states suddenly adopted tax-limitation initiatives in 1978 and approved nine out of eleven such initiatives in 1982 [Ranney, 1983]. The elite cannot always veto changes sought by the masses. The reforms of Roosevelt's New Deal era, established over the opposition of most of the elite, attest to the power of the skillfully focused discontent of the masses.

Important as the power of veto may be, it does not altogether dispel the picture of the poor as powerless to affect decisions concerning themselves. Alinsky [1965] and Piven and Cloward [1978] argue that the poor can utilize power and must be able to do so if their position is to be improved. They contend that the deliberate organization of the poor, stressing whatever grievances are most keenly felt, can lead to positive action. Through demonstrations, boycotts, and bloc voting, the poor can become one of the pressure groups in the community. They believe that, as the poor achieve power, they can prevent exploitation, formulate positive programs for their own welfare, and replace a helpless apathy with a sense of being able to control their environment.

Efforts to involve the poor in policy making and administration of the poverty programs of the late 1960s were not very successful for a variety of reasons, including lack of participation by the poor and the opposition of local political structures [Kramer, 1969; Moynihan, 1969; Brill, 1971; Helfgot, 1974]. One critic notes that despite Alinsky's dedicated and sagacious efforts to organize the poor, it was mainly the relatively prosperous and well-educated that he succeeded in mobilizing, while failing to develop real leaders from among the truly poor [Bailey, 1973]. Even one of Alinsky's favorite projects, the Woodlawn Organization, admits that it could neither maintain a persistent adversary stand nor

Single-issue voters see one issue
as paramount.

solve unaided the problem of neighborhood decay [Fish, 1973]. Some hold that organizing efforts of this type simply hamper cooperation between different groups without leading to effective participation by the poor [Roach and Roach, 1978]. Possibly the poor can be better served by organizations including members of all classes than by organizations of their own.

The mobilization of mass discontent is possible only in democracies. Elsewhere it brings a fast trip to the dungeons. A 1982 study concludes that only 54 of 165 independent nations could be considered free societies [Gastil, 1982; p. 4]. It may be that the desire to escape mass influence is a major factor in the establishment of nondemocratic governments.

POWER OF SINGLE-ISSUE VOTERS. Sometimes legislators refuse to pass a measure which receives overwhelming popular support in public opinion polls. This is often explained by the opposition of a relatively small minority of single-issue voters. These are voters for whom a single issue is so supremely impor-

tant that a candidate's stand (or earlier vote) on this one issue alone will determine their vote for or against that candidate. This gives the single-issue voters a disproportionate power. A candidate or legislator will seldom disappoint even a small bloc of single-issue voters unless there is an equal number of single-issue voters on the opposite side of the issue. A half century ago, the prohibition issue attracted many single-issue voters. Today, gun control provides a good example of single-issue politics. Several national polls have shown that gun-registration laws are favored by percentages ranging from 63 to 84 percent of the public. But one careful study finds that the opponents are twice as likely as supporters to say that this single issue would determine their vote upon a candidate [Schuman and Presser, 1978]. As long as single-issue opponents outnumber single-issue supporters by two to one, gun-registration laws are unlikely to be passed. After losing its campaign for ratification of the Equal Rights Amendment, the National Organization for Women launched a determined effort to convert its members into single-issue voters [*MS*, August 1982, p. 11].

PROPORTIONAL REPRESENTATION. Another device which increases the power of small groups is proportional representation. In the standard "winner-take-all" election, small parties have no chance. If there are ten legislative districts, the strongest party usually wins six or seven districts, the next strongest party will win three or four, while the minority parties will win none. Under proportional representation, the votes of all ten districts would be combined and each of the several parties would be given a number of representatives proportionate to its share of the total vote. Thus, a party supported by only 10 percent of the voters would still get 10 percent of the legislators, although under a majority system, such a party would elect no legislators.

Under majority (or plurality) rule, each of

the two major parties is a coalition bringing together a large number of interest groups, which in turn are forced to compromise with each other. Such parties are often criticized for straddling issues and not offering clear-cut choices to the voters, but they enable a consensus to be reached and can form a stable government. The proportional system encourages a large number of parties, often catering to single-issue voters. This, in turn, makes it hard for any party to elect a majority of the legislators. Instead, there are several small parties which join to form a government. Often the margin of control is so small that it can be upset by the defection of any one of the parties which make it up. Since each party is more concerned over a single issue than overall policies, it is easily offended and its loyalty to any coalition is shaky. The result is a weak government unable to take any action which offends even a small bloc of voters. This makes it difficult to carry out any definite government policies and even more difficult to sustain those policies for very long.

People may become so disgusted with the ineffectiveness of this form of democratic government that they become willing to accept a dictatorship as a way to get stability and decisive action [Hermens, 1978; Ebenstein and Fogelman, 1980, chap. 2]. Proportional representation is believed to have paved the way for the assumption of power by Mussolini's Fascists in Italy and to have hampered reaching a peace agreement between Egypt and Israel simply because the threat of veto by minor parties made decisive action difficult [Hermens, 1978]. Thus, a reform adopted in the name of democracy has, in the opinion of some critics, been a real threat to the effective functioning of a democratic political system.

Coercion and Disruption

Not all decisions are reached through the political processes of debate and persuasion.

Frustrated groups may resort to coercion, either when their political system is unresponsive to majority opinion or when a particular group lacks majority support and refuses to accept the majority decision.

Forceful coercion is normally a monopoly of government, but it is also used by other groups. Fascist and communist governments have normally become established after a determined, ruthless minority party bullied and shot its way into power. Political kidnappings are a recent device for revolutionary parties to coerce the release of prisoners or payment of ransom [Clutterbuck, 1978].

Nonviolent coercion has a long history [Hare and Blumberg, 1968; Gregg, 1972; Cooney and Michalowski, 1977; Bruyn and Rayman, 1979]. It consists of nonviolent ways of making a policy so costly and painful to others thay they will change it. The use of *economic coercion* through strikes, lockouts, and boycotts is far from new, but still common. Another common technique is for a protesting group to place itself in a position where the dominant group must either make a concession or take violent action against the protestors. This technique is variously called *nonresistance, passive resistance,* or *nonviolent resistance.* The object is to arouse public sympathies and to shame the dominant party into making concessions. In the late 1950s and early 1960s, groups of blacks entered segregated restaurants, parks, and other public accommodations, waited patiently for service and submitted peacefully to verbal assault and arrest [Maybee, 1961; Peck, 1962]. This emotionally moving spectacle helped change public attitudes and led to desegration of public facilities. Nationally televised pictures of peaceful civil rights marchers in Selma, Alabama, being clubbed to the ground by local police officers in 1965 may have done more to promote the civil rights movement than any other incident in our history [Garrow, 1978].

The technique of nonresistance, passive resistance, or nonviolent resistance is the historic weapon of the underdog, for it can be used by the totally powerless. Its use by American blacks declined as they developed a greater sense of "black power."

Civil disobedience is the open and public defiance of the law because of conscience or moral belief [Smith, 1968; Cohen, 1969; Murphy, 1971; Bay, 1975]. It is a technique of nonviolent coercion, resting on the powerful appeal of the spectacle of people who are willing to suffer for a moral belief. Punishment is therefore willingly accepted rather than evaded, in order to publicize and dramatize their belief that the law is unjust. This technique can be highly effective in some situations but requires great self-discipline lest its followers turn to violence. Nonviolent coercion and civil disobedience are most effective in democratic countries where protestors may be arrested but seldom will be shot. In authoritarian countries, such actions are rare [Corcoran, 1977].

Disruption, often called demonstration, is a form of coercion which is highly variable in both means and goals. It includes many ways of interrupting and paralyzing the normal day-to-day activities of a social system. Sometimes the goal is to force acceptance of the protestors' demands; sometimes it is to dramatize an issue; sometimes the motive appears to be the exhilarating experience itself, with the goals unimportant.

During the 1960s, campus disruptions became common, usually centered on administrative policies or the Vietnam war. Buildings were seized, offices packed or closed, classes disrupted, speakers heckled or shouted down, and (in a very few cases) buildings were burned [President's Commission on Campus Unrest, 1970; Kelman, 1970; Sharp, 1974; Woodward, 1974]. More recent disruptions and demonstrations have usually been directed against nuclear power plant openings.

There appear to be some periods or situations in which violence succeeds more often than nonviolence. Gamson [1975] studied fifty-three American groups and movements which promoted various social changes between 1800 and 1945. He claims that those which gained their goals were generally the ones that used violence (or, more often, had violence thrust upon them through police or mob attack), while all the nonviolent victims of attack failed to achieve their goals. But violence is a dangerous weapon. Victories may leave a legacy of bitterness which makes future victories more difficult. Majorities may move against violence in a wave of a law-and-order repression that results in minority groups becoming more powerless than ever.

TERRORISM. Most people define terrorism subjectively—one person's terrorist is another's freedom fighter [Ferencz, 1981]. More objectively defined, *terrorism* is "the use of violence or the threat of violence to coerce governments, authorities and populations by inducing fear" [Clutterbuck, 1977, p. 21]. Terrorists apply the ancient Chinese proverb: "Kill one; frighten 10 million." Television has been a godsend to terrorists and probably bears much of the responsibility for the modern escalation of terrorism [Alexander and Finger, 1977, pp. 270–282; Clutterbuck, 1977, p. 13].

Terrorism is most often used by groups with limited popular support but with sublime faith in the rightness of their cause. They believe the opposition to be so wrong, evil, and illegitimate that any means are justified. Since terrorist groups believe that they have the final truth and are working for the ultimate welfare of society, they feel justified in killing or in holding hostages until their demands are met. Terrorists are, typically, educated young people of middle- or upper-class backgrounds who see terrorism as a form of protest against social injustice [Margolin, 1977; Russell and Miller, 1978; Alexander and Gleason, 1981].

In recent years terrorist groups have often, but not always, been successful in securing the release of those in custody for assassination, bombing and kidnapping. They have also raised large sums of money through robbery and ransom and operate on an international basis [Weeks, 1978; Buckley and Olson, 1980]. Terrorists have ended civil government in places such as Northern Ireland [Bell, 1981; Moxon-Browne, 1981]. They have also forced burdensome security practices in air transportation which inconvenience everyone and add greatly to the expense of air travel [Ashwood, 1979].

Terrorists can have various goals: gaining world attention, destabilizing a government, promoting revolution, vengeance. Palestine Liberation Organization terrorism was a means—possibly the only available means—of keeping the plight of the homeless Palestinians before world attention [Alexander, 1976]. A recent wave of killings by Armenian extremists appears to be a belated revenge for Turkish genocide against Armenians over a half century ago [*Time*, 118:38, Aug. 23, 1982]. Terrorism is rare in totalitarian countries, since the detailed control of daily life makes it difficult for terrorists to move around or to collect the materials needed to operate.

In democratic countries, terrorism is a weapon of the weak. If a group cannot gain mass support through political action, terrorism permits a tiny minority to focus attention upon its grievances. It has seldom overthrown a government or brought major shifts in government policy, but terrorism can provoke a democratic government into adopting police-state methods of control, and therein lies its greatest danger [Laqueur, 1976; Wilkinson, 1977; Bell, 1978]. There is also the grim possibility that terrorists may eventually control nuclear weapons. If this ever happens, then a small group could hold the entire world hostage [Rosenbaum, 1978; Beres, 1979].

Judicial and Bureaucratic Activism

The foregoing sections discuss powers over government which are held by groups outside the government. This section considers how certain groups *within* the government may exert power of a kind not intended by the framers of the Constitution.

As stated earlier, government bureaucrats have considerable power to modify, to add to, or to veto the intent of the legislature. This is because all constitutional provisions and many laws state general objectives, leaving details to be set forth by the bureaucracy. For example, the Occupational Safety and Health Act of 1976, calling for a "safe and healthy workplace," is useless until spelled out in detailed regulations covering thousands of work situations and defining what is "unsafe." These regulations are drawn up by the bureaucracy and have the power of law, subject to court review. This gives bureaucrats a chance to write rules which go far beyond the intent of the legislature or to write rules which "water down" the intent of the legislature.

The change of administration following an election often brings persons to power who wish to make major policy changes. To change laws is difficult and time-consuming. It is faster and easier to change the bureaucrats—appoint new bureau heads who will direct a rewriting of the rules and regulations. By creative rule-writing, by starving the budget for certain programs and fattening the budget for others, and by letting the staff know which efforts will bring promotions and which will not, the effect of rewriting the laws can be achieved without changing a word of legislation. In such ways, every new administration makes policy changes.

Disagreements over bureaucratic rulings wind up in court. This gives judges their chance to modify, add to, or subtract from the intent of the legislature. "Strict-constructionist" judges believes they should stick close to the intent of the legislature; "activist" judges believe they have the duty to interpret the law according to the needs of today as they perceive them [Glazer, 1978]. For example, no legislature decreed that busing would be used for school integration or that abortions were legal. The tendency of the courts to extend vaguely worded laws and constitutional provisions into specific rules has greatly enlarged the governmental role of the judiciary.

THE EMERGENT AMERICAN CONSENSUS: FACT OR ILLUSION?

Functionalists assume that an orderly and efficient society must maintain a consensus upon basic values. Conflict theorists reply that an apparent consensus merely papers over the deep conflicts of interest and value found in modern societies. Without trying to resolve this debate, let us ask whether there *is* an American consensus.

Many commonly held values have been junked in recent years. The American people are not even close to agreement upon non-marital cohabitation, homosexuality, pornography, abortion, drug use, and many other issues, but there are a number of areas in which agreement is close to complete.

Belief in the value of the welfare state—the idea that government should maintain a "safety net" under the citizen—is shared by nearly everybody. Nearly seven out of ten Americans agree with the rather generous proposition that "the government should make sure that everyone has a good standard of living" [*Public Opinion*, 5:32, October/November 1981]. Disagreements center upon the limits and the operating procedures of the welfare system. Three national administrations (Eisenhower, Nixon, Reagan) have entered office breathing anti-welfare-state rhetoric. Each slowed the growth of welfare and "income-transfer" costs modestly, but none seriously attempted to dismantle the system. Thus, it is conventional to say that three Republican presidents "ratified" the welfare state.

Profit-making business is accepted as desirable by most Americans. If American labor unions were dedicated to class conflict along the Marxist model, they would have taken advantage of the business recession of the early 1980s by forcing corporations into bankruptcy and state ownership. Instead, they made contract concessions to help their employers survive. While business practices are often criticized, few Americans wish to see profit-making business disappear.

The work ethic is alive and strong. By more than three to one, Americans agree that "people should place more emphasis on working hard and doing a good job than on what gives them pleasure" [*Public Opinion*, 4:25, August/September 1981]. Welfare clients and poor people identify with the work ethic as strongly as the nonpoor [Goodwin, 1972, p. 112]. An occasional intellectual argues that a strong work commitment is no longer necessary in modern societies [Macarov, 1980], but few other people agree. Not all persons fully follow the work ethic for a number of reasons (we lack space to explore this here) [Yankelovich, 1982], but the acceptance of the ideology is nearly universal.

This list could be considerably extended. The functionalist can find enough value consenses to be reassured that American society is not on the verge of distintegration. The conflict sociologist can find enough conflicting interests to remain convinced that conflict is the basic social reality.

INTERRELATIONSHIP WITH OTHER INSTITUTIONS

We have already noted how other institutions—family, religion, education—are interrelated with the political and economic institutions. In the simple societies, the family is the dominant institution. In modern societies, the political-economic institutions tend to be the more dominant, although perhaps not as dominant as Marx imagined. It is far easier to show where the political-economic institutions have changed the family than to show where the family has changed the political-economic institutions. Clearly these, together

ARE ECONOMICS AND THE REST OF THE CULTURE INTERRELATED?

Joblessness causes stress that can aggravate or even cause health problems. M. Harvey Brenner, a sociologist at Johns Hopkins University, found by studying past recessions that every time the unemployment rate rose by one percentage point, deaths in the U.S. from all causes rose by 1.9 percent. Louis Ferman, a professor of social work at the University of Michigan's Institute of Labor and Industrial Relations, found an increase in infections, gastrointestinal problems and high blood pressure among the unemployed. Other problems cited are heart failure and cirrhosis of the liver.

with technology, are the main driving force in cultural change in modern societies. Whenever political-economic institutions change, the rest of the culture changes as well.

SUMMARY

Political-economic institutions are standardized ways of maintaining order in the production and distribution of goods and services. Government and economics are closely interrelated. Three patterns of political-economic institutions are: (1) the *mixed economy*, where profit and private ownership are combined with some degree of socialism and welfare statism; (2) *communism*, where profit-seeking is forbidden and all important enterprises are state-operated; and (3) *fascism*, where private enterprise operates under authoritarian state control. The mixed economies, while the most prosperous in the world, are presently struggling with recession, inflation, and conflict over the extent of the welfare functions of the state.

The manifest functions of politicoeconomic institutions are to maintain order, achieve consensus, and maximize economic production. No society is completely successful in these functions. The latent functions of politicoeconomic institutions are many, including the destruction of traditional culture and the acceleration of ecological deterioration.

There is much debate over whether human society is primarily cooperative or competitive, and governmental and economic activity is often considered in this context. We can find examples of both conflict and cooperation in all politicoeconomic systems.

Ideologies concerning governmental-economic relationships include those of Adam Smith, Karl Marx, John Maynard Keynes, and Milton Friedman. Capitalism and democracy have been under heavy attack by intellectuals for many years in Western societies. Presently, there is considerable intellectual criticism of the socialist-communist model in Western societies as being unfavorable to freedom and productivity, while in the developing countries, Marxist ideas have a strong appeal.

Power over government means the ability to control the making of decisions. Two contrasting views see the United States as: (1) ruled by a *power elite*, which may be perceived as either right-wing or left-wing; or (2) as a *pluralist* society in which decisions are reached through conflict and compromise. An alternative is the *class-dialectic model* in which dominant class groups usually prevail but can be weakened by disunity or challenged by organized competing class interests.

Unorganized masses possess a great and often unused power, especially in democratic societies. Mass power is expressed: (1) through the mass market, which determines what products, designs, and entertainment forms will succeed, and (2) in the mass veto of elite decisions through mass noncooperation. The masses also possess direct political power and can, for example, determine through voting which leaders will rule. Efforts to organize the poor into effective organizations have not been very successful.

Relatively small, single-issue voter groups wield disproportionate political power, unless directly opposed by other equally committed single-issue voters. *Proportional representation* enhances the power of single-issue voters, since it strengthens the probability that small political parties can exercise a veto. This power may prevent effective government action and encourage a resort to dictatorship.

Coercion and *disruption* have become techniques of minority groups seeking policy change. Coercion may be *forceful* or *nonviolent*.

Nonviolent coercion includes *civil disobedience* and several techniques variously known as *nonresistance*, *passive resistance*, or *nonviolent resistance*. *Disruption* is often used by very small groups to seek concessions from the majority. They are dangerous weapons which may gain victories but which often undermine democratic processes and may provoke a repressive reaction. *Terrorism* permits a small group to coerce the majority through fear of violence and is a way of destabilizing governments.

Judicial and bureaucratic activism tend to expand (or, rarely, to contract) the impact of laws and constitutional provisions beyond the intent of their makers.

An emergent American consensus carries basic agreement upon the welfare state, profit-making business, and the work ethic as basic American values.

GLOSSARY

capitalism   system based on private profit-seeking and private ownership of productive wealth.

civil disobedience   open and public defiance of a law together with willing acceptance of legal punishment.

class-dialectic model   system of social power in which dominant class groups usually prevail but can be weakened by disunity or challenged by organized competing class interests.

communism   system based on theories of Karl Marx, with state ownership of productive wealth and (supposedly) equality of all citizens.

fascist society   a one-party society ruled by a dictator stressing nationalism. Hitler's Germany, Mussolini's Italy, and Franco's Spain are examples.

feudalism   system intermediate between tribal and national societies, based upon mutual obligations between nobles and people in each locality.

judicial activism   tendency for judges to expand or enlarge upon existing laws and constitutional provisions by judicial interpretation.

mixed economy   one which combines capitalism with government enterprise and control and welfare services.

pluralist   one who believes that there is no one center of power and that decision making is the result of conflict and compromise between many different groups and individuals.

power elite   highly placed executives who are assumed to

control organizations and, thereby, the government.

proportional representation   a method of allocating legislative seats equal to the proportion of votes cast by different parties.

socialism   system in which the means of production are socially owned and controlled either by direct worker ownership or through the state.

terrorism   the use of violence or the threat of violence to coerce governments, authorities, or populations.

QUESTIONS AND PROJECTS

1   Why, over many centuries, has the relative importance

of political-economic institutions grown while the relative importance of the family declined?

2 Why do developing countries tend to adopt dictatorial rule?

3 In American political debate, the term "spenders" is often applied to those who wish generous government funding for health, education, or welfare programs but is not applied to those who wish generous government funding for defense or for producer subsidies (farm price supports, dairy market subsidies, industry "bail outs"). Explain this in terms of the functionalist perspective. The conflict perspective.

4 Have you engaged in the underground economy? How extensive do you feel it is in your community?

5 How would Friedman's economic theories be viewed by a political conservative? By a conflict theorist?

6 Must power be organized? Are there any ways for unorganized masses to express real power?

7 Despite strong official recommendation, only about 10 percent of Americans wear seat belts. What point made in this chapter does this fact illustrate?

8 Under what conditions can a relatively small number of voters have great political power?

9 Does proportional representation tend to magnify differences or to compromise them?

10 Why is terrorism more common in democratic societies than in authoritarian or totalitarian societies?

11 Do you think terrorism is ever justified? If so, when?

12 Do you believe that an activist's choice between nonviolent coercion, disruption, or terrorism is determined by the strategic realities of the situation or by the personality of the activist?

13 In G. William Domhoff, *The Higher Circles: The Governing Class in America*, Random House, Inc., New York, 1970, read pp. 281–308, in which he discusses charges that America is ruled by a left-wing group of intellectuals. Does he dispose satisfactorily of these charges? Is it more credible to charge that America is ruled by a group of managers who manipulate social policy in favor of the wealthy?

14 Read and compare the articles in the Suggested Readings by Gilder and Quinney. Which do you find the more convincing? Why?

15 On the American frontier, barn raisings were an established institution. When new settlers arrived or when a barn was burned or blown down, the entire community turned out to build a new one, topped off by a party in the evening. Why has this institution disappeared?

16 Read Joseph W. Bishop, Jr., "Lawyers at the Bar," *Commentary*, 58:48–53, August 1974. Is judicial activism an extension or a restriction of democratic political processes? Make out a case for either view.

SUGGESTED READINGS

Barnett, David L: "Communism the Great Economic Failure," *U.S. News & World Report*, 92:33–37, March 1, 1982. A brief and readable article concerning the economic difficulties of communism.

Bruyn, Severyn T. and Paula M. Rayman (eds.): *Nonviolent Action and Social Change*, Irvington Publishers, Inc., New York, 1979. Theory and practice of nonviolent action in various countries.

Collins, Randall: *Conflict Sociology*, Academic Press, Inc., New York, 1975, chap. 7; or Randall Collins and Thomas E. Ryther: *Sociology: Its Discipline and Direction*, McGraw-Hill Book Company, New York, 1975, chaps. 10–11. Conflict analyses of economic and political institutions, severely critical of capitalism and capitalist democracy.

Drucker, Peter: "Pension Fund Socialism," *The Public Interest*, 42:3–15, Winter 1976. Claims that the distinction between labor and capital is blurred by union pension funds' holdings of corporate stock.

Getschow, George: "The Day Laborer's Toil Is Hard, Pay Is Minimal, Security Nonexistant," *The Wall Street Journal*, June 22, 1983, p. 1ff. A startling exposé of the exploitation of American workers by employment agencies providing temporary manual labor—workers at the bottom of the "dual economy."

Gilder, George: "Moral Sources of Capitalism," *Society*, 18:24–27, September/October 1981. A statement by one of capitalism's most eloquent defenders.

Heilbroner, Robert L.: "Does Capitalism Have a Future?" *The New York Times Magazine*, Aug. 15, 1982, pp. 22ff. A major economist sees our economy in a serious crisis which calls for more and different government intervention not for less.

Kristol, Irving: "Ideology and Supply Side Economics,"

Commentary, 71:48–54, April 1981. A short exposition of the political implications of supply-side economics.

Phillips, Kevin: "Controlling Media Output," *Society*, 15:10–16, November/December 1977. A discussion of media personnel as constituting a "new class," with recommendations for regulation.

Quinney, Richard: "Religion and the Spirit of Capitalism," *Society*, 18:55–58, September/October 1981. A conflict sociologist rejects Gilder's "moral basis" for capitalism.

Schellenberg, James A.: *The Science of Conflict*, Oxford University Press, New York,

1082. A short, lucid analysis of conflict both as a general social process and in the form of specific hostilities. Chapters on the role of Adam Smith and Karl Marx as conflict theorists are pertinent here.

*Trounstine, Philip J. and Terry Christensen: *Movers and Shakers: The Study of Community Power*, St. Martin's Press, Inc., New York, 1982. The domination of regionally based corporate elites in Sun Belt cities is challenged by "grass-roots" politics.

*An asterisk before the citation indicates that the title is available in a paperback edition.

PART FOUR

Social Stratification

In the simplest societies, there is no social stratification. All persons (of the same age and sex) do about the same kinds of work. Some persons may be more highly respected or influential than others, but there is no group or category of persons who hold positions of greater prestige and privilege than others.

When cultures become more complex, status differences appear. As work becomes divided into specialized occupations, those doing some kinds of work become more highly respected and rewarded than others. As a society begins to produce more than the bare necessities of life, some people find ways of claiming a larger share for themselves and their children. Persons with greater prestige and more goods than others tend to band together, forming social classes. When used as a noun, stratification is the system of status differences which has developed in a society. When used as a verb, stratification is the process of developing and changing this system of status differences.

Chapter 14, "Social Class," describes the class system of modern American society and shows its effects upon the lives of people. Chapter 15, "Social Mobility," shows how people and groups change their class positions in American society. Chapter 16, "Race and Ethnic Relations," examines race and ethnic group as factors in the stratification process.

14 Social Class

343

How Americans Rank Each Other—And Themselves

People Who Have Really Made It. The man on the street subdivides this elite into four groups: the old rich (the Rockefellers), the celebrity rich (Paul Newman or Chris Evert), the anonymous rich (a millionaire land developer), and the run-of-the-mill rich (a well-heeled physician).

People Who Are Doing Very Well. If a family is to do very well, the breadwinner usually has to be a professional man— a dentist, lawyer or corporate executive. These people have very large homes with at least two cars parked in the heated garage. They fly off to Europe occasionally (sometimes at company expense) and belong to semiexclusive country clubs. When the time comes, their kids go off to private colleges or good state universities.

People Who Have Achieved the Middle-Class Dream. Although these families can count among their possessions a lot more than the necessities, they don't have a lot of luxuries. Being suburbanites, the wife has to have her own car—usually a station wagon. They live in a three-bedroom house with a family-TV room. Each summer, they pack up and head for the mountains or the beach.

People Who Have a Comfortable Life. These folks pay their bills on time and even manage to salt something away for a rainy day. They own a six-room, single-family house in a not-too-fashionable suburb.

People Who Are Just Getting Along. Often the husband is a factory worker, the wife a waitress or store clerk. They either rent a small house or large apartment. These people own a six-year-old car, two black-and-white TV sets and a clothes washer.

People Who Are Having a Real Hard Time. These men and women are proud that they are working and not on the public dole. They are likely to live in a walkup in an old apartment building. The husband could be a custodian, the wife a cleaning lady.

People Who Are Poor. Most of these families are on welfare. They call the ghetto or barrio of the inner city their home. Cockroaches come out at night in the tiny kitchens of their one-bedroom apartments and Murphy-bed rooms. They ride buses to their menial jobs, when they can find work.

(Based on interviews with 900 residents of Kansas City and Boston, reported in *Human Behavior*, 6:29, November 1977. Copyright © *Human Behavior Magazine*. Reprinted by permission.)

Aristotle observed two millennia ago that populations tended to be divided into three groups: the very rich, the very poor, and those in between. For Karl Marx the principal social classes were the wage workers (the proletariat) and the capitalists (the bourgeoisie), with a middle group (the petty bourgeoisie) which was destined to be "proletarianized." Adam Smith divided society into those who live on the rent of land, the wages of labor, and the profits of trade. Thorstein Veblen divided society into the workers, who struggle for subsistence, and a leisure class so wealthy that its main concern is "conspicuous consumption" to show how rich they are. Franklin D. Roosevelt in 1937 gave a vivid description of lower-class life when he said in his inaugural address, January 20, 1937, "I see one third of the nation ill-housed, ill-clad, and ill-nourished." All these descriptions of social class imply that money separates people into different groupings. Yet, as will be shown, social class involves more than money.

WHAT IS SOCIAL CLASS?

A *social class* may be defined as a *stratum of people of similar position in the social status continuum*. The social position of the janitor is not the same as that of the college president; a student will not greet them in exactly the same manner. Most of us are deferential toward those whose social position we believe

Differences in status, power, and income are found in all but the simplest societies. (*Peter Buckley/Photo Researchers, Inc.*)

to be above ours and are condescending to those whom we consider socially below us. These processes of snubbing and kowtowing, of trying to claw one's way in or of shouldering out the person who doesn't "belong"—provide inexhaustible material for hundreds of novels, plays, movies, and television scripts.

The members of a social class view one another as social equals, while holding themselves to be socially superior to some and socially inferior to others. In placing people in the proper social class, one asks such questions as: "To whose dinner party will

they be asked as social equals?" or "For whose daughter will their son be an 'acceptable' escort?" The members of a particular social class often have about the same amount of money, but what is much more important is that they have much the same attitudes, values, and way of life.

How many classes are there? This question is hard to answer. Classes are not sharply defined status groupings like the different ranks in an army. Social status varies along a continuum, a gradual slope from top to bottom, rather than a series of steps. As "youth," "middle age," and "old age" are points along an age continuum, social classes may be viewed as points along a status continuum. Consequently, the number of social classes is not fixed, nor do any definite boundaries and sharp status intervals separate them. Instead, persons are found at all status levels from top to bottom, just as persons are found at all weights and heights, with no abrupt gaps in the series.

Such a series can be broken up into any convenient number of "classes." Earlier students of social class broke up the status continuum into three classes—upper, middle, and lower. Later students found this division unsatisfactory for many communities, because it placed persons in the same class even when they were much too far apart to treat one another as equals. Many sociologists have used a sixfold classification by breaking each of these three classes into an upper and a lower section. The top, or *upper-upper* class, is composed of the wealthy old families, who have long been socially prominent and who have had money long enough for people to have forgotten when and how they got it. The *lower-uppers* may have as much money, but they have not had it as long, and their family has not long been socially prominent. The *upper-middle* class includes most of the successful business and professional persons, generally of "good" family background and comfortable income. The *lower-middle* class takes in the clerks, other white-collar workers and semiprofessionals, and possibly some of the supervisors and top craftspeople. The *upper-lower* class consists mainly of the steadily employed workers and is often described as the "working people" by those who feel uncomfortable about applying the term "lower class" to responsible workers. The *lower-lower* class includes the irregularly employed, the unemployable, migrant laborers, and those living more or less permanently on welfare.

This sixfold classification, used by Warner and Associates [1941, 1942] in studying an old New England town, is probably fairly typical of the large and medium-sized cities in the more settled parts of the country. In the rapidly growing Western regions, "old family" may be less important. Coleman and Neugarten (1971) use a seven-layer system much like Warner's but divide the middle classes into three levels: upper-middle (professional and managerial), comfortable middle-Americans, and marginal middle-Americans. In smaller towns, the class system is less complex. In studying a small city in the Midwest, Hollingshead [1949] used a fivefold classification in which the two upper classes were combined into one. In a small rural community, West [1945] found no agreement among the residents upon the number of classes, although the status range probably would correspond to the bottom half of the six-class system of an urban society. Lynch [1959], studying the class system of an impoverished agricultural community in the Philippines, found only two classes—the self-sustaining and the destitute.

The number of social classes, therefore, varies from place to place, it may also vary with the observer's appraisal of the number of social strata whose members have the same general status. When we speak of, for example, the middle class, we do not refer to a group of people who are clearly set off from others by a definite status interval; we refer to a group of people who cluster around a midpoint in a status scale and who view and treat one another as social equals. The fact that the terms have no distinct boundaries does not keep the terms from being useful concepts and research tools. Social class is a significant social reality not just a theoretical construct, for people *do* classify others as equals, superiors, and inferiors. Whenever people define certain other people as social equals and treat them differently from those who are not so defined, their behavior creates social classes.

Determinants of Social Class

What places one in a particular social class? Is it birth, money, education, occupation, or

The instant wealth of the lottery winner does not bring immediate upper-class status. (*United Press International*)

what? The answer to each question is yes, for all these attributes are involved.

WEALTH AND INCOME.   Money is necessary for upper-class position; yet one's class position is not directly proportional to one's income.

To understand the place of money in class determination, we must remember that a *social class is basically a way of life.* It takes a good deal of money to live as upper-class people live. Yet no amount of money will gain *immediate* upper-class status. The "new rich" have the money, but they lack the way of life of the upper-class person. They can buy the house, cars, and clothes and hire a decorator to select the proper furnishings, books, and paintings. It takes a little longer to learn the formal manners of the upper class, but some careful observation, plus intensive study of the advice of Emily Post or Amy Vanderbilt, will probably suffice. But to acquire the attitudes and feelings and habitual responses of the upper-class person takes far longer. Unless one is born and socialized in an upper-class subculture, one is almost certain to make occasional slips which betray plebeian origin. Novels and plays abound with social climbers who never quite "make it" because they occasionally use the wrong word or reflect the wrong attitude and thereby betray their humble origin. Most of the "new rich" are no more than marginal members of the upper class during their lifetimes.

Their children, however, have a better chance, and for their grandchildren, a secure upper-class status is practically assured. Money, *over a period of time*, usually gains upper-class status. People who get money begin to live like upper-class people. By the time their children mature, they are becoming "old family," and the grandchildren will have fully absorbed upper-class behavior. Thus the two requisites of upper-class status are fulfilled.

Money has other subtle overtones. Income from investments is more prestigious than income from welfare payments. Income from the professions is better than wages; money from speculating on stocks is better than

TABLE 14-1
OCCUPATIONAL PRESTIGE IN THE UNITED STATES

Occupation title	Prestige score	Occupation title	Prestige score
Member of the U.S. Senate	88.4	Locomotive engineer	47.7
State governor	84.9	Insurance agent	46.8
U.S. Supreme Court justice	84.5	Restaurant owner	46.4
Physician	81.5	Construction foreman	46.1
Ambassador to a foreign country	80.7	Skilled craftsman in a factory	45.8
College professor	78.3	IBM keypunch operator	44.9
Lawyer	75.7	Fireman	43.8
Dentist	73.5	Farm owner and operator	43.7
Colonel in the army	70.8	Automobile dealer	43.5
Airline pilot	70.1	Stenographer	43.3
Clergyman	69.0	Carpenter	42.5
Chemist	68.8	Enlisted man in the army	40.3
Sociologist	65.0	TV repairman	35.0
General manager of a manufacturing plant	63.9	Trailer truck driver	32.1
High school teacher	63.1	Semiskilled worker	31.4
Public grade school teacher	60.1	Automobile worker	30.8
Chiropractor	60.0	Used car salesman	30.6
Veterinarian	59.7	Someone who lives off social security pension	30.5
Journalist	58.8		
Computer technician	57.0	Factory worker	29.4
Official of an international labor union	55.4	Cook in a restaurant	26.0
Someone who lives off stocks and bonds	55.2	Singer in a nightclub	25.9
TV announcer	54.2	Coal miner	25.2
Trained machinist	52.4	Someone on public assistance	25.1
Computer programmer	51.3	Tenant farmer	21.5
Social worker	50.3	Waitress in a restaurant	19.6
Electrician	49.2	Migrant worker	13.7
Policeman	47.8	Garbage collector	12.6

Source: Donald J. Treiman, *Occupational Prestige in Comparative Perspective,* Academic Press, Inc., New York, 1977, pp. 318–329. Although not all the occupational titles were identical, a Gallup poll inquiry in October 1981 came out with very similar ratings [*Gallup Reports,* October 1981, p. 193].

Why would the used-car salesman rank below the automobile worker who builds the car? Why would four occupations rank below the person on public assistance?

money from gambling on horses. The nature and source of one's income carry suggestions as to one's family background and probable way of life.

Money one used to have is almost as good as money one has now. The "real" aristocracy of the South, for example, no longer has great wealth, partly because its class values prevented it from engaging in the grubby scrabbling which eventually created the oil millionaires and the industrial magnates. Yet the impoverished aristocrats can still retain upper-class status as long as they have enough money to eke out an upper class pattern of living, even though it is somewhat frayed around the edges.

Money, then, is an important determinant of social class, partly because of what it suggests about one's family background and way of life.

OCCUPATION. Occupation is another determinant of class status. As soon as people developed specialized kinds of work, they also got the idea that some kinds of work were more honorable than others. In a primitive society, the spear maker, the canoe builder, and the medicine man each hold a definite social status because of occupation. Classical China honored the scholar and despised the warrior; Nazi Germany reversed the formula. Table 14-1 gives a prestige ranking of some occupations in the United States, according to one national-opinion survey.

Just why one occupation *should* carry greater prestige than another is a question which has long fascinated social theorists. The high-prestige occupations generally receive the higher incomes; yet there are many exceptions. A popular entertainer may earn as much in a week as a Supreme Court justice earns in a year. The modestly paid clergy, diplomats, and college professors rank far above the higher-paid television stars and professional athletes in prestige and have about equal ranking with the far wealthier physicians and lawyers. The high-ranking occupations generally require advanced education, but again the correlation is far from perfect. The importance of the work is an unsatisfactory test, for how can we say that the work of the farmer or police officer is less valuable to society than the lawyer or sociologist? In fact, it has been suggested that the low-ranking garbage collector may be the most essential of all workers in an urban civilization!

Obviously, the prestige ranking of occupations cannot be easily explained on a purely rational basis; yet it can hardly be an accident that most modern societies have developed much the same hierarchy of occupational status. Surveys of data from many countries [Hodge et al., 1966; Marsh, 1971; Treiman, 1977] find that a particular occupation has about the same status rating in most urbanized, industrialized societies.[1] Apparently the industrial system usually fosters certain atti-

tudes, perceptions, and status relationships wherever it develops. In all societies, industrial or preindustrial, we see that people tend to be assigned class status according to their occupation and that people can most easily enter those occupations which are appropriate to their present class status.

Occupation is an important aspect of social class, because so many other facets of life are connected with occupations. If we know a person's occupation, we can make some guesses about the person's amount and kind of education, standard of living, associates, the hours he or she keeps, and the daily routines of his or her family life. We can even make some guesses about this person's reading tastes and recreational interests, standard of moral conduct, and religious affiliations. In other words, each occupation is part of a way of life that differs considerably from that of other occupational levels.

It is one's total way of life that ultimately determines to which class one belongs. Occupation is one of the best clues to one's way of life and, therefore, to one's social-class membership [Haug, 1972, p. 431].

The underdeveloped countries have a class structure which reflects a society that has limited use for professional, white-collar, or highly skilled workers and hence has a small middle class and a very large lower class. This pattern is changing as these countries become industrialized.

EDUCATION. Social class and education interact in at least two ways. First, a higher education requires money plus motivation. Second, the amount and kind of education affects the class rank secured. It not only brings occupational skills, it also brings changes in taste, interests, goals, etiquette, speech— in one's total way of life. In some ways, education may be even more important than occupation. De Fronzo [1973] found that blue-collar workers differed widely from white-collar workers in personal and social attitudes but that these differences largely disappeared when education was comparable.

[1] Communist societies provide some interesting exceptions, rating white-collar workers and professionals much lower than do capitalist societies (Penn, 1975).

TESTS OF CLASS RANK. Although a wealthy family background is a necessity for secure upper-class status, education may substitute for family background at the intermediate class levels. The middle classes are so large and move around so much that it is impossible to know the family background of each individual. Newcomers to a locality are likely to be accepted into whichever of the middle or lower classes their behavior fits them. Education, occupation, and expended income are three fairly visible clues, and most of the other behavior characteristics which make one "belong" are associated with these indicators.

Social scientists make great use of these three indicators—education, occupation, and income—in dividing people into social-class levels for research purposes. As we have already explained, these are useful clues to the total way of life of different social classes. Furthermore, these are easy to objectify. It would be difficult to use "crude or cultivated speech," for example as a test of class rank in a research study. While speech patterns do reveal one's social class [Labov, 1972], it would be difficult to develop an objective measure of speech usage and diction for a research study. Finally, data on education, occupation, and income are available from the census reports, broken down by "census tracts," or areas of a few blocks each. Suppose a sociologist wishes to compare death rates, or polio rates, or average family size, or practically anything as it varies among social classes. Using census data on occupation, education, and average income of the different census tracts within the community, it is easy to locate an upper-class tract, a middle-class tract, and a lower-class tract for comparison. While social class involves more than these three criteria, they are adequate to identify social classes for most research purposes.

Self-identification and Class Consciousness

Most sociologists consider social class a reality even if people are not fully aware of it.

American democratic beliefs emphasize equality and tend to inhibit a frank recognition of class lines.

Is one's class membership, then, determined by the feeling that one belongs in a particular class or by the facts of occupation, education, and income? Largely by the latter, for they determine one's overall way of life. Yet the *feeling* of class identification is of some importance, for one tends to copy the behavior norms of the class with which one identifies. Eulau [1956] found that those informants who placed themselves in a class in which they did not objectively belong shared the political attitudes of the class they claimed rather than those of the class in which they belonged. Self-identification with a social class has some effect upon behavior, whether one actually is a member of that class or not.

When asked their class identity, few Americans select either "lower class" or "upper class." They usually divide themselves between "working class" and "middle class" [Kriesburg, 1979, p. 307; Goertzel, 1979, p. 66].

Family Patterns

Many societies have at least two types of families—those with mates of each sex and children and those with only one parent and children. Each type of family in American society is found at all social levels and, by itself, does not indicate a class category. However, in recent years, the one-parent family—usually a female parent—is found much more frequently in the lower class. This is both a cause and a result of lower-class status. It is a *result* in the sense that illegitimacy, divorce, and desertion are more common in lower-class than in middle- or upper-class circles. It is a *cause* in the sense that it is very difficult for a single female parent to care for her children and, at the same time, achieve a middle-class occupation and income. Women have made many gains in recent years, but increased illegitimacy, desertion, and divorce have trapped many women and their children in a cycle of poverty

351

Social Class

> ### PEOPLE WHO ARE POOR
>
> Nearly half of the poor families are headed by women. This feminization of poverty . . . shows no sign of slowing as out-of-wedlock birth and divorce rates continue to soar. If the trend continues, warns the President's National Advisory Council on Economic Opportunity, "the poverty population would be composed solely of women and their children before the year 2000."
>
> "Life Below the Poverty Line," *Newsweek*, 98:21, April 5, 1982.
>
> Are family institutions and economic institutions interrelated?

which is hard to escape. The one-parent family is the only family poverty category which increased between 1959 and 1980 [*Statistical Abstract*, 1981, Table 748, p. 497].

Status Symbols

One of the rewards of higher social status is to be recognized as a superior. Since the rich and wellborn look like other people, they need some means of ensuring that their position is recognized. In the past, this has been found through the *status symbol,* which can be any desirable trait or object whose supply is sharply limited [Blumberg, 1974, p. 481], such as a Cadillac, mink coat, private swimming pool, and diamond. Such items were valued as much for their status shouting as for their utility or beauty.

The traditional status symbols appear to have lost some of their appeal in recent years. Incomes have risen, making these symbols available to a larger sector of the population. Most American families own automobiles, and over a third own two or more. By sacrificing other items or by using a secondhand car, it is fairly easy to get even the most expensive model. Genuine jewelry and furs may be beyond the reach of many people,

but imitations which can be detected only by experts make them available to most people.

Concern for ecology has also made some status symbols less acceptable. Does a big car indicate success or simply a callous indifference to gasoline shortage and air pollution? Sometimes the trend for fashion to filter down from the rich is reversed and the rich seem to be copying the poor. For instance, during the 1970s the work clothing of the lower classes was copied by the affluent young (and some of their elders).

Even intangible symbols are no longer as effective as formerly. Golf is played by the assembly-line worker as well as by the professional. Television brings a wide variety of cultural fare into all American homes. A great majority of youths have been graduated from high school, and so many have been graduated from college that degrees have less and less status value. The homogenizing effects of American social mobility are weakening both material and nonmaterial status symbols.

Status symbols still survive, however, as can be seen in the practice of having a conspicuous designer label or some embroidered symbol (at this writing, an alligator). Blue jeans are not lower-class garments if labeled Jordache or Calvin Klein. Shoes are more than utilitarian if made by Gucci or Bill Blass. Status symbols are still present, but the particular things which are status symbols may change over time.

SIZE OF EACH SOCIAL CLASS

Earlier studies agreed that, in a six-class ranking scale, the two lower classes included slightly over half the U.S. population [Warner and Lunt, 1941; Centers, 1949]. Later studies seemed to indicate that the lower classes were decreasing in size and the middle and upper classes were increasing. The most recent income estimates seem to indicate a reversal of that trend, but the two lower classes still represent less than half the population.

TABLE 14-2
ESTIMATES OF SOCIAL CLASS AND FAMILY INCOME*

	UNITED STATES		PHILIPPINES	
Class	Percentage of population	Income boundaries per year	Percentage of population	Income boundaries per year
Rich (upper-upper)	2.1	Over $75,000	.5	Over $20,000
Affluent (lower-upper)	10.2	$45,000–$74,999	6.0	$7,000–$20,000
Prosperous (upper-middle)	21.0	$30,000–$44,999	15.0	$4,000–$7,000
Average (lower-middle)	23.7	$20,000–$29,999	20.0	$2,500–$4,000
Below par (upper-lower)	27.0	$9,287–$19,999	15.0	$1,000–$2,500
Poor (lower-lower)	16.0	Under $9,287†	43.5	Under $1,000

*Money income only.
†Should not be equated with poverty level, since the $9,287 was for a family of four and many of these families are smaller and, therefore, would have a lower poverty figure. Also, noncash income would cut the number of families under the poverty line.
Source: U.S. data based on U.S. Bureau of the Census, *Money Income and Poverty Status of Families and Persons in the United States, 1981,* ser. P-60, no. 134, 1982, table B. Philippine data from Edita A. Tan and Virginia V. Holazo, "Measuring Poverty Incidence in a Segmented Market: The Philippine Case," *The Philippine Economic Journal,* 18:450–492, no. 4, 1979. All these are rough estimates which should be used with caution because inflation rapidly makes these figures out of date.
    Classifications adapted from Sylvia Porter, "Rich, Poor and Between," *Your Money's Worth,* Publishers House Syndicate, Feb. 1, 1974, and from Socorro C. Espiritu et al., *Sociology in the New Philippine Setting,* Alemar Phoenix, Manila, 1976.

Judging from these data, in which country do you think inequality is the greater?

A majority of the population has now finished high school, as contrasted to only about a third in 1947; the proportion in semiskilled and unskilled jobs has dropped, and proportionately fewer are living in poverty. The middle-class jobs are expanding as changes in economic life demand more technical and professional personnel. And, as technology changes the content of jobs, their status also changes. Most factory jobs used to have dirty working conditions and were filled by people who were comparatively unskilled and low-paid. Today more and more factory jobs are clean, and workers are paid better wages.

Measurement of classes is complicated because there are several criteria of membership in a given class and many families do not show *all* the characteristics of any one class level. For example, the ideal type lower-

lower-class family would live in an urban slum or rural shack; one or more adult members would drink quite heavily, and the male family head would often be absent; the family would have little education or interest in education; and its low income would come partly from occasional unskilled labor but largely from welfare. Probably comparatively few lower-class families meet all these conditions. While class differences are real, the boundaries and membership of each class cannot be clearly fixed.

Table 14-2 shows a distribution of people and income for the United States. This would be quite similar for most of the industrialized countries. The distribution for the Philippines would be fairly typical of the developing countries. The table shows a small Philippine middle and upper class and a large lower class, with massive differences in income between the lower and upper classes. In the Philippines, as elsewhere, there are arguments about government policy, but it is very hard to achieve greater equality or to elevate the lower class without major strides in economic development [Weede and Tiefenbach, 1981]. All countries are struggling to stimulate economic development, but it is a difficult process, and this contrast between the class structures of developed and underdeveloped countries is likely to persist for sometime to come.

BLUE-COLLAR AND WHITE COLLAR STATUS

The terms "blue collar" and "white collar" came into use when manual workers wore blue shirts while office workers and professionals wore *only* white shirts. Shirt-color fashions have changed, but the terms persist as labels for working class and middle class. Manual and nonmanual incomes now overlap greatly, as shown in Table 14-3. The highest incomes (among those shown) go to craftspeople and the lowest to clerical workers, with salespeople in between. A recent study finds half the clerical workers and even more (58 percent) of the craftspeople classifying themselves as either "working class" or "poor" [Jackman and Jackman, 1982]. Obviously, the boundaries of middle class and lower class are blurred, and the blue-collar/white-collar distinction is no longer a reliable guide.

Some have suggested that white-collar workers are becoming "proletarianized," that is, they are absorbing attitudes supposedly typical of blue-collar workers [Braverman, 1974; Wright et al., 1982]. The recent restudy of "Middletown" reports that the middle class became distinctly more "working class" in attitudes and life-style between 1937 and 1978 [Caplow, Bahr, and Chadwick, 1981]. The growing acceptance of unionization by white-collar workers could also be claimed as evi-

TABLE 14-3

MEDIAN WEEKLY EARNINGS IN BLUE-COLLAR AND WHITE-COLLAR OCCUPATIONS—1980

Blue-collar		White collar	
Craft	$328	Clerical	$215
Operative	$225	Sales	$279

Source: Statistical Abstract of the United States, 1981, p. 407.

Why do so many people keep low-paid white-collar jobs when many blue-collar jobs pay much better?

dence of "proletarianization" of the middle class.

Whether this is happening is disputed [Kelly, 1980]. An opposing view is that the working class has undergone "embourgeoisment" as it has assumed middle-class (bourgeois) attitudes and life-styles [Goldthrope and Lockwood, 1963, p. 133]. More recent studies also claim a growth in middle-class self-identification by blue-collar workers [Cannon, 1980].

Scholars may debate whether the working class is being "embourgeoised" or the middle class is being "proletarianized," but it is clear that their life-styles have grown less distinct. Most sociologists agree with this "convergence theory" that the classes are drawing closer together in life-style [Blumberg, 1980], yet real differences remain. LeMasters, a sociologist using the participant-observer technique, made careful notes of the conversations in a blue-collar bar and feels that blue-collar men reject much of what white-collar workers accept, although this is less true of their wives. Here is a summary description of a typical white male blue-collar worker.

He owns a nice home in a pleasant suburb. His income is squarely in the middle-class bracket. . . . He can't understand or doesn't like much of what he sees on television and so he watches little other than sports events. He loathes or fears blacks, college students, women's liberationists and homosexuals. He doesn't trust businessmen, his own union leaders, politicians or

Jews, and he is convinced that white-collar workers don't earn their money.

He doesn't like marriage, but he is married for reasons he finds difficult to explain. He would much rather be hunting, fishing or drinking with the boys than talking or watching TV with his wife. . . . "I [LeMasters] find myself somewhat surprised at the extent of the suspicion and distrust the blue-collar workers have of the white-collar middle and upper classes." (Dust jacket of E. E. LeMasters: *Blue Collar Aristocrats.* The University of Wisconsin Press, Madison, 1975. Last sentence is a direct quotation found on p. 199. Copyright © 1975 by the Regents of The University of Wisconsin.)

SOCIAL CLASS AS A SUBCULTURE

As the preceding quotation reveals, each social class is a subculture with a system of behavior, a set of values, and a way of life. This subculture serves to adapt people to the life they lead and to prepare children to assume the class status of their parents. While some overlapping and some exceptions occur, it remains true that the average middle-class child has a socialization very different from that of the average lower-class child. Let us take just one aspect of socialization—those experiences which shape ambition, education, and work habits—and see how they differ between two social-class worlds.

Typical upper-middle-class children live in a class subculture where they are surrounded by educated persons who speak the English language correctly most of the time, enjoy classical music, buy and read books, travel, and entertain graciously. They are surrounded by people who are ambitious, who go to work even when they don't feel like it, and who struggle to attain success. They are acquainted with the achievements of ancestors, relatives, and friends, and it is normal for them simply to assume that they too are going to accomplish something in the world.

When they go to school, scrubbed and expectant, they find a teacher whose dress, speech, manner, and conduct norms are much like those they already know. They are met by a series of familiar objects—picture books, chalkboard, alphabet blocks—and introduced into activities with which they are already familiar. The teacher finds them appealing and responsive children, while they find school a comfortable and exciting place. When the teacher says:

"Study hard so you can do well and become a success some day," this makes sense. Their parents echo these words; meanwhile, they see people like themselves—older brothers and sisters, relatives, family acquaintances— who actually are completing educations and moving on into promising careers. For most of them, to grow up means to complete an advanced education and launch a career.

Lower-lower-class children live in a class subculture where scarcely anyone has a steady job for very long. To be laid off and go on welfare is a normal experience, carrying no sense of shame or failure. In their world meals are haphazard and irregular, many people sleep three or four to a bed, and a well-modulated speaking voice would be lost amid the neighborhood clamor.

These children go to school often unwashed and unfed, and meet a person unlike anyone in their social world. The teacher's speech and manner are unfamiliar, and when they act in ways that are acceptable and useful in their social world, they are punished. The classroom materials and activities are unfamiliar. The teacher, who often comes from a sheltered middle-class world, is likely to decide that they are sullen and unresponsive children, while they soon conclude that school is an unhappy prison. They learn little. The school soon abandons any serious effort to teach, brands them as "discipline problems," and concentrates upon keeping them quiet so that the other children can learn. When the teacher says, "Study hard so you can do well and become a success some day," the words make no sense. They receive little reinforcement from parents, who may give lip service to educational goals but seldom persuade the children that school and learning are very important.

More important, the children see almost no one *like themsevles,* no one in their own world, who actually *is* using school as a stepping-stone to a career. In their world, the flashy cars and expensive clothes are possessed by those who picked a lucky number, or got into the rackets, or found an "angle." Thus, the school fails to motivate. For the lower-lower-class children, "growing up" too often means to drop out of school, get a car, and escape from the supervision of teachers and parents. The horizon of ambition seldom extends beyond the next weekend. Work habits are casual and irregular. Soon they marry (or cohabit) and provide for their children a life which duplicates the experiences of their own socialization. Thus, the class system operates to prepare most children for a class status similar to that of their parents.

In child socialization, the upper-lower or working class may resemble the middle class more closely than they resemble the lower-lower class. The upper-lower class usually attempts to provide children with a stable home and expects them to attend school regularly, study, and behave. Sometimes there are middle-class acquaintances or relatives to serve as models. The working-class parents may have little realization of what is involved in successful school achievement, and may not provide the home setting which makes reading or abstract conversation a natural part of growing up. Thus, their children have limited preparation for school and often fail to fulfill their parents' hopes.

Differences in the socialization of lower-class and middle-class children are lessened by two factors: (1) acquaintance across class lines and (2) the pervasive influence of television. The young of all classes spend much of their free time gazing at the television set and thus have a more homogeneous experience than was true of the children of previous generations. Television watching is now so universal a pastime that it does indeed tend to produce a greater similarity between all social groups. Some differences do remain, though, and these are probably the greatest between the very poor (the lower-lowers) and the more fortunate social classes. In fact, the lower-lowers are often considered to be living in a "culture of poverty."

The Culture of Poverty

In the past two decades, it has become fashionable to refer to a culture of poverty [Lewis, 1959, 1966*a* 1966*b*]. What this implies is that the poor form a subculture in which, as a result of their common experiences, they have developed certain attitudes and behavior patterns which have been transmitted from parent to child. These include the matrifocal family, the casual resort to physical aggression, an inability to plan for the future, a seeking of immediate gratification, weak impulse control and a fatalistic attitude toward the future. This culture-of-poverty concept has been supported by many social scientists [Kerbo, 1981] who see it as a realistic description of how the poor find it difficult, if not impossible, to break out of the cycle of generation-to-generation poverty [Galbraith, 1978; Segalman and Basu, 1979]. The concept has also been criticized [Roach and Gursslin, 1967; Glazer and Moynihan, 1971] because it does not apply to such groups as the aged poor and the ill and because it may not apply equally to all ethnic groups. Further, the

Poverty is culturally defined. What is poverty in the United States may be relative comfort in a less affluent society. (*Charles Gatewood*)

behavior patterns may not be so much norms or ideals as simply an adaptation to what appear to be unalterable circumstances [Massey, 1975, p. 604].

Social Class and Social Participation

The lower the social class, the fewer are the associations and social relations of most persons. Lower-class people participate less in organizations of any kind—clubs, civic groups, or even churches—than do middle- and upper-class people [Stone, 1960; Hyman and Wright, 1971; Curtis and Jackson, 1977, p. 215; Wilson, 1978, p. 227]. The reasons for this are unclear. Possibilities include fatigue,

the burden of more children to care for, expense, limited range of interests, less education and verbal facility, and possibly others. We are certain only that their social lives are more restricted.

THE SIGNIFICANCE OF SOCIAL CLASS

Determining Life Chances

From before one is born until one is dead, opportunities and rewards are affected by class position. Poor nutrition for the mother may affect the health and vigor of the fetus before birth, while poverty thereafter continues to handicap the poor. The lower-class person is not only likely to die prematurely but will also endure more days of illness during a lifetime. Census data on "work disability" (defined as work absences due to "serious impairment that may last a relatively long period of time") finds an annual rate of 141 disability periods per 1,000 men in the lowest income group, as compared with 56 for men in the highest income group [*Statistical Bulletin of Metropolitan Life*, 57:8, March 1976].

Happiness and Social Class

In 1974, Cameron and his colleagues asked a large sample of people to report their feelings of happiness or unhappiness. They found that happiness did not vary by the presence or absence of physical handicaps or of mental retardation. Neither was it affected by age, for the old are happy about as often as the young. Of all the factors they studied, social class seemed to have the strongest relationship. In a summary of several such studies, Easterlin [1973] found that the proportion reporting themselves as "very happy" rose steadily from 25 percent in the lowest income group to 50 percent for those with incomes of over $15,000 (comparable to about $35,000 in 1983).

The data show no relation between the wealth of a country and the happiness of its citizens. Easterlin's analysis shows that the population of the United States was no happier in 1970 than in 1940, although real income was 60 percent higher in 1970. International comparisons show that citizens of wealthier industrialized countries are no happier than those of poorer, less developed countries. It is not absolute income but the ratio between income and needs that is important. Within a given society there is some degree of consensus among most people as to their "real needs." The more prosperous people in that society are better able to meet their needs

TABLE 14-4
HAPPINESS AND INCOME
(Question: "Generally speaking, how happy would you say you are—very happy, fairly happy, or not too happy?")

Income	PERCENT RESPONDING:			
	Very happy	Fairly happy	Not too happy	Don't know
$25,000 and over	56	38	5	1
$20,000–$24,999	48	44	8	*
$15,000–$19,999	48	42	9	1
$10,000–$14,999	38	48	12	2
$ 5,000–$ 9,999	40	47	12	1
Under $5,000	35	39	26	*

*Indicates less than 1%.
Source: Gallup Reports, 189:38 39, June 1981.

Does having more money make people any happier? Or do people who are happy earn more money?

and thus more likely to be happy than those who are less prosperous. But in the more prosperous societies, the standard of "need" is higher. Thus, it is relative advantage rather than absolute amount of money which makes for happiness.

Later studies [Campbell, 1980; Fernandez and Kulik, 1981] show similar results, except that the influence of income is slightly less important than in previous years. Material success may be less important than formerly, but within each society the prosperous are happier than the poor.

Not *all* the rich are happy. The children of the rich are more likely to suffer "dysgradia," which is a constellation of ills, including severe anomie and depression. According to Wixen, who made a study entitled *Children of the Rich* [1973], dysgradia arises when middle-class values of work and family life which have been strongly held by the older generation make no sense to their children. Life has been so easy for the rich children, and their sense of security is so great, that they sometimes see no need for hard work either

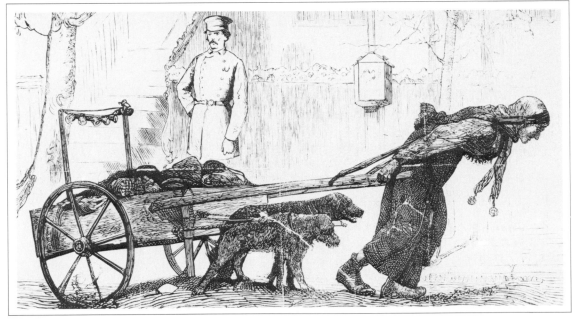

Social class determines life opportunities. (*The Bettmann Archive, Inc.*)

as a means of rising in the world or as a way of making good on their obligations to others. Not being able to participate in the satisfaction of step-by-step advancement, they fall prey to boredom. One psychiatrist claims that the children of the very rich have little contact with parents and have no clear role models and that they often lack self-esteem and develop shallow values and self-preoccupation [Grinker, 1978]. Not all children from wealthy homes suffer from dysgradia, since some gain satisfaction from their own achievement and others have internalized a sense of duty to society known as *noblesse oblige.*

Cultivating Class Ethnocentrism

There is an anecdote of a private tutor in a wealthy family who sought to teach his pupil about the life of the poor. Then the little rich girl wrote a story about the poor, beginning, "Once upon a time there was a very poor family. Everybody was poor. The Papa was poor, the Mama was poor, the children were poor, the cook was poor, the maid was poor, the butler was poor, the gardener was poor—everybody was poor."

Members of one class cannot help judging members of other classes in terms of their own class expectations and values. The middle class scorns upper-class snobbishness but strives desperately to raise its own children in a "good" neighborhood. People at every class level tend to see those above themselves as effete, snobbish, and pretentious and those beneath as either disgusting or pathetic, as either good-for-nothing or "awfully pushy." At all intermediate status levels, people tend to attribute their own status to personal achievement, the status of those above to luck, and that of those beneath them to inability and laziness. A pattern of living for the moment without trying to plan for the future is practical for a life in which one never knows how long a job will last. Similarly, the aggressiveness which keeps a lower-class child in trouble in school may be the only survival adjustment possible in a neighborhood filled with violence. Middle-class people who know little about the stress of lower-class life often wonder, "Why can't they be more like us?" This question betrays ethnocentrism, for it assumes that others *should* be like us. It also shows a failure to realize that one's own standards have grown out of one's own life situation and cannot easily be learned by those in other circumstances.

Defining the Conventional Morality

The social classes differ in etiquette as well as in moral judgments. The term "loyal worker" has one meaning in the union hall, another at the chamber of commerce.

Middle-class mores, however, tend to become the conventional mores. The church, the school, and the welfare and "uplift" agencies are middle-class institutions, staffed and run largely by middle-class persons, and dedicated to the cultivation of middle-class values. The laws are written by middle-class legislators and enforce middle-class values. Thus, the middle-class mores tend to become the official or conventional morality of the society.

This tendency creates certain strains for lower-class persons. They often find that behavior which is normal and acceptable in their class subculture is condemned and punished when they step outside this subculture, as they must do at school and in nearly all their dealings with persons in positions of authority. A good deal of resentment and class antagonism accumulates among people of the lower classes, who feel that they are constantly being prodded, scolded, and "pushed around" by middle- and upper-class people.

Explaining Many Other Group Differences

Many other kinds of group differences—racial, religious, regional—are really class differences. For example, almost any sociological black-white comparison will seem to be very flattering to whites. Blacks have proportionately more crimes, more venereal disease, more illegitimate births, more drunkenness, more desertions, more broken families, and proportionately more people on relief. If however, social-class levels are held constant, these differences between racial groups greatly decrease [Banfield, 1974, pp. 79–87]. For example, the overall black birthrate is higher than the white, but if higher income levels are compared with each other, the black birthrate is less than the white [Reed, 1975; Johnson, 1979]. And race differences in school dropout rates almost disappear if one restricts the comparison to children of white-collar parents [Coleman, 1966, pp. 454–456].

Variations in the class composition of religious groups affect comparisons between them. One would expect Baptists and Catholics to have a higher official rate of juvenile delinquency than Episcopalians and Congregationalists simply because officially recorded juvenile delinquency usually is less frequent in high-class groups. For the same reasons, exclusive residential suburbs of Long Island will have lower death rates than slum districts in New York City. Therefore, whenever data for two groups are compared, the critical observer will always wonder, "Are these groups comparable in class composition?" If not, some very misleading conclusions may be drawn.

Shaping Political Attitudes and Life-Styles

Social class affects the way people deal with virtually every aspect of reality. As space forbids examining them all, let us mention just two areas of life in which class background appears to produce contradictory tendencies: political attitudes, in which the lower classes appear to be more liberal (some would say "radical"), and social attitudes, in which the lower classes appear to be more conservative. (The terms "liberal" and "conservative" are here used to describe differing degrees of receptivity to social change.)

In political attitudes, lower-class voters more often support radical candidates who favor drastic change, especially when this includes governmental help to them. But as conflict theorists point out, American voters do not always recognize their class interest in an election and often support an attractive candidate who will not defend their class interest. In this respect, Americans seem to be less class-bound than the English. In a study of British voting, Lenski and Lenski [1982, p. 312] found a 34 percent spread between lower-class and upper- and middle-class support for a particular party in Britain as compared to 17 percent for the United States. This means that British voters divided on class lines twice as faithfully as American voters. In other words, American voters were only one-half as likely to (1) identify themselves with a particular social class and then (2) support a

FIGURE 14-1 The life-styles of older people by social class. (*Source: Diana K. Harris and William E. Cole,* Sociology of Aging, *Houghton Mifflin Company, Boston, 1980, pp. 186–187.*)

Does this seem to fit the older people you know?

	Vacation	Place for social life	Recreation	Rejuvenation aids	Retirement rite	Retirement residence	Gifts to grandchildren under 18	Gifts to grandchildren over 18
Upper class	Mediterranean cruise	Country club	Golf	Spas in Switzerland and Romania	Guest of honor at banquet	Condominiums or age-segregated apartment buildings	Money	Checking accounts and cars
Middle class	Group bus tours	Senior citizens center	Shuffleboard	Vitamins	Gold watch and group dinner	Retirement communities	Toys	Clothes
Lower class	Visit sister Dora in Detroit	Park bench	Checkers	Patent medicines	Handshake and a beer with the boys	Public housing or living with children	Cookies and pies	Cookies and pies

particular party because they believed that party would promote the interests of their class. Political scientists call this a "lack of class consciousness" among American voters.

While the lower class is often alleged to be "radical" in politics it tends to be conservative in religion, morality, taste in clothes, furniture, food, adoption of new health care practices, educational techniques, and other lifestyle matters [Dickson, 1968].

Leisure-time practices, for example, vary by social class, as shown for retired people in Figure 14-1. This variation is partly a matter of cost and partly a matter of preference. Symphony concerts, opera, and theater would die out if they depended on lower-class patronage. Churches tend to be stratified by social class, and their services reflect the social-class background of their worshippers. Reading material is class-oriented, and some magazines boast of their upper-class readership. There has been some democratization of leisure-time practices. Libraries make books available to both the poor and the rich. Sports such as golf and tennis were once rich men's pastimes and are now shared by many middle-class and quite a few working-class people. Meanwhile, proletarian art forms, such as bluegrass and country music, have spread their appeal across class lines.

In other matters of life-style and social attitude, too, the lower class appears to be more conservative than other classes. The lower class is the last to follow the trend toward democratic family decision making, permissive child training, or the use of birth control [Downs, 1970, p. 27; McNall, 1974, p. 147]. The lower class appears reluctant to accept new ideas and practices and is suspicious of innovators. Limited education, reading habits, and associations isolate lower-class people from a knowledge of the reasons for these changes, and this, together with their distrust of higher-status people, makes them suspicious of the middle- and upper-class "experts" and "do-gooders" who promote the changes. Especially in the case of health

care, using new methods may be inconvenient and even seem vaguely threatening. Such lower-class attitudes clearly constitute one of the barriers to their acceptance of new services [Dutton, 1978, p. 359].

Much of the social conservatism of the lower class is an aspect of authoritarianism. The authoritarian view is a preference for definite rules rather than for undefined, and therefore threatening, situations. It supports the idea that any change is dangerous. It tends to doubt the right of dissenters to express their views and is suspicious of minority racial, nationality, or religious groups. Surveys vary somewhat on specific items, and when education is more nearly comparable, class differences in authoritarian thinking are reduced. However, there is a general agreement upon a lower-class tendency toward authoritarianism [Grabb, 1979, 1980].

Getting the "Dirty Work" Done

A lot of unpleasant work must be done in any society, and someone must be persuaded to do it. Occasionally, special rewards may be used—honor for the warrior, or wealth and fame for the prizefighter, for example. But each complex society relies mainly upon the class system to compel someone to do the drudgery. A combination of cultural background, educational limitation, and job discrimination all work together to make the lower-class person unable to compete for the better jobs; as a result, only the poorer jobs are left. Whether it is intentional or not (and some conflict theorists would argue that it *is* intentional), the result is to get the grubby work of the world done by excluding part of the people from the nicer jobs.

The lower class also functions as a storehouse for surplus unskilled labor. Those who are not continuously needed are "stored" in the lower class, where the class subculture makes it possible to survive periods of unemployment and go on relief without guilt or sense of failure.

Fitting into the Better Spots

Middle and upper social classes also provide distinctive subcultures that prepare class members for specialized functions in society. Middle-class parents seek to impress their children with both the hope of advancement and the fear of dropping to a lower-class status. Thus, of all the social classes, the middle class is the one most noted for strenuous effort to "get ahead." The upper class need not "make a living" or struggle for status but may feel impelled to justify its status and income through some form of public service. The Roosevelts, Rockefellers, Kennedys, and many others are examples. Such patricians often promote social policies which benefit the lower classes. Their political success shows that the masses will accept leaders from the wealthy elite if they appear sensitive to lower-class needs.

The upper classes in most countries include the "jet-set," the idle rich who lead useless lives of dissipation. They may be few, but they are very conspicuous in an era of mass communication, and the envy and resentment they arouse stimulate doubts about the legitimacy of an upper class.

FUNCTIONAL AND CONFLICT THEORIES OF SOCIAL CLASS

Sociologists disagree upon whether social class stratification is useful as an efficient means of role allocation. Functionalists claim that society requires a variety of occupational roles and that the superior rewards for the upper classes are needed to persuade people to accept the responsibility and undergo the training which is required for important positions. Hence, social class is functional in terms of the total society. Davis and Moore have given the classic statement of this viewpoint:

> Social inequality is an unconsciously evolved device by which societies insure that the most important positions are filled by the most qualified persons. Hence every society, no matter how simple or complex, must differentiate persons in terms of both prestige and esteem, and must therefore possess a certain amount of institutionalized inequality. (Kingsley Davis and Wilbert Moore, "Some Principles of Stratification," *American Sociological Review*, 10:242–249, April 1945. Reprinted by permission of the authors and the *American Sociological Review*.)

Davis and Moore contend that (other things being equal) a job will be more highly rewarded according to the degree that it is disagreeable, important, and requires superior talent and training. They recognize that this would not hold true in a noncompetitive society where most occupational roles were ascribed and not achieved. Rewards include prestige and social recognition, but money is the main reward. Thus unequal pay is needed to get all the jobs filled with properly qualified people.

There has been some empirical research which lends partial support to the Davis and Moore theory. Studies find that rewards do vary with talent and training, although evidence on "importance" of the work is mixed [Lopreato and Lewis, 1963; Land, 1970; Grandjean, 1975; Grandjean and Bean, 1975; Cullen and Novick, 1979].

The Davis and Moore theory has been a favorite target of conflict scholars. They claim that inequalities of opportunity and class conditioning prevent lower-class persons from making the best use of their native abilities. Conversely, untalented upper-class persons may be kept from humble but useful work because their attitudes and expectations make such work unacceptable to them. Thus, critics charge that the class system is a dysfunctional system for distributing occupations, wasting the talents of the talented underprivileged and wasting the modest potential of the untalented overprivileged. They suggest that a better system of allocating occupational roles could be devised [Tumin, 1957; Squires, 1977]. Conflict theorists suggest that it is not functional utility but naked power which creates social stratification. Class privileges will change when lower classes challenge and change them.

It may be true, as Chambliss and Ryther claim, that "inequality is an inevitable consequence of capitalism" [1975, p. 385]. It may also be true that inequality is an inevitable consequence of cultural complexity, regardless of the politicoeconomic system. All complex societies develop some system of differential rewards. The early efforts of communist societies to operate on "equality of reward" soon foundered as they found it necessary to pay more to those who produced more [Gonzalez, 1982]. As Mao Zedong stated, "Humanity left to itself does not necessarily reestablish capitalism, but it does re-establish inequality".[2] Successful parents in any society will find ways to help their children in the competition for higher-status positions, and social classes will develop.

Does functional or conflict theory better fit the facts about social classes? This is difficult to say. Both clearly are true in part, but neither fits all the facts.

THE "NEW CLASS"

As mentioned in Chapter 13, social analysts in recent years often debate the existence of a "new class" [Briggs, 1979; Hacker, 1979]. Its members are middle- and upper-level government employees and people engaged in communication—television and radio staff, actors and actresses, journalists, professors, and clergy. They are mostly in the middle-class brackets, although some "stars" rank with the very rich. The new-class category does not quite fit the usual definition of social class but is used to indicate a group with a distinctive viewpoint.

Berger describes the role of the new class in terms of a class struggle:

[2] Quoted in *American Journal of Sociology*, 83:78, July 1977.

Social analysts debate the existence of a "new class" of upper- and middle-level government officials and communications personalities. (© *Jim Anderson, 1980/Woodfin Camp & Assoc.*)

The current class struggle is between the new knowledge class and the old business class. As in all class struggles, this one is over power and privilege . . . a large portion of the new class is economically dependent on public-sector employment or subsidization.

Once this is seen, it comes as no surprise that the new class, if compared with the business class, is more "statist" in political orientation—or, in other words, is more on the "left." Many if not most of the great liberal programs since the New Deal have served to enhance the power and privilege (not to mention the prestige) of the new class; not surprisingly, its members are devoted to these programs. (Peter L. Berger, "The Class Struggle in American Religion," *The Christian Century*, Feb. 25, 1981, pp. 197–198.)

The reason for designating them as a separate "class" [Briggs, 1979] is that their attitudes may differ from the attitudes of others with similar incomes. This communications elite is more liberal in social and political attitudes than the business elite [Rothman and Lichter, 1982]. They do not draw their money directly from business profits, and their training may lead them to take a critical view of the business society. They are seen as competing with business people for power and prestige. Therefore, they welcome "big government," which may provide them with jobs and influence, since even poverty programs use middle-class administrators. Government expansion is often justified by lower-class welfare needs, but expanding government also leads to more jobs and power for the new class. Thus the new class is an affluent group which seems to identify with lower-class political interests.

THE FUTURE OF SOCIAL CLASSES: FROM "PROLETARIAT" TO "STATUS SEEKERS"

Karl Marx, in *Das Kapital* and in the *Communist Manifesto,* stressed the importance of social class more than any other thinker in history. In the Marxist view, conflict between social classes has been continuous since the dawn of history, and the rise and fall of various social classes offer the key to the understanding of history. Prior to the industrial revolution, the top social class was a landed aristocracy which owned great estates by inheritance and noble rank. The industrial revolution forced this class to share top status with rich manufacturers, traders, and financiers.

Marx prophesied that the ultimate struggle would take place between the proletariat (wage workers) and the bourgeoisie (capitalists) and would end in the inevitable triumph of the proletariat, who would establish a classless society under the banner of communism. This interpretation of history gave to Communists a sort of "messianic hope" which enabled them to believe that, in spite of present obstacles, history was on their side and their final triumph was certain. For many years discussion of social class centered on the validity of the Marxist analysis.

The current opinion among social scientists is that Marx was only partly correct and that the class struggle is not proceeding as he predicted. Marx expected that classes would grow further apart as industrialization advanced. Hence the lower class would become more conscious of its distinct interests and more hostile to the upper class (more "class conscious"), while the middle classes would gradually be pushed down into the proletariat.

Marxist scholars would disagree with most of the content of this chapter. They reject the usual definition of social class as a status level based upon life-style, education, occupation, and income. They believe the important distinction is between those who own the means of production and control their own conditions of work and those whose means of production and conditions of work are owned and controlled by others. This would make the working class the largest class in America, since it would include most of those who are commonly viewed as middle class [Wright et al., 1982].

If one follows the definition of social class as given in this chapter, then the Marxist class predictions are not being fulfilled. The classes are coming closer together both in possessions and in attitudes. The middle class is stronger than ever in Western societies, and the workers are gaining a stake in the society which Marx wanted them to overthrow.

Marxist societies seem to follow a common pattern: After the revolution the traditional class privileges are abolished in a determined attempt at equality; then class distinctions gradually reappear. By the 1950s in the Soviet Union, the Communist party officers, factory managers, government officials, professionals, scientists, and artists formed a distinct self-perpetuating social class with special privileges, class-typed attitudes and values, and a distinct style of life [Lipset and Dobson, 1973, pp. 141–145].

Variation in money income may be less in the Soviet Union than in capitalist countries, but variation in governmentally provided privileges is greater [Connor, 1980]. Many refined techniques have developed to enable privileged Soviet citizens to escape from economic equality.

> Roomy apartments, good books, excellent schools, vital medicines, stylish clothes, automobiles, pleasant recreation resorts and even meat and vegetables are available to those who "make it." (David K. Shipley, "Making It Russian Style," *The New York Times Magazine,* Feb. 11, 1979, p. 38.)

In the Soviet Union, "equality mongering" *(uravnilovka)* is described as a form of anti-Soviet thinking far removed from true socialism [Yanowitch, 1977, pp. 23–24]. Official policies change from time to time, and recent increases in the minimum wage have reduced the size of wage differentials. Nevertheless, the existence of substantial differences in pay is a persistent part of Soviet economic life. The highest-paid 10 percent of the working force receives three to four times as much as the lowest-paid 10 percent [Yanowitch, 1977, p. 38]. This comparison refers to workers and does not include the top administrative officials and the elaborate fringe benefits they enjoy.

Many Marxists dismiss the Soviet Union as irrelevant, since it "is not truly Marxist" and point to China as a model of equality. But China appears to be repeating the Russian experience, as China is enlarging the wage differences between managers and workers, restoring exams in the colleges, and returning partway to what Marxists call "elitism" [*Business Week,* May 19, 1978, pp. 40–41; Butterfield, 1978; Gonzalez, 1982].

Far from achieving a classless society, the Communists have developed a new class system. Judged by its creed, communist society is the enemy of class privilege; judged by its results, it is class privilege's newest bastion.

SUMMARY

Social classes arise from the consequences of a division of labor. A *social class* is made up of people of similar social status who regard one another as social equals. Each class is a subculture, with a set of attitudes, beliefs, values, and behavior norms which differ from those of other classes. Social class is based on total social and economic position in the community, including wealth and income, occupation, education, self-identification, hereditary prestige, group participation, and recognition by others. Class lines are not clearly drawn but represent points along a continuum of social status. The exact size and membership of a given class is difficult to establish. Class subcultures prepare children to retain the status of their parents.

Social class is an important social reality. Social class largely determines one's life opportunities and colors personality development. Personal happiness does not depend upon the wealth of the society but is associated with being among the more affluent members of one's society. Functionalists believe that social class assigns privileges and responsibilities to individuals and thereby helps to get necessary work accomplished. Conflict theorists deny that class privileges are "functional" and see them as exploitative.

Class subcultures breed a class ethnocentrism, which prevents classes from fully understanding one another. It is mainly the standards of the middle class that are written into law and sanctioned by conventional morality. Many differences ordinarily assigned to race, religion, ethnic group, or to some other kind of group difference are actually class differences; confusion arises from the fact that racial, religious, and other groups may be unevenly distributed along the class continuum.

Social class molds the life-adjustment patterns of individuals; the lower class tends to be liberal in political action connected with economic benefits and conservative in accepting other social changes, while the opposite tends to be true of the upper class. An alleged "new class" consists of government servants and those working in some aspect of communication. This communications elite has upper-class income but is more liberal in social and political attitudes than the business elite.

Current scientific interest in class has shifted from the Marxist theory of class warfare to the struggle for individual social mobility and a lessening of the amount of inequality between classes. Social class lines have not been eliminated in socialist societies. Communist societies are not classlesss but, rather, have developed a very different kind of class system.

GLOSSARY

bourgeoisie   a French word for the middle class.

continuum   a range of variation by very small intervals (e.g., student grade-point averages) rather than by distinct categories (e.g., freshman, sophomore).

convergence theory   the theory that the classes in America are drawing closer together in life-style.

embourgeoisment theory   the theory that the working class is becoming more like the middle class.

proletarianization theory   the theory that the middle class is becoming more like the working class.

proletariat   a working class conscious of its underprivileged and landless status.

social class   a stratum of persons of similar position in the social-status continuum who regard one another as social equals.

stratification   as a noun, the system of status levels in a society; as a verb, the process of developing and changing this system of status differences.

QUESTIONS AND PROJECTS

1   Table 14-1 shows garbage collectors at the bottom of the prestige scale, but some garbage collectors earn more than assistant professors. How do you explain this discrepancy between income and status?

2   How can social classes really be subcultures when children of all class levels attend school together?

3   Read the material by Randall Collins listed in the Suggested Readings. Do you find among your friends a difference in conversational style and content which varies by social-class level? If so, give examples.

4   Is the United States primarily a middle-class country? Defend your answer.

5   Does money lead to happiness? Who is happier; the average member of a wealthy society or the affluent member of a poor society? Why?

6   Is there a relation between the problems of health and education and the attitude engendered by lower-class life? Explain.

7   How does class affect political attitudes? When a college student switches from a parent's political party, is it because of increased knowledge, youthful rebellion, or social mobility? Outline each possibility.

8   Make a chart of officers in your senior high school class (or some other organization you know well). From which social-class level does each come? Are the officers proportionately representative of the social classes present in the organization? Do members from different social classes view the group in the same way? Wherein, and why, do they differ?

9   Read the article by Peter L. Berger listed in the Suggested Readings. Do you find in his description of the "new class" the main reason many intellectuals support the expansion of government welfare programs?

10 Has the elimination of private capital led to equality of income in the Soviet Union? If not, how would you explain continuing inequality in a socialist state?

11 What is meant by the "messianic hope" of Marxism? Have recent developments supported the Marxist theory of social class?

12 Do you feel that social-class stratification is harmful or beneficial to society as a whole? Why?

13 Read and analyze the treatment of social class in one of the following novels: *Kitty Foyle*, by Christopher Morley; *Marjorie Morningstar*, by Herman Wouk; *Studs Lonigan*, by James T. Farrell; *The Forge*, by Thomas S. Stribling; *Mansfield Park*, by Jane Austen; *The Age of Innocence*, by Edith S. Wharton; *Fraternity*, by John Galsworthy; *Tobacco Road*, by Erskine Caldwell; *Hunky*, by Thomas R. Williamson; *Babbitt*, by Sinclair Lewis; *So Little Time* or *B.F.'s Daughter*, by John P. Marquand.

SUGGESTED READINGS

Berger, Peter L.: "The Class Struggle in American Religion," *The Christian Century*, 98:194–199, Feb. 25, 1981. Attributes the liberal/conservative debate to rivalry between the "new class" and the older business class.

Chalfant, H. Paul, Robert E. Beckley, and C. Eddie Palmer: *Religion in Contemporary Society*, Alfred Publishing Company, Sherman Oaks, Cal., 1981, chap. 12, pp. 371–412. A readable treatment of the relation between social class and religious affiliation and practice.

Collins, Randall: *Conflict Sociology*, Academic Press, Inc., New York, 1975, pp. 114–152. Analysis of class factors in conversation, both as indicators of class position and as products of class subcultures.

*Dobson, Richard B.: "Socialism and Social Stratification," in Jerry G. Pankhurst and Michael Paul Sachs (eds.), *Contemporary Soviet Society: Sociological Perspectives*, Praeger Publishers, New York, 1980, pp. 88–114. A readable comparison of stratification in Soviet and Western countries.

Eshleman, J. Ross: *The Family: An Introduction*, Allyn and Bacon, Inc., Boston, 1981, chap. 10, pp. 221–244. Describes how lower-, middle- and upper-class families cope with life situations.

Grabb, Edward C.: "Social Class, Authoritarianism and Racial Contact: Recent Trends," *Sociology and Social Research*, 64:208–220, January 1980. A look at social-class factors which lead to authoritarian views in race relations.

Hollander, Paul: *Political Pilgrims*, Oxford University Press, New York, 1981. Claims that intellectuals visiting communist countries tend to ignore major problems in these countries while exaggerating problems of Western countries.

Kerbo, Harold R.: "Characteristics of the Poor: A Continuing Focus in Social Research," *Sociology and Social Research*, 65:323–331, April 1981. An analysis of the tendency of social research to investigate the personal traits of the poor rather than the social factors which produce poverty.

*LeMasters, E. E.: *Blue Collar Aristocrats*, The University of Wisconsin Press, Madison, 1975. A participant-observer report on blue-collar culture as seen at a working-class tavern.

*An asterisk before the citation indicates that the title is available in a paperback edition.

15 Social Mobility

Downward Mobility

Mr. Weaver worked steadily for 20 years in Oklahoma as a truck driver and mechanic. In February of last year, he was laid off from his $16,000-a-year job. In April, his unemployment benefits ran out. He lost his house when he couldn't make the mortgage payments. For four months, he and his pregnant wife lived in their car. Just before their baby was born, they moved into a camper that lacked electricity and plumbing.

For some, like Mr. Weaver, the loss of jobless benefits can mean the difference between scraping by and losing everything. For many others, it can accelerate a painful decline in lifestyle. Thomas Harrington lost his $30,000-a-year white-collar job with a U.S. Steel mining operation in Minnesota in 1981. His unemployment benefits expired last April. His wife's salary, his temporary near-minimum-wage job and a drastically slashed budget have enabled them to keep their home, but the 37-year-old Mr. Harrington wonders if his former middle-class life is gone forever.

(Robert S. Greenberger. Reprinted by permission of *The Wall Street Journal*, March 7, 1983, p. 1. © Dow Jones & Company, 1983. All rights reserved.)

Upward Mobility

A young black woman in Boston, herself enrolled in a training program and enthusiastic about her future prospects, said, "We have more educational opportunities and many nice job programs that our parents did not have. If you improve yourself, there are better positions for you." A black man in his late 30s in Kansas City who had become a successful businessman after a childhood "close to poverty" said almost exultantly: "I can't speak for the white people, whether it's going to be harder for them to change class or not, but we have greater opportunities today than when my parents were growing up. . . . The racial barriers are down or coming down."

(Richard P. Coleman and Lee Rainwater, with Kent A. McClelland; *Social Standing in America, New Dimensions of Class*, Basic Books, Inc., Publishers, New York, 1978, p. 249)

The wish for a higher status and income than one's parents had is the American dream. The process whereby people achieve—or fail to achieve—this is called social mobility.

NATURE OF SOCIAL MOBILITY

Social mobility may be defined as the act of moving from one social class to another. An *open class* society is one in which mobility is high; a *closed class* society is one in which there is little mobility.

The *caste* system in which people are confined to the occupations and statuses of their ancestors is the most extreme example of a closed class society [Berreman, 1981]. India is often cited as the world's most caste-ridden country. Its government now is opening higher-status occupations to low-caste groups which, for centuries, have been limited to low-status work. It is trying to move India toward an open class society [Gandhi, 1980].

In the modern world, many countries are seeking to increase social mobility in the belief that this makes people happier and enables them to do the kind of work for which they are best suited. If social mobility is high, even though individuals have unequal social origins, all may believe that they are equal in having a chance of reaching a higher social-class position. If social mobility is low, then it is clear that most people are frozen into the status of their ancestors.

The Horatio Alger novels of an earlier generation helped to sustain the belief that America is a land of boundless opportunity where all positions are open to the ambitious. This belief is often derided by skeptics, but there is much in the American experience to support it. As Edmund Muskie, one-time candidate for the vice-presidency and the son of a Polish immigrant named Marciszewski, said of his father:

He had landed here with only five years of

formal education, the ability to work as a tailor and not much else. One year before he died, his son became the first of Polish ancestry to be elected governor of any state. Now this may not justify the American system to you, but I am sure it did for him. (Edmund Muskie, *Journeys*, Doubleday & Company, Inc., Garden City, N.Y., 1972, pp. 46–47.)

If desirable social statuses are actually available to all who make an effort to reach them, there will probably be little agitation for absolute social equality. If, however, the channels of social mobility are so clogged that a great many are doomed to failure, then a demand for complete equality for all is more likely. The balance of this chapter will be devoted to an analysis of how social mobility occurs, its frequency, and the factors which may accelerate or retard movement from one social stratum to another.

Individual and Group Mobility

Mobility applies to both groups and individuals. For instance, the success of the Kennedy family is an example of individual social mobility, while the Irish and Polish Catholics' march from the slums to the suburbs illustrates group mobility [Greeley, 1976].

The two kinds of mobility very often go together. A disadvantaged group may produce an occasional celebrity, but the higher the status of the group, the greater the number of high achievers.

Direction of Social Mobility

When we speak of social mobility, we usually think of an ascent from lower to higher, but social mobility runs in both directions. Some climb, some fall, and some stay at the same level as their parents held. Among a sample

---

IMMIGRANTS IN HORATIO ALGER ROLE

For many who come to its shores, America is true to its reputation as a land where hard work, luck and determination can be the key to a better life.

One such is James Kong, 39, a Korean who arrived in Chicago with his wife in 1976. Each worked two jobs at first, scrimping and saving until they could buy the small tailor shop where Mrs. Kong was a seamstress.

Kong now owns five dry-cleaning stores and a wholesale plant—enterprises that could do a million dollars' worth of business this year. How did it happen? "We have to work harder and longer hours or we wouldn't make the opportunities," says Kong.

Success on a grander scale came to Joe Nakash, an Israeli who came to New York in 1962 at the age of 19 with barely $25 in his pocket. He spent his first nights in the U.S. sleeping in subway stations. In the daytime, he looked for menial work—all he expected to find.

Nakash ended up creating Jordache Enterprises, maker of designer jeans and status-label clothing. His salary: About 1 million dollars per year. "In Israel, it was a big thing for me to think maybe I could be a driver for a rich man," says Nakash, 38. "But when I came to America, I saw it was possible for me to be a rich man."

When lawyer Luis Gomez-Dominguez, 59, came from Cuba in 1979, his first job was cutting grass in Miami parks. Today he is a city marketing manager and a prominent member of Miami's large Cuban-exile community. "My family and friends helped me," he reports. "But the real thing was that I began to work hard immediately."

U.S. News & World Report, April 12, 1982, p. 50.

About a century ago, Horatio Alger wrote a series of extremely popular novels, each telling how a poor orphan boy became prosperous through hard work and clean living. Why do you suppose his books are no longer popular?

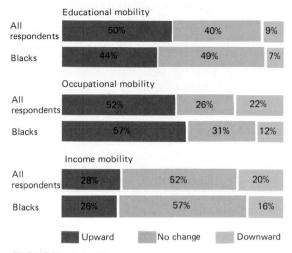

Educational mobility

| All respondents | 50% | 40% | 9% |

| Blacks | 44% | 49% | 7% |

Occupational mobility

| All respondents | 52% | 26% | 22% |

| Blacks | 57% | 31% | 12% |

Income mobility

| All respondents | 28% | 52% | 20% |

| Blacks | 26% | 57% | 16% |

■ Upward   ▨ No change   ▨ Downward

FIGURE 15-1 Upward and downward mobility in the United States. Percentage of national sample of respondents who had moved up from, made no change in, or moved down from their parents' status. (*Source: National Opinion Research Center,* General Social Surveys, 1980. *Adapted from presentation in* Public Opinion, *5:30–31, June/July 1982.*)

Are there any reasons for believing that these rates of mobility will be, or will not be, maintained for the next generation?

of Bostonians and Kansas Citians interviewed in 1971 and 1972, 60 percent felt they were in a higher socioeconomic status than their parents, 31 percent said they were the same (but thought their life easier), and only 9 percent thought they had dropped in status [Coleman and Rainwater, 1978, p. 226].

Figure 15-1 shows that there is a good deal of mobility in both directions. The extent of downward individual mobility is one of the tests of an open class society. If practically all people remain firmly fixed in the social-class rank of their parents, then we have a closed class society in which ascription (in this case, parental position) accounts for more than achievement. However, if many people drop, while many others rise, then we can assume that inherited advantages and handicaps are not great enough to keep achievement from

being a major determinant of social-class position.

COSTS AND GAINS OF MOBILITY

The idea that social mobility is good is part of our democratic ethos. We argue that a closed class society thwarts the fulfillment of individual personality and deprives society of the contributions of talented people.

While social mobility permits a society to fill its occupational niches with the most able people and offers the individual a chance to attain his or her life goal, it also involves certain costs. A mobile society arouses expectations which are not always fulfilled, thereby creating dissatisfaction and unhappiness; a traditional society in which one is born into one's appointed place arouses few hopes and few frustrations (as long as this traditional social structure remains intact). The benefits of social mobility are inseparable from its costs, since those who break the bonds which hold them back also cut the protective web which keeps them from sinking still lower. An open class society may be desirable from the viewpoint of both society and the individual, but it still has some penalties.

These penalties include the fear of falling

Occasionally a worker declines an offered promotion.

MOBILITY TENSIONS

Over a third of the students at the University of Leicester, and about half of those reading Sociology, had come from working-class homes and I became friendly with a number of them. These working-class boys had to contend with several problems not faced by the middle-class boys. They complained that middle-class girls did not consider them seriously as potential mates and they almost invariably failed to get along with the mothers of middle-class girls on the rare occasions when they met. They were ambivalent about becoming members of the middle class: they wanted the money and the status, but felt that to obtain them would be to become disloyal to their non-mobile kin and friends. They sensed that their parents, especially their fathers, were not wholeheartedly in favor of their prolonged education. It seemed to me that their fears were well grounded.

Earl Hopper, *Social Mobility, A Study of Social Control and Insatiability*, Basil Blackwell, Oxford, England, 1981, p. 2.

This is a British example. Would it also be true in other countries?

---

in status, as in downward mobility; the strain of new role learnings in occupational promotions, the disruption of primary-group relationships as one moves upward and onward. One who is passed over for promotion may envy the security of a less mobile society. Parents and children may become strangers due to changes in social attitudes. Social mobility often demands geographic mobility, with a painful loss of treasured social ties [Lane, 1977; Harris, 1981]. An offered promotion may be declined because of a fear of the burden of new responsibilities. Even marriages may be threatened when spouses are not equally interested in mobility. One mate resents the implied insult of being prodded, polished, and improved; the other resents the mate's lack of cooperation in social climbing. Some studies have even found that a high rate of mental illness may accompany either upward or downward mobility [Ellis, 1952; Hollingshead et al., 1953; Turner and Wagenfeld, 1967]. In any case, the "middle-class convert" will experience a shift of attitudes and associations which will probably be even more drastic than that involved in the process of religious conversion or of changed citizenship.

Yet there is considerable evidence that those who occupy top occupational positions are healthier and happier than others. Tropman [1971] finds that probabilities of holding high occupational rank are highest for men in continuing successful marriages; are intermediate for widowers or divorced men who are remarried; and are lowest for the unmarried, the divorced, and the separated. A Metropolitan Insurance Company study found that the death rate among top business executives was only 64 percent of that for the rest of the white population of similar ages [*Statistical Bulletin*, Feb. 1, 1974]. But these studies are open to two criticisms. They do not study *mobility*, because they do not separate those who moved up into their high rank from those who merely retained the rank into which they were born. Nor do these studies take account of the selective factor, in that those who are healthy and happily married are most likely to be promoted. Almost *any* employed group will show health levels above national averages, since persons in poor physical or emotional health tend to become unemployed and since unemployment can lead to physical or emotional health problems.

A number of studies have also reported that downward mobility is associated with many unpleasant accompaniments, such as poor health, marital discord, and feelings of alienation and social distance; but, once again, cause and effect are not identified. Such unpleasant developments could be either a cause or an effect of downward mobility. For both the individual and the society, the costs and benefits of mobility and the open class society are open to debate.

MOBILITY DETERMINANTS

The rate of mobility in modern societies is determined by (1) structural factors—those factors which determine the relative proportion of high-status positions to be filled and the ease of getting them—and (2) individual factors—those factors, including luck, which determine which people get the positions.

Structural Factors

OCCUPATIONAL STRUCTURE.   Societies differ in the relative proportion of high- and low-status positions to be filled. A society with a

primarily agricultural and extractive economy (mining and forestry) will have many low-status and few high-status positions, and mobility will be low. The rate of mobility rises with the degree of industrialization in both the capitalist and socialist countries [Simkus, 1981, pp. 225–227]. Americans principally employed in agriculture dropped from nearly 5.4 million in 1950 to 1.3 million in 1978 [*Statistical Abstract*, 1959, p. 209; 1981, p. 662], even while population was growing by about 50 percent. Most people in the developing countries are still in an agricultural and extractive economy leaving limited opportunity for upward mobility.

DIFFERENTIAL FERTILITY   Although birthrate differences have narrowed in recent years (see Chapter 17), there is still a good deal of truth in the saying, "the rich get richer, and the poor get babies." The combination of an

FIGURE 15-2   The upper- and middle-class fertility deficit and mobility. The 15 percent figure gives *net* upward mobility (upward mobiles minus downward mobiles). Since many from the upper and middle classes are downwardly mobile, the *total mobility* into the upper and middle classes is far above the 15 percent figure, and probably in excess of 20 percent. (*Source: Based on data from Richard P. Coleman and Lee Rainwater, with Kent A. McClelland,* Social Standing in America, *Basic Books, Inc., Publishers, New York, 1982, pp. 232–233.*)

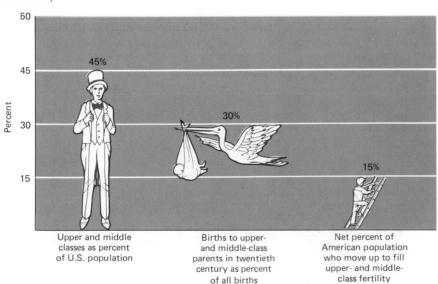

Upper and middle classes as percent of U.S. population	Births to upper- and middle-class parents in twentieth century as percent of all births	Net percent of American population who move up to fill upper- and middle-class fertility deficit

expansion of higher-status jobs and a relatively low birthrate in the upper classes means that the upper classes do not replace themselves and are constantly replenished by mobiles from the lower classes. Figure 15-2 (with its explanatory note) shows how well over 15 percent of the population moves from lower into middle and upper classes each generation.

THE DUAL ECONOMY. Many developing countries have two largely separate economies. One is the traditional economy of poor peasants consuming most of what they produce and selling little on the market. The other is a modern, cash economy in which most people produce for the market. Mobility in the modern sector may be rapid even while the traditional sector is stagnant or declining.

Some scholars believe that the United States and other industrialized societies also have a dual economy. The favored sector consists of government civil service and the highly capitalized, semimonopolistic industries with a unionized labor force. This sector pays high incomes and gives more fringe benefits. The less-favored sector consists of highly competitive, labor-intensive industries and businesses, frequently nonunion, with low wages and fewer fringe benefits. Thus, auto workers and steelworkers make high wages, not because of superior skill, ability, or training but because they are in high-wage industries. Whether this will continue to be true depends upon future changes in technology, world trade, and other factors. There also are many low-wage industries and businesses, such as textile and furniture factories, restaurant and hotel employees, and many others. One's chances for upward mobility depend to some extent upon one's success in getting into one of the favored sectors of the economy [Sorensen and Tuma, 1981; Jacobs, 1982]. Just why automobile assembly workers should be paid twice as much as textile or furniture factory workers is difficult to explain on any rational basis other than bargaining power. Conflict theory fits this case better than functionalist theory.

TABLE 15-1

AVERAGE EARNINGS OF AUTOMOBILE WORKERS AS A PERCENTAGE OF AVERAGE EARNINGS OF SELECTED WHITE-COLLAR EMPLOYEES, 1967 AND 1978

Occupation	1967	1978
Bank employee (nonsupervisory)	157%	213%
Federal civil servant (clerical)	137	178
Secretary	132	158*
Librarian	104	144*
Registered nurse	123	127*
Schoolteacher	102	121
Buyer	93	115
College professor (average all ranks)	68	88†
Personnel director	40	46
Engineer	34	44
Chemist	31	40

*1977
†1976
Source: Adapted from Paul Blumberg, *Inequality in an Age of Decline*, Oxford University Press, New York, 1980, p. 81.

In 1967, automobile workers' average income was 157% of nonsupervisory bank employees' income and 31% of chemists' income. Functionalist theory attributes income differentials largely to such factors as job importance, responsibility, skill and training required, and unpleasantness of the work. Conflict theory attributes income differences largely to bargaining power. In this case, which theory does this table support?

MOBILITY AIDS AND BARRIERS. Even in a relatively open class society, upward mobility is not open equally to everyone. As pointed out before, middle-class children typically have learning experiences which are more helpful in gaining upward mobility than the experiences of lower-class children. Conflict scholars maintain that credentials, tests, recommendations, the "old-boy network,"[1] and overt discrimination against racial and ethnic minorities and lower-class persons seriously limit upward mobility while protecting the

[1] This is the network of personal friends within a profession or business, who exchange information and recommendations on job openings, making it difficult for "outsiders" to break in.

Chances for upward mobility are affected by the sector of the economy in which one works. What factors limit these children's prospects for upward mobility? (*Marcia Keegan/Peter Arnold, Inc.*)

children of the upper classes from downward mobility. The argument over whether public schools and community colleges are an aid or barrier to upward mobility has been discussed in Chapter 12. To whatever degree opportunities are unequal, mobility chances are also unequal.

There are also structural aids to mobility. Antidiscrimination legislation is an important one, and publicly financed job training programs led to marked increases in employment and modest gains in income for many low-level workers [Hougland, Christenson, and Walls, 1982]. While the impact of various aids and barriers to mobility is difficult to measure, they are undoubtedly important factors.

Individual Factors

While structural factors may determine the proportion of high-status, well-paid positions

in a society, individual factors greatly affect which persons get them.

ABILITY DIFFERENCES. Other things being equal, the talented usually earn more than the untalented. There is still much we do not know about ability—just what it is, how to measure it, and how much of mobility can be attributed to ability differences. Yet, it is clear that not all people are equally talented. While it is impossible to measure individual ability differences satisfactorily, we assume that they are important factors in life success and mobility.

MOBILITY-ORIENTED BEHAVIOR. There is much which persons can do to increase their prospects for upward mobility.

Education Education is an important mobility ladder. Even a well-paid working-class job

A few people with limited education greatly prosper.

is hard to find unless one can read directions and do simple arithmetic. About one in five Americans is "functionally illiterate," and most of these people spend their lives on the bottom rung of the mobility ladder [Drinan, 1983]. In much of business and industry, there is not one mobility ladder but two. One stops with the job of foreman; the other begins with a job in the "executive development program" and ends with the presidency. To get on this second mobility ladder without a college degree is rare.

Education is not equally important for all careers. College and professional degrees are essential for careers as physicians, lawyers, or teachers; they are helpful but not essential in business ownership and operation; they are not at all important for careers as professional athletes or popular entertainers (many professional athletes attend college, but completing a degree has little or no effect upon their professional careers).

We are often reminded that school dropouts usually fare poorly in the job market, but much of this can be attributed to factors other than lack of formal education (such as class background, family disruption, limited ability, delinquency history and other disabilities) [Hansen, 1970; Bachman, 1972]. Some school dropouts have been highly successful. In fact, at least 3 of the 400 richest persons in the United States are reported to be dropouts [Seneker et al., 1982]. This raises the question

of whether the association between education and earnings (see Table 15-2) is causative or selective. In other words, do the educated earn more because they are educated, or is it because those who already have more advantages (greater ability, good family background, emotional stability, good work habits) are more likely to become educated? It is likely that both possibilities are true but in unknown proportions. It is possible that for many careers, the greatest value of education lies not in the particular knowledge and skills it provides but in cultivating one's ability to locate and use information as it is needed [Kohn, 1981, p. 277]. We may conclude that for a great many people, education is a prime mobility ladder but that it is possibly less necessary for all kinds of careers than has generally been assumed.

Work Habits These are sometimes overlooked as a mobility factor. One recent study concludes that work habits learned in early childhood are the most important of all predictors of eventual success and well-being [Vaillant and Vaillant, 1981]. Hard work car-

TABLE 15-2
INCOME AND EDUCATION, 1981

Education	Median income
Less than 8 years	$ 7,125
8 years	9,270
Some high school	11,936
High school graduate	16,989
Some college	19,504
College graduate	23,640
5 or more years college	27,339

Source: U.S. Bureau of the Census, *Money Income and Poverty: Status of Families and Persons in the United States, 1981*, ser. P-60, no. 134, March 1982, table 7. Students should remember that inflation rapidly makes any figures out of date and it is the relationship rather than the absolute amounts which is important.

How could we decide how much of these income differences to attribute to education and how much to other differences between the persons who do and who do not become educated?

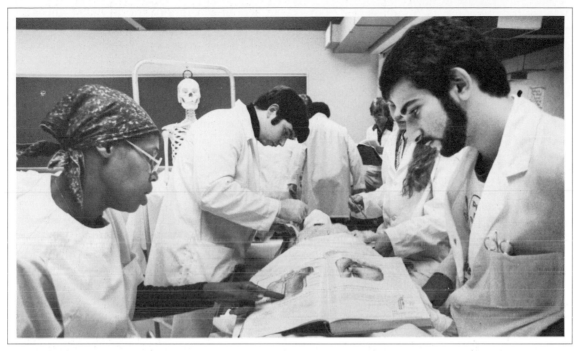

Hospital interns: a modern example of the ancient apprenticeship system. What kinds of mobility are suggested in this picture? (*Mimi Forsyth/Monkmeyer Press Photo Service*)

ries no guarantee of upward mobility, but not many achieve upward mobility without it.

The Deferred-Gratification Pattern   This consists of postponing immediate satisfaction in order to gain some later goal. Saving one's money to go to college or to start a business is an example. The students who are now studying this textbook instead of playing poker or "goofing off" are practicing the deferred-gratification pattern (DGP).

The middle class may have the most to gain through the DGP. The upper class has little need to defer gratification, for it needs only to retain positions already held. There is evidence that lower-class persons more often have a short-term perspective and less often follow the DGP [Miller, Riessman, and Seagull, 1969]. This is not surprising, for persons whose grasp upon jobs and income are short-

term are likely to have short-term plans and values. As Allison Davis noted almost a half century ago:

Ambition and the drive to attain the higher skills are a kind of luxury. They require a minimum *physical security;* only when one knows where his next week's or next month's food and shelter will come from, can he and his children afford to go in for the long-term education and training, the endless search for opportunities and the tedious apple-polishing that the attainment of higher skills and occupational status requires. (Allison Davis, quoted in William Foote Whyte (ed.), *Industry and Society,* McGraw-Hill Book Company, New York, 1946, p. 89.)

Yet judging from the upward mobility shown in Figure 15-1, there seem to be many lower-class persons who *do* defer gratification and plan for the future.

Some scholars reject the DGP as a clever

defense for inequality. Chambliss, for example, ridicules the idea that college students are deferring gratification by attending comfortable colleges instead of doing grubby work in mines, factories, and car washes [1973, pp. 10–11]. He misses the point. The deferment of gratification lies not in attending college (which can be very leisurely) but in the *long, hard study hours* of the ambitious student. Not everyone who attends college is practicing the DGP.

Mobility "Game Playing"   This has received little study, but it seems likely that a good deal of "game playing" and artful "presentation of self" (see p. 108) may be involved in upward mobility. Graduating seniors are coached on how to conduct themselves before the corporate recruiter. To be well-liked may be as important as to be competent. While not easy to measure, the ability to work smoothly with people and to impress people favorably is probably an important factor in "success." Some popular books, such as Korda's *Power* [1975], imply that success is *primarily* a matter of "front" and "one-upmanship." This is a superficial view, which underestimates the ability of corporation executives and supervisors to spot a phony. A skillful "presentation of self" will seldom take the place of competence, but it may gain one a chance to demonstrate competence and thus be a factor in mobility.

The Value-Stretch Hypothesis   This hypothesis offers one explanation for those who accept mobility values but still fail. The value-stretch hypothesis, developed by Rodman [1963, 1974], states that many people sincerely accept certain goals and values but unknowingly follow behavior which blocks attainment of their goals. The hypothesis has two tenets: (1) that these persons are not strongly enough committed to their professed goals and (2) that they fail to recognize that certain behavior is inconsistent with these goals. For example, some parents want their children to do well

in school but ignore the teachers' messages and do not insist that children do their homework. Some workers would like a better job but cannot get to work on time, or drop out of the training course which would prepare them for one.

The value-stretch pattern permits one to believe in all the approved values without having to make the effort to attain them or to accept personal blame for failing to do so [Haney et al., 1973]. We note that these persons are *not* being devious or hypocritical; they simply fail to recognize that their behavior is not consistent with their goals. Nor do we suggest that the value-stretch pattern is unique to the lower classes. It appears in all classes and includes students who think that a fast read-through is "studying" as well as ambitious parents who do not demand good work habits from their children.

THE LUCK FACTOR.   Many people who really work very hard and follow all the rules fail to succeed, while success sometimes seems to fall into others' laps. One could hardly plan or arrange for one's immediate superior to drop dead at just the moment when one is ideally qualified to move into the vacated position, but many promotions hinge on just such accidents. Anyone who tries to prove that life is always fair has assumed a difficult task. As stated earlier, some sectors of the economy are much better paid than others. A large part of "luck" probably consists of working in a favorable sector of the economy [Jencks, 1979, p. 307]. Some sectors of the economy will be expanding over the next several decades, offering job security and promotions; others will be declining, offering more layoffs than promotions. The young worker who finds a position in an expanding industry has excellent chances for lifetime job security with pleasant retirement on a good pension. Those who pick a declining industry may be on the scrap heap in later middle age, with no job, no pension, and little chance of getting either. For young people entering the job market, mobility prospects were poor in the 1930s and excellent in the 1950s and 1960s; they do not look so good in the 1980s but probably will be better in the 1990s (because of lower birthrates in the 1970s). Having the foresight to be born at the right time is helpful. The luck factor is impossible to measure and is a handy excuse for failure, yet it is undeniably a factor in mobility.

Interaction of All Factors

All of the above factors interact in ways impossible to measure. As an example, how should we interpret the findings of Jencks's study of the earnings of brothers? He found that brothers raised in the same family who made similar test scores and who had the same amount of schooling and work experience made greatly different earnings, with one brother often making twice as much as the other. This variation in earnings between these carefully matched brothers was at least 80 percent of the variation among a random sample of unrelated persons [Jencks, 1979, p. 293]. It is likely that all the above mobility determinants are involved, and luck may not be the least of them.

This discussion of mobility determinants has centered upon upward mobility. How about downward mobility? The same determinants also produce downward mobility. The structural factors—such as declining industries, a stagnating economy with declining productivity, a declining rate of economic growth and technological change—tend to increase the total number of persons who must lose class status. The individual factors—education, work habits, luck, and the others—determine which persons suffer class-status decline.

MOBILITY PROSPECTS

The increase in the proportion of higher-status jobs is the most important single factor

in the amount of upward mobility [Stolzenberg and D'Amico, 1977, p. 862]. Automation, robots, and computers are decreasing the demand for unskilled and semiskilled workers and calling for more technicians who can operate computers and complicated equipment. The multiplication of the service industries—sales and service, recreation and resort, and many others—creates openings for persons with talent and ambition, including some without college degrees. Some highly paid jobs, such as skilled crafts and locomotive engineering, have diminished, but on balance, the need for persons in high-status positions has grown. The net effect is a high rate of mobility in the United States which appears to have increased in recent years [Hauser and Featherman, 1977]. The United States may be closer to an open class society than ever, and a relatively open class society seems true of most modern industrial societies.

Mobility of Women

Women have traditionally achieved mobility mainly through marriage [Chase, 1975]. Married women might work at "suitable" occupations (subordinate to but not *too* far beneath their husbands' occupational status). But very few women gained social status through occupation. Today, however, women are claiming equal occupational opportunity, and occupation may provide women with a mobility ladder apart from marriage. Women are showing dramatic increases in the professions. Women students in law schools, for example, increased more than fivefold from 1970 to 1980 [Fossum, 1981]. A woman sociologist who has been critical of a male-dominated society has stated: "Women are clearly making the greatest progress of all American caste groups" [Duberman, 1976, p. 303].

Career and mobility patterns for men and women are growing more nearly alike, yet differences remain. The great majority of working wives still judge their class position

The number of women in law schools increased more than fivefold between 1970 and 1980. How soon will the proportion of women as judges reflect this change? (*Mimi Forsyth/Monkmeyer Press Photo Service*)

by their husbands' occupations [Jackman and Jackman, 1982], but a growing member of working wives are using *both* their own and their husbands' occupations in judging their class [Van Velsor and Beeghley, 1979]. The career mobility of married women is still greatly handicapped by household duties and childbearing with its career interruptions, as outlined in Chapters 6 and 10. True equality in career mobility will demand fundamental changes in both our familial and our politicoeconomic institutions.

SOCIETAL MOBILITY

This chapter has focused upon the mobility of individuals, but entire groups within a society may rise or fall in relative status and entire societies may become more or less prosperous. There are many groups and societies we could consider, but we will limit our discussion to the mobility of the poor and the mobility of developing countries.

Mobility of Developing Countries

The developing countries (or the Third World—a term used to distinguish these countries from both the capitalist and the communist countries) are showing both upward and downward societal mobility. Most of the nations in Africa, Asia, and South America (Japan is an outstanding exception) are classified as "developing." This means that their industrial technology and economic organizations have not yet reached the level of industrialized countries such as Japan and those in North America and Western Europe. Their per-capita income may be less than one-tenth that in the industrialized countries (see Table 15-3). This difference is not quite as great as it sounds, since many people in these countries provide their own shelter, clothing, and food and it is hard to give a cash value to these items. Record keeping is also far from perfect, and some income may not be reported.

After making due allowance for these statistical problems, the difference is still impressive. In two-thirds of the world, many people live in conditions of dire poverty. Hunger is common, and even a bicycle is an unattainable luxury. Our world has both a

TABLE 15-3
AVERAGE PER-CAPITA INCOME IN INDUSTRIALIZED AND DEVELOPING COUNTRIES, 1978

Industrialized countries		Developing countries	
United Kingdom	$4,955	Kenya	$337
Japan	8,460	Thailand	444
United States	8,612	Honduras	528

Source: World Almanac, 1982.

moderately prosperous area and an area in which malnutrition is routine and actual starvation is a constant threat. This breeds discontent within each developing country, where the prosperous are envied by the poor; and poor countries envy the prosperous countries, whom they blame for their poverty. The demand of poor countries for more of the world's wealth is the dominant theme of United Nations debate.

Governments are aware of this problem and, in the midst of much dispute as to proper methods, many programs have been launched to increase trade, improve the commercial base, and promote more efficient agriculture and industry. These programs have had modest success, and developing countries have made some gains, but most of the developing world still lives on the edge of poverty.

Even with outside help and the best possible type of economic system, can the developing countries ever reach the standard of living of the industrialized nations? One difficulty is that much of the economic improvement has been absorbed by population growth (see Chapter 17). Birthrates are falling now but must fall rapidly if prosperity is ever to be attained.

An even more difficult problem is that of the supply of necessary resources. Professor Keyfitz expressed this in vivid fashion:

> The rate and direction of development of the period 1950–1970, unsatisfactory though it may be . . . is still faster than can be sustained on present strategies. . . . One can imagine sources of energy, the capacity to dispose of wastes and substitutions for metals all doubling in the century to come, but it is not easy to conceive of such a doubling in the 15 years that would [be needed to] keep the middle class growing at 4.7 percent per year. (Nathan Keyfitz, "World Resources and the World Middle Class," *Scientific American*, 235:35, July 1976.)

There is some hope that as present raw materials grow scarce, science can provide new substitutes. Unless it does, there is no possibility that the industrialized nations can maintain their economic growth for very long. Without spectacular scientific breakthroughs that may never happen, there is no hope for the poor countries to catch up with the rich countries.

What About Poverty?

Poverty—a situation in which people lack enough money to maintain a minimum standard of health and decency—used to be the normal condition of most people. Today, there is widespread feeling that, at least in the industrialized countries, there is enough to take care of all and that no one should be desperately poor. Nevertheless, even in the world's most prosperous countries, poverty still survives.

Before we can discuss a topic profitably, it is necessary to define terms so we understand what we are talking about. The Department of Labor estimates the minimum needs of an urban family of four. This figure was set at $3,000 per year in 1960 and, because of inflation, was raised to $9,287 by 1982. This figure can be debated as either too generous or too restrictive, but at least it gives an objective base for measuring change.

Who are the poor? Many of them live at the margin of society, and many have mental, social, or physical handicaps. Many of them are children, and a disproportionate number are women. We have minimum-wage laws, but steady work at the minimum wage will not support a family. Government and private charity aid the mentally and physically handicapped but not generously. People who have other handicaps—alcoholics, for instance—are difficult to help even when society has the best of intentions. Probably the most frequent social handicap today is the broken family, usually headed by a mother with little or no support from the father. It is difficult for a woman to care for children and be the sole source of financial support, and the majority of one-parent, female-headed families live at or below the poverty line.

Extreme poverty makes upward mobility very difficult. (*Max Tharpe/Monkmeyer
Press Photo Service; Don Gestug/Photo Researchers, Inc.*)

Probably the acid test of the degree of upward social mobility is the proportion of the population who have moved above the poverty line (see Figure 15-3). Such mobility above the poverty line takes place both by overcoming individual handicaps and by making special provision for those with low incomes.

OVERCOMING HANDICAPS. Rehabilitation programs such as medical care, counseling, and vocational training may help overcome handicaps. People may be restored to health, be enabled to overcome emotional despair, or be trained for remunerative work. Many people who are poor can profit from such rehabilitative services, and many are kept

from becoming poor by such help. Accompanying these efforts are provisions to make society an easier place for the physically handicapped to function. These include the laws against discrimination and requirements that buildings be modified to permit the easy movement of those who may not be able to walk.

Many countries are giving increasing attention to such rehabilitative efforts and have had some success. However, it is a continuous struggle, and there are many of the poor whose troubles are not of the type likely to be helped by rehabilitation programs.

TRANSFER PAYMENTS. Industrialized countries have made a good deal of progress in

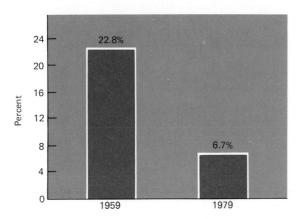

FIGURE 15-3 Percentage of Americans in poverty. (There are several different ways of calculating the poverty rate, and the rate in 1979 varies from 6.7 to 8.9 percent according to the method used.) (*Source: Timothy M. Smeeding,* Alternative Methods for Valuing Selected In-Kind Transfer Benefits and Measuring Their Effect on Poverty, *Technical Paper 50, U.S. Bureau of the Census, 1982, p. 96.*)
Does the great growth of "transfers" account for much of the decline in poverty from 1959 to 1979?

terms of spreading prosperity. In the United States, for instance, as recently as 1959, nearly a quarter of the population (22.8 percent) were classed as living in poverty, compared to 6.7 percent in 1979 [Smeeding, 1982, p. 96], yet several million people are still poor, and the number grows in economically depressed times such as the early 1980s.

The proportion of the national income received by the bottom 20 percent of the population has hovered around 5 percent for several decades, but this figure takes no account of transfer payments—called this because the intent of these payments is to transfer resources from the more affluent to the needy (financed mainly through progressive income taxes upon the more affluent; see Table 15-4). Such payments include both money and noncash items such as food stamps, subsidized housing, and Medicare. The nonmonetary payments have greatly increased in recent years, growing (in constant 1965 dollars) from $2 billion in 1965 to over $27 billion in 1980 [Smeeding, 1982, p. 3].

It should be observed that the affluent as

TABLE 15-4
WHO GETS WHAT AND WHO PAYS WHAT IN THE UNITED STATES?*

Taxpayers with incomes between	Make up ——% of all taxpayers	Get ——% of all adjusted gross income†	Pay ——% of all federal income taxes†	Pay ——% of their adjusted gross incomes
$0–$9,999	36.9	9.0	2.2	2.9
$10,000–$29,999	44.2	43.6	34.7	11.3
$30,000–$49,999	14.5	28.5	30.3	15.1
$50,000 and more	4.4	19.0	32.9	24.6

*Based on 1981 income taxed at 1982 federal income tax rates.
†Column equals more than 100%, because of rounding off.
Source: Office of Tax Analysis, Department of the Treasury (press release of Joint Economic Committee, Congress of the United States, Nov. 21, 1982.)

The federal income tax is "progressive," meaning that it taxes high incomes at higher rates than low incomes. It, together with income transfers, reduces economic inequality. Some other taxes, such as sales taxes (especially if food is taxed), are "regressive," taxing the poor relatively more heavily than the wealthy.

well as the poor receive government payments. These come in such forms as subsidized higher education (used mainly by the middle and upper classes), income tax exemptions for interest paid on housing, subsidized FHA loans, and even Coast Guard rescue operations and harbor maintenance for private boats and yachts. The total amount of subsidies to the nonpoor is somewhat greater than to the poor [Smeeding, 1982, p. 9]. However, the poor receive a larger proportion of their income in a variety of transfer payments and pay less in taxes. One estimate is that, in 1977, the net effect of transfer payments and taxes increased the income of the lowest 10 percent of the population by 55 percent. In the same year, they decreased the income of the top 20 percent by 15 percent [Meerman, 1980, p. 1247].

The combined effects of taxes and transfer payments have significantly reduced the gap between the rich and the poor. Without transfer payments (including both cash and in-kind), those in poverty in 1980, instead of being 6 or 7 percent of our people, would have been 22 percent—nearly four times as great [Murray, 1982, p. 10]. The Reagan administration reduced the amount of income redistribution, cutting the level of transfer payments to the poor and cutting taxes most greatly upon the larger incomes. A Congressional Budget Office calculation put the net effect of the 1981 Reagan administration tax and budget changes (if fully implemented) at an average loss of $240 for households under $10,000 in income and a gain of $15,130 for households over $80,000 [Bresler, 1982]. These proposed changes were based upon the belief that more of the national income should go to the affluent in order to increase savings and investment and thus restore prosperity. Before the proposals could be fully implemented, further changes were made which reduced the impact of the Reagan policy changes. The entire episode shows how the distribution of income is not purely a result

of impersonal economic forces but is also a result of conscious political decision.

MOBILITY OR EQUALITY

For years America was regarded as the land of equality because of the possibility of a "rags-to-riches" mobility. This concept has been challenged by various writers [Rawls, 1971; Jencks, 1972, 1979; Shostak et al., 1973] who insist that what matters is not equality of opportunity but equality of results.

The moral case for equality of income is well stated by Tumin [1963, p. 26]. Most already agree that inheritance of wealth alone should not guarantee a life of luxury to some while condemning others to lifelong hardship. We have, therefore, accepted the idea of equality of opportunity. A meritocracy would mean that equality of opportunity would replace an aristocracy of inherited wealth with an aristocracy of inherited talent. Is it really any more just to give wealth and status to those who pick smart parents than to those who pick rich parents?

While the moral case for equality of income is easily made, the attainment of equality poses many difficulties. For example, the many kinds of help given by parents to children are a major source of inequality. The mere fact of having parents who are hardworking, successful, self-confident, and verbally facile gives children a competitive advantage. Is there any possible way to change this?

Although absolute equality is impractical in a modern society, existing inequalities could be reduced by an expanded program of income redistribution. There are two difficulties here: political and economic. The political difficulty is in persuading middle-class people to accept the sacrifice involved. Since the top 5 percent of the country receive only 15 percent of the national income [*Statistical Abstract*, 1982–1983, p. 435], a further redistribution of income could not be financed simply by higher taxes upon the rich. It would need to reach deeply into the middle class, who are already in revolt against high taxes. There is also the politically important fact that such income redistribution would benefit the poor, most of whom do not vote regularly, at the expense of the more affluent, most of who *do* vote regularly. Thus, income transfers to the poor seem more likely to be cut than to be expanded.

The economic difficulty is that most of the investment capital which finances economic growth comes from the savings of the affluent. Many economists argue that heavy taxes on the larger incomes create capital shortages, inhibit economic growth, and promote unemployment [Okun, 1975, p. 105; Feldstein, 1977]. It is uncertain how much income redistribution a capitalist economy can support without drying up capital formation so much that the economy stagnates. To Marxists, this simply reveals the failures of a capitalist system.

Capital formation is necessary for any modern economy. Communist states set wages and prices to provide profits which can be used as capital. Regardless of the system, capital is money witheld from consumption. Which mode of capital formation is most efficient and just is a matter of continuing debate.

SUMMARY

Social mobility is movement up or down in social status and (usually) income and may be experienced by individuals or by entire groups. Upward mobility brings increased life satisfactions as well as anxieties and sacrifices. An *open class* society encourages much movement up and down the mobility ladder, while in a *closed class* or *caste* society, class status is inherited and is very difficult to change.

The amount of upward mobility is affected by structural factors, including the proportion of higher-status positions available, differential fertility, and a society's mobility aids and barriers. Individual factors in mobility include ability differences, differences in mobility-oriented behavior (education, work habits, the DGP, mobility "game playing," and value stretch), and the luck factor.

Mobility prospects depend upon the continued growth of high-status positions, and these depend upon technological change and economic growth. Mobility for married women has been determined mainly by their husbands' status, but women's own occupational status is growing more important today.

The poor Third World countries resent the affluence of the wealthy countries and demand assistance in closing the gap. Population growth and growing resource shortages and capital shortages make it difficult for them to do so.

In the capitalist (mixed-economy) countries, transfer payments with progressive taxation reduce inequalities between rich and poor. Middle-class objections to high taxes make it questionable whether there will be any further reductions in economic inequality in the capitalist countries.

GLOSSARY

capital money, or the goods which it provides, used to make other goods rather than consumed directly. Transportation equipment, factories, and warehouses are examples.
caste system a stratified social system in which social position is entirely determined by parentage, with no provision for change of position.

closed class system status system with inherited position and no provision for changes in status.
deferred-gratification pattern postponing immediate satisfaction for future gain.

entrepreneurship carrying on business.

income redistribution adjusting taxes and tax-supported benefits unequally in order to reduce inequalities of income.

open class system a status system with considerable movement up and down the mobility ladder.

social mobility movement from one class level to another.

transfer payments providing money or free services to some groups, financed by taxes paid disproportionately by other groups—thus, a transfer of income between groups.

value stretch verbal expression of values without appropriate behavior to attain them.

QUESTIONS AND PROJECTS

1 What is the difference between caste and class? Are women a caste group? Why or why not?

2 What advantages and disadvantages does a closed class system hold for a society? For the individual? Do you know of any deliberate attempts to decrease competition for status in the United States?

3 What advantages and disadvantages does an open class system hold for a society? For the individual? What makes absolute equality of opportunity impossible?

4 Do you consider yourself to be highly mobility-oriented? What factors do you think explain your own mobility orientation?

5 Assume that higher educa-

tion should become completely free of all costs and that jobs were filled strictly on merit without regard to family connections. Would you expect the same proportion of lower- and middle-class youth to reach high-status positions? Why or why not?

6 How does the value-stretch pattern among lower-class people make it difficult to evaluate their attitude toward deferred gratification?

7 Is marriage while in college an aid or a threat to the student's prospects for social mobility? Will social mobility become a threat to the marriage?

8 Describe the groups in your community showing the most rapid and least rapid rates of upward mobility. On the basis of present trends in both these groups, attempt to predict their relative position fifty years hence.

9 Analyze a pledge list in a fraternity or sorority in terms of those you would label socially mobile as contrasted to those who are simply maintaining the family status. Describe any contrasts between the personality traits of the socially mobile and the stationary pledges.

10 What is meant by transfer payments? Do they aid or discourage social mobility?

11 Read *A Tree Grows in Brooklyn*, by Betty Smith. What factors account for Francie's rejection of the slum subculture and her desire to escape it? Did she escape through luck or through her own efforts?

SUGGESTED READINGS

*Ashe, Arthur and Neil Amdur: *Off the Court*, New American Library, Inc., New York, 1981. An autobiography of a black tennis star who made good in what had been a white persons' sport. Also has observations on procedures blacks should follow to enhance social mobility.

Auletta, Ken: *The Underclass*, Random House, Inc., New York, 1982. A vivid description of the lower-lower class and the difficulties in escaping it.

Danziger, Sheldon and Robert Plotnick: "Income Maintenance Programs and the Pursuit of Income Security," *Annals of the American Academy of Political and Social Science*, 453:130–152, January 1981. A discussion of the role of transfer payments in maintaining a level of income.

*Duberman, Lucile: *Social Inequality: Classes and Caste in America*, J. B. Lippincott Company, Philadelphia, 1976. An analysis of inequality in the United States, discussing women as a "caste."

Friedan, Betty: *The Second Stage*, Summit Books, New York, 1981. A feminist leader's discussion of feminine gains and problems, showing current attitudes of women toward two-career families on pp. 260–281.

Gandhi, Raj S.: "From Caste to Class in Indian Society," *Humboldt Journal of Social Relations*, 7:1–14, Spring/Summer 1980. The effect of a changing caste system on social mobility.

*Hollander, Paul: *Soviet and American Society: A Comparison*, Oxford University Press, New York, 1978. A Hungarian sociologist goes beyond ideology to describe social-class processes in each society.

Lane, Angela Victoria: "Migration and the Processes of Occupational Mobility and Status Attainment," *Sociological Focus*, 10:43–52, January 1977. A research comparison of geographical mobility and occupational mobility finding that internal migrants (within the United States) come from a higher status than nonmigrants.

Philliber, William W. and Dana V. Hiller: "A Research Note: Occupational Attainments and Perceptions of Status Among Working Wives," *Journal of Marriage and the Family*, 41:59–72, February 1979. Contrasts the ways that working wives of working-class and middle-class husbands perceive their class status.

Piven, Frances Fox and Richard A. Cloward: *The New Class War: Reagan's Attack on the Welfare State and Its Consequences*, Pantheon Books, a division of Random House, Inc., New York, 1982. Advocates increased transfer programs to reduce inequality.

Rodman, Hyman, Patricia Voydanoff, and Albert E. Lovejoy: "The Range of Aspiration: A New Approach," *Social Problems*, 22:184–198, December 1974. Aspirations of different social classes in terms of the value-stretch concept.

Schumer, Fran R.: "Downward Mobility," *New York*, 15:20–26, 32, Aug. 16, 1982. A lively treatment of problems faced by young middle-class people who find themselves less affluent than they expected.

*An asterisk before the citation indicates that the title is available in a paperback edition.

16 Race and Ethnic Relations

388

Some would be surprised that the average black cannot be associated with poverty, welfare or unemployment. Indeed, according to the latest Urban League report on the status of blacks in America, 83 percent work for a living, 77 percent are not on welfare and 62 percent do not live in poverty. This is not to say that we should not be about the important business of reducing the 16 percent who are unemployed, the 23 percent who are on welfare or the 38 percent who do live in poverty. It is only to say that we must be careful not to leave the impression in the minds of blacks and whites, particularly the young ones, that most blacks play no productive role in the economic life of this nation. This is not true.

(Dan J. Smith, "Black Objectives for the 1980s," in Thomas Sowell et al., (eds.): *The Fairmont Papers: Black Alternatives Conference,* Institute for Contemporary Studies, San Francisco, 1981, p. 14.) © by Institute for Contemporary Studies. Used by permission.

RACIAL AND ETHNIC CLASSIFICATION

"Race" is a troublesome concept, for it has no generally agreed upon meaning. In popular usage, "race" may mean all of humanity (the "human race"), a nationality (the "German race"), or even a group which is mixed in nearly all respects but socially designated as different (the "Jewish race"). Almost any kind of category of people may be called a "race."

Even social scientists have not fully agreed in defining the term. Some have defined a race as a group of people separated from other groups by a distinctive combination of physical characteristics. As will be seen later, this poses certain difficulties because of intermixing, overlapping, and the gradual shading of physical characteristics (e.g., skin color) along a continuum without definite separations. Therefore, a "race" is not a biologically distinct grouping of people, yet many people think and act as though it were. Race is a socially significant reality, for people attach great importance to one's presumed "race." The scientist's fondness for neat scientific precision must be tempered by the need to deal with an important social reality. Perhaps an acceptable definition might read: *A race is a group of people somewhat different from other groups in its combination of inherited physical characteristics, but race is also substantially determined by popular social definition.*

It is conventional to divide the human species into three main racial stocks—the Mongoloid (yellow and brown), the Negroid (black), and the Caucasoid (white). Most groups can be placed in one of these three categories, as is shown in Figure 16-1. This figure also shows that the racial placement of some groups is uncertain because their physical characteristics overlap. For example, the Asian Indians have Mongoloid skin color but Caucasoid facial features; the Ainu of northern Japan have Caucasoid skin color and hair but Mongoloid facial features. A further complication arises from the fact that the races have been busily interbreeding for thousands of years so that nearly all racial groups are considerably intermixed. In recent years, it has become common to refer to Americans with Negroid ancestry as *blacks* rather than as Negroes. This is not very different, since *negro* is a Spanish word meaning black. In this textbook, we have generally used the term *black,* except when reproducing quotations and statistical or historical materials.

Sociologists use the term *ethnic group* to refer to *any kind of group, racial or otherwise, which is socially identified as different and has developed its own subculture.* In other words, an ethnic group is one recognized by society and by itself as a distinct group. Although the distinction is associated with a particular set of ancestors, its identifying marks may be language, religion, geographic location, nationality, physical appearance, or any combination of these. The term is properly applied whenever the group differences are consid-

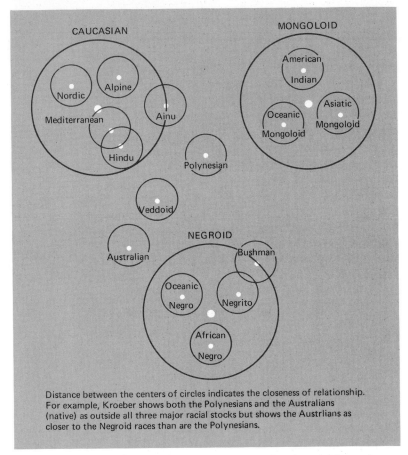

Distance between the centers of circles indicates the closeness of relationship.
For example, Kroeber shows both the Polynesians and the Australians
(native) as outside all three major racial stocks but shows the Austrlians as
closer to the Negroid races than are the Polynesians.

FIGURE 16-1 The human races. (*Source: A. L. Kroeber,* Anthropology,
Harcourt Brace Jovanovich, Inc., New York, 1948, p. 10.)

Is a *race* a biologically distinct category of people? Or is *race* a label we
apply when we think we see some similarities?

ered important enough to set off the group
from others. *The Harvard Encyclopedia of American Ethic Groups* [Thernstrom, 1980] describes
a total of 106 ethnic groups in America.

THE SCIENTIFIC VIEW OF RACE
DIFFERENCES

It is clear that the races differ in some inherited
physical characteristics. May they also vary
in their inborn intellectual and emotional
characteristics? This is a reasonable logical
possibility. Is it a fact? Is it true of nonracial
ethnic groups as well?

Physical Race Differences
Are Unimportant

All races are approximately alike in every
important physical characteristic. With a few
exceptions (such as that a dark skin is useful
under tropical sun), the differences are cos-
metic not functional. The physical differences
within the human species are very modest
compared with the differences within many
species—dogs or horses, for example.

Most scientists today are agreed that all
races are of one species, the product of a
single evolution, and that all races are about
equally "close" to the other animals. For

example, the blacks more closely resemble the apes in hair color, nose form, and facial slant; but the whites more closely resemble the apes in lip form, hair texture, and amount of body hair.

There is some evidence that allergy to different foods and susceptibility to some diseases may vary along ethnic lines. This would include the susceptibility of Jews to Tay-Sachs disease, the greater likelihood of lactose intolerance and sickle-cell anemia among blacks, and the greater probability of thalassemia, a form of anemia, among people whose ancestors came from the Mediterranean area [Zochert, 1977]. Public health workers should realize the differences in the susceptibility of ethnic groups to these specific diseases, but most diseases vary little between ethnic groups when other factors are held constant. It is primarily culture rather than heredity which produces differences between ethnic groups.

AMALGAMATION AND ASSIMILATION

Ethnic groups are not necessarily permanent and sometimes disappear through assimilation or amalgamation. *Assimilation* refers to *a cultural fusion in which two groups blend their cultures so that they become one*. There is usually an exchange of cultural traits, although this may be primarily a case of one group absorbing the other's culture. An example is "Americanization," in which immigrant groups have contributed some of their traits but mainly have adopted an English-based "core-culture." The "Americanization" of non-Anglo-Saxon names is one sign of assimilation, as shown in Table 16-1. While assimilation refers to a blending of two cultures, *amalgamation* means *a biological interbreeding of two peoples of distinct physical appearance until they become one stock*. Although distinct physical types have seldom entirely disappeared, enough inter-

TABLE 16-1
NAME CHANGING—AN ASSIMILATION TECHNIQUE

Stage name	Original name
Doris Day	Doris Kapplehoff
Tony Curtis	Bernie Schwartz
Karl Malden	Mladen Sekulovich
Judy Garland	Frances Gumm
Claudette Colbert	Claudette Chauchoin
Vic Damone	Vito Farinola
Cyd Charisse	Tula Finklea
Robert Taylor	Spengler Arlington Brough
Judy Holliday	Judy Tuvim
Rita Hayworth	Margarita Carmen Cansino
Vince Edwards	Vincent Zoino
Jane Wyman	Sarah Fulks
Kirk Douglas	Issur Danielovitch
Danny Kaye	Daniel Kaminsky
Dean Martin	Dino Crocetti
Jerry Lewis	Joseph Levitch

Source: Portion of a list in Stanley Lieberson, *A Piece of the Pie: Black and White Immigrants Since 1880*, University of California Press, Berkeley, 1980, p. 33.

Why do you think people change their names? Entertainment celebrities seem more likely to change their names than politicians. Why?

breeding has taken place so that it is difficult to find any large group of individuals who form a "pure" racial type, if, indeed, there ever have been any. England has practiced amalgamation on a grand scale. The Norman invaders of the eleventh century were soon blended with the English. Hawaii includes the descendants of the original inhabitants of the islands plus a large number of Caucasian settlers, Chinese, Japanese, Filipinos, and Koreans. All these have intermarried quite freely, the highest rates being in groups which have more males than females.

There was considerable amalgamation between whites and blacks in the United States. During the past century, it has declined for a variety of reasons: the end of slavery, the decline of the plantation, the diminishing number of white households with black servants, the rising status of blacks, a growing mutual disapproval of interracial sex contacts, and possibly the spread of contraception. But while extramarital amalgamation has declined, has ethnic intermarriage increased?

Recent data indicate that there has been an increase in intermarriage. The intermarriage rate between Jews and gentiles has showed a spectacular increase in the last two decades, showing that the tradition of Jewish endogamy, once very strong, is now greatly weakened. In the period 1900 to 1919, only 2.7 percent of Jews intermarried, but by 1971, this had grown to 41 percent. Between 1900 and 1960, fewer than 10 percent of American Jews intermarried but by 1972 almost one-third (31.7 percent) were marrying gentiles [Rosenman, 1979, p. 2].

Intermarriage between Asian-Americans and others is quite high. The 1980 census showed that nearly a quarter of Asian-Americans were married to white spouses, with the highest rate of intermarriage among those aged 16 to 24 at the time of the census count. Among the third generation Japanese-Americans, outmarriage has reached 40 percent [Montero, 1981, p. 836]. Among American married men of Hispanic origin, one-fourth had non-His-

TABLE 16-2
BLACK AND WHITE INTERMARRIAGE, 1970–1980

	1970	1980
Black husband; white wife	41,000	120,000
White husband; black wife	24,000	46,000
Total	65,000	166,000

Source: Statistical Abstract of the United States, 1981, table 56, p. 41. Figures indicate the total number of people living in mixed black-white marriages in 1970 and 1980.

Why do you think intermarriage has increased? Do you think it will continue to increase?

panic wives in 1980 [U.S. Bureau of the Census, 1981*d*, p. 162].

Black-white intermarriage has also increased (see Table 16-2), but still includes less than 2 percent of all marriages of blacks. It is difficult to know whether the increase is a minor fluctuation or a definite trend toward more black-white intermarriage [*Ebony*, 37:81–82, August 1982]. The greater popularity of racial intermarriage for black men than for black women is a consequence of men's and women's different interpretations of black liberation. In the days of slavery and even more in the discriminatory period which followed, black women were a common illicit sexual outlet for white men, while black men were threatened with death if they consorted with white women [Myrdal, 1944, p. 57]. Thus, for black women, association with white men had the stigma of oppression. Today black men see association with white women as an evidence of their liberation. Similarly, white men fear charges of exploitation if they date black women, while white women see interracial dating as an evidence of liberalism. The result is not only a lesser interracial marriage rate for black women, but an antagonism between black women and white women [Napper, 1973; Porterfield, 1978, p. 148].

In spite of a growing social acceptance, interracial marriage is still uncommon. Some of the difficulty is indicated by the divorce rates for interracial couples married in 1960, which were higher than for either all-black or all-white marriages [Heer, 1974, p. 250].

Whether there will eventually be a complete blending through intermarriage is by no means certain. Some years ago, it was estimated that 21 percent of Americans classified as white have some black ancestry, while nearly 75 percent of blacks have some white ancestry [Burma, 1946; Stuckert, 1958]. Legal equality, along with increased contact between members of different races, may bring a high rate of intermarriage. However, the rate of black-white intermarriage is still low, and participants in such marriages are likely to meet rejection from both races.

The outmarriage of Jews is high enough to raise doubts about the survival of the group, though this is a recent trend and could be reversed. The same may be said of American Indians, although outmarriage rates are lower for those living on a reservation. The outmarriage rates of both Hispanic-Americans and Asian-Americans are also high, but their effect is diminished by large-scale immigration which continuously enlarges the original ethnic group. Prediction is difficult; however, it seems likely that American ethnic groups will survive but that intermarriage may continue to increase.

PREJUDICE AND DISCRIMINATION

Whenever it is possible to assign people to different groups, there is a tendency to develop stereotypes about them (prejudice) and to treat them on the basis of these qualities (discrimination). *Prejudice* comes from two Latin words, *prae* (before) and *judicum* (a judgment). It implies *a judgment expressed before knowing all the facts*. There seem to be five main roots of prejudice. One is our ethnocentrism which inclines us to think well of those in our own group and ill of others. Another is the simple fact that every day we

make judgments of people about whom we know little; stereotypes, though never entirely accurate, are handy guides [Snyder, 1982]. Third, we generalize from our own experience with individuals of other groups. Fourth, we tend to select stereotypes which support our beliefs about what the relationships and privileges of different groups should be. Finally, we tend to develop prejudices against people who compete with us.

In ethnic relations, *discrimination* is *treating people on the basis of group classification rather than individual characteristics*. Discrimination occurs when, in hiring an employee, admitting students to school, renting a house, selecting a mate, or any one of countless situations, we accept or reject a person because of his or her ethnic identity without seriously considering personal characteristics. Discrimination has usually been practiced by a dominant group to protect its privileges. A new policy of "reverse discrimination" favors members of a subordinate group whose members may be handicapped by either past or present discrimination.

Prejudice may distort our judgment and make us unable to reach rational decisions. At one time, prejudice was a major concern of students of ethnic relations. We believed that discrimination was caused by prejudiced attitudes and that to change actions, we must first change attitudes. Later, it was recognized that this was an oversimplification and that perhaps discriminatory actions were more a *cause* than an effect of prejudiced attitudes [Blumer, 1955]. Gunnar Myrdal, a Swedish anthropologist, in his monumental study, *An American Dilemma* [1944, p. 101], refers to prejudices as "beliefs with a purpose"—the purpose being to justify prevailing racial practices.

In a classic series of research studies, Adorno [1950] found that an insecure person may be more inclined to accept prejudice uncritically and to hold to it tenaciously than one who is more self-assured. However, prejudice is not confined to the emotionally insecure and is

TABLE 16-3
TREATMENT OF BLACKS IN COMMUNITY
*(Question: "In your opinion, how well do you think blacks are treated in this
community—the same as whites are, not very well, or badly?"*)*

	PERCENT RESPONDING:			
	Same as whites	Not very well	Badly	No opinion
Whites	67	17	3	13
Nonwhites	35	41	16	8

*Question asked on Dec. 5–8, 1980.
Source: Gallup Reports, 35; 185, February 1981.

Does Professor Banton's theory about majority and minority views explain figures shown
in this table?

widespread if strongly supported by society.
A person's prejudices arise, not so much from
psychological immaturity, as from socialization in the prejudiced attitudes held in his or
her society [Bloom, 1972, p. 67]. A direct
attack on prejudice is often futile, since people
tend to develop attitudes supporting their
way of life. Hence, those who wish to change
ethnic patterns today are more concerned
about changing the ways of life embedded in
ethnic relationships. Lectures and books, even
movies and television, may have only a limited effect on prejudice, but a demonstration
that members of different groups can and do
live harmoniously should diminish the type
of prejudice which grows out of ethnic conflict
[Davis, 1978, p. 287]. A great deal of research
in the 1950s and 1960s showed that a direct
attack upon discriminatory practices was more
effective than attempts to persuade people to
change their attitudes and prejudices [Horton
and Leslie, 1981, pp. 326–328]. Little research
on prejudice has been done in recent years,
with the *Sociological Abstract* listing twenty
articles under "prejudice" during 1980 and
1981, of which only four dealt with the nature,
origins, and causes of prejudices. Most of the
rest were studies of the extent of prejudice,
showing a continued downward trend in
recent years [Tuch, 1981].

As illustrated in Table 16-3, blacks and
whites tend to take different views of the
condition of blacks, with most whites feeling
it is pretty good and many blacks finding it
unsatisfactory. Banton [1967, p. 388], a British
sociologist, points out that these are typical
majority and minority viewpoints. The majority stresses progress compared with the
past, while the minority emphasizes the distance still to go.

Discrimination remains a lively research
topic, with seventy-eight journal articles in-
dexed in the editions of the *Sociological Abstract*
for 1980 and 1981. Discrimination has greatly
declined, yet it remains. For example, a recent
study analyzes the several situations and
practices which make it more difficult for
blacks than for whites to accumulate ownership equity in housing [Parcel, 1982]. It will,
at best, be a long time before all vestiges of
discrimination disappear.

Genocide: The Ultimate Form
of Discrimination

Hitler sought to carry out the "final solution"
to what he called the "Jewish question" through
the complete extermination of all the Jews in
Europe. [Charney, 1982; Kuper, 1982]. Jews
were herded into cattle cars, transported to
concentration camps, and systematically
gassed. By the end of World War II in 1945,

IS RACISM DEAD?

The Institute for Historical Review publishes a quarterly journal, written in scholarly language, and lists on its advisory committee the names of several university professors, only one of whom has any credentials as an historian. Its articles claim that the Holocaust is a myth, that not one Jew was gassed by the Nazis, that the Nazis had no campaign to exterminate the Jewish people, and that the handful who died in the concentration camps died from disease, malnutrition, and Allied bombings.

More than 50,000 letters were sent by the Institute to college students stating that the Holocaust was a lie concocted by the Jewish people to justify the creation of Israel and that they would soon be called into the army to fight for the protection of the Jewish state.

Adapted from a promotional letter from the Simon Weisenthal Center (Los Angeles, Cal.), undated; received February 1982.

Under what circumstances might such a group as this Institute gain a following among American college students?

most of the Jews in Europe had been killed in this cold-blooded manner [Reitlinger, 1968, p. 546]. This is known as the "Holocaust" (literally, a burnt sacrificial offering), since so many people had been slaughtered on the altar of group hatred. The term *genocide* (*genos* is the Greek word for race) means the *deliberate attempt to exterminate a group,* even as homicide refers to the killing of an individual. In 1951 the United Nations adopted an agreement to outlaw genocide which, at the time of this writing, still had not been ratified by the United States. The United States shares in the moral condemnation of genocide but may fear that ratifying the agreement would authorize the United Nations to intervene in American ethnic controversies.

Genocide has been attempted many times in world history [Horowitz, 1980]. The ancient Hebrews sought to exterminate the Canaanites, American colonists massacred the Indians, and perhaps half the Armenians died at the hands of the Turks in 1915 [Dadrian, 1971, 1975]. Hindus and Muslims slaughtered each other in India after World War II [Cousins, 1954], and tribal groups in Paraguay and Burundi have been slaughtered within the past two decades [Melady, 1974; Arens, 1976]. Uganda eliminated its Indian population by expelling them from the country [Kuepper et al., 1975].

Sometimes the approximate equivalent of genocide results from ruthlessly following

policies which have the effect of destroying a people. Invading armies have often seized a country's food supply, leaving the civilian population to starve; mass deportations are usually accompanied by wholesale deaths from hunger, exposure, illness, and despair; one-sixth of the Cambodian population died in 1975 when the Cambodian Communists drove the entire urban population into the countryside with no provision for their care. [Cherme, 1975]; the "development" of forest lands in Brazil dooms most of the forest tribes to extinction [Hawrylyshyn, 1976]. Believers in automatic progress should be reminded that deaths from genocide in the twentieth century probably exceed those in all earlier centuries in the world's history.

APPROACHES TO ETHNIC POLICIES

For a period immediately following World War II, Americans engaged in bitter controversary over whether "white supremacy" and black segregation should be maintained. While this had been the prevailing pattern during previous history, a growing number of both whites and blacks advocated a "color-blind" policy of treating individuals on their own merit without regard to their ethnic identity. Demonstrations, court verdicts, and electoral victories resulted in the Civil Rights Acts of 1960 and 1964, which outlawed discrimination in the treatment of all ethnic groups. Even if all job applicants had been treated exactly alike, blacks were still at a disadvantage because of differences in education, training, family background, access to job information, and other factors. Therefore, the color-blind approach was replaced by the policy of giving active preference (affirmative action) to groups which had suffered past discrimination.

The Individual-Rights Approach

Soviet critics of the United States correctly note that, unlike the Soviet Union, the United States does not guarantee legal protection to the cultures of ethnic minorities. If ethnic art, language, religion, or literature endure, it is through voluntary effort not government support. This approach, sometimes labeled "integrationist," holds that the United States should protect the basic freedoms of all individuals but has no responsibility to maintain the identity of ethnic groups. If individuals wish, they may band together to protect ethnic identity, language, customs, and religion. This activity includes radio broadcasting and journalism in foreign tongues, churches and fraternal orders catering to an ethnic clientele, neighborhoods so ethnically concentrated they become known as "Little Italy" or "Little Poland," and even schools conducted for the sole purpose of socializing the young in an ethnic language and culture

In the individual-rights approach, there is no official recognition of race or ethnicity, but groups are allowed and even encouraged to preserve ethnic culture on a private basis [Glazer, 1972, p. 165]. If individuals allow ethnic institutions to decline or change in character, as has usually happened with immigrant groups, this is no concern of the government. Government should seek to provide individuals with equal opportunity for economic advancement, but whether all ethnic groups are equally successful is not a government concern. The United States has recently modified its individual-rights ap-

proach to include some protection based on ethnicity.

In summary, the individual-rights approach includes (1) removal of formal barriers and discriminations, (2) evaluation and treatment of persons on a basis of individual merits, and (3) no official effort to preserve ethnic cultures. The ultimate goal is an integrated society in which members of all ethnic groups participate in social life according to their talents and interests.

The Group-Rights Approach

In the United States we have assumed that all immigrants would become "Americanized" and assimilated to an "American" culture that is heavily English in flavor. In much of the rest of the world, national governments have taken it for granted that ethnic differences would persist and should be protected. An emphasis on group rights means that the government supports the survival of distinctive ethnic communities. In Yugoslavia, for instance, the government provides instruction in the mother tongue of any nationality when there are enough students to justify either a school or class. In Switzerland, there is no official language, and three major tongues have equal status. In Canada, public schools are required to offer instruction in both French and English. Such examples could be multiplied indefinitely. The point is simply that government need not promote assimilation to a common culture but can support ethnic differences. Some governments are actually more protective of the rights of ethnic groups than of individuals. We will consider two methods of protecting group rights: separatism and cultural pluralism.

SEPARATISM. Subordinate ethnic groups have often supported independence movements in an effort to withdraw completely from political involvement with another ethnic group. Many Third World representatives say that American racial minorities are essentially col-

Ethnic groups are allowed and even encouraged to preserve their ethnic culture. How do such parades do this? (© *Katrina Thomas/ Photo Researchers, Inc.*)

onies and should separate from the rule of the majority. Puerto Ricans, Chicanos, and American blacks all have separatist movements, but none has attracted a mass following. In Puerto Rican elections, the Independence party always gets a tiny vote. Black separatism in the United States is not new [Hall, 1978]; it attracted much interest in the late 1960s [Hamilton, 1972], but little is heard of it today. Black capitalism has not been very successful and now more blacks are gaining executive promotions within white corporations [Irons, 1976; Osborne, 1976; Davis and Watson, 1982]. Separatism for American blacks has been opposed by those who feel that it would leave blacks in control of a vast poverty area, with inadequate resources of their own and little support from indifferent whites [Pettigrew, 1971].

CULTURAL PLURALISM.   Cultural pluralism is a form of accommodation in which ethnic groups retain their distinct cultural differences and traditions, while cooperating peacefully and relatively equally in political, economic, and social life. The standard example of cultural pluralism is Switzerland, where Protestants and Catholics have been able to live agreeably under the same government, while speaking German, French, or Italian. Since Swiss citizens do not feel that either their religious loyalty or their ethnic identification is threatened by other Swiss, they are free to give a complete allegiance to the Swiss nation as a common government which allows for the tolerance of distinctly different cultural groups. Other examples of cultural pluralism would include Canada (English and French), Belgium (French-speaking and Flemish-speaking), Lebanon (Muslim and Christian), and Malta (Greek and Turk). Civil war in two of these countries and separatist movements in the other two show that cultural pluralism is not a perfect answer.

People who accept integration as a goal tend to diverge from cultural pluralists on many points. Some of these points of difference are shown in Table 16-4.

American religious divisions are one area of intergroup relations wherein some observers [Herberg, 1960; Greeley, 1976] believe cultural pluralism is an essential and valuable feature of American life. But it may be that cultural pluralism is only a transitional stage. Gordon [1964, p. 245] argues that one has to accept and have pride in the group of origin before one is ready to accept assimilation into the larger society. Thus, immigrants and their children may gain a sense of security and identity when encouraged to talk about the contributions which their ethnic cultures have made to American society. Similarly, black students may profit from knowing that Africa has been an historic crossroads of civilization.

Implementation of Ethnic Group Rights

Soon after the enactment of the civil rights legislation of the 1950s and 1960s, it became clear that many blacks would still be poor. Thus, the claim arose that disadvantaged ethnic minorities were entitled not only to equal oportunities but to equal rewards—the group-rights concept.

There are four main policies which American society has followed in recent years in dealing with the ethnic group rather than with individuals. These are (1) bilingual instruction, (2) affirmative action, (3) busing for racial balance, and (4) welfare and social legislation. Sociologists have played an ambivalent role in the development of these programs. Many of the programs were implemented by court orders. The testimony of sociologists was influential in the court process, although sociological findings were often misunderstood, especially when they did not support judicial decisions [Wolf, 1981].

BILINGUAL EDUCATION. In previous years, immigrant children were thrown into an English-language school system with little special help. Some had difficulty and dropped out; others mastered the language and did well. In any event, the public schools were regarded as a great assimilating agency. In recent years, this policy has been attacked as

TABLE 16-4
PATTERNS OF ETHNIC RELATIONS

	Cultural pluralism	Integration
Basic principle	Group equality	Individual legal equality
Employment policies	Group quotas	No ethnic preference
Educational policies	Bilingualism to maintain foreign language skill	English instruction only or bilingualism as a transition to English
Advantages	Preserves ethnicity	Unifies divergent peoples
	Enhances group cohesion	Enhances individual freedom
Drawbacks	Strengthens ethnic divisions	Destroys ethnic identity

Is it possible for an ethnic-relations policy to pursue both cultural pluralism and integration at the same time, or must a choice be made between them?

disrespectful to the non-English language group and as burdensome to the immigrant child. Consequently, bilingual education (for the non-English-speaking child only) has been made mandatory in every school district in which twenty or more students speak a foreign language as their native language.[1]

The program suffers from a confusion of objectives, because its advocates are divided on whether the goal of bilingual education is simply to smooth the transition to English or to maintain knowledge of a foreign language and help preserve ethnic group identity. Evidence is inconclusive as to whether bilingual education aids or delays students in learning to use the English language [Danoff, 1978, p. 14].

AFFIRMATIVE ACTION.   The Civil Rights Acts of 1960, 1964, and 1968 outlawed discrimination. Government action against discrimination was followed by a policy of affirmative action, which required not only that there be no active discrimination but that positive preference be given to groups who are victims of past discrimination. Employers must actively recruit, train, and promote minority members; universities must actively recruit students and faculty members. Quotas are outlawed, but employers must show progress in reaching "goals," which have a suspicious similarity to the forbidden quotas. Affirmative action was initiated to meet the needs of blacks and other nonwhite groups but is now more involved with upgrading the status of women.

BUSING FOR RACIAL BALANCE.   When this was introduced, it was argued that it would improve relations between black and white students, enhance the academic achievement and self-concept of black students, and advance school integration. Its success in any

¹ In 1982, the Department of Education agreed to consider special instruction in English as a second language as an alternative to bilingual education. At this writing, it is uncertain how widely this alternative program will be adopted.

of these aims is in dispute [Armor, 1972; Schellenberg and Halteman, 1974; St. John, 1975; Cohen, 1977; Epps, 1981; Daniels, 1983], and the federal government has ceased promoting busing as a means of school integration. Whether busing actually promotes integration is questionable, since busing appears to promote "white flight" (moving to the suburbs or shifting children into private schools). There is dispute over the amount of "white flight" and possible ways to prevent it [Russell and Hawley, 1981, p. 165], but it is undeniable that many large city public school systems are now too "black" to be integrated successfully. Boston's system, for example, has changed from 64 percent white in 1970 to only 30 percent white in 1983 [Harbison, 1983].

WELFARE AND SOCIAL LEGISLATION.   While America's white poor outnumber its minority poor, the *proportion* of poor persons is far higher among most nonwhite minorities. Welfare programs and social legislation affecting the poor will disproportionately affect minorities. Prime examples include AFDC (Aid to Families with Dependent Children), food stamps, Medicaid, public housing programs, and minimum-wage laws. While more whites than nonwhites are affected by these programs, a much higher *percentage* of all nonwhites is affected. There is some dispute about whether the effects are always beneficial, as discussed later in this chapter.

SEPARATISM AND TERRITORIALLY BASED MINORITIES

Most examples of cultural pluralism are found in countries where each ethnic group is concentrated in a particular territory. In Canada the French are centered in Quebec; in each of the fifteen republics of the Soviet Union, a single ethnic group is generally dominant; most of the cantons of the Swiss Confederation are composed principally of one of three nationalities—German, French, or Italian. But in the United States, each immigrant group was generally scattered rather than concentrated in a single region, and this favored assimilation and integration rather than cultural pluralism. The two major ethnic groups in the United States which do have somewhat of a territorial base—the native Americans and the Hispanic-Americans—have shown considerable resistance to assimilation.

The Native Americans

The native Americans are commonly called "Indians," as Christopher Columbus called them—his greatest mistake. In agriculture at least, Europeans assimilated Indian culture rather than the reverse. Much of the success of the European colonization was due to the colonists' adoption of the planting of corn, potatoes, tobacco, peanuts, cocoa, and several other crops. But conflict soon developed, and the colonists adopted a policy of genocide which exterminated most of the coastal and Eastern woodlands tribes. After genocide became unfashionable the surviving Indians were herded onto reservations provided by treaties, most of which the whites eventually violated.

In 1934 anthropologist John Collier became Commissioner of Indian Affairs and reversed the historic policy of encouraging tribes to disband and assimilate. He proposed that the Indians be assisted to survive as tribal units and preserve their tribal culture [Wax, 1971, p. 57]. Government policy since then has wavered between (1) promoting relocation in cities, (2) subsidizing the reservations with a wide variety of welfare programs, and (3) turning over power to tribal councils to develop reservation resources [Taylor, 1982].

Indians have known both social mobility and pervasive social disorganization. Many Indians have made distinguished careers in the arts, government, and business and are similar to other Americans in culture and life-style. Others (such as the Apache) live on reservations where efficient tribal leadership and rich mineral resources have brought them at least a degree of prosperity [MacDougall, 1982]. Still others live in bitter poverty with higher rates of alcoholism and suicide than other ethnic groups. Since Indian reservations are heavily dependent on government programs, budget cuts in these programs in the 1980s brought major problems. Unemployment was estimated at 37 percent in 1982 [Taylor, 1982].

In numbers, Indians appear to be increasing. The figures cannot be taken at face value, since census definitions and enumeration practices have often changed, yet the recorded Indian population grew from about a ¼ million in 1890 to nearly 1½ million in 1980 [U.S. Bureau of the Census, 1981c, p. 3].

While only 10 percent of the Indians were urban in 1930, 50 percent now live in cities [Deloria, 1981, p. 148]. Some hold well-paid jobs, while others survive on casual employment and welfare in urban slums. Some Indians cling to their tribal culture and, in 1970, one-third (varying from 76 percent in Arizona to 13 percent in Washington) gave an Indian language as the mother tongue

American Indians are divided upon the issue of assimilation versus cultural pluralism.

[Feagin, 1978, p. 221]. Other Indians regard their tribal background as only a dim memory, and more than one-third of Indian men have white wives [Gundlach et al., 1977, p. 465].

In the 1960s, a spirit of militant activism arose, somewhat similar to the Black Power movement among black Americans, urging that Indians reject "Euroconformity" and preserve Indian language, crafts, and religion and demanding that Indians control their own schools and economic life [Steiner, 1968, pp. 268–289; Wax, 1971, p. 176]. The image of Indians as a broken people, demoralized by helplessness and powerlessness is no longer true [Trimble, 1974]. The new Indian militance includes a trend toward increasing litigiousness, which has increased Indian power and brought them into sharp conflict with neighboring whites. Treaties upholding perpetual fishing rights have been held to exempt Indians from game laws applying to the rest of the population. Indians have won many millions of dollars in court actions. Many tribes are demanding that millions of square miles of land be returned to them.

Of all ethnic groups in the United States, Indians are the most divided on the issue of cultural pluralism versus assimilation. The larger society beckons, and its opportunities are increasingly available. Yet Indians who live in cities and work as other Americans still identify with their tribes and return to the reservation for periodic festivities. Many Indian youth are torn between the attraction of a career in the larger society and a feeling that duty demands they return "home" and work to uplift their people.

Wherever Europeans have conquered a native population and colonized their territory, the native culture has generally been seriously disrupted but the native population has not been admitted into participation in European culture. This leaves them in a cultural vacuum—unable to practice either their own traditional culture or the new European culture. The concept of *marginality* applies to

Native Americans have become militant in asserting their claims. (*Paolo Koch/Photo Researchers, Inc.*)

many American Indians. This concept, first proposed by Park [1928, p. 892] and developed by Stonequist [1937], describes the person who is on the margin of two cultures and two societies, partly assimilated into both and fully assimilated into neither. The frequent result is demoralization, alcoholism, disease, and suicide, with continuing hostility between the native people and the invaders. Occasionally, Europeans made paternalistic efforts to "take care of" the native population, and often, these efforts were equally demoralizing in effect. Social scientists are today trying to use their understanding of culture to promote more constructive relationships, but this is no easy task.

It is likely that by the year 2000 Hispanics may be America's largest ethnic minority. (© *Jim Anderson, 1980/Woodfin Camp & Assoc.*)

The Hispanic-Americans

America's second largest minority is Hispanic, numbering (officially) about 14.6 million, 6.4 percent of the population, in 1981. Since many illegal immigrants escape census count, the true number is considerably higher. The Hispanics are growing rapidly through natural increase and immigration and may be our largest minority by the year 2000 by one estimate [*Time*, 110:48, Oct. 16, 1978] or by 2020 by another [Davis, 1982]. Accurate prediction is impossible, since it is unknown how much immigration will be permitted.

MEXICAN-AMERICANS. Four-fifths of America's 8 million or more Mexican-Americans live in the Southwestern states which were taken from Mexico in 1848. The Mexicans were already established in village communities before the "Anglos" arrived, smugly contemptuous of everything Mexican in their own racial, religious, and cultural ethnocentrism. The Anglos could not care less whether the Mexicans sought assimilation or preserved their ancestral culture. The result was a cultural pluralism with few cross-cultural contacts.

While much of the traditional Mexican culture survived, the Mexicans lost most of their land to the Anglos [Feagin, 1978, p. 299]. The ancient Spanish land grants, sometimes lost and often accompanied by incomplete records, were promptly set aside by Anglo courts, presided over by Anglo judges interpreting newly enacted Anglo land laws before Anglo juries. Again, patterns of discrimination arose, with the usual dreary consequences. Today, Mexican-Americans hold little agricultural land and are heavily dependent on low-paid wage labor.

While some Mexican-Americans have achieved education and prosperity, others are powerless and alienated. Today, some reject assimilation and integration in favor of separatism and militant protest. The term *Chicano* is sometimes applied to all Mexican-Americans and sometimes only to the activist ones, while *Chicanismo* is a protest against the "cultural genocide" which they feel has destroyed their appreciation of their Mexican heritage [Moore and Pachon, 1976, pp. 151–154]. They stress group social values over individual achievement and recommend confrontation and disruption when ordinary political action fails. While "race" is perhaps an inaccurate term to apply to Mexicans, there is much rhetoric of race pride and of *la raza,* a term which refers to Mexican cultural heritage rather than to race.

The Chicano movement discourages assimilation and encourages cultural pluralism. The future is unclear. The Mexican-Americans are closing the education gap. The median years of school completed by Mexican-Americans over 25 years old is only 8.5, but for those between 20 and 24, the median is 12.2 [Brown et al., 1980, p. 102]. For the entire American population, there is less than one year difference between age groups in years of school completed [*Statistical Abstract*, 1981, p. 142]; thus the large difference in the years of school completed by younger and older Mexican-Americans show rapid educational gains. Assimilationists argue that Mexican-Americans are following the assimilationist pattern of other minorities. The children are learning English, intermarriage is increasing, the Mexican-Americans are slowly scattering, and there is increasing social mobility. Cultural pluralists, however, argue that migration from Mexico will preserve their heavy concentration in the Southwest and that most of the immigrants (along with many residents) are poor, uneducated, and Spanish-speaking, with many relatives, cultural contacts, and reasons to visit across the border—all of which discourage assimilation and promote separatism. Whether immigration remains high or low may determine the outcome of the debate between assimilation and cultural pluralism.

CUBAN-AMERICANS.   There are over a million persons of Cuban ancestry living in the United States, heavily concentrated in the Miami area of Florida. One major wave of immigration followed the overthrow of the dictatorship of Fulgencio Batista in 1959 by revolutionaries led by Fidel Castro. Castro's harsh Marxist dictatorship helped the poor but was a disaster for the middle and upper classes, whom Castro may have been willing to lose. Most of the landowners, businessmen, professionals, and government workers fled in what has been called "the biggest brain drain in the Western Hemisphere" [Cue and Bach, 1976, p. 22]. Most of these immigrants arrived with no money and no credentials recognized in the United States, but they *did* bring a personal history of work, education, self-confidence, and success. Many already spoke English, and some had American business connections. Their children did well in school, were rarely truant or delinquent, and showed high morale and self-esteem. Any such group will show high mobility in an open class society. Within slightly over one decade, national magazines were writing about the re-

markable "success story" of Cubans in the United States [e.g., *Nation's Business*, 60:78–80, March 1972].

A second wave of about 123,000 arrived within a very few months in 1979. Fewer than 10 percent of this wave had middle- or upper-class backgrounds. The majority were working-class, uneducated, non-English-speaking, and destitute. There were press reports that Castro "emptied out the jails" and dumped "the dregs of society" upon us. Since only 800 (of 123,000) were found to have criminal records, such charges were greatly exaggerated.[2] Most settled in the Miami area, where relocation facilities were swamped by the sudden influx and some unpleasant incidents developed. Having fewer personal resources than the first wave, their entry into the mainstream of the American economy will be less rapid and complete [Bach, 1980].

PUERTO-RICAN AMERICANS.   The Puerto Ricans are not technically "immigrants," since Puerto Rico is an American Commonwealth and Puerto Ricans can enter and leave the United States at will. About 1.7 million Puerto Ricans lived in the United States in 1980 [U.S. Bureau of the Census, 1981a, p. 1], most having arrived since World War II. Most have relatives in Puerto Rico, and there is a good deal of moving back and forth. Since residents of Puerto Rico pay no American income tax but receive all American health and welfare benefits, their poverty is less extreme than that of many other people.

Many of the Puerto Rican people are poor. Although the family in Puerto Rico is a close-knit extended-family unit, the Puerto Rican family in the United States shows the destabilizing effects of poverty and welfare dependency [Cordasco, 1973, p. 69]. Although the average income of all "Spanish-origin" families is about $3,000 above that of black families in the United States, that for Puerto

[2] The number found on the initial screening was 800. Subsequent investigation resulted in the detention of a total of 2,400, but the exact number with criminal records is still uncertain.

Rican families is below that for black families [Cordasco, 1973, p. 91]. It was partly upon his observations of Puerto Rican families that Oscar Lewis based his ''culture of poverty'' concept [Lewis, 1966*a*].

These brief sketches of 4 American ethnic groups leave 102 more upon which we lack space to comment. Not all are poor; some are above the national average in income. Many others share similar problems of poverty, discrimination, and assimilation difficulties. Many ethnic subcultures are being weakened by assimilation and intermarriage, but the sense of ethnic origins is not disappearing. In fact, success and acceptance seem only to intensify an ethnic group's desire to preserve its ethnic identity [Nagel and Olzak, 1982].

MINORITY MOBILITY IN THE UNITED STATES

Nearly all minorities entered the United States as poor immigrants. Some minorities have been more successful than others in upward mobility. Jews are an often mentioned example. Poles and Italians also climbed more rapidly than is generally recognized and are now among those ethnic groups with the highest average incomes [Greeley, 1976].

Sometimes it is claimed that such mobility is possible for Caucasians and not possible for nonwhites because of their visibility. The Japanese Americans challenge this claim. The Japanese came to the United States as agricultural laborers without money, connec-

During World War II Japanese-Americans were forcibly removed from their homes and placed in detention camps. (*Library of Congress*)

tions, legal protection, or a knowledge of English. For many years they were the butt of prejudice and intense discrimination. During World War II, they were considered a danger to the country and those on the U.S. mainland were forcibly removed from their homes and placed in detention centers. Virtually destitute at the end of the war, they made spectacular progress within a generation. They not only established an impressive record in California farming but were doing well in business and the professions. They have low rates of crime and mental illness [Kitano, 1976, p. 2]. As early as 1960, life expectancy of the Japanese in California was six years longer than for whites and ten years longer than for blacks [Hechter and Borhani, 1965]. The proportion of their young people in college is greater than the national average and their median income is higher than that of Caucasians. In fact, the Japanese have been so successful that they are somewhat embarrassed at being depicted as a "model minority" and sometimes seek to identify with less successful elements in American society [Kitano, 1976, p. 133]. There is a tendency to minimize the extent of their success, although one sociologist maintains that, were there no discrimination, the Japanese would have achieved even greater success because of their high educational achievement [Woodrum, 1981].

Other Asian minorities, such as those of Korean, Indian, and Filipino ancestry, also have prospered, and 1980 census reports indicate their median family income was $22,075 per year compared to $20,840 for whites [*United Press International*, April 26, 1982]. Recent Asian immigrants included highly educated professionals who moved quickly into well-paid positions. The "average" economic success of these groups masks many cases of individual poverty and frustration. Sometimes, economic activities have led to conflict. For instance, Vietnamese fishers in Texas found that their Anglo competitors burned their boats and attempted to

keep them out of the industry [Hunter, 1981]. The Vietnamese were eventually protected by court action, but the incident does illustrate that minority ethnic groups may be seen as unwelcome competitors.

Nor does economic success necessarily mean a painless accommodation to American society. Asian immigrants may remain marginal, finding it difficult either to be completely assimilated or to maintain their traditional culture. This is illustrated by the mixed reaction to former Senator Hayakawa of California. Some Asian-Americans thought of him as one of theirs who had made good, while others regarded him as a hopeless reactionary who had sold out to white society [Wilson and Hosakawa, 1980, p. 292].

Similarity in Minority Mobility

For some years, an argument has raged over whether blacks are repeating the mobility patterns of earlier Europeans immigrants or whether the black situation is unique [Hunt and Walker, 1979, pp. 346–349]. Some argue that blacks remain poor after many generations in America and claim that race discrimination has made the European immigrant model inapplicable to black Americans. They see blacks as victims of "internal colonialism" which has prevented any important black gains [Blauner, 1971, p. 236]. The differences between European immigrants and blacks before the 1964 Civil Rights Act have been adequately documented [Lieberson, 1980]. Many European and Asian immigrant groups also suffered discrimination, although in most cases it was not as intense, as firmly embedded in law, or as long lasting as discrimination against blacks. The question is: now that discrimination against blacks has eased, are they moving forward like earlier immigrant groups?

Supporters of the immigrant analogy claim that this is happening and that the recent experience of blacks resembles that of other immigrant groups [Glazer, 1971]. Most of the characteristics of inner-city blacks today were also true of many non-English immigrant groups earlier in the century. Even the black-white IQ difference (averaging about fifteen points) is similar to that between immigrant children and children of native-born parents earlier in the century.

> Extensive I.Q. data are available on white ethnic minorities around the time of World War I and in the 1920's. . . . The various data sources all led to the same conclusion: The European immigrant I.Q.'s then were virtually identical to black I.Q.'s now. What is encouraging is that the low-I.Q. immigrant groups of the past now have I.Q.'s at or above U.S. average. . . . European ancestry has not meant high I.Q.'s nor has non-European ancestry meant low I.Q.'s. The I.Q. average has varied widely with time, place and the circumstance of the groups tested. For groups with upward mobility, there has been a marked rise in I.Q.'s over time. The average I.Q.'s of Italian-Americans and Polish-Americans have risen by 20 to 25 points from the time of the surveys conducted around World War I to the surveys conducted in the 1970's. This rise is greater than the current I.Q. difference—about 15 points—between blacks and whites. (Thomas Sowell, "New Light on Black I.Q.," *The New York Times Magazine,* March 27, 1977. © 1976/1977 by The New York Times Company. Reprinted by permission.)

There is also the fact—distressing to believers in innate white superiority—that Asian children often make *higher* average IQ scores than native white Americans. Japanese children, for example, score higher than white American children by an average of eleven IQ points according to one study [Lynn, 1982] and by six points according to another [Flynn, 1983]. Most social scientists agree that the IQ is not a reliable measure of the native abilities of groups who differ in cultural background. Most social scientists agree in assuming that all racial and ethnic groups are equal in the inheritance of everything that is important for behavior and learning. It is reasonable to assume that the black-white IQ difference will

disappear with the advent of better jobs, better schools, and better housing—just as it did for the European immigrant groups earlier in this century.

Black Mobility

Blacks in the United States have had both gains and losses since the end of slavery. They made modest gains in education and land ownership, but took losses in occupational status. Before the Civil War, many of the skilled workers of the South were black slaves, but blacks were driven from all but menial work within a generation after the Civil War ended [Horton and Leslie, 1981, p. 323]. Black migration from the South accelerated after World War I, but except for a tiny black middle and upper class, most blacks were poor, propertyless, poorly educated, and unskilled, and they had no realistic prospect of upward mobility [Myrdal, 1944, chap. 9 and appendix 6]. Even as late as 1960, black college graduates could seldom find jobs except as teachers or preachers, and the lifetime earnings of black college graduates were averaging the same as those of whites with only an eighth-grade education [Horton and Leslie, 1965, p. 404]. A full recital of the facts of discrimination and inequality would fill the rest of this textbook.

History offers few examples of a group making as rapid gains as those of American blacks in recent decades, some of which are shown in Figures 16-2 and 16-3. Average earnings per worker have risen from about 50 percent of average white earnings in 1949 [Freeman, 1981, p. 251] to about 70 percent in 1976. Where earlier generations of blacks found that education did not bring higher earnings, each year of added education now brings even greater income gains to blacks than to whites [Kilson, 1981, p. 67]. By 1978, earnings of young black college graduates even exceeded those of comparable whites: $15,217 for black male graduates aged 25 to 29 and $14,013 for comparable whites, while

Many American blacks are now middle-class, with attitudes and life-styles very similar to those of other middle-class persons. (*Ron Engh/ Photo Researchers, Inc.*)

for females the corresponding figures are $9,038 for blacks and $9,012 for whites [U.S. Bureau of the Census, 1980*b*, pp. 224–225]. Blacks now hold over 15 percent of all federal government jobs [*Statistical Abstract*, 1981, p. 394]. Table 16-5 shows impressive political gains for blacks, but also shows that blacks still hold far less than their proportionate share of elective offices. Almost everywhere the picture is the same—blacks have made impressive gains, but they are still short of full equality.

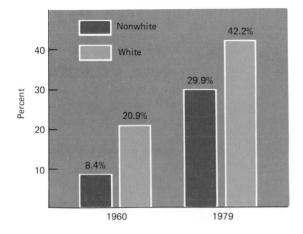

FIGURE 16-2 Percentage of white and nonwhite families with middle- or upper-class incomes. All families having an income of over $20,000 a year in 1979 dollars are considered as having middle- or upper-class incomes. (*Source:* Statistical Abstract of the United States, *1981, table 775, p. 435.*)

While the percentage of middle- and upper-income whites still exceeds that of nonwhites, the nonwhite proportion in 1979 passed the white proportion in 1960 and more than tripled in the twenty-year period. Do you think this would have happened without the passage of civil rights legislation in the 1960s?

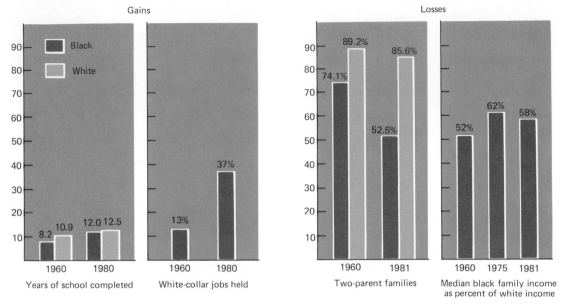

FIGURE 16-3   Black gains and losses since 1960. (*Source:* U.S. News & World
Report, *117:63, March 1, 1982, and U.S. Bureau of the Census, "Household and
Family Characteristics, March 1981," Population Characteristics, ser. P-201, no.
327, 1982.*)

Are there any figures in this graph which would explain the decline of black
family income as a percent of white family income?

TABLE 16-5
BLACK ELECTED OFFICIALS IN THE UNITED STATES, 1970 AND 1980

Elective offices	OFFICES HELD BY BLACKS		Percent increase 1970–1980	Number of such offices in U.S.	Percent held by blacks, 1980
	1970	1980			
U.S. and state legislatures	182	326	79	7,949	4.1
City and county	715	2,832	296	196,939	1.4
Law enforcement (judges, sheriffs)	213	526	147	*	*
Education (college boards, school boards)	362	1,206	233	87,062	1.4
Total	1,472	4,890	232	*	*

*Not available.
Source: Statistical Abstract of the United States, 1981, pp. 493–495.

Blacks now form about 11.7 percent of the American population. For the three categories of office shown
in the right column, how greatly would black officeholders need to increase to be proportionately represented?

The Underclass

The underclass is not entirely black. It includes many members of other minorities and many white people [Auletta, 1982]. The black underclass is, however, the most visible. Many American blacks feel that progress has passed them by, and some showed this eloquently in the Miami riots of 1980. Miami is a pleasant city where two-thirds of the black population held white-collar or well-paid blue-collar jobs [Kilson, 1981, p. 59]. For the others, Miami was a place of frustration. When police incidents touched off riots, smoldering resentment turned to violence, looting, burning, injury, and death. Both black and white businesses were burned and looted, with resentment directed against the more successful Hispanics and blacks as well as whites [Whitman, 1980].

Those left out of recent gains form the "black underclass." Their welfare payments have grown in recent decades, but unemployment among black youths has also grown to more than twice white rates, as shown in

Figure 16-4. The black poverty rate of 15 percent in 1980 would be doubled if transfer payments were not included [Smeeding, 1982, p. 101].

This growing black unemployment is part of the reason for the growth of the black underclass. Unskilled and semiskilled jobs have been leaving the central cities for the suburbs and small towns. For example, 138,000 blue-collar jobs left Chicago during the 1970s [Herbers, 1983]. Unskilled blacks cannot follow because of housing costs and lack of public transport geared to daily work in the suburbs (topic treated in more detail on pp. 471–472). Unemployment feeds on itself. The longer a young person remains unemployed, the poorer become his or her chances of ever getting and holding a job. With each additional year of unemployment, the lack of a "job history" makes one less and less employable. Meanwhile, the longer one lives on welfare and "hustling" (petty crime, drug selling, and various kinds of "con" games outlined in Liebow's *Talley's Corner* [1967]), the less likely one is to develop work habits

FIGURE 16-4 Black and white youth unemployment, 1954–1989. (*Source: U.S. Department of Labor, Bureau of Labor Statistics.*)

Why, despite civil rights legislation and affirmative action programs, has the black unemployment gap increased?

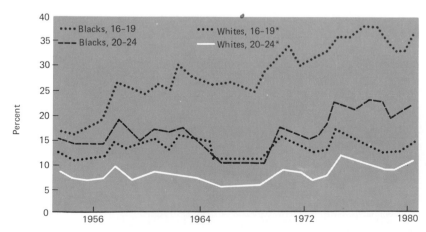

*Includes Hispanic Americans

which help in finding and holding a job. Thus the black underclass survives and grows.

The other major cause of the growth of the black underclass is the one-parent family, whose many disabilities were discussed in Chapter 10 and need not be repeated here. In 1950, only about one in six (17 percent) black families were female-headed [Moynihan, 1965*b*]. By 1981, they had grown to nearly half (47.5 percent), as compared with one in seven (14.7 percent) for white families [U.S. Bureau of the Census, 1982*a*]. In 1980, some 82 percent of all white children and only 42 percent of all black children lived with two parents. [*Statistical Abstract*, 1981, p. 49]. It is primarily this growth of female-headed families which has held the average income of black households at about 60 percent of white households [*Statistical Abstract*, 1975, p. 398; 1981, p. 432], even though individual black earnings were coming closer to those of whites. The ratio of black to white median income for male-headed households increased from 72 percent to 80 percent during the same period [Gershman, 1980, p. 98], but while married-couple black families averaged $19,368 in money income in 1981, female-headed black families averaged only $7,921 [U.S. Bureau of the Census, 1983, p. 23]. Thus, the increase in female-headed black families canceled out the improvement in black earnings by dividing them into a larger number of smaller packages.

Labor-market discrimination against blacks and other minorities has not ended, and some scholars consider it still responsible for most earnings differences [Masters, 1975]. However, discrimination has declined in recent decades and cannot be held responsible for the *growth* of the black underclass. The continuing growth of the black underclass means that there is not one black society but two: one vigorous and prospering and the other stagnant and impoverished.

FIGURE 16-5   Percentage of one-parent, female-headed families. (*Source: Statistical Abstract of the United States, 1981, p. 48, and U.S. Bureau of the Census, "Household and Family Characteristics, March 1981,"* Population Characteristics, *ser. P-20, no. 327, 1982.*)

How does the proportion of female-headed families in a population affect its average family income?

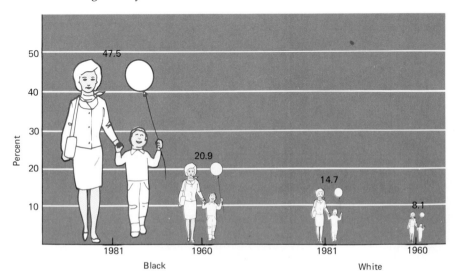

REVISIONIST THOUGHT ON MINORITY POLICIES

Since at least the mid-1960s, most of the writers on ethnic topics have shared what might be called the prevailing "orthodoxy." This orthodoxy, meaning the accepted point of view, has four main points. First, the principal problem of minority ethnic groups is discrimination. Second, the "ghetto" subculture is a constructive ethnic development. Third, the principal problem internal to the ethnic group is a lack of group pride. Finally, the way to solve these problems is through government programs countering discrimination, strengthening group pride, and improving immediate economic status through welfare.

In recent years, a number of ethnic scholars have emerged whom we will call the "revisionists," since they question the prevailing orthodoxy. The revisionists are mostly young to middle-aged; they are well-educated, and some hold academic positions. They do not agree with each other on all points, and some might reject the label, but they are included because they question one or more of the ethnic policies which had come to be taken pretty much for granted in the last two decades. In general, they feel that ghetto culture is a handicap, that welfare and civil rights measures are often counterproductive, and that factors affecting minority mobility are the same as those affecting the majority group.

Gordon Morgan [1981], for instance, considers ethnic pluralism a trap which means separation and inequality. He sees the emphasis on ethnic group identity as divisive and "black English" as a handicap to minority advance. Similarly, Richard Rodriguez [1981], attacks bilingual education as delaying assimilation. Even though assimilation may be painful, he sees it as necessary for success in American society. William Wilson [1981] claims that emphasis upon ethnic separatism and group pride helps to lock blacks in the underclass. He believes that the problems of

blacks are those of social class rather than race [1978]. This position is supported by at least one research study claiming that only 3 percent of the variance in black occupational structure from the national average could be accounted for by race discrimination [Lyon et al., 1982, p. 532]. Contrary to ethnic spokesmen and -women who attacked Moynihan [1965b] when he held family instability responsible for many black difficulties, most of the revisionists recognize the one-parent family as a major handicap. Wilson [1981] views the growth of the female-headed family as the main reason for the recent drop in black-white income ratios (that is, in the ratio of black family income to white family income).

Among those most critical of the prevailing ethnic orthodoxy are economists Thomas Sowell, Andrew Brimmer, and Walter Williams. They see affirmative action as a threat to black self-esteem, welfare programs as an inducement to avoid work, and the minimum wage as a denial of opportunity to youth. Their opposition to minimum-wage laws is based on the premise that black youth, denied a chance to work for lower wages, are kept out of any employment at all and, therefore, never learn work skills or get a toehold in the occupational world [Williams, 1981]. Most revisionists agree with Sowell that "a number of government programs—notably the minimum wage laws—have made it more difficult for blacks to find jobs and other government programs—notably welfare—have made it less necessary" [1981a, p. 223].

Busing for school desegregation is viewed as, at best, a waste of money and, at worst, a menace to education. Sowell [1976a] argues that desegregation has destroyed some schools which were doing an excellent job with black students. Columnist William Raspberry criticizes busing in his "Busing—Is It Worth the Ride?" [Raspberry, 1974].

The revisionist-orthodox argument returns to the question of whether the current situation of blacks is similar to that of the European immigrants two generations ago. The orthodox view holds that the black situation is different because continued discrimination and economic changes make it harder for the unskilled worker to advance. Most European immigrants arrived when the demand for unskilled labor was rapidly growing, while today, blacks compete in a shrinking market for unskilled labor. The revisionists claim that the black and immigrant situations would be similar if black adjustment had not been handicapped by well-meaning but counter-productive civil rights and welfare measures.

The revisionists have, in turn, been sharply attacked by defenders of the orthodox position [Willie, 1978; Clark, 1980; Oliver and Glick, 1982]. While not in complete agreement, they emphasize two main points: (1) that minorities have made real gains, which are due to the orthodox policies, and (2) remaining black poverty is due to remaining discrimination; therefore, the policies of the past two decades are still necessary and should be supported, not undermined.

The orthodox view is based upon conflict theory, seeing minority problems as mainly due to discrimination and exploitation. Supporters of this view see mobilizing minority protest as the road to mobility. They argue that recent gains by blacks in public accom-modations, housing, voting registration, college enrollment, and entry into skilled and professional job markets would not have happened without firm enforcement of civil rights legislation. They concede that earlier reports on the effects of school desegregation and busing for racial balance were inconclusive but claim that more recent studies clearly show undeniable long-term gains [Daniels, 1983, p. 97]. As for voluntary action versus government compulsion, they claim that only two school systems in the entire country desegregated without the threat of court action [Daniels, 1983, p. 97]. They see energetic government programs as necessary to prevent a revival of discrimination and to relieve continuing minority poverty and powerlessness. The revisionist position is seen as a sophisticated excuse for gutting the policies needed to continue minority advance.

The revisionists are closer to the functionalist approach. They view remaining minority difficulties as more deeply rooted in minority life-styles than in continuing discrimination. They feel that efforts to provide equal opportunity will be more beneficial than preferential treatment for minorities, and that assimilation will be more productive than separation and conflict.

SOUTH AFRICA'S NEED FOR MORE BLACK MANAGERS

There are simply not enough white managers around to support an economy that grew at 8% last year and is still burgeoning at a minimum 5% annual rate.

U.S. companies, which have the added impetus of pressure from "liberal" groups at home, have been in the forefront of efforts to train blacks (for management positions). But neither businessmen nor black leaders claim that the movement stems from moral or humanitarian reasons . . . Windsor H. Shuenyane, whose position as manager of community affairs at South African Breweries places him among the 0.2% of black workers who are currently in management spots, says coldly: "The context of economic pressure means a lot of jobs have opened to blacks. It is a change of circumstances—change of heart has had nothing to do with it."

Source: *Business Week*, June 8, 1981, p. 78.

Does this support functional or conflict theory of change? Or both? Does it support the orthodox or revisionist view of how minorities advance?

Since the passage of the Civil Rights Acts of the 1960s, the federal government has generally followed policies of strict enforcement, in accord with the orthodox view. With the Reagan administration, federal policy shifted to the revisionist view. The Reagan administration sought to limit busing for racial balance, allowed the idea to spread among employers that the federal government would not demand strict enforcement of equal-opportunity rulings [Greenberger, 1982], and issued new rules ordering employers to reduce affirmative action goals [Greenberger, 1983]. It has been accused by the Chairman of the U.S. Civil Rights Commission of "undermining our ability" to monitor enforcement of federal civil rights laws [Pear, 1983]. Seldom in history has a new national administration made so drastic a change in strategy for dealing with a social problem.

This brief outline oversimplifies many subtle aspects of ethnic problems and obscures many agreements among scholars upon ethnic policies. Although we have no recent data, your authors are of the opinion that many sociologists would support most points of the orthodox view and reject most of the revisionist ideas, and most of the "revisionist" scholars cited in this chapter are not sociologists. But there is no sure way to predict the outcome of a social policy, and honest scholars may disagree. Neither is there any sure way to isolate and measure the effects of one policy, separating them from the effects of other policies and forces that are in operation at the same time. In race and ethnic relations, as in all social problems, social policy and social programs contain large elements of hope and guesswork.

SUMMARY

A *race* is defined either as a group of people who share common physical characteristics or as a group whose boundaries are set by social definition, with no common agreement on usage. Race differences are biologically trivial but culturally important. The term *ethnic* includes not only racial groups but also other groups of common ancestry whose link is religion, language, nationality, territorial origin, or a combination of one or more of these. Different ethnic groups often exist within the same national boundaries.

Amalgamation is the biological interbreeding of racial stocks. *Assimilation* is the mutual cultural diffusion through which persons or groups come to share a common culture. *Prejudice* is a "prejudging" in which persons are treated according to the image of their group instead of according to their personal characteristics. *Discrimination* is the unequal treatment of people according to stereotyped views of them. We used to believe that prejudice caused discrimination; now we believe the opposite; discrimination creates prejudices. *Genocide* is an attempt to exterminate a people, often attempted in history but seldom completely successful.

Ethnic policy in the United States has followed several courses: (1) seeking *integration* through protecting equal individual rights; (2) protecting group rights through (*a*) *separatism* or (*b*) *cultural pluralism*, neither of which has been highly successful. Recent policy ventures include (1) *bilingual instruction,* which is of doubtful aid in learning English but helps preserve non-English language and ethnic identity; (2) *affirmative action,* which seeks, with limited success, to guarantee a group's proportionate share of desired positions, (3) *busing* for racial balance, whose effects upon racial antagonisms and upon black learning are sharply disputed, and (4) *social legislation* intended to reduce racial inequalities.

American minorities also include American Indians and Hispanic-Americans, groups which have somewhat of a territorial base and are more accepting of cultural pluralism. Some minorities, including most Europeans and Asians, have been highly mobile in the United States; others have been less mobile. The United States may be developing a growing

414

Social
Stratification

and permanent *black underclass* which does not share the recent mobility of black Americans.

The "orthodox" school of ethnic relations sees discrimination as the main problem, defends ghetto culture, lauds group pride, and advocates government action to stop discrimination, strengthen cultural pluralism, and extend welfare benefits. An opposing "revisionist" school views ghetto culture as a handicap, feels discrimination is no longer the major problem, and finds some government programs to be counterproductive.

GLOSSARY

affirmative action   programs requiring the active recruitment, hiring, and promotion of minority members.

amalgamation   biological interbreeding of racial groups until they become one stock.

assimilation   the fusion of two or more cultures so that they become one.

black underclass   poor blacks who have not shared in the upward mobility of other black Americans.

Chicano   an American of Mexican ancestry who has a strong sense of Mexican identity and resists assimilation.

cultural pluralism   toleration of cultural differences within a common society; allowing different groups to retain their distinctive cultures.

discrimination   a practice that treats equal people unequally; limiting opportunity or reward according to race, religion, or ethnic group.

ethnic group   a number of people with a common racial and cultural heritage which sets them apart from others.

genocide   a deliberate effort to eliminate an ethnic group by slaughter, expulsion, or destruction of the group's cultural heritage.

integration   condition where all racial and ethnic groups can share equally in economic and cultural life of a society.

marginality   being partly assimilated to each of two cultures and two societies and fully assimilated to neither.

orthodox   adhering to established doctrines. In this chapter, the policies of the civil rights movement.

prejudice   a bias for or against a person or group. Implies prejudging, or deciding without having sufficient facts available.

race   a group of people somewhat different from other people in a combination of inherited physical characteristics, but the meaning of the term is also substantially determined by popular social definition.

revisionist   one who favors a new interpretation of established views. In this chapter, rejection of policies of the civil rights movement.

separatism   withdrawal from contact with the dominant majority by groups which have suffered past discrimination and wish to build a separate social and economic life.

QUESTIONS
AND PROJECTS

1   Why is the term "ethnic" used in preference to "race" throughout most of this chapter?

2   What are the arguments for and against bilingual education?

3   The United States government has supported a program for relocating American Indians from their reservations to cities. What are the arguments for and against such a program?

4   Will increasing intermarriage merge all American ethnic groups? If so, is this desirable?

5   If all ethnic discrimination were ended, would all groups produce equal proportions of successful people in all occupations?

6   Read the article in the Suggested Readings by Irving Louis Horowitz. Do you know of any instances of genocide besides the ones mentioned? Do you feel that the Nazi Holocaust was unique, or is it one of several such occurrences?

7   Does your campus have a program of affirmative action? If so, interview the person in charge. To what extent does it apply to ethnic groups as contrasted to women and others? What costs and benefits seem to be involved in the program?

8 Should the United States shift to a policy of cultural pluralism similar to that in Canada, Belgium, and Switzerland? Why or why not?

9 Read the articles by Carl A. Gershman and Kenneth B. Clark in the Suggested Readings. Which one do you think makes the best case on race versus class as the basic factor in black mobility?

10 Read any of the chapters in the book by Rhoda Goldstein Blumberg and Wendell James Roye (eds.) listed in the Suggested Readings. Indicate whether or not you are acquainted with instances of interracial cooperation and describe how they worked out.

SUGGESTED READINGS

"Black Women–White Men: The Other Mixed Marriages Are Small but Growing," *Ebony*, 38:81–82, August 1982. A brief descriptive article discussing the adjustment of the black women in a mixed marriage.

*Blumberg, Rhoda Goldstein and Wendell James Roye (eds.): *Interracial Bonds*, General Hall, Inc., Bayside, N.Y., 1979. Several studies of situations in which members of different ethnic groups cooperate in joint activities, ranging from "white" Indians to interracial adoption.

Gershman, Carl A.: "A Matter of Class"; and Kenneth B. Clark, "Kenneth B. Clark Responds: The Role of Race," *The New York Times Magazine*, Oct. 5, 1980, pp. 22ff, reprinted in *Current*, 227:20–32 and 43–44, November 1980. The two argue whether class has displaced race as the most important factor affecting blacks. Gershman supports revisionist views, and Clark defends orthodox racial policies.

Gordon, Milton (ed.): "America as a Multicultural Society," *Annals of the American Academy of Political Science*, no. 454, March 1981. An issue on ethnicity, with articles on many ethnic groups and issues.

Horowitz, Irving Louis: "Many Genocides, One Holocaust? The Limits of the Rights of States and the Obligations of Individuals," *Modern Judaism*, 1:74–89, 1981. Tells how such cruelties have happened and still may happen to other peoples.

*Lieberson, Stanley: *A Piece of the Pie: Black and White Immigrants Since 1880*, University of California Press, Berkeley, 1980. A comparison of black and white immigrants, finding that conflict was due to economic competition rather than racial prejudice.

Oliver, Melvin L. and Mark A. Glick: "An Analysis of the New Orthodoxy on Black Mobility," *Social Problems*, 29:511–523, June, 1982. Maintains that discrimination is still the prime cause of black-white occupational and income differences. (Uses "orthodoxy" in the opposite sense than this textbook does.)

Rockett, Rocky L.: *Ethnic Nationalities in the Soviet Union*, Praeger Publishers, New York, 1981. Describes cultural pluralism in the Soviet Union, where half the people are non-Russian.

Rodriguez, Richard: *Hunger of Memory*, Godine Publishers, Boston, 1982. A largely autobiographical account of the costs and benefits of moving from the Mexican-American culture into the mainstream of American society.

Snyder, Mark: "Self-Fulfilling Stereotypes," *Psychology Today*, 16:60–68, July 1982. A readable article telling how ethnic stereotypes arise and are maintained.

Sowell, Thomas: *Ethnic America: A History*, Basic Books, Inc., Publishers, New York, 1981. A readable book which seeks to explain why some ethnic groups in the U.S. advanced faster and farther than others.

Sowell Thomas et al., (eds.): *The Fairmont Papers: Black Alternatives Conference*, Institute for Contemporary Studies, San Francisco, 1981. Articles by black revisionist authors challenging past policies of the civil rights establishment, including Thomas Sowell, Clarence Pendleton, Jr., Walter Williams, Maria L. Johnson, Charles V. Hamilton, Percy Sutton, and others.

*An asterisk before the citation indicates that the title is available in a paperback edition.

PART FIVE

Social Change and Social Policy

There is a legend that a great king once summoned a wise man and asked him to propound some words of wisdom that would hold true for all times and places. It is said that the wise man thought for a long time and then said, "And this, too, shall pass away."

Change is continuous in human affairs. The oft-expressed wish to "keep things just like they are" is a forlorn hope. It is never possible to do this for very long. Only by understanding change and— just possibly—by directing it can we hope that our society will change in ways to our liking.

Part Five explores some kinds of change. Chapter 17, "Population Change," examines how and why population changes and how this affects social life and social institutions. Chapter 18, "The Changing Community," surveys rural and urban communities in the United States and how they are changing. Chapter 19, "Collective Behavior and Social Movements," examines some interesting forms of social behavior and outlines some collective efforts to promote or to prevent change. Chapter 20, "Social and Cultural Change," describes the general causes and processes of change, resistance to change, and the social and personal consequences of change.

417

17 Population Change

In the past few weeks, the world's 4 billionth human being was born. Let us read the baby's horoscope, substituting our paperback sociology for astrology and statistics for stars. This baby was probably a female born to an Asian, African or Latin American family. Her father is a sharecropping farmer, her mother sweeps, draws water, fetches firewood, mends and washes the clothes, does the marketing at the village junction, cooks, looks after the children and helps out in the fields when weeding, harvesting, threshing, winnowing, pounding or stacking is the order of the day. . . .

At 10, the little girl will realize that her parents do not seem to be too worried about her and her two sisters who are in school, but that they constantly moan about their sons, one 17, one 15. The oldest one has finished his schooling and the younger one has dropped out, but they cannot find work. They could help out in the paddy field but they do not consider that sort of thing suitable for educated young men. Neither do their parents. . . .

Occasionally, ladies and gentlemen from the city and even far-off places like England and America come to the shantytown to ask questions and leave unreadable pamphlets behind. One of them, a lady who seems offensively antiseptic in that setting, makes a speech warning the people of the shantytown that the world's population has been growing rapidly for many years and that in ten or 25 years' time it will reach the "explosion point." The family's political son, his eyes bloodshot with a kind of rage, asks why this is so since people seem to have fewer children now. The antiseptic lady says it is because fewer people are dying. The political brother answers sarcastically, "That's just too bad, isn't it?" and people snicker. Another man in the crowd asks what will happen when the explosion point is reached. "Civilization will crumble" replies the lady. The crowd roars with laughter, looking around the crumbling shacks in which its members have spent so many years of their lives.

(Varindra Tarzie Vittachi, *Newsweek*, *International Edition*, March 8, 1976, p. 15.)

Population has been relatively stable throughout most of history. In the first 1,650 years after the birth of Christ, world population a little more than doubled. In the next 125 years, it doubled again. World population is now estimated at over 4 billion and is expected to be about 6 billion by the year 2000 [Haub and Heiser, 1980].

World population now grows in about 6 years by as many persons as it grew in the first 1,650 years following the birth of Christ. If 1960 rates of growth were continued for 800 years, we would have one person per square foot of land surface of the earth [Hauser, 1960].

Demographers are interested in the size, distribution, and composition of a population. There is a critical population density below which there are too few people to support modern technology. Overpopulation means too many to be comfortably supported. For each geographic area, there is an ideal population size which permits a higher per-capita production than either a higher or a lower population level. This is called the *optimum population*. The concept is easily stated, but it is difficult to determine just what is the optimum population for an area.

One person per square foot of land surface
in less than 800 years

POSSIBLE EFFECTS OF POPULATION TRENDS IN THE NEXT DECADE

Less crime
More retirement communities
Less fashion change
Slower promotion for management personnel
Fewer students and teachers
Higher retirement age
Less teenage unemployment
Rise in crude birthrates
Drop in divorce rates
Rise in relative income of young males
Strong demand for new houses and apartments
Increased use of Spanish
Need of increased investment funds

Source: Based in part on "Americans Change: Special Report on How Drastic Shifts in Demographics Affect the Economy," *Business Week,* Feb. 20, 1978, pp. 64–70, and Richard A. Easterlin, "What Will 1984 Be Like? Socioeconomic Implications of Recent Twists in Age Structure," *Demography,* 15:416–417, November 1978.

These forecasts were made in 1978. Are they coming true?

Sometimes a population will vary from the usual sex and age distribution, with certain predictable social consequences. A population with a large number of children and old people leaves a small proportion of people in productive labor to support them. If the ratio of men to women (the *sex ratio*) is markedly unequal, many people will be unable to marry (if marriage is monogamous) and may seek companionship outside marriage. Predictions of the ways in which changes in population growth and composition may affect American life are a favorite pastime of demographers. (See box above.)

CHANGING POPULATION COMPOSITION

The composition of a population refers to how it is divided according to age, sex, race, ethnic group, occupation, class, and other variables. The age and sex composition of a population is most clearly shown in a *population pyramid,* which shows the percentage of the population in each age and sex group (see Figure 17-1). Under most conditions, a population pyramid will take the shape of a perfect Christmas tree, widest at the base and tapering evenly to a point. Major changes in the birthrate (or great losses through epidemic or war) may distort this perfect tree shape, as is shown in Figure 17-1.

The composition of a population affects its social life. Washington, D.C., with its many female clerical workers, St. Petersburg, Florida, with its retired people, and Columbus, Georgia, with nearby Fort Benning—these cities are different, in part, because of differences in the age, sex, and occupational composition of the population whose needs they fill.

Why do you suppose Florida has an annual death rate of 11.0 per 1,000 people while Wyoming has a death rate of only 7.2? Can you explain why Florida's birthrate is 13.1 (births per 1,000 people) and Wyoming's is 21.7? Would it help to know that 17.3 percent of the people in Florida and only 7.9 percent of the people in Wyoming are over 65 years old? Or that 22.9 percent of the people in Florida and 40.1 percent of the people in Wyoming are between the ages of 20 and 35 [*Statistical Abstract,* 1981, pp. 28, 61, 72].

The rates above are *crude birthrates* and *death rates,* stating the number of births and deaths per 1,000 people during a year, regardless of their age composition, sex ratios, or any other characteristics. These are not very good measures for comparing health or fertility of population groups of different composition. For such comparisons, a number of *specific* or *adjusted* rates are used by demographers. Thus the crude death rate for the American population fell by 6.5 percent between 1970 and 1978, while the *age-adjusted death rate* fell by 15.1 percent [*Statistical Abstract,* 1981, p. 74]. This is a rate which makes a correction for changes in the age distribution of the population during that period. The crude rates are

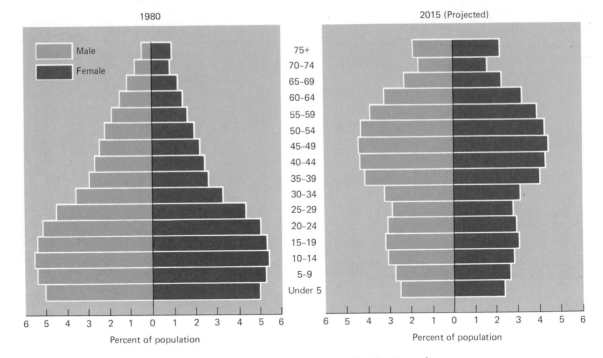

FIGURE 17-1   A population pyramid shows age and sex distribution of a population. These pyramids show how the falling birthrate has already affected the Chinese population distribution and how, if continued, it will affect the future age distribution. (*Source: 1980 pyramid: World Bank estimates. 2015 pyramid: PRB projection premised on the TFR dropping to 1.5 by 1985; increases in life expectancy at birth—females from 67.5 years [1980] to 77.5 [2015], and males from 63.6 [1980] to 73.9 [2015]; and declines in infant mortality—(females from 40.3 infant deaths per 1,000 live births [1980] to 8.9 [2015], and males from 51.9 [1980] to 13.3 [2015]. Reproduced from* Intercom, *9:13, August 1981.*)

When did the birthrate begin falling? What would the 1980 pyramid look like if the birthrate had not fallen?

the most easily available, but for many purposes, the specific or adjusted rates are more useful.

The population composition of the United States has been constantly changing. A high birthrate together with a low death rate means that the children will compose a large fraction of the total population and old people a small fraction. One possible reason for the campus activism of the sixties was that the high birthrates of the forties and fifties had given us a proportion of youth so large that it was

an unusually powerful part of society [Moynihan, 1973]. This condition is changing rapidly as current low birthrates cause the proportion of youth to shrink, while the proportion of the middle-aged and older increases. Persons under the age of 30 were 66 percent of the population in 1960 but only 50 percent in 1980 [*Statistical Abstract*, 1981, p. 26]. Between 1960 and 1980, when the total population was growing by 45 million, the number of children under 5 years old declined by 4 million. Thus, the falling birthrate gave fewer young people to balance the aging older people and increased the proportion of older people. To illustrate changing proportions: If the freshman class were to be cut in half, this would increase the proportion of seniors in the student body. Thus it is, primarily, changes in the birthrate not in the death rate that have increased the proportion of aged in our population.

This point is widely misunderstood by people who confuse life span with life expectancy. Every species has a *life span*, which is the number of years a number of a species will live until killed by aging (unless killed earlier by accident or disease, which kills most people far before their life span is complete). For some insects, the life span is only a few hours; for dogs, about 16 or 18 years; for humans, 100 to 110 years. The human life span has not increased within recorded history, but improvements in diet, sanitation, and health care enable people today to live out more of their full life span. This has increased *life expectancy*, which is the average number of years a person may reasonably expect to live given current levels of health and illness. In ancient times, life expectancy at birth is believed to have been about 20 or 25 years; today, worldwide life expectancy at birth averages about 60 years, but it is 74 years in the United States.

Life expectancy at birth in the United States has increased by 26.5 years since 1900, while life expectancy at age 65 has increased by only 4.5 years. In other words, infants today are far more likely to reach age 65 than infants at the turn of the century; but those who reach 65 today have only about 4.5 more years of life remaining than in 1900. Stated still differently, more people today live to be old, but old people today do not live very much longer than old people used to live.

Most of the increase in life expectancy after age 65 came in the later decades of this century. Between 1939 and 1979, the life expectancy after age 65 increased 2.2 years

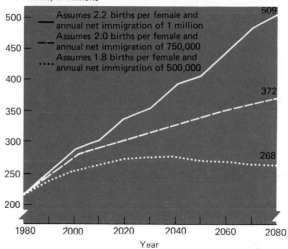

Individuals, in millions

Source: *Population Bulletin,* 27:46, June 1982.

FIGURE 17-2 U.S. population size, 1980–2080, under three different sets of assumptions. (*Source:* Population Bulletin, *27:46, June 1982.*)

Which of these projections would you rather see fulfilled?

for white males, 2.4 years for black males, 5.1 years for white females and 4.5 years for black females [*Statistical Abstract,* 1981, p. 69]. This means that the average Social Security beneficiary will draw payments for about four more years than expected when the system was designed.

Age composition has a major effect on population increase. The 1982 crude birthrate of 15.8 works out to 1.9 children per family; whereas, 2.11 children per family is generally regarded as necessary for replacement and zero population growth. This would suggest that American population growth has stopped, but the facts are far different. Because of the baby boom of the 1950s and 1960s, we now have so many women of childbearing age that even a birthrate below the "replacement" level still increases the population. Not until the age distribution returns to "normal," after perhaps three generations, will it be true that a two-child family brings no population growth. And since the rate of population growth reflects both the birth rate and the rate of immigration, which cannot be known in advance, as shown in Figure 17-2, any future population projections are little better than educated guesses.

Even though population growth continues, the declining U.S. birthrate is having some effect. The number of elementary school children decreased by about 4 million during the 1970s. The impact is more delayed on the size of the college-age population, but this will decrease in the mid-1980s. Oddly enough, a decline in the proportion of youth will have some desirable consequences (see Table 17-1). For one, the rate of crime is expected to decrease, since crime is highest among the younger age group. Likewise, teenage unemployment is expected to drop, since teenagers will then be in short supply. Also, the wages of younger workers relative to older workers should rise. This will mean that more couples can afford marriage and may increase both the marriage rate and the birthrate for the 20- to 30-year-olds.

MIGRATION

The ancestors of the American Indians are thought to have come to the North American continent over a land bridge from Asia sometime in the remote past. All other Americans trace their ancestry to relatively recent migrants. From the time of the Pilgrims, some 32 million immigrants, mostly from Europe, settled in the United States.

Push, Pull, and Channels

The forces affecting migration may be grouped under three headings; (1) push, (2) pull, and (3) channels. *Push* relates to unfavorable conditions in the homeland which make people want to leave. The shifts of national boundary lines after World War II and the rise of intolerant political states, mostly but not exclusively communist, have made life in their native lands intolerable for many people. Millions of refugees fled persecution and possible death during and immediately after World War II, and oppression since has sent millions fleeing from Cuba, Uganda, Palestine, Hungary, Czechoslovakia, Vietnam, Cambodia, Nicaragua, El Salvador, and Laos. Many of them have found new homes in the United States and elsewhere, but in 1982 there were still 10 million people living in exile, over 8 million of whom live in developing countries [U.S. Committee for Refugees, *World Refugee Survey*, 1982, p. 40].

The *pull* factor refers to the attractions in the receiving country, such as economic opportunity, climate, and type of government. This often means that many immigrants go to states already heavily populated like California, while few go to remote and sparsely peopled but less attractive places such as Alaska. *Channels* refer to the means of movement from one place to another and the presence or absence of barriers. In this respect, transportation has never been easier, but legal barriers such as emigration prohibitions and immigration restrictions have never been more formidable.

International Migration

Both increasing population and a developing nationalism encourage governments to restrict immigration to the type of immigrants they feel can most easily be assimilated and to the number the nation can easily absorb into its economy. Legal immigrants into the United States, including refugees, averaged 600,000 a year for the period 1979 to 1981, and the number of illegal immigrants was estimated at between 100,000 and 500,000 annually [*ZPG Reporter*, 1982*a*].

Immigration patterns in the United States changed with the Immigration Act of 1965. The rigid national quota system (which allowed only 100 immigrants a year from most

Asian and African countries) was replaced by a new system abolishing quotas and giving priority to relatives of American residents and to those with occupational skills useful to the United States. Meanwhile, prosperity in Northwestern Europe made migration to the United States less attractive to Europeans than in the past. The result is that immigration from the United Kingdom and Northern Europe has sharply decreased and that from Southern Europe and Asia has increased. For instance, immigration from the Philippines has increased tenfold and that from Portugal more than sixfold, while the proportion from Germany and the United Kingdom dropped by more than one-half between 1965 and 1970.

In recent years, Europe has also faced immigration problems. Some 7 million foreign workers, accompanied by wives and children, live in Western European countries. Most are from other European nations, but France, Germany, and Great Britain have sizable numbers from Asia and Africa. The migrants were welcome during periods of prosperity, but in the recession of the early 1980s, tensions arose. They are now often seen as ethnic minorities constituting a "second class society, living in economic and social deprivation that acts as a catalyst for confrontation" [U.S. News & World Report, 1982a].

Most of the rest of the world, like the United States, has also followed selective or restrictive immigration policies. The countries which encourage immigration are those like Brazil, Canada, and Australia, which are considered underpopulated. They welcome immigrants as a means of developing their resources, although even these countries have some restrictions.

Questions about U.S. policy center on the extent of illegal immigration and the effect of immigration on population increase. Illegal immigration is hard to measure, but 953,000 illegal immigrants were arrested in 1981 [Haupt, 1982]. Some of those deported return in a few days, and there are an estimated 6 to 10 million illegal aliens living in the United States. The majority of illegal immigrants are Mexicans who crossed the border illegally, but there are many other nationalities, most of whom enter the country as legal visitors and then overstay their visas. The "push" comes from Mexican society with much poverty, unemployment, and overpopulation. The "pull" comes from the prospect of wages, which, while very low by American standards, are many times higher than these workers can get in Mexico.

The 2,000-mile border with Mexico is obviously difficult to police, and the Immigration and Naturalization Service feels that its funds are inadequate. In addition, there is much business pressure to "go easy" on the illegal immigrants. Fruit growers, truck farmers, and many other business people find it difficult to get local Americans to take lower-level jobs. It is very difficult to identify the illegal immigrants without harassing legal immigrants of the same nationality. Illegal immigration is extremely difficult to control.

Not all immigrants are uneducated and unskilled [Joyce and Hunt, 1982]. Many are highly successful in business and the professions. Some 30 percent of the American Nobel Prize winners have been immigrants [Select Commission on Immigration and Refugee Policy, 1981].

The United States has traditionally welcomed refugees from oppression. In the recent case of illegal Haitian immigrants, some have sought to broaden the definition of refugee. It may be argued whether most Haitians are oppressed, but there is no denying that most Haitians are desperately poor [McGrath, 1982]. Some propose that the United States should accept "economic refugees" as well. Since a sizable proportion of the world's population could qualify as economic refugees, opening the gates to their entry would place a major strain on American resources.

Despite current restrictions, the United States is still one of the few countries taking large numbers of immigrants. At present levels of legal and illegal immigration, it would be

Illegal immigrants form an increasing part of American population growth. (*Wide World Photos*)

necessary for American citizens to cut their family size below the average of two children to achieve zero population growth. [The Commission on Population Growth and America's Future, 1972, p. 201]. As birthrates fall, immigration becomes a more significant factor in population increase; yet it is difficult to control, and both humanitarian and economic defenses can be made for allowing immigration to continue.

Internal Migration

Each year, nearly one American family in five will move. The past fifty years have seen millions of people moving to the cities of the North and the West from the agricultural areas of the South and the Middle West, plus a considerable movement of Puerto Ricans to the mainland. At present, internal migration patterns are shifting, with more people leaving metropolitan areas and moving to the South, to the West (the Sun Belt), and to small cities and rural districts.

While this internal migration is different in form from international migration, the consequences of the two shifts are much the same. The movement in a new region changes the population composition, provides new labor, and introduces a group of people ignorant of the local folkways, who have to make their adjustment to a strange cultural setting. Internal migrants thus make many of the same contributions and experience many of the same problems as did European immigrants of an earlier day.

SOCIAL AND CULTURAL ASPECTS OF POPULATION CHANGE

What causes a change in the rate of population growth? Research on birthrates concerns both *fecundity, the biological capacity to reproduce,* and *fertility, the actual rate of reproduction.* Fecundity varies greatly between individuals, but we have no evidence of fecundity differences between large population groups. Since our biological capacity to reproduce appears to be constant, social and cultural factors must explain most variations in birthrates and death rates.

Changes in Death Rates

Throughout most of history, both birthrates and death rates have been high, with only a small rate of natural increase. In the Bronze Age of ancient Greece, expectation of life at birth was an estimated 18 years. By the opening of the nineteenth century it had doubled to about 36 years. Less than two centuries later, it has doubled again, standing at 74.1 years in 1981 in the United States—

specifically, in 1980, 78.1 for white females, 74 for other females, 70.5 for white males, and 65.3 for other males, according to census data reported by the *Associated Press* [Oct. 11, 1981]. Between 1900 and 1981, the American death rate fell from 17.2 to 8.7 deaths per 1,000 people [*Metropolitan Life Statistical Bulletin*, 63:13, April/June 1982]. In the world as a whole, the death rate was between 11 and 12 per 1,000 in 1978 [*ZPG Reporter*, 1982b].

A great many factors, stretching backward for hundreds of years, have contributed to the drop in the death rate. Improved transportation made it possible to transport a food surplus and to relieve a local famine. Improvements in food preservation made it possible to preserve a food surplus. The growth of nationalism brought political institutions which were better able to cope with local crop failures and threatened famines. But preventive medicine, sanitary engineering, and public health measures were mainly responsible for the dramatic drops of the past century. After Pasteur and the germ theory of disease, many epidemic diseases quickly yielded to preventive measures. Pure food and water supply routed others. The great killers of the past—smallpox, cholera, diptheria, typhoid, and scarlet fever—have become so rare that it is hard to find cases for medical students to observe.

The decline in the death rate in Europe began about 1750 in England and France and generally preceded any decline in the birthrate. A country with a falling death rate and a stationary birthrate will show an explosive rate of population increase. This explains the rapid population growth of recent centuries.

Age at Marriage and Sex Ratios

One factor in the birthrate is the proportion of people who get married and the ages at which they marry. A study of marriages in Korea found that women married before the age of 19 had an average of 4.02 children during their childbearing years compared to 2.5 children for those married after the age of 25 [Kim et al., 1974, p. 647]. Early marriage not only increases the number of years of childbearing; it is also associated with lower social-class background, together with attitudes and practices which favor large families.

The marriage rate is also related to the sex composition of the population. One would assume that usually the number of both sexes is approximately equal and that the age distribution is "normal"; but actually this is seldom true. In the United States, the sex ratio in 1980 was 94.5 men to every 100 women, based on 110,032,000 men to 116,473,000 women. Young men wishing a wide choice of mates would be well advised to go to Washington, D.C. where a host of female office workers has reduced the sex ratio to 86 (that is, 86 men per 100 women). Those women wishing greater marital opportunities might think about Alaska, which had a sex ratio of about 115. Black men are even more scarce than white men on a relative basis, since the sex ratio for the United States for blacks was 89.6 [all sex ratios based on data in *Statistical Abstract*, 1981, pp. 25–35]. Unbalanced sex ratios mean that some people will not be able to have a monogamous marriage. A locality may attract more of one sex than another, thus there are often more women than men in cities and more men in frontier areas. For an entire nation, though, the imbalance is due to a lower death rate for females, which is cumulative through life. For the age bracket 70 to 74, the sex ratio in 1980 had fallen to 72, meaning that there were fewer than 3 males for every 4 females [based on data in U.S. Bureau of the Census, *Social Indicators III*, 1981d, p. 42].

Americans married at steadily younger ages between 1900 and 1955, when the average age at marriage turned slightly upward. The median age at marriage for men rose from 22.3 years in 1955 to 23.4 in 1979; and for women, from 20.2 to 21.6 [*Statistical Abstract*, 1981, p. 80]. It is unclear whether this is temporary or whether early marriage is be-

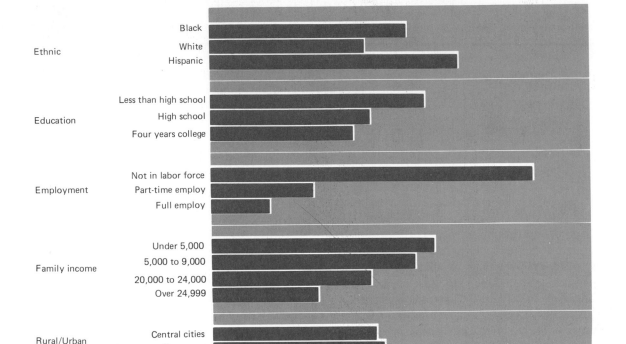

FIGURE 17-3 Fertility differentials: Number of births per 1,000 women aged 18 to 44 in the United States, 1980. Black, white, and Hispanic rates are influenced by the lower incomes of blacks and Hispanics. Employment rates are influenced by tendencies of women with young children to drop out of the labor force. Rural and urban rates seem to be almost equal. (*Source: Adapted from* Family Planning Perspectives, *14:285, September/October 1982.*)

coming less attractive. If early marriage is losing its appeal, this will be another factor reducing the birthrate.

Social Status and the Birthrate

The folk proverb that the "rich get richer and the poor get babies" describes the relationship between social status and the birthrate. In general, urbanized, well-educated, and high-income groups have lower birthrates, while rural, poorly educated, and low-income groups have higher birthrates (see Figure 17-3).

THE PLANNING ATTITUDE AND FAMILY SIZE. In the discussion of the deferred-gratification

pattern in the chapter on social mobility, we found that planning was not a typical lower-class pattern. Instead of trying to control their environment, lower-class people more often see themselves as creatures of fate, subject to forces beyond their control. Most of them do not *desire* larger families than middle-class people, but they *get* larger families because they have neither strong motivation to limit family size nor easy access to birth control and abortion services. Yet research shows that many lower-class people prefer smaller families and will use contraceptive techniques when made easily available by Planned Parenthood or other agencies [Jaffee, 1974].

The total black and Hispanic birthrate is higher than the white, but it shows the same relationship to social status. Among the college educated, the black birthrate is actually lower than the white. Women in the labor force have smaller families than those not employed. This supports a current theory that women's liberation is a vital aspect of population control.

In the United States and in many other countries as well, the birthrate differential between social categories has narrowed. Rural and urban birthrates are nearly the same. Married white women, 35 to 44 years of age with one to three years of high school, had a birthrate 141 percent of college-graduated women's birthrates in 1975, but had dropped to 128 percent in 1980 [U.S. Bureau of the Census, 1976, p. 36; 1982d, p. 60]. The Asian and the white birthrates were nearly identical in 1980 [Davis, 1982, p. 8]. Black birthrates dropped from 18.4 in 1970 to 15.9 in 1979 [*Statistical Abstract*, 1981, p. 59]. Birthrates of Hispanic women between 35 and 44 years of age dropped 19 percent in the same period [U.S. Bureau of the Census, 1976, p. 34; 1982d, p. 53]. This would seem to show that easier access to family planning clinics in recent years has lowered the birthrate of the more highly fertile groups. If this trend continues, we may see racial, regional, and economic birthrate differences disappear.

This will not happen immediately. For some years we can expect a higher fertility among lower-income groups and large ethnic minorities. Current estimates anticipate a population growth of 23 percent in the United States between 1980 and the year 2000. The black population is expected to increase 36 percent as against 10 percent for the white population. Hispanic whites, aided by immigration, are expected to increase 62 percent [calculations based on data in Davis, 1982, p. 9]. The results are indicated in Table 17-1.

There are many countries with ethnic birthrate differentials. The dominant ethnic group is usually more prosperous and has a lower birthrate than the subordinate ethnic groups.

TABLE 17-1
RACIAL-ETHNIC PERCENTAGES OF U.S. POPULATION

	1980	2000*	2040*
White (non-Hispanic)	79.9	71.9	59.1
Black	11.7	13.0	14.6
Hispanic	6.4	10.8	18.0
Asian and other	2.1	4.3	8.3

*Assuming net immigration of 1 million per year.
Source: Adapted from Leon F. Bouvier and Cary B. Davis, *The Future Racial Composition of the United States*, Demographic Information Services Center, Population Reference Bureau, Washington, D.C., August 1982.

How accurate can such population forecasts be? What variables, other than immigration, are involved in such forecasts?

This means that subordinate ethnic groups may eventually become the majority and seek greater political power. In the Soviet Union, the Russian mothers average 1.9 births, as compared with 5.8 births for mothers in the four non-Russian Republics in central Asia. In 1970, the armed forces of the Soviet Union were 56 percent Russian, but they will be only 44 percent Russian by the year 2000 [Feshbach, 1982]. The civil war in Lebanon began in part because the Moslems were outbreeding the Christians and demanding greater political power. Thus ethnic birthrate differentials may create political instability and even civil warfare.

Catholics and Population

Most Catholic pronouncements upon population policy acknowledge the existence of a population problem but denounce the most effective methods of birth control. It is often assumed that Roman Catholic teachings are a major obstacle to securing a lowered birthrate. This assumption is valid if one looks at the effect of Catholic influence on government policies. However, if one looks at the birthrates, the situation is more ambiguous. In Europe, the highest birthrate is found in Iceland, which is only 2 percent Catholic, and the lowest in Austria or Belgium, which are 99 percent Catholic. In the United States surveys several years ago found that five out of six American Catholics approved of "artificial contraception" [*Time*, 105:55, Jan. 13, 1975]. There is no longer any significant difference in birth control practices of American Catholics and non-Catholics [Westoff, 1978].

The question of government policy is another matter. Until recently, governments of many Catholic countries refused to participate in birth control programs, and Catholic influence is constantly seeking to limit the extent and effectiveness of the programs which have been adopted. Dissent from Vatican policy by many priests and bishops, as well as the laity, has not succeeded in changing the official position of opposition to any artificial means of birth control. Currently, little is heard about opposition to contraception and the major Catholic attack is on abortion [Berelson, 1978], with only 35 percent of American Catholics believing, in 1981, that legal abortions should be available to women who want them [*Public Opinion*, 4:26, April/May 1981].

THE POPULATION CONTROVERSY

Malthus on Population

The argument about population pressure still swirls around the ideas of the Rev. Thomas R. Malthus, an English clergyman whose *Essay on Population* in 1798 attracted world attention. He noted that people increase through multiplication, whereas the food supply increases only by addition and is constantly being outrun by the growth of population. Any increase in food production enables more people to survive until they have eaten up the increase. Malthus urged later marriages to keep down the birthrate, but he was doubtful that this policy would be followed. He saw no practical possibility of averting hunger, famine, and pestilence. Organized charity and relief would only en-

able a few more to survive today so that they might starve tomorrow.

In the 1920s it was popular to believe that the events of the preceding century had disproved the Malthusian hypotheses. The world had seen the greatest population growth in its history, and at the same time the standard of living had improved rather than declined. Why were Malthus's gloomy predictions not fulfilled?

One reason is that Malthus failed to foresee the widespread use of improved methods of contraception. The contraceptive devices of his day were so crude and inefficient that he and other writers paid little or no attention to them. Another reason was that Malthus did not foresee the magnitude of the industrial and agricultural revolutions of the nineteenth and twentieth centuries. Great new land areas in North and South America and Australia were brought under cultivation. Improvements in agriculture rapidly boosted output per acre. For a time, birthrates in the Western world were falling so sharply and production was rising so rapidly that Malthus began to sound like a gloomy scold instead of a gifted thinker.

By the 1960s, though, Malthus returned to fashion among scholars known as the neo-Malthusian school [Morris, 1966]. These neo-Malthusians note that the population of the world in the time of Malthus was less than 1 billion people; today, it is over 4 billion. Further, the population growth of about .5 percent a year, which alarmed Malthus, has risen to a rate of around 1.6 percent a year, or more than three times as high. Similarly, North and South America were sparsely populated at the time of Malthus, but practically all of their productive land is now in full use.[1]

---

[1] Some optimists view the "untapped tropical jungle lands" hopefully, but most jungle lands are deficient in minerals. When stripped of their forest cover, they soon form a hard, concretelike crust which absorbs little water. They are unsuitable for intensive cultivation by any presently known technology. See David W. Ehrenfeld, *Conserving Life on Earth*, Oxford University Press, New York, 1972, pp. 44–46; also F.R. Fosberg, *Tropical Africa and South America: A Comparative Study*, Smithsonian Press, Washington, D.C., 1973.

In other words, the "slack" has now been taken up so that, while the alarm of Malthus may have been premature in his day, it is quite justifiable in the current situation. Even the North American continent faces severe problems, although it is lightly populated as compared with Europe or Asia. Many areas in the United States are already short of water, and this condition is bound to worsen as population soars. Further, Americans now pay high prices for oil and other minerals, which, until recently, were abundant and cheap. In spite of these problems, it may be that the United States can maintain its present population at a high level. But can it do so for a population half again as large, or twice as large, or four times as large?

Some other parts of the world are in a better position than the United States in terms of population density, but most are worse off. In the view of the neo-Malthusians, the appearance of crisis is only a matter of time. Many countries face a real crisis now. China, for instance, has 1 billion people, as many as the whole world in 1840.

The Doomsday Debate

How many people can the earth support? The earth's "carrying capacity" involves three factors: (1) the resources available, (2) the level of technology, and (3) the standard of living at which people are supported. One estimate, for example, claims that, at our present level of technology, the entire world could support only 1 billion people at the American standard of living [Murdoch, 1975, pp. 461–462]. Thus, if the entire world is to enjoy the American standard of living (at present technology), three out of four people would have to "go away."

The neo-Malthusians believe that Malthus was not incorrect just premature. World resources are limited. We have no way to create more land, more water, more coal or oil. We shall not "run out" of oil suddenly, as when the last drop is drained from a tank. Instead,

as the huge oil fields that are easy to find and drill are drained, costs of exploration and development will rise until, at some future date, the energy costs of getting the oil will exceed the energy the oil provides.

This scenario holds for most resources: increasing costs as prime sources are exhausted and inferior sources must be used. The *acreage* of land in agricultural use is higher than ever, but the *quality* of agricultural lands is steadily declining because of soil erosion. [Eckholm, 1979]. Deforestation and overgrazing of grasslands have been enlarging the world's deserts by about 14 million acres a year, a rate which would destroy one-third of our arable land within twenty-five years [Rensberger, 1977]. The "oil shortage" has changed into a temporary "oil glut" because conservation and world recession cut oil demand while high prices encouraged oil exploration and increased supply. But the long-term prospect is for renewed oil shortages and higher prices.

This is a very brief recital of the factors which lead the doomsday school to predict a nightmare of shortages, hunger, war, revolution, pestilence, and chaos. They note that the *rate* of world population growth is slowing

TABLE 17-2
WORLD DEMOGRAPHIC SITUATION

	1965	1982
World population total	3.2 billion	4.6 billion
Average world birthrate	34 per 1,000	29 per 1,000
Average world death rate	14 per 1,000	11 per 1,000
Annual population growth rate	2.0 percent	1.7 percent
Annual increment in population	66 million	79 million

Source: Population Reference Bureau, *1982 World Population Data Sheet.*

Why has the decline in the birthrate not brought a decline in growth?

DEMOGRAPHIC TRANSITION THEORY

Stage	Birthrate	Death rate	Population
Preindustrial	High	High	Stable
Early industrial	High	Falling	Rapid growth
Mature industrial	Low	Low	Stable

but that growth measured in *numbers* of additional persons is higher than ever (see Table 17-2). Unless population growth falls very rapidly, the prediction is for a massive die-off within a very few decades [Mesarovic and Pestel, 1974; Laszlo et al., 1977; Catton, 1980; Webb and Jacobsen, 1982].

The "optimist" school claims that such doomsday predictions have been, and always will be, wrong [Vajk, 1979; Paarlberg, 1980]. The optimists are confident that science and technology can provide substitutes for scarce materials, fertilize eroded lands, and provide growing abundance for a growing population

---

IS THE U.S. EXPORTING MORE THAN FOOD?

Just as the world had come to depend heavily upon the Middle East for oil, so it now depends overwhelmingly on North America for grain. At the existing intensity of cultivation, every ton of grain exported leads to the loss of several tons of topsoil.

Lester R. Brown, "A Sustainable Society," *Environment*, 24:3, January/February 1982.

Some scholars assume that plant breeding and improved agricultural technology can indefinitely make up for continuing soil erosion. If this assumption should prove incorrect, then what?

[Kahn, 1976, 1979, 1982; Simon, 1981, 1981*a*; 1981*b*]. Population growth, according to Simon [1981*a*], is no threat, because this increases the supply of brilliant minds to invent the new technology.

The argument is bitter, but two facts are beyond argument. First, present rates of population growth cannot be maintained indefinitely. Population growth *will* greatly decline at some point in the future, either through planning or through misery. Second, without sharp declines in population growth, spectacular breakthroughs in science and technology must come quickly to avert disaster. Among the optimists who predict such breakthroughs, the names of prominent natural scientists are conspicuously absent.

Demographic Transition Theory

Throughout most of history, birthrates and death rates have both been high, with very slow population growth. In most Western nations, advances in agriculture, science, medicine, and industry brought falling death rates beginning in the seventeenth or eighteenth centuries; meanwhile, birthrates remained high and rates of population growth multiplied enormously. Before long, however, the desire for a higher standard of living led to reductions in the birthrate, so that most Western nations are approaching a new equilibrium, with both birthrates and death rates quite low and little population growth [Atkinson, 1977, p. 12]. This is explained by the theory of demographic transition—the theory that industrial and commercial development first cuts the death rate but creates a desire for smaller families and eventually cuts the birthrate as shown in Figure 17-4.

Will this same transition come to non-Western nations? This is uncertain. Brazil and Mexico are two of the most rapidly developing states in the world, but birthrates have remained high (40 and 36 respectively); at which rates, Brazil's population would double in twenty years and Mexico's in twenty-five [Coale, 1978; Peterson, 1982].

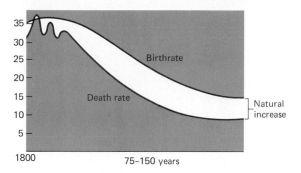

(a) Western Europe after 1800

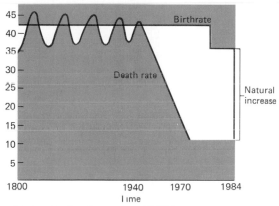

(b) Less developed countries, mid-20th century
(the sharp drop in the death rate began between
1940 and 1960, depending upon the specific country.)

FIGURE 17-4 Demographic transition in Europe; population explosion in less developed countries. Approximation of the birth rates and death rates for two different groups of nations over time. (*Source: Shirley Foster Hartley, "Our Growing Problem: Population," Social Problems, 21:194, Fall 1973.*)

Will the experience of the Western European countries be repeated by the developing countries? Why or why not?

One difficulty is that, whereas in the Western nations, "death control" *accompanied* industrialization, "death control" *preceded* the modernization and industrialization of most of the developing nations by several decades. This gave them explosive population growth before the conditions for birth control had developed. What is needed now is an approach that will reduce population growth so that economic development has a better chance.

As Shirley Hartley expresses the idea: "The gap between the rich and the poor nations continues to increase, not because there are no improvements in the less developed nations, but because they are watered down by population increase" [Hartley, 1973, p. 202]. Thus, the theory of demographic transition has yet to be demonstrated in non-Western nations [Weinstein, 1980].

The Marxist Critique

Marxists believe that the Malthusian thesis that population must exceed the food supply may hold true but *only* in exploitative social systems. They argue that capitalist colonialism has forced poor nations to produce and export specialty foods to rich countries, instead of concentrating upon producing foods needed to feed their own people [George, 1977; Lappé et al., 1977]. Marxists argue that when a social revolution ends exploitation and brings a just distribution system, improved economic conditions will bring about a reduction of population growth. Thus, overpopulation is not the cause of poverty, but poverty is the cause of overpopulation [Cereseto, 1977].

Marxists may be correct that developing countries suffer by growing export crops [Nations and Kramer, 1983]. In most communist countries, food production has lagged, and many have had to import food. The People's Republic of China, the world's largest communist country, offers an interesting example of the contrast between theory and practice. At the World Population Conference in 1974, the Chinese followed Marxist ideology and bitterly attacked efforts at population control, while demanding that references to their own birth control measures be kept off the official agenda [Hemmer, 1975]. More recently, China has officially encouraged birth control, and it now operates the most drastic population control measures found anywhere in the world. Apparently, the reality of population pressure overcame the appeal of Marxist ideology.

A growing number of people use birth control, but they are still a minority in developing countries. (*WHO Photo, by J. Abcede*)

POPULATION POLICIES

Although it is the personal decisions of men and women which determine the birthrate, governments have often tried to influence these decisions. Government policies have usually been pronatal, seeking to increase the birthrate. In recent years some governments, like China, have adopted antinatal policies and sought to discourage large families.

Pronatal Policies

Governments may try to boost the birthrate by (1) providing economic incentives for childbearing and/or (2) restricting or prohibiting contraception and abortion. There are also a number of measures having a pronatalist effect which are adopted in the belief that they promote social welfare in general, such as income tax deductions for children and family allowances which provide a cash grant for each child. Maternity-leave provisions and day-care programs reduce the conflict between work and childbearing. Welfare programs such as AFDC (Aid to Families with Dependent Children) may also be considered pronatalist, since they make it possible for women without husbands to have and keep children and still live on a level not far from that of a lower-class husband and wife family [Janowitz, 1976].

The most extreme pronatal measures have been adopted in the communist countries of eastern Europe which feel that their birthrates are too low [van der Tak, 1982*a*] with the Soviet Union not far behind [van der Tak, 1982*b*]. Cash incentives are offered for maternity. In East Germany, benefits amount to 1,000 marks (nearly $450), equal to a month's wages. Czechoslovakia spends nearly 10 percent of its national budget in direct and indirect subsidies to encourage childbearing. Abortion, which had been legalized in all the communist bloc countries except Albania, is now also restricted. After Rumania curtailed imports of contraceptives and restricted abortion, the birthrate promptly tripled to 39.9; although it has since gone down to 18.6, this is still higher than the 14.3 average for 1966 [Berelson, 1979]. This confirms Berelson's earlier observation that "making abortions legal or illegal may be one of the most effective single ways the modern state has of changing birthrates up or down" [1975, p. 6].

While efforts to ban or restrict abortion and

sterilization in noncommunist countries generally arise from moralistic motives rather than population policy goals, the effects are pronatalist. Thus, recent congressional banning of the use of federal funds for most abortions and recent restrictions upon the sterilizing of welfare clients will have the effect of increasing birthrates among the poor. The effects of pronatal policies on birthrates are difficult to measure. Some demographers suspect that the principal effect is to speed up first and second births without much effect upon the eventual size of the family.

Antinatal Policies

Governments may try to limit population growth by (1) providing facilities for contraception, abortion, and sterilization and encouraging their use; and (2) providing penalties for large families, and, less frequently, rewards for small families. Some would consider that economic development, female emancipation, and reduced economic inequality are antinatalist. These developments probably encourage a preference for smaller families.

BIRTH CONTROL FACILITIES. For many years birth control propaganda and the provision of clinics was promoted primarily by private agencies such as the Planned Parenthood Federation, which is still highly active. In recent years population control has been ac-

cepted by the United Nations and by most of the world's countries as a proper governmental concern [Salas, 1976].

Birth control clinics were usually initiated on a tentative, timid basis with a heavy medical emphasis and with little realistic effort to reach the less educated portions of the population. Often they did not provide sterilization or abortion, and sometimes their contraceptive services were limited as well. Usually they quickly reached the better-educated people but had difficulty in communicating effectively with the uneducated. The development of "the pill" was a boon to these agencies, since it was both simpler and more effective than most other contraceptive methods. With experience, the agencies became more effective both in communication and in their understanding of contraceptive methods.

BIRTH CONTROL POLICIES. It soon became apparent that it was not enough to provide people with the means to limit the size of their families. Just as crucial is the matter of motivation. If people desire large families, then no method of birth control will have much appeal. Further, even skillful propaganda may be ineffective against the traditional belief that many children are a proof of masculinity or femininity, a cheap family labor force, and insurance against poverty and isolation in old age. Presumably, these attitudes would change as countries became

Population
Change

CULTURAL FACTORS IN THE BIRTH RATE

In Zimbabwe's tribal, traditional society, everyone needs children. A woman needs children to support her if her husband dies or deserts; she hasn't any property rights of her own, not even her clothes. A man needs children to stake his claim to a farm; the chiefs allocate tribal lands only to men with families. And everyone needs

children to look after his spirit when he is dead; a spirit not properly attended will wander homeless in Zimbabwe, a sad fate indeed.

June Kronholz: "African Healing Arts Treat Saddest of Ills, an Ache in the Heart," *Wall Street Journal*, July 29, 1982, p. 1.

Is the promotion of birth control in developing countries primarily a medical or a cultural problem?

more industrialized (the demographic transition), but by that time the population might have grown to catastrophic proportions. Consequently, some governments have begun to establish penalties and rewards to motivate the acceptance of smaller families. India for several years paid men to accept a vasectomy [Bird, 1976]. Districts in Taiwan have offered savings accounts as a reward for limiting family size [Yen et al., 1973]. The Philippines, where the average woman has seven children, allows income tax deductions for only four children [Concepcion, 1973]. Singapore, which has been highly successful in reducing the birthrate, has a combination of incentives. These include delivery fees rising with consecutive children, income tax deductions for only the first three children, paid maternity leave for only two confinements, and highest priority for subsidized housing to those with two children or less [Kee and Lee, 1973].

There are critics who regard such incentives as a form of coercion. In 1977 the U.S. Congress forbade the use of foreign aid money for birth control incentives. India is the only country thus far where alleged coercion has been a domestic issue. When Mrs. Gandhi was prime minister, she greatly expanded existing birth control programs and introduced an energetic program of male sterilization which many people regarded as coercive [Bird, 1976]. This was given as one of the reasons her party lost the next election, and her successor modified the population program, removing any elements which might be regarded as coercive [Borders, 1977].

As stated earlier, the Peoples' Republic of China has established the world's most vigorous population control program. The Chinese program has adopted practically every measure tried anywhere else, as well as a few items unique to China. All contraceptive methods are made available, as well as sterilization and abortion. The one-child family is the official ideal, and the recommended minimum age for marriage is 28 for males and 25 for females [Kessen, 1975, p. 21]. The

Chinese are serious in their desire to prevent their population from rising to a second billion and, at times, have used both community pressure and direct coercion. In most areas, couples must get permission to have a child and can be ordered to abort an unapproved pregnancy [Butterfield, 1982]. They have already cut their birthrate from 37 per 1,000 in the mid-1960s to 20 in the late 1970s. However, the aim is to reduce births below the replacement level and secure an actual reduction in the size of the population [*Intercom,* 1981].

Effects of Population Stabilization

Many demographers and other scholars consider that a stable population and a relatively stable economy would be desirable (or even inevitable, either by design or by catastrophe) [Meadows, 1972; Daly, 1973; Behrens, 1978]. But there are dissenting voices. The Japanese have been highly successful in controlling population growth, but some Japanese writers now warn of the cost of a large aged population ["Concern for Welfare of Elderly Groups," *Japan Report,* June 16, 1975; Soda, 1980]. Some writers on the problems of developing countries stress the problems which come when the younger generation is smaller than the older, while they minimize the problem of population pressure [Bondestam and Bergstrom, 1980].

To stabilize population, there must be a sharp drop in the birthrate, and this disrupts the age distribution for nearly three generations (see Figure 17-1, p. 422). In the United States, this is creating problems for old-age retirement systems. The Social Security system taxes each generation of workers for the support of its elders. When it was started, there were sixteen workers paying into the system for each retiree drawing benefits. Today, there are only three workers for each beneficiary, and by the year 2025, there will be only two, as shown in Figure 17-5. It is unlikely that workers in 2025 will be willing

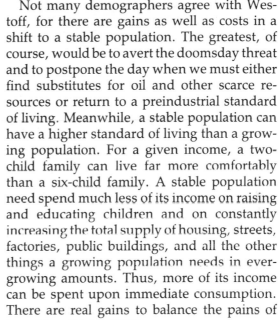

In 1950, there were 16 workers for each social security beneficiary.

In 1970, there were 4 workers for each social security beneificary.

Today, there are 3 workers for each social security beneficiary.

By 2025, there will be just 2 workers for each social security beneficiary.

Result: An increasing burden on workers whose social security taxes keep the trust funds solvent.

FIGURE 17-5 Social Security and age composition. (*Source:* U.S. News & World Report, *91:95, Dec. 27, 1981, and Jan. 3, 1982.*)

Today's college students will be retiring about the year 2025. What do you think will happen to your retirement pensions?

to give almost half their incomes to support retired persons. Policy changes to delay the retirement age and to reduce benefits have already begun and may be expected to continue. Some scholars expect the political battle between the younger and the older to become the dominant political issue of the twenty-first century [Brock, 1983].

There are other difficulties. Upward social mobility would be reduced and minorities would be at a greater disadvantage than today [Spengler, 1978]. Promotions would come more slowly, with it taking 4.5 more years to move up to middle-management positions, according to one estimate [Keyfitz, 1973, p. 335]. Thus the shift to a stable population would bring many transitional problems. We are all so accustomed to rapid growth, both in population and in the economy, that the adjustments required by a slowdown of growth are alarming. An American demographer, Charles Westoff, Director of the U.S. Commission on Population and America's Future, issued a call in 1970 for a stable population. He later decided that a stable population of

perhaps 250 million in the year 2030, followed by some decline, would be politically unacceptable and proposed a baby bonus to encourage more childbearing [Westoff, 1978].

Not many demographers agree with Westoff, for there are gains as well as costs in a shift to a stable population. The greatest, of course, would be to avert the doomsday threat and to postpone the day when we must either find substitutes for oil and other scarce resources or return to a preindustrial standard of living. Meanwhile, a stable population can have a higher standard of living than a growing population. For a given income, a two-child family can live far more comfortably than a six-child family. A stable population need spend much less of its income on raising and educating children and on constantly increasing the total supply of housing, streets, factories, public buildings, and all the other things a growing population needs in ever-growing amounts. Thus, more of its income can be spent upon immediate consumption. There are real gains to balance the pains of transition [Daly, 1973].

It appears, then, that continued population growth would lead to eventual disaster, while a shift to a stable population would call for painful adjustments lasting over two or three generations. Perhaps this simply shows how *any kind of change* has its discomforts, as will be developed in Chapter 20, "Social and Cultural Change."

PROSPECTS FOR THE FUTURE

Several of the industrialized countries have already reached or approximated a stable population. These include East and West Germany, Austria, Belgium, and the United Kingdom. By 1985 it is probable that more than a billion people, one-fourth of the present world's population, may live in countries which have ceased to have population growth. In the United States, the outlook is uncertain. Predictions for our population by the year

There is guarded optimism among agriculturalists that we may be able to feed the 6 or 7 billion people expected on earth at the end of this century. (*UN/WHO Photo*)

2030 range from 277 million to 367 million [Bouvier, 1981]. Growth is slowing, but there are factors which might reverse the current downward trend. In 1982, U.S. birthrates were up 9 percent from the 1976 figure.

In the short period of 40, 60, or 80 years—depending on how fast the Earth's population grows—world food production must be increased by at least as much as was achieved during the entire 12,000 year period from the beginning of agriculture to the year 1975!

Norman R. Borlaug (Nobel Prize-winning agricultural scientist) quoted in *USA Today*, vol. 110, no. 2439. December 1981, p. 4.

Do you think this will be achieved? If not, what then?

Notions of ideal family size are changeable, and a swing back to a larger-size family is entirely possible. In fact, over one third of adult Americans indicate that they would like a family with more than the two children which must be the norm if the United States has any chance of reaching a stable population [Gallup poll, February 1981]. Easterlin [1980] has offered the interesting suggestion that family size may be cyclical in the developed countries—that is, a generation of large families may be followed by a generation of small families, followed again by a generation of large families, with each generation reversing the family-size ideal of its parents.

The oft-predicted world famine has not arrived. In the last decade, world food production rose at between 3 and 4 percent a year while world population grew at about 2.5 percent a year. A United Nations report stated that "roughly one in ten people go hungry now, whereas as many as one in six had gone hungry two decades ago" [United Nations Department of International Economics and Social Affairs, 1982, p. 67]. Critics point out that the land base for this food supply is steadily eroding and fear that such increases in food production must someday turn into food production declines. Has doomsday been averted or merely postponed?

West and Non-West Compared

The 1974 Bucharest Conference on Population received bitter charges from the less developed countries that the real problem was not their own population increase but the "exaggerated consumerism" of the industrialized nations. As a rationale for the complacency about the population pressure in less developed countries, this is not very convincing, since there is no system under which population can double every twenty-eight years without creating human misery. However, as a reminder to the industrialized countries that

High living standards in industrialized nations make heavy demands upon natural resources. (*Karl Maslowski/Photo Researchers, Inc.; Alexander Lowry/Photo Researchers, Inc.; Joseph P. Czarnekci/Nancy Palmer Photo Agency*)

they too have a problem, the complaint has some validity. Its substance is summarized by Paul R. Ehrlich:

> Each American has roughly 50 times the negative impact on the Earth's life-support systems as the average citizen of India. Therefore, in terms of eco-system destruction, adding 75 million more Americans will be the equivalent of adding 3.7 billion Indians to the world population. (Paul R. Ehrlich, *The New York Times*, Nov. 4, 1970, p. 47. Copyright © 1970 by The New York Times Company. Reprinted by permission.)

The Population Council makes the more conservative estimate that the per-capita resource use in developing countries is one-thirteenth that of the industrialized nations [Berelson, 1975, p. 9]. Figure 17-6 shows the enormous increase in the population of developing countries but also shows that, in terms of total consumption, population increase in the industrialized countries will place an even greater demand on world resources.

It is possible that the non-Western world may be in the earlier stages of demographic transition, although it did not seem so in earlier years. Death rates plunged precipitously as non-Western lands gained epidemic control in the post–World War II years. Until recently, efforts to reduce the birthrate in the less developed areas were making little headway. In the late 1960s and the 1970s, the population control programs began to show greater promise. China, which has about a fifth of the world's population, cut its birthrate 34 percent in the last decade [*ZPG Reporter*, 14:2, July 1982]. The Indian birthrate, although still high, dropped 18 percent in a decade. Korea, Singapore, Hong Kong, and Taiwan have dropped to half of their rate of a few years ago. Other countries have made lesser, but still significant, gains, and more countries than before have started population control programs [Lightborne et al., 1982].

The drop in the annual growth rate from 2 percent to 1.7 percent has meant an actual reduction in the annual world population

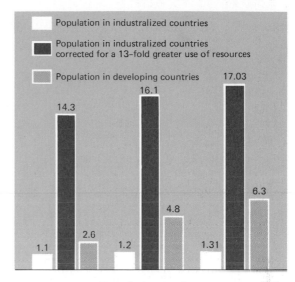

Population and resource use. The population explosion measured in terms of comparative resource use (billions). (*Source: The assumption that resource utilization is thirteen times higher in the industrialized countries is based on Bernard Berelson et al., "World Population: Status Report 1974," Reports on Population Planning, January 1974, p. 9, and 1982 World Population Data Sheet, Population Reference Bureau.*)

Is it likely that the underdeveloped countries will be able to narrow very greatly the gap between their living standards and those of the advanced countries? What is likely to happen if they fail to do so?

increase, which had been growing for several decades. Whereas the higher growth rate would have doubled the world population in thirty-six years, the lower rate will require forty-one years for doubling; or, to look at it another way, there may be a billion fewer people on earth in the year 2000 than we had previously expected.

Although the annual growth rate has been reduced from previous years, the larger world population means that, even with a lower rate, the numerical increase is greater than before (see Table 17-2, p. 431). If growth rates are to be reduced to replacement levels by the year 2000, developing countries would need to follow the Chinese example of making

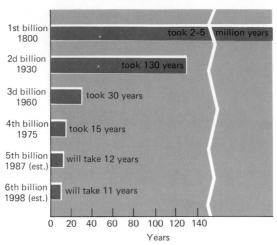

1st billion
1800 — took 2-5 million years

2d billion
1930 — took 130 years

3d billion
1960 — took 30 years

4th billion
1975 — took 15 years

5th billion
1987 (est.) — will take 12 years

6th billion
1998 (est.) — will take 11 years

0 20 40 60 80 100 120 140
Years

FIGURE 17-7 Billions added to billions. Timing of each additional billion of world population. (*Source:* U.S. News & World Report, *93:48, Aug. 2, 1981.*)

Is this situation any cause for concern? What assumptions must one make in order to answer "no" to this question?

the one-child family the ideal rather than the two- to six-child family which is desired at present [*Intercom*, 9:1, April 1982].

If world birthrates could be reduced to replacement levels by the year 2000, a very optimistic assumption, world population might stabilize at around 8.5 billion by the end of the twenty-first century [Nortman, 1972]. But world population might not stabilize; a massive die-off is a distinct possibility. As stated earlier, if present growth rates were to continue, world population would reach 20 billion by the year 2050. This will not happen, for long before this figure is reached, it is likely that famine, pestilence, war, or possibly environmental disaster will have "controlled" world population [Meadows et al., 1972; Laqueur, 1974]. The choice is clearly between family planning and famine, and it may already be too late.

SUMMARY

Demography is concerned with the age and sex composition of the population, its move-

ment, both within and across national frontiers, and its rate of growth.

The *age* and *sex composition* of a population affect its social life in many ways. Changes in age composition are due mainly to changes in birthrates and are presently increasing the proportion of the aged and reducing the proportion of children in many populations. The decreasing proportion of youth in the industrialized countries may reduce crime and teenage unemployment. An increase in the proportion of aged also reduces the proportionate number of workers and leads to heavy pension costs.

Migration is affected by the *push* given to people by unsatisfactory conditions at home, by the *pull* of attractive opportunities elsewhere, and by the *channels* or means through which they are able to migrate.

Birthrates tend to vary inversely with social status, but in recent years in the United States, the birthrates of the poor and of blacks at all income levels have been dropping sharply.

Malthus noted that population growth tends to outrun its food supply, creating overpopulation and misery unless people control population growth by postponing marriage.

Neo-Malthusians maintain that although the gloomy predictions of Malthus may have been premature, they are basically correct. The anti-Malthusians feel that the world's resources are adequate for a much larger population. Marxists and some other anti-Malthusians claim that exploitation not overpopulation is the basic cause of world hunger. The demographic transition which occurred in Western countries describes the change from a period of high birthrates and death rates and then finally to an equilibrium based on low birthrates and death rates. Whether the developing nations will repeat this demographic transition is uncertain.

Population policies may be pronatalist, antinatalist, or a mixture of both. The pronatalists reward large families and prohibit or limit the use of contraception, sterilization, and abortion. The antinatalists reward people for having smaller families and provide easy access to contraception and perhaps abortion.

The prospects for the future are uncertain. In the industrialized countries, including the United States, the trend appears to be toward eventual population stabilization, which also carries some uncomfortable adjustments.

Developing countries still have rapid rates of growth, but their rate of growth is declining. If population control efforts succeed, the world's population may eventually stabilize at about twice its present size. Whether population stability or disaster awaits us remains uncertain.

GLOSSARY

crude birthrate births per 1,000 people.
demographic transition idea that industrialization brings birthrates and death rates into balance.
demography statistical study of population composition, distribution, and trends.
fecundity biological capacity to reproduce.
fertility actual rate of reproduction.
life expectancy average years of life expected at any given age.
life span number of years that it is possible for a member of a species to survive.
optimum population the size population which will permit the highest standard of living for an area at a given level of technology.
sex ratio number of males per 100 females.

QUESTIONS AND PROJECTS

1 What has been the rate of population growth throughout most of history? Why have world rates of population growth changed recently?

2 What factors other than birth control affect the rate of reproduction?

3 Should the United States eliminate or greatly reduce immigration? Why is it difficult to control illegal immigration?

4 What were the ideas of Malthus? Do you feel that the passage of time has outdated or confirmed these ideas? Why or why not?

5 Is it true that the countries of Asia, Africa, and Latin America are now undergoing a demographic transition similar to that experienced by the United States and Western Europe at an earlier date?

6 How would you explain the tendency of inhabitants of underdeveloped areas to react more favorably to the use of sterilization and abortion than to contraception?

7 Will it be necessary to use compulsory methods of birth control to control population increase? What reason is there for thinking voluntary methods will or will not be successful? Consult the book by Stephen L. Isaacs listed in the Suggested Readings.

8 How would you explain the tendency toward an excess of females in American cities and an excess of males in the rural districts?

9 The United States seems to be moving toward lower birthrates, which will result in a smaller proportion of children and a larger proportion of the aged. What effect will this have on economic and political trends?

10 Do you think the doomsday school or the optimist school is more likely to be correct in its expectations? Compare the Suggested Readings by Julian Simon and by Lester R. Brown and Pamela Shaw in reaching your answer.

11 Do you believe that a couple has a right to bear as many children as they want and can provide for?

12 Using the most recent *Statistical Abstract of the United States*, compare the population growth of your state with others. What factors would appear to affect the relative position of your state? What adjustments do you feel your state will be required to make to meet the needs indicated by population changes?

13 Using the *United Nations Demographic Yearbook*, compare birthrates and death rates in the Philippines, India, and Mexico with those in Great Britain, France, and the United States. What conclusions would you draw about the probable future of population growth in these countries?

SUGGESTED READINGS

Appleman, Phillip: "Malthus: The Continuing Controversy," *Sierra Club Bulletin*, February 1976, pp. 9–14. A cogent treatment of neo-Malthusian and anti-Malthusian thinking. It is excerpted from the author's book *Malthus: An Essay on the Principle of Population*, W. W. Norton & Company, Inc., New York, 1976.

Brown, Lester R. and Pamela Shaw: "Putting Society on A New Path," *Environment*, 24:29–35, September 1982. A brief summary of the interrelations between population growth and environmental degradation.

Gwatkin, Davidson R., and Sarah K. Brandel: "Life Expectancy and Population Growth in the Third World," *Scientific American*, 246:57–65, May 1982. A scholarly article explaining Third World rates of population growth.

Isaacs, Stephen L.: *Population Law and Public Policy*, Human Sciences Press, New York, 1981, pp. 308–347. The incentives and penalties used by governments for both pronatal and antinatal objectives.

McGrath, Peter et al.: "Refugees or Prisoners," *Newsweek*, 99:24–29, Feb. 1, 1982. Describes Haitian refugees detained by the Immigration Service; discusses the distinction between "economic" and "political" refugees; asks whether the attitude toward the Haitians is racially motivated.

*Mohr, James C.: *Abortion in America*, Oxford University Press, New York, 1978. A historical treatment which shows that abortion became a moral issue only in the late nineteenth century.

Murdoch, William M.: "World Food Hunger," *Current*, no. 327: 6:10, December 1981. Argues that land redistribution is necessary to avert Third World hunger.

Portes, Alejandro: "Labor Functions of Illegal Aliens," *Society*, 14:31–37, September/October 1977. Tells the role of illegal Mexican migrants in the U.S. and the Mexican economy; also has articles on immigrants from China (via Hong Kong and Taiwan), Columbia, India, and the Philippines.

Simon, Julian: "Global Confusion 1980: A Hard Look at the Global 2000 Report," *The Public Interest*, 62:3–20, Winter 1980. Attack on the assumed link between population increase and shortages by a leading anti-Malthusian.

ZPG Reporter (any issue), published bimonthly by Zero Population Growth, 1346 Connecticut Avenue, N.W., Washington, D.C. Publishes articles and news items supporting the idea that no couple should bear more than two children.

*An asterisk before the citation indicates that the title is available in a paperback edition.

18 The Changing Community

If the anonymity New York grants us is a problem it is also a blessing. In small towns it is natural and easy to be passing friendly with everyone nearby, and in small towns it works. But in New York there are too many people nearby. Just try to imagine walking down Madison Avenue and being friendly to everyone you meet there! Not only would you never get where you were going, but you would be making a nuisance of yourself to thousands of people with their own errands to run. The very multitude of people makes it necessary for us to stare through and beyond one another.

. . . were I living in an apartment house, I would not care to know who lives above me, below me, or in the next apartment on either side. I want to choose my friends: I do not care to have them thrust upon me by the rental agent. And I do not want people dropping in to borrow whatever people borrow, nor to chitchat whatever neighbors chitchat . . .

It *can* be lonely at times inside that anonymity, but let a small-town friendliness echo through those canyons and the future would be chaos forever, bumper to bumper and nose to nose from here to infinity.

(John Ciardi, "Manner of Speaking," *Saturday Review*, Feb. 12, 1966, pp. 16–17).

The social life people lead is affected by the kind of community in which they live. The community is as old as humanity—or even older, for our subhuman ancestors probably shared a community life. A community can be defined either as a human group (town, city, village) or as a body of sentiment (sense of commitment, loyalty) [Gottschalk, 1975, p. 18], but there is no uniformity in the use of the term. One widely quoted definition reads: *A community is a local grouping within which people carry out a full round of life activities.* Defined in greater detail [Hillery, 1955; Jonassen, 1959, p. 20; Willis, 1977], a community includes (1) a grouping of people, (2) within a geographic area, (3) with a division of labor into specialized and interdependent functions, (4) with a common culture and a social system which organizes their activities, (5) whose members are conscious of their unity and of belonging to the community, and (6) whose members can act collectively in an organized manner. For it to qualify as a true community, its members would need to experience all or nearly all of the culture within the community's boundaries.

This definition, however, is not uniformly followed. The term is also applied to hamlets and villages with only a small cluster of houses and may be used to describe almost any subculture or category of people, whether geographical (Hickory Corners, New York City) or social (the "black community," the "community of scholars," or the "artistic community"). While sociologists like neat definitions, we must admit that a "community" is any place or category of people that is called a community.

It has been traditional to classify communities as rural or urban, depending upon whether their populations were small and agricultural, or larger and industrial or commercial. The classification was never entirely satisfactory, for it made no provision for the fishing village, the mining camp, the trading post, or many other special types of communities. Modern transportation has so eroded the boundaries between city and country that we actually have a gradual shading of one community into the other and not two distinct types of community.

THE RURAL COMMUNITY

The physical and social conditions of urban and rural life are different. Consequently there are differences in the personality and behavior of urban and rural people. These differences have provided endless source material for the novelist and the playwright and continue to interest the sociologist.

Traditional Characteristics of Rural Life

Rural communities are not all alike. Edwards [1959] distinguishes at least five types of rural communities: the town-country community with farms scattered about a village center; the open-country community without any village center; the village community, whose subtypes include the fishing village, the mining village, and the mill village; the line village, with farm homes strung along the road at the ends of long, narrow farms; and the plantation. Yet certain characteristics are common to nearly all kinds of rural communities.

ISOLATION. Perhaps the most conspicuous feature of American rural life in times past was its isolation. Throughout much of the world, rural people are clustered into small villages, within walking distance of the surrounding farmland. In the United States, the isolated homestead became the usual pattern of rural settlement, a pattern that was productively more efficient but socially isolating. Not only was the local group isolated from other groups, but each family was isolated from other families. With a thinly scattered population, personal contacts were few. Each contact involved the perception of an individual as a complete person not simply as a functionary. There were few impersonal contacts in rural societies—no anonymous bus drivers, ticket sellers, grocery clerks, or police officers. Nearly every contact was with an acquaintance who was treated not only in terms of functional role but also in terms of total personality and all the many facets of his or her status in the community.

The hospitality pattern of the American frontier, wherein the traveler was welcome to spend the night at almost any farmhouse, was a practical response both to frontier needs—where else would the traveler stay?—and to frontier loneliness. The traveler brought news, contact with the outside world, and a break in monotony. It is, therefore, no accident that the hospitality pattern developed wherever Europeans planted frontier settlements around the world [Leyburn, 1935]. Even today this hospitality pattern survives under conditions of extreme isolation. On the Alaska Highway the mores of the region require one to offer assistance to any stranded motorist. The hospitality pattern is a perfect illustration of how customs and mores arise in response to social needs, and change as these needs change.

HOMOGENEITY. Taken as a whole, American settlers were a quite heterogeneous lot. But within a given locality, the settlers were likely to be quite homogeneous in ethnic and cultural background. They generally followed earlier migrants from their home communities, so that the settlers from a particular country and district clustered together. This homogeneity, together with the comparative isolation of settlements from one another, helped to encourage the conservatism, traditionalism, and ethnocentrism of American rural communities.

FARMING. Nearly all were farmers or hired hands, while even the minister, doctor, teacher, storekeeper, and blacksmith were deeply involved in an agricultural way of life. All faced common problems, performed common tasks, and shared a common helplessness before the awesome natural forces which lie beyond human control.

SUBSISTENCE ECONOMY. The traditional American homestead tried to produce nearly everything it consumed. The bulging smokehouse, the well-stocked fruit cellar, and the shelves sagging with home-canned goods were sources of pride to the farm family. In a rapidly expanding economy with a chronic shortage of money and credit, a subsistence-and-barter economy was a socially useful adaptation. Thrift was an honored value, and conspicuous consumption was seen as an urban vice. A farm couple's status was measured by their lands, herds, barns, crops, and the inheritance they could pass on to their children—all highly visible, thus making conspicuous consumption unnecessary as symbols of success.

Living within a subsistence rather than a market economy, rural people were inclined to be suspicious of intellectuality and "book learning." Farmers were most likely to see a piece of paper when some "city slicker" was trying to do them out of something. Distrust of city people and disapproval of urban life were predictable rural attitudes.

These are some of the influences which shaped American rural personality. Although we have little empirical evidence for earlier periods, it is likely that the popular image of rural Americans as hospitable and cooperative, conservative, hard-working and thrifty, ethnocentric and intolerant was probably correct. Such characteristics were products of the physical and social conditions of American rural life until the twentieth century. Today these conditions have greatly changed, and so has the social behavior of rural people.

The Rural Revolution

REDUCED ISOLATION. Two generations ago the isolation of rural life could be measured by the contrast between the styles shown in the Sears, Roebuck catalog and those on the pages of a metropolitan newspaper. Today the styles are similar. The automobile and good roads have wrought a transformation of rural and village life which is difficult for the present generation of students to appreciate. Thousands of small villages are no longer self-contained communities, as good roads have carried their trade, their storekeepers, their professionals, and their recreation to a nearby city. If close enough to the city, they have become suburbs; if too distant, some have become the half-empty shells of decaying houses and aging people. Trans-

portation plus the press, movies, radio, and television have ended the social isolation of rural America. The true provincial today may be the urban slum dweller, who may spend years without venturing beyond one set of canyons, or possibly the suburbanite living in a one-class, one-age-group, one-race neighborhood.

COMMERCIALIZATION AND RATIONALIZATION OF AGRICULTURE. Without a revolution in agricultural productivity, there could have been little urban growth. In 1790 it required the surplus of nine farm households to support one urban household; today forty-six nonfarm households are supported by each farm household. Farming used to be a way of life which called for no special knowledge beyond that which farm youth absorbed unavoidably as they grew up. Today farming is a highly complex operation demanding substantial capital and specialized knowledge. The most successful farmers today not only use the latest farm technology but also study market trends and trade in commodities futures more actively than most readers of the *Wall Street Journal*.

The "average" American farm (in 1980) represented land and buildings worth over $250,000, plus another $60,000 or so worth of machinery, livestock, and other assets. Its operator had an "average" income of $23,800, of which only $9,000 came from farm operations. These figures do not add up. They

Today's farming is a highly complex operation.

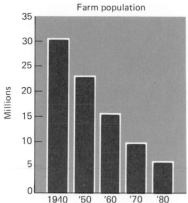

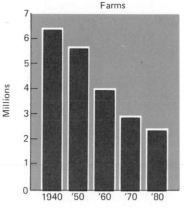

FIGURE 18-1 Farm population, farms, and farm size, 1940–1980. (*Source: Statistical Abstract, 1981, p. 654.*) How have these changes affected the political influence of farmers in the United States?

show the "average" farm returning less than 3 percent on investment with nothing for the farmer's work. The confusion arises from the census definition of a "farm" as any land under single management which produces over $1,000 worth of farm products. Thus the "average" farm includes many small part-time operations. Fewer than two out of five "farms" in 1980 produced as much as $20,000 from farm products (sales, not net income). The operators of the farms producing less than $20,000 in sales received 85 percent of their income from other sources. If only the full-time farm operations are considered, then a farm investment in the $600,000-range would be the "average." Today's successful farm is a roofless factory, using a variety of managerial skills comparable to those needed for any other business. This combination of large-scale commercialized farming with large-scale marketing is called *agribusiness.*

As farming has grown more demanding, the number of farms has fallen sharply—from 5.4 million in 1950 to 2.5 million in 1978. Meanwhile, the average size of farms has steadily increased—from 215 acres in 1950 to 415 acres in 1978 [*Statistical Abstract,* 1981, pp. 662, 664].

Farms are growing larger because of changes in farm technology. Mechanization allows one farm family to handle more acreage, and more acreage permits a more efficient use of farm machinery. Consequently, larger farms are more efficient. Production costs per unit of production on small farms are more than twice as high as on larger farms [Tweeten and Schreiner, 1970, p. 43]. There is reason to believe, however, that most full-time farm operations are now large enough to gain the "efficiencies of scale," and that continued growth in average farm size would bring no further gains [Kline, 1981].

The family farm remains the typical farm operation. Some books such as *The Myth of the Family Farm* [Vogeler, 1981] claim that corporate agribusiness is dominating American agriculture and driving out the family farm. This is debatable. Of the 51,000 corporate farms in 1978, family-held corporations accounted for 89 percent of the farms, 83 percent of their total value, and 70 percent of their total sales [*Statistical Abstract,* 1981, p. 661]. Corporation farms of all sorts accounted for only 15 percent of all farm produce in 1978, and those corporation farms which were not family-held produced only 6.5 percent of all

Farms are growing larger because of changes in farm technology. (*USDA*)

farm produce. If the family farm is a "myth," it is an extremely lively one.

Because of changes in agricultural technology, the farm population is rapidly shrinking. In 1790 the rural (farm and nonfarm) residents comprised 94.8 percent of the population. By 1920, when "farm" and "rural nonfarm" people were first separated in the census, farm people constituted 30.1 percent of the population; in 1980 they were only 2.7 percent, and they are still diminishing in proportion. We were once a nation of farmers. Today farmers are becoming one of the smallest of our major occupational groups. At present more than 1 million of our farm families are unnecessary for agricultural production and could leave the farm tomorrow without being missed. Some of these are part-time operations. About two out of five farm operators in 1978 worked two hundred days or more at nonfarm jobs. Others are "marginal" farmers, who have too little land, equipment, and capital, or too little energy and managerial skill to farm profitably. These marginal farms contribute little to our national farm product

and do not provide a decent living to their operators. Some years ago, an estimated three-fifths of the farm poor were too old, too handicapped, or too uneducated to transfer to other occupations even if offered job training [Burchinal and Siff, 1964]. Marginal farmers steadily disappear from farming through retirement and rarely through transfer to other employment. As they retire, their lands are added to other farms. Thus, the number of farmers and the farm population shrinks, while the average size of farms increases.

In 1980 American farmers entered the most serious crisis since the Depression of the 1930s. Farm prices fell sharply after 1979, with farmers caught between heavy debt, high interest payments, and falling income. Farm bankruptcies and foreclosures are approaching depression levels, and the Department of Agriculture predicts that another million farmers (not all part-time or marginal) will disappear by the end of the century [Kline, 1981]. While it is difficult to see any social benefit from it, the trend toward fewer and larger farms probably will continue.

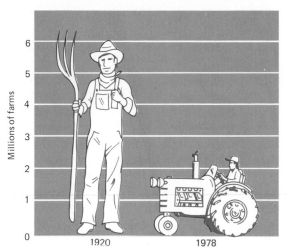

FIGURE 18-2 Farms in the United States, 1920 and 1978. The number of farms in the United States declined from 6,518,000 in 1920 to 2,479,000 in 1978. (*Source:* Statistical Abstract of the United States, *1959, p. 613; 1981, p. 662.*)

What do these data suggest about the nature of farming in the United States?

As the farm became part of the market economy, the attitudes appropriate to a subsistence economy died out. Thrift, as an

INTERRELATIONSHIP OF INSTITUTIONS

Larry Swanson . . . is an economic consultant in Lincoln, Neb., who last year completed a doctoral study of changes over a 30-year period in 27 rural Nebraska counties. "I found a direct correlation between farm sizes and conditions of rural communities," he explains. "In other words, here in the Midwest as well, when agricultural production becomes concentrated in fewer and fewer hands, the quality of community life measurably deteriorates."

From Donald Kline, "The Embattled Independent Farmer," *New York Times Magazine*, November 29, 1981, p. 145.

In what ways might agribusiness impair community life?

absolute value, seen as good in and of itself, is functionally useful in a subsistence economy. In a market economy it becomes obsolete. Farm people today appear to have as avid an appetite for new cars and color television sets as urbanites. After all, values grow out of the experience of the group. In a subsistence economy of limited productivity, where there is rarely enough of anything, especially money, the elevation of thrift to an absolute value is practical and sensible. With the development of a highly productive market economy, thrift becomes pointless as an end in itself. Instead, reasonable thrift becomes a means to an end, such as saving money on inessentials to buy a home or a new car. This and many other value changes have accompanied the technological revolution in American agriculture.

These trends are found throughout the Western world. Germany, Holland, and Belgium have less than 10 percent of their labor force in agriculture; France, about 15 percent;

FIGURE 18-3 The agricultural revolution in the United States. (*Source:* Statistical Abstract of the United States, *various dates.*)

What has made it possible for so few to feed so many?

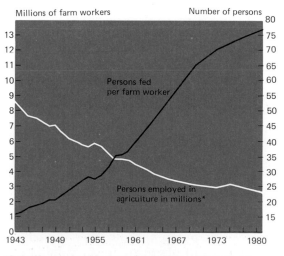

*Full-time agricultural workers, plus part-time workers equated to full-time basis.

and Italy, about 22 percent. Their rural areas face the same problems of farm unemployment and lack of training for other employment, while their cities have the same problems of congestion, housing, pollution, and taxation.

URBANIZATION OF RURAL LIFE. It is no longer possible to identify rural rustics by outmoded dress or bucolic manner. Although there are still some differences between the modal personalities, life-styles, and value systems of rural and urban dwellers, all the historic rural-urban differences are shrinking. Rural and urban people now are reached by the same media and respond to the same media personalities. Every rural activity from agriculture [Winfield,, 1973] to mate selection [Wakil, 1973] has been urbanized in that the values and norms governing the activity do not differ significantly between urban and rural people. Urban and rural people even share the same problems, as crime and drug abuse have ceased to be urban specialties. A European sociologist agrees that "we no longer have any criteria for what is urban and what is not" [Mellor, 1977, p. 49]. To a high degree, rural life is becoming urbanized, as historically urban patterns have spread into rural areas.

Taylor and Jones [1964] speak of the "urbanized social organization" of America, and every rural sociology textbook reflects this urbanization of rural life [Copp, 1964; Rogers and Burdge, 1972; Hassinger, 1978]. This process is widespread but uneven. Rural areas closer to large cities, and those where agriculture is most highly rationalized and commercialized show the highest degree of urbanization; more isolated areas and areas where farming practices are more traditional show fewer urban influences. But everywhere the steady urbanization of rural society is evident.

There are many examples of urbanization. The electric pump and the septic tank have brought urban plumbing to the rural home. The rural birthrate is approaching the urban birthrate. The rural birthrate was 77 percent higher in 1940, 40 percent higher in 1950, 34 percent higher in 1960, and 18 percent higher in 1972, when the *Statistical Abstract* ceased giving a comparison. In fact, it is becoming increasingly difficult to find any statistical data broken down into "rural" and "urban" categories. The terms still exist, with "urban" areas being defined by the U.S. Bureau of the Census as places of 2,500 or more people, and "rural" including everyone else. But most data today are classified under "metropolitan" and "nonmetropolitan" categories.

THE URBAN COMMUNITY

The Development of Cities

In order for the primitive Stone Age village to expand to a size of several hundred thousand, it needed a food surplus, a water supply, and a transportation system. Since a river valley provided all three, the first large cities arose six or seven thousand years ago in the valleys of the Nile, the Tigris, and the Euphrates. Surplus food to support an urban population was abundant in the fertile valley, and the slow-flowing rivers provided simple transportation. Although most ancient cities remained tiny by modern standards, a few reached a size of several hundred thousand, complete with problems of water supply, sewage disposal, and traffic congestion.

The growth of cities unleashed revolutionary changes. The primitive village was organized on a kinship basis and guided by custom. By contrast, a city has: (1) a division of labor into many specialized occupations, (2) social organization based upon occupation and social class rather than kinship, (3) formal government institutions based on territory rather than family, (4) a system of trade and commerce, (5) means of communication and record keeping, and (6) rational technology. These developments proceed steadily as small towns grow into large cities. Obviously the large city could not arise until the society had made a number of necessary inventions; at the same time, the development of the city proved a great stimulus to the making and improving of such inventions as carts and barges, ditches and aqueducts, writing, number systems, governmental bureaucracies, systems of occupational specialization and social stratification, and many others.

Towns and cities are of many kinds—temple towns, garrison towns, mining towns, seaports, political capitals, resort centers, industrial cities, trading centers, and others. The "company town" is a unique kind of community which has nearly disappeared [Allen, 1966]. Most large cities are diversified, carrying on a number of kinds of activity. An early sociologist, Cooley [1894], noted that cities tend to grow wherever there is a "break" in transportation so that goods must be unloaded and reloaded for transshipment. Port cities such as London, Montreal, and New Orleans are each located up a navigable river at the point where large ocean vessels can go no farther. Denver lies at the foot of a mountain range, Pittsburgh at the confluence of two rivers. The break-in-transportation theory does not necessarily apply to resort centers such as Las Vegas, Aspen, or Monte Carlo, to political capitals such as Washington or Brazilia, or to other specialized cities for which transportation was relatively unimportant, but the break-in-transportation theory still explains the location of most cities.

In the Western world, urbanization has accompanied industrialization. Commercial and industrial development provided an urban "pull," while changing agricultural technology and high rural birthrates combined to provide a rural surplus of people. In many undeveloped countries today, however, urbanization is rushing along without a proportionate industrial development. Death rates

The suburban squatter slum. Why does one appear on the outskirts of nearly every major city in the developing world? (© *Jason Laure/Woodfin Camp & Assoc.*)

in the developing countries have been falling rapidly in recent decades. Agriculture cannot absorb the population increase, so people flock to the cities, even though they have little prospect of finding jobs or housing [Ham, 1973]. In Indonesia, for example, the population of the cities has doubled every ten to fifteen years without proportionate increase in either urban industrial output or agricultural productivity.

One result of such urban growth is a type of slum practically unknown in the United States, the *suburban squatter slum*. Nearly every major city in Asia, Africa, and South America has on its outskirts a large area occupied by people living on land they do not own or rent, in flimsy shanties which they have built of scrap materials—shipping crates, scrap lumber, old signboards, flattened tin cans, old bricks, or anything else that can be scrounged. Generally there are no urban services—power, water, or sewers—and people live in a squalor which makes American slums look like castles by comparison. From one-fourth to one-half of the "urban" residents of much of the world—80 percent in Buenaventura, Colombia; 50 percent in Ankara, Turkey; 46 percent in Mexico City; 40 percent in Caracas, Venezuela—live in such wretchedness, [Juppenlatz, 1970, p. 15; Clinard, 1973; Stretton, 1978, chaps. 9–10].

Here the brutal consequences of the population explosion are evident. A falling death rate and a birthrate that remains high give a rate of population growth which exceeds the rate of expansion of the economies of the underdeveloped countries. Add to this, in most cases, a political system that is at best inefficient, and very often is both corrupt and inefficient, and often an exploitative economic system, and human misery is the inevitable result. Yet the squatter slum is not entirely dysfunctional, for it does provide—however painfully—a transitional bridge between peasant village life and the urban economy [Berry, 1973, pp. 83–91].

The Antiurban Bias

Ever since their earliest appearance, cities have been viewed with suspicion by rural peoples. The Old Testament prophets were rural men, denouncing the sins and vices of the wicked cities. Jefferson despised cities and felt that only a nation of freeholding farmers could possibly remain a democracy. Even many city people share the antiurban bias, which sees the city as a center of sin and crime, of trickery and hypocrisy, of political corruption, of frivolity and superficiality, and of vexing problems of all sorts.

The country, however, is assumed to be a haven of simple honesty and rugged integrity, where good things grow and God's own people dwell. The antiurban bias is revealed in the widespread assumption that the country or small town is a better place to raise children, that farming and raising food is more noble than other work, that "grass-roots democracy" is more genuine and rural voters more trustworthy, and that rural life and rural people are simply "better" in nearly every way. Even social research follows the antiurban bias. Most urban research shows what a mess the city is in, while funded research on rural life is generally screened to avoid any data which would challenge the assumption that "the rural community is a good place to live" [Olson, 1965].

All these assumptions are dubious, and many of them are demonstrably false. Urban and rural life are *different* in some respects, but whether one is better than the other is a question of values. The "goodness of life" in a community cannot be measured until we agree on what measures to use. If high health levels, high average incomes, higher educational levels, and many social amenities are the values chosen, then city or suburban life is better. If a quiet, uncrowded life is preferred, then the country has the edge. Obviously, this is a philosophical question not a scientific question, and it should be remembered that the assumption of rural (or urban) superiority represents a bias not a fact.

Communist revolutions outside Europe have been peasant revolutions whose leaders viewed the city as debauched and corrupt, with some reason. Cities such as Havana and Shanghai were far more unequal, exploitative, corrupt, and unproductive than any great city in the advanced capitalist countries [Stretton, 1978, p. 116]. The striking example is Phnom Penh, Cambodia (now Kampuchea), a refugee-swollen city of 2.5 million people, whose rich were corrupt and exploitative and whose poor appeared to the revolutionists as mostly useless idlers, lazy and unproductive. The Khmer Rouge leaders saw the great city as useless and parasitic. They ruthlessly drove the entire population into the countryside, with perhaps half of them dying from hardship or slaughter. The leaders decided to exterminate the educated class, abolish the great city, and return the country to an agrarian society. Phnom Penh became a near-empty shell holding a few thousand military and government officials with their families and support workers [Stretton, 1978, pp. 118–120]. The treatment of cities in Cuba and China was less draconian, since their leaders desired a modern industrial state not an agrarian society.

The Ecological Pattern of Cities

Most cities look as though they just happened—grew without plan or design—and they did. While a few major cities such as Washington, D.C., once had a plan, they have long since outgrown it. But while most city growth is not planned, neither is it entirely haphazard. Cities have structure, and there is some reason for the arrangement of their parts. Several sociologists have sought to discover the underlying pattern of modern cities. (These patterns do not fit ancient or medieval cities, nor cities in underdeveloped countries, which show a very different pattern of development [Santos, 1979]).

PATTERNS OF URBAN DESIGN. The earliest pattern of urban design was the *star pattern* of R. M. Hurd [1903]. This pictures the city as growing outward from the center along the main transportation routes, thus taking a star shape. As the automobile became a major form of urban transport, the spaces between the star points filled in, making this pattern inapplicable to modern cities.

Burgess's *concentric zone pattern*, shown in Figure 18-4, is the most famous pattern of urban design. Based upon his studies of Chicago in the early 1920s, it shows a central business district at the center, surrounded by a slum consisting of old buildings which are gradually being replaced by the expansion of the business district. This in turn is surrounded by zones of successively better-class residences.

Do real cities resemble the Burgess pattern? Most American cities have a central business district, partly or entirely surrounded by a slum. This surrounding zone contains the oldest buildings in the city, undesirable because of decay, dirt, and congestion. Housing quality tends to improve as one moves outward from this slum, and much of the choice residential area is located in the suburbs. But this pattern does not fit preindustrial cities, whose sequence of zones was reversed, with the rich living close to the center and the poor on the fringes [Sjoberg, 1960; Abbott, 1974]. Nor does the concentric zone pattern describe city growth since automobile transport became dominant. Thus, it fits some cities at a particular time and place. And even then, these zones are not unbroken bands surrounding the city, nor are they circular in shape. Instead, the various grades of residence are rather irregularly distributed and often concentrated on one side of the city.

This observation led Hoyt [1933] to frame his *sector theory of city growth*, holding that a particular kind of land use tends to locate and remain in a particular sector (a pie-shaped wedge) of the city. Thus, industry tends to

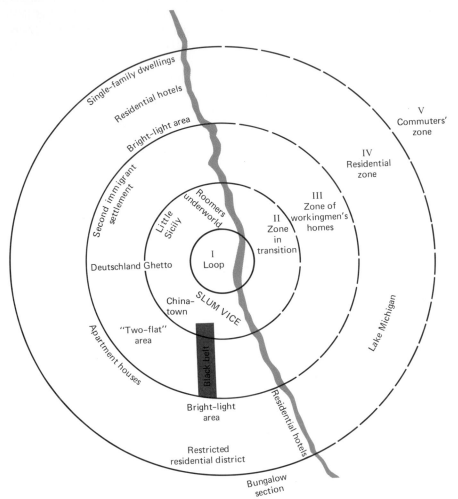

FIGURE 18-4 The concentric zone pattern: zones of Chicago, circa 1925.
(*Source: R. E. Park and E. W. Burgess,* The City, *The University of Chicago Press, Chicago, 1925, p. 55.*)
Does the city you know best bear any resemblance to this pattern?

locate in one sector, upper-class housing in an opposite sector, and working-class housing in intermediate sectors; then as time passes, each of these sectors simply expands outward until some change in topography breaks up the pattern.

The *multinuclear theory* [Harris and Ullman, 1945] holds that a number of centers—business, shopping, manufacturing—and residential areas become located early in a city's history. Topography, cost, and historical accident all enter into these early choices. These

concentrations tend to survive and fix the pattern of later city growth. Larger cities, which usually represent the growing together of once separate villages or communities, provide multiple nuclei. These three patterns are shown in comparison in Figure 18-5.

Still another pattern can be recognized—one so simple that it has not been dignified by being called a theory. It relates land use to topography. Railroads tend to follow the river valley; heavy industry locates along the railroad; upper-class residence seeks the high-

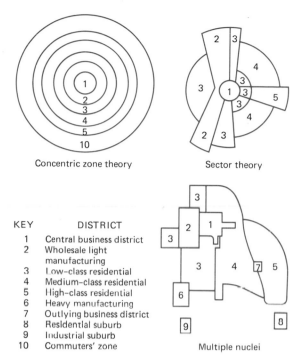

Concentric zone theory   Sector theory

KEY	DISTRICT
1	Central business district
2	Wholesale light manufacturing
3	Low-class residential
4	Medium-class residential
5	High-class residential
6	Heavy manufacturing
7	Outlying business district
8	Residential suburb
9	Industrial suburb
10	Commuters' zone

Multiple nuclei

FIGURE 18-5 Three patterns of city structure. Generalizations of internal structure of cities. The concentric zone pattern is a generalization which Burgess proposed as an ideal type to apply more or less perfectly to all cities. The arrangement of the sectors in the sector theory varies from city to city. The diagram for multiple nuclei represents one possible pattern among innumerable variations. (*Source: C. D. Harris and E. L. Ullman, "The Nature of Cities," The Annals, 242:13, November 1945.*)

Which of these most nearly fits the city you know best?

lands; and the intermediate levels of housing are scattered in between.

The existence of alternative theories shows that none of them is entirely satisfactory. None of them is perfectly illustrated by any American city, and many cities outside the United States will show very little resemblance to any of these patterns; for example, Calcutta stretches for some 35 miles along the Ganges River. Each pattern is an idea which real cities more or less perfectly resemble. Since most American cities do show some

resemblance to at least one of these patterns, the theories are helpful in revealing their prevailing structure.

City structure today has been revolutionized by transportation. In most cities the central business district has ceased to expand, and the commercial growth leapfrogs to the suburban shopping centers. A growing ring of decay is left surrounding the business district, as it no longer razes its fringe as it expands. Most of the more prosperous people flee the decay, dirt, and crime of the city for the suburbs, leaving the central city as the main reservoir for the welfare poor. The more affluent suburbs use zoning and building codes for the admitted purpose of preventing the building of low-income housing which might attract the poor [Gist and Fava, 1974, p. 614]. An aging and decaying central city is soon trapped by declining tax sources and mounting tax expenditures. This is the basic reason why nearly every city in the country has suffered a financial crisis [Robertson, 1975; Peterson, 1976; Breckenfeld, 1977; Abrahamson, 1980, chap. 14].

SLUMS. A slum is a deteriorated area of the city inhabited by poor people. Most Asian, African, and South American cities have large "shanty" slums on their outskirts as well as many slum areas within these cities. Slums in the United States are generally in the inner-city areas, the "area in transition" in Burgess's concentric zone pattern.

The slum is sometimes pictured as an area totally lacking in social organization. This is incorrect, for there *is* social organization in the slum [Whyte, 1955; Suttles, 1968; Hunter, 1975, Walter, 1977]. The slum is highly provincial, with people rarely venturing beyond the "turf" of their ethnic group. The overall pattern is one which Suttles calls "ordered segmentation" [pp. 225–227]. Each ethnic group has its boundaries, within which most social relationships are confined and socially controlled. Programs which disrupt these established boundaries therefore weaken the social controls of the area.

The oldest housing in the city is generally found in this area separating the central business district from the newer residential districts. Old buildings, however, do not cause slums. Old buildings, when structurally sound, are sometimes remodeled into highly fashionable residential districts. *It is the low income of the residents which creates a slum* [Muth, 1969].

There are several steps in the conversion of old housing into slum housing: (1) older housing units are subdivided, often through illegal makeshift conversions, so that some units lack even the facilities for cleanliness (when three families share a bathroom, who cleans it?); (2) with subdivision, there is an enormous increase in overcrowding and congestion, with buildings deteriorating through heavy use and lawns worn bare or turned into parking space; (3) building owners neglect maintenance or improvement, which are discouraged by rent control and by taxing policies which penalize improvements; (4) people who have always been poor (perhaps for generations) and have always lived in old houses generally take poor care of property. Thus, a vicious circle of cause and effect is maintained: slum landlords justify their neglect of property maintenance because slum tenants do not "take care" of property, while slum tenants typically have not developed habits of property care because they have never had any property worth taking care of.

Slumlords are often blamed for the wretchedness of the slums. The stereotype slumlord is an absentee owner who lives handsomely in a manicured suburb or a posh Florida condominium, insulated from grubby tenants by layers of realty corporations whose collectors have ingenious ways of collecting rents. Such slumlords, while doubtless real, are not numerous. In most cities, most slumlords today are minority persons who own one or two small properties, either live in one of them or in the immediate area, and get a minor part of their income from rentals [Stern-

lieb and Burchell, 1973, chaps. 2–3]. They most often became landlords because they could not afford a single-family dwelling, and they depend upon rentals to help meet the mortgage payments. Often they do not, and "residential abandonment" has become a major urban problem. Complete blocks and even entire districts are being abandoned to the rats, vandals, and squatters [Rogin, 1971; Sternlieb and Burchell, 1973]. The reason for abandonment is simple; rental income is insufficient to cover costs.

Tax policies are a prime factor in property deterioration, for property improvements bring higher tax assessments. Building code enforcement is seldom very effective in preventing deterioration. Owner-occupants are not the problem; theirs are the best-maintained slum properties. Absentee owners and realty corporations, however, may be difficult to track down, and they are experts at avoiding compliance. Finally, if fines are imposed, they are generally so small that it is cheaper to pay them than to make the repairs.

Slum clearance and low-cost housing projects had some success during the 1930s and 1940s when the program was new. Early studies showed greatly lower rates for crime and other antisocial behaviors in housing projects than in surrounding slum areas [Barer, 1946; Dee, 1956]. But as years passed, and both the levels of prosperity and the housing supply improved, the projects tended to fill up with the black welfare poor. Welfare and nonwelfare occupants do not mix well. When very many welfare tenants move in, others start moving out [Salins, 1980, p. 50]. No other residential area will accept low-income housing, for nobody wants the poor, especially when they are nonwhite. Small "scatter" public housing was also rejected, and projects became high-rise monsters located in the black ghetto (where black politicians welcomed a solid black constituency).

This isolates the project poor from the rest of society. In many projects, children lived in a world where stable families with working fathers were so few and illegitimate births and irregular families were so common that there was little chance to learn the conventional norms of study, work, marriage, and social life. Many projects became so afflicted with crime, vandalism, filth, and disorder that "normal" families fled them, rents failed to cover costs, and a cycle of abandonment and demolition began [Griffin, 1974, pp. 159–160; Cooper, 1975; Wilson and Schulz, 1978, pp. 221–223].

The early hope that better housing would bring a change toward stable (middle-class) work and family life norms has not been fulfilled. Housing alone does not "elevate" people's behavior patterns [Morris and Mogey, 1965, pp. 162–163; Weller and Luchterhand, 1973]. Public housing cannot provide

In some inner-city neighborhoods, slum dwellers are being displaced as deteriorated houses are renovated into fashionable housing for prosperous young professionals in a process called "gentrification." (*Bruce Hoertel/Camera 5*)

a decent life environment unless stable families and middle-income people are included to give a more normal population [Fuerst, 1974], and this is politically impossible. There is little realistic prospect for public housing in the United States for the near future.

Meanwhile, a *gentrification* process is developing in decaying inner-city neighborhoods. Deteriorated houses are being renovated into fashionable housing occupied by affluent young professionals. This helps to arrest urban decay and to reverse the "brain drain" to the suburbs, but it also dispossesses the inner-city poor [Fleetwood, 1979].

There has been a succession of federal approaches to slum clearance and housing improvement, none of them more than partly successful. In fact, one student of housing policy claims that virtually every intervention by federal or local governments has had the effect of promoting housing destruction instead of housing improvement [Salins, 1980]. The Reagan administration policy is to terminate practically all federally financed urban programs.

We seem to have gone full circle on the inner city, from the "no-program" of the 1920s to the "no-program" of the 1980s. As did the Nixon and Ford administrations a decade ago [Norton, 1979, p. 169], the Reagan administration implicitly accepted the inner city as a dumping ground for the minority poor.

There are rural areas which are true slums in all but location. As described in Fetterman's *Stinking Creek* [1970], rural slum housing is more dilapidated, has even fewer utility services, and has even greater room crowding. Poverty and hopelessness are equally widespread, social services are even less adequate than in the urban slum, and "welfare" is the principal source of income. The rural slum is equally grim but receives even less attention than the urban slum.

METROPOLITAN AREAS AND SUBURBS. Modern transportation is responsible for the suburb and the metropolitan area. A "standard metropolitan statistical area" is defined by the U.S. Bureau of the Census as an area with a city of at least 50,000 people (or a census-defined "urbanized area" of at least 50,000 people) and a total population of at least 100,000 people. In the 1980 census, three-fourths of the American people lived in such standard metropolitan statistical areas, with their proportion of our population showing no change since 1970. Between 1970 and 1980, the central cities lost 13.4 million people, with 10.4 million migrating to the suburbs and the rest to rural areas and small towns [U.S. Bureau of the Census, 1981*b*, p. 2].

This explosion of the suburbs is a part of what has recently come to be known as *urban sprawl*. Vast strip cities are developing from Boston to Baltimore, from Buffalo to Detroit, across Michigan and on through Chicago around to Milwaukee, and in many other places. These strip cities fit no traditional pattern of city structure. The term "megalopolis," names them and, in time, new theo-

---

THINGS ARE TOUGH ALL OVER

Decline in economic activity, loss of population, the rise of inner-city ghettos—this litany of woes so familiar in such American cities as Detroit, New York, and St. Louis—is being chanted in major cities of industrialized countries around the world. From London to Paris to Osaka, cities are facing a dramatic erosion of their economic base as business flees to suburbs or to developing countries where operating costs are much lower. The decline has spawned rising unemployment, decaying neighborhoods, racial tension, and urban violence—all virtually unknown outside the U.S. just a decade ago.

From "The World's Cities Battle a U.S.-Style Decline," *Business Week*, May 25, 1981, p. 174.

retical constructs will be developed to describe them.

Urban sprawl and strip cities bring a host of problems with them [Gottdiener, 1977; Wallace, 1980, p. 78]. Land resources are used wastefully, and the region is locked into a permanent pattern of dependence upon the automobile [McKee and Smith, 1972; Kaplan, 1976]. The existing structures of township, city, and county government are quite inadequate to organize this developing urban monstrosity. With over 1,400 separate political units in the New York metropolitan area, each with its vested interests to defend, any coherent overall planning becomes almost an impossibility. Some observers believe that the problems of these metropolitan areas are so difficult that they will not be solved, and that the largest metropolitan areas will go into a relative decline; others believe that bold planning *can* solve the problems of urban sprawl and urban blight [Jacobs, 1961; Gruen, 1964; Abrams, 1965; Erber, 1970; Griffin, 1974; Gottdiener, 1977; Birdsall, 1980]. Urban sprawl is not exclusively an American problem; it is taking place all over the world, even in the Soviet Union, despite official efforts to stem the growth of the larger cities [Anderson, 1966; Stretton, 1978, p. 194]. Urban growth proceeds for much the same reasons and has much the same consequences everywhere in the world.

The Population Turnaround

It is never safe to predict social change by simply projecting recent trends into the future. As recently as 1970, most social scientists assumed that urban growth and rural depopulation would continue indefinitely. They were dead wrong.

A 1969 Harris Poll reported that two-thirds of large-city residents wished to live elsewhere within ten years [Harris, 1970]. Many have fulfilled their wish. Rural areas and small towns are now the fastest growing parts of the United States—up by 15.5 percent, or 8.4 million people, during the 1970s. Nonmet-

TABLE 18-1

POPULATION GROWTH BY SIZE OF METROPOLITAN AREA, 1970–1980.

Size of metropolitan area	Percentage population growth, 1970–1980
3,000,000 and over	2.1
1,000,000–2,000,000	12.0
500,000–1,000,000	12.2
250,000–500,000	17.9
Under 250,000	19.0

Source: U.S. Bureau of the Census, *Current Population Reports: Population Profile of the United States, 1981*, ser. P-20, no. 374, 1982.

Why are the smaller areas growing less rapidly than the larger areas, reversing the traditional patterns of urban growth?

ropolitan counties grew much faster than metropolitan counties between 1970 and 1977 [Brown and Wardell, 1980], while the smallest metropolitan areas showed the largest growth, as shown on Table 18-1. This is the first decade since 1790 when urban areas did not grow at the "expense" of rural areas. During the 1970s, the white population of central cities fell by 6.1 million, while the black population grew by 3.6 million and the Hispanic population by 2.5 million [Bureau of the Census, 1982c, p. 23]. The developing pattern for most metropolitan areas is a minority-dominated central city surrounded by a white fringe.

Interstate migration is heavily to the "sunbelt" states of the south and southwest [Brown and Wardell, 1980, pp. 10-11]. During the 1970s, there was a *net* migration of 5.2 million persons from the northeast and north central states to the south and southwestern states [Bureau of the Census, 1981a, p. 1]. Ironically, this scattering of our population is increasing our dependence upon automobile transportation, even though the long-term outlook for gasoline supplies is uncertain.

Three reasons are given by Brown and Wardell [1980, p. 14] for this population turnaround: (1) economic decentralization, with nonfarm employment in nonmetropoli-

TABLE 18-2

POPULATION CHANGE AMONG 25 LARGEST
AMERICAN CITIES, 1970–1980

1970 rank	City	Population change	Percent change
1	New York	−824,000	−10.4
2	Chicago	−364,000	−10.8
3	Los Angeles	+155,000	+05.5
4	Philadelphia	−261,000	−13.3
5	Detroit	−311,000	−20.5
6	Houston	+361,000	+29.3
7	Baltimore	−118,000	−13.0
9	Washington	−119,000	−15.7
10	Cleveland	−177,000	−23.6
11	Indianapolis	−36,000	−04.9
12	Milwaukee	−81,000	−11.3
13	San Francisco	−37,000	−05.2
14	San Diego	+179,000	+25.8
15	San Antonio	+132,000	+20.2
16	Boston	−78,000	−12.2
17	Memphis	+22,000	+03.5
18	St. Louis	−196,000	−27.2
19	New Orleans	−35,000	−05.9
20	Phoenix	+206,000	+35.3
21	Columbus	+25,000	+04.6
22	Seattle	−37,000	−07.0
23	Pittsburgh	−96,000	−18.5
24	Denver	−23,000	−04.5
25	Kansas City, Mo	−59,000	−11.6

Source: Statistical Abstract of the United States, 1982–1983, pp. 22–24.

What patterns emerge from this table? What is common to most of the cities showing large losses? What is common to most of the cities showing large gains?

tan counties growing by 22 percent between 1970 and 1977; (2) preference for country and small-town living, as revealed by national opinion polls [Harris, 1970; Fuguitt and Zuiches, 1975; Zuiches and Carpenter, 1978]; and (3) modernization of rural life. This turn-around is definitely *not* a return to the relaxed, bucolic rural life which we imagine our ancestors to have led. Most of these rural migrants locate within commuting distance of metropolitan areas [Luloff, 1980]. They demand all the urban conveniences and soon become as involved in the organizational life of their

new communities as are the old residents [Rank and Voss, 1982]. This migration is one of the reasons for the "fading rural-urban distinction," as discussed later in this chapter.

CHANGING RACIAL STRUCTURE. Since 1940, the black population of our central cities has been growing rapidly while the white population has been fleeing to the suburbs. Between 1950 and 1980, blacks increased from 12.2 to 22.5 percent of the population of the central cities, while declining from 6.6 to 6.1 percent of the population of the suburbs. The number of black suburbanites increased, but their percentage of the total suburban population declined slightly because white suburbanites increased even faster. Most of the black suburbanites are prosperous and ambitious middle-class blacks who are leaving the inner city to the welfare poor, the unemployed and ill-employed, the broken families and the derelicts. Most black suburbanites move into the older suburbs, where they remain as segregated as they were before moving [Farley, 1970; Clark, 1979].

The growth of the black population of the central cities is slowing down, partly because the rural pool of possible black urban migrants is running low. For the nation as a whole, racial segregation has been declining. But most of this decline is in the smaller metropolitan areas and in areas of relatively low black population. In heavily black areas, residential segregation has been increasing [Van Valey et al., 1977]. Over four-fifths of American blacks are now urban, making them the most highly urbanized major segment of our population. Four central cities had black majorities in 1970—Atlanta, Gary, Newark, and Washington, D.C.—and the 1980 census added Baltimore, Birmingham, Detroit, New Orleans, and Richmond to the major cities with black majorities.

Urban Ecological Processes

Change is continuous in the American city. The means through which the distribution of

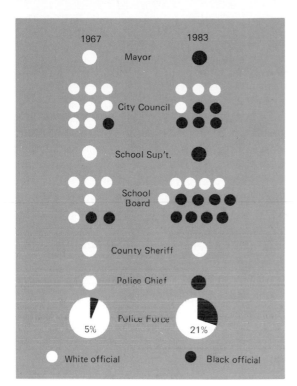

FIGURE 18-6 The changing complexion of Detroit. (*Source:* Personal letter from Office of The Mayor, City of Detroit, March 1983.)

Has this pattern been true of most major cities in the United States?

people and activities change are known as *ecological processes.* To understand them we must begin with the *natural area,* a collection of people and activities which are drawn together in mutual interdependence within a limited area. The district of flophouses and cheap hotels, cheap restaurants, pawn shops, pornography shops, taverns, and missions, all catering to the needs of low-income homeless men and women, is an example of a natural area. Other natural areas include the department-store section (formerly; most have now moved to the shopping centers), the entertainment area, the communities of recent immigrants, the rooming-house district, the college students' residential area, the warehouse district, and many others. Natural areas are unplanned. They arise from the free choices

of individuals. Persons having similar needs and preferences are drawn together into an area where these are most easily fulfilled, and this creates a natural area.

The *neighborhood,* unlike the natural area, may be either planned or unplanned. A neighborhood is an area where people neighbor, and not all areas are neighborhoods. There is very little neighboring in some areas, such as the rooming-house district, and more neighboring in the ethnic communities and family-residence areas. Some urban neighborhoods are consciously planned, with housing, communication, shopping, and recreation facilities deliberately arranged to encourage neighboring. More often the neighborhood is an unplanned product of people's need for social relations. Neighboring is greatest in family-residence areas where people face common problems of child rearing and crabgrass fighting. Neighborhoods and natural areas are constantly being formed, dissolved, and relocated through the urban ecological processes of *concentration, centralization, decentralization, segregation, invasion,* and *succession.*

Concentration is the tendency for people and activities to gather where conditions are favorable. It produces the growth of cities. *Centralization* is the clustering together of the economic and service functions within the city. People come together to work, to play, to shop; then they return to other areas to live. The shopping district; the factory district, and the entertainment district are empty of people for a part of each day or night. The central business district is a prime example of centralization. *Decentralization* is the tendency of people and organizations to desert the center of the city for outlying areas where congestion is less and land values are lower. The automobile and motor truck and electric power have greatly encouraged residential, commercial, and industrial decentralization—a tendency which greatly complicates the task of anyone who seeks to diagram the pattern of the city.

Segregation refers to the concentration of certain types of people or activities within a particular area. The "Gold Coast," the ghetto, and the produce market areas are examples, along with the hotel and banking districts, the theater district, and "used-car row." Segregation may be either voluntary or involuntary. Most immigrant groups voluntarily segregated themselves, for life was more comfortable that way. The ethnic neighborhood in the large American cities was partly voluntary and partly involuntary [Wirth, 1928]. The ghetto is an example of involuntary segregation, as low income, shortages of moderately priced housing, and a variety of threats and intimidations combine to confine most blacks to certain residential areas [Abrams, 1955; Grier and Grier, 1960; Foley, 1973].

Invasion takes place when a new kind of people, organization, or activity enters an area. Residential areas may be invaded by business, a business area may be invaded by a new kind of business residents or a different class level or ethnic group may move into a residential area. Generally the invasion is of a higher-status area by a lower-status group or activity. This direction of invasion is a normal outcome of the process of city growth and of aging. A once-exclusive residential area of homes which are no longer fashionable is invaded by people a class level below the present occupants. A generation later the same area may be invaded by persons still another class level lower, or by blacks or other ethnics, or by secondhand stores and other business houses. Occasionally the direction is reversed. As stated earlier, there are areas where dilapidated housing is being renovated or rebuilt into an upper-class residential area (gentrification). Many upper-income people have fled to the suburbs because attractive new housing is located there. Many would like to remain close to the city's center if satisfactory housing were available. Some areas have therefore traveled the complete cycle of upper-class residence to slum to upper-class residence. In all likelihood, the cycle will now be repeated.

Succession is the final stage, in which the changeover to new people or activities becomes completed. The area may remain in a disorganized and chaotic state or may become well organized around its new residents or land use.

This invasion process is continuously in operation in every American city. The processes of growth and aging make it inevitable. It is a costly process—costly in terms of human frustration and economic waste—but no one has suggested a practical alternative. Zoning is not an alternative—it is simply a technique for making invasion and succession more deliberate and orderly and for protecting vested interests in the process [Babcock, 1966; Taylor, 1980, pp. 76–77].

It is through these ecological processes that the city continues to change. City planners today are trying to control and direct the processes in order to make them less wasteful and painful.

Urban Life and Personality

The city is a place of contrasts. Cities are centers of learning, of the arts, of science and medicine, of excitement, glamor, and "progress," while rural areas have been charged with provincialism, superstition, ignorance, and bigotry. Cities are also centers of vice and crime, of frivolous extravagance, of unbridled self-indulgence, and of insincere pretension. In short, the city reveals in vivid contrast most of the dominant characteristics of the culture.

ANONYMITY. The sheer pressure of numbers makes for anonymity. Of course there are groups within which the urbanite is known as a person, but much of routine life is spent in the anonymous crowd—*The Lonely Crowd* of David Riesman [1950]. The heterogeneity of city life, with its mixture of people of all races, creeds, classes, occupations, and ethnic origins heightens this sense of anonymity. Differing interests separate people from any

In the "skid rows" are the extremes of urban anonymity—the forgotten men and women of obscure past and uncertain future. When a skid row is demolished, what happens to the skid row residents? (© *Paul Sequeira/Photo Researchers, Inc.*)

intimate acquaintance with others whom they meet in passing.

In the skid rows are the extremes of urban anonymity—the forgotten men and women of obscure past and uncertain future. They exist outside the pale of organized conventional living, their lives centered in the rooming- or flophouse, the cheap tavern, and perhaps the rescue mission. Here deviants may cluster and pursue their deviation with a minimum of interference. They are the defeated refuse of our social system, resigned, and often contented with a social role which demands little and offers little [Bogue, 1963; Wallace, 1965, 1968; Vander Kooi 1973; Blumberg et al., 1978; McSheehy, 1979].

SOCIAL DISTANCE.   City people are physically crowded but socially distant. Social distance is a product of anonymity, impersonality, and heterogeneity. Ethnic differences are one form of heterogeneity, dividing people into groups which often dislike or disdain one another. But occupational differences may be even more important sources of social distance. Unlike the agricultural community, the city has no common occupational focus which serves as a common interest for urbanites. Thus, most of the people whom one "meets" in the course of a day—neighbors, passersby, salespersons, parking lot attendants, elevator passengers—are persons with whom one has no enduring interest and only the most fleeting contact.

The city is a place of outward conformity and inner reservations, of "front" and conspicuous consumption, of "keeping up with the Joneses." When people cannot know us for what we are, they must judge us by what they see—clothing, car, jewelry, address, title, bearing.

Whether loneliness is a necessary product of city life can be debated. City people have as many primary-group associates as rural people and may see them more often [Fischer, 1976, p. 150]. But whereas *most* of the rural person's daily contacts are primary, *most* routine social contacts in the city are impersonal, segmented, and "correct." Formal politeness takes the place of genuine friendliness. With the telephone, one may contact people impersonally when necessary while keeping them at a distance. Urbanites become "nigh-dwellers," not real neighbors. Apartment dwellers may live for years with little or no acquaintance with other occupants.

Geography has always been and still remains an important basis for grouping among rural farm people, both because of scarcity of neighbors and because of the community of interests which develops from their common problems and life-styles. Urban dwellers have no such scarcity of neighbors, and one's immediate neighbors rarely share much community of interest with one. Instead, those persons with whom one shares a community of interest are likely to be scattered throughout the area. Thus, common interest replaces geographic proximity as a basis for grouping in the city. Yet urban people retain a strong sense of neighborhood identity and are not simply awash in "mass society" [Guest, Lee, and Staeheli, 1982].

REGIMENTATION. The regimentation of urban life has long been contrasted with the relaxed informality of rural life. The pressure of numbers requires that urban life be regimented. Traffic lights control the flow of traffic; subways, escalators, and elevators move on schedule. But whether urban life today is greatly more regimented than rural life is debatable. The requirements of weather conditions and the biological "clocks" of livestock may subject the farmer to a more rigidly controlled work schedule than that of many urban workers. It may be modern society, and not just urban society, that regiments us.

CROWDING. In recent years the effects of crowding upon behavior has become a favorite research topic. A number of studies of animal behavior have shown that overcrowding produces pathology and social disorganization [Calhoun, 1962; Stokols, 1976], and many have wondered if the same may be true of human beings. Crowding theory offers a very handy explanation for urban pathologies.

But animal-study findings on crowding cannot be uncritically applied to human beings, for several reasons: (1) Nowhere do human beings live under such extreme crowding as in these animal studies. (2) It is doubtful whether humans have a "territoriality" instinct which some animals seem to have [Fischer, 1976, p. 156]. (3) Humans are culture-building creatures who apparently have some capacity to adapt to conditions of high density. While some of the density studies show slight adverse effects upon some human beings [e.g, Booth and Johnson, 1975; Baldassare 1981], most of the studies do not show that high density generally has adverse effects upon people [Freedman, 1975, p. 103; Edwards and Booth, 1977]. Many high-density neighborhoods have far less pathology than many low-density neighborhoods, and there is far less crime on busy streets than on empty ones. Hong Kong is the most densely populated area on earth, yet its mortality, morbidity, and mental illness rates are low compared with most Western cities [Insel and Markowitz, 1979].

Density is an objective condition which can be measured. *Crowding* is a subjective evaluation. One is crowded if one feels a lack of desired space or privacy. (One of my friends complains that his state of Wyoming is too crowded to be livable!) There doubtless are extremes of density which would frustrate people beyond endurance. World War II veterans generally recall their crowded troopship sailings as utter nightmares. But aside from such exceptional examples, it is clear that population density need not destroy the quality of life for the inhabitants [Booth, 1976]. It is the quality of the environment inhabited and not its population density which has the greatest effect upon the quality of life.

URBAN PERSONALITY. What effects do the conditions of urban life have upon urban personality? Earlier urban sociologists, such as Park [1925], Sorokin and Zimmerman, [1929], and especially Louis Wirth in his classic essay, "Urbanism as a Way of Life" [1938], concluded that urban life created a distinct urban personality which was anomic, materialistic, self-sufficient, impersonal, hurried, superficial, manipulative, and inclined toward insecurity and personal disorganization.

Relatively little empirical research supported these impressions. Some modern studies have found that alienation and anomie are no more widespread in highly urbanized than in less highly urbanized areas [Greer and Kube, 1959, Fischer, 1973]. As urbanism increases, neighboring and participation in formal organizations decline, but primary-group relationships within kinship and friendship groups increase [Schulman, 1976]. When rural people migrate to the city, they do not enter a social vacuum but rely heavily upon relatives for social interaction [Blumberg and Bell, 1959]. Instead of the extended family declining in importance with urbanization, research finds that the extended family is an even more important unit in large cities than in rural areas [Key, 1961]. In fact, the "extended family" today might well be defined to include close friends, for they fulfill the same function as relatives. The rise of the proportion of secondary contacts with urbanism implies no absolute weakening of primary-group life.

Research has found a few differences between the urban and rural personality. For example, several studies have found rural people more likely than urban people to offer assistance, such as to a lost child [Takoosian, 1977] or a stranded motorist [McKenna, 1976]. But most recent research supports the conclusion that the anonymity and impersonality of the city were exaggerated by earlier sociologists and that any differences between urban and rural personality are not very great [Karp, Stone, and Yoels, 1977; Fischer, 1981]. Possibly the earlier urban sociologists were overly impressed by the differences between their adult urban life and the rural childhoods which most of them had known. Or perhaps some genuine urban-rural personality differences have faded as the entire society has become more urbanized.

RURAL AND URBAN CONVERGENCE

Although "rural" and "urban" are useful concepts, there has never been a sharp dividing line between them. Even before the suburban movement and the urbanization of rural life, the two life-styles converged in the *town*.

The Town

The town is intermediate between rural and urban communities. It is too large for all inhabitants to be acquainted with one another, yet small enough for informal relationships to predominate. Social behavior more closely resembles the rural than the metropolitan city pattern. There is no census definition for the town; the census classifies any settlement of over 2,500 persons as "urban" and all else as "rural." Sociological studies of the town have seldom bothered to define it, but the towns studied have never exceeded a few thousand people.

Most towns are either county seats or rural trading centers. The county-seat towns are usually stagnant, and the rural trading towns

Congestion was—and is—a common feature of urban life: Chicago, 1905; suburbia; Hong Kong; traffic in Cairo, Egypt. (*The Bettmann Archive, Inc.; Joe Munroe/Photo Researchers, Inc.; Al Lowry/Photo Researchers, Inc.; UN Photo, by B. P. Wolfe*)

are usually declining as the rural farm population falls. A great many of the youth must migrate elsewhere for employment, giving the town an abnormal population distribution and a "dead" atmosphere. The towns showing greatest growth are those close enough to cities to become commuter suburbs, or those so located as to attract industry (having water supply, labor supply, transportation, and proximity to markets), or those where tourism, recreation, or retirement living are thriving.

The local autonomy of the small town has eroded under the impact of the mass society. Martindale and Hanson [1969, p. 6] find the townspeople divided between "locals" who would like to preserve local self-sufficiency and "cosmopolitans" who would orient local life to the national economy and the mass society.

The Rural Nonfarmers

The "rural nonfarm" category has been our most rapidly growing population segment, increasing by 32 percent between 1950 and 1960, by 48 percent between 1960 and 1970, and by 20 percent between 1970 and 1980, by which time nearly one-fourth of the population fell into this category. While often called "suburbanites," either their villages are too small (under 2,500) or their settlement is too thinly scattered to be defined as "urbanized areas." These people are not engaged in farming, and many commute to urban areas for jobs, shopping, and entertainment. They are "rural" only by census definition; their life-style is more urban than rural.

The Fading Rural-Urban Distinction

Urban-rural differences of all sorts are rapidly shrinking in the Western world, and soon this will probably be true everywhere. The rural-urban distinction became secondary to the occupational distinction in importance at

The rural-urban distinction is no longer very important.

least two decades ago [Stewart, 1958; Dewey, 1960]. The distinctive rural pattern of life is more closely linked to an agricultural occupation than to mere residence in a rural area. Some years ago, a study of rural-urban differences in interpersonal relations found that farm people differed considerably from urban residents, while there was comparatively little difference between urban and rural nonfarm people [Reiss, 1959]. Clearly, occupation has become more important than rural or urban residence as a clue to one's personality and way of life. One rural sociologist concludes, "There is no *rural* society and there is no *rural* economy. It is merely *our* analytical distinction, our rhetorical device" [Copp, 1972]. We now have an *urban* culture, in which place of residence is one of the least important of all social indicators in the United States. In less developed and urbanized societies, however, the rural-urban distinction remains significant [Rosen, 1973].

THE FUTURE OF CITIES

Some of the literature on the "crisis of the cities" rebukes the present by contrasting it with a mythical Golden Age when community life was neighborly, companionable, and untroubled. But no historian has succeeded in locating such a Golden Age [Fischer et al., 1977, p. 197], and predictions of urban collapse are equally unrealistic. It is difficult to see how a modern society could operate without large cities. They may house a declining fraction of our population in the future, but it is unlikely that our "standard metropolitan statistical areas" will shrink, much less disappear [Chudacoff, 1975, p. 267].

The Inner-City Underclass

A half century of effort has failed to stop inner-city decay. It is possible that, without such effort, the inner city might be even worse, but this cannot be proved or disproved.

People, business, and industry are all deserting the central city for the suburb and smaller towns. The inner city loses many of its jobs and its better educated and more successful people. Its tax base erodes at the same time that its infrastructure (streets, bridges, sidewalks, water mains, sewers) are crumbling, sending up all kinds of urban costs.

The inner city becomes an enclave for the welfare poor and the unsuccessful. They cannot follow the jobs to the suburbs and small towns, because most residential areas deliberately zone out any new low-income housing which might attract "undesirables." Urban public transport works backwards for the inner city, for it is scheduled to bring people

into the central city in the morning and back to the suburbs at night. Any new jobs in the central city are mainly white-collar jobs which demand the good education and facility in "standard English" which most inner-city people lack. Thus inner-city poor, mostly minority poor, cannot find jobs where they live and cannot get to where the jobs are [Brunn and Wheeler, 1980, pp. 203–204]. We may be developing a permanent urban underclass, mostly minority, for whom there are no jobs and no prospects of ever getting jobs [Auletta, 1982]. The welfare cost of our inner-city underclass is our society's price for keeping the poor out of sight and out of mind.

Present federal policy is to hope that with returning prosperity, market forces will take care of inner-city problems. They will not. Most of the inner-city poor lack the job skills and the physical access needed to fill the jobs which increasing prosperity would create. A realistic program would take either of two directions: (1) *urban redevelopment*, creating new jobs within the city which inner-city people could fill, or (2) *relocation*, moving inner-city people to where the jobs are located. Some urban specialists favor redevelopment [Cassidy, 1980], and some favor relocation [Brunn and Wheeler, 1980]. Either would cost a lot of money and challenge

---

A QUESTION OF PRIORITIES

There are things that every city must do that New York, having now overcome its financial crisis, does badly or not at all. It is not hoping for the unattainable to ask that the desirable things be done—that streets and bridges be fixed, garbage be picked up, transit run dependably. There are other things we don't seem to be able to do: educate those who will not be educated, teach to work those who don't know how and

don't want to learn, reduce crime, prevent those who destroy themselves with drugs or drink from doing so.

I think it would be better if we shifted some of the enormous sums we spend on the undoable things to the doable.

Nathan Glazer, review of Charles Brecher and Raymond D. Horton, *Setting Municipal Priorities, 1982*, in *New York Times Book Review*, January 31, 1982, p. 23.

Do you agree with Glazer's view of urban priorities?

many vested interests, with no certainty of success. Our present national policy might be termed one of indifference. In the present political mood of the American people, neither program is likely to be attempted.

The New Town Movement

It is well over a century since the first "new towns" were founded in England and the United States. The idea was to avoid the dreary squalor of endless big-city growth by founding many self-contained, self-supporting new towns, pleasantly planned for efficiency and beauty. A few striking successes, such as Topiola, Finland, or Reston, Virginia, or Columbia, Maryland, show how a city can be both efficient and lovely [Clapp, 1971; Evans, 1972; Thomas and Cresswell, 1973; Campbell, 1976; Corden, 1977; Burkhart, 1981].

Most new towns in the United States have had something of a country club atmosphere. A few, such as Columbia, Maryland, included racial minorities and a mix of income levels [Burkhart, 1981], but most exclude those who are not moderately prosperous. By design, the new towns are kept to a modest size, and cannot be the magnet for artists, intellectuals, power seekers, and "happenings" which make the great city a less secure but more exciting place to live. Some residents of the new towns complain that life there is safe, efficient, and comfortable but just a bit dull. Thus, the new towns escape some urban problems while creating others; yet on balance, the new towns offer to some people a more civilized pattern of urban living than most now experience [Schaffer, 1970; Knittel, 1973; Brooks, 1974; Campbell, 1976; Klein, 1978].

New towns are no cure for the problems of existing cities. They require a huge initial investment, and most of the new town developments in the United States are in financial difficulty [Farrell, 1976; Pauley, 1976, Loomis, 1977]. Some, such as Newfield, Ohio, have completely collapsed [Steiner, 1981], and

all federal support for new towns was ended in 1978.

A new town would need to be completed every week if even half our expected urban growth were to be accommodated. Consequently, most of our urban development may be expected to follow conventional patterns.

City Planning

One commonly recommended antidote for urban problems today is city planning. Practically every city has a city planning board, although often it does little but decide upon the location of highways, public buildings, and upon zoning changes. Any comprehensive planning is certain to meet opposition from many vested interests. Yet without comprehensive planning and execution of these plans, the American city faces accelerating decay. Slums are spreading faster than they are being cleared. Uncoordinated, piecemeal development of the urban fringe and of the "strip" cities is certain to mean great waste and agonizing future problems. Sewers, water mains, and expressways, built *after* many homes and buildings are constructed, will require expensive demolition. One suburb will wind up with lots of children to educate, while another suburb will have the industrial properties which make up the tax base needed to finance good schools. Certain areas will begin to have costly floods when the development of adjacent areas alters the watershed. Quiet residential areas will become noisy thoroughfares because of developments in adjacent areas. Problems like these are the fruit of uncoordinated, unplanned regional development. There are, as yet, few planning authorities with power to make, let alone enforce, the execution of plans for an entire metropolitan area. Eventually, after the problems have become intolerable and most of the mistakes have already been made, we shall probably create the plans. They will need to include the provision of adequate public facilities such as recreation centers, public health units, and schools; necessary supplies of clean air, light, and water, along with sewage disposal; guidance and control of the restless youth of our cities; and finally ways to deal with the overwhelming problem of urban traffic. In some cases the unit of planning is an urban neighborhood, whereas other problems may demand state, regional, or even national attention.

The enormously difficult questions of how to arrest urban blight and reconstruct the social life of our cities are too complicated to be treated here. These problems fill other textbooks for other courses [Perloff et al., 1975; Cassidy, 1980; White, 1980]. Meanwhile, debate on the means and ends of urban planning and reconstruction continues [Klein, 1978; Stretton, 1978; Norton, 1979; Catonese and Snyder, 1979]. Cities are as old as recorded history, but only within the lifetime of living people have we begun to live in an urban society. And only within the memory of today's college undergraduates have we begun seriously to consider how we can organize an urban society for our comfort and contentment.

SUMMARY

A *community* is usually defined as the residents of an area within which all a group's life activities can be carried on. Rural and urban people have been different because the physical and social conditions of life were different in urban and rural communities. The traditional rural community's isolation, homogeneity, agricultural occupation, and subsistence economy all tended to develop people who were thrifty, hardworking, conservative, and ethnocentric. Changing technology has brought a rural revolution, with reduced isolation, commercialized large-scale farming, and a way of life very similar in many respects to urban patterns.

Cities become possible when an agricultural surplus develops, together with improved means of transportation, and tend to be located at "breaks in transportation." Attempts to explain the ecological pattern of American cities have produced the concentric zone, sector, and multiple nuclei theories, none of which any city perfectly fits but which many cities somewhat resemble. The most significant current developments in city structure are the *metropolitan area,* including the *suburb,* which now accounts for much of our current population growth. The present trend is for migration to rural areas and smaller towns, a turnaround which greatly lowers projections of big-city growth. The rapid growth of the black population of the central cities is now slowing down, since most blacks are now urban. As yet, there has been little black migration to the suburbs.

Slums are a product of the low income of slum residents, setting in motion a cause-and-effect circle of property neglect by landlords and property abuse by tenants. Public housing has had only limited success in arresting urban blight, in part because it intensifies the isolation of the poor from the rest of the society.

The city is a conglomeration of *natural areas,* constantly forming and shifting through the *ecological processes* of *concentration, centralization, decentralization, segregation, invasion,* and *succession.*

Urban life and personality are affected by the physical and social conditions of urban living—anonymity, density, social distance, and regimentation. These conditions were believed by earlier sociologists to cultivate a distinct urban personality—alienated, materialistic, insecure, and self-sufficient, but this conclusion is questioned by more recent research, which finds few differences between urban and rural personality. The widespread assumption that rural life and rural people are "better" is known as the *antiurban bias.* Today, urban and rural differences are rapidly shrinking. The rural-urban distinction is already less important than occupational classification as a clue to one's personality and way of life. The *town* is an example of rural-urban convergence, with townspeople divided upon whether to seek to retain small-town self-sufficiency or to seek integration into the national economy. The rapidly growing rural nonfarm population is more urban than rural in social life.

The inner-city minority poor form a growing underclass for whom there are not enough jobs within the city and who have no practical access to places where jobs might be found. The *new town movement* is an attempt to siphon people and industry into new planned communities. *City planning* is an attempt—not yet highly successful—to grapple with the increasingly grave problems of the city.

GLOSSARY

agribusiness large-scale commercialized farming and marketing.

antiurban bias assumption that city life is inferior to rural life.

community often defined as a local grouping within which people carry on a full round of life activities, but often used for any locality or category of people.

gentrification renovation of decaying urban areas for occupancy by middle- or upper-class residents.

natural area an area with a mutually interdependent cluster of a particular kind of people and activities.

urban ecological processes means whereby spatial distribution of people and activities change. They include:
  centralization clustering of economic and service functions.
  concentration tendency of people and activities to cluster together.
  decentralization flight of people and activities from the center of the city.
  invasion entrance of a new kind of people or activity into an area.
  segregation concentration of a certain type of people or activities within a particular area.
  succession completed replacement of one kind of people or activity by another.

QUESTIONS AND PROJECTS

1 Why did prehistoric people build no cities?
2 Does functional or conflict analysis better describe the rise and fall of the hospitality pattern of the frontier?
3 What has produced the rural revolution? What has this done to rural-urban differences?
4 Why has "conspicuous consumption" been more of an urban than a rural pattern? Is this relation changing today? How or why?
5 Are the "rural nonfarm" people closer to the rural or to the urban pattern in personality and life-style?
6 What causes city slums? What causes rural slums? How do rural slums resemble and differ from city slums?
7 Who is to blame for inner-city property decay and abandonment?
8 If welfare were cut off, would most of the inner-city welfare clients find jobs?
9 What are the reasons for the population turnaround? Is it a fad or an enduring change?
10 Why has crowding produced few measurable ill effects upon humans?
11 Why should urban planning be so difficult? Why can't planners devise a workable plan and carry it through?
12 Take the city you know best and apply each of the three theories of city structure. Which fits it best? How well does the theory describe the actual arrangement of this city?
13 In some college towns where 18-year-olds can vote, students could control local politics. Do they use their strength? Would the town benefit or suffer?

SUGGESTED READINGS

Booth, Alan: *Urban Crowding and Its Consequences*, Praeger

Publishers, New York, 1976. A brief summary of research.

Brunn, Stanley D. and James O. Wheeler (eds.): *The American Metropolitan System: Present and Future*, John Wiley & Sons, Inc., New York, 1980. A collection on urban problems and prospects.

Campbell, Carlos C.: *New Towns: Another Way to Live*, Reston Publishing Company, Reston, Va., 1976. An enthusiastic description of one of the more successful new towns.

Catanese, Anthony J. and James C. Snyder: *Introduction to Urban Planning*, McGraw-Hill Book Company, New York, 1979. A textbook on urban planning.

Dillman, Don A. and Daryl J. Hobbs (eds.): *Rural Society in the United States: Issues for the 1980s*, Westview Press, Boulder, Col., 1980. A collection on rural problems.

*Fischer, Claude S.: *The Urban Experience*, Harcourt Brace Jovanovich, Inc., New York, 1976. Summarizes much of our knowledge of urban life.

Fuerst, J. S.: "Class, Family, and Housing," *Society*, 12:48–53, November/December, 1974. Tells why public housing filled with welfare poor, with no stable middle-class families, is doomed to fail.

McCord, Arline and William

McCord: *Urban Social Conflict*, The C. V. Mosby Company, St. Louis, 1977. A conflict analysis of urban life, strife, and reform.

*McSheehy, William: *Skid Row*, Schenkman Publishing Co., Inc., Cambridge, Mass., 1979. A brief, readable description of skid-row life.

*Salins, Peter D.: *The Ecology of Housing Destruction: Economic Effects of Public Intervention in the Housing Market*, New York University Press for the International Center for Economic Policy Studies, New York, 1980. Argues that federal and local government intervention in housing promotes housing destruction.

*Swanson, Bert E., Richard A. Cohen, and Edith P. Swanson: *Small Towns and Small Towners: A Framework for Survival and Growth*, Sage Publications, Beverly Hills, Cal., 1979. Description and analysis of small-town life.

Van Valey, Thomas L., Wade C. Roof, and Jerome E. Wilcox: "Trends in Residential Segregation: 1960–1970," *American Journal of Sociology*, 82:826–844, January 1977. An analysis of residential segregation data, of special interest as it shows how apparently contradictory data are not necessarily incorrect but can be reconciled when the

methodology of the research studies is carefully evaluated.

Walton, John: "Toward a Synthesis of Studies of the Urban Condition," in John Walton and Donald E. Carns (eds.): *Cities in Change: Studies on the Urban Condition*, Allyn and Bacon, Inc., Boston, 1977, pp. 582–586. A very brief summary of myths and truths about American cities.

Some recent textbooks in urban sociology are: Abrahamson, Mark: *Urban Sociology*, Prentice-Hall, Inc., Englewood Cliffs, N.J., 1980; Taylor, Lee: *Urbanized Society*, Goodyear Publishing Company, Santa Monica, Cal., 1980; Wallace, Samuel E.: *The Urban Environment*, The Dorsey Press, Homewood, Ill., 1980. For textbooks in rural sociology, see Wilson, Robert A. and David A. Schultz: *Rural Sociology*, Prentice-Hall, Inc., Englewood Cliffs, N.J., 1977; Hassinger, Edward W.: *The Rural Component in American Society*, The Interstate Printers & Publishers, Inc., Danville, Ill., 1978; Bradshaw, Ted K. and Edward Blakeley: *Rural Community in Advanced Industrial Society*, Praeger Publishers, New York, 1979.

* An asterisk before the citation indicates that the title is available in a paperback edition.

19 Collective Behavior and Social Movements

Procter & Gamble Co.—tired of having its employees harassed—has enlisted the Rev. Jerry Falwell and other religious leaders to prove the company is not linked to Satanism or the Rev. Sun Myung Moon.

In recent months, P&G salesmen have had paint thrown on their cars or tires slashed. Other employees have been challenged to fights, and their children have been harassed at school because of the rumor, company officials said. Even preachers have been accusing P&G.

The rumor started with a story that linked P&G's century-old corporate symbol—a man in the moon looking out over 13 stars—to satanic worship. Another version of the rumor is that the moon symbol means P&G has been taken over by "Moonies," followers of the Rev. Sun Myung Moon.

The rumors are "preposterous" say P&G officials, who point out the symbol had its beginnings in 1851 when riverboat transporters marked P&G crates for easy identification. The design was registered in the U.S. Patent Office in 1882.

P&G now receives 12,000 calls a month about the rumors. When employees became the targets of violence, P&G decided it could no longer afford silence. The firm started an offensive against the rumors Thursday by distributing statements from five American religious leaders denouncing the rumors.

(*United Press International*, June 25, 1982.)

The rumor is just one of the fascinating kinds of collective behavior. Collective behavior is not an easy field to study scientifically. Riots and panics do not take place under the calm gaze of a visiting sociologist. Deliberately to provoke such behavior would put us in jail. Besides, just how would a sociologist conduct an interview in the midst of a mob or panic? We are limited to eyewitness accounts by observers and participants, to police records, newspaper accounts, and other scattered data. Seldom can we locate a representative sample of participants for systematic study. There have been ingenious attempts to duplicate crowd conditions of behavior in a laboratory for purposes of research, but few types of crowd behavior can be reproduced in a laboratory. Even with these limitations we have a good deal of descriptive information, together with some empirical research, from which we have developed certain insights into collective behavior.

NATURE OF COLLECTIVE BEHAVIOR

All sociologists talk about "collective behavior," but few attempt to define it. When they do, the definitions are not very useful. Smelser's definition, "mobilization on the basis of a belief which redefines social action" [Smelser, 1963, p. 8] will probably not be very clear to most students. Perry and Pugh's definition, "relatively unorganized patterns of social interaction in human groups" [1978, p. 3], has simplicity but is too broad. It covers so many kinds of behavior that it really does not define. Milgram and Toch define collective behavior as "behavior which originates spontaneously, is relatively unorganized, fairly unpredictable and planless in its course of development, and which depends upon interstimulation among participants" [1969, p. 507]. Collective behavior includes crowd behavior, mass behavior, and social movements; and the study of collective behavior includes such topics as disaster behavior, crowds, mobs, panics, rumors, crazes, mass hysteria, fads, fashions, propaganda, public opinion, social movements, and revolutions.

There are a number of theoretical formulations of collective behavior, none of them entirely adequate. Turner and Killian [1972, chap. 2] note that there are at least three different theoretical approaches. The earliest were the *contagion* theories [LeBon, 1896], which described crowd behavior as an irrational and uncritical response to the psychological temptations of the crowd situation.

This theory reflects the elitist view of common people as childish, impulsive, and irresponsible. Later came the *convergence* theories, which focus upon the shared cultural and personality characteristics of the members of a collectivity and note how these similarities encourage a collective response to a situation [Freud, 1922; Allport, 1924; Miller and Dollard, 1941]. The convergence theories view collective behavior as more than foolish impulse and admit that collective behavior can be rational and goal-directed. Finally, the *emergent norm* theories claim that in a behavior situation which invites collective behavior, a norm arises which governs the behavior [Turner and Killian, 1957, 1972]. An integrated synthesis of these theories is attempted by Smelser [1963, chap. 1]; however, it comes out as mainly an emergent norm theory. His determinants of collective behavior are:

1 *Structural conduciveness.* The structure of the society may encourage or discourage collective behavior. Simple, traditional societies are less prone to collective behavior than are modern societies.

2 *Structural strain.* Deprivation and fears of deprivation lie at the base of much collective behavior. Feelings of injustice prompt many to extreme action. Impoverished classes, oppressed minorities, groups whose hard-won gains are threatened, even privileged groups who fear the loss of their privileges—all these are candidates for collective behavior.

3 *Growth and spread of a generalized belief.* Before any collective action, there must be a belief among the actors which identifies the source of the threat, the route of escape, or the avenue of fulfillment.

4 *Precipitating factors.* Some dramatic event or rumor sets the stage for action. A cry of "police brutality" in a racially tense neighborhood may touch off a riot. One person starting to run may precipitate a panic.

5 *Mobilization for action.* Leadership emerges and begins or proposes action and directs activity.

6 *Operation of social control.* At any of the above points, the cycle can be interrupted by leadership, police power, propaganda, legislative and government policy changes, and other social controls.

Smelser's formulation has stimulated a good deal of criticism and experimentation [Oberschall, 1968; Wilkinson, 1970; Lewis, 1972; Berk, 1974a, pp. 40–46], yet it remains perhaps the most widely used theoretical approach in the study of collective behavior today.

CROWD BEHAVIOR

A *crowd* is a *temporary collection of people reacting together to stimuli.* A busload of passengers, each buried in private daydreams, is not a crowd; let the driver stop for a few drinks, and they promptly form a crowd.

Unlike most other groups, a crowd is temporary. Its members rarely know one another. Most forms of crowd behavior are unstructured, with no rules, no traditions, no formal controls, no designated leaders, no established patterns for the members to follow. Crowd behavior sometimes becomes violent, most often in response to bungling or violent attack by police or troops [Couch, 1968; Perry and Pugh, 1978, p. 19]. Crowd behavior is often called "irrational," usually by people who disapprove of the goals being sought. But crowd behavior is often goal-directed, sometimes very intelligently, and thus may be entirely "rational," even though the goals may be disapproved by others [Berk, 1974b].

Crowd behavior may appear to be spontaneous and utterly unpredictable, but as we shall see, crowd behavior is not purely a matter of chance or impulse. Crowd behavior is a part of the culture. The kinds of crowds that form and the things a crowd will do and will not do differ from one culture to another. Crowd behavior can be analyzed and understood, and to some extent predicted and controlled.

A minor incident can turn an orderly crowd into a violent one.
(*Wide World Photos*)

Contagion Theory

Social contagion is defined by Blumer as "the relatively rapid, unwitting, nonrational dissemination of a mood, impulse, or form of conduct . . ." [1975, p. 27]. Contagion theory thus emphasizes, and perhaps overemphasizes, the nonrational aspects of collective behavior. Some factors encouraging social contagion include anonymity, impersonality, suggestibility, stress, and interactional amplification.

ANONYMITY. At the county fair, many will meet their friends and neighbors; at the rock festival, most will be strangers. The more anonymous the crowd, the greater the potential for extreme action. The anonymity of the crowd removes the sense of individuality from the members. They do not pay attention to other members as individuals and do not feel that they themselves are being singled out as individuals. Thus, the restraints on a member of a crowd are reduced, and one is free to indulge in behavior which would ordinarily be controlled, because moral responsibility has been shifted from the individual to the group. At least one study [Festinger et al., 1952] claims to have confirmed these mechanisms through laboratory experimentation. Members of crowds seldom confess to any feeling of guilt after sharing in even the most outrageous atrocities, and this shift of moral responsibility to the group is part of the explanation.

IMPERSONALITY. Group behavior is typically impersonal. By this we mean that when groups interact with other groups, this interaction takes very little account of personal feelings or personal relations between members of different groups. The soldier bears no personal grudge against the enemy soldier he shoots, nor does it matter that the opposing football player is a personal friend. At the motorcycle rally, all cyclists may be perceived and feared as hoodlums by the locals, while all locals may become "the enemy" to the cyclists. The impersonality of crowd behavior is revealed in race riots where one member of the enemy race is as good or bad as another, as this incident suggests:

> We drove around for a long time. We saw a lot of colored people, but they were in bunches. We didn't want any of that. We wanted some guy all by himself. We saw one at Mack Avenue.
>
> Aldo drove past him and then said, "Gimme that gun." I handed it over to him and he turned around and came back. We were about 15 feet from the man when Aldo pulled up, almost stopped and shot. The man fell and we blew.
>
> We didn't know him. He wasn't bothering us. But other people were fighting and killing and we felt like it, too. (Alfred M. Lee and Norman D. Humphrey, *Race Riot*, Holt, Rinehart and Winston, Inc., New York, 1943, p. 38.)

It should be no surprise that peaceful passersby are attacked in race riots. If the other *group* is the enemy, then *any* member of the group is automatically a victim. But if the group setting for behavior is destroyed, then the behavior changes. For example, in the Chicago race riot of 1919, one black man outdistanced all but one of his pursuers so that the two became separated from their groups and faced each other as individuals, whereupon they quit fighting [Chicago Commission, 1922, p. 22]. Removed from their groups, they realized that fighting was pointless. Group behavior is impersonal; when interaction becomes personal, it ceases to be group behavior and changes in nature.

SUGGESTIBILITY. Since crowd situations are normally unstructured, there are no established leaders or behavior patterns for the members to carry out. Furthermore, their individual responsibility has been shifted to the group. Often the situation itself is confused and chaotic. In such a state of affairs, people sometimes act readily and uncritically upon suggestion, especially if the suggestion is made in a decisive, authoritative manner. The "unpredictability" of crowds is just another way of saying that crowds are suggestible [Lang and Lang, 1961, pp. 221–225]. This factor of suggestibility is, however, far from unlimited, and some sociologists feel that students of crowd behavior have overemphasized its importance [Couch, 1968].

STRESS. There is considerable evidence that situational stress aids social contagion [Perry and Pugh, 1978, pp. 62–65]. In other words, people under stress (fatigue, fear, anxiety, insecurity, status inconsistency, anger) are more likely to believe rumors, to panic, or to join in riots, mass hysteria, or social movements than people who are calm and untroubled.

INTERACTIONAL AMPLIFICATION. At the county fair, there is no single "crowd" most of the time; instead, there are many small groups, often family groups, drifting about with no central focus. At the rock festival, a huge, closely packed crowd surrounds a single stage from whence blasts a hypnotic beat and often a countercultural message. Most members lose themselves in a feeling of community and ecstasy somewhat like that of the great religious revivals of an earlier age.[1] This emotional buildup which crowd members give to one another is one of the most dramatic features of crowd behavior. This communi-

---

[1] See "Woodstock: Like It Was," *The New York Times*, Aug. 25, 1969, pp. 1 ff.

One can be alone in a crowd. (*Erika Stone/Peter Arnold, Inc.*)

cation of feeling is most impressive in mobs and riots, but is found in orderly crowds as well. The first one or two cheers at a football game normally fall flat; not until we hear the deep swell of voices around us will we cheer very lustily. Every professional speaker or entertainer knows that an audience thinly scattered over a large auditorium will be unresponsive. A well-filled small hall is far better. Above all, the audience must be seated close together, without many empty seats separating them. Every revivalist tries to move the audience down front so that they are close and solidly packed. The phenomenon sought has sometimes been called by the cumbersome title *interactional amplification*. This is *the process whereby the members of a crowd stimulate and respond to one another and thereby increase their emotional intensity and responsiveness.*

Contagion is increased by "milling" and "rhythm." The crowd, if unseated, may push and surge back and forth, carrying individuals along with it. The crowd may break into rhythmic clapping or shouting, with successive waves of sound carrying members to higher peaks of excitement. All these processes help to explain why crowd behavior sometimes goes further than most of the members intended. Persons who came intending to be only onlookers get caught up in the process and find themselves joining in. Many confrontations started out in a partly serious, partly festive mood but escalated through the stages of verbal abuse, rock throwing, teargassing, beating and clubbing, and sometimes shooting.

Social contagion helps to explain the great suggestibility of a crowd, once it is tuned up

The emotional buildup which crowd members give to one another is a dramatic feature of crowd behavior. (*Leif Skoogfors, 1982/Woodfin Camp & Assoc.*)

for action. A person reading in solitude a hilarious scene from a popular comedy will not find it nearly so funny as when seen as a member of an audience. Like tears, laughter is contagious. The claque, a small organized group that starts and leads the applause for a star at the right moment, is a familiar fixture in the opera house. Since our own actions are reinforced by the action of others, it takes only a few to start a wave of laughter or applause.

When a crowd becomes emotionally aroused, it needs emotional release and may act upon the first suggested action which is in line with its impulses. Lynching mobs were not always concerned about which black person they lynched; if the intended victim escaped, they might lynch any black person who was handy. In Omaha in 1919, when the mayor refused to surrender a person to be lynched, the mob attempted to lynch the mayor and very nearly succeeded. [*Literary Digest*, Oct. 11, 1919]. In a Texas town in 1930, the potential victim was hidden in the vault of the courthouse; the mob burned the courthouse, then followed by wrecking the black part of town [Cantril, 1941, pp. 97–110]. The Civil War draft riots in New York City began as protests against the draft, but soon became full-fledged antiblack riots. Any suggested action, if it is in line with the likes and dislikes of the crowd members, is likely to be acted on by an emotionally aroused crowd [Lang and Lang, chap. 8].

These characteristics of crowd behavior explain why the crowd is more than a collection of individuals. Each individual member is to some degree different in the crowd from the person he or she is when alone. As Allport [in Lindzey, 1954, vol. 1, p. 28] remarks, "It used to be said in Germany that there is no such thing as a 'single Nazi.' Only with the support of a group does the peculiar subservience to the leader and his ideology take possession of the individual." We can never fully understand crowd behavior unless we understand that the crowd, like all groups, is more than merely a collection of individuals.

Convergence Theory

According to convergence theory, crowd behavior arises from the gathering together of a number of people who share the same needs, impulses, dislikes, and purposes. The people attending a Baptist revival service share a number of characteristics which differ from those of a racetrack crowd. Why are motorcycle rallies and rock festivals so much more prone to noisy disorders than are county fairs? The people attending a rural county fair are broadly distributed by age, occupation, and social class. Most are local people, with strong ties to local groups and values, with a highly supportive attitude toward local authorities. By contrast, the motorcycle rally or rock festival attracts a quite different crowd. Most members are young and single. Most are outsiders, with no local ties or special concern for local feelings or property. Many in attendance are alienated from the dominant culture, and this alienation has been intensified by the customary local opposition to the holding of the rally or festival in their locality. Small wonder that "disorder" is more common than at county fairs.

Many more illustrations of convergence theory could be cited, showing how the gathering together of like-minded people is a major factor in crowd behavior.

Emergent Norm Theory

Crowds are never entirely like-minded, and contagion theory does not explain why the crowd takes one action rather than another. Emergent norm theorists charge that contagion theory exaggerates the irrational and purposeless components of crowd behavior. Some early riot studies showed rioters to be predominantly young, single, unsettled, and probably unstable. But studies of the riots of the 1960s found members to be relatively representative cross sections of the categories of people involved, and apparently motivated by genuine group grievances rather than by personal instabilities [Oberschall, 1968; Moinet et al., 1972; Orum, 1972, p. 76]. The burning and looting which accompanied the ghetto riots of the 1960s was not indiscriminate. Private homes, public buildings, and agencies serving the people of the area were generally spared, while those stores and offices which were perceived as exploitative were looted and burned [Oberschall, 1968; Berk and Aldrich, 1972]. These riots were not senseless outbursts of infantile or irrational rage but violent protests against perceived wrongs and injustices. This has led some observers to romanticize and idealize the rioters, picturing them as noble promoters of a higher morality [Fogelson, 1969; J. Skolnik, 1969; Rubenstein, 1970; Piven and Cloward, 1971] (provided, of course, the rioters were not KKKers, segregationists, or others with whom the observers disagreed). In opposition to this "noble crusader" image is the fact that there are some "issueless riots," which arise not from ideology, grievance, or social protest but from the desire for "fun and profit" [Marx, 1970].

The "blackout looting" in New York City in 1977, involving losses estimated at $60 million, was not ideological. The looting did not follow a protest demonstration or a "police brutality" incident. There was no anger, little physical violence, no battles with police, no general urge to "burn, burn, burn." Looting began within minutes after a widespread power failure, as the inner-city poor saw a chance to get things they wanted for free. Although spontaneous and unplanned, the looting soon became organized, with a group breaking into a store and often keeping others out until they had their pick of the "goodies" [Curvin and Porter, 1979, chap. 3; Wilson and Cooper, 1979]. Riots are not all alike. The components of serious protest and "fun and profit" appear in different proportions on different occasions. It seems that, starting with the perceptions and grievances of the members, and fed by the contagion process, a norm eventually emerges which justifies and sets limits to the crowd behavior.

A crowd in action can be a terrifying thing. A factual account of everything said and done by an aggressive mob would be unprintable. To cite just one example, lynching victims were frequently burned alive or slowly strangled and sometimes emasculated as well as being subjected to other unprintable tortures

[Raper, 1933, pp. 6–7, 144]. Some say people will do anything when caught up in the crowd. Is this true?

Limitations on Crowd Behavior

However irrational and unrestrained it may appear, crowd behavior is limited by at least four considerations: (1) the emotional needs of the members; (2) the mores of the members; (3) the leadership of the crowd; (4) the external controls over the crowd.

EMOTIONAL NEEDS OF MEMBERS.   Crowd behavior expresses the emotional needs, resentments, and prejudices of the members. In a crowd situation people may do things they ordinarily would not do, but a crowd does only those things that most of its members *would like to do.* The emotional stimulus and protection of the crowd enables its members to express the impulses, hostilities, aggressions, and rages which they are restrained from expressing in calmer moments. Many of us, for example, like to break things, but we must restrain the impulses. People in a riot can shed restraints and can tear things up without guilt feelings. If blocked from its first objective, a mob generally shifts to another. The substitute, however, still represents the hated victim or fulfills the frustrated wish.

Homogeneous audiences are the most responsive. This observation supports the convergence theory. An audience whose members have the same interests and viewpoints will respond enthusiastically to a good speaker. The political rally attracts mainly the party faithful. Its function is similar to that of a pep meeting before a football game—to arouse enthusiasm and dedication to the team. A crowd is most likely to take aggressive action when its members share a common set of prejudices and hostilities. Persons who do not share these feelings are likely to edge backward to the fringes, while the core of the crowd is made up of like-minded members.

A crowd does only those things
that most of its members would like to do.

MORES OF MEMBERS.   Crowd behavior is limited by the mores of its members. The crowd rarely if ever does anything which does not claim a measure of moral approval. Lynchings did not occur in areas where the mores of most people strongly condemned them. Lynchings took place only where a large proportion of the people felt that a lynching was morally justified, even necessary, under certain circumstances. The members of the lynching party normally considered themselves public protectors, not guilty lawbreakers. Even the lynching party, then, was expressing, rather than violating, the mores of the members and probably the dominant mores of the region. We note, furthermore, that while the victim might have been killed, burned, and mutilated, he was never crucified, nor was his body ever eaten. The crowd's mores did not support these actions.

It is true that a crowd member may confess later to have shared in acts he or she realized were morally wrong. Each person holds a number of mutually inconsistent views, and at a given moment one or another of them is operative. It may seem very "right" to shout down a platform speaker whose ideas we see as wicked and immoral; but when the speaker for *our* side is silenced, then freedom and justice have been trampled in the dust. Our mores teach us that we should be loyal to family, friends, and fellow workers and should do nothing that injures other people. When a firefighters' or police officers' strike is called, should the worker loyally support the other strikers and injure the public or stay on the job and injure fellow workers? Rarely in a behavior situation does the individual have only *one* applicable moral judgment. Which of one's several sets of mores will operate in a particular situation will be affected by the group pressures surrounding one at that moment.

The function of the crowd is not to paralyze the moral judgments of its members; the function of the crowd is to isolate and neutralize some moral judgments, so that certain others can find unrestrained expression. Thus, a crowd is doing only those things for which the mores of the participants give considerable approval.

CROWD LEADERSHIP. The leadership profoundly affects the intensity and direction of crowd behavior. Given a collection of frustrated, resentful people, a skillful leader can convert them into a vengeful mob and direct their aggression at any "enemy" whom they already hate. Likewise, a leader can sometimes calm or divert a crowd by a strategic suggestion or command.

Since most crowd behavior is unstructured, with no designated leaders, leadership is "up for grabs." Anyone may be able to assume leadership by simply calling out suggestions and commands. The most unlikely persons sometimes assume leadership. In the panic of the *Lusitania* ship disaster, it was an 18-year-old boy under whose direction a few lifeboats were successfully filled and launched [Lapiere, 1938, p. 459]. In many crowd situations, the members, frustrated by confusion and uncertainty, *want* to be directed, and the first person who starts giving clear orders in an authoritative manner is likely to be followed. An impressive appearance is helpful, but the assured manner of one who knows what to do is essential. Let us see specifically what the crowd leader does.

1 *The leader must establish rapport.* By "rapport," we mean a responsive, trusting, attentive relationship, such as any really successful speaker establishes with an audience. Rapport is most easily established by a speaker who shares the background of the crowd members, senses their feelings, and can speak their language. Affluent college students have sometimes tried to work with poor people or to promote student-worker alliances, usually with little success. A student who grew up in a working-class family and had worked in a factory might do better at establishing rapport.

2 *The leader builds emotional tensions.* For some types of crowds (mobs, riots, some audiences) the leader builds up their emotional tensions by an impassioned reminder of their problems and grievances. The revivalist convicts the sinners of their sins, the leader of the lynching mob arouses the men to defend the purity of their wives and daughters; the cheerleader focuses all history on the outcome of tomorrow's game. In some kinds of crowds (the panic, some audiences) the leader need not arouse emotional tension, for it already exists.

3 *The leader suggests action to release the tension.* The cheerleader lights the bonfire; the revivalist calls for the penitent to come to the altar; the revolutionist summons the crowd to storm the barricades.

4 *The leader justifies the suggested action.* Seldom does a crowd respond instantly to suggestion (except perhaps in panic behavior). Generally the leader makes some effort to justify the suggestion. The revivalist pictures the new life of release from sin; the looter cries, "I'm getting mine!" The repetition of the suggestion and its justifications permits social contagion to continue to operate, so that tension continues to mount and the need for release of tension continues to grow.

Leadership can function either to stimulate or to restrain a crowd, or to direct activity from one objective to another. Leadership is, therefore, one of the limiting factors in crowd behavior.

*Social
Change and
Social Policy*

EXTERNAL CONTROLS. Most mob behavior occurs in the summertime, when people are normally standing around and gathering in large outdoor assemblies. Cold weather discourages mobs; so do hard thundershowers. Mob behavior is rare on army posts, where military discipline can be invoked to maintain order. Service personnel must release their tensions off the post.

The principal external controls on crowd behavior, however, are those exerted by the police. There are practically no instances where persons were lynched in spite of a really determined effort of law-enforcement officials to prevent the lynching. Most lynchings were preceded by either the open connivance of law-enforcement officials or by their merely token resistance. The virtual disappearance of lynching in recent decades stems in large part not from any lack of persons who would enjoy a lynching but from the determination of law-enforcement officials to prevent lynchings. In recent years, shootings and "disappearances" have replaced the classic lynchings.

Some practical knowledge about crowd control is available to police officials. Some years ago, a sociologist who was also a law-enforcement official [Lohman, 1947] prepared a widely cited handbook on the handling of potential riot situations, which summarizes in simple language what social science has learned about ways of directing crowd behavior. Among the procedures used in preventing small incidents from developing into riots are: (1) preventing crowd formation by promptly arresting and carrying off noisy troublemakers and ordering the onlookers to move on; (2) meeting threatened disorder with an impressive *show of force*, bringing enough police and equipment into the area so that a *use* of force is unnecessary; (3) isolating a riot area by throwing a police cordon around it and allowing people to leave but not to enter the area; (4) diminishing a crowd by directing the persons on the fringes to "break up and go home," thus stripping the crowd down to its core and depriving the core of its mass support; (5) emphasis in police training on the officers' duty to maintain the peace, so that officers' own prejudices do not lead them into the fatal error of ignoring attacks on those whom they do not like.

With very few exceptions, serious riots are evidence of police failure. School integration disorders in the 1960s are an example. Where local police and public officials let it be known that no disorders would be tolerated, disorders were rare. Smelser [1963, pp. 261–268] cites many cases where hestitation and indecision of police and other officials, or even their open sympathizing with the rioters, encouraged riot development.

Some exceptions must be made to the proposition that police can control crowds if they wish. Small cities have no police reserves that can be shifted from place to place in an emergency. A local festival or celebration may bring people into a locality in numbers beyond the capacity of local police to handle. Campus disturbances of the 1960s were difficult to control. Students felt that the campus was "theirs," and the presence of local police or troops was more likely to provoke than to prevent a riot [Knott, 1971].

Police control of civil disturbances poses a difficult problem. Failure to use firmness early in a demonstration may encourage the crowd to grow and the disorder to become unmanageable; yet a premature police presence or use of force may "radicalize" a crowd (or a student body) and provoke an escalation of disorder. Whatever the police do is likely to be judged an error! Obviously, the capacity of police force to control crowd behavior is not unlimited [Wenger, 1973].

Some Forms of Crowd Behavior

THE AUDIENCE. An *audience* is *a crowd with interest centered on stimuli outside themselves*. The stimuli are mainly one-way. With the movie, radio, or television audience, the stimuli are entirely one-way. Every instructor, however, realizes that a performer before a "live" audience is affected by the audience reaction. An unresponsive audience will take the sparkle out of almost any sermon, lecture, or nightclub performance.

With an audience, then, there may be significant two-way stimulus and response, even though the audience situation discourages the communication. The most successful performers cultivate a two-way communication which seems to make the performer a part of the group [Berger, 1971]. There is also a certain amount of communication between members, as they cheer, applaud, boo, whisper, mutter, doze, or snore. Social contagion still operates, usually at a more subdued level than in other crowds—highly subdued at a sedate church service, more freely expressive at a political rally or a sports event. Audiences may become unruly and may even become riotous.

THE RIOT. A *riot* is *the action of a violently aggressive, destructive crowd.* It may be a religious riot, like that between the Hindus and the Moslems in India in 1947 [Duncan, 1947; McGinty, 1947] or between Catholics and Protestants in Northern Ireland. It may be a nationality riot, like that between American servicemen and Mexicans in Los Angeles in 1943, or the so-called "zoot-suit" riot [Turner and Surace, 1956], or the many mob actions against European immigrants in the United States during the nineteenth and early twentieth centuries [Higham, 1955]. Race, religion, or nationality—no matter what the cause, the crowd behavior is much the same. A group is disliked because it is different; or it serves as a convenient scapegoat; or it is hated because it competes too successfully. With suitable stimulating incidents and without effective police discouragement, persons who are individually frustrated and insecure start action; it builds and grows; the attacked group strikes back, and the riot is under way.

Civic officials sometimes blame a riot upon "outside agitators" or "communist conspirators." By implication, this denies the importance of underlying grievances or of community failure to deal with them. But numerous riot investigations have found remarkably little evidence of riot planning or riot direction. Most riots are spontaneous outbursts by aggrieved groups reacting to a stimulus incident or rumor [Knopf, 1975, p. 104].

Riots are of many kinds. In the classic race riot, members of two races indiscriminately hunt down and beat or kill one another, as in Chicago in 1919 [Chicago Commission, 1922] or in Detroit in 1943 [Lee and Humphrey, 1943]. One study of many race riots [Lieberson and Silverman, 1965] finds that they were usually precipitated by a report of dramatic violence by one race against the other—rape, murder, assault, police brutality—in a society where race problems have not been—and perhaps cannot be—resolved by existing social institutions, and were most likely to occur in communities that had been unresponsive to black needs and appeals [Downes, 1968].

There are other kinds of riots. The protest riot, common in colonial countries, had the object of dramatizing grievances and wringing concessions from the governing powers. The black riots in many American cities beginning in 1965 were not conventional race riots—not primarily a clash between races—but protest riots. A decade of civil rights "victories" had brought few gains to lower-class blacks, who remained outside the "affluent society." While skilled and educated blacks were gaining, lower-class blacks were falling steadily further behind, growing more frustrated than ever. Usually precipitated by reports of police brutality (often untrue), large-scale violence, burning, and looting exploded across the country [Moynihan, 1965a; Blauner, 1966; Cohen and Murphy, 1966; Rustin, 1967; *Ebony,* special issue, August 1967; National Advisory Commission on Civil Disorder, 1968; Boskin, 1969; Urban America, Inc.,

1969; Oberschall, 1975, pp. 329–332]. Any riot provides the support of the crowd and a release from moral responsibility, so that one may express any impulse. Many riots include all these elements—flaunting of authority, attack upon disliked groups, and looting and wrecking of property, especially property belonging to the hated group.

Some campus riots, notably at Berkeley, California, in 1964 and 1965, and at Kent State in 1970, were disturbing to many Americans. As riots go, they were pretty tame affairs, involving only a small fraction of the students plus some nonstudents who "hung around" the larger campuses. There was a lot of noise and some seizing of campus buildings and disruption of campus activities but little property destruction. Virtually all physical injuries or deaths were inflicted by police or troops. With the end of the draft for service in Vietnam, the greatest source of student protest was removed, and campus demonstrations soon ended.

Student disorders are, of course, as old as the university. A wave of them in the 1880s hit many colleges, with Amherst's rebellion led by Calvin Coolidge and (later Chief Justice) Harlan Fiske Stone (after Stone was thrown out of another college for leading a demonstration) [Feuer, 1966]. These nineteenth-century rebellions were staged by students who were alienated from their college administrations but who were not alienated from their society. More recent campus disorders have typically been led by students and nonstudents who were deeply alienated from Establishment society and who would not be placated by anything less than major changes in contemporary social institutions [Knott, 1971].

THE ORGY. *Revelry of a crowd which transgresses the normal mores* is an *orgy*. Like other crowd actions, the orgy releases tensions; but where the riot is mad with anger, the orgy is mad with joy. One cannot have an orgy by oneself; revelry must be shared, or it falls flat. But a

very creditable orgy may be promoted by anywhere from a handful of persons to a crowd of thousands. Exactly where "decent recreation" leaves off and the orgy begins is, perhaps, a value judgment. But to be effective in the release of tension, the orgy must involve behavior which exceeds the ordinary daily restraints and inhibitions. Yet not all restraints are lifted, for some of the taboos remain in force. The orgy is *unrestrained behavior within recognized limits*. Listiak refers to these partial but limited relaxations of normal restraints as "Time Outs" [1974, p. 13].

In the orgy we see the factors which operate in all crowd behavior—leadership, social contagion, suggestibility, and transfer of moral responsibility to the group. Since it takes time for these forces to begin to operate, the party takes a while to get going. Before long, inhibitions are diluted, and interaction becomes less restrained. Thus, many a motel party, after-the-game celebration, or convention get-together winds up as an orgy.

All societies create frustrations in their members, and all societies provide in some way for the release of tensions. In some societies the orgy is an institutionalized way for members to release their accumulated tensions. One sociologist describes the orgy as "legitimate deviance" [Listiak, 1974, p. 13]. Many primitive societies had periodic festivals or holidays in which ceremonial and orgiastic behavior were combined [MacAndrew and Edgerton. 1969]. Games, feasting, drinking, orgiastic dancing, and the suspension of some of the sex taboos were common features of primitive festivals. Among the Incas, for example:

> Holidays might last for a day or for a week; there might be public dancing, such as when hundreds of radiantly clothed "Chosen Women" danced with Huaschar's chain; there could be games and sports; there was always drinking, of a sort one writer calls "approved license." For the Indian [Inca] was expected to get drunk, which he did, quaffing immense quantities of fermented chìcha; for ritual drunkenness was as

essential to a good festival as agriculture discipline to a good harvest.

Games at the festivals differed from those played by the Indian boy. . . . On the day fixed for the [December] feast, men and girls came to a predetermined place among the ripened fruit gardens, whose ripening they were to celebrate. Men and women were completely naked. At a given signal they started on a race, upon which bets were placed, toward some hill at a distance. Each man that overtook any woman in the race "enjoyed her on the spot." (Victor W. von Hagen, *Realm of the Incas*, Mentor Books, New American Library of World Literature, Inc., New York, 1957, pp. 96–97. From the series, *The Ancient Sun Kingdoms of the Americas*, The World Publishing Company, Cleveland.)

Students of revelry have assumed that the greater the accumulated tensions, the greater the temptation to find release through orgy. Casual observation would seem to support this idea. Whenever men are isolated from female company or family life and subjected to harsh discipline, monotonous work, and unsatisfactory living conditions for long periods of time, most of them promptly go on a spree at the first opportunity. Army camps, naval stations, construction camps, lumber camps, and mining camps are classic examples. Presumably, the greater the frustrations and tensions, the more riotous the release. Ernie Pyle [1943, p. 3], the perceptive war correspondent, observed that infantry men often endured mud, rain, and dirt, and continuous chaos and uncertainty even as to where they would eat and sleep, whereas sailors ordinarily had clean clothes, good food, and a ship to call home. He then remarked that ". . . sailors didn't cuss as much or as foully as soldiers. They didn't bust loose as riotously when they hit town."

Today the automobile and the mobile home have largely destroyed the isolation of the construction camp, lumber camp, or mining camp, and the orgy has largely faded from their fringes. What no amount of moralizing could do, changing technology has accom-

plished. The armed services have attempted to make military life more comfortable and less frustrating, and the row of taverns, gambling places, and houses of prostitution in the nearest town is shortened, if not gone.

American society has many approved forms of recreation—dancing, moviegoing, participation sports, spectator sports, and many others—which doubtless serve to release tensions. A few events, such as the football victory celebration or the Christmas office party show in very mild form some of the features of the institutionalized orgy. Some community festivals, such as New Orleans' Mardi Gras, Cheyenne's Frontier Day, the Calgary Stampede, or Canada's Grey Cup Week,[2] come closer to being institutionalized orgies. But with relatively few exceptions, our society has not permitted instutionalized orgies, and even the office Christmas party has largely disappeared in recent years.

Orgies are fairly safe outlets in primitive societies. In a nonmechanical society, drunkenness which is limited to a few scheduled occasions may be harmless. In a society with a consanguine family system, collective property ownership, and a serene unconcern with exact biological paternity, an occasional period of sexual license creates no problems. But in our society, the price of an orgy may be a painful accident, a costly fire, or a "problem" pregnancy. Our society's inability to provide safe, harmless orgies, however, also carries a price tag. In a society which produces a great many tensions within individuals, these tensions must find release in one way or another. Blocking one dangerous outlet does not guarantee that the substitute outlet will be less offensive. Lapiere comments:

That the cause of the drunken spree lies in social circumstances which demand an occasional es-

---

[2] The Grey Cup is awarded annually to the winner of the Canadian National Football League Championship. Grey Cup Week is held in the city in which the championship game is played [Listiak, 1974].

cape, rather than, as moralists assume, in the commercial provision of opportunities for such indulgence, is illustrated by the history of an attempt to check the week-end sprees of English industrial workers. Motivated, no doubt, by the best of intentions, the stringent closing of the "pubs" in the depressing East End of London some years ago had, however, such unanticipated consequences that it was soon found advisable to remove the harsh restrictions. Withholding alcohol from workers who were accustomed to a week-end drunk reduced drunkenness and disorderly conduct, but it caused a striking increase in the frequency of wife beating, murder, and suicide. (Richard Lapiere, *Collective Behavior*, McGraw-Hill Book Company, 1938, p. 484. © 1938. Used with permission of McGraw-Hill Book Company.)

The persistent question of how to reconcile our appetite for revelry with our need for individual safety and social order is not likely to be settled in the near future.

THE PANIC. Panic has sometimes been defined as an emotional state of desperate, uncontrollable fear [Cantril, 1943; Janis, 1951].

More recent definitions include collective flight as a necessary feature of panic [Quarentelli, 1954]. Most widely quoted, however, is Smelser's definition of panic as "a collective flight based on a hysterical belief." [1963, p. 131].

Panic involves the familiar elements of crowd behavior, blossoming suddenly under the stress of crisis. There is little empirical research on panic, since we dare not produce panics to order for study. There are, however, many descriptive accounts and theoretical formulations [Strauss, 1944; Foreman, 1953; Smelser, 1963; Schultz, 1964; Perry and Pugh, 1974, pp. 108–116]. Panic appears to be most likely to seize a group which is fatigued by prolonged stress, although many panics have spread through perfectly relaxed groups. Smelser [1963, chap. 6] sees panic as likely when people feel in great danger with a very limited escape route. Where there are ample escape routes, there is little perceived danger, little fear, and little likelihood of panic. Where there is *no* escape, the usual response is a calm acceptance of fate.

A perceived crisis produces fear, uncertainty, confusion, and a lack of decisive lead-

---

WHOSE FAULT?

There was no enemy, no anger, no panic. Just thousands of people eager to hear The Who at Cincinnati's Riverfront Coliseum. Only a few held reserved seats. Over 15,000 held "general admission" tickets, inviting each to try to beat the others to a good seat.

The crowd started building shortly after noon. By mid-afternoon the police were called. By 7:00 P.M. the crowd was pressing forward impatiently. When the doors finally opened, the crowd surged forward. Inevitably, some fell and could not rise, trampled under foot by others irresistibly pushed forward by those pressing from behind. Moments later, eleven persons were dead and seven seriously injured.

Who was to blame? Only those on the outer edges of the crowd had any choice, but they were too far back to sense any problem so they pressed forward. Was it their fault?

A Cincinnati editor called the youthful audience "animals." Was he correct?

When 15,000 people are sold "general admission" tickets to hear popular celebrities, crowd control problems may be expected. It had happened before at the Coliseum—at concerts by Elton John in 1976 and Led Zepplin in 1977.

Crowd control problems are always a possibility. Lack of foresight by responsible officials makes them a predictable certainty.

Adapted from "Stampede to Tragedy," *Time*, Dec. 17, 1979, pp. 88–89.

What suggestions might a sociologist give upon how to avert such a tragedy?

ership. The role of leadership is crucial in panic prevention, for panic spreads when members lose faith in organized, cooperative effort, and each takes individual defensive action [Mintz, 1951]. In a burning building, one person shouting "Fire!" or "Let me out!" may be enough to start a panic. When a crowd is leaving in an orderly manner, if there is any interruption—if someone stumbles and momentarily blocks the aisle—somebody may break out of line in a dash and touch off a panic. Often a panic is precipitated by a "front to rear communication failure." Those in front see that the escape route is blocked, and seek to turn back to find another; those in back cannot see this and push forward harder and harder as the delay lengthens. This is the usual explanation for the suffocating pileup.

In panic prevention, a leader does at least two things: (1) organizes the crowd so that cooperative activity can proceed, and (2) relieves uncertainty by specific directions and reassurances. Marshall [1947, p. 130] has pointed out that when an army unit is under heavy fire, if the unit leader says, "Let's get out of here!" panic is likely; but if he says, "Follow me to that fence," panic is unlikely. Once panic has spread, it generally continues until the crisis is past or the members are exhausted (or dead). Panic prevention depends upon a decisive leader who assumes direction quickly enough to organize action before panic begins.

MASS BEHAVIOR

A *mass* is not the same as a crowd. The spectators at a football game are a crowd; those watching the game at home on television are a mass. Hoult [1969, p. 194] defines a mass as a "relatively large number of persons, spatially dispersed and anonymous, reacting to one or more of the same stimuli but acting individually without regard for one another."

Mass behavior is *the unorganized, unstructured, uncoordinated, individually chosen behavior of masses*. It differs from crowd behavior in that crowd behavior is brief and episodic and is acted out by people as a group, whereas mass behavior is more enduring and arises from the sum total of many individual actions. Also, crowds are aggregations of people in immediate social interaction with one another; masses are scattered and in no direct, continuous contact with one another. Masses cannot mill and interact as crowds do. When many people, acting individually rather than as a group, move in the same direction, this is mass behavior. A flight of refugees or the popularity of videogames are examples.

The Rumor

At last count, the Federal Communications Commission had received over 11 million angry letters over a seven-year period protesting Madalyn Murray O'Hair's petition to remove religious broadcasting from the airwaves. Mrs. O'Hair's battle against school prayers is well remembered, but her campaign against religious broadcasting is strictly imaginary. Neither she nor anyone else filed such a petition. But despite repeated FCC corrections, thousands of letters a day were still arriving [Castelli, 1976; Koza, 1982]. Such is the power of rumor.

A *rumor* is *a rapidly spreading report unsubstantiated by fact*. Rumors may be spread by mass media or by word of mouth. Much of our casual conversation consists of rumor-mongering. Every topic, from neighbors' morals to the fate of the nation, attracts interesting and disturbing rumors. Whenever there is a social strain, rumors flourish. Wherever accurate and complete facts on a matter of public concern are not available or are not believed, rumors abound. Since rumors can ruin reputations, discredit causes, and undermine morale, the manipulation of rumor is a common propaganda device.

In a classic work on rumor, Allport and Postman [1947, p. 46] point out that a great amount of rumormongering springs from nothing more complicated than the desire for interesting conversation or the enjoyment of a salacious story. Public celebrities attract rumors like honey draws flies. Thus, a rumor of the mysterious death of one of the Beatles spread among young people in 1971 and persisted despite repeated denials [Suczek, 1972]. People are most likely, however, to believe and spread a rumor *if it will justify their dislikes or relieve their emotional tensions.* People who dislike Republicans, hate blacks, or despise welfare clients will remember and repeat damaging rumors about these groups. The rumor changes continuously as it spreads, for people unconsciously distort it into the form that most perfectly supports their antagonisms. People uncritically accept and believe a rumor if it fits in with their pattern of beliefs and dislikes, or if it provides an emotionally satisfying explanation of something.

Every presidential assassination has produced a flood of rumors of assassination conspiracies [Belin, 1973]. The conspiracy rumor is especially satisfying. It gives one the flattering feeling of having "inside" knowledge, along with a delicious sense of fearlessly denouncing evildoers.

Rumors are not very effectively dispelled by truthful correction. The "rumor control centers" established in many cities during the 1960s' urban riots were of doubtful effectiveness [Knopf, 1975, pp. 301–315]. Such centers often spread the rumor rather than the correction [Ponting, 1973]. Some scholars claim that more effective techniques of rumor control are now available [Rosnow and Fine, 1976], but other scholars question whether this is true [Weinberg and Eich, 1978]. Rumors are believed and spread because people need and like them. As Shibutani [1966, p. 139] proposes: "The process of rumor construction is terminated when the situation in which it arose is no longer problematic." This means,

for example, that rumors flourish where people feel they cannot trust government officials to tell them the truth, but rumors will subside if confidence in their officials is restored.

An unusually persistent rumor often becomes a legend, accepted as true by many who hear it. According to Brunvand [1981, p. 10], a rumor may pass into a legend if it: (1) has strong story appeal, (2) is founded in public belief about what could happen, (3) teaches a moral "lesson." Brunvand traces many such legends back into folklore history, such as the "vanishing hitchhiker" (who enters a car or carriage or chariot and then mysteriously disappears). Many such legends have been around for generations, updated from time to time to fit changing technology.

The Fad or Fashion

A *fad* is *a trivial, short-lived variation in speech, decoration, or behavior.* The fad apparently originates in the desire to gain and maintain status by being different, by being a leader, and dies out when it is no longer novel. Bogardus [1950, pp. 305–309] studied 2,702 fads over many years, finding that most of them deal with trivia. They typically grow rapidly, have a two- or three-month plateau, and then decline, although some last longer, and a few become permanent parts of the culture. The pet rock fad of 1977, which included the marketing of diplomas, easy chairs, and burial lots for one's pet rock, may have owed its brief popularity to its audacious absurdity. It is doubtful that many pet rock owners viewed it as anything but a cute joke.

Fashions are similar to fads, but *change less rapidly, are less trivial, and tend to be cyclical.* Women's hemlines go up, down, up, down. Men's beards luxuriated, withered, and luxuriated again over a cycle of about a hundred years, as calculated by Robinson [1976]. The popularity of beards spreads until nearly all young men wear them as symbols of youth and masculinity. They remain popular until, as these young men age, they are replaced by clean-shaven young men who now associate beards with doddering senility.

According to Konig [1974], fashion originates in the desire to decorate one's body for greater sexual attractiveness. Fashion is important only in societies with a class system. In a homogeneous, undifferentiated society, distinction through fashion does not arise, since all adorn themselves and act much alike. In a rigidly stratified society, fashion consciousness is unnecessary, for distinction is already firmly assigned [Blumer, 1969a, p. 117]. It is in the open class society with considerable mobility that fashion is important. The upwardly mobile middle class are the most fashion conscious. Those who already are securely upper class can afford to show little concern for fashion and sometimes dress as though clothes were only to keep off the rain.

Fashions do not always originate among the elite and diffuse downward but may originate at any class level. In the early 1970s, working-class garb became fashionable, and faded blue denims became too costly for the poor. Fashions spread as people who wish to be up to date make their collective selections from many competing models [Blumer, 1969b].

Fashion may involve almost any aspect of group life—manners, the arts, literature, philosophy, even the methodologies of science—but is most often seen in clothing and adornment. As this is written, small alligators embroidered on clothing are popular—probably already peaked and soon to fade [Ingrassia, 1981]. Yet fashions are not entirely trivial or whimsical, for they reflect the dominant interests and values of a society at a particular time [Harris, 1973]. Throughout most of history, to be fat was fashionable, for fatness was a sign of health and wealth in a world where hunger lurked everywhere [Hollander, 1977]. In the eighteenth century, elaborate clothing reflected an ornate and decorative upper-class culture, and the confining styles of the Victorian era reflected Victorian prudishness [Flugel, 1930].

Fashion changes often reflect changes in needs, attitudes, and values. When dark-skinned slaves did most of the menial work, a sickly pallor was fashionable; now that most work has shifted indoors, an evenly distributed tan is desired (even though it is now known to be not entirely healthy). During the political conservatism and relative indifference to social problems of the placid 1950s, the popular song lyrics were personal and romantic; as concern over social problems and competing life-styles grew in the later 1960s, the popular song lyrics assumed a sharp tone of social criticism [Rosenstone, 1969]; in the later 1970s, protest songs declined in popularity as the campus became calm and the political atmosphere grew more conservative. Thus, fashion reflects the currents of change in a society.

There is much speculation, but little scientific research, on the possibility that fashion changes and choices arise from unconscious emotional needs and impulses. In one of the very few research studies, Becker [1971] concluded that those women who were first to wear miniskirts were women who had negative self-images, while the women who accepted the midiskirt craved attention so badly as to wear something ugly and sexless to attract it. Reed [1974] claimed that from the personality profiles of women college students she could predict their fashion preferences with 72 percent accuracy. Fashion choices are a form of "presentation of self," for "all choices of clothing, particularly the quick and simple, involve allying oneself with others who have made the same kind of choice" [Hollander, 1982].

Although unconscious motivation may be involved, fashion choices meet genuine social needs as defined by social-class, age, and sex groups, and other group affiliation. Fashion consciousness aids the middle-class social climber, and a distinct mode of dress or hairstyle fills the early teenager's need to "belong" in a private world not run by adults. [Barber and Tobel, 1952]. Long hair and untrimmed beards for men in the early 1960s were a symbol of social protest, for a deliberate sloppiness in dress and grooming was a way to shock and express contempt for the Establishment. But a decade later, beards and long hair no longer expressed social protest. Instead they had become so fashionable that experimental studies found that bearded men were rated as more handsome, masculine, and virile than their shaven compatriots [Pellegrini, 1973]. Whatever becomes fashionable is perceived as beautiful.

Fashion changes may be deliberately manipulated by the apparel industry, but only to a limited degree, for there is evidence that consumers will not passively accept everything labeled fashionable [Jack and Schiffer, 1948; Lang and Lang, 1961, chap. 15]. Determined efforts of the women's wear industry to promote the midiskirt in 1970 met with failure, mainly because women felt that midiskirts made them look older [Reynolds and Darden, 1971]. Here, again, fashion reflects the dominant cultural values.

The Craze

Where the panic is a rush away from a perceived threat, the craze is a rush toward some satisfaction. As Smelser observes [1963, chap. 7], the craze may be superficial (miniature golf, Monopoly, Hula-Hoops, Frisbees, celebrity fan clubs, skateboards, videogames) or serious (war crazes, nomination of a President); it may be economic (speculative boom), political (bandwagons), expressive (dance steps), or religious (revivals), to mention only a few types. Flagpole sitting, dance marathons, jigsaw puzzles, canasta, and chain letters have all had their moments.

The craze differs from the ordinary fad in that *it becomes an obsession for its followers*. As this is written, the videogame is a craze, but

it may no longer be a craze by the time students read this.

Many crazes involve some kind of get-rich-quick scheme. The Holland tulip craze of 1634 bid up the price of tulip bulbs until their value exceeded their weight in gold. The Florida land boom of the 1920s pushed land prices to levels fantastically beyond any sound economic valuation. In the craze, the individual gets caught up in a mass hysteria and loses ordinary caution. Speculators sell to one another at climbing prices until some bad news pricks the bubble or until so many susceptible persons have joined that no new money is entering the market; then confidence falters, and the market collapses in a frenzy to unload holdings [Mackay, 1932].

Since the craze seizes only a fraction of the population and is a time-consuming preoccupation, it generally wears itself out quite quickly. Some crazes disappear completely; others subside and endure as a less frenzied activity of some people.

Mass Hysteria

Mass hysteria is *some form of irrational, compulsive belief or behavior which spreads among people.* It can be a brief crowd incident, as when a wave of uncontrollable twitching spread through a Louisiana high school [Schuler and Parenton, 1943]. *The New York Times* [Sept. 14, 1952] reported that at a Mississippi football game, 165 teenaged girls in a cheering section became excited and "fainted like flies." Or mass hysteria may extend beyond a single collection of people at a single moment in time. In one town, dozens of people over several weeks reported being attacked by a "phantom anesthetist" who sprayed them with an unknown drug which caused paralysis and other symptoms [Johnson, 1945]. The Salem witchcraft trials are an interesting historical example of mass hysteria [Starkey, 1949].

Recurrent waves of flying-saucer reports,

The craze differs from the ordinary fad by becoming an obsession for its followers. (© *Jim Anderson, 1983/Woodfin Camp & Assoc.*)

together with an elaborate pseudoscientific literature on flying saucers, are a more modern example of mass hysteria [Hackett, 1948; Gardner, 1957, chap. 5; Menzel and Taves, 1977]. From an analysis of the reports, it can be suspected that flying-saucer reports were often the main cause of flying-saucer reports; that is, publicity about flying saucers aroused a series of new "sightings." It is, of course, a scientific possibility that some of the "unidentified flying objects" are from outer space. As stated earlier, a negative proposition (e.g., "there are no flying saucers") is impossible to prove; but the present evidence for them is most unconvincing [Condon, 1969; Klass, 1975; Menzel and Taves, 1977; Shaeffer, 1981].

During the late summer of 1974, nearly a hundred reports of mysterious "cattle mutilations" spread through Nebraska and South Dakota. Some officials attributed these mutilations (ears, lips, and sex organs most often

missing) to such exotic causes as bloodthirsty cultists or visitors from outer space, and residents were advised to band together for night patrols. Before long, however, veterinarians' prosaic conclusion that the cattle had died of natural causes and had been nibbled by small predators [Stewart, 1977] should have ended the matter—but it did not. Cattle-mutilation stories continued to circulate [Frazier, 1979]. Given a choice between a factual, scientific explanation and an exotic, mysterious explanation, many people prefer the latter.

Mass hysteria often takes the form of physical illness "epidemics." In the most famous case study of mass hysteria, women working in a textile factory claimed to have been bitten by June bugs. Investigators found no bugs but did find acute worker resentment of required overtime work [Kerckhoff and Back, 1968]. Many similar "epidemics" have been reported, usually in high schools or factories during periods of unusual stress [Herbert, 1982b].

Why do some people succumb to mass hysteria while others seem to be immune? Our very limited research suggests that physical and psychological stress increases susceptibility. In a junior high school, there was a sudden wave of illnesses and fainting spells from a "gas" which proved to be nonexistent. A comparative study found that, in contrast to the "immunes," the "hysterics" had a record of more absences, more visits to the school nurse for trivial reasons, and more deviations of several kinds [Goldberg, 1973]. In another case of "gas" hysteria in a data-processing center where the work (keypunching and sorting) was exacting but monotonous and the working conditions unsatisfactory, the women who were most dissatisfied with the work situation were the most susceptible to the phantom fumes [Stahl and Lebedun, 1974]. It thus appears that there are some personality differences between those who "keep their cool" and those who are prone to panic or hysteria, but no personality profile of the susceptible person has yet been established.

Do we, then, have satisfactory explanations for mass behavior? Not entirely. All the forms of mass behavior herein discussed seem to arise from some form of frustration or discontent. Periods of social crisis seem to foster a profusion of fads and crazes [Turner and Killian, 1972, p. 130]. Possibly recreational fads and crazes offer an escape from serious problems which appear unsolvable. All forms of collective behavior may serve to release tensions and provide some form of wish-fulfillment. We can venture some forecasts of when and where the more extreme forms of collective behavior are likely to appear and have some knowledge of how they may be controlled. With further study, we should know more.

Disaster Behavior

A relatively recent field of sociological study is *disaster behavior*. It is difficult to classify, for it includes both crowd and mass behavior, and may include rumor, panic, orgy, mass hysteria, and possibly other forms. A new journal, *Mass Emergencies*, was founded in 1975 at the Disaster Research Center of Ohio State University. A considerable body of research knowledge is being collected, destroying many popular myths about behavior in disaster [Barton, 1969; Dynes, 1970; Wenger et al., 1975; Perry and Pugh, 1978, chap. 4]. For example, looting is widely believed to be common following a disaster but is actually quite rare. Disaster studies are useful in showing officials what to expect when disaster strikes and how best to mobilize their resources.

PUBLICS AND PUBLIC OPINION

The term "public" is used in several senses. In popular use, "the public" is synonymous with "the people" or with practically everybody—not a very useful concept. Sociologists use the term in two senses: (1) A *public* may be defined as a *scattered number of people who share an interest in a particular topic*. There is a baseball public, an opera public, an investment public, a political-affairs public, and many others. (2) A *public* may be defined as *a number of people who are concerned over, divided upon, and in discussion about an issue*. Each important issue thus has its public, and there is no such thing as *the* public under these two definitions.

The members of a public are not gathered together like the members of a crowd. Each member of a public can communicate directly with only a handful of the other members. A public is reached mainly through the mass media. The titles of many magazines reveal the public for which each is published—*House*

& Garden, Field & Stream, Guns & Ammo Magazine, Western Horseman, Cats Magazine, U.S. Camera, Stamps Magazine, Motor Trend Magazine, The Theater, Workbench, Audio, National Geographic Magazine, Holiday, Pacific Affairs, and hundreds more. Since the members of a public can communicate effectively only through such mass media, it follows that those who control the media have considerable power to influence the opinions of that public.

Publics are created by cultural complexity. In a simple culture there would be few if any publics. A complex culture produces many interest groups with rival axes to grind and develops many issues over which people differ. For example, one group wishes to keep our national parks and wilderness areas in their unspoiled condition with a minimum of development; another group wants to develop them into recreation centers with resorts, airstrips, and ski lifts; still other groups wish to hunt the game, log the timber, mine the minerals, graze the grassland, or dam the streams in the parks and wilderness areas. Such interest clashes multiply as a culture become more complex.

Few issues arise in a simple, stable culture; that is, few situations develop which cannot be handled by following the traditional folkways and mores of the society. But in a complex, changing culture, issues are constantly arising. In other words, situations are constantly developing which our traditional folkways and mores either will not handle at all or will handle only in a way that leaves some groups dissatisfied. For example, should "hard" pesticides which remain poisonous for a long time (such as DDT) be banned in order to protect the environment, or are they necessary for food production and disease control? Tradition gives no clear answer.

In these ways a complex changing culture creates a great many publics, each concerned with an activity, interest, or issue. As the

The elite are no longer separated from the nonelite.

members of a public consider the issue and form opinions concerning it, *public opinion* is developed.

Public opinion also has two definitions: (1) *an opinion held by a substantial number of people;* (2) *the dominant opinion among a population.* According to the first usage, there can be many public opinions; according to the second, public opinion refers to a public *consensus* upon an issue. Both usages are common in the literature, and the particular meaning must be inferred from the way the term is used.

Public opinion is a creation of the complex society and the mass media. In traditional societies, gemeinschaft relations predominate, while an elite rules according to established traditions without very much concern for anything such as public opinion. If the ordinary people had been questioned about current "issues," their usual response would have been one of bewilderment. True enough, there were differences of interest and viewpoint in earlier societies, but these were typically thrashed out *within* the elite without involving the ordinary people (except as they suffered the consequences). The elite are no longer separated from the nonelite and must consider nonelite views. Public opinion depends upon having a mass whose opinions are important to the elite, whereupon different sections of the elite seek to propagandize and manipulate this mass in support of elite interests. Democracies differ from dictatorships in that in democracies different groups among the elite compete vigorously for mass support, whereas in a dictatorship some faction among the elite gains dominance, removes or neutralizes its competitors, and enjoys a monopoly of propaganda.

Measurement of Public Opinion

The leaders of a group or a nation cannot lead wisely unless they know which way the people are willing to be led. The public opinion poll is a recent invention for finding out what people are thinking. A poll is simple in concept but difficult to carry out because, as is shown above, an opinion is a rather complicated phenomenon. The pollsters prepare a set of questions on an issue, seeking to phrase the questions in such a way that the wording does not prejudice the informant's answer. Then these questions are offered to a small number of people (from a few hundred to a few thousand) so that each group or class in the total population is represented in the sample in its correct proportion. If all these preliminary arrangements are made without serious error, opinion is measured quite accurately. The Gallup Poll, for example, has predicted the vote on recent elections with an average error of less than 2 percent of the total population vote. But there are many pitfalls in public opinion polling which a pollster must guard against in trying to attain this level of accuracy. One of the greatest is the tendency of people to state firm opinions on issues which they know nothing about, have not thought about, and really have no opinion upon. A sample of Hamilton County, Ohio, citizens were asked the question, "Some people say that the 1975 Public Affairs Act should be repealed. Do you agree or disagree with this idea?" One-third of the people stated a firm opinion, which is remarkable, since there was no "1975 Public Affairs Act" [Cory, 1979].

The accuracy of public opinion polls is diluted by such "pseudo-opinions." This error can be reduced by "filter" questions, such as, "Have you heard much about . . .?" [Bishop et al., 1980]. Other pitfalls surround the wording of questions, the selection of the sample, and the weighing or interpreting of responses [Parten, 1950; Phillips, 1966; Hennessy, 1970; Sonquist and Dunkelberg, 1977]. Despite their limitations, polls are so important today that a new journal, *Public Opinion*, devoted entirely to presenting and commenting upon opinion polls, made its debut in 1978.

Manipulation of Public Opinion

The main emphasis in public opinion research has been upon ways of manipulating public opinion. *Propaganda* includes all efforts to persuade people to a point of view upon an issue; everything from Sunday school lessons to billboards are propaganda; advertising, sales promotion, and fund-raising drives are prime examples.

The usual distinction between education and propaganda is that education seeks to cultivate one's ability to make discriminating judgments, while propaganda seeks to persuade one to the undiscriminating acceptance of a ready-made judgment. In practice, education often includes a good deal of propaganda. Teachers sometimes propagandize for their own opinions; interest groups seek to get their own propaganda, disguised as "educational materials," into the school; society virtually forces the school to propagandize for the approved moral and patriotic values. Conservatives wish the schools to propagandize for the status quo, while Marxists and other radicals insist that teachers should propagandize for the revolution. To draw a clear distinction between education and propaganda is not always possible. And it should be repeated that propaganda is not necessarily "bad"; it is merely a term applied to *all* attempts to influence other peoples' opinions

Brad Tufts made no speeches, no personal appearances, but still garnered enough write-in votes to win a recent primary election for student body president at San Diego State University. His candidacy was an experiment by members of a class called Advertising Campaigns. The class flooded the campus with Brad Tufts posters, T-shirts, bumperstickers. "We set out to see if formally educated students would vote for a candidate solely on basis of advertising image," says Asst. Prof. Jack Haberstroh. Brad Tufts is two years old.

Behavior Today, May 1, 1972, p. 3. Copyright © Ziff-Davis Publishing Company, All rights reserved.

"Image" seems to be all that mattered in this election. Is this true of all elections?

and actions. The common propaganda techniques (name-calling, glittering generality, testimonial, plain folks, card-stacking, bandwagon), first outlined by Lee and Lee [1939], have been reprinted in countless textbooks, where most students have probably seen them.

LIMITS OF PROPAGANDA. If the powers of propaganda were unlimited, the side with the most money and the best public relations agency would always win. Since this does not always happen, the power of propaganda must be limited in various ways.

1 *Competing propagandas* are probably the greatest limitation. With a monopoly of propaganda, a propagandist can suppress and manufacture facts, and no effective rebuttal is possible. The mere *existence* of competing propagandas in a democratic state exerts a restraining influence both upon the propagandist and upon the receiver.

2 *The credibility of the propagandist* in the eyes of the receivers limits what they will accept. Credibility is reduced where the propagandist has a vested interest, so propaganda is often conducted under the name of a noble-sounding organization (Fundamental Freedoms Foundation, Tax Equality Association, Homeowners' Association) which conceals the interests of the propagandists.

3 *The sophistication of the receiver* limits the effects of propaganda. In general, those who are well educated or well informed on the issue are less affected by propaganda than the poorly educated and the poorly informed.

4 *The beliefs and values of the recipient* limit the propaganda he or she will believe. Most people accept uncritically any propaganda which fits in with their established attitudes and values and usually reject, equally uncritically, any which conflict. Like the person who said, "I've read so much about the dangers of smoking that I've decided to give up reading," one may simply "tune-out" anything which conflicts too sharply with one's beliefs and desires. For this reason, a propagandist rarely tries to change the basic attitudes of recipients; instead, he or she tries to get them to accept a new definition of the issue that will call up those attitudes and images which support the propagandist's cause.

5 *Cultural drifts and trends* limit the effectiveness of propaganda. A cultural drift is not stopped by propaganda. Propaganda may accelerate or retard a cultural trend, reinforce or weaken a value. But it is doubtful if propaganda in a democratic society can either initiate or halt a cultural trend, destroy a well-established value, or instill a new value which the society is not already developing.

SOCIAL MOVEMENTS

The social movement is one of the major forms of collective behavior. A social movement is formally defined as "a collectivity acting with some continuity to promote or resist change in the society or group of which it is a part [Turner and Killian, 1972, p. 246]. Stated less formally, a *social movement is a collective effort to promote or resist change.*

Social movements originate as unplanned, unorganized, undirected groupings of people who are dissatisfied with things. People talk, share ideas, and grumble; intellectuals publish learned articles; citizens write letters to the editor; people experiment with novel forms of expression. In most movements, leadership and organization emerge before long. After an active life which seldom exceeds a decade or two, the movement passes out of the active phase. Sometimes the movement leaves permanent organizations (YMCA) or changes (women's suffrage), and sometimes it disappears with scarcely a trace (the Esperanto movement for a universal language).

Theories of Social Movements

PSYCHOLOGICAL THEORIES. The psychological theories find the roots of social movements in the personalities of the followers.

Discontent Theory This theory holds that movements are rooted in discontent. People who are comfortable and contented have little interest in social movements. Discontent can be of many kinds, ranging from the searing anger of those who feel victimized by outrageous injustice to the mild annoyance of those who do not approve of some social change.

It is probably true that, without discontent, there would be no social movements. But discontent is an inadequate explanation. There is no convincing evidence of any close association between the level of grievance and discontent in a society and its level of social movement activity [Muller, 1972; Snyder and Tilly, 1972]. People may endure great discontent without joining a social movement. Many societies have endured great poverty, in-

equality, brutality, and corruption for centuries without serious social protest. And all modern societies always have enough discontent to fuel many social movements [Turner and Killian, 1972, p. 271]. Discontent may be a necessary condition but not a sufficient condition for social movements.

Personal Maladjustment Theory This theory sees the social movement as a refuge from personal failure. Many scholars believe that movements find their supporters among the unhappy, frustrated persons whose lives lack meaning and fulfillment. A widely read book written by a self-educated manual laborer, *The True Believer* [Hoffer, 1951], describes the kinds of people drawn to social movements: the bored, the misfits, the would-be creative who cannot create, the minorities, the guilty sinners, the downwardly mobile, and others who for any reason are seriously dissatisfied with their lives. They add meaning and purpose to their empty lives through movement activity.

It is plausible that people who feel frustrated and unfulfilled should be more attracted to social movements than those who are complacent and contented. Those who find their present lives absorbing and fulfilling are less in need of something to give them feelings of personal worth and accomplishment, for they already have these. Thus the movement supporters—and especially the *early* supporters—are seen as mainly the frustrated misfits of society.

While plausible, the misfit theory is not well substantiated. It is difficult to measure a person's sense of nonfulfillment, although some inferences may be drawn from career histories, such as Hitler's expressed resentment at his rejection as a serious artist. It is another theory which sounds reasonable but which cannot easily be proved or disproved.

SOCIOLOGICAL THEORIES. The sociological theories study the society, rather than the personality of individuals.

Relative Deprivation Theory Relative deprivation is a concept developed by Stouffer [1949]. It holds that one *feels* deprived according to the gap between expectations and realizations. The person who wants little and has little feels less deprived than the one who has much but expects still more.

Relative deprivation is increasing throughout most of the underdeveloped world. The world's poor are deciding that poverty, hunger, and illness are not necessary. They long for bicycles, radios, refrigerators, and all the other things that glitter along the slope of endlessly ascending desires. They hunger for these treasures but have little real understanding of what it takes to produce them. Even where people are beginning to get some of the things they covet, these satisfactions come with an unbearable slowness.

A weakening of traditional and tribal controls generally accompanies this enormous inflation of desires. The recently established independent governments of Third World countries have little hope of keeping up with their peoples' expectations. Revolutions seem most likely to occur not when people are most miserable but after things have begun to improve, setting off a round of rising expectations [Brinton, 1938; Street and Street, 1961]. The outbreak most often happens after a downturn has interrupted a period of improvement, creating an intolerable gap between rising expectations and falling realizations [Davies, 1962; Geschwender, 1968].

Relative deprivation theory is plausible but unproved. Feelings of deprivation are easy to infer but difficult to measure, and still more difficult to plot over a period of time. And relative deprivation, even when unmistakably severe, is only one of many factors in social movements [Gurney and Tierney, 1982].

Resource Mobilization Theory This theory stresses techniques rather than causes of movements. It attributes importance to the effective use of resources in promoting social movements, since a successful movement demands effective organization and tactics. Resource mobilization theorists see leadership, organization, and tactics as major determinants of the success or failure of social movements [Oberschall, 1973; Wilson, 1973; Gamson, 1975; McCarthy and Zald, 1977; Zald and McCarthy, 1979; Walsh, 1981]. Resource mobilization theorists concede that without grievances and discontent, there would be few movements but add that mobilization is needed to direct this discontent into an effective mass movement.

The resources to be mobilized include: supporting beliefs and traditions among the population, laws that can provide leverage, organizations and officials that can be helpful, potential benefits to be promoted, target groups whom these benefits might attract, any other possible aids. These are weighed against personal costs of movement activity, opposition to be anticipated, other difficulties to be overcome, and tactics of operation to be developed.

As an example, the ghetto riots of the 1960s occurred when the civil rights movement was gaining momentum, effective black leaders had won national recognition, and a sympathetic national administration was in power. During the summer of 1982, black discontent was probably far greater than during the 1960s. Decades of black gains seemed to be slipping away as black unemployment rose, the black-white income gap widened, social services were being slashed, and affirmative action programs were being undermined. Ghetto riots were expected but failed to materialize [Blum, 1982]. Why? In 1982, no black leaders of Martin Luther King's stature were available, the civil rights movement had wound down to a stall, and an unsympathetic national administration had taken power. Discontent was probably greater, but resources were fewer. As one black leader lamented, "Last time, the president [Lyndon Johnson] was on our side, looking for social equality. This time the president [Ronald Reagan] is against us." [Banks, 1982].

Resource mobilization theory does not fit expressive or migratory movements, which can succeed without organization or tactics. Evidence for resource mobilization theory is largely descriptive and is challenged by some scholars [e.g., Goldstone, 1980]. It is likely that societal confusion, personal maladjustment, relative deprivation, discontent, and resource mobilization are all involved in social movements, but in undetermined proportions.

As usual, we have several theories, each plausible, each supported by some evidence, but none clearly proved. Social movements are of so many kinds, with so many variables involved, that possibly no one theory will ever be conclusively established.

Kinds of Social Movements

MIGRATORY MOVEMENTS.   Discontented people may wish to move. When many move to the same place at the same time, they create a migratory social movement. Migration of Irish to the United States following the great potato famine, the back-to-Israel movement of the Jews known as Zionism, the flight of the East Germans to West Germany before the Berlin Wall locked them in, the escape of Cuban refugees to the United States, and the American migratory turnaround (from big cities to small towns and country) are examples.

EXPRESSIVE MOVEMENTS.   When people cannot easily move and cannot easily change things, they may change themselves. In expressive movements, *people change their reactions to reality* instead of trying to change the reality itself. Expressive movements range from the relatively trivial (forms of dance, art, music, dress) to the serious (religious movements, occultism). Expressive movements may help people to accept a reality they despair of changing. "Gallows humor" is common among oppressed peoples. Yet some change may result. The protest songs of the 1960s

and early 1970s may have helped to promote some social reforms. In Jamaica, where poverty and inequality are extreme and economic distress has been growing, a music of social protest called reggae has seized the popular imagination. It has created millionaire superstar performers who live the good life while singing impassioned lyrics of anger and injustice [Bradshaw, 1977; DeVoss, 1977; Roberts and Kloss, 1979, pp. 111–113]. It is not yet clear whether reggae serves to arouse and mobilize popular discontent or to drain off discontent into a politically "harmless" emotional outlet.

UTOPIAN MOVEMENTS.   These are attempts to create a perfect society in miniature. Then this model can be copied and perhaps transform the entire society. There have been dozens of utopian communities in the United States, few of which lasted more than a very few years [Gardner, 1978]. Perhaps the most successful utopian movement in recent history is the Israeli kibbutz [Spiro, 1958; Tiger and Shepher, 1975].

REFORM MOVEMENTS.   These are attempts to improve the society without greatly changing its basic social structure. They are common in democratic societies and rare in societies where dissent is not tolerated. U.S. history shows dozens of reform movements—abolitionists, prohibitionists, feminists, environmentalists, gay liberationists, and many others. Hundreds more would-be reform movements never get past the one-person-with-mailing-list stage.

REVOLUTIONARY MOVEMENTS.   A social revolution is a sudden, sweeping, and usually violent change in a social system. (The "palace revolt" in which the faces change, with no change in the class system or the distribution of power and income among the groups in the society, is not included as a social revolution.) Revolutionists generally oppose reformers because they believe that significant

"Gallows humor" appears where open political criticism of the government earns one a fast trip to the salt mines. It permits an oppressed people to express hostility and release tension in relative safety. These jokes have been told in Poland by Polish people.

Did you hear that Soviet scientists have bred a new animal by crossing a cow with a giraffe? It can graze in Poland and be milked in the Soviet Union.

Why do ZOMOs (riot police) travel in threes? One can read, one can write, and the third keeps an eye on these two intellectuals.

What is a Polish string quartet? A Polish symphony orchestra just back from a Western concert tour.

China's leader Deng and Soviet leader Brezhnev agree to resolve their differences, but Deng makes three Chinese demands. "We must have 100 million tons of coal." "Done," Brezhnev replies. "And 20 new cargo ships," Deng asks. "Agreed," Brezhnev assents. "And a million bicycles," Deng adds. "Impossible," Brezhnev snaps. "Why?" asks Deng. Brezhnev replies, "Because the Poles don't make bicycles."

President Reagan asks God, "How long before my people are happy?" God replies, "One hundred years." Reagan weeps and leaves. President Mitterand asks God, "How long until the French people are happy?" "Two hundred years," God replies. Mitterand weeps and leaves. Gen. Jaruzelski asks God, "How long until the Polish people are happy?" God weeps and leaves.

Adapted from Frederick Kempe, "Warsaw Wit Shows the Poles Aren't Totally Disarmed," *Wall Street Journal*, Sept. 24, 1982, p. 1.

Why is gallows humor not very common in the United States?

---

reform is impossible under the existing social system. They see basic change as possible only after the existing system is overthrown and the elite classes are deposed, often through execution or exile. In most revolutions, several factions unite to overthrow the existing regime, after which there may be a bloody struggle for power among these factions.

The course of revolution is illustrated in the recent Iranian revolution: (1) growing discontent and erosion of support for the old regime (Iranians at home and abroad demonstrating against the Shah); (2) increasing disorder, riots, and bombings, with growing inability of the government to maintain order despite harsh repression; (3) overthrow of the government (flight of the Shah) as armed forces join the revolution; (4) temporary rule of moderates (Bani-Sadr, Ghotbzadeh), soon overthrown as revolutionists contend for power among themselves; (5) rule of extremists (Khomeini government of Moslem fundamentalists); (6) reign of terror, with harsh repression of those revolutionists who lost out in bid for power (numerous executions, including Ghotbzadeh); (7) invasion from abroad (either to end revolution, as in American, French, and Russian revolutions, or just to settle old scores, as in Iraq's attack on Iran); (8) revolutionary armies fight well and repel invaders; (9) eventual return to stability, perhaps with *partial* restoration of prerevolutionary order (which does not always happen). Most successful revolutions follow this pattern more or less closely [Edwards, 1927; Brinton, 1938; Salert, 1976; Welch, 1980].

RESISTANCE MOVEMENTS.   The Ku Klux Klan appeared in the South to keep the blacks "in their place" after the Civil War [Mecklin, 1924]. It has reappeared at intervals in various parts of the country as a nativist movement to protect the "real Americans" against blacks, Catholics, foreigners, atheists, and liberals [VanderZanden, 1960; Alexander, 1965].

The many social and cultural changes of

A resistance movement expresses opposition to recent change. Do you think the antinuclear movement will succeed in blocking nuclear weapons development? (© *Rick Smolan/Contact*)

recent decades have been profoundly disturbing to many Americans who feel that our national virtues are being eroded by sexual permissiveness, secularism, feminism, pacifism, and welfare statism. A great many contemporary resistance movements express their dismay at the directions in which our nation has been moving. These include the prolife movement to restrict legal abortion, the antipornography movement, the effort to legalize school prayers, the "creationist" movement to require teaching of the biblical account of creation in schools wherever the evolutionist account is presented, and the antifeminist movement, among others.

The Moral Majority is a group attempting to mobilize fundamentalist Christians in organized opposition to many national developments and in support of balanced budgets and a more powerful and aggressive national defense. Its success, as this is written, remains to be determined.

Life Cycles of Social Movements

Some scholars have posed a life cycle which many movements follow [Dawson and Gettys, 1934, pp. 708–709; Zald and Ash, 1969; Blumer, 1969*a*, pp. 65–122]. The stages include: (1) the *unrest* stage of growing confusion and discontent; (2) the *excitement* stage, when discontent is focused, causes of discontent are identified, and proposals for action are debated; (3) the *formalization* stage, when leaders emerge, programs are developed, alliances are forged, and organizations and tactics are developed; (4) an *institutionalization* stage, as organizations take over from the early leaders, bureaucracy is entrenched, and ideology and program become crystallized, often ending the active life of the movement; (5) the *dissolution* stage, when the movement either becomes an enduring organization (like the YMCA) or fades away, possibly to be revived at some later date. This life cycle fits poorly the expressive and migratory movements but is more applicable to the utopian, reform, revolutionary, and resistance movements.

SUMMARY

Collective behavior is a characteristic of complex cultures and is usually absent in simple societies. It includes crowd behavior, mass behavior, and social movements.

A *crowd* is a temporary gathering of people who are acting together. Three principal theories attempt to explain crowd behavior. *Contagion theories* emphasize the psychological processes of suggestion and manipulation; *convergence theories* stress the like-mindedness of crowd members; *emergent norm theories* show how, in crowd situations, a norm develops which sanctions and limits behavior. Crowd behavior is characterized by: (1) anonymity—the individual loses customary restraints and sense of personal responsibility, (2) impersonality—only the group affiliation of the person is important, (3) suggestibility—crowd members act uncritically upon suggestions, (4) stress, and (5) interactional amplification—crowd members build up one another's emotional involvement. Crowd behavior is limited, however, by: (1) emotional needs and attitudes of the members; (2) the mores of the members, who rarely do anything which is not condoned by certain of their mores; (3) crowd leaders, who must establish rapport, build emotional tensions, suggest action to relieve these tensions and justify this action; and (4) external controls,

mainly the police, whose ability to control crowd behavior depends partly upon skill and partly upon the nature of the particular crowd.

Crowd behavior takes many forms. The *audience* is largely, but not entirely, a one-way crowd responding to a single stimulus. In the *riot*, members of a violently aggressive crowd release their accumulated hostilities, sometimes irrationally and sometimes purposefully. In the *orgy*, a good-natured crowd enjoys itself through uninhibited indulgence. In the *panic*, people become a crowd in sudden, disorganized flight from danger.

A *mass* is a separated number of people responding individually to the same stimuli. *Mass behavior* is the unorganized, unstructured, uncoordinated behavior of masses. Forms of mass behavior include the *rumor*, a rapidly spreading report unsubstantiated by fact; the *fad* or *fashion*, a temporarily popular variation in speech, manners, dress, or behavior; the *craze*, a short-lived mass preoccupation with a particular satisfaction; *mass hysteria*, some form of irrational compulsion which spreads among a people; and possibly others. *Disaster behavior* is a relatively recent field of study which includes a variety of forms of collective behavior.

The term *public* is defined by sociologists both in terms of those people sharing a common interest and of people sharing a common concern over an issue. *Public opinion* includes both the different opinions held by substantial numbers of people and the consensus opinion held by most people.

Practically every interest group today is trying to manipulate public opinion. Propaganda, often called "public relations," is one of our largest businesses. Propaganda may be less powerful than it sometimes appears to be, for its effects are limited by competing propagandas, by the credibility of the propagandists, by the sophistication of its receivers, by the established beliefs and values of the receivers, and by the existing trends within the culture.

Social movements are collective ways of promoting or resisting change. Psychological theories attribute social movement activity to *personal discontents* or to *personal maladjustments* which make people receptive; sociological theories stress *relative deprivation*, when people's expectations outrun their realizations, or *resource mobilization*, with effective organization, tactics, and movement leaders. There are several types of social movements: *migratory movements*, in which people move to a new place; *expressive movements*, in which people change themselves rather than change the society; *utopian movements*, which are efforts to create a perfect society on a small scale; *reform movements*, which seek to correct some imperfections in the society; *revolutionary movements*, which seek to replace the existing system with a new one; and *resistance movements*, which seek to reverse some recent social change. Many movements pass through the stages of *unrest, excitement, formalization, institutionalization*, and *dissolution* in their life cycle.

GLOSSARY

audience a crowd with members' interest centered upon stimuli outside themselves.

collective behavior behavior which originates spontaneously, is relatively unorganized, fairly unpredictable, and depends upon interstimulation between a number of participants.

craze a temporary obsessive interest shared by a number of people.

crowd behavior behavior of temporary collection of people reacting together to stimuli; such behavior is brief and episodic.

fad a trivial, short-lived, popular variation in speech, decoration, or behavior.

fashion a variation in speech, decoration, or behavior, of temporary duration but less trivial or brief than a fad.

mass behavior the unorganized, unstructured, uncoordinated, individually selected behavior of masses in a mass society.

mass hysteria an irrational, compulsive belief or behavior which spreads among a number of people.

orgy joyous revelry of a crowd which transgresses normal mores.

panic a collective flight based upon a hysterical belief.

propaganda all efforts to persuade others to an acceptance of a point of view.

public a number of people who share an interest in a particular topic or activity, or who are concerned about and divided upon an issue.

public opinion an opinion held by a significant number of people; the dominant opinion among a population.

riot action of a violently aggressive, destructive crowd.

rumor a rapidly spreading report unsubstantiated by fact.

social movement a collective effort to promote or resist change.

QUESTIONS AND PROJECTS

1 When we say that crowd behavior is "unstructured," what do we mean? Of what importance is its unstructured character?

2 Which has the greater potential for extreme crowd behavior—the class reunion or the family reunion? Why?

3 Why do crowd members seldom feel guilty about their mob actions?

4 Are there any situations in our culture which contain elements of the institutionalized orgy?

5 Should we fully institutionalize the orgy in American society? What benefits might accrue? What difficulties would arise?

6 Why do colleges no longer have student demonstrations as in the 1960s?

7 Do you think you are immune to panic? To crazes? To mass hysteria? What makes you think so?

8 Can you think of any propaganda efforts or causes which have failed in the United States because they conflicted with our cultural values? With prevailing cultural trends?

9 Suppose that a major disaster (fire, flood, explosion)

were to happen. What do you think you would do? Assume a leadership role? Huddle in paralysis? Wait to follow others? Panic? What reason have you to give for your expected behavior?

10 Write up a description of a campus pep rally as an example of crowd behavior.

11 Research studies (such as Neil Vidmar and Milton Rokeach: "Archie Bunker's Bigotry: A Study in Selective Perception and Exposure," *Journal of Communication*, 24:36–47, Winter 1974) show that the TV show "All in the Family" was perceived by liberals as a devastating exposé of bigotry, while conservatives and bigots heard Archie "telling it like it is." What implications has this for opinion manipulations?

12 Try an experiment in rumor. Select a harmless rumor (such as that a new parking ramp will be built) and set it going by a specified number of tellings. Then record the time, frequency, and form in which it "comes back" to you as it spreads over the campus.

13 Recall and describe a crowd situation in which the behavior lagged dispiritedly for a time. Show how each of the characteristics of crowd behavior come into operation and kindled a proper enthusiasm in the members. Or, if you have the opportunity, attend and observe a crowd situation for your analysis.

14 Prepare a list of aggressive actions which you think you could engage in if placed in a suitably encouraging crowd situation. Prepare a list of actions in which you think you could not possibly share, no matter what the crowd situation. Give your reasons for each listing.

15 Run a campus public opinion poll on a fictious proposition such as "Do you favor or oppose one board member's proposal to tie students' tuition fees to their point averages?" See how many will admit that they do not know of the proposal, and how many state firm opinions on it.

SUGGESTED READINGS

Blumer, Herbert: "Collective Behavior," in Alfred McClung Lee (ed.): *Principles of Sociology*, Barnes & Noble, Inc., New York, 1969. Chapters 7–12 are a classic treatment of this topic in one of the College Outline Series handbooks.

Brenton, Myron: "Studies in the Aftermath," *Human Behavior*, 4:56–61, May 1975. A brief popularized summary of disaster research studies.

Brown, Michael and Amy Golden: *Collective Behavior*, Goodyear Publishing Company, Pacific Palisades, Cal., 1973. A textbook containing perceptive chapters (3–6) on collective behavior in disasters and (11–13) on student protest.

Brunvand, Jan Harold: *The Vanishing Hitchhiker: American Urban Legends and Their Meanings*, W. W. Norton & Company, Inc., New York, 1981. An entertaining account of the origin and meanings of many current legends. (Condensed in *Psychology Today*, 14:50–62, June 1980).

Colligan, Michael L. et al. (eds.): *Mass Psychogenic Illness: A Social Psychological Analysis*, Lawrence Erlbaum Associates, Publishers, Hillsdale, N.J., 1982, A collection on mass hysteria.

*Curvin, Robert and Bruce Porter: *Blackout Looting*, Gardner Press, Inc., New York, 1979. An analysis of the power blackout looting in New York City, correcting many popular misconceptions.

Herbert, Wray: "An Epidemic in the Works," *Science News*, 122:188–190, Sept. 18, 1982. A brief treatment of mass hysteria.

Isaacson, Walter: "The Battle over Abortion," *Time*, 116:20ff, April 6, 1981. A popular account of a current resistance movement.

Knopf, Terry Ann: *Rumors, Races and Riots*, Transaction Books, New Brunswick, N.J., 1975. A study of rumor as a factor in race riots.

*Lee, Alfred McClung and Norman D. Humphrey: *Race Riot*, Octagon Press, New York, 1967. A classic description and analysis of the Detroit race riot of 1941.

Listiak, Alan: "'Legitimate Deviance' and Social Class: Bar Behavior During Gray Cup Week," *Sociological Focus*, 7:13–44, Summer 1974. De-

scription of an institutionalized orgy in a Canadian city.

Morin, Edgar, "Rumor in a
City in Central France," *Psychology Today*, 6:77ff., October
1972. A sociologist's account
of a vicious, titillating rumor.

Perry, Joseph B., Jr., and Meredith David Pugh: *Collective
Behavior: Response to Social
Stress*, West Publishing Company, St. Paul, Minn., 1978.
A textbook on collective behavior and social move-
ments.

*Roberts, Ron E. and Robert
Marsh Kloss: *Social Movements: Between the Balcony and
the Barricade*, 2nd ed., The
C. V. Mosby Company,
St. Louis, 1979. A brief textbook on social movements.

Salert, Barbara: *Revolutions and
Revolutionaries*, Elsevier Scientific Publishing Company,
New York, 1976. Four theories of revolution.

Stewart, James R.: "Cattle Mutilations: An Episode of Collective Delusion," *The Zetetic*
(later *The Skeptical Inquirer*),
1:55–66, Spring/Summer
1977. An account of a recent
example of mass hysteria.

Turner, Ralph H. and Lewis M.
Killan: *Collective Behavior*,
Prentice-Hall, Inc., Englewood Cliffs, N.J., 1972,
chaps. 3–12. An interestingly
written textbook, about half
of which is devoted to the
topics covered in this chapter.

White, Theo: "Building the Big
Dam," *Harper's Magazine*,
June 1935, pp. 112–121. An
entertaining explanation of
how and why construction
camp workers used to go on
payday sprees.

*An asterisk before the citation indicates
that the title is available in a paperback
edition.

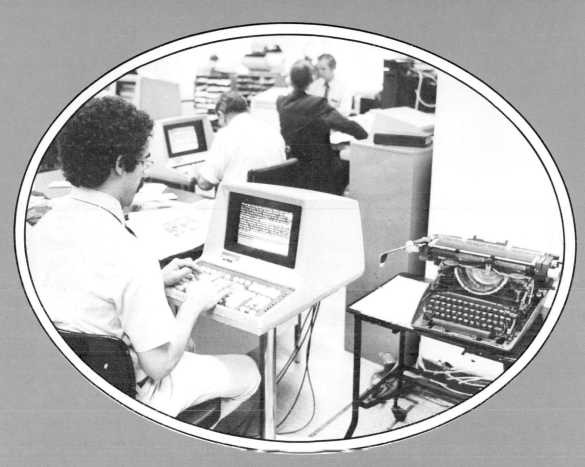

20 Social and Cultural Change

Beka, Sudan—This tiny village between the Blue and White Niles lies in an expanse of farmland that, six years ago, produced an average of roughly five "kentars," or bales, of cotton per acre a year.

But that was before modern agricultural methods were adopted. Now, the yield is just two kentars per acre. The reasons for the decline are debated, but one thing is clear: While trying to get more out of the land, the Sudanese ended up getting less.

That a step forward in technology should be followed by a step backward in production is an anomaly of economic life in poor countries such as Sudan, where the simple ways of the past sometimes work better than expensive new ways. . . .

The problems started in the 1970s, when the government decided to adopt modern farming methods to increase output at Gezira. The idea was to use fertilizers, pesticides, crop rotations and more frequent irrigation to improve yields. It all made sense in principle.

But the new farming techniques undermined the traditional balance in the Gezira. The initial dose of pesticides, for example, killed predators of the white fly and left the cotton crop more vulnerable than before. Worse, the Sudanese found themselves locked into ever-rising costs. Where they had initially planned only one spraying of pesticides annually, Gezira agronomists soon found it necessary to spray up to seven times a year. They didn't have enough money for the required crop-dusting planes.

The increased use of irrigation also backfired. Every time water flowed through the canals and ditches, it carried silt and other debris. Soon, some of the ditches were so full of mud and water weeds that the simple gravity-flow system wouldn't work any more. But the Sudanese couldn't afford the excavation equipment to reopen the blocked waterways. . . .

The Sudanese appreciate Western help in rehabilitating their economy after the disastrous development binge of the 1970s. But several officials privately grumble that it was Western experts who helped persuade them to put aside the traditional farm economy—and rush headlong into a future they couldn't afford.

(Reprinted by permission from *The Wall Street Journal*, Nov. 27, 1981, pp. 1ff. © Dow Jones & Company, Inc., 1981. All rights reserved.)

Although we know a good deal about the conditions and processes of change, we have no satisfactory explanation of *why* change occurs. Possibly the explanation lies in the human capacity for becoming bored. Most of the higher species, whenever not hunting, eating, or mating, simply go to sleep—as much as twenty hours a day. Humans cannot sleep that much, and human boredom may be the true cause of social change [Hirschman, 1982].

Another answer is simply to assume that change is a *constant* in the universe, which needs no explanation. A constant is something which is always present. Populations grow and decline; fashions come and go; mountains are pushed upward and erode away; even the sun is gradually burning itself out.

No society exactly copies and transmits the culture to each new generation. This is shown by language changes. English has changed so greatly that most students have their troubles with Shakespeare and are hopelessly lost in Chaucer. In 1755 Samuel Johnson published his dictionary in the hope that it would stabilize word meanings and stop language changes but soon confessed that he had failed. None of the historic efforts to protect a culture from change or "foreign influences" has succeeded for very long. Social and cultural change is continuous and irresistible. Only its speed and direction vary.

There is a distinction between *social change*—changes in the social structure and social relationships of a society—and *cultural change*—changes in the culture of a society. Some social changes might include changes in the age distribution, average educational level, or birthrate of a population; or the decline of informality and personal neighborliness as people shift from village to city; or the change in the relationship between workers and employers when unions become organized; or the change of the husband from the boss to a partner in today's democratic family. Cultural changes might include such things as the invention and popularization of the automobile; the addition of new words to our language; changing concepts of propriety and morality; new forms of music, art, or dance; or the general trend toward sex equality. Yet the concepts overlap. The trend toward sex equality involves both a changing set of cultural norms concerning male and female roles and some changing social relationships as well. Nearly all important changes involve both social and cultural aspects. In practice, therefore, the distinction is seldom a very important one, and the two terms are often used interchangeably. Sometimes the term *sociocultural change* is used to include changes of both kinds.

There is an important distinction between social change and *progress*. The term "progress" carries a value judgment. Progress means change in a desirable direction. Desirable as measured by whose values? Are taller buildings, higher incomes, or easy divorce and abortion desirable? Not all Americans are agreed. Since progress is an evaluative term, social scientists prefer the neutrally descriptive term "change."

THEORIES OF SOCIAL CHANGE

Dozens of writers—social scientists, theologians, even novelists—have advanced grand theories of social change. A "grand theory" is a broad, sweeping theory covering some important phenomena over all times and places. We shall outline a few of the more important ones. (Each of the scholars listed was a prolific writer, from whose extensive scholarly writings only a tiny fraction is summarized.)

Evolutionary Theories

All evolutionary theories assume that there is a consistent direction of social change carrying all societies through a similar sequence of stages from the original to the final stage of development. Also, evolutionary theories imply that when the final stage is reached, evolutionary change will end.

Auguste Comte (1798–1857), a French scholar sometimes called the founder of sociology, saw societies passing through three stages of growth: (1) the *theological stage*, guided by supernatural wisdom; (2) the *metaphysical stage*, a transitional stage in which supernatural beliefs are replaced by abstract principles as cultural guidelines, and (3) the *positive, or scientific, stage*, in which society is guided by evidence-based scientific laws.

Herbert Spencer (1820–1903) was an English scholar who wrote the first book entitled *Principles of Sociology* (1896). Like most scholars of his day, he was excited by Darwin's theories of organic evolution. He saw a parallel social evolution, with societies moving through a series of stages from homogeneous and simple tribal groups to complex modern societies. He applied Darwin's "survival of the fittest" to human societies, where he felt that the struggle for survival rewarded the talented and energetic and eliminated the lazy and unfit. This view came to be called "social Darwinism," and was eagerly embraced by the affluent.

Lewis Henry Morgan (1818–1881) an American anthropologist, saw a series of seven fixed technological stages through which societies passed from savagery to civilization.

Karl Marx (1813–1883) was a German social philosopher who spent much of his life in England. While he is classed as a conflict theorist, his theory of change is clearly evolutionary. Like other evolutionists, he saw a series of successive changes of increasing technological complexity, from primitive hunting to modern industrialism. Each stage had its appropriate "mode of production," while all other elements of the culture were brought into harmony with it. Each stage contained within itself "the seeds of its own destruction," for each stage inevitably created the conditions which destroyed it and led into the next stage. Marx thus viewed capitalism as brutal and exploitative but as a necessary preparation for the transition into communism. He saw the eventual overthrow of capitalism and the emergence of communism as absolutely inevitable, despite anything which capitalists might do to prevent it.

All evolutionary theories have certain weaknesses: (1) the data supporting the location of societies along the series of stages were often inaccurate, with a society being placed in whatever stage best fitted the theory; (2) the sequence of stages was not truly fixed, as some societies leapfrog over intermediate stages directly into the industrial or communist stage and some have even moved "backward" to an earlier stage; and (3) the assumption that major social change ends when a society reaches the "final" stage seems naïve. If change is a constant, will any set of arrangements ever be "final"?

Yet evolutionary theory contains much accurate description. Most societies *have* moved from simple to complex forms. To some extent, there *are* stages of development, in each of which the various elements of a culture fit together in an integrated system. With modernization, certain other social changes have

become necessary, such as transport and banking systems, labor specialization, and role-based rather than kinship-based social organization. All societies which modernize must accept much the same series of other changes. Thus the theory of successive stages, while not entirely correct, is not entirely wrong.

Cyclical Theories

The cyclical theorists also see a series of stages through which societies must pass. But, instead of ending in a "final" stage of perfection, they see a return to the starting point for another round.

Oswald Spengler (1880–1936), a German philosopher, saw each great civilization passing through successive stages of birth, growth, and decline, with the completed cycle covering about a thousand years. He attracted attention mainly because of his colorful doomsday predictions in *The Decline of the West* [1926].

Pitirim Sorokin (1889–1968) was a Russian sociologist who fled to the United States after the revolution. He saw all great civilizations in an endless cycle of three cultural systems: (1) the *ideational culture*, guided by supernatural beliefs and values; (2) the *idealistic culture*, in which a blend of supernatural beliefs and evidence-based rationality creates the ideal society; and (3) the *sensate culture*, in which sensations are the test of reality and the goal of life. In his *Social and Cultural Dynamics* [1941], he viewed modern Western civilization as rotten and soon to collapse, to be followed by a new ideational culture.

Arnold Toynbee (1889–1975), an English historian, also viewed the fate of great civilizations as birth, growth, decay, and death. The twenty-one great civilizations all arose in response to some challenge, and all have died except Western civilization, which is moving into the later stages of decay [1935–1961].

All these cyclical theories are interesting, and all are supported by mountains of supporting detail. But to identify, accurately date, and compare thousands of items showing changes in art, literature, music, law, morals, trade, religion, and other elements of a culture over thousands of years involves so many dubious records and so much selection and guesswork that the data base for the theories is untrustworthy. And these theories do not explain *why* civilizations change as they do, or why different societies respond so differently to a challenge. The theories are entertaining but not entirely convincing.

Functional and Conflict Theories of Change

Neither functional nor conflict theory includes any grand theories of change such as those above. Functionalists accept change as a constant which does not need to be "explained." Changes disrupt the equilibrium of a society, until the change has been integrated into the culture. Changes which prove to be useful (functional) are accepted and those which are useless or dysfunctional are rejected.

Many conflict theorists follow the Marxist pattern of evolutionary change, but conflict theory itself has no special theory of change. Instead of viewing change as the constant, conflict theory views social conflict as the constant, and change as the result of this conflict. Since conflict is continuous, change is continuous. Change produces new interest groupings and classes, and conflict between these produces further change. Any particular change represents the success of victorious groups or classes in imposing their preferences upon others. As shown in Table 20-1, functional and conflict theories of change are differences in emphasis and are not in fundamental opposition.

By this time, most students may have decided that theories of change are not very satisfactory. Perhaps the study of conditions and processes of change will be more rewarding.

PROCESSES OF SOCIAL CHANGE

Unlike earlier scholars who thought up grand theories of social change, William F. Ogburn, an American sociologist, was the first scholar to devote detailed study to the actual processes of change. His work still forms the basis for much of the recent theory and research on social change, including even such popular best-sellers as Alvin Toffler's *Future Shock* [1970] and *The Third Wave* [1981].

Discovery

A *discovery* is *a shared human perception of an aspect of reality which already exists.* The principle of the lever, the circulation of the blood, and the conditioned reflex existed long before

TABLE 20-1
FUNCTIONAL AND CONFLICT VIEWS OF CHANGE

	Functional view	Conflict view
Each society is	relatively stable	constantly changing
Each part of a society normally contributes to	its survival	its change
Each society is normally	relatively integrated	in tension and conflict
Social stability depends upon	consensus among members	constraint of some by others

Source: Adapted from Bryce F. Ryan, *Social and Cultural Change*, The Ronald Press Company, New York, 1969, p. 48.

Are all the above propositions correct? Is it possible for all to be correct?

they were discovered by human beings. A discovery is an addition to the world's store of verified knowledge. A discovery adds something new to the culture because, although this reality may always have existed, it becomes part of the culture only after its discovery.

A discovery becomes a factor in social change only when it is put to use. For two hundred years after the cause of scurvy was discovered, sailors continued to die because people were cheaper than lime juice.

When new knowledge is used to develop new technology, vast changes generally follow. The ancient Greeks knew about the power of steam, and before A.D. 100 Hero of Alexandria had built a small steam engine as a toy, but steam power produced no social changes until it was put to serious use nearly two thousand years later. Discoveries become a factor in social change when new knowledge is put to new uses.

Invention

An *invention* is often defined as *a new combination or a new use of existing knowledge.* Thus, George Selden in 1895 combined a liquid-gas engine, a liquid-gas tank, a running-gear mechanism, an intermediate clutch, a driving shaft, and a carriage body and patented this contraption as an automobile. None of these ideas was new; the only novelty was the combined use of them. The Selden patent was attacked and eventually revoked by the courts on the ground that he did not originate the idea of combining these items.

While existing elements are used in a new invention, it is the *idea* of combining them in a useful way that produces something which never before existed. Thus, iron, with the addition of small amounts of other metals, became steel, an alloy with properties which no metal known at that time could equal. Likewise, a round slice of tree log or stone and a length of tree limb were not new, but the wheel and axle were new. The wheel did

not exist until someone had the idea of using a limb and a slice of a tree log or stone in this manner.

Inventions may be classified as *material inventions,* such as the bow and arrow, telephone, or airplane, and *social inventions,* such as the alphabet, constitutional government, or the corporation. In each case, old elements are used, combined, and improved for a new application. Invention is thus a continuing process, with each new invention the last in a long series of preceding inventions and discoveries. In a popularly written book, Burlingame [1947] analyzed a number of familiar inventions, showing how each began hundreds or thousands of years ago and passed through dozens of preliminary inventions and intermediate stages. Invention is not strictly an individual matter; it is a social process involving an endless series of modifications, improvements, and recombinations. As Gillin [1948, pp. 158–163] pointed out, each invention may be new in *form, function,* and *meaning.* "Form" refers to the shape of the new object or the actions of the new behavior trait; "function" refers to what the invention does; "meaning" refers to the long-range consequences of its use. To these three we might also add that an invention may be new in *principle,* that is, in the basic scientific law upon which it is based.

The jet engine and the piston engine use the same principle (expansion of burning gases) but differ in form (one uses expanding gases directly for thrust, the other to push a piston in a cylinder). The steam engine and the piston gasoline engine are similar in form but differ in principle (one creates expanding gases by boiling water, the other by burning gasoline). The bow and arrow differ in both principle and form from the primitive spear but have the same function and meaning. The wheeled cart was new in all respects (in principle, since the load was carried by wheel and axle instead of being dragged or packed; in form, since it was new in design; in function, since it carried both people and possessions; in meaning, since it made large-scale, long-distance overland transport possible). Very few inventions are new in all four respects.

Most of the important inventions have been made by people working alone or in small groups [Jewkes et al., 1969]. Inventions typically passed through long periods of development, covering many decades, before becoming marketable products. Most inventors were not scientists but, contrary to the "backyard tinkerer" image, worked closely with scientists and were well informed about the scientific knowledge of the time. They were inspired mainly by the excitement of making something new, not by the desire for wealth, and most inventors made little or nothing on their inventions. Edison, for example, claimed that he *lost* money on his inventions and made money only on his manufacturing operations. [Jewkes et al., 1969, p. 94].

Invention today increasingly is accomplished through team research at large corporate, government, or university laboratories. Most corporate research and development activity aims at "product improvement" rather than at new inventions, while government funding is heavily concentrated upon weapons development. Thus, despite the "institutionalization of research," the single inventor or small independent team still supplies many of the useful new inventions.

Diffusion

Even the most inventive society invents only a modest proportion of its innovations. Most of the social changes in all known societies have developed through *diffusion, the spread of culture traits from group to group.* Diffusion operates both within societies and between societies. Jazz originated among black musicians of New Orleans and became diffused to other groups within the society. Later it spread to other societies and has now been diffused throughout the civilized world.

Diffusion takes place whenever socieites

come into contact. Societies may seek to prevent diffusion by forbidding contact, as with the Old Testament Hebrews:

> When the Lord thy God shall bring thee into the land whither thou goest to possess it, and hath cast out many nations before thee . . . thou shalt smite them and utterly destroy them; thou shalt make no covenant with them, nor shew mercy unto them; neither shalt thou make marriages with them. . . . For they will turn away thy son from following me, that they may serve other gods. . . . But . . . ye shall destroy their altars, and break down their images, and cut down their groves, and burn their graven images with fire. (Deut. 7:1–5.)

Like most efforts to prevent intercultural contacts, this prohibition failed. The Old Testament tells how the Hebrews persisted in mingling and intermarrying with the surrounding tribes, adopting bits of their cultures in the process. Whenever cultures come into contact, some exchange of culture traits always takes place.

Most of the content of any complex culture has been diffused from other societies. Ralph Linton has written a famous passage which tells how 100 percent Americans have actually borrowed most of their culture from other societies:

> Our solid American Citizen awakens in a bed built on a pattern which originated in the Near East but which was modified in Northern Europe before it was transmitted to America. He throws

Most of the content of any complex culture has been diffused from other societies.

back covers made from cotton, domesticated in India, or linen, domesticated in the Near East, or silk, the use of which was discovered in China. All of these materials have been spun and woven by processes invented in the Near East. He slips into his moccasins, invented by the Indians of the Eastern woodlands, and goes to the bathroom, whose fixtures are a mixture of European and American inventions, both of recent date. He takes off his pajamas, a garment invented in India, and washes with soap invented by the ancient Gauls. He then shaves, a masochistic rite which seems to have been derived from either Sumer or Ancient Egypt.

Returning to the bedroom, he removes his clothes from a chair of Southern European type and proceeds to dress. He puts on garments whose form originally derived from the skin clothing of the nomads of the Asiatic steppes, puts on shoes made from skins tanned by a process invented in ancient Egypt and cut to a pattern derived from the classical civilizations of the Mediterranean, and ties around his neck a strip of bright-colored cloth which is a vestigial survival of the shoulder shawls worn by seventeenth century Croatians. Before going out for breakfast he glances through the window, made of glass invented in Egypt, and if it is raining puts on overshoes made of rubber discovered by the Central American Indians and takes an umbrella, invented in southeastern Asia. Upon his head he puts a hat made of felt, a material invented in the Asiatic steppes.

On his way to breakfast he stops to buy a paper, paying for it with coins, an ancient Lydian invention. At the restaurant a whole new series of borrowed elements confronts him. His plate is made of a form of pottery invented in China. His knife is of steel, an alloy first made in southern India, his fork a medieval Italian invention, and his spoon a derivative of a Roman original. He begins breakfast with an orange, from the eastern Mediterranean, a cantaloupe from Persia, or perhaps a piece of African watermelon. With this he has coffee, an Abyssinian plant, with cream and sugar. Both the domestication of cows and the idea of milking them originated in the Near East, while sugar was first made in India. After his fruit and first coffee

he goes to waffles, cakes made by a Scandinavian technique from wheat domesticated in Asia Minor. Over these he pours maple syrup, invented by the Indians of the Eastern woodlands. As a side dish he may have the egg of a species of bird domesticated in Indo-China, or thin strips of the flesh of an animal domesticated in Eastern Asia which have been salted and smoked by a process developed in northern Europe.

When our friend has finished eating he settles back to smoke, an American Indian habit, consuming a plant domesticated in Brazil in either a pipe, derived from the Indians of Virginia, or a cigarette, derived from Mexico. If he is hardy enough he may even attempt a cigar, transmitted to us from the Antilles by way of Spain. While smoking he reads the news of the day, imprinted in characters invented by the ancient Semites upon a material invented in China, by a process invented in Germany. As he absorbs the accounts of foreign troubles he will, if he is a good conservative citizen, thank a Hebrew deity in an Indo-European language that he is a 100 percent American. (Ralph Linton, *The Study of Man*, Prentice-Hall, Inc., Englewood Cliffs, N.J., pp. 326–327. © 1936, renewed 1964. Reprinted by permission.)

Diffusion is always a two-way process. Traits cannot diffuse unless there is some kind of contact between peoples, and these contacts always entail some diffusion in both directions. Europeans gave horses, firearms, Christianity, whiskey, and smallpox to the Indians in exchange for corn, potatoes, tobacco, venereal disease, and the canoe. Yet the exchange is often lopsided. When two cultures come into contact, the society with the simpler technology generally does the more borrowing. Within societies, low-status groups generally borrow more than high-status groups. Slave groups generally absorb the culture of their masters, while their own is forgotten or deliberately extinguished.

Diffusion is a selective process. A group accepts some culture traits from a neighbor, at the same time rejecting others. We accepted much Indian food but rejected Indian religion.

Function often changes when an artifact diffuses into another society. (*American Museum of Natural History*)

Indians quickly accepted the white people's horse, but few accepted the white people's cow.

Diffusion generally involves some modification of the borrowed element. As noted earlier, each cultural trait has *principle, form, function,* and *meaning.* Any or all these may change when a trait is diffused. When Europeans adopted Indian tobacco, they smoked it in a pipe somewhat like the Indian pipe, thus preserving the form, although they also added other forms—cigars, cigarettes, chewing tobacco, and snuff. But they entirely changed function and meaning. Indians smoked tobacco as a ceremonial ritual; Europeans used it first as a medicine and later for personal gratification and sociability. The outward forms of Christianity have been diffused more readily than the functions and meanings. In missionary areas many converts have accepted the forms of Christian worship while retaining many of their traditional supernatural beliefs and practices. Non-Western peoples have put tin cans and other Western artifacts to a variety of uses, both utilitarian and aesthetic. American colonists accepted maize (corn) from the Indians unchanged; it traveled to Europe, where it was used as food for animals but not for people; it was then diffused to West Africa, where it became a favorite food and even an offering to the gods. Endless examples could be cited to show how traits are nearly always modified as they are diffused.

Sociologists and anthropologists have made many research studies of the diffusion process [Allen, 1971, chap. 12]. Most of our aid programs in underdeveloped countries, as well as those for "underprivileged" groups in our own country, are primarily efforts to promote diffusion. Consequently, it is one of the most important topics in sociology.

FACTORS IN THE RATE OF CHANGE

Discovery, invention, and diffusion are processes of change. But what causes them to happen? We cannot answer this question without first examining the meaning of the term *cause*. A cause is sometimes defined as a phenomenon which *is both necessary and sufficient* to produce a predictable effect. It is *necessary* in that we never have this effect without this cause, and *sufficient* in that this cause, alone, always produces this effect. Thus defined, very few causes have been established in social science. Does drunkenness cause divorce? Many spouses endure a drunken mate, while others divorce mates who are bone-dry. Obviously, drunkenness is neither a necessary nor a sufficient condition to produce a divorce. Most causation in social science is multiple—that is, a number of factors interact in producing a result. What factors interact in producing a social change?

First of all, we note that the factors in social change are mainly social and cultural not biological or geographic. Not everyone accepts this view. Some people would attribute the rise and fall of great civilizations to changes in the biological characteristics of nations. Often these theories have a racial twist; a great civilization is said to arise from a vigorous, creative race and to fall when the race mixes with lesser breeds and dilutes its genius. According to an opposite version, a great burst of creativity follows a fortunate intermixture of races and dies out as the hybrid strain runs out. Most scientists reject all such theories. During the period of recorded history, our biological attributes appear to have been a constant, not a variable, in human behavior.

Physical Environment

Major changes in the physical environment are quite rare but very compelling when they happen. The desert wastes of North Africa were once green and well-populated. Climates change, soil erodes, and lakes gradually turn into swamps and finally plains. A culture is greatly affected by such changes, although sometimes they come about so slowly that they are largely unnoticed. Human misuse can bring very rapid changes in physical environment which, in turn, change the social and cultural life of a people. Deforestation brings land erosion and reduces rainfall; overgrazing destroys the vegetation cover and promotes erosion. Much of the wasteland and desert land of the world is a testament to human ignorance and misuse [Mikesell, 1969; Horton and Leslie, 1981, chap. 19]. Brazil today appears to be repeating the deforestation which turned much of the border of the Mediterranean Sea into wasteland two thousand years ago (decimating their Indians much as we did two centuries ago) [Davis, 1977]. Environmental destruction has been at least a contributing factor in the fall of most great civilizations.

Many human groups throughout history have changed their physical environments through migration. Especially in primitive societies, whose members are very directly dependent upon their physical environment, migration to a different environment brings major changes in culture. Civilization makes it easy to transport a culture and practice it in a new and different environment. The British colonial in the jungle outposts usually took afternoon tea and dressed for dinner. Yet no one would suggest that people were unaffected by the jungle environment; all cultures are affected by a change of physical environment [Hoffman, 1973].

Population Changes

A population change is itself a social change,

but also becomes a casual factor in further social and cultural changes. When a thinly settled frontier fills up with people, the hospitality pattern fades away, secondary-group relations multiply, institutional structures grow more elaborate, and many other changes follow. A stable population may be able to resist most change, but a rapidly growing population *must* either migrate, improve its productivity, or starve. Great historic migrations and conquests—of the Huns, the Vikings, and many others—have arisen from the pressure of a growing population upon limited resources. Migration encourages further change, for it brings a group into a new environment, subjects it to new social contacts, and confronts it with new problems. No major population change leaves the culture unchanged. As this is written, many scholars are gravely wondering whether overpopulation or nuclear war is the more likely to destroy modern civilization.

Isolation and Contact

Societies located at world crossroads have always been centers of change. Since most new traits come through diffusion, those societies in closest contact with other societies are likely to change most rapidly. In ancient times of overland transport, the land bridge connecting Asia, Africa, and Europe was the center of civilizing change. Later, sailing vessels shifted the center to the fringes of the Mediterranean Sea, and still later to the northwest coast of Europe. Areas of greatest intercultural contact are the centers of change. War and trade have always brought intercultural contact, and today tourism is adding to the contacts between cultures [Greenwood, 1972].

Conversely, isolated areas are centers of stability, conservatism, and resistance to change. Almost without exception, the most primitive tribes have been those who were the most isolated, like the polar Eskimos or the Aranda of Central Australia. Even among

"civilized" peoples, isolation brings cultural stability. The most "backward" American groups have been found in the inaccessible hills and valleys of the Appalachians [Sherman and Henry, 1933; Surface, 1970].

Leyburn [1935] has shown how European groups who migrated to remote, isolated frontiers often retained many features of their native culture long after they had been discarded by their parent society. Thus, by the nineteenth century, the social life of the Boers in the South African Transvaal resembled the life of the seventeenth-century Dutch more than that of the nineteenth-century Dutch in the Netherlands.

Ethnic enclaves, whose isolation is social and voluntary rather than geographic, show a similar conservatism, whether it be Americans in Spain [Nash, 1967], Amish in America [Hostettler, 1964], or Tristan Islanders in England [Munch, 1964, 1970]. Isolation invariably retards social change.

Social Structure

The structure of a society affects its rate of change in subtle and not immediately apparent ways. Inkeles and Smith [1974] conducted in-depth interviews in six developing countries, seeking to find out what made some persons receptive to change. They found that some persons had "a general modernity syndrome" [p. 225] and that such persons were likely to have worked in a factory, to have had several years of education, and to read newspapers.

A society which vests great authority in the very old people, as classical China did for centuries, is likely to be conservative and stable. A society which stresses conformity and trains the individual to be highly responsive to the group, such as the Zuñi, is less receptive to change than a society like the Ileo, who are highly individualistic and tolerate considerable cultural variability [Ottenberg, 1959].

A highly centralized bureaucracy is very

favorable to the promotion and diffusion of change [Dowdy, 1970], although bureaucracies have sometimes been used in an attempt to suppress change, usually with no more than temporary success.

When a culture is very highly integrated, so that each element is rightly interwoven with all the others in a mutually interdependent system, change is difficult and costly. Among a number of Nilotic African peoples, such as the Pakot, Masai, and Kipsizis, the culture is integrated around the cattle complex. Cattle are not only a means of subsistence; they are also a necessity for bride purchase, a measure of status, and an object of intense affection [Schneider, 1959]. Such a system is strongly resistant to social change. But when the culture is less highly integrated, so that work, play, family, religion, and other activities are less dependent upon one another, change is easier and more frequent. A tightly structured society, wherein every person's roles, duties, privileges, and obligations are precisely and rigidly defined, is less given to changes than a more loosely structured society, wherein roles, lines of authority, privileges, and obligations are more open to individual rearrangement.

The structure of American society is highly conducive to social change. Our individualism, our lack of rigid social stratification, our relatively high proportion of achieved statuses, and our institutionalization of research all encourage rapid social change. Today tens of thousands of workers are engaged in finding new discoveries and inventions. This exploration is something new in the world's history. Our dazzling and sometimes upsetting rate of change is one consequence.

Attitudes and Values

To us change is normal, and most Westerners pride themselves upon being progressive and up to date. Children in Western societies are socialized to anticipate and appreciate change. By contrast, the Trobriand Islanders off the

Children in our society are socialized to anticipate and appreciate change.

coast of New Guinea had no concept of change and did not even have any words in their language to express or describe change [Lee, 1959, pp. 89–104]. When Westerners tried to explain the concept of change, the islanders could not understand what they were talking about. Societies obviously differ greatly in their general attitude toward change. A people who revere the past, worship their ancestors, honor and obey their elders, and are preoccupied with traditions and rituals will change slowly and unwillingly. When a culture has been relatively static for a long time, the people are likely to assume that it should remain so indefinitely. They are intensely and unconsciously ethnocentric; they assume that their customs and techniques are correct and everlasting. A possible change is unlikely even to be seriously considered. Any change in such a society is likely to be too gradual to be noticed.

A rapidly changing society has a different attitude toward change, and this attitude is both cause and effect of the changes already taking place. Rapidly changing societies are aware of social change. They are somewhat skeptical and critical of some parts of their traditional culture and will consider and experiment with innovations. Such attitudes powerfully stimulate the proposal and ac-

The Amish have accepted new farming techniques but are slow to accept new machinery. (*Jane Latta/Photo Researchers, Inc.*)

ceptance of changes by individuals within the society.

Different groups within a locality or a society may show differing receptivity to change. Every changing society has its liberals and its conservatives. Literate and educated people tend to accept changes more readily than the illiterate and uneducated [Nwosu, 1971; Waisanen and Kumata, 1972]. The Amish in the United States have resisted change of nearly every kind except, sometimes, in farming techniques. Although the Amish may never have heard of the "integration of culture," they realize that if their young people had easy access to movies, television, motorcycles, and fast food, their traditional values would soon fade.

A group may be highly receptive to changes of one kind and resistant to changes of other kinds. The Amish quickly accepted new farming procedures (seeds, crop breeds, crop rotation, field management), slowly accepted new farm machinery, and rejected practically all new consumer products. Many religious groups readily accept new church architecture but not new religious doctrines. Some changes are more threatening to a group's major values than are other changes.

Attitudes and values affect both the amount and the direction of social change. The ancient Greeks made great contributions to art and learning but contributed little to technology. Work was done by slaves; to concern oneself with a slave's work was no proper task for a Greek scholar. No society has been equally dynamic in all aspects, and its values determine in which area—art, music, warfare, technology, philosophy, or religion—it will be innovative.

Perceived Needs

A society's rate and direction of change are greatly affected by the needs its members perceive. "Needs" are subjective; they are real if people feel that they are real. In many underdeveloped and malnourished parts of the world, people not only have objective needs for *more* food, they also need *different* foods, especially vegetables and legumes. Agricultural changes which bring *more* food are more readily accepted than those bringing *different* foods, for which they feel no need [Arensberg and Niehoff, 1971, p. 155]. Until people feel a need, they resist change; only the perceived needs of a society count.

Some practical inventions languish until the society discovers a need for them. The zipper fastener was invented in 1891 but ignored for a quarter century. The pneumatic tire was invented and patented by Thompson in 1845 but was ignored until the popularity of the bicycle created an awareness of need for it; then it was reinvented by Dunlop in 1888.

It is often stated that changing conditions create new needs—genuine, objective needs not just subjectively "felt" needs. Thus, urbanization created a need for sanitary engineering; the modern factory system created a need for labor unions; and the high-speed automobile created a need for superhighways. A culture is integrated, and, therefore, changes in one part of the culture create a need for adaptive changes in related parts of the culture.

It is doubtless true that failure to recognize an objective need may have unpleasant consequences. For centuries, sickness and death were the price of our ancestors' failure to recognize that urban growth made sewers necessary. A more recent failure to recognize that death control creates a need for birth control has brought half the world to the brink of starvation. All this does not alter the fact that it is only those "needs" which are perceived as needs which stimulate innovation and social change.

The concept of perceived need as herein outlined is largely a functionalist concept. Functionalists see many "needs" as objective

realities growing from survival necessities and from the constant development of new technology. Conflict theorists would reply that a majority of our "needs" are perceived as a result of skillful promotion by those who profit from creating and then meeting them. Thus we "need" new gadgets because they are cleverly advertised, and we "need" trillions for defense because the military-industrial complex finds it profitable in money and power to promote war scares and international tensions. The disagreement is one of emphasis. Both functionalists and conflict theorists agree that some "needs" are created and some are objective necessities.

Necessity, however, is no guarantee that the needed invention or discovery will be made. At present, we perceive that we need cures for cancer and for the common cold, a pollution-free power source, and effective disposal of nuclear wastes. These is no certainty that we shall develop any of these. Necessity may be the "mother of invention," but invention also needs a father—a cultural base to provide the necessary knowledge and technique.

The Cultural Base

Prehistoric cave dwellers could make exceedingly few material inventions, for they had very little to work with. Even the bow and arrow include a number of inventions and techniques—notching the bow ends, tying the bowstring, hafting and pointing the arrow, plus the idea and technique of shooting it. Not until these components were invented was it possible to invent the bow and arrow. By the *cultural base*, we mean *the accumulation of knowledge and technique* available to the inventor. As the cultural base grows, an increasing number of inventions and discoveries become possible. The invention of the geared wheel provided a component which has been used in countless inventions. The discovery of electromagnetism and the invention of the vacuum tube, the transistor, and the microchip provided necessary components for hundreds of more recent inventions.

Unless the cultural base provides enough earlier inventions and discoveries, an invention cannot be completed. Leonardo da Vinci in the late fifteenth century sketched many machines which were entirely workable in principle and detail, but the technology of his day was incapable of building them. His drawings for the aerial bomb, hydraulic pump, air-conditioning unit, helicopter, machine gun, military tank, and many others were clear and workable, but the fifteenth century lacked the advanced metals, the fuels, the lubricants, and the technical skills necessary to carry his brilliant ideas into practical reality. Many inventive ideas have had to wait until the supporting gaps in knowledge and technique were filled in. The recent "knowledge explosion" is often cited as the source of modern innovation. This is another way of saying that the cultural base is rapidly growing and is accessible to a growing portion of our people.

When all the supporting knowledge has been developed, the appearance of an invention or discovery becomes almost a certainty. In fact, it is quite common for an invention or discovery to be made independently by several persons at about the same time. Ogburn [1950, pp. 90–102], a sociologist who specialized in the study of social change, listed 148 such inventions and discoveries, ranging from the discovery of sun spots, independently discovered by Galileo, Fabricius, Scheiner, and Harriott, all in 1611, to the invention of the airplane by Langley (1893–1897), Wright (1895–1901), and perhaps others. In fact, disputes over who was first with an invention or a scientific discovery are common and sometimes acrimonious [Merton, 1957c]. When the cultural base provides all the supporting items of knowledge, it is very probable that one or more imaginative persons will put these items together for a new invention or discovery.

This is one reason new weapons systems are developed endlessly. It is in the nature of science and technology that anything we can build, *any* advanced people can build. And, so the rationale goes, our enemies *will* build such weapons whether we do or not, so let's get on with it. Of course, this leads to an endless and fruitless arms race which can be limited only by international agreements which we seem unable to reach.

CROSS-FERTILIZATION. The great importance of the cultural base is revealed by the principle of *cross-fertilization*, which states that discoveries and inventions in one field became useful in an entirely different field. Pasteur's germ theory of disease grew out of his efforts to tell France's vintners why their wine turned sour. The vacuum tube, developed for radio, made possible the electronic computer, which now aids research in nearly everything from astronomy to zoology. Certain radioactive materials, by-products of the search for more deadly weapons, are now invaluable in medical diagnosis, therapy, and research. Image intensifiers, developed for night fighting in Vietnam, are now widely used by naturalists for field research. Most of the present uses of computers and lasers were not even imagined when they were invented. Stouffer's studies [1949], designed to show the armed services how to get more effective fighting men, also provided knowledge that was useful to students of group dynamics, race relations, and several other fields of sociology.

THE EXPONENTIAL PRINCIPLE. This principle states that, as the cultural base grows, its possible uses tend to grow in a geometric ratio. To illustrate: If we have only two chemicals in a laboratory, only one combination (A-B) is possible; with three chemicals, four combinations are possible (A-B-C, A-B, A-C, and B-C); with four chemicals, ten combinations; with five chemicals, twenty-five; and so on. As the size of the cultural base grows by addition, the possible combinations of these elements grow by multiplication. This helps to explain today's high rate of discovery and invention [Hamblin et al., 1973]. A vast accumulation of scientific technical knowledge is shared by all the civilized societies, and from this base new inventions and discoveries flow in a rising tide.

RESISTANCE TO AND ACCEPTANCE OF SOCIAL CHANGE

Not all proposed innovations are accepted by the society. Some years ago, Spicer suggested that proposed changes meet resistance when (1) the change is imposed by others, (2) the change is not understood, or (3) the change is seen as a threat to people's values [Spicer, 1952 p. 18]. A process of *selective acceptance* operates as some innovations are accepted instantly and some only after long delay; some are rejected entirely, and others are accepted in part. Thus we accepted completely the Indians' corn; accepted and modified their tobacco; accepted in a very small, highly modified way their totemic clans (Boy Scout "beaver" and "wolverine" patrols); and totally rejected their religion. Acceptance of innovations is never total and is always selective according to several considerations.

Specific Attitudes and Values

Aside from its general attitude toward change, each society has many specific attitudes and values which cling to its objects and activities. When government agents introduced hybrid corn to the Spanish-American farmers of the Rio Grande Valley some years ago, the farmers readily adopted it because of its superior yield, but within three years, they had all returned to the old corn. They did not like the hybrid corn because it did not make good tortillas [Apodaca, 1952]. People's established likes and dislikes are important factors in social change.

If an object has a purely utilitarian value—

> A 1913 car-owner's manual states: "The automobile has now developed to the point where it is not anticipated that there will be further developments or changes, and this manual should be a reliable guide for the motorist of the future."
>
> Samuel M. Inman, quoted by Leo Aikman in the *Atlanta Constitution*.
>
> Can you think of any other examples of failure to anticipate future change?

that is, if it is valued because of what it will do—change may be accepted quite readily. If some feature of the traditional culture is valued intrinsically—valued for itself, aside from what it will do—change is less readily accepted. To the American farmer, cattle are a source of income, to be bred, culled, and butchered whenever most profitable. But to many of the Nilotic peoples of Africa, cattle represent intrinsic values. The owner recognizes and loves each cow. To slaughter one would be like killing one of the family. A Pakot with a hundred cattle is rich and respected; one with only a dozen is poor; one with no cattle is ignored as though dead. Efforts of Western officials to get such peoples to manage their herds "rationally"—to cull their herds, breed only the best, and stop overgrazing their lands—have generally failed.

The average American, who usually takes a coldly rational, relatively unsentimental view of economic activities, finds it hard to appreciate the sentiments and values of non-Western peoples. He or she is irritated by the Biaga of Central India, who refused to give up their primitive digging sticks for the far superior moldboard plow. Why? The Biaga loved the earth as a kindly and generous mother; they would gently help her with the digging stick to bring forth her yield but could not bring themselves to cut her "with knives" [Elwin, 1939, pp. 106–107]. The American is annoyed by the Ettwah Indians' unwillingness to adopt green manuring (plowing under a crop of green sanhemp as fertilizer). But to this Indian, "green manuring involves a very cruel act of plowing under the sanhemp leaf and stalk before they are ripe. This act involves violence" [Mayer, 1958, p. 209]. Yet is there any basic difference between these illustrations and American refusal to eat horse meat because it conflicts with our values? How about those American groups who condemn homosexuality, sexual permissiveness, abortion, divorce, alcoholic beverages, or the eating of meat because these conflict with their values? To each of us, it seems right to reject any innovation that conflicts with our mores or values; when others do likewise, their refusal often impresses us as ignorant superstition or stubbornness. Such is ethnocentrism!

Demonstrability of Inventions

Not all inventions are very useful. U.S. Patent No. 3,423,150 was issued for a "toilet bowl lock," to "prevent unauthorized access to the toilet bowl," while U.S. Patent No. 3,580,592 protects the inventor of the "combination deer carcass sled and chaise lounge." Only a tiny fraction of all patents are issued for inventions which prove to be useful.

An innovation is most quickly accepted when its usefulness can be easily demonstrated. The American Indians very eagerly accepted European guns but have not accepted European religion. Many inventions work so poorly in their earlier stages that most people wait until they are perfected. The early automobile owner was often advised to "Get a horse!" Early imperfections delay the acceptance of workable inventions.

Some innovations are easily demonstrated on a small scale; others cannot be demonstrated without costly, large-scale trials. Most mechanical inventions can be tested cheaply in a few hours or days. Most social inventions, such as the corporation, social organization based on role rather than on kinship, or

Fear of change arises from uncertainty about its effects. This handbill appeared in Philadelphia more than a century ago. (*The Bettman Archive, Inc.*)

nuclear arms control, are not easily tried out in the laboratory or testing bureau. Many social inventions can be tested only through a long-term trial, involving at least an entire society. We hesitate to adopt an innovation until we have been shown how it works; yet we can determine the practical value of most social inventions only by adopting them. This dilemma slows their acceptance.

Compatibility with Existing Culture

Innovations are most readily accepted when they fit in nicely with the existing culture. The horse fitted easily into the hunting culture of the Apache, as it enabled them to do better what they were already doing. Not all innovations mesh so well. Innovations may be incompatible with the existing culture in at least three ways.

First, *the innovation may conflict with existing patterns.* In many developing countries, the idea of appointment and promotion on a merit basis clashes with the traditional family obligation to take care of one's relatives. Many current environmental proposals in the United States conflict with our traditional concepts of land use, property rights, and personal liberties.

When an innovation conflicts with existing culture patterns, there are at least three possible outcomes: (1) It may be rejected, as most Americans have rejected chopsticks, nude beaches, and communism; (2) it may be accepted, and the conflicting cultural traits may be modified to fit it, as we have altered our child-labor practices to permit compulsory public education; (3) it may be accepted and its conflict with the existing culture may be concealed and evaded by rationalization, as in those areas (including France and, until recently, five of the United States) where contraceptives were freely sold "for prevention of disease," although the sale of contra-

ceptives was forbidden by law. While not always decisive, conflict with the existing culture discourages acceptance of an innovation.

Sometimes an apparent conflict can be avoided by role compartmentalization. As an example, the Kwaio of the Solomon Islands had chiefs every Tuesday! Their social organization included no chiefs, but it became necessary to invent some to handle dealings with white officials after World War II. To avoid conflict between these new "chiefs" and the traditional holders of authority and influence, they simply agreed that the chiefs would "reign" only on Tuesdays when the white officials called [Keesing, 1968]. In this way, a potentially disruptive innovation was fenced off from the rest of the culture.

Second, *the innovation may call for new patterns not present in the culture.* The American Indians had no patterns of animal husbandry into which the cow could be fitted. When

In the early days of the last war when armaments of all kinds were in short supply, the British, I am told, made use of a venerable field piece that had come down to them from previous generations. The honorable past of this light artillery stretched back, in fact, to the Boer War. In the days of uncertainty after the fall of France, these guns, hitched to trucks, served as useful mobile units in the coast defense. But it was felt that the rapidity of fire could be increased. A time-motion expert was, therefore, called in to suggest ways to simplify the firing procedures. He watched one of the gun crews of five men at practice in the field for some time. Puzzled by certain aspects of the procedure, he took some slow motion pictures of the soldiers performing the loading, aiming, and firing routines.

When he ran these pictures over once or twice, he noticed something that appeared odd to him. A moment before the firing, two members of the gun crew ceased all activity and came to attention for a three-second interval extending throughout

the discharge of the gun. He summoned an old colonel of artillery, showed him the pictures, and pointed out this strange behavior. What, he asked the colonel, did it mean. The colonel, too, was puzzled. He asked to see the pictures again. "Ah," he said when the performance was over, "I have it. They are holding the horses."

This story, true or not, and I am told it is true, suggests nicely the pain with which the human being accommodates himself to changing conditions. The tendency is apparently involuntary and immediate to protect oneself against the shock of change by continuing in the presence of altered situations the familiar habits, however incongruous, of the past.

Elting E. Morrison, *Men, Machines, and Modern Times*, The M.I.T. Press, Cambridge, Mass., 1966, p. 17. Reprinted by permission of The M.I.T. Press.

Can you think of any similar examples where a procedure has been continued after it is no longer useful?

they were first given cows by government agents, they hunted them as game animals. A society generally tries to use an innovation in old, familiar ways. When this fails, the society may develop new ways of making effective use of the new element. Thus, we have disguised each new building material to make it look like an old, familiar material. Early concrete blocks were faced like rough-finished stone; asphalt and asbestos shingles were finished to look like brick or wood; aluminum siding is still made to look like wood. Then, after some years, these materials begin to be used in designs and ways which make full use of their own properties and possibilities. Most innovations call for some new patterns in the culture, and it takes time to develop them.

Third, *some innovations are substitutive, not additive*, and these are less readily accepted. It is easier to accept innovations which can be added to the culture without requiring the immediate discard of some familiar trait complex. American baseball, popular music, and the "western" movie have been diffused throughout most of the world. Each could be added to almost any kind of culture without requiring surrender of any native traits. But sex equality, democracy, or merit-based recruitment and promotion have diffused more slowly; each requires the surrender of traditional values and practices. Many non-Western peoples have readily accepted the procedures and materials of scientific medicine—inoculations, antibiotics, analgesics, and even surgery—for these could coexist with their traditional folk medicine. The ill Navaho could swallow the government doctor's pill while the Navaho healing dance continued. But many of these people neither understand nor accept the scientific foundations of medicine, such as the germ, virus, and stress theories of disease or the rest of the medical subculture, for these conflict with their traditional belief system. Whenever the nature of the choice is such that one cannot have *both* the

new and the old, the acceptance of the new is usually delayed.

Costs of Change

The very poor generally resist all change, because they cannot afford to take *any* risk [Arensberg and Niehoff, 1971, pp. 149–150]. Change is nearly always costly. Not only does change disrupt the existing culture and destroy cherished sentiments and values, but it also involves some specific costs.

TECHNICAL DIFFICULTIES OF CHANGE. Very few innovations can simply be added to the existing culture; most innovations require some modification of the existing culture. Only recently did England replace an awkward and clumsy monetary system with a decimal currency, while the United States has been resisting a switch to the metric system of measures for two centuries. Why have such clumsy systems been retained for so long? Because the changeover is so difficult [Guillen, 1977]. England's switch to a decimal currency in 1967 proved to be far more complicated than simply learning a new system. Changes in cash registers, coin machines, bookkeeping records, standardized merchandise sizes, and arguments over pound fractions were all involved. Learning the metric system would be very simple, but the task of making and stocking everything from window frames to nuts and bolts in both size ranges for a half century or so is overwhelming. Railroads would be more efficient if the tracks were a foot or two farther apart to permit wider cars, but the cost of rebuilding the tracks and replacing the rolling stock is prohibitive. The standard typewriter keyboard is very inefficient, making the left hand do two-thirds of the work, but a new keyboard would require typists to relearn to type. New inventions often make present machinery obsolete and destroy the market for skills which workers have spent years developing.

528

*Social
Change and
Social Policy*

VESTED INTERESTS AND CHANGE. The costs of social change are never evenly distributed. The industry which is made obsolete and the workers whose skill is made unmarketable are forced to bear the costs of technical progress, while others enjoy the improved products. Those to whom the status quo is profitable are said to have a *vested interest.* Communities with an army post or navy yard nearby find that all this government money is good for business, so these communities have a vested interest in retaining these military establishments. Students attending state universities have a vested interest in tax-supported higher education. President Reagan's efforts to trim student loan funds met with strong opposition from both the colleges and the students. Nearly everyone has some vested interests—from the rich with their tax-exempt bonds to the poor with their welfare checks and food stamps.

Most social changes carry a threat, real or imaginary, to some people with vested interests, who then oppose these changes. Examples are almost endless. In 1579 the Council of Danzig, acting in response to pressure from weavers, ordered the strangulation of the inventor of an improved weaving machine; and the spinsters of Blackburn, Eng-

land, invaded Hargreave's home to destroy his spinning jennies [Stern, 1937]. The Japanese learned to produce and use guns in the sixteenth century but renounced them about 1637 because the warrior elite preferred to retain their sword-wielding supremacy [Perrin, 1979]. The early railroads were opposed by landowners who did not want their lands cut up and by canal owners and toll-road companies; and then in turn the railroads became vigorous opponents of the automobile and helped to block construction of the St. Lawrence seaway. Employer opposition to the organization of labor unions was long and bitter and still continues in some places, while unions resort to "featherbedding" in the effort to retain jobs made unnecessary by technical change. Each group is an ardent advocate of progress in general but not at the expense of its own vested interests.

Those with vested interests, however, appear as promoters of change whenever they believe the proposed change will be profitable to them. American corporations spend billions of dollars each year to develop new products which they can sell profitably. Many business groups in the Great Lakes area energetically supported the St. Lawrence seaway proposal. Such government enterprises

---

**VESTED INTERESTS
AND SOCIAL
CHANGE**

Although returnable beverage containers [instead of throwaways] would be of enormous benefit to society, practical politics is always biased toward the status quo. For example; the 40,000 people who would lose jobs if all bottles had to be returnable have a clear idea of who they are; the 165,000 people who would acquire jobs are not easily identified, and have no union looking out for their prospective interests. Moreover, a returnable beverage container law would cut into the profits and growth potential of man-

ufacturers of bottles and cans alike, and the two have forged a potent political alliance to defeat such legislation. The problem, in this case, lies not so much in determining what policies would promote the public interest as in assembling the political muscle to overcome the opposition of those to whom change would not necessarily represent an improvement.

Denis Hayes, "The Unfinished Agenda: Goals for Earth Day '80," *Environment,* 22:7, April 1980. A publication of the Helen Dwight Reid Educational Foundation.

Do most changes benefit some while injuring others? How do we decide whose interests should prevail?

are normally denounced as socialism by those who are not enriched thereby, while those whom the proposal benefits will find other terms to describe it. (Apparently, *socialism* operates when the government spends money to benefit *you*, not *me!*)

Business interests have sought and obtained many kinds of government regulation and "interference" when it seemed in their interest to do so. Labor unions have been most eloquent supporters of laws to limit child labor. The great Chicago fire of 1871 showed the weakness of competing private fire-fighting companies, and more important, imposed such heavy losses upon fire insurance companies that they threw their support behind the proposal for tax supported municipal fire departments. Most social reforms are not secured until powerful people with vested interests redefine their interests and decide that the reform would benefit them.

Unfortunately, there are instances in which the change is so profitable to some that the harmful consequences are ignored. In many Third World countries, baby food formulas have successfully been promoted as "modern" in contrast to "old-fashioned" breast feeding, thus enriching American and European corporations at the expense of infant health in these countries [*Science News,* 113:357, June 3, 1978].

Role of the Change Agent

Who proposes a change, and how does this person go about it? The identity of the originator greatly affects acceptance or rejection. A Nigerian government effort to introduce new fertilizer failed because of the peasants' bad past experiences with government officials [Lauer, 1977, p. 10]. Any proposal identified as "communist" is doomed to certain defeat in the United States. Opponents of all sorts of proposals often label them communist in order to defeat them. Innovations which are first adopted by persons at the top of the prestige scale and power system are likely to filter downward quite rapidly; those first adopted by low-status persons are likely to percolate upward more slowly, if at all.

Successful change agents often seek to make the change appear innocuous by identifying it with familiar cultural elements. King Ibn-Saud introduced radio and telephone to Saudi Arabia by quoting the Koran over them. Christian missonaries in Venezuela had little success with the Warao tribe until they rewrote the Christian doctrines in the form of chants, which the Warao then sang with great enthusiasm [Wilbert, 1977]. Franklin D. Roosevelt's leadership rested partly upon his ability to describe major reforms in terms of homespun American sentiments and values.

How well a village water project succeeds relates directly to the villagers' view of the technology used: Is it superimposed on their way of life, or is it integrated into village mores?

When a water system is placed in a village by outsiders—without any local involvement—it is likely to be underused, misused, and soon forgotten. Compare this with the Milange development project in Malawi, in which villagers helped plan, locate, and build a perennial gravity flow water system—complete with simply made and conveniently located pumps that have remained in good working condition.

Many water systems do not work properly because virtually no local resident knows how they operate. The logical solution is to institute a training program for operating the system *at the same time* it is being installed. A cadre of barefoot engineers could keep water supply systems functioning well over a large rural area.

Jane Stein, "Fumbled Help at the Well," *Environment,* 19:17, June/July 1977. A publication of the Helen Dwight Reid Educational Foundation.

How does this illustrate the concept of the integration of culture?

Change agents must know the culture in which they work. This point is stressed in the many guidebooks for aid officials working in development programs in underdeveloped countries [Arensberg and Niehoff, 1971; Leagins and Loomis, 1972; Loomis and Beagle, 1975], or for business executives preparing to operate in an unfamiliar culture [Whiting, 1977], or even for change agents working to promote change in our own society [Rothman, Erlich, and Teresa, 1976].

The thoughtless ethnocentrism of Western social scientists and technicians has often doomed their efforts to failure [Alatas, 1972; Selwyn, 1973]. Government attempts to settle Navaho Indians as individual families on irrigated land were unsuccessful, for the Navaho were accustomed to work land cooperatively along extended kinship lines. An amusing illustration of how ignorance and ethnocentrism handicapped a change agent is found in Micronesia, where an American labor relations expert sought to recruit Palauan workers for a mining operation. He first demanded to see the "chief"—a request which posed a problem since they had no chief in their social structure. Finally they produced a person with whom the American expert sought to establish rapport by throwing an arm around his shoulder and laughingly tousling his hair. In Palauan culture this was an indignity roughly equivalent, in our culture, to opening a man's fly in public [Useem, 1952]. Needless to add, this expert was not very successful.

Many of our "foreign aid" programs have made conditions worse not better in the lands we sought to help. Due partly to American ethnocentrism and partly to the egomania of some Third World leaders, much of the development money was wasted on impractical heavy industry or showy buildings while agriculture was often neglected [Warren, 1979; Kronholz, 1982]. The agricultural development programs were often ethnocentric efforts to export American high-technology agriculture to underdeveloped countries which had a shortage of land and capital and a

surplus of labor. This was a policy of sheer madness. Mechanized agriculture increases output per worker not per acre. This high-technology agriculture failed to use the resource these countries had in abundance—labor—but created needs for expensive imported machinery, repair parts, fuel, fertilizers, and pesticides which they could not afford [Crittenden, 1982]. Thus our "aid" programs often enriched the prosperous and impoverished the poor, who were pushed off their land to make room for large mechanized farms [McInerney and Donaldson, 1975; Bauer and Yamey, 1982; Tucker, 1982]. The result was a decline in local food production and an increase in economic inequality and hunger. A more rational aid program would have sought to improve the traditional labor-intensive agriculture and to improve the native strains of plants and animals which were already adapted to the local climate and did not demand expensive imports of fertilizer and pesticide.

Not all foreign aid programs have been such dismal failures; many have been highly successful. Enough have failed, in the manner described above, to be a warning against the baleful effects of ethnocentrism.

The efforts of the change agent are not always appreciated. The inventor is often ridiculed; the missionary may be eaten; and the agitator or reformer is usually persecuted. Radicals are likely to be popular only after they are dead, and organizations (like the Daughters of the American Revolution) dedicated to the memory of dead revolutionists have no fondness for live ones. Those who sought to change the segregated racial patterns of American society may become heroes in the history books, but they faced jail and physical violence during their lifetime. Change agents do not always observe all laws, but even careful law observance is no protection. It was impossible to be a labor organizer in the 1930s or a civil right worker in the 1950s without being beaten, jailed, or even worse.

Persecution of change agents and social reformers has a long history. Huss and Ser-

THE UNANTICIPATED CONSEQUENCES OF CHANGE

Traditionally in Kenya, a man had no sex relations with his wife for four or five years while she nursed their baby. He either lived with another wife or returned to his family. And for a woman to have another child after her first child had married was scandalous. Thus most wives had four or five children, spaced about five years apart.

Christian missionaries, seeking to end polygamy, encouraged men to remain living with their nursing wives. This failed to end polygamy, for about a third of all marriages are still polygamous. But wives now bear children less than three years apart, for an average of more than eight children each. Together with other changes, this now gives Kenya the most rapid rate of population growth in the world, doubling in just 18 years.

Adapted from *The Wall Street Journal*, April 11, 1983, pp. 1, 18.

Have other change agents been more successful than missionaries in anticipating the consequences of change?

vetus were burned at the stake, while Luther and Wycliffe narrowly escaped. Florence Nightingale fought against family opposition, public ridicule and scorn, and official jealousy, intrigue, and slander in her efforts to change the image of nurse from slattern to professional. The actions for which Jane Adams was persecuted and reviled in her youth brought her showers of honors in her old age. Change agents are likely to be honored only when they are very old or very dead.

THE DEVIANT AS CHANGE AGENT. Many change agents are deviants of some sort. The nonconformist may unwittingly launch a new fashion, speech form, or dance step. Inventors are people who love to tinker; they are more excited by the challenge of a new idea than by the possibility of riches [Barnett, 1953, pp. 150–156]. Social reformers are necessarily people who are disenchanted with some aspect of the status quo. Without deviants, there would be many fewer social changes.

THE CONSEQUENCES OF CHANGE

Social Effects of Discovery and Invention

No social change leaves the rest of the culture entirely unaffected. Even an "additive" innovation draws time and interest away from other elements of the culture. Some innovations are shattering in their impact. When the Europeans passed out steel axes to the Yir Yoront of Australia, the gift appeared to be an innocuous gesture, but the stone ax was so tightly integrated into the culture that a chain reaction of disruption spread through the social structure [Sharp, 1952]. The stone ax was a symbol of adult masculinity. It might be lent to women and to youths, and the lines of ax borrowing were very important features of the social organization. When superior steel axes were passed out indiscriminately and owned by women and youths, the symbol of authority was so undermined that authority itself became clouded, relations were confused, and reciprocal obligations became uncertain. The stone for the axes was quarried far to the south and traded northward along trade routes through an established system of trading partners, who also shared in important ceremonials. With the substitution of the steel ax, trading relationships languished, and this rich ceremonial sharing was lost. Deep and serious disturbance of Yir Yoront culture is traced to the single innovation of the steel ax. The illustration is dramatic; but have the effects of the automobile or the radio upon American culture been less far-reaching? Ogburn [1933, pp. 153–156] compiled a list of 150 social changes which he attributes to the radio, while Pool has collected a series of essays which attribute to the telephone consequences ranging from the strengthening of police power to rearranging the spatial pattern of cities [Pool, 1977].

Ogburn distinguished three forms of the social effects of invention. (1) *Dispersion, or the multiple effects of a single mechanical invention,* is illustrated by the many effects of the radio, or the automobile, which shortens travel time; supports a huge manufacturing and servicing industry; provides a market for vast quantities of gasoline and oil, steel, glass, leather, and other materials; requires a massive road-building program; alters courtship and recreational behavior; promotes suburbs and shopping centers; and has many other consequences. (2) *Succession, or the derivative social effects of a single invention,* means that an invention produces changes, which in turn produce further changes, and so on. The inventor of the cotton gin (*a*) simplified cotton processing and made cotton more profitable; this result (*b*) encouraged the planting of more cotton; and the planting (*c*) required more slaves; the increase in slavery and growing Southern dependence upon cotton export (*d*) helped to provoke the Civil War, which (*e*) greatly stimulated the growth of large-scale industry and business monopoly; these in turn (*f*) encouraged antitrust laws and labor unions; and the chain still continues. While these developments were not entirely due to the cotton gin, it helped to produce them all. (3) *Convergence, or the coming together of several influences of different inventions,* may be variously illustrated. The six-shooter, barbed wire fencing, and the windmill aided in the settlement of the great American plains. The automobile, the electric pump, and the septic tank made the modern suburb possible. Nuclear warheads, intercontinental missiles, and radar detection systems have, in the opinion of many military theorists, made total war obsolete.

Much has been written about the social effects of invention. It does not matter whether the new trait has been invented within the society or diffused into it; the social effects are equally great from either method. Guns "made all men the same size" and ended the power advantage of the horsed knight in armor, cannons ended the defensive strength of the medieval castle and strengthened the king at the expense of the provincial nobility. A diffused trait often finds a society quite unable to cope with it successfully. For example, primitive societies which brew their own alcoholic beverages generally have cultural controls over their use, but primitive societies which received alcohol from whites had no such controls, and the effects were generally devastating [Horton, 1943]. To cite one instance, the Eskimo of St. Lawrence island, when first introduced to alcohol, promptly went on a month-long drunk and missed the annual walrus migration; the following winter most of them died of starvation [Nelson, 1899]. Innovations, whether discovered, invented, or diffused, can be equally disruptive.

Unequal Rates of Change

Since a culture is interrelated, changes in one aspect of the culture invariably affect other aspects of the culture. The affected traits will usually be adapted to this change, but only after some time has passed. This time interval between the arrival of a change and the completion of the adaptations it prompts is called *cultural lag,* a concept developed by Ogburn [1922, pp. 200–213]. As an illustration, he pointed out that about 1870, workers in large numbers began entering factories, where they were often injured in unavoidable accidents. But not until another half-century had passed did most states get around to enacting workers' compensation laws. In this instance, the cultural lag was about fifty years.

A cultural lag exists wherever any aspect of the culture lags behind another aspect to which it is related. Probably the most pervasive form of cultural lag in present Western societies is the lag of institutions behind changing technology. For example, in most states the size of a county was based upon the distance one could travel to the county seat and return in the same day; despite improved transportation, the county unit still remains at its old size, inefficient for many of its functions.

Some cultural lags involve the lag of one part of the material culture behind a related part of the material culture. For a quarter century after we replaced the horse with the automobile, we continued to build the garage out behind the house, back where the smelly stables used to go. Today in some developing areas where mechanized market agriculture has replaced subsistence agriculture, the building of good transport, storage, and market facilities has lagged, and a lot of food rots in the fields because it cannot be brought to market. Sometimes the material culture lags behind changes in the nonmaterial culture. For example, educational research has long since discovered that movable classroom furniture aids in organizing learning activities, yet thousands of classrooms still have inflexible rows of desks screwed to the floor. Finally, one aspect of nonmaterial culture may lag behind other related aspects of nonmaterial culture. As shown in Figure 20-1, the world's lag in the use of birth control following our brilliant success in death control has produced the population explosion, probably the world's most catastrophic cultural lag.

The concept of cultural lag applies to differing rates of change *within* a society not to rates of change between societies. It describes the disharmony between related parts of a single culture, produced through unequal rates of change. Cultural lags are most numerous in a rapidly changing culture. They are symptoms not of a backward society but of a highly dynamic and increasingly complex society. But even if all people were wise, objective, and adaptable, they would still need some time to discover what adaptations a new change would require and more time to work out and complete those adaptations. Most of us, however, are pretty ignorant

Social and Cultural Change

Sociocultural change is uneven. (© *Georg Gerster/ Photo Researchers, Inc.*)

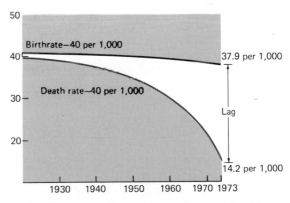

FIGURE 20-1 Cultural lag: death control and birth control in developing countries. (*Source: Based on data in Dorothy Nortman and Elizabeth Hofstatter, "Population and Family Planning Programs: A Factbook,"* Reports on Population Planning, *6:2, December 1974.*)

Which change requires the greater degree of active cooperation by the masses of the people: the drop in the death rate or the birthrate?

about matters outside our specialty, are prejudiced and swayed by vested interests, and are not nearly so adaptable as we like to imagine. Cultural lags are numerous and persistent.

Social Change and Social Problems

A social problem is often defined as a condition which many people consider undesirable and wish to correct [Horton and Leslie, 1981, pp. 4–6]. By this definition, a perfectly integrated society would have no social problems, for all institutions and behavior would be neatly harmonized and defined as acceptable by the values of the society. A changing society inevitably develops problems. Either the conditions themselves change and become unacceptable (population growth, soil erosion, and deforestation create a conservation problem) or the society's changing values define an old condition as no longer tolerable (child labor, poverty, racism, or sex inequality). Social problems are part of the price of social change. The detailed analysis of social problems, however, belongs in another textbook and another course.

Disorganization and Demoralization

Modern technology is spreading all over the world. As suggested earlier in this chapter, all new elements disrupt the existing culture to some extent. If a culture is tightly integrated, with all its traits and institutions fitting closely together, change in any one of them will disorganize this arrangement. In today's world, change is most rapid in the developing countries; as a country approaches full "modernization," the rate of change slows down [Fierabend and Fierabend, 1972]. Thus, it is the developing countries that are suffering the greatest disorganization, both because of their high rate of change and because of their relative unfamiliarity with the change process. Modernization and "progress" bring new

hardship to many of the poor, who endure the resultant price inflation without sharing in the benefits [Scott and Kerkvliet, 1973]. Modernization promotes new systems of social stratification and encourages increased ethnic competition within developing countries [Bates, 1974]. "Progress" is a mixed blessing.

When a culture becomes highly disorganized, the people's sense of security, morale, and purpose in life are damaged. When people are confused and uncertain, so that their behavior is also inconsistent, hesitant, and contradictory, they are described as *personally disorganized*. If their disorganization proceeds until they lose their sense of purpose in life and become resigned and apathetic, we describe them as *demoralized*. They have lost their morale, and often their behavior controls are lost as well. A demoralized people is likely to suffer population decline, through a lowered birthrate, a higher death rate, or both. The capacity of a thoroughly demoralized people simply to die out has attracted the attention of a number of anthropologists [Rivers, 1922; Maher, 1961].

The extermination of the buffalo demoralized the American Indians of the Great Plains [Lesser, 1933; Wissler, 1938; Sandoz, 1954; Deloria, 1970]. The buffalo provided food, clothing, and shelter, in all, over fifty separate parts of the buffalo carcass were used by the Indians. The buffalo hunt provided the principal object of the Indian's religious ceremonials, the goal of maturing, and a road to status and recognition. The other avenue to status—warfare—was also dependent upon an ample supply of dried buffalo meat. When the government exterminated the buffalo in order to pacify the Indians, it demoralized them as well. The integrating and status-giving functions of the war party and the buffalo hunt were lost. Religious ceremonials were now empty and meaningless. The hunting economy was totally destroyed, and the Indians lived, and sometimes starved, on government handouts. The traditional goals and values

Modern technology is spreading to all parts of the world. (*Will McIntyre/Photo
Researchers, Inc.*)

which gave zest and meaning to life were
now unavailable, and to substitute white
goals and values was an almost impossible
task of learning. In the few instances where
Indians did successfully adopt the white economy, this, too, was soon destroyed by white
hunger for the Indians' land [Foreman, 1932;
Collier, 1947, pp. 199–219; Deloria, 1970].
Suffering from the destruction of their own
culture, denied access to white culture, rav-
aged by white diseases, and corrupted by
alcohol, many Indian tribes became deeply
demoralized. Depopulation was almost universal, and only in this century has Indian
population begun to rebuild. This story of
devastatingly disruptive social change, disorganization of the culture, and personal
disorganization and demoralization of the
people has been repeated hundreds of times
in the world's history.

Not all native peoples, however, have been
demoralized by their contacts with Western
societies. The Palauans of Micronesia worked
out an interdependent blend of traditional
culture and Western commercialism. They
happily drove trucks and pounded typewrit-
ers to earn money to buy the traditional clan
gifts and used motor launches to carry their
sweet potatoes to traditional festivals [Mead,
1955, p. 128]. Whether changes disrupt a
society to the point of demoralization depends
upon the nature of the changes, the way they
are introduced, and the structure of the society upon which they impinge.

Pains and Gains of Change

Much is written about the pains of change,
but less about the gains of change. Those
who wistfully contrast the troubled present
with the "good old days" do not know their
history very well. Those on the glorious and
free American frontier endured discomforts
we moderns would consider unbearable. They

536

*Social
Change and
Social Policy*

were bothered by flies and suffered terribly from mosquitos (rare in most parts of Europe); they lost entire crops to grasshoppers, hail, or drought; they froze in winter and baked in summer; their only relief from toothache was a crude extraction; a broken bone almost always brought a misshapen or useless limb, while a compound fracture brought certain infection and amputation without anesthesia; most people suffered dietary deficiencies; about one in four women died in childbirth, and most parents saw some of their children die in infancy or childhood. While adapting to change is sometimes painful, failure to accept and adapt to change is far more painful.

Is change least painful when it comes slowly? Not necessarily. Since culture involves interrelations, it is generally easier to accept a cluster of related changes than to accept them one at a time. For example, if a primitive people acquires clothing without soap, then filth and disease are predictable; if they get clothes without sewing machines, then they will be clothed in tatters. With mud floors to sit upon and no place to store clothing and these other artifacts, filth and clutter are a certainty. But if all these elements—clothes, soap, sewing machines, and floored houses with shelves and closets—are adopted together within a single generation, these changes can be made far more easily than if they are spaced over several generations. The harmful effects of bottle feeding upon infant health in Third World countries is due largely to their lack of pure water for the formula and sterilizing facilities for the bottles. This is another example in which introducing one change without the related changes has been disastrous. (It is also an instance where the Marxist image of the greedy corporation seeking profits at all costs seems fully justified.)

Western cultural diffusion generally converts the native village into a depressing slum, not because the people adopt too many new traits but because they adopt too few. It may even be psychologically easier to make a lot of changes than a few. As Margaret Mead

[1956, pp. 445–446] has observed, "A people who choose to practice a new technology or enter into drastically new kinds of economic relationships will do this more easily if they live in different houses, wear different clothes and eat different, or differently cooked food." Much of the social disorganization which accompanies social change stems from the fact that a people who are willing to adopt new trait complexes are blocked from doing so. Sometimes they are blocked by their own limited resources and sometimes by the unwillingness of the dominant whites to admit them into full participation in Western civilization [Bascom and Herskovitz (eds.), 1959, p. 4].

We need, therefore, to revise the notion that slow change is necessarily more comfortable than rapid change. In some situations, the rapid wholesale change of a way of life may be infinitely less disturbing than piecemeal changes, as Mead [1956, chap. 18] has shown in her study of the Manus, who moved from the Stone Age into Western civilization in a single generation. The reason may be that slow change allows cultural lags to accumulate, not to be corrected until they become painful. Rapid change may actually produce fewer lags, because many of the related items of the culture may be changed at the same time.

Change has come with dazzling speed upon contemporary Western societies. Within a few short generations, the Western peoples have shifted from life in rural, agricultural folk societies to life in an immensely complex urban, industrial, impersonal mass society. Are contemporary Western societies disorganized? Certainly! Cultural lags are numerous at every point. The school is constantly straining to prepare children for a society which changes even before they become adult. A century ago husband and wife could each assume a quite clearly defined role; today neither can be at all sure what he or she will be expected to be and do in their marriage. Every level of government is struggling with tasks which few of our grandfathers would have guessed it would ever assume. Although the traditional informal controls of the gemeinschaft society are failing to regulate the behavior of individuals in this impersonal urban world of ours, we are still hunting for effective substitutes.

A popular writer [Toffler, 1970] has given the term "future shock" to the stresses and anxieties provoked by rapid change. Recent research provides some support for the thesis that stress and anxiety are linked with the perceived rate of change [Lauer, 1974]. Some social scientists are doubtful that we shall make the changes necessary to grapple with such problems as the population explosion, pollution, and resource exhaustion. They fear that civilization may collapse in depression, famine, pestilence, warfare, and chaos [Heilbroner, 1974; Laqueur, 1974; Catton, 1980]. Such pessimism is far from new. The fifteenth century, for example, was an epoch of profound pessimism [Huizinga, 1924, p. 22]. Time will tell whether today's "men of good fear" are any more correct.

SOCIAL PLANNING: CAN CHANGE BE DIRECTED?

Is it possible to predict and control the direction of social change? To do this demands that we know what changes are going to take place. All of the major changes of the 1960s—the New Left, the youth counterculture, the black nationalist movement, the new feminist movement—caught most social scientists by surprise. Most attempts to predict future change are little more than projections of recent trends into the future. By this technique, one could have predicted two centuries ago that today's streets would be hip-deep in horse manure and that today's American population would exceed a billion people. Obviously, by projecting recent trends, we cannot accurately predict the future. One scholar [Rosen, 1976] has published a book

carrying the confident title, *Future Facts: A Forecast of the World as We Will Know It Before the End of the Century*, and a magazine called *The Futurist* carries many forecasts. But most social scientists are more modest. Some feel that social change is caused by social forces beyond our effective control [Sorokin, 1941, 1948; Lapiere, 1965]. For example, when the necessary supporting knowledge is developed, an invention will be made by someone, even if this invention is most troublesome to human existence. The hydrogen bomb is an example. Although we fear it may destroy us, we go on advancing it because others will do so anyway. Could the Indian wars possibly have been avoided? The Indians had land the settlers wanted for a growing population, and their advance was certain to destroy the Indian's way of life. The many brutal episodes were merely the symptoms, not the cause, of a conflict which was unavoidable, given these groups with their respective needs and cultural backgrounds. Practically any great social change can be thus described in terms of blind social forces, so that we conclude that what *did* happen was about the only thing that *could* happen in that situation.

Some social scientists, however, believe that we *can* exert *some* influence over the course of social change [Mannheim, 1949; Bottomore, 1962, pp. 283–284; Horowitz, 1966]. Social planning is an attempt at the intelligent direction of social change [Riemer, 1947; Adams, 1950; Gross, 1967; Bennis et al., 1969, chap. 1; Kahn, 1969; Havelock, 1973; Friedmann, 1973; Gil, 1973; Kramer and Specht, 1975]. But just how the conflicting wishes of different publics are to be reconciled remains a perplexing problem.

Elite direction of social planning is characteristic of communist societies. Decision making has been highly centralized, and plans have been exceedingly intricate and detailed. Planning which attempts to program practically all the activities of a society is less successful than planning that is limited to only one, or a small number, of activities or goals. This kind of social planning is an old American tradition. When the framers of our Constitution rejected primogeniture (the European provision that the lands pass intact to the eldest son) and entail (the provision that prevents him from selling them), these American planners were seeking to construct a society of small, landowning farmers instead of a society of landed estates. This purpose was reinforced by the Homestead Act of 1862, which gave public lands in small parcels to individual farmers instead of selling it in large blocks to the highest bidders. Zoning ordinances, building codes, public education, and compulsory school attendance laws are examples of social planning. Some problems which call for planning at the national or international level include the use of the world's water resources and fishing rights, use of mineral resources under international waters, the acid rain problem, and many others.

A critic of planning would contend that such planning efforts do not really change anything but are merely slightly more orderly ways of carrying out changes that are inevitable anyway. The comment perhaps sums up the matter. Certainly, no social planning will prevent or reverse a change which present knowledge and longtime trends are creating. There is, for example, no way of returning to the "simple life," nor is it possible by planning to steer social change in a direction contrary to most people's wishes and values. The major social changes are probably uncontrollable, but social planning may be able to reduce the delays and costs of integrating them into the culture.

We would always like to know—and can never be sure we know—what the future holds. A flood of books and articles are telling us how computers and robots will transform society as greatly as did the industrial revolution [e.g., Chamberlin, 1982; Kidder, 1982; Osborne, 1982; Papert, 1982]. Whether they are any more correct than yesterday's forecasters remains to be seen.

SUMMARY

All societies change continuously. Evolutionary theories see all societies passing through quite similar stages of development until some final (presumably ideal) stage is reached, when social evolution ends. Cyclical theories see societies passing through a cycle of changes, returning to the starting point and repeating the cycle. Functional and conflict theories concentrate upon explaining, somewhat differently, the conditions and processes of change.

New traits appear through *discovery* and *invention* or through *diffusion* from other societies. The rate of social change varies enormously from society to society and from time to time. *Geographic changes* can produce great social change. More often, *migration* to a new environment brings changes in social life. *Changes in population size* or *composition* always produce social changes. Since *isolation* retards change and *cross-cultural contacts* promote change, physically or socially isolated groups show fewer changes. The *structure of the society* affects change: A highly conformist, traditional society or a highly integrated culture is less prone to change than the individualistic, permissive society with a less highly integrated culture. A society's *attitudes and values* greatly encourage or retard change. The *perceived needs* of a people affect the speed and direction of change. Perhaps most important of all, the *cultural base* provides the foundation of knowledge and skill necessary to develop new elements; as the cultural base expands, the possibilities of new combinations multiply in an *exponential* manner, while knowledge in one area often *cross-fertilizes* other areas of development.

Not all innovations are accepted. The attitudes and values of a group determine what kind of innovations a group is likely to accept. If an innovation's usefulness can be demonstrated easily and cheaply, the proof is helpful; but many social inventions cannot be tested except through a complete acceptance.

Compatible innovations are more readily accepted than those which clash with important features of the existing culture. Technical difficulties of fitting a change into the existing culture often cause great economic cost and personal inconvenience. People with vested interests normally oppose change, but they occasionally discover that a proposed change is to their advantage. The change agent's ingenuity and social position affect his or her success in introducing changes. Unless change agents know the culture very well, they may fail in their efforts, because the consequences of changes and the techniques needed to promote them are generally miscalculated.

The consequences of change are endless. Discoveries and inventions, as well as diffused new traits and complexes, often set off a chain reaction of change which disrupts many aspects of the culture. The different parts of the culture, interrelated and interdependent though they are, do not change at the same rate of speed. The time interval between the acceptance of a new trait and the completion of the adaptations it forces is called *cultural lag*. All rapidly changing societies have many cultural lags and are somewhat *disorganized*. In a disorganized society, persons who may have greater difficulty in finding a comfortable behavior system become disorganized themselves. When they lose hope of finding a rewarding way of conducting their lives and cease trying, they have become *demoralized;* and may actually die out as a group. While change is sometimes painful, refusing to change can be even more painful, for change brings gains along with pains. *Social planning* attempts to reduce the pains of change, but its success is debatable.

GLOSSARY

cause a phenomenon which is both necessary and *sufficient* to produce a predictable effect.

cross-fertilization in social change use in one field of discoveries and inventions from an entirely different field.

cultural base for invention the accumulation of knowledge and techniques available to the inventor.

cultural change changes in the culture of a people, often used interchangeably with social change.

cultural lag the time lag between a change or innovation and accomplishment of the social and cultural adjustments which the innovation makes necessary.

demoralization loss of morale and sense of purpose; resignation and apathy.

diffusion the spread of culture traits from group to group.

discovery a shared human perception of an aspect of reality which already exists.

exponential principle the idea that as a cultural base grows, its possible uses tend to grow in a geometric ratio.

invention a new combination or a new use of existing knowledge.

personal disorganization loss of sense of certainty and direction, with confused and inconsistent behavior.

progress social or cultural change of a kind defined as desirable according to some set of values.

social change change in the social structure and relationships of a society, often used interchangeably with cultural change.

social planning attempt at the intelligent direction of social change.

QUESTIONS AND PROJECTS

1 Why are social scientists hesitant to use the term "progress"?

2 Will social evolution ever reach a "final" stage where future evolutionary change will end?

3 What kind of difficulties would face a corporation which tried to suppress a highly useful invention?

4 Is knowledge of the diffusion process likely to reduce ethnocentrism?

5 What are some of the change-promoting features of American society? What are some of its change-resisting features?

6   Is the rate of invention likely to continue rising or to fall off? Why?

7   Why will a person who insists upon the latest cars, fashion, and gadgets often be entirely satisfied with ancient social philosophies?

8   How many of those persons whom we now consider "great" were noncontroversial during their lives? How many achieved greatness by promoting changes and how many by preventing changes?

9   Is it possible for a change agent to promote a major change without arousing violent hostilities?

10   How do the difficulties of modernization in developing countries illustrate the concept of cultural integration?

11   How has American ethnocentrism impaired the effectiveness of our foreign aid programs in developing countries?

12   What are some recent social changes in our society which you consider undesirable? Some which you consider desirable? What values are you using in making these judgments?

13   Why should social change be so difficult? Why can't people simply get together, decide what changes are desirable, and then promote them?

14   Evaluate this statement: "The more successfully we progress, the fewer cultural lags and social problems we shall have."

15   Read one of the following novels, which describe Americans operating as change agents in other societies, and explain the agents' success or failures in that capacity: Ronald Hardy, *The Place of the Jackals;* Graham Greene, *The Quiet American;* James Ullman, *Windom's Way;* Kathryn Grondahl, *The Mango Season;* Margaret Landon, *Never Dies the Dream;* Thomas Streissguth, *Tigers in the House.*

SUGGESTED READINGS

*Bascom, William R. and Melville J. Herskovits (eds.): *Continuity and Change in African Cultures,* The University of Chicago Press, Chicago, 1959. Two essays—Simon Ottenberg, "Ibo Receptivity to Change," and Harold K. Schneider, "Pakot Resistance to Change"—describe the opposite reactions of two societies to proposed change.

Bettman, Otto: *The Good Old Days—They Were Terrible,* Random House, Inc., New York, 1974. Pictures and text showing what the old days were like.

Conger, D. Stuart. "Social Inventions," *The Futurist,* August 1973, pp. 149 ff. An interesting history of dozens of social inventions.

Crittenden, Ann: "Foreign Aid," *The New York Times Magazine,* June 6, 1982, pp. 66ff. A critical article on the effects of foreign aid in developing countries.

Davis, Shelton H.: *Victims of the Miracle: Development and the Indians of Brazil,* Cambridge University Press, New York, 1977. A depressing account of how Brazil's "development" is, in the author's opinion, damaging the land and destroying the Indians.

Friedman, J. and M. J. Rowlands (eds.): *The Evolution of Social Systems,* The University of Pittsburgh Press, Pittsburgh, 1978. A collection of evolutionary theories of social change.

Guillen, Michael A.: "U.S. Metric Conversion: Rough Road Ahead," *Science News,* 112:42–43, July 16, 1977. A very brief illustration of the technical difficulties of change.

Hanson, Mark: "The Improbable Change Agent and the PhB," *Rural Sociology,* 38:237–242, Summer 1973. An entertaining account of how a patient change agent works to promote change in a poor rural American county.

Hayes, Denis: "The Unfinished Agenda: Goals for Earth Day '80," *Environment,* 22:6–14, April 1980. A brief article proposing certain changes in environmental policy as necessary for survival.

*Jewkes, John et al.: *The Sources of Invention,* W. W. Norton & Company, Inc., New York, 1969. An interesting study of the invention process, with case histories of many inventions.

*Lassey, William R. and Richard P. Fernandez (eds.): *Leadership and Social Change,* University Associates, La Jolla, Cal., 1976. A collection on leadership in social change.

Lauer, Robert H.: *Perspectives on Social Change,* Allyn and Bacon, Inc., Boston, 1977. A textbook on social change.

Lee, Dorothy: "The Cultural Curtain," *Annals of the American Academy of Political and Social Science*, 323:120–128, May 1959. An interesting article showing, with many illustrations, the need for change agents to understand the culture in which they promote change.

Mechlin, George F.: "Seven Technologies for the 1980's," *USA Today*, 111:62–65, January 1983. A brief look at promising technologies which may help solve many of our nation's problems.

Mihanovich, Clement S.: "Forecasting the Future," *USA Today*, 110:23–25, March 1982. An article culling twenty-one "scientific" predictions of social change from such journals as *Daedelus* and *The Futurist*.

Morgan, Chris and David Langford: *Facts and Fallacies: A Book of Definitive Mistakes and Misguided Predictions*, Webb and Bower, Exeter, England, 1982. An entertaining list of predictive bloopers by famous persons.

Rosen, Stephen: *Future Facts: A Forecast of the World as We Will Know It Before the End of the Century*, Simon & Schuster, Inc., New York, 1976. An interesting effort to predict our future technology, social organization, and daily life.

*An asterisk before the citation indicates that the title is available in a paperback edition.

Glossary

Academic freedom The freedom of scholars and teachers to search for and teach the truth as they perceive it.

Acculturation Acquisition by a group or individual of the traits of another culture.

Achieved role or status A role or status attained by individual choice, effort, action, or accomplishment.

Affirmative action Programs requiring the active recruitment, hiring, and promotion of minority members and women.

Aggregation A gathering of people without conscious interaction.

Alienation An emotional separation from a society or group, combining feelings of powerlessness, normlessness, and social isolation.

Amalgamation Biological interbreeding of two or more peoples of distinct physical appearance until they become one stock.

Androgyny Having both masculine and feminine personality characteristics in the same person, with neither set dominant.

Anomie Condition of a society with no single, consistent set of norms and values for people to internalize and follow.

Antiurban bias Assumption that city life is inferior to rural life.

Applied science Scientific methodology applied to the search for knowledge which will be useful in solving practical problems.

Argot The special language terms of a subculture.

Ascribed role or status A role or status assigned according to hereditary traits without regard to individual preference, ability, or performance.

Assimilation The fusion of two or more cultures so that they become one.

Association Organized group of people pursuing some common interest.

Audience A crowd with interest centered on stimuli outside itself.

Autonomy Self-government and freedom from outside direction.

Bias A tendency, usually unconscious, to see facts in a certain way because of one's wishes, interests, or values.

Black underclass Poor blacks who have not shared in the upward mobility of other black Americans.

Bourgeoisie The middle class.

Bureaucracy A pyramid of officials who conduct rationally the work of a large organization.

Capital Money or the goods which it provides, which are used to make other goods rather than consumed directly; e.g., transportation equipment, factories, and warehouses.

Capitalism System based on private profit-seeking and private ownership of productive wealth.

Case study A detailed study of a single event, place, person, group, or institution.

Caste Social status, including occupation assigned by heredity.

Caste system A stratified social system in which social position is entirely determined by parentage, with no provision for change of position.

Category A number of people who share some common characteristics.

Cause A phenomenon which is both *necessary* and *sufficient* to produce a predictable effect.

Charismatic expression Highly emotional religious expression, including speaking in tongues (glossolalia).

543

Chicano An American of Mexican background who has a strong sense of Mexican identity.

Civil disobedience Open and public defiance of a law with willing acceptance of legal punishment.

Civil religion Religious beliefs that are widely held throughout a society.

Class-dialectic model System of social power in which dominant class groups usually prevail but can be weakened by disunity or challenged by organized competing interests.

Clique A small group of intimates with strong in-group feelings based upon common sentiments and interests.

Closed class system Status system with inherited position and no provision for changes in status.

Collective behavior Behavior which originates spontaneously, is relatively unorganized, fairly unpredictable, and depends upon interstimulation among participants.

Collectivity A physical collection of people.

Communism System based on theories of Karl Marx, with state ownership of productive wealth and (supposedly) equality of all citizens.

Community Often defined as a local grouping within which people carry on a full round of life activities, but often used for any locality or category of people.

Compartmentalization Isolating roles from one another so that one is unaware of role conflicts.

Conflict perspective Views society as in a continuous state of conflict between groups and classes, tending toward dissent, tension, and change.

Conjugal family Family of the married couple and their children.

Consanguine family Family with a group of married sisters and their children, or a group of married brothers and their children, as its core, with a fringe of spouses and other relatives.

Conservative One who may accept minor reforms but who believes that the existing social system is essentially sound.

Contest education Relatively open admission to higher education with expectation of many failures and dropouts.

Continuum A range of variation by very small intervals (e.g., student grade-point averages) rather than by distinct categories (e.g., freshman, sophomore).

Contractual Relating to a formal listing of joint privileges and duties, as distinct from informal, traditional arrangements.

Control group A group of subjects who resemble the experimental group in all respects except the variable(s) being studied.

Convergence theory The theory that classes in America are drawing closer together in life-style.

Counterculture A subculture not merely different from but in opposition to the conventional and approved culture of the society; e.g., the drug subculture.

Craze A temporary obsessive interest shared by a number of people.

Cross-fertilization in social change Use in one field of discoveries and inventions from an entirely different field.

Cross-sectional study One which covers a wide range of phenomena or a widespread sample of people at a single moment.

Crowd A temporary collection of people reacting together to stimuli.

Crowd behavior Behavior of a temporary collection of people reacting together to stimuli; such behavior is brief and episodic.

Crude birthrate Births per 1,000 people per year.

Cult A religious group, usually of small membership, that stresses the ecstatic emotional experience of its members and may promote new religious ideas.

Cultural base for invention The accumulation of knowledge and techniques available to the inventor.

Cultural change Changes in the culture of a people; often used interchangeably with social change.

Cultural integration The degree to which the traits, complexes, and institutions of a culture are harmoniously adjusted to one another.

Cultural lag The time lag between a change or innovation and the accomplishment of the social and cultural adjustments which the innovation makes necessary.

Cultural pluralism Toleration of cultural differences within a common society; allowing different groups to retain their distinctive cultures.

Cultural relativism Concept that the function, meaning, and "desirability" of a trait depend upon its cultural setting.

Cultural trait Smallest unit of culture as perceived by a given observer.

Culture Everything that is socially learned and shared by the members of a society; social heritage which the individual receives from the group; a system of behavior shared by members of a society.

Culture complex A cluster of related culture traits.

Deferred gratification pattern Postponing immediate satisfactions in order to have some future gain.

Demographic transition theory Idea that industrialization eventually stabilizes a population through a decline in the death rate, followed by a decline in the birthrate.

Demography Statistical study of population composition, distribution, and trends.

Demoralization Loss of morale and sense of purpose, leaving one resigned and apathetic.

Denomination A fairly large religious group, usually supported by private gifts, and therefore not as pressured as the ecclesia to accept all majority social norms.

Deviant subculture A subculture whose norms are in opposition to those of the dominant culture.

Deviation Behavior which is defined as a violation of the norms of a group or a society.

Deviation, primary The deviant behavior of one who is conformist in the rest of his or her life organization.

Deviation, secondary Deviant behavior which follows from one's public identification as a deviant.

Diffusion The spread of culture traits from group to group or from society to society.

Discontinuity in socialization Experiences at one life stage which do not aid or even hinder transition to a later stage.

Discovery A shared human perception of an aspect of reality which already exists.

Discrimination A practice that treats equal people unequally; limiting opportunity or reward according to race, religion, or ethnic group.

Dramatic role presentation A conscious effort to play a role in a manner which will create a desired impression upon others.

Drive Hereditary urge which temporarily disappears when it has been satisfied.

Ecclesia A church to which virtually all members of a society belong, at least nominally; receives state support and generally supports cultural norms.

Ecumenical Literally worldwide; usually refers to efforts to promote understanding, cooperation, or even a merger among religious associations.

Ego, superego, and id Freudian concepts; the *id* is the instinctive, antisocial, selfish desires and impulses of the person; the *superego* is the social ideals and values which the person has internalized and which form the conscience; the *ego* is the conscious and rational part of the self which oversees the restraint of the id by the superego.

Embourgeoisment theory The theory that the working class is becoming more like the middle class.

Endogamy Practice of choosing mates within some specified group.

Ethclass A group sharing both class position and ethnic background.

Ethnic group A number of people with a common racial and/or cultural heritage which sets them apart from others.

Ethnocentrism Tendency of each group to take for granted the superiority of its own culture.

Ethos Unifying spirit of a particular society; set of major values shared by all.

Evaluation study One which seeks to determine the effects of a program or policy.

Evolution Theory that present forms of life have developed from earlier, simpler forms.

Evolutionary perspective View that different societies show many similarities in their development.

Exogamy Practice of choosing mates from outside some specified group.

Experimental group Subjects whose responses to various experimental influences are observed.

Experimental study One in which the researcher tries out different variables in a controlled situation.

Exponential principle The idea that as the cultural base grows, its possible uses tend to grow in geometric ratio.

Extended family The nuclear family plus any other kin with whom important relationships are maintained.

Fad A trivial, short-lived, popular variation in speech, decoration, or behavior.

Family A kinship grouping which provides for the rearing of children and for certain other human needs.

Fascist society An authoritarian society ruled by a dictator stressing nationalism; e.g., Hitler's Germany, Mussolini's Italy, and Franco's Spain.

Fashion A variation in speech, decoration, or behavior, of temporary duration but less trivial or brief than a fad.

Fecundity Biological capacity to reproduce.

Feral children Children supposedly reared apart from human beings and therefore unsocialized.

Fertility Actual rate of reproduction.

Feudal society A society based upon the mutual obligations between a landowning nobility and the other social classes; e.g., tenth-to-seventeenth century Europe, and China and Japan until recent times.

Folkways Customary, normal, habitual behavior characteristics of the members of the group.

Functionalist perspective View of society as an organized network of cooperating groups, tending toward consensus and stability.

Fundamentalists Those who stress the importance of religious beliefs they regard as "fundamental," including the virgin birth of Christ, the physical resurrection of Jesus, and the accuracy of the Scriptures in every detail.

Gemeinschaft A society in which most relationships are either personal or traditional.

Gender Often used interchangeably with *sex*, although some scholars distinguish between sex and gender, with sex being the biological part and gender the socially learned part of sexuality and sex roles.

Generalized other The totality of values and standards of one's community or one's social group, whose judgments one applies to one's own behavior in forming the concept of self.

Genocide A deliberate effort to eliminate an ethnic group by slaughter, expulsion, or destruction of the group's cultural heritage.

Gentrification Renovation of decaying urban areas for occupancy by middle- or upper-class residents.

Gesellschaft A society based on contractual as contrasted with traditional relationships

Glossolalia Speaking in tongues; a religious experience in which one speaks syllables which form no known language.

Group Any number of persons who share a consciousness of membership and of interaction; often used incorrectly to denote aggregation, collectivity, or category.

Group deviant One who conforms to the norms of a deviant group or subculture.

Group dynamics The interaction within small groups.

Hominids One of the species consisting of early humans and/or their ancestors.

Homosexual A term applied to persons with a strong preference for sex partners of the same sex and to persons who, regardless of sex preference, engage in sex relations with a person of the same sex.

Hypothesis Tentative, unverified statement of the possible relationship of known facts; a reasonable proposition worthy of scientific testing.

Identity crisis For Erikson, one of eight major turning points in life when important directions in personality development are taken. Popularly applied to any period of uncertainty.

Ideology A system of ideas which sanctions a set of norms.

Impressionistic study One which is a systematic collection of the investigator's impressions, without using measuring instruments, control groups, collections of statistics, or other more formal procedures.

Income redistribution Adjusting taxes and tax-supported benefits unequally in order to reduce inequalities in income.

Individual deviant One who deviates from the norms of the subcultures he or she shares.

In-group A group or category toward which one has a feeling of identity or belonging.

Instinct An inborn behavior pattern characteristic of all members of the species.

Institution An organized cluster of folkways and mores centered around a major human activity; organized system of social relationships which embodies certain common values and procedures and meets certain basic needs of society.

Integration Process of developing a society in which all racial and ethnic groups can share equally in the cultural and economic life.

Intellectual One whose work is dealing mainly with ideas.

Interactionist perspective The view of society that concentrates upon the interaction between persons and groups.

Internalize To learn something so thoroughly

that it becomes an automatic, unthinking part of our response.

Interview study   One in which informants answer a series of questions asked by the interviewer.

Invention   A new combination or a new use of existing knowledge.

Judicial activism   Tendency for judges to expand or enlarge upon existing laws and constitutional provisions by judicial interpretation.

Labeling   Identifying one as a deviant; often followed by a change in one's treatment by others.

Latent functions   Unintended effects of a policy, program, or institution.

Liberal   One who accepts the social system as basically sound but feels that extensive reforms may be needed; in religion, a religious person who rejects many fundamentalist beliefs.

Life expectancy   Additional years of life expected at a given age.

Life span   Number of years which it is possible for a member of a species to live.

Longitudinal study   A study of the same phenomena over a period of time.

Looking-glass self   Perception of the self that one forms by interpreting the reactions of other people to oneself.

Mainline church   A denomination which seeks to harmonize religious and scientific views; includes (in the United States) such denominations as Catholic, Presbyterian, Methodist, American Baptist, Episcopalian, the United Church of Christ, Disciples of Christ, Reform and Conservative Judaism, and perhaps others.

Manifest functions   Intended purposes of a policy, program, association, or institution.

Marginality   Being partly assimilated to each of two cultures and two societies and fully assimilated to neither.

Marriage   The approved social pattern whereby two or more persons establish a family.

Masculinity/femininity   Feeling and acting in the ways expected of males or females at a particular time and place.

Mass   A relatively large number of people, spatially dispersed and anonymous, acting independently in response to the same stimuli.

Mass behavior   The unorganized unstructured, uncoordinated, individually selected behavior of masses in a mass society.

Mass hysteria   An irrational, compulsive belief or behavior which spreads among a number of people.

Matched-pair technique   One which matches each member of an experimental group with a person in the control group who is similar in all respects except the variable(s) being studied.

Matrilocal marriage   Social pattern in which the married couple live with the wife's family.

Median   The midpoint in a series of items arranged according to size.

Meritocracy   A social system in which status is assigned according to individual merit.

Mixed economy   An economy which is a mixture of capitalism and governmental ownership and control.

Mob   An emotionally aroused crowd taking violent action.

Modal personality   A personality configuration which is typical of most members of a group or society.

Mode   Value which appears most frequently in a series.

Monogamy   Marriage form permitting only one mate (at a time).

Mores   Strong ideas of right and wrong which require certain actions and forbid others.

Multivariate analysis   Statistical procedures which allow a researcher to work with two or more variables at one time.

Mutation   A change in the genes and hence in the nature of inherited characteristics.

Nativism   Rejection of contemporary culture, with a desire to return to traditional patterns; rejection of "foreign" groups and influences.

Natural area   An area with a mutually interdependent cluster of a particular kind of people and activities.

Neanderthal   Pertaining to a race of prehistoric people who lived between 60,000 and 300,000 years ago.

Neolocal marriage   Social pattern in which the married couple set up a household apart from other relatives.

Norm   A standard of behavior. A statistical norm is a measure of actual conduct; a cultural norm states the expected behavior of the culture.

Normative investigation   Research which seeks to confirm a conclusion already reached.

Norms of evasion   Recognized and sanctioned patterns through which people indulge their wishes without openly challenging the mores of a society.

Nuclear family   Also called the "conjugal family"; consists of a husband and wife and their children.

Objectivity   Observing and accepting facts as they are, not as one would wish them to be.

Observational study   One in which the investigator does nothing but watch, record, and interpret what is happening.

Ombudsperson (ombudsman)   An official empowered to investigate and sometimes adjust complaints against officials.

Open class system   A status system with considerable movement up and down the mobility ladder.

Optimum population   The population size which permits the highest standard of living for an area at a given level of technology.

Orgy   Joyous revelry of a crowd which transgresses the normal mores.

Orthodox   Adhering to established doctrines.

Out-group   A group or category toward which one has no feeling of identify or of belonging.

Panic   A collective flight based on a hysterical belief.

Participant-observer study   One in which the researcher takes part in the behavior he or she is studying.

Patrilocal marriage   Social pattern in which the married couple live with the husband's family.

Peer group   A group of one's "equals," usually similar persons with whom one habitually associates.

Personal disorganization   Loss of sense of certainty and direction, with confused and inconsistent behavior.

Personality   The totality of behavior of an individual with a given tendency system interacting with a sequence of situations.

Pluralist   One who believes that there is no one center of power and that decision making is the result of conflict and compromise between many different groups and individuals.

Polyandry   A form of polygamy in which the wife has two or more husbands.

Polygamy   A plurality of mates

Polygyny   A form of polygamy in which the husband has two or more wives.

Popular sociology   Treatment of sociological topics in popular media, usually by nonsociologists.

Position   The rank one holds in a hierarchical series.

Power elite   Interlocking network of corporate executives and military, governmental, or educational officials, which is alleged to make most of the important decisions in American society.

Prejudice   A bias for or against a person or group; implies "prejudging," or deciding without sufficient facts.

Primary group   Small group in which people come to know one another intimately, as individual personalities; distinct from the impersonal, formal, utilitarian secondary group.

Progress   Social or cultural change of a kind defined as desirable according to some set of values.

Proletariat   A working class which is conscious of its underprivileged and propertyless status.

Proletarianization theory   The theory that the middle class is becoming more like the working class.

Propaganda   All efforts to persuade others of an acceptance of a point of view.

Proportional representation   Each party receives legislative seats equal to the proportion of votes received by that party.

Prospective study   One that begins with the present and carries observations forward over a period of time.

Public   A number of people who share an interest in a particular topic or activity, or are concerned about and divided upon an issue.

Public opinion   An opinion held by a significant number of people; the dominant opinion among a population.

Pure science   Search for new knowledge without major concern for its practical uses or effects.

Questionnaire study   One in which data are obtained as informants fill in answers to a series of written questions.

Race   A group of people somewhat different from other people in a combination of inherited physical characteristics, but the meaning of the term is also substantially determined by popular social definition.

Radical   One who believes the social system is unjust and drastic changes are needed.

Random-assignment technique   One which builds experimental and control groups by assigning members at random to each group.

Random sample   One in which every person has

an equal chance to appear, as when every fifth, or tenth, or hundredth name is selected.

Rationalization Redefining a painful situation in terms which are personally and socially acceptable.

Reference group Any group accepted as model or guide for one's judgments and actions.

Replication Repetition by other researchers to see whether findings are confirmed.

Representative sample One in which all kinds of people appear in the same proportions as they appear in the total population studied.

Resocialization The unlearning and relearning needed for a major role transition.

Retrospective study One which works backward from the present moment, usually by examining records.

Revisionist One who favors a new interpretation of established views.

Riot Action of a violently aggressive, destructive crowd.

Rite of passage Any ritual which marks movement from one status to another, such as the ceremonies attending birth, death, puberty, or marriage.

Role Expected behavior of one who holds a certain status.

Role behavior The actual behavior of one who fills a role.

Role conflict Contradictory demands within a role; competing demands of two different roles.

Role personality A pattern of personality traits which a particular role requires.

Role playing Acting out the behavior of a role which one actually holds, as when a couple marry and set up a household.

Role relinquishment Giving up one role in order to accept another.

Role set A cluster of associated roles that together form a social status.

Role strain Difficulty in meeting one's role obligations.

Role taking Assuming or acting out the behavior of a role which one does not actually hold, as when children "play house."

Role transition Changing from one role to another.

Rumor A rapidly spreading report unsubstantiated by authenticated fact.

Science A body of organized, verified knowledge which has been secured through scientific in-

vestigation; a method of study whereby a body of verified knowledge is discovered.

Secondary group Group in which contacts are impersonal, segmental, and utilitarian, as distinct from the small, intimate, highly personal primary group.

Sect A small religious group seeking to return to a strict observance of earlier religious values and doctrines.

Secularization Movement from a sacred to a rationalistic, utilitarian, experimental viewpoint.

Secular society Ruled by rational or scientific rather than religious values.

Segregation Separation of two or more groups based on a desire to avoid equal-status social contact.

Self A person's awareness of, and attitudes toward, his or her own person.

Self-fulfilling prophecy A prediction which starts a chain of events which make the prediction come true.

Self-selected sample One in which members become included by voluntary action, such as returning a questionnaire or letter.

Separatism Withdrawal from contact with the dominant majority by groups which have suffered past discrimination and wish to build a separate social and economic life.

Sex A biological quality distinguishing male from female (or, rarely, some intermixture of both).

Sex drive A predisposition, probably biological, for persons to seek sexual and sex-related response from one or more others, usually of the opposite sex.

Sexism/sexist Beliefs in or policies of male superiority or sex inequality; uncritical acceptance of sex-role stereotypes.

Sex ratio Number of males per 100 females.

Sex role/gender role The expected behavior of males and females at a particular time and place.

Sexual identity/gender identity One's awareness and acceptance of being male or female.

Sexuality All the feelings and behaviors linked to sex through either biology or social learning.

Significant others Those individuals whose approval one desires and whose judgments will affect one's attitudes and behavior.

Slum A deteriorated area of the city inhabited by poor people.

Social change Change in the social structure and

relationships of a society; often used interchangeably with *cultural change*.

Social class A stratum of persons of similar position in the social-status continuum who regard one another as social equals.

Social contagion Process whereby members of a crowd stimulate and respond to one another and thereby increase their emotional intensity and responsiveness.

Social control All the means and processes whereby a group or a society secures its members' conformity to its expectations.

Social Darwinism The belief that social arrangements developed gradually on the basis of a competitive struggle in which the fittest humans and social forms survived.

Social disorganization Disruption of existing culture by social change, as shown by failure of traditional social controls, role confusions, and conflicting moral codes.

Social distance Degree of closeness to, or acceptance of, members of other groups.

Social gospel The belief that religion has a major concern with social justice.

Socialism System in which the means of production are publicly owned and controlled either by direct worker ownership or through the state.

Social isolates Organisms lacking normal social contacts with other members of their species.

Socialization Process by which a person internalizes the norms of his or her groups so that a distinct self emerges unique to the individual.

Social mobility Movement from one class level to another.

Social movement Collective effort to promote or resist change.

Social order A system of people, relationships, and customs operating smoothly together to accomplish the work of a society.

Social planning Attempt at the intelligent direction of social change.

Society A relatively independent, self-perpetuating human group which occupies a particular territory, shares a culture, and has most activities within this group.

Sociobiology The systematic study of the biological basis of human behavior.

Sociocultural change Changes in either the social structure and relations or in the culture of a society.

Sociogram A diagram showing attractions and rejections among a small group of persons.

Sociology The scientific study of human social life.

Sociometry A method of studying and diagramming social relationships and making sociograms.

Sponsored education Restrictive admission to advanced education, with the expectation that nearly all will be graduated.

Statistical comparative study One which compares collected statistical data for different groups, places, or times.

Status Position of an individual in a group, or of a group in relation to other groups.

Status inconsistency Some disparity between one's several statuses.

Stereotype A group-shared image of another group or category of people.

Stratification The system of status levels of a society; the process of developing and modifying this system of status differences.

Stratified random sample A random sample that includes members of each of the various categories of people in the population studied.

Subculture A cluster of behavior patterns related to the general culture of a society and yet distinguishable from it; behavior patterns of a distinct group within the general society.

Symbol Anything which represents something beyond itself; such as a word, a gesture, or a flag.

Symbolic communication Exchanging meanings through words and other symbols which have no meaning in themselves but to which agreed meanings have become attached; distinguished from exchange of meanings through instinctive barks and growls.

Technology Use of scientific discoveries to solve practical problems.

Tenure The right to retain a position unless it is abolished or one is removed because of misconduct or incompetence.

Terrorism The use of violence or the threat of violence to coerce governments, authorities, or populations.

Tracking Grouping students according to ability.

Transfer payments The provision of money or free services to some groups that is financed by taxes paid disproportionately by other groups—

thus a transfer of income between groups or classes.

Unique experience The total experience of a person, which no other person exactly duplicates.

Urban centralization Clustering of economic and service functions.

Urban concentration Tendency of people and activities to cluster together.

Urban decentralization Flight of people and activities from the center of the city.

Urban ecological processes Means whereby spatial distribution of people and activities changes.

Urban invasion Entrance of a new kind of people or activities within a particular area.

Urban segregation Concentration of a certain type of people or activities into an area.

Urban succession Completed replacement of one kind of people or activity by another.

Utilitarian Useful in practical ways, or distinct from ornamental, aesthetic, or emotional.

Values Ideas about what is important and what is unimportant.

Value stretch Holding and expressing the belief that something has value but failing to follow through with appropriate behavior to attain it.

Variable Anything which varies from case to case, such as age, sex, and education among human beings.

Verifiable evidence Factual observations which other trained observers can see, weigh, count, and check for accuracy.

Voluntary association Formal organization directed toward some definite function which one supposedly enters voluntarily rather than by ascription.

Xenocentrism A preference for foreign ideas or products; the opposite of ethnocentrism.

Bibliography

Abbott, Walter F.: "Moscow in 1897 as a Preindustrial City: A Test of the Inverse Burgess Zonal Hypothesis," *American Sociological Review,* 39:542–550, August 1974.

Abell, George O., and Barry Singer (eds.): *Science and the Paranormal: Probing the Existence of the Supernatural,* Charles Scribner's Sons, New York, 1981.

Abrahamson, Mark: *Urban Sociology,* Prentice-Hall, Inc., Englewood Cliffs, N.J., 1980.

Abrams, Charles: *Forbidden Neighbors: A Study of Prejudice in Housing,* Harper & Row, Publishers, Inc., New York, 1955.

————: *The City Is the Frontier,* Harper & Row, Publishers, Inc., New York, 1965.

Abt, Clark C. (ed.): *The Evaluation of Social Programs,* Sage Publications, Beverly Hills, Calif., 1977.

Adams, E. M.: "The Logic of Planning," *Social Forces,* 28:419–423, May 1950.

Adams, Margaret: *Single Blessedness: Observations on the Single Status in a Married Society,* Basic Books, Inc., Publishers, New York, 1976.

Adorno, T. W., Else Frankel-Brunswick, D. J. Levinson, and R. N. Sanford: *The Authoritarian Personality,* Harper & Row, Publishers, Inc., New York, 1950.

Ageton, Suzanne S., and Delbert S. Elliott: "The Effect of Legal Processing on Delinquent Orientation," *Social Problems,* 20:87–100, October 1974.

Akers, Ronald L.: *Delinquent Behavior: A Social Learning Approach,* Wadsworth Publishing Company, Inc., Belmont, Calif., 1973.

Alatus, Seyd Hussein: "The Captive Mind in Developmental Studies: Some Neglected Problems and the Need for an Autonomous Social Science Tradition in Asia," *International Social Science Journal,* 24:9–25, no. 1, 1972.

Alba, Richard D., and David E. Lavin: "Community Colleges and Tracking in Higher Education," *Sociology of Education,* 54:223–237, October 1981.

Alexander, Charles C.: *The Ku Klux Klan in the Southwest,* University of Kentucky Press, Lexington, 1965.

Alexander, Yonah: *International Terrorism: National, Regional and Global Perspectives,* AMS Press, Inc., New York, 1976, chap. 10, "Palestinian Terrorism."

———— and Seymour Maxwell Finger (eds.): *Terrorism: Interdisciplinary Perspectives,* John Jay Press, New York, 1977.

———— and John M. Gleason: *Behavioral and Quantitative Perspectives on Terrorism,* Pergamon Press, New York, 1981.

Alinsky, Saul D.: "The War on Poverty—Political Pornography," *Journal of Social Issues,* 21:41–47, January 1965.

Allen, Francis R.: *Socio-Cultural Dynamics: An Introduction to Social Change,* The Macmillan Company, New York, 1971.

Allen, James B.: *The Company Town in the American West,* University of Oklahoma Press, Norman, 1966.

Allport, Floyd H.: *Social Psychology,* Houghton Mifflin Company, Boston, 1924.

Allport, Gordon W., and Leo Postman: *The Psychology of Rumor,* Holt, Rinehart and Winston, Inc., New York, 1947.

Alspach, Steven: "Women's Sex Role Attitudes and Life Satisfaction," *Sociological Focus,* 15:279–287, August 1982.

Alt, Herschel, and Edith Alt: *Russia's Children*, Bookman Associates, Inc., New York, 1959.

Amalrik, Andrei: *Will the Soviet Union Survive Until 1984?* Harper & Row, Publishers, Inc., New York, 1969.

Amneus, Daniel: *Back to Patriarchy*, Arlington House Publishers, New Rochelle, N.Y., 1979.

Anderson, Charles H.: *The Political Economy of Social Class*, Prentice-Hall, Inc., Englewood Cliffs, N.J., 1974.

Anderson, Raymond H.: "Soviet Urban Sprawl Defies Official Efforts to Curb the Growth of Cities," *The New York Times*, Nov. 13, 1966, p. 122.

Apodaca, Anadeto: "Corn and Custom: The Introduction of Hybrid Corn to Spanish American Farmers in New Mexico," in Edward H. Spicer (ed.), *Human Problems in Technological Change*, Russell Sage Foundation, New York, 1952, pp. 35–39.

Appelbaum, Richard P.: *Theories of Social Change*, Markham Publishing Company, Chicago, 1970.

Appelbaum, Ronald L., et al.: *The Process of Group Communication*, Science Research Associates, Inc., Chicago, 1979.

Apple, Michael W.: *Ideology and Curriculum*, Routledge & Kegan Paul, Ltd., New York, 1979.

Andrey, Robert: *The Territorial Imperative*, Atheneum Publishers, New York, 1966.

Arens, Richard: *Genocide in Paraguay*, Temple University Press, Philadelphia, 1976.

Arensberg, Conrad M., and Arthur M. Niehoff: *Introducing Social Change: A Manual for Community Development*, Aldine-Atherton, Inc., Chicago, 1971.

Argyris, Chris: "We Must Make Work Worthwhile," *Life*, May 5, 1967, pp. 56ff.

Armbruster, Frank E.: "The More We Spend, the Less Children Learn," *The New York Times Magazine*, Aug. 28, 1977, pp. 9ff.

Armor, David J.: "The Evidence on Busing," *The Public Interest*, 28:90–126, Summer 1972.

Aron, Raymond, in collaboration with Jessie Bernard, T. H. Pear, Raymond Aron, and Robert C. Angell: *The Nature of Conflict*, International Sociological Association, UNESCO, Paris, 1957.

Asch, S. E.: "Effects of Group Pressure Upon the Modification of Judgments," in Heinz Guetzkow (ed.): *Groups, Leadership, and Men*, U.S. Office of Naval Research, Carnegie Institute of Technology, Pittsburgh, 1951.

Ashwood, Thomas M.: "The Airline Response to Terrorism," in Yonah Alexander and Robert A. Kilmarx (ed.), *Political Terrorism and Business: The Threat and the Response*, Praeger Publishers, Inc., New York, 1979, pp. 129–139.

Atchley, Robert C.: *The Social Forces in Later Life: An Introduction to Social Gerontology*, Wadsworth Publishing Company, Inc., Belmont, Calif., 1980.

Atkinson, L. Jay: *World Population Growth: Analysis and New Projections of the United Nations*, Foreign Research Service, U.S. Department of Agriculture, Foreign Agricultural Economic Report 129, Washington, February 1977.

Auger, James G.: quoted in *Business Week*, April 4, 1983, p. 10.

Auletta, Ken: *The Underclass*, reviewed in *Washington Post*, June 27, 1982.

Babcock, Richard F.: *The Zoning Game: Municipal Practices and Policies*, The University of Wisconsin Press, Madison, 1966.

Bach, Robert L.: "The New Cuban Immigrants: Their Background and Prospects," *Monthly Labor Review*, 103:39–46, October 1980.

Bachman, Jerald B., et al.: *Dropping Out—Problem or Symptom*, Insitute for Social Research, Ann Arbor, Michican, 1972.

Bailey, Robert, Jr.: "Urban Radicals: Activists in an Alinsky Community Organization," *Growth and Change*, 4:3–9, July 1973.

Bailey, William C.: "Inequality in the Legal Order: Some Further Analysis and Commentary," *Social Problems*, 29:51–61, October 1981.

Bain, Read: "The Self- and Other-words of a Child," *American Journal of Sociology*, 41:767–776, May 1936.

Baldassare, Mark: "The Effects of Household Density on Subgroups," *American Sociological Review*, 46:110–118, February 1981.

Bales, Robert F.: *Interaction Process Analysis: A Method for the Study of Small Groups*, The University of Chicago Press, Chicago, 1950.

——— and Fred L. Strodtbeck: "Phases in Group Problem-Solving," *Journal of Abnormal and Social Psychology*, 46:485–495, October 1951.

Baltes, Paul B.: "Longitudinal and Cross-Sectional Sequences in the Study of Age and Generation Effects," *Human Development*, 11:145–171, no. 1, 1968.

——— and Warner K. Schaie: "Aging and IQ: The Myth of the Twilight Years," *Psychology Today*, March 1974, pp. 35–38ff.

Bane, Mary Jo: *Here to Stay: American Families in the Twentieth Century*, Basic Books, Publishers, Inc., New York, 1978.

———— and Christopher Jencks: "Schools and Equal Opportunity," excerpt from "Inequality: A Reassessment of the Effect of Family and Schooling in America," *Saturday Review of Education*, Sept. 16, 1972, pp. 37–42.

Banfield, Edward C.: *The Unheavenly City Revisited*, Little, Brown and Company, Boston, 1974.

Banks, Joseph: Quoted in David J. Blum: "The Long Hot Summer Ends Without Riots that Some Predicted," *The Wall Street Journal*, Sept. 23, 1982, p. 1.

Banks, Olive, and Douglas Finlayson: *Success and Failure in the Secondary School*, Methuen & Co., Ltd., London, 1973.

Banton, Michael P.: *Race Relations*, Basic Books, Inc., Publishers, New York, 1967.

Bar, Michael: Research reviewed in "The Stereotype Could Be True," *Time*, 110:36, Sept. 12, 1977.

Barber, Bernard, and Lyle S. Tobel: " 'Fashion' in Women's Clothes and the American Social System," *Social Forces*, 31:124–131, December 1952.

Barber, Theodore X., and William B. Meeker: "Out of Sight, Out of Mind," *Human Behavior*, August 1974, pp. 56–60.

Barer, Naomi: "Delinquency Before, After Admission to New Haven Housing Development," *Journal of Housing*, 3:27, January 1946.

Barnett, David L.: "Communism the Great Economic Failure," *U.S. News & World Report*, 92:33–37, March 1, 1982.

Barnett, H. G.: *Innovation: The Basis of Social Change*, McGraw-Hill Book Company, New York, 1953.

Barton, Allan H.: *Disaster: A Sociological Analysis of Collective Stress Situations*, Doubleday & Company, Inc., Garden City, N.Y., 1969.

Bascom, William R., and Melville J. Herskovitz (eds.): *Continuity and Change in African Cultures*, The University of Chicago Press, Chicago, 1959.

Bassis, Michael S.: "The Campus as a Frog Pond: A Theoretical and Empirical Reassessment," *American Journal of Sociology*, 82:1318–1326, May 1977.

Bates, Robert H.: "Ethnic Competition and Modernization in Contemporary Africa," *Comparative Political Studies*, 6:457–484, January 1974.

Bauer, Peter, and Basil Yamey: "Foreign Aid: What Is at Stake?" *The Public Interest*, 68:53–69, Summer 1982.

Bavelas, Alex: "Communication Patterns in Task-Oriented Groups," in Dorwin Cartwright and Alvin F. Zander (eds.), *Group Dynamics*, 2nd ed., Harper & Row, Publishers, Inc., New York, 1962, pp. 669–682.

Baxter, Sandra, and Marjorie Lansing: *Women and Politics: The Invisible Majority*, The University of Michigan Press, Ann Arbor, 1980.

Bay, Christian: *Civil Disobedience: Theory and Practice*, Black Rose Books, Montreal, 1975.

Bayley, David H.: "Learning About Crime: The Japanese Experience," *The Public Interest*, 44:55–68, Summer 1976.

Becker, Howard S.: *Outsiders*, The Free Press, New York, 1963.

————: "Whose Side Are We On?" *Social Problems*, 14:239–247, Winter 1967.

Becker, John: Research note in *Behavior Today*, Feb. 22, 1971, p. 2.

Beckman, Leonard: "Clothes Make the Person: Social Roles and Uniforms," *Psychology Today*, 7:49–51, April 1974.

Beglis, Jeanne F., and Anees A. Sheikh: "Development of Self-Concept in Black and White Children," *Journal of Negro Education*, 43:104–110, Winter 1974.

Behrens, Steve: "Baby Bonuses—or Boom," *Zero Population Growth National Reporter*, 10:1, May 1978.

Belin, Daniel W., Esq.: *You Are the Jury*, Quadrangle Books, Inc., New York, 1973.

Bell, Alan P., et al.: *Sexual Preference: Its Development in Men and Women*, Indiana University Press, Bloomington, 1981.

Bell, Daniel: "The Power Elite—Reconsidered," *American Journal of Sociology*, 64:238–250, November 1958.

————: *The Coming of Post-Industrial Society: A Venture in Social Forecasting*, Basic Books, Inc., Publishers, New York, 1973.

Bell, J. Bowyer: *A Time of Terror: How Democratic Societies Respond to Revolutionary Violence*, Basic Books, Inc., Publishers, New York, 1978.

————: "The Irish Republican Army," in David Carlton and Carlo Scharf (eds.), *Contemporary Terror: Studies in Sub-State Violence*, St. Martin's Press, Inc., New York, 1981, pp. 215–226.

Bellah, Robert N.: "American Civil Religion in the 1970s," in R. E. Richey and D. G. Jones (eds.),

American Civil Religion, Harper & Row, Publishers, Inc., New York, 1974, pp. 255–272.

———: *The Broken Covenant: American Civil Religion in Time of Trial*, Seabury Press, Inc., New York, 1975.

——— and Phillip E. Hammond: *Varieties of Civil Religion*, Harper & Row, Publishers, Inc., New York, 1980.

Bem, Sandra Lipsitz: "Androgyny vs the Tight Little Lives of Fluffy Women and Chesty Men," *Psychology Today*, 9:58–62, September 1975a.

———: "Sex Role Adaptability: One Consequence of Psychological Adaptability," *Journal of Personality and Social Psychology*, 31:634–643, no. 4, 1975b.

——— et al.: "Sex Typing and Androgyny: Further Explorations of the Expressive Domain," *Journal of Personality and Social Psychology*, 34:1016–1023, no. 5, 1976.

Benbow, Camilla Persson, and Julian C. Stanley: "Sex Differences in Mathematical Ability: Fact or Artifact?" *Science*, 210:1262–1264, Dec. 12, 1980.

Benedict, Ruth: *Patterns of Culture*, Houghton Mifflin Company, Boston, 1934.

———: "Continuities and Discontinuities in Cultural Conditioning," *Psychiatry*, 1:161–167, 1938.

Bennett, William J., and Edwin J. Delattre: "Moral Education in the Schools," *The Public Interest*, 50:81–98, Winter 1978.

Bennis, Warren G., Kenneth D. Benne, and Robert Chin: *The Planning of Change*, Holt, Rinehart and Winston, Inc., New York, 1969.

Berelson, Bernard: "Romania's 1966 Anti-Abortion Decree: The Demographic Experience of the First Decade," *Population Studies*, 33:209–222, July 1979.

——— et al.: *Family Planning and Population Programs: A Review of World Development*, The University of Chicago Press, Chicago, 1966.

——— et al.: "World Population: Status Report 1974," *Reports on Population Family Planning*, January 1975, pp. 1–47.

——— et al.: "1966–1977: A Look at the Record," *Family Planning Perspectives*, 10:20–23, January/February 1978.

Beres, Luis Rene: *Terrorism and Global Security: The Nuclear Threat*, Westview Press, Boulder, Col., 1979.

Berg, Ivar: "Rich Man's Qualifications for Poor Man's Jobs," *Trans-action*, March 1969, pp. 45–50.

Berger, Bennett M.: "Audiences, Art and Power," *Trans-action*, May 1971 pp. 26–30.

Berger, Peter L.: *Pyramids of Sacrifice*, Basic Books, Inc., Publishers, New York, 1974.

———: "The Class Struggle in American Religion," *The Christian Century*, 98:194–199, Feb. 25, 1981.

——— and Thomas Luckmann: *The Social Construction of Reality: A Treatise on the Sociology of Knowledge*, Doubleday & Company, Inc., Garden City, N.Y., 1966.

Berk, Bernard: "Face: Saving at a Singles Dance," *Social Problems*, 24:530–544, June 1977.

Berk, Richard A.: *Collective Behavior*, Wm. C. Brown Company Publishers, Dubuque, Iowa, 1974a.

———: "A Gaming Approach to Collective Behavior," *American Sociological Review*, 39:355–373, April 1974b.

——— and Howard E. Aldrich: "Patterns of Vandalism During Civil Disorders as an Indicator of Selection of Targets," *American Sociological Review*, 37:533–547, October 1972.

Berkman, Lisa F.: Reviewed in *Science News*, 118:392, Dec. 20, 1980.

Bernstein, Basil: "Elaborated and Restricted Codes: An Outline," *Sociological Inquiry*, 36:254–261, Spring 1966.

Berreman, Gerald D.: *Caste and Other Inequalities*, South Asia Books, Columbia, Mo., 1981.

Berry, Brian J. L. (ed.): *The Human Consequences of Urbanization*, Macmillan & Co., Ltd., London, 1973.

Berscheid, Ellen, and Elaine Walster: "Physical Characteristics," in Leonard Berkowitz (ed.), *Advances in Experimental Social Psychology*, 7:158–215, Academic Press, Inc., New York, 1974.

Bettelheim, Bruno: "Does Communal Education Work? The Case of the Kibbutz," *Commentary*, 33:117–125, February 1962; reprinted in Edwin M. Schur (ed.), *The Family and the Sexual Revolution*, Indiana University Press, Bloomington, 1964, pp. 293–307.

———: *The Children of the Dream*, The Macmillan Company, New York, 1969.

Bickman, Leonard: "Clothes Make the Person: Social Rules and Uniforms," *Psychology Today*, 7:49–51, April 1974.

Biderman, Albert D.: "Social-Psychological Needs and 'Involuntary' Behavior as Illustrated by Compliance in Interrogation," *Sociometry*, 23:120–147, 1960.

Bieber, I. et al.: *Homosexuality: A Psychiatric Study*,

Basic Books, Publishers, Inc., New York, 1962.

Bierstedt, Robert A.: *The Social Order*, McGraw-Hill Book Company, New York, 1974.

Birch, Herbert G., and Joan Dye Gussow: *Disadvantaged Children: Health, Nutrition, and School Failure*, Harcourt Brace Jovanovich, Inc., New York, 1970.

Bird, Kai: "Sterilization in India; Indira Gandhi Uses Force," *Nation*, 222:747–749, June 19, 1976.

Birdsall, Stephen S.: "Alternative Prospects for America's Urban Future," in Stanley D. Brunn and James O. Wheeler (eds.), *The American Metropolitan System: Present and Future*, John Wiley & Sons, Inc., New York, 1980, p. 201–211.

Birnbach, Lisa (ed.): *The Official Preppie Handbook*, Workman Publishing Company, New York, 1980.

Bishop, George F., et al.: "Pseudo-Opinions of Public Affairs," *Public Opinion Quarterly*, 44:198–209, Summer 1980.

Black, Hal: "Navajo Sheep and Goat Guarding Dogs," *Rangelands*, 3:335–337, December 1981.

Blaine, Graham B., Jr., et al.: "Does Living Together Before Marriage Make for a Better Marriage?" *Medical Aspects of Human Sexuality*, 9:32–39, January 1975.

Blank, Blanche D.: "Degrees: Who Needs Them?" *AAUP Bulletin*, 58:261–266, Autumn 1972.

Blauner, Robert: *Alienation and Freedom: The Factory Worker and His Industry*, The University of Chicago Press, Chicago, 1964.

———: "Whitewash over Watts," *Trans-action*, 3:3–9, March/April 1966.

———: "Internal Colonialism and Ghetto Revolt," in James A. Geschwender (ed.), *The Black Revolt*, Prentice-Hall, Inc., Englewood Cliffs, N.J., 1971.

Blechman, Elaine A.: "Are Children With One Parent at Psychological Risk?" *Journal of Marriage and the Family*, 44:179:195, February 1982.

Blood, Robert O., Jr., and Donald M. Wolfe: *Husbands and Wives*, The Free Press, New York, 1960.

Bloodworth, Dennis: "How Mao Rides the Dragon," *The Observer*, Sept. 11, 1966; reprinted in *Current*, October 1966, pp. 48–50.

Bloom, B. S.: "The Thought Process of Students in Discussion," in Sidney J. French (ed.), *Accent on Teaching*, Harper & Row, Publishers, Inc. New York, 1954.

Blum, David J.: "The Long Hot Summer Ends Without Riots That Some Predicted," *Wall Street Journal*, Sept. 23, 1982, pp. 1ff.

Blumberg, Leonard V., and Robert R. Bell: "Urban Migration and Kinship Ties," *Social Problems*, 6:328–333, Spring 1959.

———, Thomas E. Shipley, Jr., and Stephen F. Barsky: *Liquor and Poverty: Skid Row as a Human Condition*, Rutgers University Center of Alcohol Studies, New Brunswick, N.J., 1978.

Blumberg, Paul: "The Decline and Fall of the Status Symbol: Some Thoughts on Status in a Post-Industrial Society," *Social Problems*, 21:480–498, April 1974.

———: *Inequality in an Age of Decline*, Oxford University Press, New York, 1980.

Blumer, Herbert: "Attitudes and the Social Act," *Social Problems*, 3:59–64, October 1955.

———: "Symbolic Interaction," in Arnold M. Rose (ed.), *Human Behavior and Social Process*, Houghton Mifflin Company, Boston, 1962, pp. 19–22.

———: "Collective Behavior," in Alfred McClung Lee (ed.), *Principles of Sociology*, Barnes & Noble, Inc., New York, 1969a, pp. 65–122.

———: "Social Movements," in Alfred McClung Lee (ed.), *Principles of Sociology*, Barnes & Noble, Inc., New York, 1969b, pp. 99–120.

———: "Outline of Collective Behavior," in Robert E. Evans (ed.), *Readings in Collective Behavior*, 2nd ed., Rand McNally & Company, Chicago, 1975, pp. 22–45.

Blundell, William E.: "Natural Enemies: To Loggers, the Woods Are Dark and Deep—But Far From Lovely," *Wall Street Journal*, Dec. 8, 1981, pp. 1ff.

Bogardus, Emory S.: *Fundamentals of Social Psychology*, Appleton-Century-Crofts Inc., New York, 1950.

———: "Racial Distance Changes in the United States During the Past Thirty Years," *Sociology and Social Research*, 43:127–135, November/December 1958.

———: "Racial Reactions by Regions," *Sociology and Social Research*, 43:286–290, March/April 1959.

Bogue, Donald J.: *Skid Row*, The Community and Family Study Center, Chicago, 1963.

Bohen, Halcyone H., and Anamaria Viveros-Long: *Balancing Jobs and Family Life: Do Flexible Work Schedules Help?* Temple University Press, Philadelphia, 1981.

Bolling, Landrum S.: "Islamic Fundamentalism on

the Move," *Saturday Evening Post*, 252:52–57, September 1980.

Bondestam, Lars, and Staffan Bergström: *Poverty and Population Control*, Academic Press, Inc., New York, 1980.

Boorstin, Daniel J.: "Political Revolutions and Revolutions in Science and Technology," in Daniel J. Boorstin, *The Republic of Technology*, Harper & Row, Publishers, Inc., New York, 1978, pp. 22–33.

Booth, Alan: *Urban Crowding and Its Consequences*, Frederick A. Praeger, Inc., New York, 1976.

———: "Does Wives' Employment Cause Stress for Husbands?" *The Family Coordinator*, 28:445–449, October 1979.

——— and David Richard Johnson: "The Effect of Crowding on Child Health and Development," *American Behavior Scientist*, 18:736–749, July/August 1975.

Borders, William: "India Will Curb Birth Control Program," *The New York Times*, April 3, 1977, p. 8.

Boskin, Joseph: "The Revolt of the Urban Ghettos," *Annals of the American Academy of Political and Social Science*, 382:1–14, March 1969.

Bottomore, T. B.: *Sociology: A Guide to Problems and Literature*, George Allen & Unwin, Ltd., London, 1962, pp. 283–284.

Bouma, Gary D.: "Assessing the Impact of Religion: A Critical Review," *Sociological Analysis*, 31:172–179, Winter 1970.

———: "A Critical Review of Recent 'Protestant Ethic' Research," *Journal for the Scientific Study of Religions*, 12:141–155, June 1973.

———: "The Real Reason One Conservative Church Grew," *Review of Religious Research*, 20:127–137, Spring 1979.

Bouvier, Leon F.: *The Impact of Immigration on U.S. Population Size*, Population Trends, and Public Policy, ser. 1, Population Reference Bureau, Washington, 1981.

Bowles, Samuel, and Herbert Gintis: *Schooling in Capitalist America: Educational Reform and the Contradictions of Economic Life*, Basic Books, Inc., Publishers, New York, 1976.

Boyer, L. Bryce, et al.: "Ecology, Socialization, and Personality Development Among Athabascans," *Journal of Comparative Family Studies*, 5:61–73, Spring 1974.

Bradshaw, Jon: "The Reggae Way to Salvation," *The New York Times Magazine*, Aug. 14, 1977, pp. 24ff.

Brady, Thomas F.: "French Worker-Priests Must Abandon Politics," *New York Times*, Jan. 13, 1954, sec. 4, p. 7.

Brand, David: "Russia's Private Farms Show State-Run Ones How to Raise Output," *Wall Street Journal*, March 3, 1981, pp. 1ff.

Braverman, Harry: "Labor and Monopoly Capital: The Degradation of Work in the 20th Century," *Monthly Review*, 26:1–134, July 1974.

Brazziel, William F.: "Letter From the South," *Harvard Educational Review*, 39:348–352, no. 2, 1969.

Breckenfeld, Gurney: "It's Up to the Cities to Save Themselves," *Fortune*, August 1977, pp. 144ff.

Bresler, Robert J.: "The Reagan Budget: Making Choices—All of Them Wrong," *USA Today*, 110: 8–9, May 1982.

Briggs, B. Bruce: "An Introduction to the Idea of the New Class," in B. Bruce Briggs (ed.), *The New Class*, Transaction Books, New Brunswick, N.J., 1979, pp. 1–18.

Brill, Harry: *Why Organizers Fail*, University of California Press, Berkeley, 1971.

Brim, Orville G. (ed.): *The Dying Patient*, Transaction Books, New Brunswick, N.J., 1979.

Brinton, Crane: *The Anatomy of Revolution*, W. W. Norton & Company, Inc., New York, 1938.

Brock, Horace W.: "Social Security Inequity: Picking the Pockets of Tomorrow's Elderly," *USA Today*, 111:10–13, March 1983.

Bronfenbrenner, Urie, with the assistance of John C. Condry, Jr.: *Two Worlds of Childhood: U.S. and U.S.S.R.*, Basic Books, Inc., Publishers, New York, 1970.

Brooks, Richard Oliver: *New Towns and Communal Values: A Case Study of Columbia, Maryland*, Frederick A. Praeger, Inc., New York, 1974.

Broom, Leonard: *The Social Psychology of Race Relations*, Schenkman Publishing Co., Inc., Cambridge, Mass., 1972.

———, and F. Lancaster Jones: "Status Consistency and Political Preference: The Australian Case," *American Sociological Review*, 35:989–1001, December 1970.

Brown, David L., and John M. Wardwell: *New Directions in Urban-Rural Migration: The Population Turnaround in Rural America*, Academic Press, Inc., New York, 1980.

Brown, George H., et al.: *Education of Hispanic Americans*, National Center for Education Statistics, Washington, 1980.

Brown, Robert L.: "Social Distance as a Function

of Mexican-American and Other Ethnic Identity," *Sociology and Social Research*, 57:273, 287, April 1973.

Bruck, Connie: "Professing Androgyny," *Human Behavior*, October 1977, pp. 21–31.

Brunn, Stanley D., and James O. Wheeler (eds.): *The American Metropolitan System: Present and Future*, John Wiley & Sons, Inc., New York, 1980.

Brunvand, Jan Harold: *The Vanishing Hitchhiker: American Urban Legends and Their Meanings*, W. W. Norton & Company, Inc., New York, 1981.

Bruyn, Severyn: *The Human Perspective in Sociology: The Methodology of Participant Observation*, Prentice-Hall, Inc., Englewood Cliffs, N.J., 1966.

——— and Paula Rayman: *Nonviolent Action and Social Change*, Westview Press, Boulder, Col., 1979.

Bryan, Clifford E., and Robert L. Horton: "School Athletics and Fan Aggression," *Educational Researcher*, 5:2–11, July/August 1978.

Brym, Robert J.: *Intellectuals and Politics*, George Allen & Unwin, Ltd., London, 1980.

Buchanan, Patrick: "Reflections on '74: Power of the Press and a Departing Star," *TV Guide*, Jan. 11, 1975, pp. 5–6.

Bucher, G. R.: "Liberation Theology," *Intellect*, 105:278–280, February 1977.

Buckhout, Robert, et al.: "Eyewitness Identification: Effects of Suggestion and Bias in Identification from Photographs," *Bulletin of the Psychonomic Society*, 6:71–74, July 1975.

Buckley, Alan D., and Daniel Olson (eds.): *International Terrorism: Current Research and Future Trends*, Avery Publishing Co., Inc., Wayne, N.J., 1980.

Budd, L. S.: *Problems, Disclosure, and Commitment of Cohabiting Couples and Married Couples*, unpublished Ph.D. dissertation, University of Minnesota, 1976.

Bunzel, John H.: "To Each According to Her Worth," *The Public Interest*, 67:77–93, Spring 1982.

Bunzel, Ruth: "Economic Organization of Primitive Peoples," in Frank Boaz (ed.), *General Anthropology*, D.C. Heath and Company, Boston, 1938.

Burchard, Waldo: *The Role of the Military Chaplain*, University of California Press, Berkeley, 1963.

Burchinall, Lee G., and Hilda Siff: "Rural Poverty," *Journal of Marriage and the Family*, 26:399–405, November 1964.

Burger, Amy L., and Neil S. Jacobson: "The Relationship Between Sex Role Characteristics, Couple Satisfaction, and Couple Problem Solving Skills," *The American Journal of Family Therapy*, 4:52–60, Winter 1979.

Burkhart, Lynne C.: *Old Values in a New Town*, Praeger Publishers, Inc., New York, 1981.

Burlingame, Roger: *Inventors Behind the Inventor*, Harcourt Brace Jovanovich, Inc., New York, 1947.

Burma, John H.: "The Measurement of Negro Passing," *American Journal of Sociology*, 52:18–22, July 1946.

Burstein, Leigh, Kathleen B. Fischer, and M. David Miller: "The Multilevel Effects of Background on Science Achievement: A Cross-National Survey," *Sociology of Education*, 53:215–225, October 1980.

Burton, Nancy W., and Lyle V. Jones: "Recent Trends in Achievement Levels of Black and White Youth," *Educational Researcher*, 11:10–14, April 1982.

Butterfield, Fox: "Settling a Score with Mao," *The New York Times Magazine*, Dec. 10, 1978, pp. 42ff.

———: "How the Chinese Police Themselves," *The New York Times Magazine*, April 18, 1982, pp. 32ff.

Cain, Pamela S., and Donald J. Treiman: "The Dictionary of Occupational Titles as Source of Occupational Data," *American Sociological Review*, 46:253–278, June 1981.

Calhoun, John B.: "Population Density and Social Pathology," *Scientific American*, 106:39–148, February 1962.

Calvin, A. D., and Wayne H. Holtzman: "Adjustment to the Discrepancy between Self-Concept and the Inferred Self," *Journal of Consulting Psychiatry*, 17:39–44, no. 1, 1953.

Cameron, Paul: "Social Stereotypes: Three Faces of Happiness," *Psychology Today*, 8:63–64, August 1974.

Campbell, Angus: "The American Way of Mating: Marriage Si, Children Only Maybe," *Psychology Today*, 8:37–44, May 1975.

———: *The Sense of Well-Being in America*, McGraw-Hill Book Company, New York, 1980.

———, Phillip E. Converse, and Willard L. Rodgers: *The Quality of Life in America: Perceptions, Evaluations, and Satisfactions*, Russell Sage Foundation, New York, 1976.

Campbell, Carlos C.: *New Towns: Another Way to Live*, Reston Publishing Company, Reston, Va., 1976.

Cannon, Lynn Weber: "Normative Embourgeoisement Among Manual Workers: A Reexamination Using Longitudinal Data," *Sociological Quarterly*, 21:185–195, Spring 1980.

Cantril, Hadley: *The Psychology of Social Movements*, John Wiley & Sons, Inc., New York, 1941.

———: "Causes and Control of Riot and Panic," *Public Opinion Quarterly*, 7:669–679, Winter 1943.

Caplow, Theodore: *Principles of Organization*, Harcourt, Brace, and World, New York, 1964.

———, Howard M. Bahr, and Bruce A. Chadwick: *Middletown Families: Fifty Years of Change and Continuity*, The University of Minnesota Press, Minneapolis, 1982.

Carden, Maren Lockwood: *The New Feminism*, Russell Sage Foundation, New York, 1974.

Carnoy, Martin: *Education and Cultural Imperialism*, David McKay Company, Inc., New York, 1975.

Cary, Charles D.: "Peer Groups in the Political Socialization of Soviet Schoolchildren," *Social Science Quarterly*, 55:451–461, September, 1974.

Cash, Thomas F., and Ronald F. Salzbach: "Beauty of Counseling: Effects of Counselor Physical Attractiveness and Self-disclosure on Perceptions of Counselor Behavior," *Journal of Counseling Psychology*, 25:283–291, July 1978.

Cassidy, Robert: *Liveable Cities: A Grassroots Guide to Rebuilding Urban America*, Holt, Rinehart and Winston, Inc., New York, 1981.

Castelli, Jim: "The Curse of the Phantom Petition," *TV Guide*, July 24, 1976, pp. 4–6.

Catanese, Anthony, and James C. Snyder (eds.): *Introduction to Urban Planning*, McGraw-Hill Book Company, New York, 1979.

Catlin, Nancy, et al.: "MMPI Profiles of Cohabiting College Students," *Psychological Reports*, 38:407–410, April 1976.

Catton, William R., Jr.: *Overshoot: The Ecological Basis of Revolutionary Change*, The University of Illinois Press, Urbana, 1980.

Centers, Richard: *The Psychology of Social Classes*, Princeton University Press, Princeton, N.J., 1949.

Cereseto, Shirley: "World Starvation: Causes and Solutions," *The Insurgent Sociologist*, 7:33–52, Summer 1977.

Chamberlin, Leslie J.: "Facing up to Robotation," *USA Today*, 111:31–33, November 1982.

Chambliss, William J. (ed.): *Sociological Readings in the Conflict Perspective*, Addison-Wesley Publishing Company, Inc., Reading, Mass., 1973.

——— and Milton Mankoff (eds.): *Whose Law,*

What Order? John Wiley & Sons, Inc., New York, 1976.

——— and Thomas E. Ryther: *Sociology: The Discipline and Its Direction*, McGraw-Hill Book Company, New York, 1975.

Chandler, Michael: Research note in *Behavior Today*, Dec. 14, 1970, p. 2.

Chao, Paul: *Women Under Communism: Family in China and Russia*, General Hall, Inc., Bayside, N.Y., 1977.

Chappell, Neena L.: "The Social Process of Learning Sex Roles," in Hilary M. Lips and Nina Lee Colwell (eds.), *The Psychology of Sex Differences*, Columbia University Press, New York, 1978, pp. 103–124.

Charney, Israel W., with Chanan Rapaport: *How Can We Commit the Unthinkable? Genocide: The Human Cancer*, Westview Press, Boulder, Col., 1982.

Chase, Ivan D.: "A Comparison of Men's and Women's Intergenerational Mobility in the United States," *American Sociological Review*, 40:483–505, August 1975.

Chase-Dunn, Christopher K.: "Socialist States in the Capitalist World Economy," *Social Problems*, 27:505–525, June 1980.

Che, Wai-Kin: *The Modern Chinese Family*, R and E Research Associates, Palo Alto, Cal., 1979.

Cherne, Leo: "Into a Bottomless Hole," *Freedom at Issue*, 32:10, September/October, 1975.

Chicago Commission on Race Relations: *The Negro in Chicago*, The University of Chicago Press, Chicago, 1922.

Chudacoff, Howard P.: *The Evolution of American Urban Society*, Prentice-Hall, Inc., Englewood Cliffs, N.J., 1975.

Clapp, James A.: *New Towns and Urban Policy*, Dunellen Publishing Company, New York, 1971.

Clark, Kenneth B.: "Kenneth B. Clark Responds: The Role of Race," *The New York Times Magazine*, Oct. 5, 1980, pp. 22ff.; reprinted in *Current*, 227:33–42, November 1980.

Clark, Robert A., F. Ivan Nye, and Viktor Gecas: "Work Involvement and Martial Role Performance," *Journal of Marriage and the Family*, 40:9–21, February 1978.

Clark, Thomas A.: *Blacks in Suburbs: A National Perspective*, Center for Urban Policy Research, Rutgers University, New Brunswick, N.J., 1979.

Clark, Thomas P.: "Homosexuality as a Criterion Predictor of Psychopathology in Non-patient

Males," paper presented at Annual Meeting of the Western Psychological Association, Sacramento, Calif., 1975.

Clary, Jack: "Stop the Fans!" *TV Guide*, Nov. 19, 1977, pp. 2–4.

Clausen, Connie: *I Love You, Honey, but the Season's Over*, Holt, Rinehart and Winston, Inc., New York, 1961.

Clements, Barbara Evans: *Bolshevik Feminist: The Life of Aleksandra Kollontai*, Indiana University Press, Bloomington, 1979.

Clifton, Rodney A.: "Ethnicity, Teachers' Expectations and the Academic Achievement Process in Canada," *Sociology of Education*, 54:291–301, October 1981.

Clinard, Marshall B.: *Crime in Developing Countries*, John Wiley & Sons, Inc., New York, 1973.

————: *Cities With Little Crime: The Case of Switzerland*, Cambridge University Press, New York, 1978.

———— and Robert F. Meier: *The Sociology of Deviant Behavior*, Holt, Rinehart and Winston, Inc., New York, 1979.

Clutterbuck, Richard: *Guerrilas and Terrorists*, Faber & Faber, Ltd., London, 1977.

————: *Kidnap and Ransom: The Response*, Faber & Faber, Ltd., London, 1978.

Coale, Ansley J.: "Population Growth and Economic Development: The Case of Mexico," *Foreign Affairs*, 56:412–420, Winter 1978.

Cohen, David K.: "Social Science and Social Policy," *The Educational Forum*, 41:393–414, May 1977.

Cohen, Jerry, and William S. Murphy: *Burn, Baby, Burn*, E. P. Dutton & Co., Inc., New York, 1966.

Cohen, Marshall: "Civil Disobedience in a Constitutional Democracy," *Massachusetts Review*, 10:211–216, Spring 1969.

Cole, Stewart G., and Mildred Weise Cole: *Minorities and the American Promise*, Harper & Row, Publishers, Inc., New York, 1954.

Coleman, James S.: *Public and Private Schools*, National Opinion Research Center, Chicago, 1981.

———— et al.: *Equality of Educational Opportunity*, U.S. Department of Health, Education and Welfare, Washington, 1966.

———— et al.: *Youth: Transition to Adulthood: Report of the Panel on Youth of the President's Science Advisory Committee*, The University of Chicago Press, Chicago, 1974.

————, Thomas Hoffer, and Sally Kilgore: "Cognitive Outcomes in Public and Private Schools," *Sociology of Education*, 55:65–70, April 1982.

Coleman, Richard P., and Bernice L. Neugarten: *Social Status in the City*, Jossey-Bass, Inc., San Francisco, 1971.

———— and Lee Rainwater, with Kent A. McClelland: *Social Standing in America: New Dimensions of Class*, Basic Books, Inc., Publishers, New York, 1978.

Colfax, J. David, and Jack L. Roach (eds.): *Radical Sociology*, Basic Books, Inc., Publishers, New York, 1971.

College Board: *On Further Examination*, New York, 1977.

Collier, John: *Indians of the Americas*, W. W. Norton & Company, Inc., New York, 1947.

Collins, Glenn: "A New Look at Life with Father," *The New York Times Magazine*, June 17, 1979, pp. 30ff.

Collins, Randall: *Conflict Sociology*, Academic Press, Inc., New York, 1975.

————: *The Credential Society: A Historical Sociology of Education and Stratification*, Academic Press, Inc., New York, 1979.

Comte, Auguste: *Positive Philosophy*, translated by Harriet Martineau, C. Blanchard Company, New York, 1855.

Concepcion, Mercedes: "Philippines," *Studies in Family Planning*, 4:114–116, April 1973.

Condon, Edward U.: "UFO's I Have Found and Lost," *Bulletin of the Atomic Scientists*, 35:6–8, December 1969.

Conger, Rance D.: "Social Control and Social Learning Models of Delinquent Behavior: A Synthesis," *Criminology*, 14:17–40, May 1976.

Conley, John A., and Russell Smiley: "Drive Licensing Tests as Predictor of Subsequent Violations," *Human Factors*, 18:565–573, December 1976.

Connor, Walter D.: Foreword to Jerry G. Pankhurst and Michael Paul Sacks, *Contemporary Soviet Society: Sociological Perspectives*, Praeger Publishers, Inc., New York, 1980.

Converse, Phillip E.: "Country Differences in Use of Time," in Alexander Szalas (ed.), *Use of Time: Daily Activities of Urban and Suburban Populations in 12 Countries*, Mouton and Company, The Hague, 1972.

Cook, Thomas D.: *Evaluation Studies Review Annual*, Sage Publications, Beverly Hills, Calif., 1978.

Cooley, Charles Horton: "The Theory of Transportation," *Publications of the Americal Economic Association*, vol. 9, no. 3, 1894.

———: *The Nature of Human Nature*, Charles Scribner's Sons, New York, 1902.

———: "A Study of the Early Use of Self Words by a Child," *Psychological Review*, 15:339–357, 1908.

Cooney, Robert, and Helen Michalowski: *The Power of the People: Active Non-Violence in the United States*, Peace Press, Inc., Culver City, Calif., 1977.

Cooper, Clare C.: *Easter Hill Village*, The Free Press, New York, 1975.

Cooper, John L.: *The Anti-Gravity Force: A Study of the Negative Impact of Public Bureaucracy on Society*, Kendall-Hunt Publishing Co., Dubuque, Iowa, 1981.

Copp, James H. (ed.): *Our Changing Rural Society: Perspectives and Trends*, The Department of Publications, State University of Iowa, Iowa City, 1964.

———: "Rural Sociology and Rural Development," *Rural Sociology*, 37:515–538, 1972.

Corcoran, Edward A.: *Dissention in the Soviet Union*, unpublished Ph.D. dissertation, Columbia University, New York, 1977.

Cordasco, Francesco (ed.): *The Puerto Ricans, 1493–1973*, Oceana Publications, Inc., Dobbs Ferry, N.Y., 1973.

Corden, Carol: *Planned Cities: New Towns in England and America*, Sage Publications, Beverly Hills, Calif., 1977.

Cornell, George W.: "Agreement Hailed by Church Scholars," Associated Press, Feb. 6, 1982.

Cory, Christopher T.: "The Prevalence of 'Pseudo-Opinion' in Polls," *Psychology Today*, 13:21ff., November 1979.

Coser, Lewis A.: *The Functions of Social Conflict*, The Free Press, New York, 1956.

———: "Some Functions of Deviant Behavior and Normative Flexibility," *American Journal of Sociology*, 69:172–181, September 1962.

———: *Greedy Institutions: Patterns of Undivided Commitment*, The Free Press, New York, 1974.

Cote, William: "MEA Has Troubles of Its Own," *Kalamazoo Gazette*, Sept. 7, 1977, p. C-4.

Couch, Carl J.: "Collective Behavior: An Examination of Some Stereotypes," *Social Problems*, 15:310–322, Winter 1968.

Council on Environmental Quality and the Department of State: *The Global 2000 Report to the President of the United States: Entering the 21st Century*, Pergamon Press, New York, 1980.

Coursey, Robert D.: "Clothing Doth Make the Man, in the Eye of the Beholder," *Perceptual and Motor Skills*, 36:1259–1264, June 1973.

Cousins, Norman: "Where Violence Begins," *Saturday Review*, 37:22–25, January 1954.

Crampton, C. Gregory: *The Zuñis of Cibola*, University of Utah Press, Salt Lake City, 1977.

Crane, John A.: *The Evaluation of Social Policies*, Kluwer-Nijhoff Publishing, Boston, 1982.

Crittenden, Ann: "Foreign Aid," *The New York Times Magazine*, June 6, 1982, p. 66ff.

Crosbie, Paul V. (ed.): *Interaction in Small Groups*, The Macmillan Company, New York, 1975.

Crosby, Faye, and Linda Nyquist: Research reported in *Psychology Today*, 13:27, March 1980.

Cue, Renaldo A., and Robert L. Bach: "The Return of the Clandestine Worker and the End of the Golden Exile: Recent Mexican and Cuban Immigration in the United States," paper presented at Conference on the New Immigration, Smithsonian Institution, Washington, Sept. 15–17, 1976.

Cullen, John B., and Shelley M. Novick: "The Davis-Moore Theory of Stratification: A Further Examination and Extension," *American Journal of Sociology*, 84:1424-1437, May 1979.

Currie, Robert: *Methodism Divided: A Study in the Sociology of Ecumenicalism*, Faber & Faber, Ltd., London, 1968.

Curtis, Patricia: "Our Pets, Ourselves," *Psychology Today*, 16:66–67, August 1982.

Curtis, Richard F., and Elton F. Jackson: *Inequality in American Communities*, Academic Press, Inc. New York, 1977.

Curtis, Russell L., Jr., and Louis A. Zurcher, Jr.: "Voluntary Associations and the Social Integration of the Poor," *Social Problems*, 18:339–357, Winter 1971.

Curvin, Robert, and Bruce Porter: *Blackout Looting*, Gardner Press, Inc., New York, 1979.

Cushing, Frank H.: *My Adventures in Zuñi (1882–1883)*, American West Publishing Co., Palo Alto, Calif., 1790.

Dadrian, Vahakan: "Factors of Anger and Aggression in Genocide," *Journal of Human Relations*, 19:394–417, Fall 1971.

———: "A Typology of Genocide," *International Review of Modern Sociology*, 5:201–212, Autumn 1975.

Dahl, Robert A.: "A Critique of the Ruling Elite Model," *American Political Science Review*, 52:463–469, June 1958.

———: *Who Governs?* Yale University Press, New Haven, Conn., 1961.

———: *Modern Political Analysis*, Prentice-Hall, Inc., Englewood Cliffs, N.J., 1976.

Dahrendorf, Ralf: "Conflict Groups, Group Conflicts and Social Change," in *Class and Industrial Society*, Stanford University Press, Stanford, Calif., 1959, p. 202–223.

———: "Towards a Theory of Social Conflict," in Amitai Etzioni and Eve Etzioni (eds.), *Social Change*, Basic Books, Inc., Publishers, New York, 1964, pp. 100–123.

Dai, Bingham: "Obsessive-Compulsive Disorders in Chinese Culture," *Social Problems*, 4:313–321, 1957.

Daly, Herman E. (ed.): *Toward a Steady-State Economy*, W. H. Freeman and Company, San Francisco, 1973.

Daniels, Lee A.: "In Defense of Busing," *The New York Times Magazine*, April 17, 1983, pp. 34ff.

Danoff, Michael N.: *Evaluation of the Impact of ESEA Title VII Spanish/English Bilingual Education Program: Overview of Study and Findings*, prepared for U.S. Office of Education by American Institutes for Research, Palo Alto, Calif., March 1978.

Darwin, Charles: *On the Origin of Species* (1859), (introduction by Ernst Mayr), Harvard University Press, Cambridge, Mass., 1964.

David, Deborah S., and Robert Brannon: *The Forty-Nine Percent Majority: The Male Sex Role*, Addison-Wesley Publishing Company, Inc., Reading, Mass., 1976.

Davies, Christie: "Crime, Bureaucracy, and Equality," *Policy Review*, 23:89–105, Winter 1983; reprinted in *Current*, 251:35–46, March/April 1983.

Davies, James C.: "Toward a Theory of Revolution," *American Sociological Review*, 27:5–19, February 1962.

Davis, Alan G., and Philip M. Strong: "Working Without a Net: The Bachelor as a Social Problem," *Sociological Review*, 25:109–120, February 1977.

Davis, Cary: "The Future Racial Composition of the United States," *Intercom* (Population Reference Bureau), 10:8–10, September/October 1982.

Davis, F. James: *Minority-Dominant Relations: A Sociological Analysis*, AHM Publishing Corporation, Arlington Heights, Ill., 1978.

Davis, George, and Glegg Watson: *Black Life in Corporate America: Swimming in the Mainstream*, Anchor Books, Doubleday & Company, Inc., Garden City, N.Y., 1982.

Davis, Keith: *Human Relations at Work*, McGraw-Hill Book Company, New York, 1972.

Davis, Kingsley: *Human Society*, The Macmillan Company, New York, 1937.

——— and Wilbert E. Moore: "Some Principles of Stratification," *American Sociological Review*, 10:242–249, April 1945.

Davis, Peter: *Hometown*, Simon and Schuster, New York, 1981.

Davis, Shelton H.: *Victims of the Miracle: Development and the Indians of Brazil*, Cambridge University Press, New York, 1977.

Dawson, Carl, and W. E. Gettys: *Introduction to Sociology*, The Ronald Press Company, New York, 1934, 1948.

Deaux, Kay, and Tim Enswiller: "Explanation of Successful Performance in Sex-linked Tasks: What Is Skill for the Male Is Luck for the Female," *Journal of Personality and Social Psychology*, 29:80–85, January 1974.

Deckard, Sinclair: *The Woman's Movement*, Harper & Row, Publishers, Inc., New York, 1979.

Dee, William L. J.: "The Social Effect of a Public Housing Project on the Immediate Community," in Meyer Weinberg and Oscar E. Shabat (eds.), *Society and Man*, Prentice-Hall, Inc., Englewood Cliffs, N.J., 1956, pp. 329–339.

DeFronzo, James: "Embourgeoisement in Indianapolis," *Social Problems*, 21:260–283, Fall 1973.

Deloria, Vine, Jr.: *Custer Died for Your Sins: An Indian Manifesto*, The Macmillan Company, New York, 1970.

———: "Native Americans: The American Indian Today," *Annals of American Academy of Political and Social Science*, 454:139–149, March 1981.

Dempewolff, J. A.: "Some Correlates of Feminism," *Psychological Reports*, 34:671–676, April 1974.

DeVoss, David: "The Reggae Message," *Human Behavior*, 6:65–70, January 1977.

Dewey, Richard: "The Rural-Urban Continuum: Real but Relatively Unimportant," *American Journal of Sociology*, 66:60–66, July 1960.

Dichter, Ernest: *Motivating Human Behavior*, McGraw-Hill Book Company, New York, 1971.

Dickson, Stewart: "Class Attitudes to Dental Treatment," *British Journal of Sociology*, 19:206–211, June 1968.

Dittes, James E., and Harold H. Kelley: "Effects of Different Conditions of Acceptance upon Conformity to Group Norms," *Journal of Abnormal and Social Psychology*, 53:100–107, July 1956.

Djilas, Milovan: *The New Class*, Frederick A. Praeger, Inc., New York, 1957.

Dobson, Richard B.: "Mobility and Stratification in the Soviet Union," in Alex Inkeles, James Coleman, and Neil Smelser (eds.), *Annual Review of Sociology, 1977*, Annual Reviews, Inc., Palo Alto, Calif., 1978.

Dollard, John, et al.: *Frustration and Aggression*, Yale University Press, New Haven, Conn., 1939.

Domes, Jurgen: "New Policies in the Communes: Notes on Rural Societal Structures in China, 1976–1981," *Journal of Asian Studies*, 41:253–267, February 1982.

Domhoff, G. William: *The Higher Circles*, Random House, Inc., New York, 1970.

———: *Who Really Rules: New Haven and Community Power Reexamined*, Transaction Books, New Brunswick, N.J., 1978.

——— (ed.): *Power Structure Research*, Sage Publications, Beverly Hills, Calif., 1980.

Dorn, H. F. M.: "Tobacco Consumption and Mortality from Cancer and Other Diseases," *Public Health Reports*, 74:581–593, 1959.

Douglas, Jack D. (ed.): *The Relevance of Sociology*, Appleton Centry Crofts, New York, 1970.

Douglas, John H., and Julie Ann Melter: "Record Breaking Women," *Science News*, 112:172–174, Sept. 10, 1977.

Dowdy, Edwin: "Aspects of Tokugawa Bureaucracy and Modernization," *Australian Journal of Politics and History*, 16:375–389, December 1970.

Downes, Bryan T.: "The Social Characteristics of Riot Cities: A Comparative Study," *Social Science Quarterly*, 49:504–520, December 1968.

Downs, Anthony: *Who Are the Urban Poor?* Committee for Economic Development, New York, 1977.

Doyle, Richard: *The Rape of the Male*, Poor Richard's Press, St. Paul, Minn., 1970.

Draper, Lt. Theodore: "The Psychology of Surrender," *Atlantic Monthly*, 176:62–65, August 1945.

Dresen, Sheila: "Adjusting to Single Parenting," *American Journal of Nursing*, 76:1286–1289, August 1976.

Drinan, Robert F.: "Education: To Cherish?" *New York Times*, February 27, 1982, sec. 4, p. 19.

Drucker, Peter: "Pension Fund Socialism," *The Public Interest*, 42:3–15, Winter 1976.

———: "Working Women: Unmaking the 19th Century," *Wall Street Journal*, July 6, 1981, p. 12.

Druckman, Daniel, et al.: *Nonverbal Communication: Synthesis, Theory and Research*, Sage Publications, Beverly Hills, Calif., 1982.

Duberman, Lucile: *Social Inequality: Classes and Caste in America*, Harper & Row, Publishers, Inc., New York, 1976.

Dubois, Cora: *The People of Alor*, The University of Minnesota Press, Minneapolis, 1944.

Duncan, Beverly, and Otis D. Duncan: *Sex Typing and Social Roles*, Academic Press, Inc., New York, 1978.

Duncan, David Douglas: "In the Middle of an Indian Massacre," *Life*, Oct. 6, 1947, pp. 6ff.

Duncan, Greg, and James Morgan: Research reported in "Divorced Mothers, Unite," *Psychology Today*, 16:73, November 1982.

Duncan, Otis D.: "Indicators of Sex Typing: Traditional, Egalitarian, Situational and Ideological Responses," *American Journal of Sociology*, 85:25–60, September 1980.

Duncan, R. Paul, and Carolyn Cummings Perucci: "Dual Occupation Families and Migration," *American Sociological Review*, 41:252–261, April 1976.

Dunphy, Dexter C.: *The Primary Group: A Handbook for Analysis and Field Research*, Appleton Century Crofts, New York, 1972.

Durant, Will: *The Age of Faith*, Simon and Schuster, New York, 1950.

Durkheim, Émile: *On the Division of Labor* (1893), trans. by George Simpson, The Free Press, New York, 1960.

———: *Le Suicide: Etude de Sociologie* (1897), trans. by J. A. Spaulding and G. Simpson, the Free Press, New York, 1951.

———: *The Elementary Forms of Religious Life: A Study of Religious Sociology* (1912), trans. by J. W. Swan, The Free Press, New York, 1947.

Dutton, Diana B.: "Low Use of Health Services by the Poor," *American Sociological Review*, 43:348–367, June 1978.

Dynes, Russell R.: *Organized Behavior in Disaster*, Heath Lexington Books, Lexington, Mass., 1970.

Easterlin, Richard J.: "Does Money Buy Happiness?" *The Public Interest*, 30:3–11, Winter 1973.

———: *Birth and Fortune: The Impact of Numbers on*

Personal Welfare, Basic Books, Inc., Publishers, New York, 1980.

Eastland, Terry: "In Defense of Religious America," *Commentary*, 71:39–45, June 1981.

Ebenstein, William, and Edwin Fogelman: *Today's Isms*, 8th ed., Prentice-Hall, Inc., Englewood Cliffs, N.J., 1980.

Eckholm, Eric: *Planning for the Future: Forestry and Human Needs*, Worldwatch Institute, Washington, 1979.

Edgerton, Robert B.: *Deviance: A Cross-Cultural Perspective*, Cummings Publishing Company, Menlo Park, Calif., 1976.

Edwards, Allen A.: "Types of Rural Communities," in Marvin B. Sussman (ed.), *Community Structure and Analysis*, Thomas Y. Crowell Company, New York, 1959.

Edwards, John N., and Alan Booth: "Crowding and Human Sexual Behavior," *Social Forces*, 55:791–808, March 1977.

Edwards, Laura E., et al.: "Adolescent Pregnancy Prevention Services in High School Clinics," *Family Planning Services*, 12:6–14, January/February 1890.

Edwards, Lyford P.: *The Natural History of Revolution*, The University of Chicago Press, Chicago, 1927.

Efron, Edith: "So This Is Adversary Journalism," *TV Guide*, Jan. 18, 1975, pp. 5–6.

Eggan, Dorothy: "The General Problem of Hopi Adjustment," *American Anthropologist*, 45:357–373, July 1943.

Erlich, Paul, and Anne H. Ehrlich: *Population, Resources, Environment: Issues in Human Ecology*, Prentice-Hall, Inc., Englewood Cliffs, N.J., 1970.

Eisenstein, Zillah: "Constructing a Theory of Capitalist Patriarchy and Socialist Feminism," *The Insurgent Sociologist*, Summer 1977, pp. 3–17.

Ekman, Paul, and Wallace V. Friesen: "Detecting Deception from the Body or Face," *Journal of Personality and Social Psychology*, 19:288–297, March 1974.

Ellis, Evelyn: "Social Psychological Correlates of Upward Social Mobility among Unmarried Career Women," *American Sociological Review*, 17:588–563, October 1952.

Elwin, Varrier: *The Biaga*, John Murray (Publishers), Ltd., London, 1939.

Epps, Edgar G.: "Minority Children: Desegregation, Self-Evaluation, and Achievement Orientation," in Willis D. Hawley (ed.), *Effective School Desegregation: Equity, Quality and Feasibility*, Sage Publications, Beverly Hills, Calif., 1981, pp. 85–106.

Erber, Ernest (ed.): *Urban Planning in Transition*, Grossman Publishers, New York, 1970.

Erikson, Erik: *Childhood and Society*, 2nd ed., W. W. Norton & Company, Inc., New York, 1963.

———: *Youth and Crisis*, W. W. Norton & Company, Inc., New York, 1968.

Erikson, Kai T.: *Wayward Puritans: A Study in the Sociology of Deviance*, John Wiley & Sons, Inc., New York, 1966.

———: *Everything in Its Path: Destruction of Community in the Buffalo Creek Flood*, Simon & Schuster, Inc., New York, 1976.

Erskine, Hazel: "The Polls: Pacifism and the Generation Gap," *Public Opinion Quarterly*, 36:616–627, Winter 1972–1973.

Etzioni, Amitai: Quoted in John Leo, "The Hollowing of America," *Time*, 118:85, Dec. 20, 1982.

Eulau, Hans: "Identification with Class and Political Role Behavior," *Public Opinion Quarterly*, 20:515–529, Fall 1956.

Evans, Sue L., et al.: "Failure to Thrive: A Study of 45 Children and Their Families," *Journal of Child Psychiatry*, 11:440–457, July 1972.

Fanfani, Amintore: *Catholicism, Protestantism and Capitalism*, Sheed & Ward, Inc., New York, 1955.

Farb, Peter: *Man's Rise to Civilization as Shown by the American Indians from Primeval Times to the Coming of the Industrial State*, E. P. Dutton, Inc., New York, 1968.

Farley, Reynolds: "The Changing Distribution of Negroes Within Metropolitan Areas: The Emergence of Black Suburbs," *American Journal of Sociology*, 75:512–529, January 1970.

———, Toni Richards, and Clarence Wurdock: "School Desegregation and White Flight: An Investigation of Competing Models and Their Discrepant Findings," *Sociology of Education*, 53:123–139, July 1980.

Farnsworth, Beatrice: *Aleksandra Killontai: Socialism, Feminism, and the Bolshevik Revolution*, Stanford University Press, Stanford, Calif., 1980.

Farrell, Warren: *The Liberated Male: Beyond Masculinity: Freeing Men and Their Relationship With Women*, Random House, Inc., New York, 1975.

Farrell, William C.: " 'New Towns' Facing Growing

Pains," *The New York Times*, June 13, 1976, p. 26.

Fast, Julius: *Body Language*, M. Evans and Company, Philadelphia; distribution in association with J. B. Lippincott Company, Philadelphia, 1970.

Feagin, Joe R.: *Racial and Ethnic Relations*, Prentice-Hall, Inc., Englewood Cliffs, N.J., 1978.

Featherman, David L., and Robert M. Hauser: "Sexual Inequalities and Socioeconomic Achievement in the United States, 1962–1973," *American Sociological Review*, 41:462–483, June 1976.

Feldstein, Martin S.: "The U.S. Saves Too Little," *Society*, 14:76–78, March/April 1977.

———: "The Retreat From Keynesian Economics," *The Public Interest*, 64:92–105, Summer 1981.

Ferencz, B. B.: "When One Person's Terrorist Is Another Person's Hero,"*Human Rights*, 9:38–42, Summer 1981.

Ferman, Louis A.: Quoted in "A New Layer of Structural Unemployment," *Business Week*, Nov. 14, 1977, p. 149.

Fernandez, Roberto M., and Jane C. Kulik: "A Multilevel Model of Life Satisfaction: Effects of Individual Characteristics and Neighborhood Composition," *American Sociological Review*, 46:840–850, December 1981.

Fernandez, Ronald (ed.): *The Future as a Social Problem: A Reader*, Goodyear Publishing Company, Santa Monica, Calif. 1977.

Ferree, Myra Marx: "Working-Class Jobs: Housework and Paid Work as Sources of Satisfaction," *Social Problems*, 23:431–441, April 1976.

Ferrell, Mary Zey, O. C. Ferrell, and Quentin Jenkins: "Social Power in a Rural Community," *Growth and Change*, 4:3–6, April 1973.

Feshbach, Murray: "Between the Lines of the 1979 Soviet Census," *Problems of Communism*, 31:27–37, January/February 1982.

Festinger, L., A. Pipestone, and T. Newcomb: "Some Consequences of Deindividuation in a Group," *Journal of Abnormal and Social Psychology*, 47:382–389, April 1952.

Fetterman, John: *Stinking Creek: A Portait of a Small Community in Appalachia*, E. P. Dutton & Co., Inc., New York, 1970.

Feuer, Lewis S.: "The Risk is 'Juvenocracy'," *The New York Times Magazine*, Sept. 18, 1966, pp. 56ff.

Fierabend, Ivo, and Rosalind L. Fierabend: "Coerciveness and Change: Cross-national Trends," *American Behavioral Scientist*, 15:911–927, July 1927.

Finkelhor, David, Richard J. Gelles, Gerald T. Hotaling, and Murray A. Straus (eds.): *The Dark Side of Families: Current Family Violence Research*, Sage Publications, Beverly Hills, Calif., 1983.

Finnie, William C.: Cited in research note in *Society*, January 1974, p. 11.

First, Elsa: Review of Peter Tompkins and Christopher Bird, "The Secret Life of Plants," *The New York Times Book Review*, Dec. 30, 1973, p. 15.

Fischer, Claude S.: "On Urban Alienation and Anomie: Powerlessness and Social Isolation," *American Sociological Review*," 38:311–326, June 1973.

———: *The Urban Experience*, Harcourt Brace Jovanovich, Inc., New York, 1976.

———: "The Public and Private Worlds of City Life," *American Sociological Review*, 46:306–316, June 1981.

——— et al.: *Networks and Places: Social Relations in the Urban Setting*, The Free Press, New York, 1977.

Fischer-Galati, Stephen: "Facist-Communist Convergence," *Society*, 18:30–31, May/June, 1981.

Fish, John Hall: *Black Power–White Control: The Struggle of the Woodlawn Organization in Chicago*, Princeton University Press, Princeton, N.J., 1973.

Fisher, B. Aubrey: *Small-Group Decision Making: Communication and the Group Process*, McGraw-Hill Book Company, New York, 1980.

Fisher, Seymour, and Roger P. Greenberg: *The Scientific Credibility of Freud's Theories and Therapy*, Basic Books, Inc., Publishers, New York, 1977.

Fisk, Norman M.: Quoted in "The Ultimate Proof of Sex Discrimination," *Business Week*, Jan. 25, 1982, p. 12.

Fleetwood, Blake: "The New Elite and an Urban Renaissance," *The New York Times Magazine*, Jan. 14, 1979, pp. 16ff.

Flugel, J. C.: *The Psychology of Clothes*, The Hogarth Press, Ltd., London, 1930.

Flynn, James R.: "Now the Great Augmentation of the American I.Q.," *Nature*, 301:655, Feb. 24, 1983.

Fogelson, Robert E.: "Violence as Protest," in Robert H. Connery (ed.), *Urban Riots: Violence and Social Change*, Random House, Inc., New York, 1969.

Foley, Donald L.: "Institutional and Contextual

Factors Affecting Housing Choices of Minority Residents," in Amos H. Hawley and V. P. Rock (eds.), *Segregation in Residential Areas: Papers on Racial and Socioeconomic Factors in Choice of Housing*, National Academy of Sciences, Washington, 1973, pp. 85–147.

Ford, Brian J.: *Patterns of Sex: The Mating Urge and Our Sexual Future*, St. Martin's Press, Inc., New York, 1980.

Ford, Clellan S., and Frank A. Beach: *Patterns of Sexual Behavior*, Harper & Row, Publishers, Inc., New York, 1951.

Foreman, Grant: *Indian Removal*, University of Oklahoma Press, Norman, 1932.

Foreman, Paul B.: "Panic Theory," *Sociology and Social Research*, 37:295–304, May/June 1953.

Forgey, Donald G.: "The Institution of *Berdache* Among the North American Plains Indians," *The Journal of Sex Research*, 11:1–15, February 1975.

Fortune, R. F.: *The Sorcerers of Dobu*, E. P. Dutton & Co., Inc., New York, 1932.

Fosberg, Lacey: "The Make-Believe World of Teen-Aged Maternity," *The New York Times Magazine*, Aug. 7, 1977, pp. 29ff.

Fossum, Donna: "Women in the Legal Profession: A Progress Report," *American Bar Association Journal*, 67:579–581, May 1981.

Fowlkes, Martha R.: *Behind Every Successful Man: Wives of Medicine's Academe*, Columbia University Press, New York, 1981.

Fox, Richard G.: "The XYY Offender: A Modern Myth," *Journal of Criminal Law, Criminology and Police Science*, 62:59–73, March 1971.

Frazier, Kendrick: "Cattle Mutilations in New Mexico," *Skeptical Inquirer*, 4:10–11, Fall 1979.

Frederichs, Robert W.: *A Sociology of Sociology*, The Free Press, New York, 1970.

Frederick, Otto: "The Computer Moves In," *Time*, 119:14–24, Jan. 3, 1983.

Freedman, Jonathan L.: *Crowding and Behavior*, The Viking Press, Inc., New York, 1975.

Freeman, M. D. A.: *Violence in the Home*, Saxon House, Westmead, England, 1979.

Freeman, Richard B.: "Black Economic Progress after 1964: Who Has Gained and Why?" in Sherwin Rosen (ed.), *Studies in Labor Markets*, The National Bureau of Economic Research, The University of Chicago Press, Chicago, 1981, pp. 247–294.

Freilich, Morris, and Lewis A. Coser: "Structural

Imbalances of Gratification: The Case of the Caribbean Mating System," *British Journal of Sociology*, 12:1–19, March 1972.

Freud, Sigmund: *Group Psychology and the Analysis of the Ego*, The Hogarth press, Ltd., London, 1922.

Friday, Paul C., and Gerald Hage: "Youth Crime in Postindustrial Societies," *Criminology*, 14:347–368, November 1976.

Friedan, Betty: *The Feminine Mystique*, W. W. Norton & Company, Inc., New York, 1963.

Friedmann, John: *Retracking America: A Theory of Transitional Planning*, Anchor Books, Doubleday & Company, Inc., Garden City, N.Y., 1973.

Friedrichs, Jurgen, and H. Ludke: *Participant Observation: Theory and Practice*, Lexington Books, Lexington, Mass., 1975.

Fromm, Erich: "Individual and Social Origins of Neurosis," *American Sociological Review*, 9:380–384, 1944.

———: *The Art of Loving*, Harper & Row, Publishers, Inc., New York, 1956.

Fuerst, J. S.: "Class, Family and Housing," *Society*, November 1974, pp. 48–53.

Fuguitt, Glenn V., and James J. Zuiches: "Residential Preference and Population Distribution," *Demography*, 12:491–504, August 1975.

Furstenberg, Frank F., Jr.: *Unplanned Parenthood: The Social Consequences of Teen-Age Parenthood*, The Free Press, New York, 1976.

Galbraith, John Kenneth: *The Nature of Mass Poverty*, Harvard University Press, Cambridge, Mass., 1978.

Gallese, Liz Roman: "Marriage by Long Distance," *Wall Street Journal*, May 4, 1978, pp. 1ff.

Gamson, William A.: *The Strategy of Social Protest*, The Dorsey Press, Homewood, Ill., 1975.

Gandhi, Raj S.: "From Caste to Class in Indian Society," *Humboldt Journal of Social Relations*, 7:1–14, Summer 1980.

Gans, Herbert J.: "The Positive Functions of Poverty," *American Journal of Sociology*, 78:275–289, September 1972.

Gardner, Hugh: "Dropping into Utopia," *Human Behavior*, March 1978, pp. 43–47.

Gardner, Martin: *Fads and Fallacies in the Name of Science*, Dover Publications, Inc., New York, 1957.

———: *Science: Good, Bad and Bogus*, Prometheus Books, Buffalo, N.Y., 1981.

Gardner, R. Allen, and Beatrice T. Gardner:

"Teaching Sign Language to a Chimpanzee," *Science*, 165:664–672, August 15, 1969.

Garino, David P.: "They Write a Lot More Than a Ticket for Drunken Driving," *Wall Street Journal*, July 12, 1982, p. 1.

Garrow, David J.: *Protest at Selma: Martin Luther King and the Voting Rights Act of 1965*, Yale University Press, New Haven, Conn., 1978.

Gastil, Raymond D.: "The Comparative Survey of Freedom," *Freedom at Issue*, 84:3–14, January/February 1982.

Gelles, Richard: *The Violent Home*, Sage Publications, Beverly Hills, Calif., 1972.

———: *Family Violence*, Sage Publications, Beverly Hills, Calif., 1979.

Gellhorn, Walter: *Ombudsmen and Others: Citizens' Protectors in Nine Countries*, Harvard University Press, Cambridge, Mass., 1967.

George, Jean Craighead: "Consider the Ones Who Lead," *International Wildlife*, September/October 1979, pp. 38–45.

George, Linda K.: *Role Transitions in Later Life*, Brooks/Cole Publishing Company, Monterey, Calif., 1980.

George, Susan: *The Real Reasons for World Hunger*, Allanheld, Osmun and Company, Montclair, N.J., 1977.

Gershman, Carl: "A Matter of Class," *The New York Times Magazine*, Oct. 5, 1980, pp. 22ff., reprinted in *Current*, 227:20–32, November 1980.

Gerson, Menachem: *Family, Women, and Socialization in the Kibbutz*, Lexington Books, Lexington, Mass., 1978.

Geschwender, James A.: "Explorations in the Theory of Social Movements," *Social Forces*, 47:127–135, December 1968.

Geyer, R. Felix: *Alienation Theories: A General Systems Approach*, Pergamon Press, New York, 1980.

Gil, David G.: *Unraveling Social Policy Analysis and Political Action Towards Social Equality*, Schenkman Publishing Co., Inc., Cambridge, Mass., 1973.

Gilbert, Lucia A., et al.: "Feminine and Masculine Dimensions of the Typical, Desirable, and Ideal Man and Woman," *Sex Roles*, 4:76–78, October 1978.

Gilder, George: *Sexual Suicide*, Quadrangle Books, Inc., New York, 1973.

———: "Moral Sources of Capitalism," *Society*, 18:24–27, September/October, 1981.

Gillin, John P.: *The Ways of Men*, Appleton-Century-Crofts, Inc., New York, 1948.

Gist, Noel P., and Sylvia Fleis Fava: *Urban Society*, Harper & Row, Publishers, Inc., New York, 1974.

Glazer, Nathan: "Blacks and Ethnic Group: The Difference and the Political Difference It Makes," *Social Problems*, 18:444–461, Spring 1971.

———: "America's Race Paradox," in Peter I. Rose (ed.), *Nation of Nations*, Random House, Inc., New York, 1972, pp. 165–180.

———: "Should Judges Administer Social Services?" *The Public Interest*, 50:64–80, Winter 1978.

———: "Towards a Self-Service Society?" *The Public Interest*, 70:66–90, Winter 1983.

——— and Daniel P. Moynihan: "The Culture of Poverty: The View from New York City," in Alan Winter (ed.), *The Poor: A Culture of Poverty or a Poverty of Culture?* Wm. B. Eerdmans Publishing Co., Grand Rapids, Mich., 1971, pp. 20–48.

Glenn, Norval, and Sara S. McLanahan: "Children and Marital Happiness: A Further Specification of the Relationship," *Journal of Marriage and the Family*, 44:63–72, February 1982.

Glick, Paul C., and Arthur J. Norton: "Marrying, Divorcing, and Living Together in the U.S. Today," *Population Bulletin*, 32, no. 5, 1979, pp. 36–37.

Glock, Charles Y., and Robert N. Bellah (eds.): *The New Religious Consciousness*, University of California Press, Berkeley, 1976.

Glueck, Sheldon, and Eleanor Glueck: *Predicting Juvenile Delinquency and Crime*, Harvard University Press, Cambridge, Mass., 1959.

Goertzel, Ted G.: "Class in America: Qualitative Distinctions and Quantitative Data," *Qualitative Sociology*, 1:53–76, January 1979.

Goffman, Erving: *Presentation of Self in Everyday Life*, Social Science Research Center, University of Edinburgh, 1956; reprinted by Anchor Books, Doubleday & Company, Inc., Garden City, N.Y., 1959.

———: *"Asylums*, Anchor Books, Doubleday & Company, Inc., Garden City, N.Y., 1961.

———: *Where the Action Is: Three Essays*, Doubleday & Company, Inc., Garden City, N.Y., 1967.

———: *Forms of Talk*, University of Pennsylvania Press, Philadelphia, 1981.

Gold, Martin: *Delinquent Behavior in an American*

City, Brooks/Cole Publishing Company, Monterey, Calif., 1970.

Goldberg, Evelyn L.: "Crowd Hysteria In a Junior High School," *Journal of School Health,* 43:362–365, June 1973.

Goldberg, Herb: *The Hazards of Being Male: Surviving the Myth of Male Privilege,* New American Library, Inc., New York, 1976.

Goldberg, Stephen: *The Inevitability of Patriarchy,* William Morrow & Company, Inc., New York, 1973.

Goldman, Marshall I.: *The Spoils of Progress: Pollution in the Soviet Union,* The M.I.T. Press, Cambridge, Mass., 1972.

Goldstone, Jack A.: "The Weakness of Organization: A New Look at Gamson's 'The Strategy of Social Protest'," *American Journal of Sociology,* 85:1017–1042, March 1980.

Goldthorpe, John H., and David Lockwood: "Affluence and the British Class Structure," *Sociological Review (New Series),* 11:133–163, July 1963.

Goleman, Daniel: "We Are Breaking the Silence About Death," *Psychology Today,* September 1976, pp. 44–47ff.

Gonzalez, Nanci L.: "The Organization of Work in China's New Communes," *Science,* 218:898–903, September 1982.

Goodall, Jane (Baroness Jane Van Lawick): "Chimp Killings: Is It the Man in Them?" *Science News,* 113:276, April 1978.

Goode, William J.: *World Revolution and Family Patterns,* The Free Press, New York, 1963.

Goodwin, Leonard: *Do the Poor Want to Work? A Social Psychological Study of Work Orientation,* The Brookings Institution, Washington, 1972.

Gordon, Leonid A., and Eduard V. Klopov: *Man After Work,* trans. by John Bushness and Kristine Bushness, Progress Publishers, Moscow, USSR.,1975.

Gordon, Milton: *Assimilation in American Life: The Role of Race, Religion and National Origins,* Oxford University Press, New York, 1964.

———: *Human Nature, Class and Ethnicity,* Oxford University Press, New York, 1978.

Gottdiener, Mark: *Planned Sprawl: Private and Public Interests In Suburbia,* Sage Publications, Beverly Hills, Calif., 1977.

Gottlieb, Anne: "Feeble Human Beings," *The New York Times Book Review,* Feb. 21, 1971, pp. 1ff.

Gottschalk, Shimon S.: *Communities and Alternatives: An Exploration of the Limits of Planning,* John Wiley & Sons, Inc., New York, 1975.

Gouldner, Alvin: "Anti-Minotaur: The Myth of a Value-Free Sociology," *Social Problems,* 9:190–213, Winter 1962.

———: "Toward the Radical Reconstruction of Sociology," *Social Policy,* May/June 1970, pp. 18–25.

Gove, Walter J. (ed.): *The Labeling of Deviance: Evaluating a Perspective,* John Wiley & Sons, Inc., New York, 1975.

Grabb, Edward G.: "Working Class Authoritarianism and Tolerance of Outgroups: A Reassessment," *Public Opinion Quarterly,* 43:36–47, Spring 1979

———: "Social Class, Authoritarianism and Racial Contact: Recent Trends," *Sociology and Social Research,* 64:208–220, January 1980.

Graff, Harvey J.: *The Literacy Myth: Literacy and Social Structure in the Nineteenth-Century City,* Academic Press, Inc. New York, 1979.

Grandjean, Burke P.: "An Economic Analysis of the Davis-Moore Theory of Stratification," *Social Forces,* 53:543–552, June 1975.

———: and Frank D. Bean: "The Davis-Moore Theory and Perceptions of Stratification: Some Relevant Evidence," *Social Forces,* 54:166–180, September 1975.

Greeley, Andrew M.: *Religion In the Year 2000,* Sheed & Ward, Inc., New York, 1969.

———: "Intellectuals as an Ethnic Group," *The New York Times Magazine,* July 12, 1970; reprinted in Robert K. Yin (ed.), *Race, Creed, Color, or National Origin,* F. E. Peacock Publishers, Inc., Itaska, Ill., 1973, pp. 113–123.

———: "The Ethnic Miracle," *The Public Interest,* 45:20–36, Fall 1976.

———: *Religion: A Secular Theory,* The Free Press, New York, 1982.

——— and Peter H. Rossi: *The Education of American Catholics,* Aldine Publishing Company, Chicago, 1966.

Green, Richard: "Sexual Identity of 37 Children, Raised by Homosexual or Transsexual Parents," *American Journal of Psychiatry,* 135:692–697, June 1978.

Greenberg, Edward S.: "Black Children, Self-Esteem and the Liberation Movement," *Politics and Society,* 2:293–307, Spring 1972.

Greenberg, Ellen F., and W. Robert Nay: "The

Intergenerational Transmission of Marital Instability Reconsidered," *Journal of Marriage and the Family*, 44:335–347, May 1982.

Greenberg, Joel: "Who Loves You?" *Science News*, 112:139–141, Aug. 17, 1977.

Greenberger, Robert S.: "Firms Prod Managers to Keep Eye on Goal of Equal Employment," *Wall Street Journal*, May 17, 1982, pp. 1ff.

———: "Federal Shift in Hiring Rules Stirs Criticism," *Wall Street Journal*, March 15, 1983, p. 27.

Greenwood, Davydd J.: "Tourism as an Agent of Change: A Spanish Basque Case," *Ethnology*, 11:81–91, January 1972.

Greer, Colin: *The Great School Legend*, Basic Books, Inc., Publishers, New York, 1972.

Greer, Scott, and Ella Kube: "Urbanism and Social Structure: A Los Angeles Study," in Marvin B. Sussman (ed.), *Community Structure and Analysis*, Thomas Y. Crowell Company, New York, 1959.

Gregg, Richard B.: *The Psychology and Strategy of Gandhi's Nonviolent Resistance*, Garland Publishing Company, New York, 1972.

Grier, Eunice, and George Grier: "Discrimination in Housing," *Anti-Defamation League*, New York, 1960.

Griffin, C. W.: *Taming the Last Frontier: A Prescription for the Urban Crisis*, Pitman Publishing Corporation, New York, 1974.

Griffin, John H.: *Black Like Me*, Houghton Mifflin Company, Boston, 1961.

Grinker, Roy R., Jr.: "The Poor Rich: The Children of the Superrich," *American Journal of Psychiatry*, 135:913–916, August 1978.

Gross, Neil: "Some Contributions of Sociology to the Field of Education," in Ronald M. Pavalko (ed.), *Sociology of Education: A Book of Readings*, F. E. Peacock Publishers, Inc., Itaska, Ill., 1976, pp. 19–31.

Gruen, Victor: *The Heart of Our Cities*, Simon & Schuster, Inc., New York, 1964.

Guba, Egon G., and Yvonne S. Lincoln: Effective Evaluation, Jossey-Bass, Inc., San Francisco, 1981.

Guest, Avery M., Barrett A. Lee, and Lynn Staeheli: "Changing Locality Identification in the Metropolis: Seattle: 1920–1978," *American Sociological Review*, 47:543–549, August 1982.

Guhl, A. M.: *Social Behavior of the Domestic Fowl*, Technical Bulletin No. 73, Kansas Agricultural Experiment Station, Manhattan, Kan., 1953.

Guillen, Michael A.: "U.S. Metric Conversion: Rough Road Ahead," *Science News*, 112:42–43, July 16, 1977.

Gundlach, James H., P. Nelson Reid, and Alden E. Roberts: "Migration, Labor Mobility and Relocation Assistance: The Case of the American Indian," *Social Service Review*, 51:464–473, September 1979.

Gurney, Joan Neff, and Kathleen J. Tierney: "Relative Deprivation and Social Movements: A Critical Look at 20 years of Theory and Research," *Sociological Quarterly*, 23:33–47, Winter 1982.

Guttentag, Marcia, and Helen Bray: *Undoing Sex Stereotypes*, McGraw-Hill Book Company, New York, 1976.

——— et al. (eds.): *The Mental Health of Women*, Academic Press, Inc., New York, 1980.

Hacket, Andrew: "Two New Classes or None," in B. Bruce Biggs (ed.), *The New Class*, Transaction Books, New Brunswick, N.J., 1979, pp. 155–168.

Hackett, Herbert: "The Flying Sauce," *Sociology and Social Research*, 32:869–873, May/June 1948.

Hadden, Jeffrey K.: *The Gathering Storm in the Churches*, Doubleday & Company, Inc., Garden City, N.Y., 1969.

——— and Charles E. Swann: *Prime-Time Preachers: The Rising Power of Fundamentalism*, Addison-Wesley Publishing Company, Inc., Reading, Mass., 1981.

Hall, Florence Turnbull, and Marguerite Paulson Schroeder: "Effects of Family and Housing Characteristics on the Time Spent on Household Tasks," *Journal of Home Economics*, 62:23–29, January 1970.

Hall, Raymond L.: *Black Separatism in the United States*, University Press of New England, Hanover, N.H., 1978.

Ham, Eviyoung: "Urbanization and Asian Lifestyles," *The Annals of the American Academy of Political and Social Science*, 405:104–113, January 1973.

Hamblin, Robert L., R. Brooke Jacobsen, and Jerry L. Miller: *A Mathematical Theory of Social Change*, John Wiley & Sons, Inc., New York, 1973.

Hamilton, Charles V.: "The Nationalist vs. the Integrationist," *New York Times*, October 1, 1972, pp. 37ff.

Hamilton, Richard: "Liberal Intelligentsia and White Backlash," in Irving Howe (ed.), *The World of the Blue Collar Worker*, Quadrangle Books, Inc., New York, 1972.

Haney, C. Allen, Robert Michielutte, Clark E. Vincent, and Carl M. Cochrane: "The Value Stretch Hypothesis: Family Size in a Black Population," *Social Problems*, 21:206–219, Fall 1973.

Haney, Craig, Curtis Banks, and Philip Zimbardo: "Interpersonal Dynamics in a Simulated Prison," *International Journal of Criminology and Penology*, 1:69–97, February 1973.

Hansen, W. Lee, et al.: "Schooling and Earnings of Low Achievers," *American Economic Review*, 60:409–418, June 1970.

Hanson, David J.: "A Note on Sociology and Infrahuman Culture," *International Journal of Contemporary Sociology*, 10:121–124, June 1973.

Harbison, Georgia: "Reforming Boston's Schools," *Time*, 121:72, March 7, 1983.

Hardin, Garrett: *Nature and Man's Fate*, Rinehart & Company, Inc., New York, 1959.

Hare, A. Paul, and Herbert H. Blumberg (eds.): *Non-Violent Direct Action; American Cases; Social-Psychological Analyses*, Corpus Books, Washington, 1968.

Hareven, Tamara K. (ed.): *Transitions: The Family and the Life Course in Historical Perspective*, Academic Press, Inc., New York, 1978.

Harlow, Harry F.: Research reviewed in "Love among the Monkeys," *Science News*, 108:389–390, Dec. 20, 1975.

——— and Margaret K. Harlow: "A Study of Animal Affection," *Natural History*, 70:48–55, 1961.

Harmon, Harry H., et al.: *Evaluation of Driver Education Programs*, Educational Testing Service, Princeton, N.J., 1969.

Harris, C. C.: *The Sociological Enterprise: A Discussion of Fundamental Concepts*, St. Martin's Press, Inc., New York, 1980.

Harris, C. D., and E. L. Ullman: "The Nature of Cities," *Annals of the American Academy of Political and Social Science*, 242:7–17, November 1945.

Harris, Diana K., and William E. Cole: *Sociology of Aging*, Houghton Mifflin Company, Boston, 1980.

Harris, Louis: "A Life Poll," *Life*,, 68:102, Jan. 9, 1970.

Harris, Marvin: "What Goes Up May Stay Up," *Natural History*, 81:18–25, January 1973.

———: Quoted in "A Conversation with Carol Tavris," *Psychology Today*, 8:61–69, January 1975.

Harris, Richard J.: "Rewards of Migration for Income Change and Income Attainment, 1968–73," *Social Science Quarterly*, 62:275–292, June 1981.

Hart, John, and Diane Richardson: *The Theory and Practice of Homosexuality*, Routledge and Kegan Paul, Boston, 1981.

Hartley, Shirley Foster: "Our Growing Problem: Population," *Social Problems*, 21:190–205, Fall 1973.

Hassett, James, and John Houlihan: "Different Jokes for Different Folks," *Psychology Today*, 12:64–71, January 1979.

Hassinger, Edward W.: *The Rural Component in American Society*, The Interstate Printers & Publishers, Inc., Danville, Ill., 1978.

Haub, Carl, and Douglas W. Heiser: *1980 World Population Data Sheet*, Population Reference Bureau, Washington, 1980.

Haug, Marie: "Social Class Measurement: A Methodological Critique," in Gerald W. Thielbar and Saul D. Friedman (ed.), *Issues in Social Inequality*, Little, Brown and Company, Boston, 1972, pp. 423–451.

Haupt, Arthur: "The U.S. and Mexico's Blurring Border," *Intercom* (Population Reference Bureau), 10:1ff., September/October 1982.

Hauser, Philip M.: *Population Perspectives*, Rutgers University Press, New Brunswick, N.J., 1960.

Hauser, Robert M., and David L. Featherman: *Occupations and Social Mobility in the United States*, The University of Wisconsin Press, Madison, 1975.

——— and ———: *The Process of Stratification: Trends and Analysis*, Academic Press, Inc., New York, 1977.

Havelock, Ronald G., and Mary C. Havelock: *Training for Change Agents*, Center for Research on Utilization of Scientific Knowledge, The University of Michigan, Ann Arbor, 1973.

Hawrylyshyn, G.: "No Match for Progress," *International Wildlife*, 6:41–47, January/February 1976.

Hayanagi, Tadashi: "The Mother's Child-Bearing Attitudes and Her Child's Socialization—A Clinical Aspect in Child Socialization," *Journal of Educational Sociology*, 23:110–123, October 1968.

Hearst, Patricia, and Alvin Moscow: *Every Secret Thing*, Doubleday & Company, Inc., Garden City, N.Y., 1982.

Hechter, H. H., and N. O. Borhani: "Longevity in Racial Groups Differs," *California Health*, 20:3–5, Feb. 1, 1965.

Heckman, Norma A., et al.: "Problems of the Professional Couple: A Content Analysis," *Journal of Marriage and the Family*, 39:323–330, May 1977.

Heer, David M.: "The Prevalence of Black-White Marriage in the United States, 1960 and 1970," *Journal of Marriage and the Family*, 36:246–258, May 1974.

Heilbroner, Robert L.: *An Inquiry into the Human Prospect*, W. W. Norton & Company, Inc., New York, 1974.

———: "Does Capitalism Have a Future?" *The New York Times Magazine*, Aug. 15, 1982, pp. 21ff.

——— and Lester C. Thurow: *Five Economic Challenges*, Prentice-Hall, Inc., Englewood Cliffs, N.J., 1981.

Heilbrun, Alfred B., Jr.: *Human Sex Role Behavior*, Pergamon Press, New York, 1981.

Helfgot, Joseph: "Professional Reform Organizations and the Symbolic Representation of the Poor," *American Sociological Review*, 39:475–491, August 1974.

Hemmer, Carl: "World Population Conference: Bucharest in Retrospect," *War on Hunger*, 9:8–16, no. S18.34, January 1975 (monthly publication of the Agency for International Development, U.S. Department of State, Office of Public Affairs).

Henley, Nancy M.: *Body Language: Power, Sex and Nonverbal Communication*, Prentice-Hall, Inc., Englewood Cliffs, N.J., 1977.

Hennessy, Bernard C.: *Public Opinion*, Wadsworth Publishing Company, Inc., Belmont, Calif., 1970.

Henning, Margaret, and Anne Jardim: *The Managerial Woman*, Anchor Books, Doubleday & Company, Inc., Garden City, N.Y., 1977.

Herberg, Will: *Protestant, Catholic, Jew*, Doubleday & Company, Inc., Garden City, N.Y., 1960.

Herbers, John: "Will the 1980s Witness a New Surge of Black Political Gain?" *The New York Times*, Feb. 27, 1983, sec. 4, p. 5.

Herbert, Muriel: *The Snow People*, G. P. Putnam's Sons, New York, 1973.

Herbert, Wray: "Sources of Temperament: Bashful at Birth?" *Science News*, 121:36, Jan. 16, 1982*a*.

——— "An Epidemic in the Works," *Science News*, 122:188–190, September 1982*b*.

Hermens, Ferdinand A.: "The New Dilemma of Democracy," *Freedom at Issue*, 47:13–17, September/October 1978.

Herzog, Elizabeth: *Children of Working Mothers*, Children's Bureau Publication No. 382, U.S. Department of Health, Education and Welfare, 1960.

Herzog, Frederick: *Justice Church*, Orbis books, Maryknoll, N.Y., 1981.

Heyneman, Stephen T., and William A. Loxley: "Influence on Academic Achievement Across High and Low Income Countries: A Reanalysis of IEA Data," *Sociology of Education*, 55:13–21, January 1981.

Higham, John: *Strangers in the Land: Patterns of American Nativism, 1860–1925*, Rutgers University Press, New Brunswick, N.J., 1955.

Hilbary, William E.: "Race, Deprivation, and Adolescent Self-Images," *Social Science Quarterly*, 56:105–114, June 1975.

Hill, W. W.: "The Status of the Hermaphrodite and Transvestite in Navaho Culture," *American Anthropologist*, 37:273–279, 1935.

Hillery, George A.: "Definitions of Community: Areas of Agreement," *Rural Sociology*, 20:111–123, 1955.

Hindus, Maurice: "Historical Trends in American Historical Association, New York, December 1971.

Hirschi, Travis: *Causes of Delinquency*, University of California Press, Berkeley, 1969.

———: "Intelligence and Delinquency: A Revisionist Review," *American Sociological Review*, 42:571–587, August 1977.

Hirschman, Albert O.: *Private Interest and Public Action*, Princeton University Press, Princeton, N.J., 1982.

Hite, Shere: *The Hite Report: A Nationwide Study of Female Sexuality*, The Macmillan Company, New York, 1976.

———: *The Hite Report on Male Sexuality*, Alfred A. Knopf, Inc., New York, 1981.

Hodge, Robert W., Donald J. Treiman, and Peter H. Rossi: "A Comparative Study of Occupational Prestige," in Reinhard Bendix and Seymour M. Lipset (eds.), *Class, Status and Power*, The Free Press, New York, 1966, pp. 309–321.

Hoebel, E. Adamson: *Man in the Primitive World*, McGraw-Hill Book Company, New York, 1949.

Hoffer, Eric: *The True Believer*, Harper & Row, Publishers, Inc., New York, 1951.

———: *Working and Thinking on the Waterfront*, Harper & Row, Publishers, Inc., New York, 1969.

————: *In Our Time*, Harper & Row, Publishers, Inc., New York, 1976.

Hoffman, George W.: "Migration and Social Change," *Problems of Communism*, 22:16–31, November 1973.

Hoffman, Lois Wladis: "Research Findings on the Effects of Maternal Employment on the Child," in F. Ivan Nye and Lois W. Hoffman (eds.), *The Employed Mother in America*, Rand McNally & Company, Chicago, 1963, pp. 190–212.

Hoffreth, Sandra L., and Kristin A. Moore: "Women's Employment and Marriage," in Ralph E. Smith (ed.), *The Subtle Revolution: Women at Work*, The Urban Institute, Washington, 1979.

Hofstadter, Richard: *Anti-Intellectualism in American Life*, Alfred A. Knopf, Inc., New York, 1964.

Hoge, Dean R., and J. W. Carroll: "Religiosity and Prejudice in Northern and Southern Churches," *Journal for the Scientific Study of Religion*, 12:181–197, June 1973.

———— and Gregory H. Petrillo: "Development of Religious Thinking in Adolescence: A Test of Goldman's Theories," *Journal for the Scientific Study of Religion*, 17:139–154, June 1978.

Hollander, Anne: "When Fat Was in Fashion," *The New York Times Magazine*, Oct. 23, 1977, pp. 36ff.

————: Quoted in Harris Diensterey, "Clothes Power," *Psychology Today*, 122:71, December 1982.

Hollander, Paul: *Soviet and American Society*, The University of Chicago Press, Chicago, 1978.

Hollingshead, August B.: *Elmtown's Youth*, John Wiley & Sons, Inc., Inc., New York, 1949.

———— and Frederick C. Redlich: "Social Stratification and Psychiatric Disorders," *American Sociological Review*, 18:163–169, April 1953.

Holmstrom, Lynda Lyttle: *The Two Career Family*, Schenkman Publishing Co., Inc., Cambridge, Mass., 1973.

Homans, George C.: *The Human Group*, Harcourt, Brace and Company, Inc., New York, 1950.

Hooker, Evelyn: "Parental Relations and Male Homosexuality in Patient and Nonpatient Samples," *Journal of Consulting and Clinical Psychology*, 33:140–142, April 1969.

Hooton, E. A.: *Crime and the Man*, Harvard University Press, Cambridge, Mass., 1939.

Hopkins, Jane, and Priscilla White: "The Dual-Career Couple: Constraints and Supports," *The Family Coordinator*, 27:253–259, July 1977.

Horn, Joseph M., et al.: "Texas Adoption Project,"

paper presented at the Fifth Annual Meeting of the Behavior Genetics Association, 1975; abstracted in *Behavior Genetics*, 6:109, January 1976a.

———— et al.: Heritability of Personality Traits in Adult Male Twins," *Behavior Genetics*, 6:17–30, January 1976b.

Hornung, Carlton A.: "Social Status, Status Inconsistency, and Phychological Stress," *American Sociological review*, 42:623–638, August 1977.

Horoszowski, Pawel: "Women's Status in Socialistic and Capitalistic Countries," *International Journal of Marriage and the Family*, 1:1–18, March 1971, and 1:160–180, April 1971.

————: *Economic Special-Opportunity Conduct and Crime*, Lexington Books, Lexington, Mass., 1980.

Horowitz, Allan, and Michael Wasserman: "The Effect of Social Control on Delinquent Behavior: A Longitudinal Test," *Sociological Focus*, 12:53–70, January 1979.

Horowitz, David (ed.): *Radical Sociology: An Introduction*, Canfield Press, San Francisco, 1971.

Horowitz, Irving Louis (ed.): *The New Sociology: Essays in Social Science and Social Theory in Honor of C. Wright Mills*, Oxford University Press, Fair Lawn, N.J., 1964.

———— (ed.): *Three Worlds of Development: The Theory and Practice of World Stratification*, Oxford University Press, New York, 1966.

————: *Taking Lives: Genocide and State Power*, 3rd ed., Transaction Books, New Brunswick, N.J., 1980.

————: "Many Genocides, One Holocaust? The Limits of the Rights of States and the Obligations of Individuals," *Modern Judaism*, 1:74–89, 1981.

Horton, Donald: "The Functions of Alcohol in Primitive Societies," *Quarterly Journal of Studies on Alcohol*, 4:293–303, 1943.

Horton, Paul B., and Donald H. Bouma: "The Sociological Reformation: Immolation or Rebirth," *Sociological Focus*, 4:25–41, Winter 1970–1971.

———— and Gerald R. Leslie: *The Sociology of Social Problems*, 3rd. ed., Appleton Century Crofts, New York, 1965; 7th ed., Prentice-Hall, Inc., Englewood Cliffs, N.J., 1981.

Horton, Robert L.: *The Value-System of the High School Adolescent*, unpublished M.S. thesis, Western Michigan University, 1967.

Hostettler, John A.: "Persistence and Change Patterns in Amish Society," *Ethnology*, 3:185–198, April 1964.

————: *Hutterite Society*, The Johns Hopkins Press, Baltimore, 1974.

Hotchkiss, Sandy: "Peaceful Dying," *Human Behavior*, April 1978, pp. 32–33.

Houck, Oliver A.: "Lenin's Trees," *Audubon*, 82:114–119, March 1980.

Hougland, James G., Jr., James A. Christenson, and David S. Walls: "The Impact of Job Training on Occupational Mobility: The Experience of Former CETA Participants," paper presented at the 77th Annual Meeting of the American Sociological Association, San Francisco, 1982.

Hoult, Thomas Ford: *Dictionary of Modern Sociology*, Littlefield, Adams, and Company, Totowa, N.J., 1969.

House, James S., and Elizabeth Bates Harkins: "When and Why Is Status Inconsistency Stressful?" *American Journal of Sociology*, 81:395–412, September 1975.

Howard John R.: *The Cutting Edge: Social Movements and Social Change in America*, J. B. Lippincott Company, Philadelphia, 1974.

Howell, Joseph T.: *Hard Living on Clay Street*, Anchor Books, Doubleday & Company, Inc., Garden City, N.Y., 1973.

Hoyt, Homer: *One Hundred Years of Land Values in Chicago*, The University of Chicago Press, Chicago, 1933.

Huang, L. J.: "Some Changing Patterns in the Communist Chinese Family," *Marriage and Family Living*, 23:137–146, May 1961.

Huff, Darrell: *How to Lie with Statistics*, W. W. Norton & Company, Inc., New York, 1954.

Huizinga, J.: *The Waning of the Middle Ages*, Edward Arnold (Publishers) Ltd., London, 1924.

Humphreys, Laud: *Tearoom Trade: Impersonal Sex in Public*, Aldine Publishing Company, Chicago, 1970, 1975.

Hunt, Chester L.: "The Phillippine Compact Farm: Right Answer or Wrong Question?" *Journal of Rural Cooperation*, 5:121–140, no. 2, 1977.

————: "Liberation Theology in the Philippines: A Test Case," *Christianity Today*, 26:24–26, March 5, 1982.

———— and Lewis Walker: *Ethnic Dynamics: Patterns of Intergroup Relations in Various Societies*, Learning Publications, Holmes Beach, Fla., 1979.

Hunt, Janet G., and Larry L. Hunt: "Dilemmas and Contradictions of Status: The Case of the Dual-Career Family," *Social Problems*, 24:407–416, April 1977.

Hunt, Larry L., and Janet G. Hunt: "A Religious Factor in Achievement Among Blacks: The Case of Catholicism," *Social Forces*, 53:595–605, June 1975.

Hunt, Morton: *Sexual Behavior in the Seventies*, Playboy Press, Chicago, 1974.

Hunter, Albert: "The Loss of Community: An Empirical Test Through Replication," *American Sociological Review*, 40:537–552, October 1975.

Hunter, Gordon: "Judge Bans Any Intimidation of Vietnamese," *Houston Chronicle*, May 15, 1981.

Hurd, Richard M.: *Principles of City Land Values*, Record and Guide, New York, 1903.

Hurley, John R., and Donna P. Palonen: "Marital Satisfaction and Child Density Among University Student Parents," *Journal of Marriage and the Family*, 29:483–484, August 1967.

Huxley, Aldous: *Brave New World*, Doubleday & Company, Inc., Garden City, N.Y., 1932.

————: *Brave New World Revisited*, Harper & Row, Publishers, Inc., New York, 1958.

Hyman, Herbert H., and Charles R. Wright: "Trends in Voluntary Association Memberships of American Adults: Replication Based on Secondary Analysis of National Sample Surveys," *American Sociological Review*, 36:191–206, April 1971.

Hymowitz, Carol: "Women Coal Miners Fight for Their Right to Lift Shovel," *Wall Street Journal*, Sept. 10, 1981, p. 1.

Illich, Ivan D.: *Deschooling Society*, Harper & Row, Publishers, Inc., New York, 1972.

Imbus, Sharon H., and Bruce E. Zawacki: "Autonomy for Burned Patients When Survival Is Unprecedented," *New England Journal of Medicine*, 297:308–311, Aug. 11, 1977.

Inglitzin, Lynn B., and Ruth Ross (eds.): *Women in the World: A Comparative Study*, Clio Press, Santa Barbara, Calif., 1976.

Ingrassia, Lawrence: "Those Little Alligators on Clothes Still Beg, Breed Imitators and Detractors," *Wall Street Journal*, Dec. 11, 1981, p. 29.

Inkeles, Alex, and David H. Smith: *Becoming Modern: Individual Changes in Six Developing Countries*, Harvard University Press, Cambridge, Mass., 1974.

Insel, Paul M., and Frank Markowitz: "The Hazards of Crowding," *USA Today*, 108:25–28, July 1979.

Intercom (Population Reference Bureau): "China's One Child Population Future," 9:1–12, August 1981.

Intercom (Population Reference Bureau): "The 1982 Data Sheet: World Population Now (and 38 Years From Now)," 10:1–11, April 1982.

Irons, Edward D.: "Black Entrepreneurship: Its Rationale, Its Problems, Its Prospects," *Phylon*, 37:12–25, March 1976.

Jack, Nancy Koplin, and Betty Schiffer: "The Limits of Fashion Control," *American Sociological Review*, 13:730–738, December 1948.

Jackman, Mary R., and Robert W. Jackman: *Class Awareness in the United States*, University of California Press, Berkeley, 1982.

Jackson, Maurice: *Their Brothers' Keepers*, (mimeo.), Pacific School of Religion, cited in Alfred H. Katz and Eugene I. Bender: *The Strength in Us*, Franklin Watts, Inc., New York, 1974, p. 25.

Jacobs, Alan H.: "Volunteer Fireman: Altruism in Action," in W. Arens and Susan P. Montague (eds.), *The American Dimension: Cultural Myths and Social Realities*, Alfred Publishing Company, New York, 1976, pp. 194–205.

Jacobs, David: "Inequality and the Legal Order: An Ecological Test of the Conflict Model," Social Problems, 25:514–525, June 1978.

———: "Some Fundamental Misuses of Multiple Regression: A Response to Bailey," *Social Problems*, 19:61–64, October 1981.

———: "Competition, Scale of Political Explanations for Inequality: An Integrated Study of Sectoral Explanations at the Aggregate Level," *American Sociological Review*, 47:600–614, October 1982.

Jacobs, Jane: *The Death and Life of Great American Cities*, Random House, Inc., New York, 1961.

Jacques, Jeffrey M., and Karen J. Chason: "Cohabitation: Its Impact on Marital Success," *The Family Coordinator*, 28:35–39, January 1979.

Jaffe, Frederick S.: "Low Income Families: Fertility in 1971–1972," *Family Planning Perspectives*, 6:107–112, Spring 1974.

Janis, Irving: *Air War and Emotional Stress*, McGraw-Hill Book Company, New York, 1951.

Janowitz, Barbara A.: "The Impact of AFDC on Illegitimate Birth Rates," *Journal of Marriage and the Family*, 38:485–494, August 1976.

Japan Society, Inc.: *The Police and The People: A Comparison of Japanese and American Police Behavior*, Japan Society, Inc., New York, 1977.

Jeffery, Clarence R.: *Crime Prevention Through Environmental Design*, Sage Publications, Beverly Hills, Calif., 1977.

Jencks, Christopher: *Who Gets Ahead: The Determinants of Success in America*, Basic Books, Inc., Publishers, New York, 1979.

——— et al.: *Inequality*, Basic Books, Inc., Publishers, New York, 1972.

Jensen, Arthur E.: *Bias in Mental Testing*, The Free Press, New York, 1979.

Jewkes, John, et al.: *The Sources of Invention*, W. W. Norton & Company, Inc., New York, 1969.

Johnson, Benton: "Taking Stock," *Journal for the Scientific Study of Religion*, 21:189–200, September 1982.

Johnson, Coleen Leahy, and Frank Arvid Johnson: "Attitudes Towards Parenting in Dual-Career Families," *American Journal of Psychiatry*, 134:391–395, April 1977.

Johnson, Donald M.: "The 'Phantom Anesthetist' of Mattoon: A Field Study of Mass Hysteria," *Journal of Abnormal and Social Psychology*, 40:175–186, 1945.

Johnson, Frank (ed.): *Alienation: Concept, Terms, and Meanings*, Seminar Press, New York, 1973.

Johnson Lloyd, and Jerald B. Bachman: *Understanding Adolescence*, Allyn and Bacon, Inc., Boston, 1973.

Johnson, Nan E.: "Minority Group Status and the Fertility of Black Americans, 1970: A New Look," *American Journal of Sociology*, 84:1386–1389, May 1979.

Johnson, Norris R., and William E. Feinberg. "Youth Protest in the 1960s: An Introduction," *Sociological Focus*, 13:173–177, August 1980.

Johnstone, Ronald: *Religion and Society in Interaction: The Sociology of Religion*, Prentice-Hall, Inc., Englewood Cliffs, N.J., 1975.

Jonassen, Christen T.: "Community Typology," in Marvin B. Sussman (ed.), *Community Structure and Analysis*, Thomas Y. Crowell Company, New York, 1959.

Jones, James H.: *Bad Blood: The Tuskegee Syphilis Experiment*, The Free Press, New York, 1981.

Joyce, Richard, and Chester L. Hunt: "Philippine Nurses and the Brain Drain," *Social Science and Medicine*, 16:1223–1233, Summer 1982.

Juel-Nielson, Neils: *Individual and Environment: Monozygotic Twins Reared Apart*, International Universities Press, Inc., New York, 1980.

Jung, L. Shannon: *Identity and Community: A Social Introduction to Religion*, John Knox Press, Atlanta, Ga., 1980.

Juppenlatz, Morris: *Cities in Transformation: The*

Urban Squatter Problem of the Developing World, University of Queensland Press, St. Lucia, Queensland, Australia, 1970.

Kadushin, Charles: *The American Intellectual Elite,* Little, Brown and Company, Boston, 1974.

Kagan, Jerome: *The Second Year: The Emergence of Self-Awareness,* Harvard University Press, Cambridge, Mass., 1981.

Kagan, Robert William: "God and Man at Yale Again," *Commentary,* 73:48–51, February 1982.

Kahn, Alfred J.: *Theory and Practice of Social Planning,* Russell Sage Foundation, New York, 1969.

Kahn, H. A.: "The Dorn Study of Smoking and Mortality among U.S. Veterans: Report on 8½ years of Observation," *National Cancer Institute Monographs,* no. 9, January 1966, pp. 1–125.

Kahn, Herman: *World Economic Development,* Westview Press, Boulder, Col., 1979.

———: *The Coming Boom,* Simon and Schuster, New York, 1982.

——— et al.: *The Next 200 Years: A Scenario for America and the World,* William Morrow & Company, Inc., New York, 1976.

Kahn, Robert L., et al.: "Americans Love Their Bureaucrats," *Psychology Today,* 9:66–70, June 1975.

Kane, John J.: "The Irish Wake: A Sociological Appraisal," *Sociological Symposium,* 1:21–27, Fall 1968.

Kanter, Rosabeth Moss: *Men and Women of the Corporation,* Basic Books, Publishers, Inc., New York, 1977.

Kaplan, Bert: "A Study of Rorschach Responses in Four Cultures," *Papers of the Peabody Museum of American Archaeology and Ethnology,* vol. 42, no. 2, Harvard University Press, Cambridge, Mass., 1954.

Kaplan, Howard B.: "Increase in Self-Rejection as an Antecedent of Deviant Responses," *Journal of Youth and Adolescence,* 4:281–292, September 1975.

———: "Increase in Self-Rejection and Continuing/Discontinued Deviant Response," *Journal of Youth and Adolescence,* 6:77–87, March 1977.

——— and Alex D. Pokorny: "Self-Attitudes and Suicidal Behavior," *Suicide and Life-Threatening Behavior,* 6:23–25, Spring 1976.

Kaplan, Roy H., and Curt Tautsky: "The Meaning of Work Among the Hard-Core Unemployed," *Pacific Sociological Review,* 17:185–198, April 1974.

Kaplan, Samuel: *The Dream Deferred: People, Politics and Planning in Suburbia,* Seabury Press, Inc., New York, 1976.

Karp, David A., Gregory P. Stone, and William C. Yoels: *Being Urban: A Social Psychological View of Urban Life,* D. C. Heath and Company, Lexington, Mass., 1977.

Kasselbaum, Gene: *Delinquency and Social Policy,* Prentice-Hall, Inc., Englewood Cliffs, N.J., 1974.

Kastenbaum, Robert: "Is Death a Life Crisis?" in Nancy Daton and Leon H. Ginsberg (eds.), *Life-Span Developmental Psychology: Normative Life Crises,* Academic Press, Inc., New York, 1976, p. 45.

Katchadourian, Herant A.: *Human Sexuality,* University of California Press, Berkeley, 1979.

Katz, Alfred H., and Eugene I. Bender (eds.): *The Strength in Us,* Franklin Watts, Inc., New York, 1976.

Katz, J.: "Past and Future of the Undergraduate Woman," paper presented at Radcliffe College, Cambridge, Mass., April 1978.

Katz, Jay, et al.: *Experimentation with Human Beings,* Russell Sage Foundation, New York, 1972.

Katz, Michael B.: *Class, Bureaucracy and Schools: The Illusion of Educational Change in America,* Praeger Publishers, Inc., New York, 1971.

Kee, Wan Fook, and Ann Sarah Lee: "Singapore," *Studies in Family Planning,* 4:117–118, April 1973.

Keesing, Roger M.: "Chiefs in a Chiefless Society: The Ideology of Modern Kwaio Politics," *Oceania,* 38:276–280, June 1968.

Keller, Suzanne: "Does the Family Have a Future?" *Journal of Comparative Family Studies,* 2:1–14, Spring 1971.

Kelley, Dean M.: "Why Conservative Churches Are Still Growing," *Journal for the Scientific Study of Religion,* 17:165–172, June 1978.

Kelly, Michael P.: *White-Collar Proletariat,* Routledge & Kegan Paul, Ltd., Boston, 1980.

Kelman, Herbert C.: "Deception in Social Research," *Trans-action,* 3:20–24, July/August 1966.

Kelman, Steven: *Push Comes to Shove: The Escalation of Student Protest,* Houghton Mifflin Company, New York, 1970.

Keniston, Kenneth, and the Carnegie Council on Children: *All Our Children: The American Family Under Pressure,* Harcourt, Brace and World, Inc., New York, 1977.

Kephart, William H.: *Extraordinary Groups: The Sociology of Unconventional Life-Styles,* St. Martin's Press, Inc., New York, 1982.

Kerbo, Harold R.: "Characteristics of the Poor: A

Continuing Focus in Social Research," *Sociology and Social Research*, 65:323–331, April 1981.

Kerckhoff, Alan C., and Kurt W. Back: *The June Bug*, Appleton Century Crofts, New York, 1968.

Kessen, William (ed.): *Childhood in China*, Yale University Press, New Haven, Conn., 1975.

Kessner, Thomas: *The Golden Door: Italian and Immigrant Mobility in New York City, 1880–1915*, Oxford University Press, New York, 1977.

Key, William H.: "Rural-Urban Differences and the Family," *Sociological Quarterly*, 2:49–56, no. 1, 1961.

Keyfitz, Nathan: "Individual Mobility in a Stationary Population," *Population Studies*, 7:335–352, July 1973.

Kidder, Tracy: *The Soul of the Machine*, Atlantic Monthly Press, Little, Brown and Company, Boston, Mass., 1982.

Kiernan, Bernard P.: *The United States, Communism, and the Emergent World*, Indiana University Press, Bloomington, 1972.

Kilson, Martin J.: "Black Progress? Black Social Classes and Intergenerational Poverty," *The Public Interest*, 64:58–78, Summer 1981.

Kim, Mo-Im, et al.: "Age at Marriage, Family Planning Practices, and Other Variables as Correlates of Fertility in Korea," *Demography*, 11:641–656, November 1974.

Kinsey, Alfred C., et al.: *Sexual Behavior in the Human Male*, W. B. Saunders Company, Philadelphia, 1948.

―――― et al.: *Sexual Behavior in the Human Female*, W. B. Saunders Company, Philadelphia, 1953.

Kirkpatrick, Jeane: "Politics and the New Class," *Society*, 16:42–48, January/February 1979.

Kitano, Harry H. L.: *Japanese Americans: The Evolution of a Subculture*, 2nd ed., Prentice-Hall, Inc., Englewood Cliffs, N.J., 1976.

Klass, Philip J.: *UFOs Explained*, Random House, Inc., New York, 1975.

Klein, Donald C. (ed.): *Psychology of Planned Community: The New Town Experience*, Human Sciences Press, New York, 1978.

Kline, David: "The Embattled Independent Farmer," *The New York Times Magazine*, Nov. 29, 1981, pp. 138ff.

Kluckhohn, Florence Rockwood, and Fred L. Strodtbeck: *Variations in Value Orientations*, Row, Peterson & Company, Evanston, Ill., 1961.

Knittel, Robert E.: "New Towns, Knowledge, Ex-

perience, and Theory: An Overview," *Human Organization*, 32:27–48, Spring 1973.

Knopf, Terry Ann: *Rumors, Race and Riots*, Transaction Books, New Brunswick, N.J., 1975.

Knott, Paul D. (ed.): *Student Activisim*, Wm. C. Brown Company Publishers, Dubuque, Iowa, 1971.

Kodera, James T.: "Toward an Asianization of Christianity: Demise of Metamorphosis?" in Herbert Richardson (ed.), *Ten Theologians Respond to the Unification Church*, The Rose of Sharon Press, Inc., New York, 1981, pp. 75–88.

Kohlberg, Lawrence: "Development of Moral Character and Moral Ideology," in Martin L. Hoffman and Lois Wladis Hoffman (eds.), *Review of Child Development*, Russell Sage Foundation, New York, 1964, pp. 383–431.

Kohn, Melvin: "Personality, Occupation and Social Stratification: A Frame of Reference," in Donald J. Treiman and Robert V. Robinson (eds.), *Research in Social Stratification and Mobility*, 1:267–297, JAI Press, Greenwich, Conn., 1981.

―――― and Carmi Scholler: "Occupational Experience and Psychological Functioning: An Assessment of Reciprocal Effects," *American Sociological Review*, 38:97–118, February 1973.

Kon, Igor S.: "The Concept of Alienation in Modern Sociology," in Peter L. Berger (ed.), *Marxism and Sociology*, Appleton Century Crofts, New York, 1969, pp. 146–167.

Konig, René: *A La Mode: On the Social Psychology of Fashion*, Seabury Press, Inc., New York, 1974.

Korda, Michael: *Power: How to Get It; How to Use It*, Random House, Inc., New York, 1975.

Kornblum, William: *Blue-Collar Community*, The University of Chicago Press, Chicago, 1974.

Koza, Patricia: United Press International, May 31, 1982.

Kramer, Ralph M.: *Participation of the Poor: Comparative Community Case Studies in the War on Poverty*, Prentice-Hall, Inc., Englewood Cliffs, N.J., 1969.

―――― and Harry Specht (eds.): "Processes of Directed Change: Social Planning," in *Readings in Community Organization Practice*, part 11, sec. D, Prentice-Hall, Inc., Englewood Cliffs, N.J., 1975.

Kranowitz, Leo: *Equal Rights: The Male Stake*, The University of New Mexico Press, Albuquerque, 1981.

578

Bibliography

Kretschmer, Ernest: *Physique and Character,* Harcourt, Brace & World, Inc., New York, 1925.

Kriesberg, Louis: *Social Inequality,* Prentice-Hall, Inc., Englewood Cliffs, N.J., 1979.

Krisberg, Barry: *Crime and Privilege: Toward a New Criminology,* Prentice-Hall, Inc., Englewood Cliffs, N.J., 1975.

Kronholz, June: "Ghana's Economic Skid Illustrates Bleak Spiral of Poverty in Africa," *Wall Street Journal,* Jan. 4, 1982, pp. 1ff.

Krout, Maurice A.: *Introduction to Social Psychology,* Harper & Row, Publishers, Inc., New York, 1942.

Kubler-Ross, Elizabeth: *Death—The Final Stage of Growth,* Prentice-Hall, Inc., Englewood Cliffs, N.J., 1975.

Kuepper, William G., et al.: *Ugandan Asians in Great Britain: Forced Migration and Social Absorption,* New Viewpoints, New York, 1975.

Kuhn, Manford H., and Thomas S. McPartland: "An Empirical Investigation of Self-Attitudes," *American Sociological Review,* 19:68–75, February 1954.

Kuper, Leo: *Genocide: Its Political Use in the Twentieth Century,* Yale University Press, New Haven, Conn., 1982.

Kutner, Nancy G.: "Low Income Ethnicity and Voluntary Association Involvement," *Journal of Sociology and Social Welfare,* 3:311–321, January 1976.

Labov, William: *Sociolinguistic Patterns,* University of Pennsylvania Press, Philadelphia, 1972.

Ladd, Everett Carl, Jr.: "Clearing the Air: Public Opinion and Public Policy on the Environment," *Public Opinion,* 5:16–20, February/March 1982.

———— and Seymour Martin Lipset: "The 1977 Survey of the American Professoriate," reported in *Public Opinion,* 1:37, May/June 1978.

LaFeber, Walter: "Inevitable Revolutions," *Atlantic,* 249:74–83, June 1982.

LaMott, Kenneth: "The Mao Solution," *Human Behavior,* August 1977, pp. 20ff.

Lampe, Philip E.: "The Acculturation of Mexican Americans in Public and Parochial Schools," *Sociological Analysis,* 39:57–66, Spring 1975.

Lancaster, Jane B.: *Primate Behavior and the Emergence of Human Culture,* Holt, Rinehart and Winston, Inc., New York, 1975.

Land, Kenneth C.: "Path Models of Functional Theories of Social Stratification as Representations of Cultural Beliefs on Stratification," *Sociological Quarterly,* 11:474–484, Fall 1970.

Landers, Donald, and Donna M. Landers: "Socialization via Interscholastic Athletics: Its Effects on Delinquency," *Sociology of Education,* 51:299–303, October 1978.

Landis, Paul H.: *Social Control,* J. B. Lippincott Company, Philadelphia, 1956.

Lane, Angela Victoria: "Migration and the Processes of Occupational Mobility and Status Attainment," *Sociological Focus,* 10:43–52, January 1977.

Lane, Robert: *Political Ideology,* The Free Press, New York, 1962.

Lang, Kurt, and Gladys Engel Lang: *Collective Dynamics,* Thomas Y. Crowell Company, New York, 1961.

Langer, John: "Drug Entrepreneurs and Dealing Culture," *Social Problems,* 24:377–386, February 1977.

Lapidus, Gail Warshofsky: *Women in Soviet Society: Equality, Development, and Social Change,* University of California Press, Berkeley, 1978.

Lapiere, Richard T.: *Collective Behavior,* McGraw-Hill Book Company, New York, 1938.

————: *A Theory of Social Control,* McGraw-Hill Book Company, New York, 1954.

————: *Social Change,* McGraw-Hill Book Company, New York, 1965.

Lappe, Frances Moore, et al.: *Beyond the Myth of Scarcity,* Houghton Mifflin Company, Boston, 1977.

Laqueur, Walter: "The Gathering Storm," *Commentary,* August 1974, pp. 22–33.

————: "The Futility of Terrorism," *Harper's,* 252:99–111, March 1976.

Lasswell, Harold D.: *Politics: Who gets What, When, How,* The World Publishing Company, Cleveland, 1958.

Laszlo, Ervin (ed.): *Goals for Mankind: A Report to the Club of Rome on the New Horizons of the Global Community,* E. P. Dutton & Co., Inc., New York, 1977.

Laubach, Gerald D.: "Growing Criticism of Science Impedes Progress," *USA Today,* 109–51–54, July 1980.

Lauer, Robert H.: "Rate of Change and Stress: A Test of the 'Future Shock' Thesis," *Social Forces,* 52:510–516, June 1974.

————: *Perspectives on Social Change,* Allyn and Bacon, Inc. Boston, 1977.

Leagins, J. Paul, and Charles P. (eds.): *Behavioral Change in Agriculture*, Cornell University Press, Ithaca, N.Y., 1971.

LeBon, Gustav: *The Crowd: A Study of the Popular Mind*, Ernest Benn, Ltd., London, 1896.

Lee, Alfred McClung: *Multivalent Man*, George Braziller, Inc., New York, 1966.

———: *Toward A Humanist Sociology*, Prentice-Hall, Inc., Englewood Cliffs, N.J., 1973.

———: *Sociology for Whom?* Oxford University Press, New York, 1978.

——— and Norman D. Humphrey: *Race Riot*, Holt, Rinehart and Winston, Inc., New York, 1943.

——— and Elizabeth Briant Lee: *The Fine Art of Propaganda*, Harcourt, Brace and World, Inc., and the Institute for Propaganda Analysis, New York, 1939.

Lee, Dorothy: *Freedom and Culture*, Prentice-Hall, Inc., Englewood Cliffs, N.J., 1959.

LeMasters, E. E.: *Blue Collar Aristocrats: Life Styles at a Working Class Tavern*, The University of Wisconsin Press, Madison, 1975.

Lemert, Edwin M.: *Social Pathology*, McGraw-Hill Book Company, New York, 1951.

Lenski, Gerhard M.: "Status Crystallization: A Non-vertical Dimension of Social Status," *American Sociological Review*, 19:405–413, June 1954.

——— and Jean Lenski: *Human Societies: An Introduction to Macrosociology*, McGraw-Hill Book Company, New York, 1982.

Leo, John: "Getting Tough With Teens," *Time*, 115:47, June 8, 1981.

Leon, Dan: *The Kibbutz: A New Way of Life*, Pergamon Press, New York, 1970.

Lerner, Barbara: "American Education: How Are We Doing?" *The Public Interest*, 69:59–82, Fall 1982.

Lerner, Michael: "Respectable Bigotry," *American Scholar*, 38:606–617, Autumn 1969.

Leslie, Gerald R.: *The Family in Social Context*, Oxford University Press, New York, 1982.

Lesser, Alexander: "Cultural Significance of the Ghost Dance," *American Anthropologist*, 35:108–115, January 1933.

Leventman, Seymour (ed.): *Countercultures and Social Transformation: Essays on Negativistic Themes in Sociological Theory*, Charles C Thomas, Publisher, Springfield, Ill. 1981.

Lever, H.: "Changes in Ethnic Attitude in South Africa," *Sociology and Social Research*, 56:202–210, January 1972.

Levine, Daniel U., and Jeanie Keeney Meyer: "Level and Rate of Desegregation and White Enrollment Decline in a Big City School District," *Social Problems*, 24:451–462, April 1977.

Levine, Robert, and Donald C. Campbell: *Ethnocentrism: Theories of Conflict, Ethnic Attitudes and Group Behavior*, John Wiley & Sons, Inc., New York, 1972.

——— et al.: "Individual Differences or Sex Differences in Achievement Orientation," *Sex Roles*, 8:455–466, April 1982.

Levinson, Daniel J., et al.: *The Seasons of a Man's Life*, Alfred A. Knopf, Inc., New York, 1979.

Levitan, Sar A., and Richard S. Belous: *What's Happening to the American Family?* The Johns Hopkins Press, Baltimore, 1981.

Leviton, Jarvey: "The Implications of the Relationship Between Self-Concept and Academic Achievement," *Child Study Journal*, 5:24–35, no. 1, 1975.

Levitt, Theodore: *The Third Sector: New Tactics for a Responsive Society*, American Management Association, New York, 1973.

Levy, Marion J.: "Social Patterns (Structures)," in Wilbert E. Moore and Robert M. Cook (eds.), *Readings on Social Change*, Prentice-Hall, Inc., Englewood Cliffs, N.J., 1967.

Lewis, Jerry M.: "A Study of the Kent State Incident Using Smelser's Theory of Collective Behavior," *Sociological Inquiry*, 42:87–96, Spring 1972.

Lewis, Oscar: *Five Families: Mexican Case Studies in the Culture of Poverty*, Basic Books, Inc., Publishers, New York, 1959.

———: *La Vida: A Puerto Rican Family in the Culture of Poverty, San Juan and New York*, Random House, Inc., New York 1966a.

———: "Culture of Poverty; with Biographical Sketch," *Scientific American*, 215:19–25, October 1966b.

Lewis, Sinclair: *Babbitt*, Harcourt, Brace and World, Inc., New York, 1922.

———: *Arrowsmith*, Harcourt, Brace and World, Inc., New York, 1933.

Leyburn, James G.: *Frontier Folkways*, Yale University Press, New Haven, Conn., 1935.

Lieberman, E. James: "The Case for Small Families," *The New York Times Magazine*, March 8, 1970, pp. 86–89.

Lieberson, Stanley: *A Piece of the Pie*, University of California Press, Berkeley, 1980.

——— and Arnold R. Silverman: "Precipitants and

Conditions of Race Riots," *American Sociological Review*, 30:887–898, December 1965.

Liebow, Elliot: *Tally's Corner: A Study of Negro Streetcorner Men*, Little, Brown and Company, Boston, 1967.

Lightborne, Robert, Jr., and Susheela Singh, with Cynthia P. Green: "The World Fertility Survey: Charting Global Childbearing," *Population Bulletin*, 37:1–55, March 1982.

Link, Bruce: "Mental Patient Status, Work, and Income," *American Sociological Review*, 47:202–215, April 1982.

Lindesmith, Alfred E.: "Social Problems and Sociological Theory," *Social Problems*, 8:98—102, Fall 1960.

Lindsay, William R.: "The Effects of Labeling: Blind and Non-blind Ratings of Social Skills in Schizophrenic and Non-schizophrenic Control Subjects," *American Journal of Psychiatry*, 139:216–219, February 1982.

Lindzey, Gardner (ed.): *Handbook of Social Psychology*, Addison-Wesley Press, Inc., Cambridge, Mass., 1954.

Linton, Ralph: *The Study of Man*, Appleton-Century-Crofts, Inc., New York, 1936.

Lips, Hilary M., et al.: "Masculinity, Femininity, and Androgyny," and "Sex Differences in Ability," in Hilary M. Lips and Nina Lee Colwell (eds.), *The Psychology of Sex Differences*, Prentice-Hall, Inc., Englewood Cliffs, N.J., 1978, pp. 125–144, 145–176.

Lipset, Seymour Martin: "Social Mobility and Equal Opportunity," *The Public Interest*, 29:90–108, Fall 1972.

——— and Richard B. Dobson: "Social Stratification and Sociology in the Soviet Union," *Survey: A Journal of East-West Studies*, 88:114–185, Summer 1973.

——— and Everett Carl Ladd, Jr.: "The Politics of American Sociologists," *American Journal of Sociology*, 78:67–104, July 1972.

Liska, Allen E.: *Perspectives on Deviance*, Prentice-Hall, Inc., Englewood Cliffs, N.J., 1981.

Listiak, Alan: " 'Legitimate Deviance' and Social Class: Bar Behavior During Grey Cup Week," *Sociological Focus*, 7:13–44, Summer 1974.

Lloyd, Cynthia B., and Beth T. Niemi: *The Economics of Sex Differentials*, Columbia University Press, New York, 1979.

Loftus, Elizabeth F.: "The Incredible Eyewitness," *Psychology Today*, 8:116–119, December 1974.

———: *Eyewitness Testimony*, Harvard University Press, Cambridge, Mass., 1979.

Lohman, Joseph D.: *The Police and Minority Groups*, Chicago Park District, Chicago, 1947.

Lombroso, Cesare: *Crime, Its Causes and Remedies*, trans. by H. P. Horton, Little, Brown and Company, Boston, 1912.

Loomis, Charles P., and J. Allan Beagle: *A Strategy for Rural Change*, Halstead Publishers, New York, 1975.

Loomis, Donald: "White Paper Calls New Town Program 'Poorly Organized'," *Architectural Record*, 161:38, March 1977.

Lopreato, Joseph, and Lionel S. Lewis: "An Analysis of Variables in the Functional Theory of Stratification," *Sociological Quarterly*, 4:301–310, Autumn 1963.

Lowie, Robert H.: *Introduction to Cultural Anthropology*, Holt, Rinehart and Winston, Inc., New York, 1940.

Lowry, Ritchie P.: *Who's Running This Town? Community Leadership and Social Change*, Harper & Row, Publishers, Inc., New York, 1965.

Lubeck, Steven G., and Vern L. Bengtson: "Tolerance for Deviance: Generational Contrasts and Continuities in the Study of Socal Problems," paper presented at 72nd Annual Meeting of the American Sociological Association, Chicago, 1977.

Lubin, Joann S.: "Big Fight Looms Over Gap in Pay for Similar 'Male', 'Female' Jobs," *Wall Street Journal*, Sept. 16, 1982*a*, p. 33.

———: "White Collar Cutbacks Are Falling More Heavily on Women Than Men," *Wall Street Journal*, Nov. 9, 1982*b*, p. 31.

Luloff, A. E.: *New Hampshire's Changing Population*, New Hampshire Agricultural Experiment Station, Research Report #87, Durham N.H., 1980.

Lurie, Nancy: "Winnebago Berdache," *American Anthropologist*, 55:707–712, December 1953.

Lyles, Jean Caffey: "New Language for Liturgy," *Christian Century*, 98:1358–1359, Dec. 30, 1981.

Lynch, Frank: *Social Class in a Bicol Town*, Philippines Studies Program, The University of Chicago Press, Chicago, 1959.

Lynch, James J.: *The Broken Heart: The Medical Consequences of Loneliness*, Basic Books, Inc., Publishers, New York, 1977.

Lynd, Robert S., and Helen M. Lynd: *Middletown*, Harcourt, Brace and World, Inc., New York, 1929.

—— and ——: *Middletown in Transition*, Harcourt, Brace and World, Inc., New York, 1937.

Lynn, Robert: "IQ in Japan and the United States Shows a Growing Disparity," *Nature*, 297:222–223, May 20, 1982.

Lyon, Larry, Troy Abell, Elizabeth Jones, and Holley Rector-Owen: "The National Longitudinal Surveys Data for Labor Market Entry: Evaluating the Small Effects of Racial Discrimination and the Large Effects of Sexual Discrimination," *Social Problems*, 29:524–539, June 1982.

MacAndrew, Craig, and Robert B. Edgerton: *Drunken Comportment: A Social Explanation*, Thomas Nelson & Sons, Don Mills, Ontario, 1969.

Macarov, David: *Work and Welfare: The Unholy Alliance*, Sage Publications, Beverly Hills, Calif., 1980.

MacAvoy, Paul W.: "The Underground: No Recess," *The New York Times*, Aug. 4, 1982, sec. 4, p. 3.

Maccoby, Eleanor Emmons, and Carol Nagy Jackson: *The Psychology of Sex Differences*, Stanford University Press, Stanford, Calif., 1974.

MacDougall, William: "Apaches Make Their Peace with the Modern World," *U.S. News & World Report*, 87:64–65, April 5, 1982.

Mackay, Charles: *Extraordinary Popular Delusions and the Madness of Crowds*, L. C. Page & Company, Boston, 1932.

Macklin, Eleanor: "Review of Research on Nonmarital Cohabitation in the United States," in Bernard I. Murstein (ed.), *Exploring Intimate Lifestyles*, Springer Publishing Co., Inc., New York, 1978, pp. 196–243.

Maher, Robert F.: *The New Man of Papua: A Study in Cultural Change*, The University of Wisconsin Press, Madison, 1961.

Mahoney, Anne Rankin: "The Effect of Labeling Upon Youth in a Juvenile Justice System," *Law and Society Review*, 8:583–614, Summer 1974.

Malinowski, Bronislaw: *Crime and Custom in Savage Society*, Routledge & Kegan Paul, Ltd., London, 1926.

Malone, Patrick: "Major Breakthroughs in Genetic Research," *Washington Post*, Aug. 27, 1973, D-3.

Mann, James T.: "New Life Ahead for Christian Unity," *U.S. News & World Report*, 93:57, Dec. 27/Jan. 3, 1982 (combined issue).

Mannheim, Karl: *Man and Society in an Age of Reconstruction: Studies in Modern Social Structure*, Verry, Fischer, and Co., Inc., New York, 1949.

Mantell, David Mark: "Doves vs Hawks: Guess Who Had the Authoritarian Parents?" *Psychology Today*, 8:56–62, September 1974.

Marcuse, Herbert: *One Dimensional Man*, Beacon Press, Boston, 1964.

——: *An Essay on Liberation*, Beacon Press, Boston, 1969.

——: *New Theories of Revolution*, International Publications Service, N.Y., 1972.

Margolin, Joseph: "Psychological Perspectives on Terrorism," in Yonah Alexander and Seymour Maxwell Finger (eds.), *Terrorism: Interdisciplinary Perspectives*, John Jay Press, New York, 1977, pp. 270–282.

Mariani, John: "Television Evangelism: Milking the Flock," *Saturday Review*, 6:22–25, Feb. 3, 1979.

Marotz-Baden, Ramona, et al.: "Family Form and Family Process? Reconsidering the Deficit Family Model Approach," *The Family Coordinator*, 28:5–14, January 1979.

Marsh, Robert M.: "The Explanation of Occupational Prestige Hierarchies," *Social Forces*, 50:214–222, December 1971.

Marshall, S. L. A.: *Men Under Fire*, William Morrow & Company, Inc., New York, 1947.

Martin, Julie: "Most Teen-agers Would Register Republican," *Phoenix Gazette*, May 29, 1982, p. 4.

Martindale, Don, and R. Galen Hanson: *Small Town and the Nation: The Conflict of Local and Translocal Forces*, Greenwood Publishing Company, Westport, Conn., 1969.

Marx, Gary T.: "Issueless Riots," *Annals of the American Academy of Political and Social Science*, 391:21–33, September 1970.

Massey, Garth: "Studying Social Class: The Case of Embourgeoisement and the Culture of Poverty," *Social Problems*, 22:595–608, June 1975.

Masters, Stanley K.: *Black-White Income Differentials*, Academic Press, Inc., New York, 1975.

Matza, David: *Becoming Delinquent*, Prentice-Hall, Inc., Englewood Cliffs, N.J., 1969.

Maybee, Carlton: "Evolution of Non-Violence," *Nation*, 193:78–81, Aug. 12, 1961.

Mayer, Albert J., et al.: *Pilot Project: India*, University of California Press, Berkeley, 1958.

Mayer, Jean: "Networks Are Accused of Neglecting Childen in Era of Deregulation," *Wall Street Journal*, March 17, 1983, pp. 1ff.

Mayeske, George W.: "On the Explanation of

Racial-Ethnic Group Differences in Achievement Test Scores," Office of Education, Washington, (mimeo), 1973.

Mayrl, William W.: "The Christian-Marxian Encounter: From Dialogue to Detente," *Sociological Analysis*, 39:84–90, Spring 1978.

McBirnie, William S.: *Who Really Rules America: A Study of the Power Elite*, Center for American Education and Research, Glendale, Calif., 1968.

McCarthy, James B.: *Fearful Living: The Fear of Death*, Halsted Press, Somerset, N.J., 1980.

McCarthy, John D., and Mayer N. Zald: "Resource Mobilization and Social Movements: A Partial Theory," *American Journal of Sociology*, 82:1212–1241, May 1977.

McClelland, David C.: "The Power of Positive Drinking," *Psychology Today*, 4:40ff, January 1971.

McClosky, Herbert, and John H. Schaar: "Psychological Dimensions of Anomy," *American Sociological Review*, 30:14–40, February 1965.

McGinty, Alice B.: "India: A House Divided," *Current History*, 13:288–291, November 1947.

McGrath, Peter, et al.: "Refugees or Prisoners," *Newsweek*, 99:24–29, Feb. 1, 1982.

McInerney, John P., and Graham F. Donaldson: *The Consequences of Farm Tractors in Pakistan*, World Bank, Washington, 1975.

McIntosh, William Alex, and Jon P. Alston: "Religion and the New Immigrants: Initial Observations Concerning Lao Refugees in America," paper presented at the Association for the Sociology of Religion, Toronto, 1981.

McKee, David L., and Gerald H. Smith: "Environmental Diseconomies in Suburban Expansion," *American Journal of Economics and Sociology*, 31:181–188, April 1972.

McKenna, Richard J.: "Good Samaritans in Rural and Urban Settings: A Nonreactive Comparison of Helping Behavior of Clergy and Control Subjects," *Representative Research in Social Psychology*, 7:58–65, 1976.

McKinney, William J.: "America's Religious Recession," *USA Today*, 109:26–28, September 1981.

McLanahan, Sara S., et al.: "Network Structure, Social Support, and Psychological Well-Being in the Single-Parent Family," *Journal of Marriage and the Family*, 43:601–612, August 1981.

McNall, Scott G.: *The Sociological Experience*, Little, Brown and Company, Boston, 1974.

McPartland, James M., and Edward L. McDell: "Control and Differentiation in the Structure of American Education," *Sociology of Education*, 55:77–88, April 1982.

McSheehy, William: *Skid Row*, Schenkman Publishing Co., Inc., Cambridge, Mass., 1979.

McVay, Frank L.: "The Social Effects of the Eight Hour Day," *American Journal of Sociology*, 8:521–530, January 1903.

Mead, George Herbert: *Mind, Self and Society*, The University of Chicago Press, Chicago, 1934.

Mead, Margaret: *Cultural Patterns and Technical Change*, UNESCO, Mentor Books, New American Library, Inc., New York, 1955.

———: *New Lives for Old*, William Morrow & Company, Inc., New York, 1956.

Meadows, Donella H., et al.: *The Limits to Growth*, Universe Books, New York, 1972.

Mecklin, John H.: *The Ku Klux Klan*, Harcourt, Brace and World, Inc., New York, 1924.

Mednick, Martha T. Shuch: "Social Change and Sex-Role Inertia: The Case of the Kibbutz," in Mednick et al. (eds.), *Women and Achievement*, Hemisphere, Washington, 1975, pp. 85–103.

Meerman, Jacob: "The Incidence of Sales and Excise Taxes and Where Do We Put The Transfer?" *Journal of Political Economy*, 88:1242–1248, December 1980.

Melady, Thomas Patrick: *Burundi: The Tragic Years*, Orbis Books, Maryknoll, N.Y., 1974.

Mellor, J. R.: *Urban Sociology in an Urbanized Society*, Routledge & Kegan Paul, Ltd., Boston, 1977.

Menzel, Donald H., and Ernest H. Taves: *The UFO Enigma: The Definitive Explanation of the UFO Phenomenon*, Doubleday & Company, Inc., Garden City, N.Y., 1977.

Mercy, James A., and Lala Carr Steelman: "Familial Influence on the Intellectual Attainment of Children," *American Sociological Review*, 47:532–542, August 1982.

Merton, Robert K.: "Social Structure and Anomie," *American Sociological Review*, 3:672—682, October 1938.

———: "Bureaucratic Structure and Personality," in *Social Theory and Social Structure*, The Free Press, New York, 1949*a*, pp. 151–160.

———: "Spheres of Influence: Monomorphic and Polymorphic," in Paul B. Lazarsfeld and Frank R. Stanton (eds.), *Communications Research*, Harper & Row, Publishers, Inc., New York, 1949*b*, pp. 148–149.

———: *Social Theory and Social Structure*, The Free Press, New York, 1957*a*.

———: "Manifest and Latent Functions: Toward a Codification of Functional Analysis in Sociology," in *Social Theory and Social Structure*, The Free Press, New York, 1957*b*, pp. 19–84.

———: "Priorities in Scientific Discovery: A Chapter in the Sociology of Science," *American Sociological Review*, 22:635–659, December 1957*c*.

———: *The Sociology of Science*, edited and with an introduction by Norman W. Storer, The University of Chicago Press, Chicago, 1973.

Mesarovic, Mihaljo, and Eduard Pestel: *Mankind at the Turning Point: The Second Report of the Club of Rome*, E. P. Dutton & Co., Inc., Reader's Digest Books, Inc., New York, 1974.

Meyers, William R.: *The Evaluation Enterprise*, Jossey-Bass, Inc., San Francisco, 1981.

Miale, Florence R., and Michael Selzer: *The Nuremburg Mind: The Psychology of Nazi Leaders*, Quadrangle/The New York Times Book Co., New York, 1976.

Michels, Robert: *Political Parties: A Sociological Study of the Oligarchical Tendencies in Modern Democracy*, The Free Press, New York, 1949.

Mikesell, Marvin W.: "The Deforestation of Mount Lebanon," *The Geographical Review*, 59:1–28, January 1969.

Milgram, Stanley, and Hans Toch: "Collective Behavior: Crowds and Social Movements," in Gardner Lindzey and Elliott Aronson (eds.), *Handbook in Social Psychology*, vol. IV, Addison-Wesley Publishing Company, Inc., Reading, Mass., 1969, pp. 507–610.

——— and ———: *Obedience to Authority: An Experimental View*, Harper & Row, Publishers, Inc., New York, 1974.

Miller, Delbert C.: *International Community Power Structures: Comparative Studies of Four World Cities*, Indiana University Press, Bloomington, 1970.

Miller, Niel E., and John Dollard: *Social Learning and Imitation*, Yale University Press, New Haven, Conn., 1941.

Miller, S. M., Frank Riessman, and Arthur Seagull: "Poverty and Self-Indulgence: A Critique of the Non-Deferred Gratification Pattern," in Louis A. Ferman, Joyce L. Kornbluh, and Alan Haber (eds.), *Poverty In America*, The University of Michigan Press, Ann Arbor, 1968, pp. 416–432.

Miller, Walter B.: "Lower Class Culture as a Generating Milieu of Gang Delinquency," *Journal of Social Issues*, 14:5–19, no. 3, 1958.

Mills, C. Wright: *The Power Elite*, Oxford University Press, Fair Lawn, N.J., 1956.

———: *The Sociological Imagination*, Oxford University Press, New York, 1959.

Mintz, Alexander: "Non-Adaptive Group Behavior," *Journal of Abnormal and Social Psychology*, 46:150–158, no. 1, 1951.

Mitchell, G.: *Human Sex Differences: A Primatologist's Perspective*, Van Nostrand Reinhold, New York, 1981.

Mitchell, G. Duncan: *A Dictionary of Sociology*, Aldine Publishing Company, Chicago 1968.

Mitchell, Robert Edward: "Methodological Notes on a Theory of Status Crystallization," *Public Opinion Quarterly*, 28:315–325, Summer 1964.

Mitford, Jessica, *The American Way of Death*, Simon and Schuster, New York, 1963.

Miyamoto, S. Frank, and Sanford M. Dornbusch: "A Test of Interactionist Hypothesis of Self-Conception," *American Journal of Sociology*, 61:399–403, 1956.

Moinet, Sheryl M., et al.: "Black Ghetto Residents and Rioters," *Journal of Social Issues*, 28:45–62, no. 4, 1972.

Monroe, Keith: "The New Gambling King and the Social Scientists," *Harper's Magazine*, January 1962, pp. 35–41.

Montague, Ashley: "Chromosomes and Crime," *Psychology Today*, 2:43–49, October 1968.

Montero, Darrel: "The Japanese Americans: Changing Patterns of Assimilation Over Three Generations," *American Sociological Review*, 46:829–840, December 1981.

Moore, Joan W., and Harry Pachon: *Mexican Americans*, Prentice-Hall, Inc., Englewood Cliffs, N.J., 1976.

Moore, Kristin A., and Steven F. Caldwell: "The Effect of Governmental Policies on Out-of-Wedlock Sex and Pregnancy," in Frank F. Furstenberg, Jr., Richard Lincoln, and Jane Menken (eds.), *Teenage Sexuality, Pregnancy, and Childbearing*, University of Pennsylvania Press, Philadelphia, 1981, pp. 126–135.

Moore, Wilbert E.: *Social Change*, Prentice-Hall, Inc., Englewood Cliffs, N.J., 1963.

Moreno, J. L.: "Psychodramatic Treatment of Marriage Problems," *Sociometry*, 3:2–23, 1940.

———: *Sociometry: Experimental Method and the Science of Society*, Beacon House, Inc., Beacon, N.Y., 1951.

Morgan, Gordon D.: *America Without Ethnicity*,

584

Bibliography

National University Publications, Kennikat Press, Port Washington, N.Y., 1981.

Morgan, Robin (ed.): *Sisterhood Is Powerful*, Random House, Inc., New York, 1970.

Morris, Judy K.: "Professor Malthus and His Essay," *Population Bulletin*, 22:7–27, February 1966.

Morris, R. N., and John Mogey: *The Sociology of Housing*, Routledge & Kegan Paul, Ltd., London, 1965.

Moxon-Browne, E.: "Terrorism in Northern Ireland: The Case of the Provisional IRA," in Juliet Lodge (ed.), *Terrorism: A Challenge to the State*, St. Martin's Press, Inc., New York, 1981, pp. 146–163.

Moynihan, Daniel P.: "Behind Los Angeles: Jobless Negroes and the Boom," *The Reporter*, Sept. 9, 1965a, p. 31.

———: *The Negro Family: The Case for National Action*, U.S. Department of Labor, Washington, 1965b.

———: *Report of the Secretary's Advisory Committee on Traffic Safety*, U.S. Department of Health, Education, and Welfare, Washington, 1968.

———: *Maximum Feasible Misunderstanding: Community Action in the War on Poverty*, The Free Press, New York, 1969.

———: "Equalizing Education—In Whose Benefit? *The Public Interest*, 29:66–89, Fall 1972.

———: " 'Peace'—Some Thoughts on the 1960's and 1970's," *The Public Interest*, 32:3–12, Summer 1973.

Muller, Edward N.: "A Test of a Partial Theory of Potential for Political Violence," *American Political Science Review*, 66:928–959, September 1972.

Munch, Peter A.: "Culture and Super-Culture in a Displaced Community: Tristan deCunha," *Ethnology*, 3:369–376, October 1964.

———: *Crisis in Utopia*, Thomas Y. Crowell Company, New York, 1970.

Munsinger, Barry: "The Adopted Child's I.Q.: A Critical Review," *Psychological Bulletin*, 86:623–659, September 1975.

Murdoch, William M.: *Environment*, Sinauer, Sunderland, Mass., 1975.

Murdock, George, P.: *Our Primitive Contemporaries*, The Macmillan Company, New York, 1936.

———: *Social Structure*, The Macmillan Company, New York, 1949.

———: "Sexual Behavior: A Comparative Anthropological Approach," *Journal of Social Hygiene*, 36:133–138, April 1950.

Murphy, Jeffrie G.: *Civil Disobedience and Violence*, Wadsworth Publishing Company, Inc., Belmont, Calif., 1971.

Murphy, Michael J., et al.: "Rated and Actual Performance of High School Students as a Function of Sex and Attractiveness," *Psychological Reports*, 48:103–106, February 1981.

Murray, Charles A.: "The Two Wars Against Poverty: Economic Growth and the Great Society," *The Public Interest*, 69:3–16, Fall 1982.

Mussen, Paul Henry, et al.: *Child Development and Personality*, Harper & Row, Publishers, Inc., New York, 1974.

Muth, Richard F.: *The Spatial Pattern of Urban Residential Land Use*, The University of Chicago Press, Chicago,1969.

Myrdal, Gunnar: *An American Dilemma*, Harper & Row, Publishers, Inc., New York, 1944.

Nagel, Joane, and Susan Olzak: "Ethnic Mobilization in New and Old States: An Extension of the Competition Model," *Social Problems*, 30:127–143, December 1982.

Napper, George: *Blacker Than Thou*, Wm. B. Eerdmans Publishing Co., Grand Rapids, Mich., 1973.

Nash, Dennison: "The Fate of Americans in a Spanish Setting: A Study of Adaptation," *Human Organization*, 26:157–163, Fall 1967.

Nations, James D., and Daniel I. Kramer: "Rainforests and the Hamburger Society," *Environment*, 25:12–20, April 1983.

Nelson, Edward W.: "The Eskimo about Bering Straits," *18th Annual Report, Bureau of American Ethnology*, Part I, Washington, D.C., 1899, pp. 268–270.

Newman, William H.: *American Pluralism*, Harper and Row, Publishers, Inc., New York, 1973.

Nichols, Robert C.: "Heredity and Environment: Major Findings from Twin Studies of Ability, Personality and Interests," paper presented at Annual Meeting of the American Psychological Association, Washington, Sept. 4, 1976; abstracted in *Human Behavior*, September 1977, p. 61.

Nilson, Alleen Pace, et al.: *Sexism and Language*, National Council of Teachers of English, Urbana, Ill., 1977.

Nixon, Howard L., II: *The Small Group*, Prentice-Hall, Inc., Englewood Cliffs, N.J., 1979.

Nortman, Dorothy: "Population and Program Planning: A Fact Book," *Reports on Population Planning*, September 1972, p. 2.

Norton, R. D.: *City Life Cycles and American Urban Policy*, Academic Press, Inc., New York, 1979.

Novak, Michael: "Arms and the Church," *Commentary*, 77:37–41, March 1982.

Noyes, Russell, Jr., and Kevin John Clancy: "The Dying Role: Its Relevance to Improved Patient Care," *Psychiatry*, 40:41–47, February 1977.

Nwosu, S. N.: "Education and Economic Development," *African Studies*, 30:75–90, n. 2, 1971.

Nye, F. Ivan: "Adolescent-Parent Adjustment: Age, Sex, Sibling Number, Broken Homes, and Employed Mothers as Variables," *Marriage and Family Living*, 14:327–332, November 1952.

——, John Carlson, and Gerald Garrett: "Family Size, Interaction, Affect, and Stress," *Journal of Marriage and the Family*, 32:216–226, May 1970.

—— and Lois W. Hoffman: *The Employed Mother in America*, Rand McNally & Company, Chicago, 1963.

Oakes, Jeannie: "Classroom Social Relationships: Exploring the Bowles and Gintis Hypothesis," *Sociology of Education*, 55:197–211, October 1982.

Oakley, Ann: *Subject Women: Where Women Stand Today—Politically, Economically, Socially, Emotionally*, Pantheon Books, a division of Random House, Inc., New York, 1981.

Oberschall, Anthony: "The Los Angeles Riot of 1965," *Social Problems*, 15:322–341, Winter 1968.

——: *Social Conflict and Social Movements*, Prentice-Hall, Inc., Englewood Cliffs, N.J., 1973.

Oberstone, Andrea Kincses, and Harriet Sukoneck: "Psychological Adjustment and Style of Life of Single Lesbians and Single Heterosexual People," paper presented at Annual Meeting of the Western Psychological Association, Sacramento, Calif., 1975.

Oden, Sherri L.: "Coaching Low-Accepted Children in Social Skills," paper presented at 48th Annual Meeting of Midwestern Psychological Association, Chicago, 1976; reviewed in *Human Behavior*, November 1976, pp. 37–38.

Ogburn, William F.: "The Influence of Invention and Discovery," in President's Research Committee on Social Trends, *Recent Social Trends*, McGraw-Hill Book Company, New York, 1933, pp. 122–166.

——: *Social Change*, The Viking Press, Inc., New York, 1922, 1950.

——: "The Wolf Boy of Agra," *American Journal of Sociology*, 46:499–554, March 1959.

Okun, Arthur M.: *Equality and Efficiency: The Big Tradeoff*, The Brookings Institution, Washington, 1975.

Oliver, Melvin L., and Mark A. Glick: "An Analysis of the New Orthodoxy on Black Mobility," *Social Problems*, 29:511–523, June 1982.

Olson, Philip: "Rural American Community Studies: The Survival of Public Ideology," *Human Organization*, 23:342–350, Winter 1964–1965.

O'Nell, Carl W.: "An Investigation of Reported 'Fright,' as a Factor in the Etiology of Susto, 'Magical Fright'," *Ethos*, 1:41–63, Spring 1975.

Orcutt, James D.: "Societal Reaction and the Response to Deviation in Small Groups," *Social Forces*, 52:256–267, December 1973.

——: "The Impact of Student Activism on Attitudes Toward the Female Sex Role," *Social Forces*, 54:382–392, December 1975.

Orleans, Leo A., and Richard B. Suttmeier: "The Mao Ethic and Environmenal Quality," *Science*, 170:1173–1176, Dec. 11, 1970.

Orlofsky, Jacob L., and Michael T. Windle: "Sex Role Differentiation and Personal Adjustment," *Sex Roles*, 4:805–811, December 1978.

Orthner, Dennis K., et al.: "Single-Parent Fathering: An Emerging Life Style," *The Family Coordinator*, 25:429–437, October 1976.

Orum, Anthony M.: *Black Students in Protest: A Study of the Origins of the Black Student Movement*, American Sociological Association, Washington, 1972.

Osborne, Adam: *Running Wild: The Next Industrial Revolution*, McGraw-Hill Book Company, New York, 1979.

Osborne, Albert E., Jr.: "The Welfare Effect of Black Capitalism on the Black Community," *Review of Black Political Economy*, 6:477–483, Summer 1976.

O'Shaughnessy, Thomas J.: "Christian-Muslim Empathy in an Hour of Crisis," *The Ecumenist*, 12:87–90, September/October 1974.

Ostrander, Susan: "A Marxian Theory of Sexual Stratification," *Case Western Reserve Journal of Sociology*, 5:38–58, July 1973.

Ottenberg, Simon: "Ileo Receptivity to Change," in William R. Bascom and Melville J. Herskovitz (eds.), *Continuity and Change in African Cultures*, The University of Chicago Press, Chicago, 1959, pp. 130–143.

Otto, Luther B.: "Girl Friends as Significant Others: Their Influence on Young Men's Career Aspirations and Achievements," *Sociometry*, 40:287–293, 1977.

Ouchi, William G.: *Theory Z: Now American Business Can Meet the Japanese Challange*, Addison-Wesley Publishing Company, Inc., Reading, Mass., 1981.

Paarlberg, Don: *Farm and Food Policy: Issues of the 1980s*, University of Nebraska Press, Lincoln, 1980.

Packard, Vance: *The Hidden Persuaders*, David McKay Company, Inc., New York, 1957.

Papert, Seymour: *Mindstorms: Children, Computers, and Powerful Ideas*, Basic Books, Inc., Publishers, New York, 1980.

Parcel, Toby L.: "Wealth Accumulation of Black and White Men: The Case of Housing Equity," *Social Problems*, 30:199–211, December 1982.

Park, Robert E.: "Human Migration and the Marginal Man," *American Journal of Sociology*, 33:881–893, May 1928.

———, Ernest W. Burgess, and R. D. McKenzie: *The City*, The University of Chicago Press, Chicago, 1925.

Parker, Robert Nash: "Structural Constraints and Career Earnings," *American Sociological Review*, 46:884–892, December 1981.

Parsons, Talcott: *The Structure of Social Action*, McGraw-Hill Book Company, New York, 1937.

———: *The System of Modern Societies*, Prentice-Hall, Inc., Englewood Cliffs, N.J., 1971.

Parten, Mildred: *Surveys, Polls, and Samples: Practical Procedures*, Harper and Row, Publishers, Inc., New York, 1950.

Pascale, Richard Tanner, and Anthony G. Athos: *The Art of Japanese Management: Applications for American Executives*, Simon & Schuster, Inc., New York, 1981.

Pastor, Robert A.: "Our Real Interests in Central America," *Atlantic*, 249:27–39, July 1982.

Patterson, Michelle, and Donileen R. Loseke: Review of Margaret Henning and Ann Jardim, *The Managerial Woman*, and Rosabeth Moss Kanter, *Men and Women of the Corporation*, in *Contemporary Sociology*, 7:256–259, May 1978.

Pauly, David, et al.: "New Towns: Lost Dream?" *Newsweek*, 89:90–92, Nov. 29, 1976.

——— et al.: "A Deregulation Report Card," *Newsweek*, 98:5ff., Jan. 11, 1982.

Peal, Ethel: " 'Normal' Sex Roles: An Historical Analysis," *Family Process*, 14:389–409, September 1975.

Pear, Robert: "Rights Panel Says Reagan Officials Are Impeding Law," *The New York Times*, March 20, 1983, p. 1ff.

Pearson, Karl: *The Grammar of Science*, A. & C. Black, Ltd., London, 1900.

Peck, James: *Freedom Ride*, Simon & Schuster, Inc., New York, 1962.

Pedrick-Cornell, Claire, and Richard J. Gelles: "Elder Abuse: The Status of Current Knowledge," *Family Relations*, 31:457–465, July 1982.

Peek, Charles W.: "Family Structure and Violence Towards Parents: Examination of Neglected Variables in the Study of Family Violence," paper presented at Annual Meeting of the Society for the Study of Social Problems, Toronto, August 1982.

Pellegrini, Robert J.: "Impressions of Male Personality as a Function of Beardedness," *Psychology*, 10:29–33, February 1973.

Pelton, Leroy H.: "Child Abuse and Neglect: The Myth of Classlessness," *American Journal of Orthopsychiatry*, 48:608–618, October 1978.

Penn, Roger: "Occupational Prestige Hierarchies: A Great Empirical Invariant?" *Social Forces*, 54:352–364, December 1975.

Pepinsky, Harold E.: *Crime and Conflict: A Study of Law and Society*, Academic Press, Inc., New York, 1976.

Pepitone-Rockwell, Fran (ed.): *Dual-Career Couples*, Sage Publications, Beverly Hills, Calif., 1980.

Perlman, Daniel: "Self-Esteem and Sexual Permissiveness," *Journal of Marriage and the Family*, 36:470–473, August 1974.

Perloff, Harvey S., et al.: *Modernizing the Central City: New Towns Intown . . . and Beyond*, Ballinger Publishing Company, Cambridge, Mass., 1975.

Perrin, Noel: *Giving Up the Gun: Japan's Reversion to the Sword, 1543–1879*, David R. Godine, Publishers, Inc., Boston, 1979.

Perry, Joseph B., Jr., and Meredith David Pugh: *Collective Behavior: Response to Social Stress*, West Publishing Company, St. Paul, Minn., 1978.

Peters, John Fred: "Mate Selection Among the Shirishna," *Practical Anthropology*, 18:19–23, January/February 1971.

Peterson, George E.: "Finance," in William Gorham and Nathan Glazer (eds.), *The Urban Predicament*, Urban Institute, Washington, 1976, pp. 35–118.

Peterson, James C., and Gerald Markle: "Politics and Science in the Laetrile Controversy," *Social Studies of Science*, (9:139–166, May 1979.

Peterson, William: "The Social Roots of Hunger and Over-population," *The Public Interest*, 68:37–52. Summer 1982.

Pettigrew, Thomas R.: *Racially Separate or Together*, McGraw-Hill Book Company, New York, 1971.

Pfohl, Stephen J.: "The 'Discovery' of Child Abuse," *Social Problems*, 24:310–323, February 1977.

Pfuhl, Erdwin H., Jr.: *The Deviance Process*, D. Van Nostrand Company, Inc., New York, 1979.

Pheterson, Gail I., et al.: "Evaluation of the Performance of Women as a Function of Their Sex, Achievement, and Personal History," *Journal of Personality and Social Psychology*, 19:114–118, July 1971.

Phillips, Bernard S.: *Social Research*, The Macmillan Company, New York, 1966.

Phillips, Kevin: "Controlling Media Output," *Society*, 15:10–16, November/December 1977.

Piaget, Jean: *Play, Dreams and Imitation in Childhood*, W. W. Norton & Company, Inc., New York, 1951.

———: *The Moral Judgment of the Child*, Kegan Paul, Trench, Trubner & Co., Ltd., London, 1932; 2nd ed., The Free Press, New York, 1965.

——— and Barbel Inhelder: *The Psychology of the Child*, Basic Books, Inc., Publishers, New York, 1969.

Pierce, Kenneth: "A Case for Moral Absolutes: Christian Schools Go Forth and Multiply," *Time*, 117:54–56, June 1981.

Pincus, Lily: *Death and the Family: The Importance of Mourning*, Pantheon Books, a division of Random House, Inc., New York, 1975.

Pine, Vanderlyn R. et al.: *Acute Grief and the Funeral*, Charles C Thomas, Publisher, Springfield, Ill., 1976.

Piven, Frances Fox, and Richard A. Cloward: *Regulating the Poor: The Functions of Public Welfare*, Pantheon Books, a division of Random House, Inc., New York, 1971.

——— and ———: *Poor People's Movements: Why They Succeed, How They Fail*, a division of Random House, Inc., Pantheon Books, New York, 1977.

——— and ———: "Social Movements and Societal Conditions: A Response to Roach and Roach," *Social Problems*, 26:172–178, December 1978.

Pleck, Joseph H.: "Men's Family Work: Three Perspectives and Some New Data," *The Family Coordinator*, 28:481–488, October 1979.

———: *The Myth of Masculinity*, The M.I.T. Press, Cambridge, Mass., 1981.

Podhoretz, Norman: "The New Defenders of Capitalism," *Harvard Business Review*, 59:96–106, March/April 1981.

Pogrebin, Letty Cottin: *Growing Up Free: Raising Your Children in the 1980s*, McGraw-Hill Book Company, New York, 1980.

Polsby, Nelson W.: *Community Power and Political Theory*, Yale University Press, New Haven, Conn., 1980.

Ponting, J. Rick: "Rumor Control Centers: Their Emergence and Operations," *American Behavorial Scientist*, 16:391–401, January 1973.

Pool, Ithiel deS.: *The Social Impact of the Telephone*, MIT Press, Cambridge, Mass., 1977.

Porter, Cathy: *Aleksandra Kollontai: The Lonely Struggle of the Woman Who Defied Lenin*, The Dial Press, Inc., New York, 1980.

Porterfield, Austin L.: *Youth in Trouble*, Leo Potishman Foundation, Fort Worth, Tex., 1946.

Porterfield, Ernest: *Black and White Mixed Marriages*, Nelson Hall Company, Chicago, 1978.

Portwood, Doris: "A Right to Suicide?" *Psychology Today*, 11:66–76, January 1978.

Premack, David: "Language in Chimpanzees," *Science*, 182:808–822, May 21, 1971.

Prescott, James W.: "Alienation of Affection," *Psychology Today*, 13:124, December 1979.

President's Commission on Campus Unrest: *Report*, Washington, 1970.

Pryce-Jones, David: "The Bete Noire of France's Left," *The New York Times Magazine*, Dec. 11, 1977, pp. 55ff.

Pyle, Ernie: *Brave Men*, Holt, Rinehart and Winston, Inc., New York, 1943.

Quarentelli, Enrico: "The Nature and Conditions of Panic," *American Journal of Sociology*, 60:267–275, November 1954.

Queen, Stuart A., Robert W. Habenstein, and John B. Adams: *The Family in Various Cultures*, J. B. Lippincott Company, Philadelphia, 1975.

Quinn, Robert P., and Martha S. Baldi de Mandilovitch: *Education and Job Satisfaction: A Questionable Payoff*, Survey Research Center, University of Michigan, Ann Arbor, 1975.

Quinney, Richard: *Class, State, and Crime*, David McKay Company, Inc., New York, 1977.

———: *Class, Status and Crime*, Longmans, Green & Co., Ltd., New York, 1980.

Rafky, David M.: "Blue Collar Power: The Social Impact of Urban School Custodians," *Urban Education*, 6:349–372, January 1972.

Ramey, James W.: "Alternative Lifestyle," *Society*, July/August 1977, pp. 43–46.

Rand, Ayn: *For the Intellectual: The Philosophy of Ayn Rand*, Random House, Inc., New York, 1961.

————: *An Introduction to Objectivist Epistomology*, Mentor Books, New American Library, Inc., New York, 1979.

Randi, The Amazing (stage name of James A. Randi): *The Magic of Uri Geller*, Ballantine Books, Inc., New York, 1975.

Randi, James A.: *Flim-Flam!* Prometheus Books, Buffalo, N.Y., 1982.

Rank, Mark R., and Paul R. Voss: "Patterns of Rural Community Involvement: A Comparison of Residents and Recent Immigrants," *Rural Sociology*, 47:197–219, Summer 1982.

Ranney, Austin: "The Year of the Referendum," *Public Opinion*, 5:12–14, December/January 1983.

Raper, Arthur F.: *The Tragedy of Lynching*, The University of North Carolina Press, Chapel Hill, 1933.

Rapoport, Rhona, and Robert N. Rapoport: *Dual-Career Families Reexamined*, Harper & Row, Publishers, Inc., New York, 1976.

Raspberry, William: "Busing—Is It Worth the Ride?" *Reader's Digest*, 105:141–142, September 1974.

Ravitch, Diane: *The Revisionists Revised*, Basic Books, Inc., Publishers, New York, 1978.

Rawls, John: *A Theory of Justice*, The Belknap Press, Harvard University Press, Cambridge, Mass., 1971.

Ray, J. J.: "Ethnocentrism: Attitudes and Behavior," *Australian Quarterly*, 43:89–97, June 1971.

Reed, Fred W., et al.: "Relative Income and Fertility: The Analysis of Individual Fertility in a Biracial Sample," *Journal of Marriage and the Family*, 37:799–805, November 1975.

Reed, Julia Ann: "Clothing as a Symbolic Indicator of the Self," unpublished study; abstracted in *Human Behavior*, July 1974, pp. 34–35.

Rehberg, Richard A., and Evelyn R. Rosenthal: *Class and Merit in the American High School: An Assessment of the Revisionist and Meritocratic Argument*, Longmans, Green & Co., Ltd., New York, 1978.

Reiss, Albert J., Jr.: "Rural-Urban Status Differences in Interpersonal Contacts," *American Journal of Sociology*, 65:182–195, September 1959.

Reissman, Leonard: Review of C. Wright Mills, *The Power Elite*, *American Sociological Review*, 21:513–514, August 1956.

Reiter, Rayna E. (ed.): *Toward an Anthropology of Women*, Monthly Review Press, New York, 1975.

Reitlinger, Gerald: *The Final Solution: The Attempt to Exterminate the Jews of Europe*, Thomas Yoseloff, Ltd., South Brunswick, N.J., 1968.

Rensberger, Royce: "14 Million Acres a Year Vanishing as Deserts Spread Around the Globe," *The New York Times*, Aug. 28, 1977, pp. 1ff.

Reyburn, Wallace: *The Inferior Sex*, Prentice-Hall, Inc., Englewood Cliffs, N.J., 1972.

Reynolds, Fred D., and William R. Darden: "Why the Midi Failed," *Journal of Advertising Research*, 12:39–44, August 1972.

Ribble, Margaret A.: *The Rights of Infants*, Columbia University Press, New York,, 1943.

Richardson, James T.: "People's Temple and Jonestown: A Comparison and Critique," *Journal for the Scientific Study of Religion*, 19:239–255, September 1980.

Richardson, Laurel Walum, *see* Walum, Laurel Richardson.

Riding, Alan: "Latin Church in Siege," *The New York Times Magazine*, May 6, 1979, pp. 32ff.

Ridker, Ronald K. (ed.): *Population and Development: The Search for Selective Intervention*, The Johns Hopkins Press, Baltimore, 1976.

Riemer, Svend: "Social Planning and Social Organization," *Amerian Journal of Sociology*, 52:508–516, March 1947.

Riesman, David, with Nathan Glazer and Reuel Denney: *The Lonely Crowd: A Study in the Changing American Character*, Yale University Press, New Haven, Conn., 1950.

Risman, Barbara J., and Charles T. Hill et al.: "Living Together in College: Implications for Courtship," *Journal of Marriage and the Family*, 43:77–84, February 1981.

Rivers, W. H. R.: "On the Disappearance of Useful Arts," in *Festkrift Tillagnad Edward Westermarck, Helsingfors*, 1922, pp. 109–130; summarized in A. L. Kroeber, *Anthropology*, Harcourt, Brace and World, Inc., New York, 1949, p. 375.

Roach, Jack L., and Orville R. Gursslin: "An Evaluation of the Concept of the Culture of Poverty," *Social Forces*, 45:383–391, March 1967.

———— and Janet E. Roach: "Organizing the Poor: Road to a Dead End," *Social Problems*, 26:160–171, December, 1978.

Roazen, Paul: *Erik Erikson: The Power and Limits of a Vision*, The Free Press, New York, 1976.

Robbins, Thomas, and Dick Anthony: "New Religions, Families and Brainwashing," *Society*, 15:77–83, May/June 1978.

Roberts, Paul Craig: "The Breakdown of the Keynesian Model," *The Public Interest*, 52:21–33, Summer 1978.

Roberts, Ron E.: *The New Communes*, Prentice-Hall, Inc., Englewood Cliffs, N.J., 1971.

———, and Robert Marsh Kloss: *Social Movements: Between the Balcony and the Barricade*, 2nd ed., The C. V. Mosby Company, St. Louis, 1979.

Robertson, Wyndham: "Going Broke in the New York Way," *Fortune*, August 1975, pp. 141ff.

Robinson, Dwight H.: "Fashions in Shaving and Trimming of the Beard: The Men of the *Illustrated London News*, 1842–1972," *American Journal of Sociology*, 81:1133–1139, March 1976.

Rodman, Hyman: "The Value Stretch," *Social Forces*, 42:205–215, December 1963.

———, Patricia Voydanoff, and Albert E. Lovejoy: "The Range of Aspirations: A New Approch," *Social Problems*, 22:188–198, December 1974.

Rodriguez, Richard B.: *Hunger of Memory*, David R. Godine, Publishers, Inc., Boston, 1982.

Roebuck, Julian B., and Wolfgang Frese: *The Rendezvous: A Case Study of an After Hours Club*, The Free Press, New York, 1976.

——— and S. Lee Spray: "The Cocktail Lounge: A Study in Heterosexual Relations in a Public Organization," *American Journal of Sociology*, 72:388–395, January 1967.

Rogers, Everett M., and Rabel I. Burdge: *Social Change in Rural Society*, Prentice-Hall, Inc., Englewood Cliffs, N.J., 1972.

Rogin, Richard: "This Place Makes Bedford Stuyvesant Look Beautiful," *The New York Times Magazine*, March 28, 1971, pp. 30ff.

Rose, A. J.: *Patterns of Cities*, Thomas Nelson, Ltd., Melbourne, Australia, 1967.

Rose, Arnold: *The Power Structure: Political Process in American Society*, Oxford University Press, New York, 1967.

Rosen, Bernard C.: "The Reference Group Approach to the Parental Factor in Attitude and Behavior Formation," *Social Forces*, 34:137–144, December 1955.

———: "Social Change, Migration, and Family Interaction in Brazil," *American Sociological Review*, 38:198–212, April 1973.

Rosen, Stephen: *Future Facts: A Forecast of the World as We Will Know It Before the End of the Century*, Simon and Schuster, New York, 1976.

Rosenbaum, David: "Nuclear Terror," in John D. Elliott and Leslie K. Gibson (eds.), *Contemporary Terrorism: Selected Readings*, International Association of Chiefs of Police, Gaithersburg, Md., 1978, pp. 81–95.

Rosenhan, D. L.: "On Being Sane in Insane Places," *Science*, 179:250–258, January 1973.

Rosenman, Yehuda: Introduction to Egon Mayer and Carl Sheingold, *Intermarriage and the Jewish Future: A National Study in Summary*, Institute of Human Relations, American Jewish Committee, New York, 1979, pp. 1–4.

Rosenstone, Robert A.: "The Times They Are A-Changing: The Music of Protest," *The Annals of the American Academy of Political and Social Science*, 382:131–144, March 1969.

Rosnow, Ralph L., and Gary Alan Fine: *The Social Psychology of Rumor*, American Elsevier Publishing Company, Inc., New York, 1976.

Rossi, Alice: "Sex Equality: The Beginning of Ideology," in Betty Roszak and Theodore Roszak (eds.), *Masculine/Feminine*, Harper & Row, Publishers, Inc., New York, 1970, pp. 173–186.

Rossi, Peter H.: Review of C. Wright Mills, *The Power Elite*, in *American Journal of Sociology*, 62:232–233, September 1956.

Rossman, Parker: *Hospice: Creating New Models of Care for the Terminally Ill*, Association Press, New York, 1977.

Rothman, Jack, *Planning and Organizing for Social Change: Action Principles from Social Science Research*, Columbia University Press, New York, 1974.

———, John L. Erlich, and Joseph G. Teresa: *Promoting Innovation and Change in Organizations and Communities*, John Wiley & Sons, Inc., New York, 1976.

Rothman, Stanley, and S. Robert Lichter: "Media and Business Elites: Two Classes in Conflict?" *The Public Interest*, 69:117–125, Fall 1982.

Rubenstein, Richard E.: *Rebels in Eden: Mass Political Violence In the U.S.*, Little, Brown and Company, Boston, 1970.

Rubin, Kenneth H., and Terrence L. Maioni: "Play Preference and Its Relationship to Egocentrism, Popularity, and Classification Skills in Preschoolers," *Merrill-Palmer Quarterly*, 21:171–179, July 1975.

Rubin, Lillian B.: Reviews of Margaret Hennig and Anne Jardim, *The Managerial Woman*, and Rosabeth Moss Kanter, *Men and Women of the Corporation*, in *Contemporary Sociology*, 7:259–263, May 1978.

Ruesch, Hans: *The Top of the World*, Pocket Books, a division of Simon & Schuster, Inc., New York, 1977.

Rule, Sheila: "The Follow Through On Head Start," *The New York Times*, Jan. 10, 1982, sec. 13, p. 42.

Russell, Charles A., and Bowman H. Miller: "Profile of a Terrorist," in John D. Elliott and Leslie K. Gibson (eds.), *Contemporary Terrorism: Selected Readings*, International Association of Chiefs of Police, Gaithersburg, Md., 1978, pp. 81–95.

Russell, Christine H., and Willis D. Hawley: "Understanding White Flight and Doing Something About It," in Willis D. Hawley (ed.), *Effective School Desegregation: Equity, Quality and Feasibility*, Sage Publications, Beverly Hills, Calif., 1981, pp. 157–184.

Rustin, Bayard: "A Way Out of the Exploding Ghetto," *New York Times Magazine*, August 13, 1967, pp. 16ff.

Ryden, Hope: "On the Trail of the West's Wild Horses," *National Geographic*, 139:94–109, January 1971.

Sacks, Michael Paul: *Women's Work in Soviet Russia: Continuity in the Midst of Change*, Frederick A. Praeger, Inc., New York, 1976.

———, "Sexual Equality and Soviet Women," *Society*, July/August 1977, pp. 48–51.

Sagarin, Edward (ed): *Deviance and Social Change*, Sage Publications, Beverly Hills, Calif., 1977.

Sage, Wayne: "The War on the Cults," *Human Behavior*, 5:40–49, October 1976.

Saghir, Marcel T., and Eli Robins: *Male and Female Homosexuality: A Comprehensive Investigation*, The Williams and Wilkins Company, Baltimore, Md., 1973.

St. John, Nancy H.: *School Desegregation Outcomes for Children*, John Wiley & Sons, Inc., New York, 1975.

Sakharov, Andrei: *My Country and the World*, Alfred A. Knopf, Inc., New York, 1975.

Salas, Rafael M: *People, An International Choice: The Multilateral Approach to Population*, Pergamon Press, Elmsford, N.Y., 1976.

Salert, Patricia: *Revolutions and Revolutionists*, Elsevier Scientific Publishing Company, New York, 1976.

Salins, Peter D.: *The Ecology of Urban Destruction: Economic Effects of Public Intervention in the Housing Market*, New York University Press for the International Center for Economic Policy, New York, 1980.

Salomone, Jerome J.: "An Empirical Report on Some Aspects of American Funeral Practices," *Sociological Symposium*, 1:49–56, Fall 1968.

Samuels, Shirley C.: *Enhancing Self-Concept in Early Childhood: Theory and Practice*, Human Sciences Press, New York, 1977.

Samuelson, Kurt: *Religion and Economic Action: A Critique of Max Weber*, Harper & Row, Publishers, Inc., New York, 1961.

Samuelson, Robert: "Badmouthing the Bureaucracy," *New Republic*, 174:10–14, May 15, 1976.

Sandy, Peggy Reeves: *Female Power and Male Dominance: On the Origins of Female Inequality*, Cambridge University Press, New York, 1981.

Sandoz, Mari: *The Buffalo Hunters*, Hastings House, Publishers, Inc., New York, 1954.

SanGiovanni, Lucinda: *Ex-Nuns: A Study of Emergent Role Passage*, Ablex Publishing Company, Norwood, N.J. 1978.

Santos, Milton: *The Shared Space: The Two Circuits of Urban Economy in Underdeveloped Countries*, Methuen, Inc., New York, 1979.

Scanlon, Arlene, et al.: "Attitudes Toward Woman Physicians in Medical School," *Journal of the American Medical Association*, 247:2803–2807, May 28, 1982.

Scanzoni, John: *Sex Roles, Women's Work, and Marital Conflict*, Lexington Books, Lexington, Mass., 1978.

Scarf, M.: "Goodall and Chimpanzees at Yale," *The New York Times Magazine*, Feb. 18, 1973, pp. 14ff.

Scarr, Sandra, and Richard A. Weinberg: "I.Q. Test Performance of Black Children Adopted by White Families," *American Psychologist*, 31:726–739, October 1976.

Schachter, Stanley: "Deviation, Rejection, and Communication," *Journal of Abnormal and Social Psychology*, 46:190–207, April 1951.

Schaffer, Frank: *The New Town Story*, MacGibbon & Kee, London, 1970.

Scheff, Thomas J.: *Being Mentally Ill*, Aldine Publishing Company, Chicago, 1966.

Scheflen, Albert E.: *Body Language and the Social Order*, Prentice-Hall, Inc., Englewood Cliffs, N.J., 1973.

Schein, Edgar H.: "Interpersonal Communication, Group Solidarity and Social Influence," *Sociometry*, 23:148–161, June 1960.

Schellenberg, James A., and John Halteman: *Effects of Busing Upon Academic Achievement and Attitudes of Elementary School Children*, Center for Educational Studies, Western Michigan University, Kalamazoo, June 1974.

Schindler, John A.: *How to Live 365 Days a Year*, Prentice-Hall, Inc., Englewood Cliffs, N.J., 1954.

Schlafly, Phyllis: *A Choice Not an Echo*, Pere Marquette Press, Alton, Ill., 1964.

Schlesinger, Benjamin: *The One-Parent Family: Perspectives and Annotated Bibliography*, University of Toronto Press, Toronto, 1978.

Schmemann, Serge: "Moscow: Jobs Are There but the Problem Is Productivity," *The New York Times*, Feb. 14, 1982, sec. 12, p. 11.

Schmidt, Gunter, and Wolkmur Sigursch: "Changes in Sexual Behavior among Young Males and Females between 1960–1970," *Archives of Sexual Behavior*, 2:27–45, June 1972.

Schneider, Harold K.: "Pakot Resistance to Change," in William R. Bascom and Melville J. Herskovitz (eds.) *Continutiy and Change in African Cultures*, The University of Chicago Press, Chicago, 1959.

Schoenherr, Richard A., and Andrew M. Greeley: "Role Commitment Process and the American Catholic Priesthood," *American Sociological Review*, 39:407–426, June 1974.

Schooler, Carmi: "Childhood Family Structure and Adult Characteristics," *Sociometry*, 35:255–269, June 1972.

Schreiber, E. M.: "Enduring Effects of Military Service? Opinion Differences Between U.S. Veterans and Nonveterans," *Social Forces*, 57:824–839, March 1979.

Schuler, Edgar A., and V. J. Parenton: "A Recent Epidemic of Hysteria in a Louisiana High School," *Journal of Social Psychology*, 17:221–235, 1943.

Schulman, Norman: "Role Differentiation in Urban Networks," *Sociological Focus*, 9:149–158, April 1976.

Schultz, Duane P.: *Panic Behavior, Discussion and Readings*, Random House, Inc., New York, 1964.

Schuman, Howard: "The Religious Factor in Detroit: Review, Replication and Reanalysis," *American Sociological Review*, 36:30–48, February 1971.

———— and Stanley Presser: "Attitude Measurement and the Gun Control Paradox, *Public Opinion Quarterly*, 41:427–430, Winter 1977–1978.

Schumer, Fran R.: "Downward Mobility," *New York*, 15:20–26, Aug. 16, 1982.

Schur, Edwin M.: *Labelling Deviant Behavior: Its Sociological Implications*, Harper & Row, Publishers, Inc., New York, 1971.

Schwartz, Michael, and Sandra S. Tangri: "A Note on Self-Concept as an Insulator against Delin-quency," *American Sociological Review*, 30:922–934, December 1965.

Schwebbe, Gudrun, and Michael Schwebbe: "Judgment and Treatment of People of Varied Attractiveness," *Psychological Reports*, 48:11–14, February 1981.

Scott, James, and Ben Kerkvliet: "The Politics of Survival: Peasant Response to 'Progress' in Southeast Asia," *Journal of Southeast Asian Studies*, 4:241–267, September 1973.

Seabury, Paul: "Trendier Than Thou," *Harper's*, 257:39–60, October 1978.

Seeman, Melvin: "The Alienation Hypothesis," *Psychiatry and Social Science Review*, 3:1–6, 1969.

Segalman, Ralph, and Asake Basu: "Aid to the Families of Dependent Children—a Case for a Transgenerational Poverty," testimony to the House Ways and Means Committee, Subcommittee of Welfare Reform Committee, U.S. Congress, Los Angeles, Nov. 18, 1977.

Select Commission on Immigration and Refugee Policy: *U.S. Immigration Policy and the National Interest*, 97th Congress, First Session, May 1981.

Selwyn, Percy: "The Tyranny of the Technician," *Internatinal Development Review*, 15:17–20, no. 1, 1973.

Seneker, Harold, with Jonathan Greenberg and John Dorfman: "The Forbes Four Hundred," *Forbes*, 130:100–140, Sept. 13, 1982.

Sewell, William H.: "Infant Training and the Personality of the Child," *American Journal of Sociology*, 58:150–159, September 1952.

Shaeffer, Robert: *The UFO Verdict: Examining the Evidence*, Prometheus Books, Buffalo, N.Y., 1981.

Shaffer, David, and Judy Dunn: *The First Year of Life: Psychological and Medical Implications of Early Experience*, John Wiley & Sons, Inc., New York, 1982.

Sharp, Gene: *The Politics of Nonviolent Action*, Porter Sargent, Boston, 1974.

Sharp, Lauriston: "Steel Axes for Stone Age Australians," in Edward L. Spicer (ed.), *Human Problems in Technological Change*, Russell Sage Foundation, New York, 1952, pp. 69–90.

Shaver, Philip, and Jonathan Friedman: Your Pursuit of Happiness," *Psychology Today*, 19:26–32, August 1976.

Shaw, Clifford: *The Jackroller: A Delinquent Boy's Own Story*, The University of Chicago Press, Chicago, 1930.

———— and H. D. McKay: *Juvenile Delinquency in*

Urban Areas, The University of Chicago Press, Chicago, 1942.

———, ———, and J. F. McDonald: *Brothers in Crime,* The University of Chicago Press, Chicago, 1938.

——— and M. E. Moore: *The Natural History of Delinquent Career,* The University of Chicago Press, Chicago, 1931.

Sheehy, Gail: *Passages: Predictable Crises of Adult Life,* E. P. Dutton & Co., Inc., New York, 1976.

Sheldon, William H.: *Varieties of Delinquent Youth,* Harper & Row, Publishers, Inc., New York, 1949.

Shepher, Joseph: "Familism and Social Structure: The Case of the Kibbutz," *Journal of Marriage and the Family,* 31:567–573, August 1969.

Sherif, Muzafer A.: "A Study of Some Social Factors in Perception," *Archives of Psychology,* no. 187, 1935.

Sherman, Mandell, and Thomas R. Henry: *Hollow Folk,* Thomas Y. Crowell Company, New York, 1933.

Shibutani, Tamotsu: *Improvised News: A Sociological Study of Rumor,* The Bobbs-Merrill Company, Inc., Indianapolis, 1966.

Shils, Edward A: *The Intellectuals and the Powers and Other Essays,* The University of Chicago Press, Chicago, 1972.

——— and Morris Janowitz: "Cohesion and Disintegration in the Wehrmacht in World War II," *Public Opinion Quarterly,* 12:280–315, Summer 1948.

Short, James F., Jr., and Fred L. Strodtbeck: *Group Process and Gang Delinquency,* The University of Chicago Press, Chicago, 1965.

Shorter, Edward: "Illegitimacy, Sexual Revolution and Social Change in Modern Europe," *Journal of Interdisciplinary History,* 2:237–272, Autumn 1971.

———: *The Making of the Modern Family,* Basic Books, Inc., Publishers, New York, 1975.

Shostak, Arthur B. (ed.) *Putting Sociology to Work: Case Studies in the Application to Modern Social Problems,* David McKay Company, Inc., New York, 1974.

———, John Van Til, and Sally Van Til: *Privilege in America: An End to Inequality,* Prentice-Hall, Inc., Englewood Cliffs, N.J., 1973.

Shupe, Anson D., and David G. Bromley: *The New Vigilantes: Deprogrammers, Anti-Cultists and the New Religions,* Sage Publications, Beverly Hills, Calif., 1980.

Sieber, Sam D.: "Toward a Theory of Role Accumulation," *America Sociological Review,* 39:567–578, August 1974.

Siegal, Harvey: "Creationism, Evolution, and Education: The California Fiasco," *Phi Delta Kappan,* 63:95–101, October 1981.

Silcock, T. H.: *Southeastern University: A Comparative Account of Some Development Problems,* The Duke University Press, Durham, N.C., 1964.

Silverman, Matthew: "Toward a Theory of Criminal Deterrence," *American Journal of Sociology,* 41:442–461, June 1976.

Simis, Konstantin: "Russia's Underground Millionaires," *Fortune,* 103:36–50, June 29, 1981.

———: *U.S.S.R.: The Corrupt Society,* Simon and Schuster, New York, 1982.

Simkus, Albert A.: "Comparative Stratification and Mobility," *International Journal of Comparative Sociology,* 22:213–236, September/December 1981.

Simmons, John, and Leigh Alexander: "The Determinants of School Achievement in Developing Countries: A Review of Research," *Economic Development and Cultural Change,* 26:341–357, January 1978.

Simon, Julian L.: *The Ultimate Resource,* Princeton University Press, Princeton, N.J., 1981*a*.

———: "Global Confusion 1980: A Hard Look at the Global 2000 Report," *The Public Interest,* 62:3–20, Winter 1981*b*.

Simon, William, and John Gagnon: "Psychosexual Development," in Don Byrne and Lois A. Byrne (eds.), *Exploring Human Sexuality,* Thomas Y. Crowell Company, New York, 1977, pp. 117–129.

Singh, J. A. L., and Robert M. Zingg: *Wolf Children and Feral Men,* Harper & Row, Publishers, Inc., New York, 1942.

Singh, Jyoti Shanker (ed.): *World Population Policies,* Praeger Publishers, Inc., New York, 1979.

Sjoberg, Gideon: *The Preindustrial City,* The Free Press, New York, 1960.

Skodak, Marie, and Harold M. Skeels: "A Final Follow-up Study of One Hundred Children," *The Journal of Genetic Psychology,* 75:85–125, 1949.

Skolnik, Arlene: *The Intimate Environment: Exploring Marriage and the Family,* Little, Brown and Company, Boston, 1973.

Skolnik, Jerome (ed.): *The Politics of Protest*, Ballantine Books, Inc., New York, 1969.

Smeeding, Timothy M.: *Alternative Methods for Valuing Selected In-Kind Transfer Benefits and Measuring Their Effect on Poverty*, U.S. Bureau of the Census, Technical Paper No. 50, 1982.

Smelser, Neil J.: *Theory of Collective Behavior*, The Free Press, New York, 1963.

———: "The Mechanization of Social Relations," in Myron Weiner (ed.), *Modernization*, Basic Books, Inc., Publishers, New York, 1966, p. 111.

———: *The Sociology of Economic Life*, Prentice-Hall, Inc., Englewood Cliffs, N.J., 1976.

Smith, Betty: *A Tree Grows in Brooklyn*, Harper and Row, Publishers, Inc., New York, 1943.

Smith, Constance E., and Anne Freedman: *Voluntary Associations: Perspectives on the Literature*, Harvard University Press, Cambridge, Mass., 1972.

Smith, Delbert D.: "The Legitimacy of Civil Disobedience as a Legal Concept," *Fordham Law Review*, 336:707–730, May 1968.

Smoot, Dan: *The Invisible Government*, The Dan Smoot Reports, Inc., Dallas, Tex., 1962.

Smullen, Ivor: "The Chimp That Went Fishing," *International Wildlife*, 8:16–19, May/June 1978.

Snyder, David, and Charles Tilly: "Hardship and Collective Violence in France, 1830–1960," *American Sociological Review*, 37:520–532, October 1972.

Snyder, Mark: "Self Fulfilling Stereotypes," *Psychology Today*, 16:60–68, July 1982.

Soda, Takemune: "Quantity and Quality of the Aged Population in Japan: The Use of Life Tables for the Assessment of Group Vitality," *Journal of Population Studies*, 3:1–7ff., April 1980.

Somit, Albert: "Brainwashing," in David L. Sells (ed.), *International Encyclopedia of the Social Sciences*, The Macmillan Company, New York, 1968, vol. 2, pp. 138–142.

Sonquist, John A., and William C. Dunkelberg: *Survey and Opinion Research: Procedures for Processing and Analysis*, Prentice-Hall, Inc., Englewood Cliffs, N.J., 1977.

Sorensen, Aage B., and Nancy Bradendon Tuma: "Labor Market Structures and Social Mobility," in Donald J. Treiman and Robert V. Robinson (eds.), *Research in Social Stratification and Social Mobility*, 1:67–94, JAI Press, Greenwich, Conn., 1981.

Sorokin, Pitirim A.: *Contemporary Sociological Theories*, Harper & Row, Publishers, Inc., New York, 1928.

———: *Social and Cultural Dynamics*, American Book Company, New York, 1941.

———: *The Revolution of Humanity*, Beacon press, Boston, 1948.

——— and Carle C. Zimmerman: *Principles of Rural-Urban Sociology*, Holt, Rinehart and Winston, Inc., New York, 1929.

Sowell, Thomas: "Patterns of Black Excellence," *The Public Interest*, 43:26–58, Spring 1976a.

———: "A Black Conservative Dissents," *The New York Times Magazine*, Aug. 8, 1976b, pp. 14–15.

———: "New Light on Black I.Q." *The New York Times Magazine*, March 17, 1977, pp. 65–61.

———: *Ethnic America: A History*, Basic Books, Inc., Publishers, New York, 1981a.

———: "False Assumptions About Black Education," in Thomas Sowell et al., (eds.), *The Fairmont Papers*, Institute for Contemporary Studies, San Francisco, 1981b, pp. 63–80.

Spector, Paul E.: "Population Density and Unemployment: The Effects on the Incidence of Violent Crime in America," *Criminology*, 12:399–401, February 1975.

Spence, Janet T., and Robert L. Helmreich: *Masculinity and Femininity: Their Psychological Dimensions, Correlates, and Antecedents*, University of Texas Press, Austin, 1978.

Spengler, Joseph J.: *Facing Zero Population Growth: Reactions and Interpretations, Past and Present*, The Duke University Press, Durham, N.C., 1978.

Spengler, Oswald: *The Decline of the West*, translated by Charles Francis Atkinson, Alfred A. Knopf, Inc., New York, 1926–1928.

Spicer, Edward H. (ed.): *Human Problems in Technological Change*, Russell Sage Foundation, New York, 1952.

Spiro, Melford E.: *Children of the Kibbutz*, Harvard University Press, Cambridge, Mass., 1958.

———: *Gender and Culture: Kibbutz Women Revisited*, The Duke University Press, Durham, N.C., 1979.

Spitz, René: "Hospitalism," in *The Psychoanalytic Study of the Child*, vol. 1, International Universities Press, Inc., New York, 1945, pp. 53–74.

———: *The First Year of Life*, International Universities Press, Inc., New York, 1965.

Spock, Benjamin: *The Pocket Book of Child Care*, Pocket Books, a division of Simon & Schuster, Inc., New York, 1945, 1957, 1974.

Bibliography

————: *Raising Children in a Difficult Time*, W. W. Norton & Company, Inc., New York, 1974.

————: *Babies and Child Care*, Pocket Books, Inc., a division of Simon & Schuster, Inc., New York, 1977.

Spradley, James P.: *Participant Observation*, Holt, Rinehart and Winston, Inc., New York, 1980.

Sprung, Barbara (ed.): *Perspectives on Non-Sexist Early Childhood Education*, Teachers College Press, Columbia University, New York, 1976.

Squires, Gregory D.: "Education, Jobs and Inequality: Functional and Conflict Models of Stratification in the United States," *Social Problems*, 42:436–450, April 1977.

Stacey, Judith: "Toward a Theory of Family and Revolution," *Social Problems*, 26:499–508, June 1979.

Stacy, Frank A.: *Ombudsmen Compared*, Oxford University Press, New York, 1978.

Stafford, Rebecca, et al.: "The Division of Labor Among Cohabiting and Married Couples," *Journal of Marriage and the Family*, 39:43–57, February 1977.

Stahl, Sidney M., and Morty Lebedun: "Mystery Gas: An Analysis of Mass Hysteria," *Journal of Health and Social Behavior*, 14:44–50, March 1974.

Stark, Rodney, and William Sims Bainbridge: "Of Churches, Sects and Cults," *Journal for the Scientific Study of Religion*, 18:117–131, June, 1979.

———— and ————: "Secularization and Cult Formation," *Journal for the Scientific Study of Religion*, 20:33–34, December 1981.

Starkey, Marion L.: *The Devil in Massachusetts*, Alfred A. Knopf, Inc., New York, 1949.

Stein, Maurice, and Arthur Vidich: *Sociology on Trial*, Prentice-Hall, Inc., Englewood Cliffs, N.J., 1964.

Stein, Peter J. (ed.): *Single Life: Unmarried Adults in Social Context*, St. Martin's Press, Inc., N.Y., 1981.

Steiner, Frederick: *The Politics of New Town Planning: The Newfields, Ohio Story*, Ohio University Press, Athens, 1981.

Steiner, Stanley: *The New Indians*, Harper & Row, Publishers, Inc., New York, 1968.

Steinhart, Peter: "A Plague of Coyotes," *The New York Times Magazine*, March 28, 1982, pp. 21ff.

Steinmetz, Suzanne K.: *The Cycle of Violence: Assertive, Aggressive, and Abusive Family Interaction*, Praeger Publishers, Inc., New York, 1977.

Stephens, William A.: "A Cross-Cultural Study of Modesty and Obscenity," in *Technical Report of the Commission on Obscenity and Pornography*, Washington, vol. IX, 1970.

Stern, Bernhard J.: "Resistance to the Adoption of Technological Inventions," in U.S. National Resources Committee, *Technological Trends and National Policy*, 1937, pp. 39–66.

Sternberg, David Joel: *Radical Sociology*, Exposition Press, Hicksville, N.Y., 1977.

Sternlieb, George, and Robert W. Burchell: *Residential Abandonment: The Tenement Landlord Revisited*, Center for Urban Policy Research, Rutgers University Press, New Brunswick, N.J., 1973.

Stevenson, Matilda: "The Zuñi Indians," *23rd Annual Report of the Bureau of American Ethnology, 1901–1902*, Washington, 1902.

Stewart, Charles T., Jr.: "The Rural-Urban Dichotomy: Concepts and Uses," *American Journal of Sociology*, 64:152–158, September 1958.

Stewart, James R.: "Cattle Mutilations: An Episode of Collective Delusion," *The Zetetic* (now *The Skeptical Inquirer*), Spring/Summer 1977, pp. 55–66.

Stiglin, Laura E.: "A Classic Case of Over-Reaction: Women and Social Security," *New England Economic Review*, January/February 1981, pp. 29–40.

Stockard, Jean, and Miriam M. Johnson: *Sex Roles: Sex Inequality and Sex Role Development*, Prentice-Hall, Inc., Englewood Cliffs, N.J., 1980.

Stokols, David: "The Experience of Crowding in Primary and Secondary Environments," *Environment and Behavior*, 8:49–86, March 1976.

Stoltz, Lois Keek: "Effects of Maternal Employment upon Children: Evidence from Research," *Child Development*, 31:749–782, 1960.

Stolzenberg, Ross M., and Ronald J. D'Amico: "City Differencs and Nondifferences in the Effect of Race and Sex on Occupational Distribution," *American Sociological Review*, 42:937–986, December 1977.

Stone, Carol: "Some Family Characteristics of Socially Active and Inactive Teenagers," *Family Life Coordinator*, 8:53–57, 1960.

Stonequist, Everett H.: *The Marginal Man*, Charles Scribner's Sons, New York, 1937.

Stoner, Caroll, and Jo Anne Parke: *All God's Children*, Chilton Books, Radnor, Pa., 1977.

Stouffer, Samuel A., et al.: *Studies in the Social*

Psychology of World War II, vol. 2, "The American Soldier: Combat and Aftermath," Princeton University Press, Princeton, N.J., 1949.

Strange, Heather, and Joseph McCrory: "Bulls and Bears in the Cell Block," *Society*, 11:51–59, July/August 1974.

Straus, Murray A., Richard Gelles, and Suzanne Steinmetz: *Behind Closed Doors: Violence in the American Family*, Anchor Books, Doubleday & Company, Inc., Gaden City, N.Y., 1980.

Strauss, Anselm L.: "The Literature on Panic," *Journal of Abnormal and Social Psychology*, 39:317–328, July 1944.

———, Barney G. Glasser, and Jeanne C. Quint: "Religion, American Values and Death Perspective," *Sociological Symposium*, 1:30–36, Fall 1968.

Street, Peggy, and Pierre Street: "In Iran a New Group Challenges Us," *The New York Times Magazine*, July 23, 1961, pp. 11ff.

Stretton, Hugh: *Urban Planning in Rich and Poor Countries*, Oxford University Press, Oxford, 1978.

Stryker, Robin: "Religio-Ethnic Effects on Early Career," *American Sociological Review*, 46:222–231, April 1981.

Stuckert, Robert P.: "African Ancestry of the White American Population," *Ohio Journal of Science*, 58:155–160, May 1958.

Suchman, Edward A.: *Evaluation Research: Principles and Practice in Public Service and Social Action Programs*, Russell Sage Foundation, New York, 1967.

Suczek, Barbara: "The Curious Case of the 'Death' of Paul McCartney," *Urban Life and Culture*, 1:61–76, April 1972.

Sulzberger, C. L.: "How Many Divisions Has the Pope?" *The New York Times*, Oct. 8, 1958, p. 34.

Sumner, William Graham: *Folkways* (1906), Ginn and Company, Boston, 1940.

Surface, Bill: *The Hollow*, Coward-McCann, Inc., New York, 1970.

Suter, Larry E., and Herman P. Miller: "Incomes of Men and Career Women," *American Journal of Sociology*, 78:962–974, January 1973.

Sutherland, Edwin H.: *White Collar Crime*, The Dryden Press, Inc., New York, 1949.

Suttles, Gerald D.: *The Social Order of the Slum*, The University of Chicago Press, Chicago, 1968.

Swatos, William H.: "Beyond Denominationalism?" *Journal for the Scientific Study of Religion*, 20:217–227, September 1981.

Syzmanski, Albert: "The Inauthentic Sociology: A Critique of Etzioni's Activist Society," *Human Factor*, 9:53–63, Spring 1960.

———: "The Socialization of Women's Oppression: A Marxian Theory of the Changing Position of Women in Advanced Capitalist Society," *The Insurgent Sociologist*, 6:31–58, Winter 1976.

Szasz, Thomas S.: *The Manufacture of Madness*, Dell Publishing Co., Inc., New York, 1970.

Takoosian, Harold, et al.: "Who Wouldn't Help a Lost Child? You, Maybe," *Psychology Today*, 10:67ff., February 1977.

Talmon, Yonina: *Family and Community in the Kibbutz*, Harvard University Press, Cambridge, Mass., 1972.

Tavris, Carol, and Carole Offir: *The Longest War: Sex Differences in Perspective*, Harcourt Brace Jovanovich, Inc., New York, 1977.

Taylor, Lee. *Urbanized Society*, Goodyear Publishing Company, Santa Monica, Calif., 1980.

Taylor, Miller Lee, and A. R. Jones: *Rural Life in Urbanized Society*, Oxford University Press, Fair Lawn, N.J., 1964.

Taylor, Ronald A.: "Where Tribes Fit Into Reagan's Plan," *U.S. News & World Report*, 87:68, March 15, 1982.

Taylor, Telford: *Nuremberg and Vietnam: An American Tragedy*, Quadrangle Books, Inc., Chicago, 1970.

Terkel, Louis (Studs): *Working*, Pantheon Books, a division of Random House, Inc., New York, 1974.

Terrace, Herbert S.: *Nim, A Chimpanzee Who Learned Sign Language*, Alfred A. Knopf, Inc., New York, 1979.

Thernstrom, Stephen (ed.): *Harvard Encyclopedia of American Ethnic Groups*, Harvard University Press, Cambridge, Mass., 1980.

Thomas, Michael C., and Charles C. Flippen: "American Civil Religion: An Empirical Study," *Social Forces*, 51:218–225, December 1972.

Thomas, Ray, and Peter Cresswell: *The New Town Idea*, The Open University Press, Milton Keynes, England, 1973.

Thomas, W. I.: *The Unadjusted Girl*, Little, Brown and Company, Boston, 1923.

———: *Primitive Behavior: An Introduction to the Social Sciences*, McGraw-Hill Book Company, New York, 1937.

——— and Florian Znaniecki: *The Polish Peasant in*

Europe and America, Alfred A. Knopf, Inc., New York, 1918, 1927.

Thompson, Victor A.: *Modern Organization,* University of Alabama Press, Tuscaloosa, 1977.

Thorman, George: *Family Violence,* Charles C Thomas, Publisher, Springfield, Ill., 1980.

Thurow, Lester C.: "Why Women Are Paid Less Than Men," *The New York Times,* March 3, 1981, sec. III, p. 2.

Tiger, Lionel, and Joseph Shepher: *Women in the Kibbutz,* Harcourt Brace Jovanovich, Inc., New York, 1975.

Tittle, Charles R.: "Deterrents or Labeling," *Social Forces,* 53:399–410, March 1975.

———: *Sanctions and Social Deviance: The Question of Deterrence,* Praeger Publishers, Inc., New York, 1980.

Toffler, Alvin: *Future Shock,* Random House, Inc., New York, 1970.

———: *The Third Wave,* Bantam Books, Inc., New York, 1981.

Togerson, Ellen: "TV Watching," *TV Guide,* April 23, 1977, p. 4.

Tomasson, Richard F.: "Religion Is Irrelevant in Sweden," in Jeffrey K. Hadden (ed.), *Religion in Radical Transition,* Transaction Books, New Brunswick, N.J., 1971, pp. 111–127.

Tompkins, Peter, and Christopher Bird: *The Secret Life of Plants,* Harper & Row, Publishers, Inc., New York, 1973.

Tönnies, Ferdinand: *Community and Society* (1887), trans. and ed. by Charles A. Loomis, The Michigan State University Press, East Lansing, 1957.

Toynbee, Arnold: *A Study of History,* Oxford University Press, London, 1935–1961.

Treiman, Donald J.: "Status Discrepancy and Prejudice," *American Journal of Sociology,* 71:651–664, May 1966.

———: *Occupational Prestige in Comparative Perspective,* Academic Press, Inc., New York, 1977.

——— and Kermit Terrell: "Sex and the Process of Status Attainment: A Comparison of Working Women and Men," *American Sociological Review,* 40:174–200, April 1975.

Trimble, Joseph E.: "Say Good-bye to the Hollywood Indian," paper presented at Annual Meeting of American Psychological Association, New Orleans, August 1974.

Troeltsch, Ernst: *The Social Teachings of the Christian Churches,* vols. 1 and 2, trans. by Olive Wyon, The Macmillan Company, New York, 1931.

Troll, Lillian: Research reported in "More Motivated, but No Happier," *Science News,* 121:43, Jan. 16, 1982.

Tropman, John E.: "Social Mobility and Marital Stability," *Applied Social Studies,* 3:165–173, 1971.

Trost, Jan: *Unmarried Cohabitation,* International Library, Vasteros, Sweden, 1979.

Trotter, Robert J.: "Aggression: A Way of Life for the Quolla," *Science News,* 103:65–80, Feb. 3, 1973.

Tuch, Stephen A.: "Analyzing Recent Trends in Prejudice toward Blacks: Insights from Latent Class Models," *American Journal of Sociology,* 87:130–142, July 1981.

Tucker, Jonathan B.: "Biomass Systems in India: Is the Technology Appropriate?" *Environment,* 24:13ff., October 1982.

Tuddenham, Read D.: "The Influence of a Distorted Group Norm upon Judgments of Adults and Children," *Journal of Psychology,* 52:231–239, July 1961.

Tumin, Melvin: "Some Unapplauded Consequences of Social Mobility," *Social Forces,* 36:21–37, September 1957.

———: "On Inequality," *American Sociological Review,* 28:19–26, February 1963.

Turnbull, Colin: *The Mountain People,* Simon & Schuster, Inc., New York, 1973.

Turner, Jay R., and Morton O. Wagenfeld: "Occupational Mobility and Schizophrenia: An Assessment of the Social Causation and Social Selection Hypothesis," *American Sociological Review,* 32:104–113, February 1967.

Turner, Ralph H., and Samuel J. Surace: "Zoot-Suiters and Mexicans: Symbols in Crowd Behavior," *American Journal of Sociology,* 62:14–20, July 1956.

——— and Lewis M. Killian: *Collective Behavior,* Prentice-Hall, Inc., Englewood Cliffs, N.J., 1957, 1972.

Tweeten, Luther, and Dean Schreiner: "Economic Impact of Public Policy and Technology in Marginal Farms and on the Non-Farm Population," in Iowa State University Center for Agricultural and Economic Development, *Benefits and Burdens of Rural Development,* The Iowa State University Press, Ames, 1970, pp. 41–76.

Tylor, Edward: *Primitive Culture: Researches into the Development of Mythology, Philosophy, Religion, Language, Art and Custom,* vol. 1, John Murray (Publishers), Ltd., London, 1871.

Udry, J. Richard: "Marital Alternatives and Marital Disruption," *Journal of Marriage and the Family*, 43:889–897, November 1981.

United Nations Department of International Economics and Social Affairs, *Report on the World Situation*, no. E-821V.2, United Nations, New York, 1982.

U.S. Bureau of the Census: "Fertility of American Women, June 1975," *Current Population Reports*, ser. P-20, no. 301, 1976.

———: "Projections of the Population of the United States," *Current Population Reports*, ser. P-25, no. 704, 1977.

———: "Families Maintained by Female Householders, 1970–1979,"*Current Population Reports*, ser. P-23, no. 10, 1980*a*.

———: "Money Income of Households, Families and Persons in the United States, 1978," *Current Population Reports*, ser. P-60, no. 123, 1980*b*.

———: "Persons of Spanish Origin in the United States, March 1980." *Current Population Reports*, ser. P-20, no. 361, 1981*a*.

———: "Geographic Mobility, March 1975 to March 1980," *Current Population Reports*, ser. P-20, no. 368, 1981*b*.

———: "Population Profile of the United States, March 1980," *Current Population Reports*, ser. P-20, no. 363, 1981*c*.

———: *Social Indicators III*, 1981*d*.

———: "Household and Family Characteristics, March 1980," *Current Population Reports*, ser. P-20, no. 366, 1981*e*.

———: "Household and Family Characteristics, March 1981," *Current Population Reports*, ser. P-20, no. 371, 1982*a*.

———: "Marital Status and Living Arrangements, March 1981," *Current Population Reports*, ser. P-20, no. 372, 1982*b*.

———: "Population Profile of the United States, 1981," *Current Population Reports*, ser. P-20, no. 374, 1982*c*.

———: "Fertility of American Women, June 1980," *Current Population Reports*, ser. P-20, no. 375, 1982*d*.

———: "Money Income of Households, Families, and Persons in the United States, 1981," *Current Population Reports*, ser. P-60, no. 137, 1983.

U.S. Bureau of Labor Statistics: *Summary of the Report on Conditions of Women and Children Wage Earners in the United States*, Bulletin No. 175, 1908.

U.S. Commission on Population Growth and the American Future: *Final Report: Population Growth and the American Future:* New American Library, New York, 1972.

U.S. Department of Labor: *Negroes in the United States: Their Economic and Social Situation*, Bulletin 1511, June 1966.

Unni, K. P.: "Polyandry in Malabar," *Sociological Bulletin* (India), 7:62–79, 1958.

Urban America, Inc.: *One year Later*, Frederick A. Praeger, Inc., New York, 1969.

Useem, John: "South Sea Island Strike: Labor-Management Relations in the Caroline Islands, Micronesia," in Edward H. Spicer (ed.), *Human Problems in Technological Change*, Russell Sage Foundation, New York, 1952, pp. 149–164.

Vaillant, George E., and Caroline O. Vaillant: "Natural History of Male Psychological Health: Work as a Predictor of Positive Mental Health," *American Journal of Psychiatry*, 138:14333–1440, November 1981.

Vajk, J. Peter: *Doomsday Has Been Cancelled*, Peace Press, Inc., Culver City, Calif., 1979.

Van den Berghe, Pierre L.: *Man in Society: A Biosocial View*, Elsevier, New York, 1975.

Vander Kooi, Ronald: "The Main Stem: Skid Row Revisited," *Society*, September 1973, pp. 64–71.

van der Tak, Jean: "East Europe's Drive to Raise Birth Rates: A Temporary Success," *Intercom* (Population Reference Bureau), 10:1–11, February 1982*a*.

———: "USSR's Demographics Pose Challenges to the Kremlin," *Intercom* (Population Reference Bureau), 10:1–11, July/August 1982*b*.

VanderZanden, James W.: "The Klan Revival," *American Journal of Sociology*, 65:456–462, March 1960.

Vanek, Joanne: "Time Spent in Housework," *Scientific American*, 321:119–120, November 1974.

van Gennep, Arnold: *Rites of Passage*, The University of Chicago Press, Chicago, 1960.

Van Valey, Thomas L., Wade C. Roof, and Jerome E. Wilcox: "Trends in Residential Segregation: 1960–1970," *American Journal of Sociology*, 82:826–844, January 1977.

Van Velsor, Ellen, and Leonard Beeghley: "The Process of Class Identification Among Employed Married Women: A Replication and Reanalysis," *Journal of Marriage and the Family*, 41:771–791, November 1979.

Veevers, Jean E.: *Childless by Choice*, Butterworths, Toronto, 1980.

Vernon, Glenn: *The Sociology of Death: An Analysis of Death Related Behavior*, The Ronald Press Company, New York, 1978.

Villadsen, L. A.: "Unwed Mothers in Our Midst," Wall Street Journal, Feb. 11, 1982, p. 25.

Vincent, Clark E.: "An Open Letter to the 'Caught Generation'," *The Family Coordinator*, 1:143–150, April 1972.

Vogeler, Imgolf: *The Myth of the Family Farm: Agribusiness Dominance of the U.S. Agriculture*, Westview Press, Boulder, Col., 1981.

Vogt, Evon Z., and Ethel M. Albert: *People of Redrock: A Study of Values in Five Cultures*, Harvard University Press, Cambridge, Mass., 1966.

Von der Muhll, George: "Robert A. Dahl and the Study of Contemporary Democracy," *American Political Science Review*, 71:1079–1096, September 1977.

Von Frank, April: *Family Policy in the USSR Since 1944*, R and E Research Associates, Palo Alto, Calif., 1979.

Von Hentig, Hans: "Redhead and Outlaw," *Journal of Criminal Law and Criminology*, 38:1–6, May/June 1947.

Voorhies, Barbara: "Supernumerary Sexes," paper presented at 71st Annual Meeting of the American Anthropological Association, Toronto, November 1973.

Waisanen, F. B., and Hideya Kumata: "Education, Functional Literacy, and Participation in Development," *International Journal of Comparative Sociology*, 13:21–35, March 1972.

Wakil, S. Parvez: "Campus Mate Selection Preferences: A Cross-National Comparison," *Social Forces*, 51:471–476, June 1973.

Wallace, A. F. C.: "The Modal Personality Structure of the Tuscarora Indians as Revealed by the Rorschach Test," *Bureau of American Ethnology*, Bulletin No. 150, 1952*a*.

————: "Individual Differences and Cultural Uniformities," *American Sociological Review*, 17:747–750, December 1952*b*.

Wallace, Samuel E.: *Skid Row as a Way of Life*, Harper & Row, Publishers, Inc., New York, 1965.

————: "The Road to Skid Row," *Social Problems*, 16:92–105, Summer 1968.

————: *The Urban Environment*, The Dorsey Press, Homewood, Ill., 1980.

Wallerstein, Immanuel: *The Modern World System*, Academic Press, Inc., New York, 1974.

————: *The Capitalist-World Economy*, Cambridge University Press, Cambridge, Mass., 1979.

Wallerstein, James S., and Clement J. Wyle: "Our Law-Abiding Law Breakers," *National Probation*, pp. 107–112, March/April 1947.

Walsh, Edward J.: "Resource Mobilization and Citizen Protest in Communities Around Three Mile Island," *Social Problems*, 29:1–21, October 1981.

Walter, E. V.: "Dreadful Exposures: Detoxifying an Urban Myth," *Archives Européennes de Sociologie*, 18:151–159, 1977.

Walum, Laurel Richardson: *The Dynamics of Sex and Gender: A Sociological Perspective*, Rand McNally College Publishing Co., Chicago, 1977.

Warner, L.: "Running Battle of the Library Shelves," *Times Educational Supplement*, 3377:14, March 13, 1981.

Warner, W. Lloyd, and Paul S. Lunt: *The Social Life of a Modern Community*, Yale University Press, New Haven, Conn., 1941.

———— and ————: *The Status System of a Modern Community*, Yale University Press, New Haven, Conn., 1942.

Warren, Bill: "The Postwar Economic Experience of the Third World," in Rotho Chapel Colloquium, *Toward a New Strategy for Development*, Pergamon Press, New York, 1979, pp. 144–168.

Warriner, Charles K.: "The Nature and Functions of Official Morality," *American Journal of Sociology*, 64:165–168, September 1958.

Wax, Murray L.: *Indian Americans: Unity and Diversity*, Prentice-Hall, Inc., Englewood Cliffs, N.J., 1971.

Webb, Maryla, and Judith Jacobsen: *U.S. Carrying Capacity: An Introduction*, Carrying Capacity, Inc., Washington, 1982.

Webbe, Stephen: "U.S. Army May Use British System to Boost Morale," *Christian Science Monitor*, Nov. 13, 1980, pp. 1ff.

Weber, Max: *The Protestant Ethic and the Spirit of Capitalism* (1904), trans. by Talcott Parsons, George Allen & Unwin, Ltd. London, 1930.

————: *Essays in Sociology* (1904), trans. and ed. by Talcott Parsons, Charles Scribner's Sons, New York, 1956.

Weede, Erich: "Beyond Misspecification in Sociological Analysis of Income Inequality, *American Sociological Review*, 45:497–501, June 1980.

———— and Horst Tiefenbach: "Some Recent Explanations of Income Inequality," *International Studies Quarterly*, 25:255–282, June 1981.

Weeks, Albert L.: "Terrorism: The Deadly Tradition," *Freedom at Issue*, 46:2–11, May/June 1978.

Weil, Andrew: "Andrew Weil's Search for the True Uri Geller," *Psychology Today*, 8:45–50, June 1974; 8:74–82, July 1974.

Weinberg, Sanford B., and Ritch K. Eich: "Spreading Fire with Fire: Establishment of a Rumor Control Center," *Communications Quarterly*, 16:26–31, Summer 1978.

Weinstein, Jay: "Do We Need A Theory of Demographic Transition?" *Humboldt Journal of Social Relations*, 7:71–86, Spring/Summer 1980.

Weitz, Shirley: *Sex Roles: Biological, Psychological, and Social Foundations*, Oxford University Press, New York, 1977.

Welch, Claude E., Jr.: *Anatomy of Rebellion*, State University of New York Press, Albany, 1980.

Weller, Leonard, and Elmer Luchterhand: "Effects of Improved Housing on the Family Functioning of Large, Low-Income Black Families," *Social Problems*, 20:382–389, Winter 1973.

Wenger, Dennis E.: "The Reluctant Army: The Functioning of Police Departments During Civil Disturbances," *American Behavioral Scientist*, 16:326–342, January/February 1973.

———— et al.: "It's a Matter of Myths: An Empirical Examination of Individual Insight into Disaster Response," *Mass Emergencies*, 1:33–46, October 1975.

West, James: *Plainville, U.S.A.*, Columbia University Press, New York, 1945.

Westie, Frank F.: "Social Distance Scales: A Tool for the Study of Stratification," *Sociology and Social Research*, 43:251–258, March/April 1959.

Westoff, Charles: "Some Speculations on Marriage and Fertility," *Family Planning Perspectives*, 10:79–83, March/April 1978.

Whimby, Arthur, with Laura Shaw Whimby: *Intelligence Can Be Taught*, E. P. Dutton & Co., Inc., New York, 1975.

White, Burton L.: *The First Three Years of Life*, Prentice-Hall, Inc., Englewood Cliffs, N.J., 1975.

White, D. M., and R. L. Francis: "Title VII and the Masters of Reality: Eliminating Credentialism in the American Labor Market," *Georgetown Law Review*, 64:1213–1244, 1976.

White, Michael J.: *Urban Renewal and the Changing Residential Structure of the City*, Community and Family Center, The University of Chicago, 1980.

Whiting, Robert: *The Chrysanthemum and the Bat*, Dodd, Mead & Company, Inc., New York, 1977.

Whitman, David: "Class Conflict Behind the Miami Riot," *USA Today*, 109:23–25, November 1980.

Whitt, J. Allen: "Towards a Class Dialectic Model of Power: An Empirical Assessment of Three Competing Models of Political Power," *American Sociological Review*, 44:81–100, February 1979.

Whyte, Martin King: *The Status of Women in Preindustrial Societies*, Princeton University Press, Princeton, N.J., 1978.

Whyte, William F.: *Street Corner Society*, The University of Chicago Press, Chicago, 1955.

Wilbert, Johannes: "To Become a Maker of Canoes: An Essay in Warao Enculturation," in Johannes Wilbert (ed.), *Enculturation in Latin America: An Anthology*, Latin American Center Publications, University of California, 1977, pp. 303–358.

Wilkie, Jane Ribbett: "The Trend Toward Delayed Parenthood," *Journal of Marriage and the Family*, 43:583–591, August 1981.

Wilkinson, Doris Y.: "Collective Behavior Theory and Research: A Critique of Smelser's Approach," paper presented at American Sociological Association, Washington, 1970.

Wilkinson, Paul W.: *Terrorism and the Liberal State*, John Wiley & Sons, Inc., New York, 1977.

Williams, Allen J., Jr., Nicholas Babchuck, and David R. Johnson: "Voluntary Associations and Minority Status: A Comparative Analysis of Anglo, Black, and Mexican Americans," *American Sociological Review*, 38:637–646, October 1973.

Williams, Juanita H.: *Psychology of Women: Behavior in a Biosocial Context*, W. W. Norton & Company, Inc., New York, 1977.

Williams, Walter E.: "Legal Barriers to Economic Gains: Employment and Transportation, in Thomas Sowell et al., (eds.), *The Fairmont Papers*, Institute for Contemporary Studies, San Francisco, 1981, pp. 23–30.

Willie, Charles: Increasing Significance of Race," *Society*, 15:10–12, July 1978.

Willis, Cecil L.: "Definitions of Community II: An Examination of Definitions of Community Since 1950," paper presented at Southern Sociological Society, Atlanta, 1977.

Wilson, Basil, and John L. Cooper: "Ghetto Reflections and the Role of the Police Officer,"

Journal of Police Science and Administration, 7:28–35, 1979.

Wilson, Edmund O.: *Sociobiology, The New Synthesis*, Harvard University Press, Cambridge, Mass., 1975.

Wilson, Glenn, and David Nias: "Beauty Can't Be Beat," *Psychology Today*, 10:97–99, September 1976.

Wilson, John: *Introduction to Social Movements*, Basic Books, Inc., Publishers, New York, 1973.

———: *Religion in American Society: The Effective Presence*, Prentice-Hall, Inc., Englewood Cliffs, N.J., 1978.

Wilson, Robert A., and Bill Hosakawa: *East to America: A History of the Japanese in the United States*, William Morrow & Company, Inc., New York, 1980.

——— and David A. Schulz: *Urban Sociology*, Prentice-Hall, Inc., Englewood Cliffs, N.J., 1978.

Wilson, Stephen: *Informal Groups: An Introduction*, Prentice-Hall, Inc., Englewood Cliffs, N.J., 1978.

Wilson, Warner, et al.: "Authoritarianism Left and Right," *Bulletin of the Psychonomic Society*, 7:271–274, March 1976.

Wilson, William Julius: *The Declining Significance of Race*, The University of Chicago Press, Chicago, 1978.

———: "The Black Community in the 1980's: Questions of Race, Class and Public Policy," *Annals of the American Academy of Political and Social Science*, 454:26–41, March 1981.

Wimberly, Ronald C.: "Testing the Civil Religion Hypothesis," *Sociological Analysis*, 37:341–352, Winter, 1976.

——— and James A. Christenson: "Civil Religion and Other Religious Identities," *Sociological Analysis*, 42:91–101, December 1981.

Winfield, Gerald F.: "The Impact of Urbanization on Agricultural Process," *The Annals of the American Academy of Political and Social Science*, 405:65–74, January 1973.

Wirth, Louis: *The Ghetto*, The University of Chicago Press, Chicago, 1928.

———: "Urbanism as a Way of Life," *American Journal of Sociology*, 44:3–24, July 1938.

Wise, James: "A Gentle Deterrent to Vandalism," *Psychology Today*, 16:31–38, September 1982.

Wisnewski, Robert L.: "Carrying Capacity: Understanding Our Biological Limitations," *Humboldt Journal of Social Relations*, 7:55–70, Spring/Summer 1980.

Wissler, Clark: "Depression and Revolt," *Natural History*, 41:108–112, February 1938.

Wittfogel, Karl A.: *Oriental Despotism*, Yale University Press, New Haven, Conn., 1957.

Wixen, Burton N.: *Children of the Rich*, Crown Publishers, Inc., New York, 1973.

Woelfel, Joseph, and Archibald O. Haller: "Significant Others: The Self-Reflective Act and the Attitude Formation Process," *American Sociological Review*, 36:74–87, February 1971.

Wolcott, Robert, and Adam Rose: "Economic Effects of the Clean Air Act," reviewed in *Science News*, 122:58, July 24, 1982.

Wolf, Eleanor: *Trial and Error*, Wayne State University Press, Detroit, 1981.

Wolock, Isabel, and Bernard Horowitz: "Child Maltreatment and Maternal Deprivation among AFDC Recipients," *Social Service Review*, 53:175–182, June 1979.

Wood, Allen W.: *Karl Marx*, Routledge & Kegan Paul, Ltd., London, 1981.

Woodrum, Eric: "An Assessment of Japanese American Assimilation, Pluralism, and Subordination," *American Journal of Sociology*, 87:157–169, July 1981.

Woodward, C. Vann: "What Became of the 1960's?" *New Republic*, 171:18–25, Nov. 9, 1974.

Wren, Christopher S.: "China Unleashes a Capitalist Tool," *The New York Times*, April 25, 1982, sec. 3, pp. 1ff.

Wright, Eric Olin, et al.: "The American Class Structure," *American Sociological Review*, 47:709–726, December 1982.

Wright, James D.: "Are Working Wives Really More Satisfied? Evidence from Several National Surveys," *Journal of Marriage and the Family*, 40:301–313, May 1978.

Wright, Janey D.: "The Socio-Political Attitudes of White, College-Educated Youth," *Youth and Society*, 6:251–296, March 1975.

Wrong, Dennis H.: *Skeptical Sociology*, Columbia University Press, New York, 1976.

Wynder, E. L., and A. Graham Evarts: "Tobacco as a Possible Etiological Factor in Bronchogenic Carcinoma: A Study of Six Hundred and Eighty-four Proved Cases," *Journal of the American Medical Association*, 143:329–336, May 27, 1950.

Yang, C. K.: *The Chinese Family in the Communist Revolution*, The M.I.T. Press, Cambridge, Mass., 1959.

Yankelovich, Daniel: *The Changing Values on Cam-*

pus: A Survey for the JDR Fund, Pocket Books, a division of Simon & Schuster, Inc., New York, 1972.

———: "The Hidden Appeal of the Moral Majority," *Psychology Today*, 15:23–24, November 1981.

———; "The Work Ethic Is Underemployed," *Psychology Today*, 16:5–8, May 1982.

Yankelovich, Skelley, and White, Inc.,: Cited in "The New Morality," *Time*, Nov. 21, 1977, pp. 111–118.

Yanowitch, Murray: *Social and Economic Equality in the Soviet Union*, M. E. Sharpe, White Plains, N.Y., 1977.

Yen, C. H., C. M. Wang, and Y. T. Wang: "Taiwan," *Studies in Family Planning*, 4:118–123, April 1973.

Yinger, J. Milton: *Sociology Looks at Religion*, The Macmillan Company, New York, 1963.

———: *Toward a Field Theory of Behavior*, McGraw-Hill Book Company, New York, 1965.

———: "Countercultures and Social Change," in J. Milton Yinger and Stephen J. Cutler (eds.), *Major Social Issues: A Multidisciplinary View*, The Free Press, New York, 1978, pp. 476–498.

———: *Countercultures*, The Free Press, New York, 1982.

Yoon, Won K.: "Organizational Aspects of Korean Immigrant Churches in North America," paper presented at the Association for the Sociology of Religion, Toronto, 1981.

Young, Kimball and Raymond W. Mack: *Sociology and Social Life*, American Book Company, New York, 1959.

Youniss, James: *Parents and Peers in Social Development: A Sullivan-Piaget Perspective*, The University of Chicago Press, Chicago, 1980.

Zablocki, Benjamin: *Alienation and Charisma: A Study of Contemporary American Communes*, The MacMillan Company, New York, 1980.

Zahn, G. D.: *The Military Chaplaincy: A Study of Role Transition in the Royal Air Force*, University of Toronto Press, Toronto, 1969.

Zald, Mayer N., and Roberta Ash: "Social Movement Organizations," in Barry McLaughlin, *Studies in Social Movements*, The Free Press, New York, 1969, pp. 461–485.

——— and John D. McCarthy (eds.): *The Dynamics of Social Movements: Resource Mobilization, Social Control, and Tactics*, Winthrop Publications, Cambridge, Mass., 1979.

Zelditch, Morris, Jr.: "Cross-Cultural Analysis of Family Structure," in Harold T. Christensen (ed.), *Handbook of Marriage and the Family*, Rand McNally & Company, Chicago, 1964, pp. 462–500.

Zelnik, Melvin, and John F. Kantner; "Contraceptive Patterns and Premarital Pregnancy Among Women Aged 15–19 in 1976," *Family Planning Perspectives*, 10:135–142, May/June 1978.

Zimbardo, Philip, et al.: "A Pirandellian Prison," *The New York Times Magazine*, May 8, 1973, pp. 38ff.

Zimmerman, Carle C.: "The Future of the American Family, II, The Rise of Counterrevolution," *International Journal of the Sociology of the Family*, 2:1–9, March 1972.

Zochert, Donald: "Ethnic Diseases Getting New Attention," *Los Angeles Times*, May 4, 1977, p. 1.

ZPG Reporter: "Demographer Reassess Earlier Projections, 14:4, July/August, 1982*a*.

ZPG Reporter: "World Population Growth Rate Declines Slightly," 14:8, March/April 1982*b*.

Zuiches, Glenn V., and Edwin H. Carpenter: "Residential Preferences and Rural Development Policy," *Perspectives*, 1:12–17, November 1978.

Zumbo, Jim: "Coyote Control: No Easy Answers," *American Forests*, 87:46–53, September 1981.

Name Index

Subject Index